RED LIGHT WOMEN
OF THE ROCKY MOUNTAINS

© 2009 by the University of New Mexico Press

All rights reserved. Published 2009

14 13 12 11 10 09   1 2 3 4 5 6

Library of Congress Cataloging-in-Publication Data

MacKell, Jan, 1962–

Red light women of the rocky mountains / Jan MacKell.

p. cm.

Includes bibliographical references and index.

ISBN 978-0-8263-4610-0 (hardcover : alk. paper)

1. Prostitution—United States—History.

I. Title.

HQ144.M27 2009

306.740978´09034—dc22

2008046797

Book design and type composition by Melissa Tandysh

Composed in 10/14.25 ScalaOT

Display type is Serlio LT Std

RED LIGHT WOMEN
OF THE ROCKY
MOUNTAINS

JAN MACKELL

FOREWORD BY THOMAS J. NOEL

UNIVERSITY OF NEW MEXICO PRESS
ALBUQUERQUE

FOR COREY, WHO GOT HERE JUST IN TIME.

CONTENTS

LIST OF ILLUSTRATIONS

FOREWORD

MS. JAN MACKELL AND I MET ON ONE OF HER CRACKERJACK WALKING tours of Cripple Creek, Colorado, once the richest of all the Rocky Mountain cities of gold. Jan, who also directs the Cripple Creek District Museum, led us into the Old Homestead, a landmark brothel museum. Her eyes twinkled, and her smile widened. She treated the topic with wit and color, but also with a respect for these women. She emphasized there, as in this book, that they were human beings with unique stories and personalities—not just stereotypical whores.

Jan, formerly a sparkplug driving Cripple Creek's historic preservation commission, has helped save the Old Homestead from being "casinoized." She also takes a keen interest in the other surviving Rocky Mountain region sex shops of yesteryear. Modern-day brothel museums, reenactments, bed races, and other celebrations of whoredom are listed by state in this book's last chapter.

Landmarking red light venues for preservation has proven controversial. Some people question whether we want our children and grandchildren to remember all the sin and sorrow. Fortunately, individuals such as Jan have insisted we not forget this chapter of western and women's history. Yet opposition often arises when brothels come up for local or national register designation. Devout preservationists, of course, insist that it is best to keep a landmarked building in its original usage. Ideally, a cute Carnegie Library should remain a library, a school a school, a church a church. But law enforcement and stricter, more puritanical moral enforcement make it difficult if not impossible to reincarnate bordellos as bordellos except in the lucky state of Nevada.

At one very heated brothel landmark public hearing, it was decided after much debate that bordellos might be appropriately recycled as law offices. When the word spread, however, the next public hearing attracted a woman purporting to represent the world's oldest profession. She declared that law offices besmirched her business. At one point, she stood and fairly screamed, "Gol darn it" (or some such words), "there are some things a whore won't do for money!"

None of the attorneys there had an answer for her.

So the story goes, and in that spirit this book explores the good among the bad girls. Jan's research comes up with some surprising and engaging characters and conclusions. She starts with Native Americans and includes other nonwhite Americans. A few went into prostitution just for kicks, but many women did it because it seemed the best if not the only way to support themselves and their families. Such was the case with a prostitute who lost her job when Salt Lake City's notorious Stockade closed, leaving her to lament, "I can't support my child with wages paid girls for honest work in this city."

MacKell even addresses an issue most of us try to avoid—aging. A bright, attractive woman in her prime, she takes interest in brides of the multitude who are "well past their prime, with some being almost fifty years old." These fallen angels, she finds, were sometimes less interested in feminine finery and dressed more casually, including in parts of soldier uniforms they had acquired in years of dealing with the military. As a very young man down south, I found one such matronly madam dressed very casually. She wore nothing below the waist, saying it just got in the way. For Chinese prostitutes in San Francisco, MacKell finds that aging could mean being locked away to die.

Sad and touching stories await you in these pages. Herein you will find a red light stop called the Green Lantern run by a former circus "fat lady," Big Alma. She ran the Green Lantern in Rawlings, Wyoming, so authoritatively that Silver City Millie of New Mexico fame asked her to run a brothel in Laramie also. There, Big Alma outlawed dancing in a campaign to make this "a clean, well-run whorehouse."

This book is a popular, narrative history that will not bore readers with politically correct academic sermonizing and gender studies strutting. You will have to look elsewhere for those things. My only complaint is that the book ends too soon. I hope Jan is planning a sequel and will get a green light on continuing her red light researches.

—Professor Tom "Dr. Colorado" Noel, Denver

PREFACE

IN 1989, I WAS SUPPLEMENTING MY COLLEGE LIFESTYLE BY BARTENDING in Colorado Springs. One of my customers was a dear old man named Richard "Red" Buss, a former Colorado College professor who traveled a daily barhopping circuit via public transit. Red grew up on the infamous Westside, once known as a separate, rip-roaring town called "Colorado City." Over Jack Daniels and water, while smoking a cigar, Red would tell me in his gruff but gentle manner all about the old days. Having been born in 1907, Red remembered lots of old-timers, including the famous madam Laura Bell McDaniel. Though he was only eleven when she died, he remembered seeing her on the street and commented on the fine way she had carried herself. His description of her made me wish I could travel back in time and meet her myself.

In the time since then, Laura Bell and her contemporaries have become a favorite obsession of mine. Each and every one of the ladies I have discovered—and they number well into the thousands now—has an amazing story to tell. No matter how much or how little information is available, whether they were wonderful women or slovenly wenches you would not want to pass on the street today, all of them dared to do something incredibly outrageous and totally against social norms: they sold, traded, and gave their bodies for sex.

This is my second book about the history of prostitution. Unlike my first book, *Brothels, Bordellos, and Bad Girls: Prostitution in Colorado 1860–1930* (University of New Mexico Press, 2004), which I took the leisure of researching for years, this manuscript was on a much more timely deadline of only a little more than a year. It was Luther Wilson's idea that I write a manuscript covering the entire Rocky Mountains. In my mind's eye, I pondered that great scar of vast, unforgiving mountain ranges that runs from the Mexican border all the way up through Canada. On either side and sometimes right on top of them, several different states have the privilege of viewing these majestic peaks.

Although I have traveled and lived in many of these states, it has taken time to realize the importance of the Rockies in the development of the American West. Within their crevices lurk the most precious metals sought after by man. Settlements, from tiny camps and whistle stops to military forts and thriving metropolises, sprang up everywhere during the early 1800s and into the 1900s. Windblown mountaintops above timberline, thick forests, high mountain prairies, rocky cliffs, desert plains—no place was too harsh for pioneers to try to settle. Their courage in doing so is the reason we have the privilege of enjoying the pleasures and amazing scenery in many of those same places today.

In the course of writing this book, I traveled to each state in search of its wicked women. The endeavor ranged from exhausting (Arizona and Utah in one week) to disappointing ("I've never heard of a 'redline' [sic] district," said a Heritage Center docent in New Mexico) to delightful ("You're researching prostitution? Wonderful!" exclaimed a librarian in Mormon Utah) to great fun ("Would a person researching this subject want her picture taken on the madam's bed?" queried the owner of the Oasis Bordello Museum in Idaho). Each trip resulted in a beer box full of notes and a backseat full of books.

Out of this pleasant and often frustrating mess, I found out that the historical dichotomy making up the attitudes toward prostitution in the Rocky Mountains was simply amazing. Each of the seven states represented here contained its own unique geographic, social, economic, and cultural standards with regards to the industry. Even the profession's terminology varied from one place to another. Some states and cities have preserved— or at least have declined to destroy—the landmarks making up their red light district history. Others would just as soon those landmarks went away altogether. Many big cities have lost their grasp on the industry as it was in the early days. Most satisfying was the information I gleaned in little, out-of-the-way places from people who obviously respect their history and truly enjoy talking of the shady ladies from long ago.

Montana proved by far to be the most open about its prostitution history, probably because the industry flourished there well into the 1980s. Librarians and museum docents in Idaho, Colorado, and Arizona, each cashing in on their notorious characters of the past, also provided much useful information. Wyoming is still such an rural state that its red light history is still presented as a matter of fact. Utah was a pleasant surprise; queries about its prostitution history brought sheer delight to the faces of librarians, who willingly ran to their back rooms and brought forth stacks of files as if they had been waiting for someone like me to come along. New Mexico proved to be the most difficult to research; much brothel history has been buried under modern office buildings, and few people remain who know much about it. The state's ghost towns remain the greatest testimony to its bawdy past.

In my first book, I also had the delight of researching the names and stories of more than two thousand ladies of the lamplight. During my research, I got to know as many of them as I could, as intimately as I could. They literally became integrated into my life, and the drop of any one name brought instant memory of whatever I knew about her. It gave me great satisfaction to write about every one of them, save for two women about whom I could find nothing but their names.

That is what made this book so much more difficult to write. In Montana alone, I found thousands upon thousands of working girls. Less but equally mind-boggling numbers of prostitutes from the past were unearthed in Arizona, New Mexico, Utah, Idaho, and Wyoming. Even Colorado, where my original research was focused, brought forth a slew of new women I had never before heard of. I often felt—and still feel—as if the old gals were literally after me, popping out at the most unusual times even when I was researching something else. It was as if they knew that if their spirits made themselves known to me, I could help give them salvation by remembering who they really were.

Likewise, certain famous events that took place in the Rocky Mountains were essential to my research. The hanging of Henry Plummer in Montana, the gunfight at the O.K. Corral in Arizona, the murders of Colonel Henry Fountain and his son in New Mexico, the great Idaho fire of 1910 that wiped out so many towns—all are intriguing enough in their own right. All are also covered in other well-known annals of history. Knowing what happened is important to realizing how these events affected the West's development. But this book is about the history of prostitution and its effects. There is no doubt that although some major events played a part in the prostitution industry's success, the industry also had its own role in shaping the West.

Thus came the most difficult decisions in writing about prostitutes throughout the Rocky Mountains. Aside from the fact that prostitutes witnessed certain historic events, was it so important to record such moments for this book if prostitutes were not directly involved in them? What should I leave out? Then there were the ladies of the lamplight themselves. Who had the least interesting story to tell? Who had the best? These dilemmas boiled down to one question: Who and what would my readers most like to know about? The answer was an enigma to me. It was like going to the pound and picking out only one pet, knowing you have to leave the rest behind to an uncertain fate. Who would save the ones that I could not?

Another problem, I quickly found, is that the states composing the Rocky Mountains have incredible histories in their entirety. In my research, I inevitably unearthed the history of prostitution not just along the Rockies, but elsewhere in each state. These stories are included as a matter of record and because I felt they simply shouldn't be left out.

I learned early on that writers have to make choices. That knowledge was certainly of use in the writing of this book. The choices were often difficult to make, but here they are. The ladies in this book have great stories to tell, sometimes sad and tragic, sometimes happy and funny. Their race for a hard-earned place in these pages has been well run, but I selected every single one of them because she was special in some way and best suited to give a good understanding of the prostitution industry's place in the American West. Maybe other historians will pick up the trail and discover those I had to leave out. In the meantime, I can only hope that you, the reader, will enjoy my choices and find these women worthy of the stories they relate.

—Jan MacKell

FIGURE I ✻ *A typical prostitute of the early twentieth century. Viewers of this photo were likely more shocked by the cigarette hanging from the girl's mouth than by the amount of skin showing. Courtesy of Jay Moynahan.*

Acknowledgments

As always, an amazing number of people came forward during my research and subsequent writing of this book to make my work easy, pleasant, and a heck of a lot of fun. I had a blast in Arizona and thank Bonnie at the Gila County Historical Museum in Miami; the employees of the Copper Queen Hotel as well as Jack Riddle and the very helpful ladies at the Bisbee Historical Society in Bisbee; Joe Meehan and his staff at the Arizona Historical Society in Flagstaff; and Karen Underhill at the Cline Library of Northern Arizona University at Flagstaff.

In Colorado, I am indebted to several people. Mr. Art Tremayne of Cripple Creek shared memories of his grandma, Lelia Loveless, with me. Madams Lodi Hern and Charlotte Bumgarner of the Old Homestead House Foundation in Cripple Creek, as well as Bob Jeffries, Todd Fred, and Valerie Flournoy of the Wild Horse Casino—owners of the Old Homestead Museum in Cripple Creek—all worked with me and allowed me to fulfill my dream of running the museum beginning in the summer of 2007. Thanks also go to the excellent staff at the Denver Public Library, including Steve and Barbara in the Magazine and Newspaper Department, as well as to Mary Davis and her wonderful staff at Penrose Library in Colorado Springs. Mike Yurich of Oak Creek knew some of the ladies and shared their diaries and other information with me. I am also grateful to Yale Fyler of Cortez, who always helps me dig up books when I am down his way.

Jack and Michele Mayfield gave me a personal tour of their Oasis Bordello Museum in Wallace, Idaho. During my time in Montana, Ann Butterfield at the Pioneer Museum in Bozeman, Ellen Crain at the wonderful Butte–Silver Bow Public Archives in Butte, Kathy at the Jefferson County Courthouse, and Ray at the Montana Valley Bookstore in Alberton were of immense help. Special thanks go to Rudy Giecek, owner of the fabulous

Dumas brothel in Butte, who gave my friend and me an extensive tour of his museum and spent several hours telling us about its fascinating history.

Thanks go to several people in New Mexico: Barry Drucker of the State of New Mexico State Records Center and Archives in Santa Fe, Dennis O'Keefe of Silver City, Mr. George Schafer at the wonderfully preserved Pinos Altos Museum, and Molly Healy at the Silver City Museum and Gift Shop. In Utah, Ben at the Park City Museum in Park City was of great help. I also had fun working with Ellen Kiever, archivist at Uintah County Library in Vernal and thank Robin at the Special Collections section of the Provo County Library in Provo.

On a more personal note, the most important person I must thank is my mom, who was overseeing this project even as she was dying in the winter of 2006–2007. My dad, with his incredible business sense and way of seeing the logic in things, comes next. Special thanks also go to my aunt Barbara, who was a great help and comfort—more than she even knows—during the writing of this book. My good e-pal Jan Koski has graciously featured me on her Soiled Doves Web site (www.soiled-doves.com), and her friend Professor Jay Moynahan provided an amazing amount of help during all of my research. It seemed as if everywhere I went, Jay had already been there, and the notes he left behind saved me an incredible amount of time.

I also thank the very best of my friends and family for their support, inspiration, and assistance: Amos, Birdie, and Buddy; Kerry McKenna and Mark Rathgeber, who have supported me from the "git"; Kim Tulley, Lori Sewald, and Mark Gregory; Missie, Jeff, and Stubby Trenary; Nolon Mick, Ray Javernick, Terri Stierhoff, Steve Mackin, Bonnie Mackin, and the rest of the staff and board of the Cripple Creek District Museum; and Uncle Howard, whose talks with my mother as they were related to me were priceless.

Last but certainly not least are my great friends and colleagues, my publisher Luther Wilson at the University of New Mexico Press, and Professor "Dr. Colorado" Tom Noel, without whom I never would have come this far.

The Pioneering of Prostitution

≋ BECAUSE THE EARLIEST INHABITANTS OF THE WEST WERE NATIVE Americans, it can be said that the prostitution industry actually began with them. In actuality, however, the earliest prostitution in the West was not considered prostitution at all, but merely the tradition of selling, lending, and trading women to others for sex. In a society that agreed with multiple wives and the use of them for entertainment of guests and trading, there was little need for promiscuous women to sell themselves.[1] Sex in general was regarded as a very healthy and integral part of life, and there was no shame in it. Whereas certain tribes encouraged their adolescent girls to keep their virginity until marriage, or at least to project themselves as innocent, others allowed their teenagers to engage openly in courtship. All Native Americans largely frowned upon extreme promiscuity, however.[2]

Attitudes toward the lending or trading of women varied among Native American tribes. Among the Assiniboine, it was common for parents to lend out their daughters for sex, always in trade for goods. The more the girls brought, the greater the respect for them and their families. Furthermore, the girls in many Indian societies often expressed their anticipation and desire for such transactions to occur. Only the rare *wittico-weeon*, or "fool woman," of the Assiniboine plied her trade on her own, for pay. Such women "were considered lost beyond redemption."[3]

It is interesting to speculate whether the coming of Spanish explorers increased the number of *wittico-weeons* or any other prostitutes among Indian tribes. Spanish archives reveal very few references to the sex trade, although the records are rife with instances of concubinage, rape, and kidnapping. Many historians agree that it was the immigration of the French from Canada and later of the whites from the East that put prostitution into the commercial category, where it remains even today. Prostitution provided another way to procure food and goods from the white men, but it also unfortunately brought the spread of venereal disease, which up until that time was foreign to most native nations.[4]

Prostitution was certainly no stranger to explorers Meriwether Lewis and William Clark, who during their journey along the Columbia River near the Pacific Coast in 1805–1806 were treated to six Chinook maidens. A Chinook leader's wife oversaw the "regular prices proportioned to the beauty of each female." The endeavor was largely unsuccessful because the men of the party had been warned of disease and illness resulting from intercourse with Indian women.[5] At least one of the men, however, contracted syphilis, and Lewis noted that another of his party came down with it as well. Lewis treated both men with mercury, which proved to be a limited success.[6] Both patients died young, leading to the assumption that they had succumbed to the disease.

Lewis and Clark also witnessed venereal disease among the Mandan in North Dakota.[7] Later, when they encountered a tribe of Sioux, the men were amazed at how many wives were offered up for their entertainment, commenting, "[W]e observed among them some women who appeared to be held in more respect than those of any nation we had seen."[8] Lewis and Clark notably held that same respect for the famed Sacajawea. This strong and courageous woman who gave birth along the trail while leading the men West may actually have functioned as a part-time prostitute for them as well. Although it has never been proved that Sacajawea carried venereal disease, historians do suspect that Meriwether Lewis himself may have contracted syphilis, perhaps from the Indian maiden herself. The illness may explain what led to Lewis's psychotic behavior a few years after the expedition and subsequently his suicide in 1809.[9]

With the coming of white men and later of their wives, white prostitution became a tolerable alternative for women who wished to keep their husbands from the clutches of Indian prostitutes. Back east, larger cities already had established houses of prostitution. Visiting a brothel was socially acceptable in most male circles. Single men who yearned for companionship were frequent customers, and more than a few of them probably shopped for wives. Married men, however, were also known to frequent brothels if only pursuing the cliché idea that they enjoyed cheating on their wives. Women's attitudes toward prostitution in this era appear surprisingly open by today's standards, but their reasoning seems sound enough. During the 1800s, a woman's personal toilet was quite complex. Daily dress, no matter the weather, involved yards of petticoats, slips, pinafores, pantaloons, stockings, bustles, and tight, breath-stealing corsets. All were skillfully hidden beneath dresses made of heavy material. In short, Victorian dress was downright uncomfortable. In some cases, corsets could even cause internal injuries or an abortion. One store catalog advertised an instrument devised to push organs back where they belonged by inserting it into the vagina.[10]

Complicating the issue of dress was a lack of knowledge by doctors and people in general about such anatomical issues as premenstrual syndrome, menopause, and lack of estrogen. Society forbade frank discussion of sex, especially recreational or pleasurable sex. Proper girls were brought up believing sex was bad unless undertaken to produce children. Talk of contraception was also taboo, although some wives quietly discussed it with each other over the back fence. Some husbands, however, refused to let their wives practice contraception at all, so the fear of having too many children and of death during childbirth frightened many women into abstinence.[11]

Thus, many wives left their husbands in frustration. Men who visited brothels discreetly kept it from their wives, who in turn pretended not to know about it if such visits came to their attention. In the case of wives who knew about these indiscretions, the recrimination could range from divorce to no reaction whatsoever. A woman with a husband who visited the occasional whorehouse was better off than a woman with no husband at all, and the fear of contracting venereal disease from one's husband simply put an end to marital sex for good.[12] As a child, Clarabelle Decker moved with her family to Oatman, Arizona, in 1909. She later remembered that at the time the town had a sizeable red light district: "There was a well worn path from the mine shafts below the Tom Reed Mine to a large saloon where they cashed their paychecks. It was almost on old Highway 66 and had a large porch where the men and the 'girls' visited in warm weather. Oatman had a large 'Red Light' district, and we kids knew not to go around certain houses. On paydays my mother usually took one of us children and met my father as he came off shift so he would get home with his paycheck, which she would cash at Lavon & Withers store."[13]

By the time the West was being settled by whites between 1840 and 1880, prostitution was a given profession. Some speculate that prostitutes may have comprised the second-largest group of working women in the West, right behind domestic servants.[14] Nevertheless, the population of women on the early frontier was slow to grow. The mining camps, military forts, and ranching districts of the early West were filled with woman-hungry men. Living for months without seeing a woman was a common malady before the fairer sex drifted west after their male counterparts. One lonely bachelor, it was said, actually managed to get his hands on some lady's lingerie and charged his friends to look at it. The cost was more for those wanting to touch it.[15] When word got out that a female waitress was serving drinks in a Georgia Gulch, Colorado, saloon, the miners broke their necks going to see her like "boys who go to see a monkey."[16]

In 1860, the ratio of men to women in Colorado was sixteen to one. In California Gulch near Leadville alone, there were 2,000 males and only 36 females. South Park boasted an amazing 10,519 men to 91 women! Most of the gentler sex were well admired, respected, and obeyed. In their absence, the men, desperate for companionship, held dances anyway and designated "female" dance partners by tying ribbons or handkerchiefs on their arms. If by some miracle a woman did attend a dance or other social gathering, she could rely on being treated with the utmost kindness despite wearing out her dance slippers with dozens of partners. Married men were fully expected to permit their wives to attend such social gatherings rather than keeping them at home. To prevent other men from feasting their eyes upon the rare and coveted female was considered downright rude.[17]

Backgrounds

Ruth Rosen's book *The Lost Sisterhood* lists a turn-of-the-century survey regarding how women came to be prostitutes. One study identified the top reasons as bad home conditions; betrayal, deception, or seduction; death or desertion by husband; choice; bad friends; desire for more money; desire for pleasure; alcohol and drugs; a "naturally bad" character; and economic necessity.[18] Indeed, many women worked as "occasional" prostitutes, taking up the profession to subsidize other income they earned as seamstresses, laundresses, domestics, and factory workers. Even a temporary layoff from any of these legitimate professions could mean starvation during a harsh winter. Prostitution was a viable way to make extra cash. But women also had other reasons for turning to prostitution. The *Albuquerque Morning Journal* commented on one young harlot in 1885: "Dashing along Railroad Avenue yesterday on a handsome horse was a good looking young girl residing in a house of ill-fame in this city, and to all appearances there was not a care upon her features, but she has a history. Her father, mother, two brothers and sister have all died violent deaths at the hands of other parties, and she, the only one in the family left, says that she lives only for vengeance."[19]

It is interesting how false advertising fooled many women into the profession. Two young women of Montana, for instance, verified in 1881 that they had merely answered an ad in Eureka asking for "a young lady to play piano and sing for a country place of amusement; steady place; $150 a month, fare paid." The girls should have been suspicious when they learned the travel fare would not be paid in advance, and one of them had to hawk a diamond ring to get the money for passage. The place of their employment turned out to be a beer hall, from which the girls departed as soon as they were able. Despite being well brought up and educated, even "smart" girls could fall victim to deceit.[20] Another fallen woman in Colorado told a group of admirers in 1860 that she had been lured into the profession in St. Louis at the age of fifteen when she ran off with a "gay and dashing city youth." The man took her to his aunt's house, where under the influence of drugs she drank some wine. "When I awoke to consciousness at about noon of the next day, I found this residence miraculously transformed into a house of shame."[21]

Women who were tricked into being working girls usually found a way to escape back to their hometowns. For others, turning to prostitution was the only choice they had to get the money in order to return home. A case in point was a woman known only as "Lady Gay," who first came to Tombstone, Arizona, with her miner husband. Soon after their arrival, he set out alone for the Dragoon Mountains to prospect, despite warnings that Apaches were there in abundance. When he didn't return, his wife was left alone in a strange country with no means of support. Turning to prostitution was the only way Lady Gay could gather enough money to leave Arizona and return to her family in Rhode Island. A similar fate befell another Tombstone woman known as Jessie Jo, whose husband drank and gambled away their money.[22]

Yet other women found their places in life just plain boring. A woman known only as "Miss Evie," a former schoolteacher, quit her job to go to work at Blonde Marie's parlor house in Tombstone. The future career of another Tombstone prostitute was set in stone when her husband placed the following classified: "I hereby warn the public not to trust my wife Flossie on my account, as she has left my bed and board, and I will not be responsible for any debts she may contract. Louis Blonberg."[23]

There were other reasons for entering the profession. In Salt Lake City, Utah, Rose Watkins testified that she was forced into prostitution when her father died penniless and her mother became ill. Rose's coworker, Alma Baxley, claimed she had been a prostitute in Texas before going straight upon arriving in Salt Lake. After a few months, however, word of Alma's former occupation caused her to lose her job and resume working in a bordello. Another woman declined honest work in 1911 when Salt Lake City's infamous Stockade closed. "I can't support my child with the wages paid girls for honest work in this city," she said.[24] This woman and countless others had discovered the ultimate bottom line when it came to deciding to take up prostitution as a career: it paid much more than menial jobs. One woman in Leadville, Colorado, complained to a reporter in 1880 that she was forced to work in a dance hall by her husband's inability to make adequate money. "You saw that tough, half-drunken brute embrace me. I submitted to his caresses. I floated gaily with him through the dance. I half supported him as he staggered to the bar for drinks. And you ask if I like to do all this. Haven't I loathed this accursed life from the first?"[25]

An early Colorado census taker later verified what historians are finding today: ladies of easy virtue suffered unease at giving personal information about themselves. When a count of the ladies at Salt Lake City's Stockade was taken, sixteen of forty women were identified by name only. Census supervisor Hugh McMillin noted that "[t]hese persons represent 'the Underworld' of Salt Lake City and repeated calls of the enumerator and special agents failed to elicit any further information than that given above."[26] Two particularly sticky questions, what their real names were and where they were born, proved especially problematic. It was also not unusual for prostitutes in such situations to claim they were really dressmakers, milliners, teachers, or salesladies, and there was a tendency to give

FIGURE 2 ❧ *Although hundreds of photographs of prostitutes have surfaced in recent years, not all women enjoyed being photographed. In this early 1900s scene, a Butte, Montana, harlot appears to flee from the photographer. Courtesy of the Timothy Gordon Collection.*

varying places and dates of birth from one census to the next. Like any other pioneers, female easterners coming West could reinvent themselves into whoever or whatever they wanted to be.

Ethnicity

The majority of working girls in the Rocky Mountains were white, but a number of them varied in race and place of birth. Foreign women came to America three ways: either on their own volition, as the hired employees of American brothel or saloon owners, or by force as purchased or kidnapped slaves. In Silver City, Idaho, business owners and "procuresses" made trips to Germany to recruit girls.[27] In Cripple Creek, Colorado, saloon owner Morris Durant hired French immigrant "French Blanche" LeCoq to migrate from New Orleans.[28] In most situations, the girls who were hired came to America of their own accord and agreed to the terms of paying off their passage to the men who paid for their ticket.

The case was very different for Chinese women, though, whose plight necessitates further study. The Chinese culture largely frowned on women's migration abroad from China. Hence, a number of pioneer Chinese men arrived in America alone. Many left wives behind in China out of respect for their traditions, an inability to afford their wives' passage, or fear of bigotry that could turn violent in the new land. Young Chinese girls, however, were regarded as a viable way to provide financial assistance to their families. This trend was especially popular among the poorer-class families, who saw their daughters as entering prostitution for the good of the family. These most put upon emigrants were as young as ten or eleven years of age. They were sold and brought to the United States with their families' understanding that the girls would be able to live their lives freely once there. In most cases, the girls' families received only a few pennies or dollars, but were relieved to think that their daughters were being sent to a better life. Many were under the impression that the girls were serving as mail-order or "picture brides" who would marry an American or Chinese man when they arrived.[29]

In reality, these girls were sold into virtual slavery. One young prostitute, nineteen-year-old Gon Sing, testified that she was purchased in China by a man for 680 Mexican dollars. "I was told that when I came here I would be married to a respectable, wealthy Chinese merchant." Instead, upon reaching America, Gon was sold again for $1,680 worth of gold and forced into a San Francisco house of prostitution. Another girl, Chun Ho, said the Chinese mistress of a "procurer" in San Francisco talked both Chun and her mother into letting Chun move to California. "She painted that life so beautiful that I was seized with an inclination to go there," said Chun, whose mother received $200 in Mexican money.[30]

Americans were as guilty as the Chinese themselves, but soon the Chinese prostitution industry became monopolized by the Tongs—a Chinese mafia who owned their prostitutes and imported them from China.[31] Once the girls were in America, there was no way to return home, and most of them were forced into prostitution in order to work off the cost of their passage. They had arrived in America without knowing English, but they were forced to sign contracts written in English promising to prostitute their bodies until their debt was paid to their benefactor. Per the contract, a sick day, menstrual cycle, or pregnancy meant additional time would be tacked on to their debt. To these unfortunate, illiterate girls, there was no end in sight and no law that could save them. Even if they did marry, their husbands usually ended up pimping them to the Tongs anyway.[32]

Before the Tongs got a hold on the industry, the Chinese view of prostitution as an economic opportunity initially led to a number of freelance prostitutes during the California gold rush between 1848 and 1854. The first Chinese prostitutes, among them the famous courtesan Ah Toy of San Francisco, could run their own businesses and hope to marry out of the profession, much like any American woman. These women were called "Baak Haak Chai" in their homeland language, which literally means "one hundred men's wife."[33] By 1852, however, when some ten thousand Chinese migrated to San Francisco, their passage was being overseen mostly by an organization known as the Six Companies. Composed of important celestial businessmen, the Six Companies lent money to both men and women seeking passage to America, got them jobs upon their arrival, and saw to it the loan was repaid, with interest. In short, the Six Companies literally ruled over immigrants' lives before, during, and after they made the trip to the new land.[34]

The sudden increase in the Chinese population made these new immigrants largely noticeable. Their culture, religion, eating habits, and strangely different way of life tended to repulse Americans. Ignorance of the ancient Chinese philosophies and Old World thinking caused most whites to express extreme prejudice against these people. "Of different language, blood, religion, and character, inferior in most mental and bodily qualities," noted *The Annals of San Francisco* in 1854, "the Chinaman is looked upon by some as only a little superior to the negro, and by others as somewhat inferior." Their natural patience was mistaken for submission to ill treatment. The men's willingness to work hard in the mines for less pay and under near slave conditions did little to endear them to the money-greedy white miners of the goldfields.[35] And despite the Chinese immigrants knowledge of natural medicine, passed down through thousands of years, few except prostitutes of all ethnic backgrounds dared use it.[36]

As much as Americans disliked the Chinese in their midst, they were not beyond having sex with them. A reporter for the *Owyhee Avalanche* in Idaho noted in 1875 a Chinese working girl who held a baby in her arms. The child was about six months old, with looks that led the writer to believe "there had been a successful attempt round her to 'cross the breed.'" American authorities frowned on the prostitution business even as they did little to assist the women. They knew that most Chinese girls were being transported by ships leaving Canton, Hong Kong, and Macao.[37] They also knew, usually by the complaints of others, that such girls were subjected to abuse and enslavement. Occasional raids by San Francisco authorities, sometimes at the request of the Six Companies, netted girls as young as eight years of age. The girls were taken to mission homes or asylums until work could be found for them, but many ended up in houses of prostitution anyway. Many more girls were taken from San Francisco by Tongs or white traders and brought to the mining camps of the Rocky Mountains, where men could auction or sell them with considerably less interference from authorities. Even Ah Toy did her share of buying, selling, and enslaving "Chinagirls."[38] Between 1852 and 1873, the "Hip Yee" Tong imported an estimated six thousand girls from China and netted around $200,000 for them.[39] By 1860, there were more Chinese prostitutes in Sacramento, California, than prostitutes of any other race.[40]

Chinese women in America could fall into various classes as wife, concubine, or prostitute. The higher their virtue, the more valuable they were. In China, concubines were considered more valuable if they had avoided sexual contact with Euro-Americans. As companions solely to Chinese men, these women lived well and provided companionship and domestic services to several men. Even after their arrival in America, Chinese concubines and prostitutes were considered to be of a lower status if they had slept with Americans prior to their arrival.[41] Over time, the prevailing attitude became the opposite simply because of the prejudices against the Chinese; sex with Chinamen was not as profitable or as acceptable as sex with whites.

If not kept prisoner in an underground basement, lower-status Chinagirls were likely to find themselves living and working in the back of gambling halls, opium dens, brothels, and cribs. They were often abused by their masters or madams and were seldom allowed to turn away customers who had venereal diseases or were drunk or abusive. Thus, many women succumbed to disease, violence, and suicide during the terms of their contracts. The average career—and life—expectancy for a Chinese prostitute was no more than five years.[42] The Tongs tended to rule not just

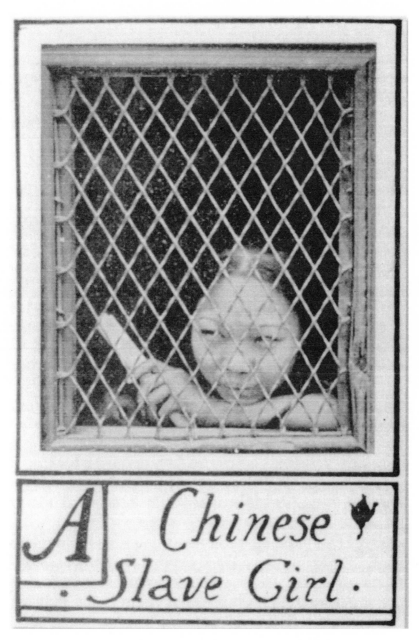

FIGURE 3 A Chinese prostitute looks out on the world from her prison
in the late 1800s. Literally slaves, such girls had no hope for their futures,
only the prospect of illness and an early death. Courtesy of the Bancroft Library,
University of California, Berkeley, XFFF850.WI86V.20: No. 30: 04.

over the girls, but also over the gambling and the opium dens whose services included prostitution. Much like their white counterparts, the girls were divided into classes by looks and talent. Some Chinese brothel girls dressed well and had painted faces, a clean working environment, and a better opportunity to be purchased for exclusive use by a client or married man. Many more, however, were kept prisoner, operating behind barred windows and doors in tiny rooms with no more than a bed. Those who tried to escape were beaten, branded, and sometimes chained to their beds.[43]

Inhumane treatment of Chinagirls was extreme by 1869. Especially in larger cities, most Chinese dens of prostitution were underground, away from the public eye, and were rife with filth and disease. Their prisoners were frightened, ill, and broken in spirit. Girls who lost their attractiveness under such conditions were sometimes allowed to "escape" to mission homes, but more often they were taken to an even dingier den and left to die. One such place was described in San Francisco in 1869: "The place is loathsome to the extreme. On one side is a shelf four feet wide and about a yard above the dirty floor, upon which there are two old rice mats. . . . When any of the unfortunate harlots is no longer useful and a Chinese physician passes his opinion that her disease is incurable, she is notified that she must die." Such girls were led to these places, forced through the door, and left with a cup of water, some rice, and a small oil lamp. "Those who have immediate charge of the establishment know how long the oil should last, and when the time is reached they return to the 'hospital,' unbar the door and enter. . . . Generally the woman is dead, either by starvation or from her own hand; but sometimes life is not extinct; the spark yet remains when the 'doctors' enter; yet this makes little difference to them. They come for a corpse, and they never go away without it."[44]

By 1870, thousands of Chinese women populated the northern states of the Rocky Mountains, especially Idaho and Montana, but other places as well. It is interesting to note that Silver City, Idaho, had a Chinese population that was larger than the population of the average western town in 1870. The city very well may have served as a cultural gathering place for establishing residency in America and importing goods from the Far East. Notably, Silver City supported two Buddhist temples, and Chinese prostitutes typically outnumbered white working girls. Newspapers and other historical documentation also note a number of conflicts among the Tongs of Silver City.[45] The presence of so many Chinese might be an indication that the Six Companies, despite Americans' prejudices, had gained a strong foothold in the West.

In 1874, after several years of American authorities' lambasting the Chinese for leaving their wives in the homeland while importing girls for immoral purposes, the Six Companies finally made a formal reply. In their statement, they argued that several Chinese families did live in America, but that "pure and chaste" women had not come to America out of fear of defying their old customs. The document openly admitted that the companies brought prostitutes to the United States, but "at the instigation and for the gratification of white men." The Six Companies had even tried to send some of the women back to China, but were stopped by a white lawyer who maintained the girls' rights to be in America.[46] The Six Companies and American authorities came to a standoff as immigration of prostitutes continued. In the mid-1870s, Portland, Oregon, and Vancouver, Canada, joined San Francisco as major ports of entry for girls being imported from China, for the most part because California had enacted an immigration code forbidding "lewd or debauched women" from entering the country.[47]

In a more concerted effort to quell prostitution immigration, the Chinese Exclusion Act of 1882 decreed that female immigrants coming from China must be limited to U.S. citizens, women married to Chinese men, or daughters of "domiciled merchants" who were born outside of America. In response, the Tongs merely resorted to smuggling girls, bribing customs officials, forging birth certificates and papers, and coaching their charges into lying to officials to procure entry to the United States. Lee Yow Chun, who was brought to America in 1897, remembered being taken from her parents' house and told exactly what to say to officials before boarding the steamer ship *China* for California.[48]

Throughout the 1880s, thousands of girls were induced to leave China as indentured servants and to sign contracts binding their sexual services for four to five years upon their arrival in the United States. Such contracts continued to be loaded with double standards. Prostitute Xin Jin's contract stipulated that should she run away, she would pay all costs incurred in finding her and returning her to her brothel. Ah Kam's contract contained a clause that should she attempt to escape or resist, she could be sold.[49] A typical contract during the 1880s read as follows: "For the consideration of [whatever sum had been agreed upon], paid into my hands this day, I, [name of girl], promise to prostitute my body for the term of [number] years. If, in that time, I am sick one day, two weeks shall be added to my time; and if more than one day, my term of prostitution shall continue an additional month. But if I run away, or escape from the custody of my keeper, then I am to be held as a slave for life." Most girls had little knowledge of the document's legality or what it actually implied.[50]

Anti-Chinese sentiments also continued throughout the 1880s. Certain towns did not like the "yellow eyes" in their midst, and bigotry ran strong. In Mineral Park, Arizona, in 1884, it came to the attention of white saloon owners and madams that more and more young people were turning to Chinese opium dens for entertainment. The anger at money being spent in such places was further enflamed by the growing number of addicts. The white madams issued an edict that opium smokers were to stay away from their girls, and beginning in July that year the *Mohave Miner* took up a crusade against the dens.[51] Worse yet, young boys who would be turned away at a white parlor house were welcome into Chinese cribs. By 1885, physicians in San Francisco were noting that boys as young as ten and twelve years of age were infected with venereal disease that they had contracted from Chinagirls.[52]

The 1882 Chinese Exclusion Act was amended in 1888 to prohibit reentry of Chinese who had recently departed American shores. Again, many women's papers were simply falsified, but the rising costs of illegal immigration only resulted in an increase in the kidnapping of Chinese women within the United States. Nevertheless, the Chinese Exclusion Act worked to an extent. At least in Idaho by around 1890, the Chinese population appears to have been declining. The number of Chinese in Owyhee County, for instance, was only 245, although it had been larger in previous years.[53]

Despite this decline, anti-Chinese sentiments continued. In Butte, Montana, a committee was formed in 1893 that demanded that all Chinese prostitutes be fired. In response, the madams of houses of prostitution accordingly instructed their male employees to throw the committee members down the stairs. The group next threatened to boycott such houses and publish the names of anyone employing or patronizing Chinese places. Intolerance against the Chinese in Montana came to a head in 1894 when Chinese residents at Anaconda were successfully driven out of town. In 1897, a group of Chinese businessmen filed suit against twenty-four Butte labor unions. They were represented by the state's first U.S. senator, Colonel Wilbur Fisk Sanders, who successfully obtained a restraining order

FIGURE 4 ❦ *In this 1871 engraving, the symbolic figure of Columbia stands between a Chinese man and an angry mob. The wall in the background is riddled with anti-Chinese slogans. Courtesy of the Denver Public Library, Western History Collection, Z-3811.*

against the unions. Bigotry toward the Chinese nevertheless continued, especially when large groups of them fought among themselves over control of Chinatown's gambling dens, drugs, and prostitutes.[54]

By then, Donaldina Cameron had been working in San Francisco for two years to free Chinese slaves. Mrs. Cameron assisted the police in actively staging raids. Her mission home provided medical aid, education opportunities, and jobs, and many of her rescued girls even married.[55] This effort encouraged authorities to take a firmer stand against the industry. In 1898, Lieutenant of Police William Price testified to the Commission of Immigration that 90 percent of Chinese immigrant women were prostitutes. "They are sold as fast as they can be brought over," said Price, who also verified that most of these women were purchased for about $3,000 each.[56] The Chinese prostitution industry was still clearly out of control, but at least authorities were finally taking steps to abolish it. It was not until 1910, however, that Congress passed the Mann Act, which forbade, under heavy penalties, the transportation of women from one state to another for immoral purposes. Well more than a decade passed before at least Colorado's Chinese prostitutes ultimately freed themselves from the clutches of enslaved prostitution, though.[57]

Japanese women who came to America to ply their trade were in deep contrast to the Chinese. Although both races are Asian in origin, Japanese girls did not appear in the West in nearly the large numbers that their Chinese counterparts did. The vast difference between Chinese and Japanese prostitutes remains largely unexplained. Salt Lake City is notable for the number of Japanese courtesans working there who appeared in court.[58] Author Jay Moynahan has also noted that a number of Japanese prostitutes worked in Alaska during the 1800s. Those who have remained in history's eye appear to have worked independently and done well for themselves.[59] Moynahan speculates that the difference between Chinese and Japanese girls was basically cultural: Japanese women came to America to marry Japanese men, only to find they were indentured prostitutes instead; Chinese women were sold outright by their families with the knowledge that they were to serve as sex slaves.[60]

Cripple Creek, Colorado, documented only one known Japanese prostitute, whereas Denver sported a "Japanese Quarter" in 1894 with six known girls.[61] Among them was Kiku Oyama, who was murdered by the "Market Street Strangler" in 1894. Two other women, Lena Tapper and

Marie Contassot, were the first to die during the short-lived but terrifying serial murder spree that never was solved. Kiku's case is interesting not just because she was a victim of the Strangler, but also because it gives a good view into the life of a Japanese courtesan. Kiku was employed by a parlor house. She also did well enough to send $50 to her mother in Japan each month. Kiku had also recently bailed out all five of her coworkers for $33 dollars when the Japanese Quarter was raided. Mamie Sheehan, Kiku's white neighbor, called the girl "the brightest Japanese on the row."[62]

Lifestyles

College student Jimmy Harold Smith may have said it best when in his 1977 thesis he explained that a prostitute "could be mother, sister, lover, selfless confidant, entrepreneur, card shark, woman-child. She could become, by turns, fragile, loving, tender, tough, hard nosed, shrewd, incisive, bold. She was, in fact, a Cheshire cat."[63] Indeed, in looking at the life of frontier prostitutes as a whole, we can easily see common traits among them. They were usually single women with or without children who plied their trade as employees of a house or on their own. They had constant brushes with the law consistent with local ordinances and were subject to segregation and persecution. Their ages varied from as young as fourteen to as old as forty or more years of age. All battled such potential hazards as venereal disease, alcohol and drug addiction, physical abuse, pregnancy, and the results of abortion. They strived to leave the business eventually and did so by marriage, retirement, or death. Many, such as restaurant owner and middle-aged widow Amelia Rucker of Tombstone, Arizona, supplemented their main income by working part time as a prostitute.[64]

The average lifestyle of a prostitute varied according to geographic region, social norms, economic trends, and amount of discrimination in the town or camp where she lived.[65] Most paid rent or a portion of their earnings to a landlord, madam, or pimp. In Albuquerque, the girls could either pay for room, board, and laundry on a weekly basis or keep a quarter of their weekly earnings and give the remainder to the madam.[66] Madam Millie Cusey-Clark of Silver City, New Mexico, exacted half of her girls' earnings.[67] Many red light districts served as their own private communities. Within their boundaries, prostitutes worked, ate, slept, confided in each other, fought with and stole from one another, and established rank among themselves. In these small and often forlorn-looking neighborhoods, women hoped, dreamed, and tried to see around the present dimness of their futures. Their place of employment was also their home, where they were treated for illness, looked after the sick, and dressed the dead. Drug overdoses and alcohol poisoning were common. Most experienced girls and madams knew how to handle funeral arrangements. Even if the family of the dead could be found, they often refused to claim the body.[68] The prostitute's closest friends were limited to those she knew in her profession, usually fellow soiled doves and madams as well as male customers, pimps, and saloon owners.[69]

Although documentation is practically nonexistent, there are indications that a few women turned to lesbianism to make up for the lack of love among their male customers. In March 1892, two of Denver madam Mattie Silks's girls, Effie Pryor and Allie Ellis, were found lying nude together after a double suicide attempt via morphine. Effie was saved, but Allie died.[70] When Dora Forrest died of an accidental morphine overdose in Butte, Montana, in 1896, she was in bed with fellow prostitute Madge Dawe.[71] Cripple Creek, Colorado, madam Pearl DeVere was lying next to one of her girls, Maud Stone, when it was discovered she had overdosed on morphine in 1897.[72] During the 1930s, madam Millie Cusey-Clark of New Mexico briefly employed a brothel manager named Vera who was bisexual. Millie recalled that Vera had boyfriends, but also "kept a pet among the girls, and would make love to her too." Jealous fits over a woman who did not return Vera's advances eventually resulted in too many problems, and Millie fired Vera.[73]

Lack of love and public shunning often resulted in depression that ran high among the girls, many of whom became addicted to various vices to escape their problems. Many standard medicines contained potentially lethal doses of such drugs as laudanum, morphine, cocaine, opium, and alcohol. Wyeth's New Enterius Pills, Feeley's Rheumatic Mixture, and Godfrey's Cordial contained morphine. Laudanum, a liquid form of opium, was applied to sprains and bruises or consumed straight from the bottle. Combinations of morphine and cocaine relieved colds. Visiting opium dens in the back of Chinese laundries or brothels was also a popular pastime. Almost all of these drugs could be obtained without a prescription or over the counter from any local pharmacy. Prostitutes often sent messengers and newsboys to buy their drugs for them at the local pharmacy. In the interest of remaining discreet, the girls would send the boy with a certain

FIGURE 5 ❧ *A group of prostitutes poses at a Nebraska brothel during the late 1800s or early 1900s. As housemates, the women were forced to form friendships with each other. Note the presence of the madam's pet dog, which many women kept to battle their own loneliness. Courtesy of the Old Homestead Parlour House Museum at the Wild Horse Casino, Cripple Creek, Colorado.*

playing card and money to the drug store. The pharmacist, upon receiving the card, knew what the girls were ordering. The boys usually received a good tip upon completing the mission.[74]

It is safe to assume that most ladies of the evening, no matter where they were, were in general as clean as they could be and regular in their bathing habits. If they could get ammonia, they sometimes applied it to bathwater to help clean the pores. In the absence of lip powder, the girls would give their lips a brisk rubbing to bring out their color. Tar or oatmeal soap and glycerin kept the skin toned and soft.[75] Belladonna leaves applied to the eyelids dilated the pupils to create "bedroom eyes." Hair, teeth, and facial makeup were other important facets of everyday life. Many women bleached their hair, a very dangerous process during which one could suffer burns to the skin as well as to the eyes. An unfortunate fact easily forgotten is that many girls also had poor teeth because they didn't have the luxury of a toothbrush or lessons on how to use it. Thus, many girls had missing, gold-filled, or gold-capped teeth.[76]

In their manner of dress, those women who could afford it used any means available to enhance their appearance. Remedies often included such accoutrements as "false calves" and false bosoms shaped into "breasts" made of fine wire to "really look and feel quite natural."[77] Sears & Roebuck's Catalog for 1909 offered the "Princess Bust Developer and Bust Cream or Food." The kit contained a concoction made into cream to rub on the bosom and a plunger-type tool made of aluminum to help "expand and fill out" the breasts.[78] In the absence of teeth or in the case of gaunt faces, the girls also inserted "plumpers" into their mouths to make their faces appear rounder and healthy.[79]

The prostitute's overall appearance was important, even if her way of dress and her looks were only enough to entice a customer for a few minutes' time. Thomas Dimsdale, publisher of Montana's first newspaper in Virginia City, described the typical dance hall girls, who were "sometimes dressed in uniform, but, more generally, habited according to the dictates of individual caprice, in the finest clothes money can buy, and which are fashioned in the most attractive styles they can suggest." The average dance hall girl he encountered was "middle height, of rather full and rounded form; her complexion as pure as alabaster, a pair of dangerous looking hazel eyes, a lightly Roman nose, and a small and prettily formed mouth. Her auburn hair is neatly banded and gathered in a tasteful, ornamental net, with a roll and gold tassels at the side."[80] A young woman who lived in both Montana and Colorado recalled that the prostitutes she encountered "were easily recognizable by their painted cheeks and the flaunting of their gaudy clothes on the streets. They were always to be seen either walking up and down or clattering along on horseback or in hacks. . . . These women were so in evidence that I felt no curiosity about them. I knew that besides being so much upon the streets, they went to hurdy-gurdy houses and to saloons and that they were not 'good women.'"[81]

Thomas Dimsdale also described the typical partner to these women as a man who "stands six feet in his boots, which come to the knee, and are garnished with a pair of Spanish spurs, with rowels and balls like young water wheels. His buckskin leggings are fringed at the seams and gathered at the waist with a U.S. belt, from which hangs his loaded revolver and his sheath knife. His neck is bare, muscular, and browned from exposure, as is also his bearded face, whose somber expression is relieved by a pair of piercing black eyes. His long black hair hangs down beneath his wide felt hat and in the corner of his mouth is a cigar, which rolls like the lever of

FIGURE 6 ᴄᴀ *Ready for a night on the town. Two working girls in Helena, Montana, sport fancy Parisian outfits, early 1900s. Most prostitutes aspired to look as nice as they could. Courtesy of the Timothy Gordon Collection.*

an eccentric, as he chews the end in his mouth. . . . No wonder that a wild mountaineer, with leather breeches, would be willing to pay—not one dollar, but all that he has in his purse, for a dance and an approving smile from so handsome a woman."[82] Although Dimsdale's description is of a typical mountain man, other brothel customers could include cowboys, gamblers, miners, and businessmen whose attire matched that of their respective professions.

The workday for a typical prostitute began around noon and ended as late as six o'clock the next morning. During these hours, the girls turned as many tricks as they could while drinking, dancing, and playing cards with their customers. The idea was to make as much money during the shift as possible. Timing was important: more customers meant more money. The typical fee in the Victorian era ranged from fifty cents to $50, but time with a girl was especially short in the cheaper houses.[83] The average transaction lasted only a few minutes, but others as long as twenty minutes, and the girls averaged four to six customers per night.[84] One customer remembered the transaction of sex itself as quick and very businesslike: "She'd lay on her back and get you on top of her so fast, you wouldn't even know you'd come up there on your own power. She'd grind so that you almost felt like you had nothing to do with it. Well, after that, she had you. She could make it get off as quickly as she wanted to . . . and she didn't waste any time, I'll tell you . . . I'd say the whole thing, from the time you got in the room until the time you came didn't take three minutes."[85]

Being a woman of the night meant frequently moving as economics and the law dictated. Prostitutes tended to travel together or with a trusted male friend, perhaps a companion even, for increased safety. A number of girls tended to travel a circuit as weather, mining booms, cattle shipping, and railroad construction demanded.[86] Pioneer Anne Ellis recalled encountering a traveling prostitute camped near the town of Bonanza, Colorado. "We went over to investigate, and found a course, red-faced woman, her straw colored hair hanging in her eyes. She was one who had fallen so low that she drove from one camp to another, plying her trade in these tents." Ellis did note that the woman later married an Englishman and moved into "one of the best houses in town." A visit to her revealed "diamonds, very red plush furniture, and her very pale blue and bright pink tea gowns; also a parrot and a cage of parakeets."[87] In Wyoming and other cattle states, prostitutes were known to appear mysteriously in "cat wagons" in June, remain only until fall, then move on.[88] Other women served as "camp followers" to troops traveling among the military forts of the West.

The Business

During the Victorian era, the prostitution industry saw many changes. The initial pioneers to the Rocky Mountains were primarily men exploring rough, uncharted country with little information as to what lay in those vast mountain ranges. The untamed terrain was certainly no place for a lady. Success among the gold camps, however, spelled certain wealth for those shady ladies who dared traipse along the trails in search of their own proverbial gold mine. In the early West, houses of ill fame were primitive and unregulated, and they sprang up sporadically in the mining camps of the Rocky Mountains. They could be anything from a tent to a shanty to a shed to a building to rooms above a saloon or even actually a house. In these early days, working girls of the boom camps could often call their own shots, sometimes charging an ounce of gold just to sit with a man in a gambling house. Others could charge anywhere from twenty to hundreds of dollars for sex.[89] As cities and towns became more civilized, the industry evolved into a caste system. Courtesans and mistresses were higher up than parlor house ladies. Madams did not always have sex with clients, and those who did could increase their profits by functioning as a "working madam." Parlor house ladies made more than brothel girls, who rated above crib girls. Crib girls made more money and gained more respect than dance hall and saloon girls. Washed-up saloon girls were destined to become street-walkers if they were unable to leave the profession.[90]

As the population increased, so did the number of laws limiting where and when bawdy houses could operate and regulating the girls who worked in them. Nearly every town and city in the West eventually had strict ordinances prohibiting girls from entering or working in saloons, gambling houses, and brothels. In certain places, women could not even be hired as musicians or performers. In other places, they were barred during certain hours. But laws could be violated as much by police officers themselves as by the girls of the night. In Salt Lake City in 1891, police captain William B. Parker appeared drunk at Hattie Wilson's brothel one evening after midnight. He wanted to hear piano music, but because the only girl available did not know how to play, he left. A few minutes later he heard singing coming from the house, returned, and attempted to drag Hattie to jail. A male customer later testified that he tried to interfere and was struck by another officer. A third policeman, George Albright, testified that Parker was profane and played favorites among his employees, but the captain was acquitted for his actions. He was, however, released from duties under the pretext that there was no longer a need for a police captain. In another case, Salt Lake City councilmen who were supposed to be investigating the brothels were in fact making the rounds, drinking and dancing as they went. When they caught a Salt Lake policeman "stretched on a couch smoking a cigar," he quipped, "I plead guilty to the charge and will fine myself $25.00."[91]

Whether by legal or illegal means, fines and fees paid by the shady ladies filled city coffers. Hundreds of harlots deserve forgotten or long past due credit for their contributions to schools, churches, the poor, the homeless, children, injured and sick miners, and countless other people and causes. When it was finally decided that a church should be erected in Kingston, New Mexico, for example, madam Sadie Orchard and her friends passed a hat among the saloons and brothels. Gold nuggets, jewelry, and cash netted $1,500, an ample amount to build the house of worship.[92] Colorado City, Colorado, madam Laura Bell McDaniel gave her blind friend Dusty McCarty a job bartending.[93] Madam Lea Perry of Silver City, New Mexico, was remembered as a kind-hearted woman who helped those in need, purchasing coats for poor children and grubstaking miners.[94] Colorado's legendary Silver Heels risked her own life and became permanently pockmarked while helping during a smallpox epidemic.[95] In Jerome, Arizona, madam Lil Douglas and her girls bought presents for the local children at Christmastime.[96] The ladies of the row willingly shared their wealth, sometimes by law, sometimes by unwritten law, and sometimes by their own volition.

The geographic location of red light districts tended to follow a trend. They were usually to be found near the railroad tracks, the nearer the depot the better. Most districts were generally located within a block or so of the main thoroughfare, easily accessible by discreet alleys or passageways. In many cases, the houses of ill repute backed up to saloons or gambling houses located in the respectable part of the downtown area. Fancy parlor houses were more prevalent in the early years, before the ratio of men to women began to equalize. As more women arrived in the West, the need

FIGURE 7 ❧ *Neglect in the red light district. Although Madam Mary Gleim's former bordellos are well maintained on Front Street in Missoula, buildings directly across the street have suffered considerably, as illustrated in this photograph taken in 2006. From the author's collection.*

for parlor houses slowly diminished, and the number of single-girl cribs rose. In Albuquerque between 1891 and 1893, the number of parlor houses dwindled from seven to four. Cribs, which had been practically nonexistent in 1891, numbered up to ten by 1893. These small places generally measured twenty-four by fourteen feet and were built together like tiny rowhouses. The rooms were usually only big enough for a bed, stove, and dresser, but their designs varied.[97] From the outside by day, many red light districts may have appeared poor, rundown, and dirty. Once the sun set, however, they came alive with bright twinkling lights, gay music, plush furnishings, and the sounds of laughter. As the industry matured, many districts were located near ethnically diverse or lower-class neighborhoods as the general public dictated. Today, many of these places are identifiable as warehouse districts because once the prostitution industry was shut down, nobody wanted to be associated with the former houses of shame.

During the late 1800s and into the 1900s, bawdy houses employed advertising tactics in a variety of unique and interesting ways. Because prostitutes and madams were largely prohibited from advertising in newspapers, they had to resort to other means. Some of the less expensive forms of advertising included offering discount nights, hiring bands to parade the streets and solicit, driving new girls in a buggy around town, or conducting supposed "Virgin Auctions." Sometimes the girls would wear their fanciest dresses on the streets as a form of advertising. A common pitch was for the girls to sit, invitingly dressed, in second-story windows and call to prospects down below. In the cribs, usually located in the poorer section of the district, women were not beyond leaning in their doorways and inviting a passerby to "C'mon in, baby." A more drastic measure of advertising was "hat snatching." A girl would grab a man's hat from his head and escape into the brothel with it. The hapless male would then attempt to go inside and retrieve his hat without falling victim to the pleasures within. Larger cities published a directory of dance halls, gambling dens, and brothels that was easily obtainable if one knew who to ask. Elite parlor houses often requested letters of recommendation from satisfied customers, which they displayed for new prospects. Engraved invitations were occasionally sent to prospective clients for grand openings or special parties. Other times, madams took their employees on excursions to nearby mining camps. Under the guise of a "vacation," the girls could thus drum up new or temporary business.[98]

It was not uncommon for prostitutes to give out business cards with such information as their location, price, and special skills. One such card in Tombstone, Arizona, read, "Elderly gentlemen would do well to ask for Maxine. She is especially adept at coping with matters peculiar to advanced age and a general rundown condition."[99] Especially in Montana and Idaho, larger parlor houses were specially designed to allow soliciting from within. Each of the forty-three rooms at the Dumas brothel in Butte, Montana, featured a window in which the girl could sit to entice customers coming down the hall. At the Red Onion Saloon, which was built in Skagway, Alaska, in 1897, ten dolls representing the girls upstairs were kept on the back of the bar. When one of the soiled doves was engaged with a client, her doll was accordingly laid on its back. Each room upstairs included a copper tube that was utilized to send the money for each transaction down to the bar. When the bartender received the money, he would stand the corresponding doll upright again so customers knew the girl was available.[100]

Hazards of the Profession

By far, the most dreaded malady for any prostitute was disease. Gonorrhea, syphilis, and chlamydia ran rampant during the Victorian era. Catching any one of these dreaded diseases could mean the end of a girl's career, not to mention serious illness and death. A hospital report in Idaho City, Idaho, in 1865 stated that one out of every seven patients was suffering from venereal disease.[101] Such illnesses were typically treated or at least suppressed with urethral injections, irrigations, calomel, and mercurial ointments.[102] In 1874, it was estimated that one out of every 18.5 persons in the United States had syphilis.[103] In the Rocky Mountains, Dr. Robert Shikes asserted that upwards of half of all mining camp prostitutes had suffered from the illness.[104] These statistics show that many people did not know how to reduce the risk of venereal disease, although there were exceptions. Madam Laura Evens of Salida, Colorado, showed her employees how to check their clients for venereal disease prior to having sex. One customer recalled how a girl approached him and "seized my genital organ in one hand, wringing it in such a way as to determine whether or not I had gonorrhea. She did this particular operation with more knowledge and skill than she did anything else before or after."[105] There were many drugstore remedies for venereal disease, but in fact mercury had long been considered the most effective treatment for syphilis if the patient did not die from gangrene or lockjaw.[106] In the late nineteenth century, injections of arsenic or bismuth helped cure or at least treat the diseases. It was not until the invention of penicillin during the 1940s, however, that patients saw any real or lasting cure.[107]

Although prostitutes were often blamed for spreading such diseases, few studies were conducted on how many male customers spread it to their wives. Because the male clientele of any given brothel included married men, discretion upon an outbreak of venereal disease was important. Depending on the town, attitudes toward the discovery of such outbreaks could vary from a public outcry to a quiet spreading of the word. In September 1880, Minnie Bennett, a married thirty-seven-year-old woman, succumbed to syphilis in Fremont County, Colorado. Minnie was probably a housewife and very likely caught the disease from her husband.[108] In Prescott, Arizona, one doctor illustrated his sense of humor when, upon finding one of the denizens of a local brothel to be infected, he merely put a sign on the door reading "Closed for repairs."[109]

Another danger of being a prostitute was drug or alcohol addiction. There are many references to prostitutes and dance hall girls drinking only colored water or tea while on duty, but alcohol consumption was a part of daily life at any bordello. In 1880, Yavapai County, Arizona, prostitute B. Pennybacker died from drinking whiskey.[110] In 1886, in Ouray, Colorado, newspapers reported a drunken prostitute who was seen "reeling along the sidewalk, scattering school children—on their way from dinner to school— right and left, in her wild flight." At last, the girl fell and "wallowed all over the sidewalk" until someone helped her up.[111] The Coroner's Docket in Butte, Montana, reflects the 1896 death of prostitute Josie Davis, who accidentally killed herself by drinking nearly a pint of whiskey and Jamaican ginger at the Cottage Hotel.[112]

There is no doubt that prostitutes were indeed victims, even though some of them chose to be so. Society as a whole looked at them as wicked no matter what their contributions to any given community, event, or persons were. They were victimized by the double standards of a government that punished and fined them for their deeds while at the same time realizing a healthy profit from their work. Their clients were mostly users who satisfied their own needs in a time when women were chastised for feeling any form of passion. In the event of an incident, the female guilty parties were usually named outright in the local papers, but the men escaped persecution. Madams, landlords, pimps, and even husbands utilized these women at a profit for themselves. A prostitute could hope to make herself less of a victim only by working her way up in the profession or leaving it altogether, but even madams and former working girls were forever slaves to a society that bound them to a certain realm.

Abuse by landlords, madams, male consorts, and customers was unfortunately common in the underworld. A shining example is "Buckskin Frank" Leslie, who began his penchant for violence by shooting bartender Mike Killeen in Tombstone in 1880.[113] The subject of their dispute was Killeen's wife, May. One night Killeen heard that Leslie had taken May from a dance to the Cosmopolitan, a local brothel. The disheartened husband had threatened to kill both Leslie and May if she attended the dance. Sure enough, Killeen went to the hotel and found the couple sitting on the porch. During the ensuing pistol and fistfight among Killeen, Leslie, and another man named George Perine, Killeen was shot in the face and died. Leslie claimed self-defense and got off.[114] May married Leslie just a few days after her husband was interred at Boothill Cemetery.[115] In 1882, six months after being hired to work at the Oriental Saloon, Leslie killed William "Billy the Kid" Claiborne outside the front door.[116] Claiborne had in fact just recently escaped harm at the infamous gunfight at the O.K. Corral.[117] Leslie had apparently thrown Billy out of the bar earlier, and the young man was returning with his own gun to have it out with Leslie when the shooting occurred. Leslie was again acquitted when testimony showed that the shooting was in self-defense.[118]

May remained married to Leslie through 1887, but soon found him to be a real brute. Not only did he beat and choke his new wife, but he also got into the drunken habit of making her stand against a wall while he fired an outline of bullets around her. Also, May claimed, Leslie failed to provide for her and had "illicit relations" with Mrs. Birdie Woods in 1886. May successfully filed for divorce and was awarded $650.[119] Leslie next set his sights on a Bird Cage Theatre employee named Mollie Bradshaw, also known as "Mollie Williams" and "Blonde Mollie." Blonde Mollie, however, was living with E. L. Bradshaw, her common-law husband. The latter was not much better than Frank Leslie. When Bradshaw was found dead in an alley with a bullet through his head, Leslie was suspected but never arrested due to lack of evidence.[120] With Bradshaw out of the way, Frank Leslie took Mollie to his ranch in the Swisshelm Mountains. There followed a pattern by which the two of them would get drunk and fight every night. Leslie soon became jealous of ranch hand James "Six-shooter Jim" Neal. One day in 1889 Leslie spent the day fighting off and on with Mollie, slapping and knocking her to the ground.[121] When he found Mollie and Jim talking on the front porch, he blew up yet again.[122] This time he went into the house and brought out a pistol, "took deliberate aim at the woman and fired." He then turned on Neal and shot him in the chest.[123]

Having killed Mollie and thinking he had killed Neal, Leslie apparently left the ranch. But Neal had only suffered a bad wound. Neighbors helped bandage him up and hid him in a cave. Thus, the ranch hand lived to testify that Frank Leslie killed Mollie. Although Leslie originally pleaded not guilty, his lawyers convinced him to confess, and he was sentenced to life at the Territorial Prison in Yuma. While there, he managed to get a San Francisco newspaper to run an article about him that exonerated him from the shooting of Mollie Williams and made him look as if he were innocent. The story was picked up by a Mrs. Belle Stowell, a San Francisco

FIGURE 8 ❧ *Blonde Mollie, circa 1880s. A fallen woman of Tombstone, Mollie was perhaps seeking respectability when she hooked up with Frank Leslie. The unfortunate woman instead became Leslie's last victim of domestic violence. Courtesy of Ben T. Traywick, Tombstone, Arizona.*

divorcée who began corresponding with Leslie. Soon Belle was negotiating with Yuma prison officials, and in 1896 Leslie was pardoned. He and Belle Stowell married in December at Stockton, California. What became of them after that is unknown.[124]

Tombstone's criminal element eventually held no bounds for women of the underworld. In 1882, prostitute Mollie Kingsman was standing in front of her crib at Allen and Sixth streets when a Mexican man suddenly appeared and began dragging her by her head and hair. Pulling her into a nearby gulch, the man tried to stone her. When the rocks weren't large enough to kill Mollie, he bit her ear off instead. Mollie escaped and ran screaming back toward her house with the man in pursuit. Constable Frank Broad heard Mollie's screams and caught the culprit as he tried to escape. Mollie suffered a lifelong scar, and the paper noted that a portion of her ear was found in the street the morning after her assault. Another story is told of a madam in Tombstone whose unruly and drunken customer began pushing her girls around and throwing furniture. The madam ordered the man out, but he grabbed her, and the two fell to the floor. During the tussle, the man bit the madam on the backside. She pressed charges, and the fellow was arraigned in court to answer charges of assault. During her testimony, the madam thoroughly convinced the judge and jury that the man had indeed bit her. When the customer was called to testify, however, he marched over to the jury, opened his mouth and displayed an entirely toothless grin.[125]

Abuse by madams was another common malady. During the mid-1880s in Globe, Arizona, Justice of the Peace John Wentworth heard the case of a young prostitute who charged that her madam had hit her on the head with a water pitcher. The madam answered the charges and demanded a jury trial. She was found guilty and fined $100. Undaunted, the madam paid the fine on protest and swore revenge, "embarrassing all of the jurors before they could leave the courtroom and then hounding Wentworth for several weeks."[126]

A number of skirmishes also erupted among the girls. In 1907, Arizona prostitute Francisca Robles stabbed Ignacia Pina and Jose Garcia in a fit of jealousy. Francisca was under the impression that her lover, Ramon Moreno, was seeing Ignacia. Although Ignacia was living with Garcia, Francisca's temper flared when the two couples encountered each other near the alley. Francisca whipped out a seven-inch knife and stabbed Ignacia in the shoulder. Garcia received the worst wound with a stab to the lungs. When officers located Francisca and Moreno at the Porto Rico saloon, Francisca denied knowing anything about the incident. Moreno, however, piped up and offered to show officers where his lady fair had hidden the knife under the floor of the saloon. Francisca Robles's notoriety in the red light district as well as her long line of lovers and numerous frays with the police were no secret. Her trial was set for November, where she pled guilty and was sentenced to two years in the state pen at Yuma. She was released twenty months into her sentence and disappeared.[127]

Even customers were not immune to violence. In Wallace, Idaho, in 1893, Ella Tolson, a black prostitute, shot her lover. Howard Johnson, also black, was found nearly dead behind the Troy laundry near Fifth and Cedar. Johnson was taken to his room. When he was examined, it was found that five shots had been fired at him. Three of the shots had passed through his clothing, and one had hit him in the forearm, but one had entered his chest. Johnson recovered enough to name Ella as the culprit, from whom he had just confiscated a pistol the previous night. Ella was arrested at the house of R. H. Allen after she confessed to the shooting.[128] Violence sometimes entered an affair because of the local red light district. In 1889, the *Wallace Free Press* (Wallace, Idaho) reported on the death of gunman Charles Skeels at the hands of his wife in Spokane, Washington. Skeels had recently received a gunshot wound to the thigh in a Murray, Idaho, bawdy house. Upon hearing her injured husband had visited such a place, Mrs. Skeels shot him. "Counsel have brought out a pretty strong case of justifiable homicide for Mrs. Skeels," commented the newspaper. What the paper did not reveal for another week was that Mrs. Skeels was also known as "Broncho Liz," a notorious woman of Idaho's Silver Valley. Liz had given up the profession upon meeting Skeels, and initially was masquerading as a male farm laborer on his family ranch while plotting with him to desert his wife. A divorce was secured in 1888, and Skeels married Liz. All was well until Liz found out Skeels had slept with Frankie Howard, a variety actress in Murray. When summoned from Frankie's room, Skeels hit Liz, whereupon she shot him three times. She was acquitted.[129]

In April 1908, at Kofa, Arizona, a black prostitute called "Pinkie Dean" took a knife to miner Billy Hennessy in her apartment in the back of a local saloon. Little is known about Pinkie except that she had been educated in Kansas and had a sister, Mrs. Celia Williams, living in Shawnee, Oklahoma. Why she decided to slice up Billy Hennessy is unknown, but it was acknowledged that she was drunk at the time. Six "ugly, fearsome wounds—one of them exposing much of the man's intestines"—landed Pinkie in jail without bond. Hennessy recovered, and Pinkie was found guilty of attempted murder. She was sentenced to two and a half years in the state pen at Yuma beginning in October. During her incarceration, Pinkie spent five days in solitary confinement for fighting. She was also transferred to the newly built Florence Penitentiary, where she was released on October 9, 1910.[130]

Another malady to the profession was pregnancy, which not only put prostitutes out of work for a time, but could also be expensive, especially if they declined an abortion. Women long ago learned certain trade secrets for preventing pregnancy. Some methods, used as early as the late 1700s, included douching with water and vinegar, alcohol, salt, soda, or any number of other disinfectants. Saturating a sponge with such ingredients and inserting it into the vagina was another method. Diaphragms were fashioned from half of a hallowed-out lemon or orange or from beeswax.[131] By the 1840s, commercial birth control and abortion products were available to women. Madame Restell's Preventative Powders provided birth control, and Portuguese Female Pills caused stillbirths. Condoms were brought to America by the French, but were hard to obtain, and, besides, men generally did not favor using them.[132] According to a Colorado prostitute named LaVerne, however, men sometimes brought rubbers with them, or the girls provided them and insisted they be used.[133] Unfortunately for many women, commercial means of preventing pregnancy were held up considerably by the Comstock Law of 1873, which forbade interstate mailing of birth control literature or devices. Thus, women all over America had to come up with their own birth control concoctions.[134] Women of the West passed recipes among themselves for contraceptives made out of plants such as pennyroyal or Queen Anne's lace.[135] Although suppositories made from cocoa butter or Vaseline could offer some protection, douching was far more common. Warm or cold water mixed with alum, bicarbonate of soda, bichloride of mercury, borax, ceolin, diluted vinegar, Lysol, or potassium biartate were used, but douches could just as easily push sperm farther into the womb rather than washing it out. Diaphragms, also called "womb veils," were not available until 1880.[136] Opiates, a favorite drug of shady ladies, were found to disrupt or stop menstruation altogether and so made an even more handy, but equally dangerous form of birth control.[137]

Finding herself pregnant was often devastating to a soiled dove's career. Abortion was a common and dangerous alternative to pregnancy but was in fact employed more than contraception.[138] In America, a few white women might have been privy to Indian women's methods for abortion. Mixtures of cedar sprouts, Seneca snakeroot, juniper, or mugwort could be used.[139] More dangerous chemicals included cotton rust, ergot, iodine, oil of tansy, prussic acid, saffron, savin, and even strychnine. Some of these ingredients were even offered in professional patent medicines, and several of them could mean illness or death to the user.[140] And these remedies oftentimes failed to perform. Ergot, for instance, usually only resulted in cramps.[141] The services of professional abortionists could be procured, but were just as unsafe. Back-room abortions were generally performed by unskilled midwives and could have disastrous results.[142] When these methods failed, pregnancy was dealt with on a case-to-case basis. Most women dreaded the idea of hindering their work with a pregnancy. Those who did give birth raised their babies in the brothels, pawned them off on relatives or friends, or sent them away to school or orphanages if they lived.[143]

Census records are most revealing in identifying the children living in the bordellos of the West at various times, but even so it is difficult to pinpoint any exact numbers regarding children in brothels, largely because they were unnoticed, hidden, or ignored by the general public.[144] Children in brothels were more common in the lower-class houses. When Boulder, Colorado, madam Sue Fee died from her drug habits in 1877, she left behind a son guessed to be about four or five years old. The Denver census for 1880 lists three women, Ella Cree, Hellen McElhany, and Miss Doebler as having six children between them. Likewise, four-year-old Elizabeth Franklin was living with her mother, Mary Franklin, in 1900 at Colorado City, Colorado. In Trinidad, Colorado, Margarita Carillo had a three-and-a-half-year-old Italian boy living at her brothel. The census notes the boys' parents were deceased.[145]

Being raised in a brothel was not the easiest childhood. Mothers, especially those working in cribs or rented rooms, sometimes had no choice but to keep their babies in their rooms. During business hours, the child was kept quiet or sleeping as much as possible, sometimes with a dose of laudanum.[146] The children often had little contact with the outside world, relying on the confines of the brothel for entertainment, education, care, and feeding. Many prostitutes were illiterate, so their children tended to be illiterate as well because sending them to public schools was often out of the question. Without an education or chances for advancement outside of the bordellos in which they were raised, most of these children faced dim futures with limited career opportunities—unless they learned the brothel or bar-room trade. Daughters of prostitutes were especially susceptible to following in their mothers' footsteps. Mrs. Jane Ryan is one of many who began a family operation in Cripple Creek with her three daughters before

FIGURE 9 *Mrs. Jane Ryan and her prostitute daughters, Julia, Mona, and Annie, circa 1890s. Jane in fact appears to have run a respectable operation, considering her profession. Nevertheless, Annie was arrested in 1929 for shooting a former police officer. Courtesy of the Colorado Historical Society, Denver, F-51, 401.*

moving to Denver. The authorities and society in general frowned upon such actions, especially in situations involving preteenage girls.[147]

Another, much more ugly facet of the presence of children in brothels concerns the use of them as sexual slaves. Young girls, especially virgins, were enticing to certain men. Although houses of prostitution would sometimes stage fake "Virgin Auctions," a number of children—usually those kidnapped or sold into virtual slavery—were also offered at high prices for the pleasure of deflowering them. Such practices were present in England, but also in America in the early West. Men who purchased such girls did so to heighten their own pleasure. "Pain became an essential ingredient for pleasurable sex . . . and since the defloration of very young virgins can be excruciating, Victorians were obsessed with a 'defloration mania.' The screams of children became indispensable, shrill torture was the 'essence of delight' and many gentlemen would not silence a single note." Worse yet, such actions usually guaranteed the girls' official introduction into the prostitution industry as a career.[148]

Accurate numbers of the deaths of children, either as the offspring of prostitutes or as sex slaves, will never be known. Stillborn and aborted fetuses were often quietly disposed of or buried without record. In February 1877, Mary Kean, Mr. Thomas Wicks, and Mrs. Wicks were charged in Laramie, Wyoming, with failing to provide a proper burial for a fetus. The child was probably Mary's.[149] In Butte, Montana, coroner's records indicate an unusual number of deceased infants found in the prospect holes around town. Similarly, dead babies were often found just beyond the outskirts of the red light district. A dead infant female was once found in a vault in the back of a Meaderville, Montana, saloon.[150] In Leadville, Colorado, Stillborn Alley was so named for the number of dead infants found along the alley. Rescuing these poor children was often the goal of crusades led by the Women's Christian Temperance Union and even by police officers themselves.[151]

End of Career or Life

One prostitute put it pretty bluntly: "Death is the only retirement from prostitution."[152] Unfortunately, for the most part she was right. If prostitutes did not die at the hands of someone else or from disease, they tended to end their own lives. One such case was Fay Anderson, a Salida, Colorado, prostitute who killed herself by drinking an ounce of carbolic acid. She died in agony. Ettie Barker, once a favorite actress at the Theater Comique in Pueblo, Colorado, committed suicide by morphine in Denver in 1877. In 1900, Blanch Garland, employee of the Bon Ton Dance Hall in Cripple Creek, Colorado, committed suicide with two ounces of chloroform after a quarrel with her lover. Likewise, Nellie Rolfe was found dead of an apparent morphine overdose in her room at 377 Myers, Cripple Creek, in 1903.[153] In a most unusual circumstance, when prostitute Malvina Lopez of Tombstone, Arizona, decided to end her life, her companion, John Gibbons, decided to join her. The two were found dead in a closed room. Fumes from a pan of burning charcoal were sufficient to kill them.[154]

Another unusual story comes from Albuquerque, where in 1881 two soiled doves named Belle and Maud decided to do themselves in. Just a few weeks earlier, Belle had tried to overdose on laudanum, but succeeded only in making herself sick. Then, according to the *Albuquerque Morning Journal*, the girls were sharing a novel written by May Agnes Fleming, which apparently influenced their decision to commit mutual suicide. The two procured a fatal dose of "Tr. Opii," which they intended to share and were discussing their pending funeral when Maud's favorite customer came in. Maud immediately forgot the suicide pact and "set herself about entertaining her lover" while Belle drank her half of the vial. In fact, Maud expressed no concern even as her consort suggested calling a doctor. Maud "was satisfied that her friend wanted to die." Her lover, however, summoned a doctor anyway. Belle was revived and was expected to live.[155]

More often than not, prostitutes who chose suicide did so because of a man. Many others, however, did find a way out of the profession by marrying. Cockeyed Liz of Colorado once summed up how most women of the profession felt: "A parlor house is where the girls go to look for a husband and where the husbands go to look for a girl."[156] Furthermore, history records that in general prostitutes were regarded as decent prospects for marriage. "They made good wives," remembered one pioneer of Jerome, Arizona. "They had to try so much harder than those who had no brands to blot."[157] Likewise, Mattie Silks of Denver recalled that some of her girls married their clients and that most of them were satisfied with the union. "They understood men and how to treat them and they were faithful to their husbands. Mostly the men they married were ranchers. I remained friends with them, and afterwards with their husbands, and I got reports.

So I knew they were good wives."[158] Some girls, however, encountered the prospect of marriage with caution. When young Tim Kinerk talked of his dream farm to a hurdy-gurdy girl in Bozeman, Montana, she was quick to warn him against taking her there. "No, Tim," she said, "you would not want me when you get that farm."[159]

Given the trials and tribulations any budding relationship must endure, matrimonial unions were certainly complicated by the fact that one of the parties had been and might continue to be a prostitute. Even in the Victorian era, the average union spawned from a tavern or bordello was bound to be a soap opera of the highest drama. Court records from the time confirm that romance in the prostitution industry was a whirlwind of spurned affections, fits of jealousy, threats of suicide, and hazy incidents during which one or both parties were under the influence of alcohol or drugs. An abusive lover might find himself under arrest, only to have the object of his affection drop the charges once things cooled off. In Albuquerque, Judge Sullivan refused to file charges against "Dandy Pat" in July 1883 for breaking up his prostitute mistress's furniture. The woman, identified only as Maud, had already filed and subsequently dropped charges against Pat so many times that the judge simply grew sick of the whole affair. Ever determined, Maud simply procured the services of a different judge and had Pat arrested anyway.[160]

A month later, a well-known citizen of Albuquerque decided to scare his prostitute mistress by swallowing a vial of poison right in front of her. The frightened woman cried for help and sent for a doctor before throwing herself at her lover's feet, atoning for her mistakes, and promising to love him forever. Only then did the man admit that the "poison" he had swallowed was nothing more than powdered sugar.[161]

Women tried to leave the profession in other ways without success. The *Boulder County News* in Colorado reported in 1876 on a disgruntled soiled dove who wished to reform, but was being kept from doing so by lack of public sentiment and aid. The paper ended its commentary by encouraging the Christian ladies of the town to do the right thing.[162]

2

AMAZONS OF ARIZONA

BECAUSE ARIZONA DID NOT BECOME A STATE UNTIL 1912, ITS citizens enjoyed a fairly lawless lifestyle long after its western counterparts had been somewhat civilized by the government. Desert forts and mountain mining camps survived here as early as the 1850s, primarily after the Gadsden Purchase of 1853–54, which deeded part of Arizona south of the Gila River to the United States.[1] Thus, for many years pioneers enforced their own codes of law and ethics. Lawbreakers could easily escape to the cozy confines of Mexico to the south, New Mexico to the east, California to the west, and Utah to the north. In between those borders were empty land, vast canyons, and lonely trails that outlaws and prostitutes alike could traverse with little trouble from the law.

A prime example of the lawlessness in early Arizona was Canyon Diablo, located between present-day Flagstaff and Winslow and north of Two Guns. In its time, Canyon Diablo was labeled a "rip-snorting, hell-roaring gun town." The place was first named by one Lieutenant Whipple in 1853.[2] By 1880, a town had sprung up when the railroad was constructed through the area and across the canyon. The nearest law enforcement was at Flagstaff, and the place subsequently became "meaner than Tombstone and Dodge City combined." The main drag was known as "Hell Street,"

39

where fourteen saloons, ten gambling halls, four houses of prostitution, and two dance halls operated twenty-four hours a day.[3]

Given the roughness of such a place, the women were likely pretty tough themselves. The favorite dance hall was the Cootchy-Klatch, and sex could be found for sale at Clabberfoot Annie's and B. S. Mary's. Annie and Mary kept up a healthy rivalry, often engaging in all-out catfights. On a typical fight night, the two would hurl epithets and insults at each other while the men egged them on. After several minutes of caterwauling, the two would lunge at each other, rolling in the dirt, one pummeling the other. At fight's end, both staggered away with bloody noses, black eyes, bite marks, and considerably less hair. Even at six feet tall, Mary had little advantage over Annie's hour-glass figure. On at least one occasion, Annie filled Mary's derriere with buckshot.[4]

When Canyon Diablo finally acquired a marshal, he was allegedly dead by the end of his first day, and five successors fared no better.[5] The old Canyon Diablo began fading in about 1882, and the coming of the Atlantic & Pacific Railroad changed the town completely. The buildings of Hell Street were disassembled and taken elsewhere.[6] By 1905, the community was becoming a ghost town.[7]

Some of Arizona's earliest prostitution also likely occurred in Tucson, originally an ancient Indian village that became part of Arizona with the Gadsden Purchase. Tucson was also capital of Arizona Territory between 1867 and 1877.[8] The 1880 census identifies nine "courtesans" in Tucson, although there were probably many more. The known prostitutes occupied three houses. In one house, Eva Clayton oversaw two other girls and employed a sixteen-year-old male Chinese servant. Monie Powers also employed two girls. Three women shared a house with three blacksmiths, an indication that they may have been romantically involved. Interestingly, four of the women were listed as married. But the real heyday of Tucson's red light district was the period from 1891 to 1917. The district was located along two blocks in Gay Alley, which was actually named for pioneer Mervin Gay. According to pioneer Roy Drachman, who grew up near Gay Alley, the street was "about twenty feet wide, with a narrow sidewalk on each side" and several adobe houses and apartments. The wealthier madams lived "on McCormack across from where Gay Alley ended." Drachman and his friends were forbidden from entering Gay Alley, but they did have to go by the entrance on the way to and from school. "We walked right past the home where the 'madame of madames' lived," said Drachman, "and often heard some rather colorful language."[9]

Upwards of 250 women worked in Gay Alley at its height, where no less than ten houses of ill repute flourished. The girls were subject to monthly fees and Friday health exams. Infected girls were required to leave the alley until they were cured.[10] Despite their confinement to Gay Alley, however, working girls intermingled with people from other walks of life. Eve Blanchard was one of the madams who each Christmas donated $500 to a local orphanage anonymously. She was aided by Mrs. Jennie Drachman, a respectable cigar merchant's wife. One madam, who may or may not have been Eve, had some sort of a monopoly over the district; new women were required to check in with her, and she collected their $5 monthly "civic license" fees.[11] Two of the saloons in Tucson were the Legal Tender and Congress Hall, which saw nightly shootings.[12] Congress Hall may have been associated with the Congress Hotel on East Broadway, which was later home to at least one prostitute. The woman had a small boy, whom the bell-boy would watch while his mother worked. Today the child's spirit allegedly continues to play in the elevator, and his mother's high heels can be distinctly heard crossing the lobby.[13]

In 1910, police officer Jesus Comacho, who grew up in a neighborhood close to Gay Alley, was assigned to patrol the red light district. Before long, Comacho was nicknamed "the Mayor of Meyer Street" after one of the thoroughfares in the district. Prostitution was finally outlawed in Tucson in 1917, however. The general public was fed up with Gay Alley being in the midst of their downtown. Many prostitutes from Gay Alley simply took up residence in other parts of the city, but others refused to budge. In answer, barriers made of red corrugated iron were constructed around the red light district during the 1920s.[14] This action apparently diminished the attraction of the red light district, and the girls lost enough business to merit leaving. Roy Drachman did remember, however, that a few of the girls stayed in town with their families or favorite paramours.[15]

During its heyday, Tucson was in hot competition with Prescott, which was also one of the earliest towns in Arizona and had one of the largest red light districts. The city served as the first capitol of Arizona Territory in 1864.[16] Prostitution was obviously present before 1871, when Madam Mollie Shepherd sold her brothel for an alleged $40,000. Mollie boarded a stagecoach with her cash, but between Wickenburg and Ehrenberg the

FIGURE 10 ᓚ *In Tucson, Arizona, and many other places, most prostitutes aspired to be adept at poker. This gal, circa 1928, appears to be having lots of fun doing card tricks. Courtesy of Exhibit Supply Company, Library of Congress, Washington, D.C.*

stage was robbed. The driver and five passengers were killed, but Mollie and an army paymaster named William Kruger survived. In giving their accounts of the incident, however, Mollie and Kruger's stories didn't match up. Further investigation resulted in the couple's being suspected of pulling off the robbery themselves. Lack of evidence set them free, and they went to California, where they received celebrity status because of newspaper reports about the robbery. All was well until Kruger claimed in an interview that Mollie had died of wounds she had received during the robbery (Mollie had initially shown only powder burns on her arm). When reporters could not find any record of Mollie's death, they returned to Kruger, only to find he had suddenly checked out of his hotel. Nothing was ever heard of the couple again, save for a report that a man named William Kruger was killed by a stray bullet in Phoenix in 1872.[17]

Mollie Shepherd's disappearance was quickly forgotten. By 1873, there were more than seven thousand mines around Prescott, creating numerous opportunities for saloon owners and prostitutes. The girls of the town were soon pulling shenanigans worthy of the newspaper's attentions. In February 875, the local newspaper published a tongue-in-cheek review of a scuffle, reporting that "Tommasita, the 'forsook,' shot at Julia Granee, the new love, and chawed one of her digits as she would the developed resources of a tomale [sic]. Julia carved her antagonist as you would a 'spitted' fowl, while the bone of contention viewed this national pastime with complacency and inwardly resolved to devote the remainder of his days to the survivor. Constable Leonard arrived at this juncture and brought the festivities to an abrupt termination." Tommasita pressed charges, and Julia had to appear before a grand jury. The outcome of the appearance was not reported, although it was noted that Julia was "the same who cut Pancha Burnett badly some time since."[18]

When the territorial capital moved to Tucson in the 1870s, the population of Prescott dipped for a time, but soon picked back up as more pioneers traveled to Arizona. Before long, the town's red light district was wilder than ever and had earned the nickname "Whoretown." By 1880, Whoretown was located along Leroux Street. Cribs measuring ten by twelve feet were also located along Goodwin and Granite streets. Women of the town were also free to service soldiers from nearby Fort Whipple. The men paid around a dollar a visit, and, according to the 1880 census, approximately seventeen girls were there to serve their needs.[19]

The most famous madam of Prescott was Lydia (Lidia, Lyda) Carlton. Born in 1860 in New York, Lydia ran her brothel between 1880 and 1900 but may have been in business as late as 1910. Her place was built like a hotel, with bedrooms upstairs and social rooms downstairs, and she charged about twice as much as other brothels. Lydia's girls were also referred to as "sporting girls" or "caterers." Her house served liquor, and customers were expected to purchase a drink while they chose their company for the evening. Once the client chose a girl, he was expected to buy her a drink, which was usually iced tea disguised as something stronger. Lydia was also noted for requiring her customers to be inspected for venereal disease. Anyone found to be unfit physically or financially was asked to leave. Her girls were also required to wash their customers after transacting with them, resulting in the local joke that "a Peter Pan was a wash basin in a brothel." There is little doubt that Lydia's parlor house was among the most popular in Prescott. An employee named Thelma was once noted as having turned in ninety-seven towels, one for each customer, to the local Chinese laundry.[20] Other notable women of Prescott were Dirtie Girtie and Laura Montgomery.[21]

By 1900, between fifty and one hundred prostitutes were still working in Prescott. Following some brief disputes over the law requiring bordellos to stay outside the limits of schoolhouses and public buildings, there was a curious lack of any arrests for prostitution.[22] Rather, the city apparently welcomed entertainers such as Grace "Little Egypt" Bartell, who first introduced her legendary belly dance at the World's Columbia Exposition in Chicago in 1893 and performed on Prescott's Whiskey Row in 1910.[23] For all intents and purposes, the industry was allowed to operate and flourish until the district, like the rest of Arizona, received orders from Fort Whipple and the U.S. military to close in 1917. As in many other towns, Prescott's prostitution industry made a much more discreet return after World War I. The former Golden Eagle Saloon, which had been turned into a rooming house called the Rex Arms, was said to be a clandestine bordello. Nothing of Prescott's red light district remains today.[24]

The antics at Prescott were nothing compared to those in Phoenix, whose origins date to 1868 after Jack Swilling of Wickenburg passed through and noticed the potential for ranching.[25] Phoenix was unusual in that it was founded primarily by and for Anglo-Americans. Segregation between whites, Mexicans, Chinese, and blacks was present from neighborhoods and lodges to churches and cemeteries.[26] This standard was also no doubt applied to the red light districts. Of 240 women listed in the 1880 census for Phoenix, however, none fit the typical makeup of a prostitute. There is absolutely no doubt that such women were present, so the census taker may purposely have omitted them. The city was considered a garden spot during the 1890s, but the growing metropolis soon bloomed into a large melting pot of people with a variety of backgrounds—and ethics. By 1899, Phoenix sported some of the largest and fanciest gambling halls in the United States, complete with plush carpets, elaborate wallpaper, chandeliers, and "costly paintings of women in all degrees of nudity." They had real women, too, "handsome young women in gorgeous and décolleté gowns, who sing ballads and snatches of opera for the entertainment of the throngs of men."[27]

Phoenix's vice element suffered the usual ups and downs, arrests intermingling with merriment for several decades. The red light district eventually came to be centralized between Jackson, Jefferson, First, and Third streets. Gambling and prostitution were still very much present in Phoenix throughout the 1920s and even later. Following the military closures of red light districts throughout the state in 1917, a number of illicit joints operated throughout town, especially in the southern portion. Although raids were frequently staged, the inhabitants merely paid a fine more often than they were closed down. City authorities enjoyed the extra income not only from such fines, but also from the money paid for police protection. In 1934, the chief of police vowed to put an end to the brothels that at the time operated primarily on Jefferson, Madison, and Jackson between Central and Fourth streets, but because prostitution was also flourishing in many other parts of the city, it was hard to control. If one house closed in one part of the city, another opened elsewhere. In addition, police officers were enjoying all sorts of kickbacks for letting such places run. A private investigator concluded in 1935 that the only way to get rid of the gambling halls and bordellos would be to reorganize the police department and root out the crooks.[28]

By 1940, the city was still making much money from fines. "The operators used to pay a flat $50," explained the *Arizona Republic*, "but lately the 'fines' have been changed to a basis of $25 for each 'resident' of their hotels, making some of the levies $150 per month. A city that a year ago said it would not tolerate prostitution collected in excess of $9,000 in 'fines' from these women in the last six months." Added to this discovery was the fact that just a week earlier, eighteen new cases of syphilis and eleven cases of gonorrhea had been reported to Phoenix health officials. Nevertheless, many citizens continued to view Phoenix's skin trade as a necessary evil that was better operated under control.[29]

The only solution seemed to be to tone down the red light district as much as possible. The district was "officially" closed in early 1942, but the brothels were allowed to reopen discreetly, minus their "glaring neon signs." All remained quiet until November, when Colonel Ross Hoyt, commander of Luke Field, publicly forbade his personnel from visiting Phoenix, citing fears of venereal disease. There were nine bordellos in town with fifty working girls, plus two bars out of which prostitutes worked and a "disorderly" massage parlor. Colonel Hoyt's actions at last had an effect on city officials, especially when it was revealed that the incidence of venereal disease at Luke Field had tripled in the previous four months. Accordingly, the city promised to round up its wayward women, inspect them for disease, and admit for treatment those who tested positive to a newly formed clinic for such illnesses. As usual, however, the promise never came to fruition, and local citizens began demanding the resignation of city administrators and law officials. The battle among good citizens, Phoenix's bad girls, Luke Field, and the corrupt city hall continued for several years.[30]

The battles over corruption in Phoenix served to divert attention away from the number of satellite towns between there and Flagstaff, at least in later years. In the early years, copper discoveries near the base of the Pinal Mountains resulted in several mining camps including Globe.[31] Soon after the town was founded in 1873, ladies of the night began drifting over the mountains from other places to take up business.[32] Globe's red light district was accessed via a bridge over Pinal Creek on Yuma Street and was located behind the businesses along Broad Street.[33] By 1882, Judge A. H. Hackney, publisher of the *Arizona Silver Belt* newspaper, was attacking Globe's many lawless citizens and the Five Points brothel, among other illicit businesses. By then, the number of saloons and the number of bordellos were about equal, with some of the taverns serving as a front for illegal activities in back or upstairs.[34] Ladies of the line included Big Bertha, the Hobo Queen, Jennie Scott, Jew Rose, and Texas Jenny.[35] Entertainment at the St. Elmo Saloon included female acrobats and singers who doubled as prostitutes between their acts.[36]

During the 1890s, County Surveyor Alex Pendleton became known for his stand against madam Jennie Scott. In 1891, Jennie was arrested for "offenses against good morals." Surprisingly, she was found not guilty by a jury of twelve men. A few months later, however, Jennie was arrested again for firing a pistol in the streets. This time she was fined $50. Shortly afterward, one of Jennie's brothels burned. In the ruins were the charred remains of Bertie Lee, a black prostitute employed by Jennie. An investigation revealed that another black prostitute, Alena Jasper, had thrown a kerosene lamp at Bertie, resulting in the subsequent fire and her death. Amazingly, the jury found Alena not guilty of murder after hearing testimony that Bertie Lee had been "a cantankerous and ill-tempered person." Bertie's death, however, further marred Jennie Scott's reputation in the eyes of Alex Pendleton, who ultimately convinced the county board of supervisors to pass a resolution ordering that "no house of prostitution shall operate within the boundary of Globe Township."[37]

Before the law could take effect, however, the territorial legislature passed a different law decreeing that houses of ill fame could not operate within 400 yards of a courthouse or public building or within 250 yards of a school. As a result, prostitution remained technically legal in Globe.[38] In answer, Globe officials, probably led by Pendleton, chose to build the new Central School in close proximity to Jennie's place.[39] When the school was completed, Pendleton himself measured off the distance between the school and Jennie's. To his disappointment, the boundary rule fell within three feet of the front parlor. Jennie was accordingly told to conduct her business in her back room, which she was probably already doing anyway. Jennie had had enough, however. Instead of adhering to the new rule, she closed her brothel altogether and erected some new cribs farther down the street, safely out of range of any public buildings. In 1917, when soldiers were being stationed at Globe during World War I and prostitution was outlawed, Jennie Scott closed her doors. She declined to reopen after the war.[40] Maps as late as 1929 do show six adobe and fourteen frame bordellos in the red light district, and some historians maintain that prostitution was alive and well in Globe until the 1960s.[41] Today, only some crumbling adobe ruins remain at the site. Since 1873, Globe had dealt with soldiers from Fort Grant, located forty miles south. The fort was meant to be an improvement over the old Fort Grant, which was plagued by Apache attacks and malaria. Conditions at the new Fort Grant were better, save for two notorious brothels masquerading on the outskirts of the post. Unregulated, the houses were often the culprits when venereal disease broke out at the post.[42]

If Globe and Fort Grant did not match Phoenix in the size and notoriety of its red light district, Flagstaff did. When the Atlantic & Pacific Railroad announced it would be cutting through a flat area below the San Francisco Peaks in 1876, enterprising pioneers lost little time in scurrying to accommodate railroad workers. Old Town, as it was later called, soon sprang up on the southeastern slope of Observatory Hill with supplies and entertainment. The numerous business houses included twenty-one saloons along the rough main street. There was also at least also one "dance house in which the proprietor has a large platform erected which he has furnished with several pistols and guns. When a valiant gets a little troublesome he picks him off at a single shot and that is the end of the creature." Most, however, seemed to welcome such businesses to town. When a dance hall was established in September 1881, the *Prescott Miner* rejoiced, "Here is another revenue of $100 per month for the county."[43]

Indeed, Flagstaff's soiled doves appear to have had free reign for well more than a decade. In 1893, their cheekiness was illustrated by a newspaper article wherein each of three prostitutes was fined $16.50 for "keeping a disorderly house." But the girls "refused to pay their fine, preferring to spend sixteen days in the county jail where, they said, they could have a 'good time.'"[44] When the city was incorporated a year later, new ordinances dealt with garbage removal, stray animals, disorderly noises and fights—but not with the prostitution industry, which was merely required to pay the high fee of $15 per month for a business license. The red light ladies of Flagstaff initially refused to pay the high "tax" and actually threatened to leave town, a proposal that did not go over well with a large portion of the male population. Accordingly, the city council compared the fee to that levied in other towns across the territory and lowered it to $5 per brothel. The girls stayed.[45]

The victory of Flagstaff's fallen sisters was short-lived. The attention they drew to themselves enticed the city council to better regulate their behavior. In February 1895, Flagstaff's tenth ordinance decreed that women "would no longer be allowed to flaunt themselves and their cigarettes in the streets, and they must not enter a saloon at any time of the day or night." Women could, however, use a saloon or gambling hall as a means to pass through on their way to eat in a restaurant, so long as they kept moving and did not drink anything, alcoholic or otherwise, as they went. Furthermore, prostitutes were instructed to keep their doors closed while doing business and were not allowed to accompany males anywhere in public. Flagstaff's new ordinance was put to the test a mere five months later when singers Agnes Nelson and Bella Raymond were arrested for performing in a saloon. The women's attorney argued that the girls had a right to sing wherever they wished so long as they behaved. The court initially ruled against the women, and an appeal was filed. Bella left town, but Agnes was still in Flagstaff when it was decided to bend the ordinance for performers who paid the monthly tax.[46]

Agnes Nelson likely did leave town about a year later when reformists urged the city council to up the monthly tax, which by this time was $10, to a whopping $55. Two years later the reformists succeeded in enticing the city council to demand $500 per month in advance for each female employed by a saloon. Although the new fee discouraged women from working in saloons, it did little to quell the soiled doves of Flagstaff. Another tactic used to thin the prostitution population in 1900 was to ban working girls from the new "fire district," an area designated as more flammable than the rest of the town. As a result, the girls of the red light district dispersed themselves throughout town, making them even harder to track. In 1901, being a prostitute was declared a misdemeanor, which would result in fines or jail time or both. When Thomas Pollock was elected mayor later that year, he designated an official red light district south of the railroad tracks on San Francisco Street.[47]

Sanborn Fire Insurance maps for 1901 through 1904 identify only six houses of prostitution along San Francisco Street and Cottage Avenue. The largest was at 29–30 San Francisco, but other bordellos appear to have been big enough for only one or two girls.[48] The district grew larger in 1908 with the mayoral election of Benjamin Doney, who lifted the hefty laws imposed on the bawdy houses, saloons, and gambling dens and expanded the red light district to a ten-block area. The fee for a business license for a bordello was in fact lowered even as respectable businesses were required to pay more. Doney's actions were appalling to state legislators and reformists, and by 1910 he was out. Flagstaff's red light district was shrunk back to the size it had been in 1901, and liquor licenses were banned south of the tracks. When the district ignored those laws aimed at them, the city council discontinued issuing business licenses in 1913 and outlawed prostitution altogether in 1915.[49] But the girls simply continued operating out of the Hotel Paso Del Norte at South San Francisco and Benton Avenue, as well as at two nearby dance halls and behind several saloons along San Francisco Street.[50]

This time, the ladies' plans backfired with the tragic and gory murder of Annie Marie "Dutch May" Sutter-Peters and her husband, Fred Prescott. Born in 1886, May was thought to have been formerly married to one Harry Peters.[51] She had also been a part of Flagstaff's red light district for some time and owned three brothels. Only recently, she had married Prescott while on a trip to Kansas City to see her family, who knew nothing of her profession. May also saw a unique peep show there that she decided to duplicate in Flagstaff. Upon returning home, she created a makeshift stage in one of her houses, and "Dutch May's Shimmy Shakers" were ready for their first performance. In it, three girls identified as Ethel, Rose, and Irene appeared on stage wearing nothing but ankle-length, loosely fitting muslin dresses. The girls would dance seductively for several minutes, pulling the muslin tightly over various parts of their anatomy and suggestively lifting the dresses as high as their knees. As customers threw coins onto the stage, the girls would ultimately strip altogether. Then May would step up on stage and auction the girls off one by one. After the auction, three more girls would appear on stage, and so on. By rotating her girls, May could keep the show going all night long.[52]

The entertainment didn't stop there. At the door, Prescott would entice the big spenders to come back at 2:00 A.M. for a special show that cost only $10. At the appointed time, the men would show up, sleepy and drunk but anxious to see what was in store. This time, in a carefully choreographed act, one of May's girls would come shrieking into the room stark naked with other girls chasing her and pretending to beat her with whips. As the pretend melee heightened among the girls, one of them would be forced to perform sexual acts, after which May would auction them off all over again. The highest bidder got to take the whip for an additional $10; May's girls knew to submit to services before the customer could use it.[53]

Although Dutch May thus put on what was considered the lewdest of shows, she relaxed in the relative comfort that few, if any, men would admit to witnessing such an act, let alone talk about it anywhere except among themselves. Her only real trouble was a man named Arley Downs, who had enticed one of the girls, Ethel, to move in with him. Ethel had already snuck out once to dance in the Shimmy Shaker show. When May went to the house to ask Ethel to participate again, however, Downs allegedly slapped her and made her leave. Ethel still managed to perform more shows, even while Downs thundered around and even accosted Fred Prescott in the street.[54]

Then in August 1916, some of May's friends proposed having a party in the woods. Five local businessmen met up with May and her girls, and the party was on. After several libations, it was decided to record the occasion, and a photographer was sent for. Two known photographs were made: one of the group with their clothes on, and another with the girls wearing nothing. When the partygoers sobered up, one of them found the photographer and destroyed the glass negatives—but not before the shutterbug managed to make several prints and distribute them among friends. The news infuriated the businessmen involved, as well as Arley Downs and others. Some of them even tried to get the marshal to run May and Prescott out of town, but the attempt was futile.[55] Thus, the insulted parties apparently took care of business their own way. On Wednesday, August 30, Everett Hanna, who was building a house for May, went to the home where she was living and knocked on the door. Hanna smelled a "peculiar" odor and notified coroner Judge Harrington that something was amiss at the Prescott household.[56]

The scene inside the house was chilling. May and Prescott lay in a bed that had been set on fire. Prescott's throat had been cut from ear to ear, and he had been shot through the head. He also had several deep cuts in his back. May's throat was also cut, and she, too, had been shot in the head, twice. Her dog had also been shot, and a canary was dead in its cage. Bullet holes scarred the ceiling, and the room was splattered with blood. In Prescott's hand was a loaded six-shooter with one bullet fired. On the dresser was a blood-smeared note written in his hand, reading, "To the public: May and I quarrel [sic] over a P.I. [private investigator?] that always came here and tried to break up our home. She attacked me with a razor which is around here somewhere. I shot her then myself. Notify Mrs. ___-___ Prescott, 325 Garfield Ave. K.C., Mrs. C. M. Prescott, Santa Barbara, Cal." The writing was smooth and perfectly formed, illustrating that Prescott was relatively calm when he wrote the note. May's trunk had been opened and contained additional letters that showed no sign of trouble.[57] But more blood was found splattered on clothing inside the trunk, and there was a second gun, also covered with blood. Valuable jewelry in the trunk remained undisturbed.[58] In another part of the house was a bloody razor, and it appeared as though someone had tried to clean up some of the blood with water. A second razor was found in the yard along with several bullet shells. Blood was smeared on the doorknob leading into the house and on the screen door.[59] In a corrugated iron shack in back of the house, investigators also found "blood clots" on the floor and a bloody handprint on the side of the door.[60]

Police began looking at the last-known whereabouts of May and Prescott. The latter had returned from out of town on August 26. May had last been seen August 28 by two fellow prostitutes who spoke with her.[61] Neighbors testified they heard the couple arguing the afternoon and night before the murders, but amazingly nobody had heard any shots being fired.[62] Witnesses in the case included Everett Hanna, Sheriff W. G. Dickinson, Dr. T. P. Manning, and several other men. Prostitute witnesses included Babe Park, Bessie Jackson, Ethel Simmons, Erma Williams, Fay Dalton, Irene Smith (a.k.a. Mrs. Starkey), Mildred Williams, and Rosie Harkabus. Arley Downs was questioned, as were Harry Peters and another man, but all were released.[63] There was much speculation that anger over the tainted photographs had inspired someone to murder May and Prescott, but there was no proof.[64] Following an investigation by a coroner's jury, it was concluded that May and her husband were killed by "parties unknown." The killer was never caught. Neither Prescott's sister nor his parents or ex-wife went to the double funeral, nor did May's father in Portland. The couple was buried in the city cemetery, and the case was never solved.[65]

Dutch May's death may have been the end of the red light district south of the tracks in Flagstaff, but the girls moved on. During the 1940s, a handful of prostitutes worked out of the Hotel Monte Vista on North San Francisco Street. Two such women were supposedly murdered on the third floor of the hotel during the 1940s and their bodies thrown out of the window. Today, their ghosts reputedly walk the third-floor hallways.[66] Former police officer Wally Smith, who worked at Flagstaff in the early 1960s, recalled one 2:00 A.M. call to a domestic situation. The man of the house had just discovered that his wife and her girlfriend were actually turning tricks during their weekend excursions to Las Vegas. "A lot of those kinds of girls from Flagstaff did that," Smith commented, adding,

FIGURE 11 ⚜ *As of 2007, much remains of the 100 block of San Francisco Street in Flagstaff, Arizona, where brothels and saloons once flourished. Stand-alone bawdy houses such as Dutch May's, however, no longer stand. From the author's collection.*

"They may not have gambled much, but they sure did come home big winners." Smith also remembered another call, this one to a hotel where officers found a woman beating mercilessly on a hotel room door. Inside the room was the woman's husband and a local lady of the evening. "The gal was trying to escape out the bathroom window," Smith said of the young prostitute. "Her bottom got stuck and the officers had to come around to the other side and pull her out."[67] Even as late as the 1970s, local rumor was that Flagstaff's shady ladies frequented the lounge at the Little America Hotel, sitting close to the dance floor and waiting for men to ask them to dance so they could be propositioned.[68]

South of Flagstaff, the high-mountain town of Jerome established its own notorious reputation. Settled in 1876, Jerome quite literally hangs off Cleopatra Hill on Mingus Mountain above the Verde Valley. It wasn't until 1883 that Jerome was so named, but ladies of the night invaded the camp even before the first buildings were erected.[69] Like everyone else, the women first lived in tents. Those who had no tent could still conduct business on blankets behind trees, earning them the name "blanket whores." As the town grew, the ladies set up shop on Jerome Avenue. By the 1890s,

Jerome's red light ladies were operating smack dab in the middle of the business district. Respectable citizens were soon subjected to more than one spectacle. Old-timers remembered a night when a young prostitute wearing a French gown and carrying a green umbrella strolled up Main Street. A drunken burro, whom miners were feeding beer in a bar across the street, wandered up to the woman and attempted to take a bite of the umbrella. The resulting tug of war caused quite a stir as amused miners poured out of nearby saloons to watch. C. A. Brown, who lived in Jerome from 1896 to 1900, remembered a Fourth of July celebration during which a madam paraded her twelve girls around town in an elegantly outfitted carriage. The girls were dressed beautifully and were shaking hands with some of the men. One girl, Trudy, pressed a bonbon into Brown's hand. "When I opened the bonbon," Brown later recalled, "there was a little note, 'I hope you come to see me.'"[70]

Jerome's wanton women were also subject to violence, as illustrated by the 1894 murder of a woman known only as "Bohemia" by her lover.[71] When Jerome suffered the first of several fires in 1897, the cause was a woman at Japanese Charlie's who threw a kerosene lamp at a man. "It missed the mark," recalled eyewitness Oscar Wager, who was drinking next door at Connor's Saloon, "but broke against the wall and almost instantly the interior of the flimsy building was a mass of flames." Everyone escaped save for one prostitute who "was lying dead drunk in a back room. My partner went in and carried her out and dumped her in the snow." A second prostitute, named Charlotte, was trapped in her room above Alex Cordiner's Peerless Saloon and was rescued by one Dan Slaughter.[72]

Among Jerome's fanciest bawdy houses was the Fashion, which by 1898 was being called "the Leading Sporting House in all of Northern Arizona." Amenities included eleven different games of chance, live music performed from a stage in the rear, and a German beer and lunch hall with separate dining facilities for respectable folks. The plush décor was updated often and included new chandeliers.[73] But the Fashion had barely left its mark before Jerome burned again in 1898.[74] This time the culprit was not a prostitute, but Jennie Bauters's (or Banters's) bordello was among the casualties. Jennie immediately rebuilt a two-story affair on Main Street. In fact, "Belgian Jennie," as she was sometimes known, lost her brothel to fire on three different occasions and rebuilt each time. In the 1897 fire, Jennie's losses amounted to $5,500, more than for anyone else in town.[75] During

FIGURE 12 *A couple of Jerome beauties drum up business from their bordello, circa 1920s or 1930s. Ladies of the evening aspired to look, smell, and feel their best at all times. Courtesy of the Jerome Historical Society, Jerome, Arizona.*

another fire, Jennie actually offered the firemen free passes if they would save her place, and it was said that "the men rose to superhuman efforts that day."[76]

Between fires, Jennie bought and sold other brothels. One of them was simply known as "Jennie's Place," possibly the same place Jennie built after the fire of 1898. The two-story building had a glass front door covered with lace. Inside was a large reception area with another draped doorway leading to a long hallway with rooms on either side.[77] Jennie's Place was also the first main-street business to have a sidewalk in front of it. Jennie's houses of pleasure offered exceptional service. C. A. Brown reported that customers were greeted "by a trim maid in spangled short skirt and a revealing bodice. Net stockings, whose tops were hidden up underneath her waistline. She would take the customer's hat and coat and brush the snow or dust off with a little whisk broom bearing around its handle a big bow of vivid pink ribbon. The ribbon matched the one in her hair." The customer was then led to a reception room and asked which of Jennie's girls he wished to see. If the girl was available, the man was led through a door covered with a velvet drape and down a hallway to the proper room. If she was otherwise engaged, the gentleman was asked to wait in one of a handful of easy chairs, discreetly concealed by a folding screen. Jennie would sometimes come and visit with the client, chatting or buying him another drink while he waited.[78]

FIGURE 13 ❧ *Jennie Banters and her girls pose on the balcony of her parlor house in the 1890s. Jennie did quite well in Jerome before meeting a cruel end at the hands of her drug-addicted lover. Courtesy of the Jerome Historical Society, Jerome, Arizona.*

It was not always so quiet at Jennie's; one time her house made the papers after a client knifed one of her girls to death and committed suicide.[79] In time, though, Jennie became extremely wealthy and was at one point among the richest women in Arizona. Sometime after 1899, she moved to Goldroad, south of Kingman. In 1905, she was murdered by her opium-addicted boyfriend, Clement Leigh. The two had recently broken up, but a drunken Leigh announced his intentions to get some money from Jennie early one morning. He kicked in the door and shot her as she ran from the room. The helpless woman managed to get to the street, begging Leigh to spare her life as he chased her. He shot Jennie twice more and left her lying in the street while he went to reload his gun. According to the *Mohave County Miner*, he then returned to where she lay. "Observing that she was not yet dead he moved her head so that he could get a better shot, and then deliberately fired the pistol." Leigh's antics were not over. He next shot himself in the chest, lay down next to Jennie's lifeless body, placed his hat over his face, and was apparently waiting to die. A crowd gathered around the pair before Constable Fred Brown appeared and took Leigh to jail. Leigh was hanged for the murder in 1907.[80] Jennie's entire estate was willed to her son, twenty-three year old Philippe Bauters of Chicago.[81]

Another elite bordello in Jerome was the O.K. Rooming House. Whereas most girls charged a dollar or two, the price at the O.K. was $5. Anne Johnson, also known as the "Cuban Queen," was another bordello owner. Described as tall and dark, Anne was known to employ women with features similar to hers, including mulatto women. She also offered gambling at her place, whereas other brothels did not.[82] Many of Anne's girls married, and Anne herself married a local mine foreman.[83] Other Jerome women, including one known only as Lily, worked out of cribs. As an independent crib woman, Lily was respected more than common brothel girls. She also charged less than the fancier parlor houses and was remembered as "a very lonely woman who would go to the last picture show of the evening."[84] Like Lily, two other women of the time were remembered only by their first name: Rose and Madam Pearl. Pearl was remembered as a kind and generous woman, as well as a heavy smoker. When she died young, her body lay in state for twenty-four hours so her admires could come say good-bye.[85]

Jerome burned a third time in 1899.[86] The town was soon back on its feet yet again, however, with the usual assortment of fights and brawls occurring in the red light district. In around 1900, one resident recalled, a young man of the town entered a raffle for a gold watch. At two different times, he told two different girls from the Fashion that if he won the watch, he would give it to them. Quite by some luck, the boy did win the prize, at which time the two girls engaged in a free-for-all over who would get it. The crowd stood cheering them on for some time before finally breaking up the fight, but the man and his prize watch had long disappeared from the scene. Most unfortunately, this amusing incident was countered by more serious crimes. By 1903, newspapers as far away as New York were calling Jerome the wickedest city in the West, and it was no wonder.[87] In 1904, L. W. Watson slashed prostitute Fannie Howard's face. Fannie testified that she and Watson had made a circuit among the local bars before retiring to her place. The couple had been asleep about four hours when Fannie awoke to find one of Watson's hands inexplicably on her throat, the other holding a knife. Watson got several severe slashes in before Fannie succeeded in kicking him to the floor. He then sat down in a chair, and when Fannie pleaded with him to call a doctor, he demanded his $5 back and cut her again. Watson finally left, and Fannie summoned help, but severe cuts through her cheeks and across her throat required ninety-one stitches. Watson was arrested at the Montana Hotel, and it was thought he was guilty of committing similar crimes against prostitutes in Tucson, Phoenix, and Los Angeles.[88]

Following this and other crimes, Mayor George Hull outlawed women from saloons in 1905 and demanded that all prostitutes leave town. The new law was enforced by Marshal Fred Hawkins, who duly reported that Hull's wishes had been carried out. In fact, though, the red light district was still in full swing from all appearances. Hawkins may simply have asked the ladies of the row to be more discreet, and his actions became tradition among Jerome's law officers. When the district was ordered closed, Hawkins or his successors would simply talk to the local madams, who agreed to close their doors for a day or two before quietly reopening.[89] Mayor Hull was not to be outdone, though. In January 1906, he outlawed gambling, but this decree had the same results as his efforts to close the red light district. Besides, the gambling houses were backed by the county attorney, and gambling remained legal.[90] The ladies of the row, numbering about forty and incensed that they were being discriminated against but the gambling halls were not, took a stand against the city council. A

FIGURE 14 ❧ *The Cuban Queen brothel. This building is one of only two or three still standing, although it was abandoned and deteriorating as of 2008. Courtesy of the Jerome Historical Society, Jerome, Arizona.*

compromise was reached. If the ladies would be subject to bimonthly health exams, pay their fines and fees, and restrict themselves to an official red light district, they could stay. This they did, establishing their own neighborhood on none other than Hull Avenue.[91]

Jerome's skin trade was still active in 1913.[92] The brothels were restricted to Hull Avenue, and an alleyway between there and Main Street was dubbed "Husband's Alley."[93] The alleyway was accessible via a false store front on the west end of the Connor Hotel. The rooms at the Connor proved too expensive for Jerome's ladies of the night to utilize, but it was commonly known that men playing cards or billiards could access Husband's Alley from the hotel.[94] When the War Department closed the district in 1917, the girls of the row were given until March 1 to clear out.[95] To that effect, the city hired John Crowley to be the police chief and run Jerome's prostitutes out of town. Crowley's job wasn't easy. At the Fourth of July parade, he noticed three women of the night, each wearing a beautiful French gown, boldly marching in the parade. When Crowley approached the women, one of them escaped, but the remaining two girls took him by the arms and continued marching. Not wishing to make a scene, he compliantly marched along too. In the following months, however, Crowley continued ousting the bad girls of Jerome, and some forty women eventually packed their bags and left town.[96]

Following World War I, prostitution infiltrated Jerome once more. In 1922, the city ordered a cleanup campaign, but only two women were arrested. In the meantime, the city hired nurse Mattie Leyel to assist the health officer with exams. Leyel displayed a fondness for some of the girls in later years. "There was one that was a very pretty lady," she recalled. "She had a daughter that was around nine years old. She went into prostitution to keep the little girl in school." Leyel also remembered that the madams kept their own health standards. Once, when a man was checked into the hospital with venereal disease, one of the madams came to make sure he hadn't been to her place. Despite these efforts, the general public continued their tirade against lewd women. During the late 1920s, John Sullivan of the Sullivan Hotel (formerly Jennie Bauters's bordello) complained to the city that prostitutes were continuing to operate on Hull Avenue behind his building.[97] But the United Verde Mine was still working, and for a short time Jerome was the fifth-largest city in Arizona.[98] Jerome's shady ladies were reaping in the profits of this boom, but they received a scare in July 1931 with the murder of a young woman named Juanita Marie "Sammie" Dean.

Sammie had previously worked in Texas and Colorado. She also had a gambler husband named George, whose whereabouts were unknown. In the early evening, according to the *Verde Valley News* of July 10, Sammie was found strangled in her home. She had last been seen by a neighbor early in the morning on the day of her death, but some friends who came by at noon said she didn't answer her door. At six o'clock that evening, one Leo Portillo went to Sammie's place and found her. Her front doors were locked, but the back doors stood open. Sammie's purse was empty, and a gun was missing, but her jewelry was in place. Police found evidence of a struggle,

FIGURE 15 ❧ *Juanita Marie "Sammie" Dean, circa 1920s. Sammie was
a well-known prostitute in Jerome until her murder in 1931. In a rare act
for a prostitute's family, her sister came to town and claimed the body.
Courtesy of the Jerome Historical Society, Jerome, Arizona.*

numerous fingerprints around the room, and bruises on Sammie's right
arm, left shoulder, and neck. They had few suspects, although some interesting information was found in some letters Sammie had written to her
family back home. She claimed that the mayor's son wanted to marry her
and had vowed revenge when she refused his proposal. Whether he was
questioned is unknown. Sammie also had a boyfriend, "a hard miner and
fighter," who likewise does not appear to have been questioned. Sammie's
sister, who lived in Dallas, came to Jerome and took Sammie back to Texas
for burial.[99]

Prostitution continued thriving in Jerome during the 1930s, with Police Chief Tom Cantrell acquiescing to the presence of the shady ladies of Hull Avenue. In fact, it was common to see prostitutes dressed in their finest and dining at the Connor Hotel or the New York Café. The Wigwam, located on Hull Avenue next to the cribs, rented rooms and sold liquor as well.[100] During those years, Dr. Frank Brown tended to the ladies of the row. His patients paid $3 a week to be tested for venereal disease, and problems occurred only when a stranger carrying it came to town. Brown remembered Lil Douglas, who employed three or four girls, most of whom would be in town only a couple of months before moving on.[101] Despite running a clean house, Lil and her girls were often subject to fines for loitering— possibly because Lil liked to drum up business by parading her girls past the bars on Main Street.[102] Lil did more than loiter, however. In time, local citizens gained much respect for her. On one occasion, Lil's daughter, who had no idea what her mother did for a living, came to visit. For the duration of the visit, Lil closed her place and masqueraded as a store clerk, and the townspeople kindly did not give her away.[103] Lil and her girls also enjoyed the rare luxury of dining with their law-abiding neighbors, and they were in the habit of buying presents for the local children at Christmastime. Lil operated in Jerome into the 1940s.[104] It was understood that any man looking for sexual favors had to go to Lil's; sex crimes were not tolerated.[105] People eventually began moving away, though, and Jerome evolved into an engaging tourist destination.

By far the most notorious town in Arizona was Tombstone, founded in 1878. Tombstone's male population initially respected women to a great degree. In 1879, John Ringo shot a man named Hancock for making "a disparaging remark about some women."[106] But the town's soiled doves were by this time already making a name for themselves as nuisances to the city, as evidenced by the 1880 arrest of a prostitute for stealing a man's revolver. She was fined $15, and when she couldn't pay, she was remanded to the city jail.[107] Despite such incidents, bar women were hard to find in those early days. Some saloon owners went so far as to advertise in Los Angeles newspapers in their desperation to find singers and hostesses. It was a good deal; women answering the ad received 20 percent of the money their clients spent.[108] In 1881, when Tombstone was the seat of Cochise County, city officials enacted the Code of City Ordinances. Several amendments were made as necessary, including limiting the red light district to certain parts of the

FIGURE 16 ❧ *Very little remained of Jerome's red light district in 2007; even much of Hull Avenue was devoid of the old houses of ill repute. The alley still contained remnants of the district's bawdy past, however. From the author's collection.*

city and declaring that "[i]t shall be unlawful for any lewd woman to appear upon the street except in decent costume, to sprawl about the doors of any bagnio, or to solicit prostitution by calling or requesting persons passing upon the streets to enter their houses or rooms, or to talk loudly or in any manner expose themselves indecently, or in any manner solicit prostitution within the city limits."[109]

Such declarations may have been prompted by Tombstone's respectable women, one of whom made her feelings known in the *Tombstone Epitaph* newspaper. "It seems from your issue of the 9th that the city fathers have extended in the demimonde the liberties of the city," the woman blasted. "Allen Street was virtually theirs, to such an extent that a respectable woman would hesitate to even cross it. But this was not enough. Hitherto, although it has been impossible to pass along the streets provided with sidewalks without our ears being stunned with a multitude of oaths 'at every turn.'" Soon afterward, the city began requiring that the girls purchase monthly licenses, as illustrated by a $4 payment made by Emma Parker in 1881.[110] Emma also ran a boardinghouse while plying her trade on the side, both in her own house and at the local bordellos.[111] Emma and a Mrs. McDonald were once brought into court for keeping houses of ill fame. Both pled not guilty. A few days later Emma went on a binge at the Occidental Saloon and was arrested for being drunk and disorderly, for using vulgar language, and for fighting.[112]

In December 1881, another Tombstone ordinance decreed that madams and lone prostitutes were to pay the city $10 per month, plus another $20 if they sold liquor. None of the ordinances outlawed prostitution, however, and the town permitted women to operate as long as they purchased a monthly license to do so. The process ran quite smoothly at first, with few complications, save for at least one complaint filed by prostitute Mattie Ervin, who stated that she had not started doing business until October 20, 1881, and thus refused to pay for any license dating before that. Early on, both sides of the law found numerous loopholes in the ordinances. When Police Chief Virgil Earp requested that the city council allow him to fire Officer Bronk for demanding police protection money from a prostitute called Miss Amanda, it was the madams who came to Bronk's rescue. Three bordello proprietresses signed a letter stating that Officer Bronk was "respected by the brutal class that impose upon us" and emphasizing that "[i]f we see fit to pay officers for extra duty it is our affair."[113]

By then, Tombstone was quite busy, the south side of Allen Street bustling with a variety of businesses. Women of the night were now prohibited from walking on that side of the street, but the north side of Allen Street was the locale of several saloons, dance halls, and gambling halls, including the Crystal Palace Saloon, the Oriental Saloon, and Ritchie's Dance Hall.[114] Soon, the north side of Allen Street was alternately known as "Rotten Row."[115] Tombstone had burned in June 1881 when a bartender along Rotten Row got too close to a whiskey barrel with a lit cigar in his mouth. The resulting inferno destroyed sixty saloons, restaurants, and other businesses.[116] Citizens were quick to rebuild and start over, but the men of Tombstone really needn't have worried about prosperity among their prostitutes. At least four women who made their way to Tombstone have become legends as the consorts of the famous Earp brothers and Doc Holliday, and therefore are linked to the historic shoot-out at the O.K. Corral: Big Nose Kate, Bessie Earp, Mattie Blaylock, and Josephine Marcus.

The Earp and Holliday affairs with prostitutes began in 1872 with Big Nose Kate. During her lifetime, Kate used several names, including

"Cummings," "Elder," "Fisher," "Holliday," "Horony," "Melvin," and "Kerris."[117] She was Mary Katharine Harony when she was born in 1850 in Budapest, Hungary.[118] Her family came to America in 1860 and was living in Davenport, Iowa, when her parents died in 1866.[119] The girl and her siblings were placed with a guardian, a farmer who made the children work hard. He also once tried to rape Kate, at which time she whacked him on the head with an ax handle and ran away. Stranded on the banks of the Mississippi River with no money, she stowed away on the steamship *Ulysses*, which was headed for St. Louis. Captain Burlington Fisher found her, heard her story, and promised her safe passage. During the journey, the two had intimate relations, but there appeared to be no love lost when Kate disembarked at St. Louis. Fisher in fact helped place Kate in the Ursuline Convent, which had been her original destination. Life in the convent was not what Kate had in mind, however, and she left after only a few days.[120]

Around this time, Kate adopted one or more aliases, including "Kate Fisher" and "Kate Elder"—possibly because she kept running away. She also picked up her infamous nickname, "Big Nose Kate."[121] Around 1869, she was working for St. Louis madam Blanc Tribolet. When Blanc was killed by a customer, Kate allegedly avenged her death by shooting the man and then left St. Louis.[122] She claimed to have married Silas Melvin in St. Louis in 1872 and possibly moved to Atlanta.[123] Most historians maintain that the newlyweds settled in Missouri, and Kate had a son. When both the child and her husband died, she returned to prostitution.[124] In time, her trademark sales pitch became, "I'll give two ups to your one down."[125] She apparently drifted to Fort Griffin, Texas, where she was destined to meet John Henry "Doc" Holliday.[126] Holliday was born just a year after Kate in Griffin, Georgia. His mother died of tuberculosis when he was fifteen, and in 1870, at age nineteen, he shot a man during an altercation over a watering hole. His father sent him to dental school in Pennsylvania.[127] Holliday graduated dental school but returned home with tuberculosis. His brother died of the disease, and doctors advised Holliday to move to Texas, which he did.[128] Thus, Doc Holliday met Big Nose Kate at Fort Griffin sometime around 1872.[129] Kate may have been working at an outpost, serving soldiers at the fort when she met Holliday. Although their relationship got off to a slow start, Kate was persistent and eventually became Holliday's only girl. He appreciated her self-sufficiency, her dark looks, and her spunk.[130]

FIGURE 17 ❧ *Although most historians have agreed that this undated photograph is of Big Nose Kate, controversy has risen over its authenticity over recent years. Judging by her features, this woman definitely fits the description of Kate. Courtesy of the Mazzulla Collection, Colorado Historical Society, Denver.*

Holliday also met Wyatt Earp at Fort Griffin, and a lifelong friendship was formed. Wyatt, born in 1848 in Illinois, was already a widower when he met Holliday.[131] In fact, it may have been because of Wyatt that Holliday met Kate. In later years, Kate claimed that Wyatt was one of her frequent customers until he "went back to [prostitute] Mattie Blaylock." Whether Kate made this statement regarding her time in Texas or later, when she was working for madam Bessie Earp in Dodge City, Kansas, is unclear.[132] Little is known about Mattie except that she was born Celia Ann Blaylock in Fairfax, Iowa or Wisconsin, between 1848 and 1850.[133] A number of researchers believe she ran away from home at age sixteen and made her way to Scott City, Kansas, where she first worked as a prostitute before moving to Dodge City. Speculation runs amuck as to when Mattie met Wyatt and when or if the two ever married.[134]

Equally puzzling is the story that one night Holliday got in a fight over a card game, stabbed a man to death, and was arrested. In the dark of night, Kate allegedly set fire to the hotel where he was incarcerated in and broke him out while authorities were occupied fighting the blaze.[135] What is known for sure is that when Wyatt went to Dodge City, Holliday and Kate went too. The couple registered at Deacon Cox's Boarding House as "Mr. and Mrs. J. H. Holliday," and Doc set up a dental practice. He mostly spent his time playing cards with Wyatt and another new friend, Bat Masterson, and began drinking a great deal. Kate would stay by Holliday's side during his coughing fits, but he began resenting her good health and often fought with her. He also voiced his disapproval of Kate's continuing to work as a prostitute, but she did it anyway. Kate countered with Holliday's confession that he had once been madly in love with his first cousin. One night after yet another drunken fight, and Holliday had gone back to the hotel room to sleep it off, Kate busted down the door with a Colt pistol in her hand. "You are a lousy son of a bitch!" she screamed, "I'm going to shoot you so full of holes you won't float in brine!" Kate fired the gun into the mattress, at which Holliday leaped up, grabbed the gun, and hit her in the head with it. The two apparently made up, for when they were seen together the next day, they "were holding hands and behaving like newlyweds."[136]

Also in Dodge City, or nearby, was Wyatt's brother James. The oldest of the Earp brothers had served in the Civil War and traveled the West before marrying prostitute Nellie Bartlett Ketchum, better known as "Bessie," in Kansas or Illinois in 1873.[137] By 1874, Big Nose Kate was working at Bessie's parlor house.[138] In June of that year, Bessie "Errp" (as spelled in the arrest report) was arrested, along with one Sallie "Erp," for running a bawdy house. Who Sallie was is unknown.[139] Kate also continued her frequent battles with Holliday. Wyatt witnessed several fights between the two and frequently advised his friend to "belt her one."[140] In truth, however, many historians surmise that Holliday loved Kate so much he even enjoyed fighting with her. But it was probably a relief to Kate when she and Holliday temporarily left Earp's company. In 1876, according to Kate, she and Holliday married in Valdosta, Georgia. The newlyweds have also been documented as visiting or temporarily living in Deadwood, South Dakota; Fort Griffin, Texas; Trinidad, Colorado; and Las Vegas, New Mexico.[141] Authors JoAnn Chartier and Chris Enss claim the couple were in Trinidad when Holliday became ill and they decided to move to Las Vegas. There, Holliday set up his dental practice again and ran a saloon at night. The Hollidays remained there for two years.[142] Kate may also have worked at a dance hall in Santa Fe.[143]

Kate was definitely at Las Vegas in 1879 when Wyatt visited and talked Holliday into going with him to Arizona. She was not happy about the decision. "I wanted Doc to stay with me. I told Doc that, but Wyatt told him that Arizona was the better place to be."[144] Wyatt was probably right, considering that Holliday had just shot a man to death during an altercation in Las Vegas some months earlier.[145] Kate also noted that "Wyatt had his wife and brother James and his wife and daughter with him." Whether Wyatt's wife was Mattie Blaylock is up for speculation. Kate further remembered that "Doc and I went to the hotel. Virgil Earp, the oldest brother, was already in Prescott. Was there two years ahead of us." In Prescott, Doc got on a winning streak and decided to stay there until it played out. Kate went on to Globe because she heard there was good money to be made there and in time purchased a hotel.[146] Holliday, meanwhile, stayed on in Prescott through June 1880. According to the 1880 census, he shared a boarding-house apartment with two other men on Montezuma Street and listed his occupation as "dentist."

The Earps, meanwhile, had moved on to Tombstone. In 1879, the Earp clan in Tombstone included Wyatt and Virgil, plus Bessie and James, the latter of whom went to work for the saloons and gambling houses.[147] When the census was taken on June 2, 1880, the family was sharing an apartment in a large boardinghouse at 120 Allen Street. Mattie Blaylock was there, too, listed as "Mattie Earp," wife of Wyatt, and keeping house. The family also

FIGURE 18 ❧ *Mattie Blaylock, circa 1873. Mattie was Wyatt Earp's first love after the death of his wife, Urilla. When Wyatt threw her over for Josephine Marcus, Mattie remained with the Earp family for a couple of years before moving back to Arizona. Courtesy of Glenn Boyer, Tucson, Arizona.*

included Virgil's wife, Alvira, better known as "Allie." Although Allie never worked as a prostitute, she seems to have accepted Bessie and Mattie as a part of her family. Various sources have identified her especial fondness for Mattie, who, due to severe headaches, became addicted to laudanum.[148] When the census enumerator visited number 4 Allen Street on June 3, he found that James and Bessie had moved there. Sometime after the census was taken, Holliday's lucky streak in Prescott ended, and he joined the Earps in Tombstone. Big Nose Kate remembered that "the Earps had such a power I could not get Doc away from them."[149]

Although Wyatt is listed as a farmer in the 1880 census, he in fact owned property in Tombstone, which he leased to prostitute Dutch Annie. The madam constructed her own houses on the property.[150] It was probably through his dealings with the red light district that Wyatt met Josephine Sarah "Josie" Marcus. Although Josie denied she was ever a prostitute, much evidence suggests she was. She was born in 1861 in Brooklyn, New York, but by 1880 the Marcus family had relocated to San Francisco. In May 1880, Josie ran away from home at the age of nineteen. She had heard about Tombstone on the docks in San Francisco and yearned for some excitement. She took a job with some friends performing in *H.M.S. Pinafore* at the Adelphi Theater, and the tour went on the road. After performing in Santa Barbara, Los Angeles, and San Bernardino, the tour turned east and performed at Prescott before landing in Tombstone. On the way, Josie's coach was accosted by some Apaches. She later claimed that Sheriff Johnny Behan of Tombstone, later her lover, was among the men who shooed the natives away.[151] Behan had married in San Francisco back in 1869, but by 1873 it was obvious to his wife, Victoria, that Behan "openly and notoriously visited houses of ill-fame and a prostitute at said town of Prescott."[152]

Victoria was particular in naming one Sada Mansfield as a favorite of Johnny. She successfully filed for divorce in 1875, and Johnny moved to Tombstone, becoming sheriff in 1879. There, it was said, he would often tax the brothels twice: once for the city coffers and again for his own pocket.[153] By early 1881, Josie was performing in plays in Tombstone and was engaged to Behan, but she also appears to have been providing sexual services.[154] Working under the names "Sadie Jo" and "Shady Sadie," the actress-prostitute worked in various bordellos and theaters. In June 1881, Sadie Jo paid $7.50 for a license to ply her trade at the southwest corner of Sixth Street and Allen Street. Wyatt Earp, who was now deputy marshal,

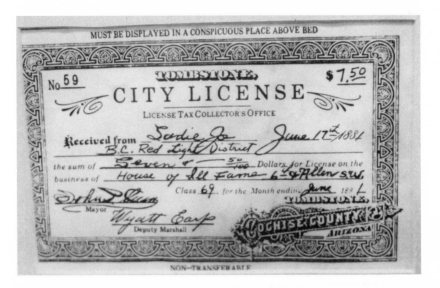

FIGURE 19 Prostitute Sadie Jo's alleged tax license, dated June 17, 1881, and signed by Wyatt Earp. If Sadie was indeed Josephine Marcus, this early business transaction with Wyatt was likely the beginning of their romance. Courtesy of Tombstone City, Tombstone, Arizona.

signed the license, which may explain how the two met. Earp was still living with Mattie Blaylock, supposedly in a covered wagon no more than fifty feet from Sadie's house of ill repute.[155] When it became obvious Wyatt was smitten with Josie, Mattie stubbornly remained with the rest of the family in hopes he would come back to her. Wyatt, however, now saw his common-law wife as a clingy, dependent laudanum addict, and there are indications that Mattie's temperament may have had something to do with his change of heart. "If Mattie had a temper like her sister," the daughter-in-law of Mattie's sister once said, "I don't blame [Wyatt] for leaving her."[156]

But Wyatt's actions especially appalled Allie Earp, who made her feelings known some years later to author Frank Waters. Although various manuscripts have claimed Allie and the other Earp women knew nothing of Wyatt's affair with Josie in Tombstone, Waters interviewed Allie and apparently found out otherwise. In his book *The Earp Brothers of Tombstone*, Waters reveals Allie's view of the love triangle among Wyatt, Josie, and Mattie. "We all knew about it and Mattie did too," Allie said. "That's why we never said anything to her. We didn't have to. We could see her with her eyes all red from cryin', thinkin' of Wyatt's carryin' on. I didn't have to peek out at night to see if the light was still burnin' in her window for Wyatt. I knew it would still be burnin' at daylight when I got up." Allie also recalled horrible fights between Mattie and Wyatt, as well as being with Mattie when she once spotted Josie in a local store.[157]

Wyatt seemed to be blatantly indifferent to his family's opinions. Although thirteen years his junior, Josie coddled Wyatt like a child, and he let her. Something about her bewitching dark eyes and lustrous hair intrigued him. And Josie thought Wyatt was the best-looking man in Tombstone. In time, theirs became one of the most torrid and talked-about love affairs in the West. It was no secret to anyone, even Josie, that Wyatt was a known skirt-chaser. Despite her love for him, her quick temper no doubt surfaced when he displeased her. "Wyatt and Josie had their ups and downs like any other relationship between two strong-minded people," said Terry Earp of Arizona, wife of Wyatt's great-nephew who claimed he was named after his famous uncle. "They were, however, devoted to one another and their love survived their temperaments." It was said that to please Wyatt, Josie learned to cook all of his favorite dishes and to overcome a tendency toward emotional displays. Wyatt affectionately called her "Sadie," perhaps from her short-lived days as a harlot.[158]

Doc Holliday, meanwhile, was suffering through his own woman trouble. Although he refused to move to Globe, he was soon sending Kate letters telling her how badly he missed her. Kate finally gave in, paid a friend to look after her hotel, and went to Tombstone. Upon her arrival there in March 1881, she was alarmed at how sickly Holliday looked.[159] His condition convinced her to stay. Kate's first home was a place Holliday found, located between a funeral parlor and a winery on the north side of Allen Street at Sixth Street.[160] The reunion was hardly blissful; when armed robbers held up a stage near the town of Contention and killed the driver and a passenger, a drunken and angry Kate told Sheriff Johnny Behan that Holliday was responsible and signed an affidavit to that effect. Holliday was arrested, but when Kate sobered up, she recanted her story, and the charges were dropped.[161]

When Holliday got out of jail, he gave Kate a stagecoach ticket and some money and sent her back to Globe.[162] There, Kate took a job working at a hotel restaurant, possibly her own.[163] News of Holliday's alleged involvement in the stagecoach incident might have circulated as far away

FIGURE 20   *As with the photograph of Big Nose Kate, the authenticity of this portrait of Josephine Marcus, probably taken while she was part of a troupe of performers in 1879 or 1880, has recently been questioned. For several decades, however, most historians have agreed that it is authentic. Courtesy of Glenn Boyer, Tucson, Arizona.*

as New Mexico; in July 1881, the *Las Vegas Optic* recalled how happy Las Vegas had been to see the couple leave two years earlier: "It will be remembered, especially by pioneers of the East Side, that Doc Holliday was at one time the keeper of a gin mill on Centre Street, near the site of the Centre Street Bakery. Doc was always considered a shiftless, bagged legged character—a killer and a professional cut-throat and not a wit too refined to rob stages or even steal sheep . . . the woman, Elder . . . was a Santa Fe tidbit and surrounded her habiliments with a detestable odor before leaving the 'ancient' [city] that will in itself make her memory immortal." Whatever their reputation in the public eye, Holliday and Kate remained inseparable. In October 1881, Holliday wrote to Kate again and asked her to come back to Tombstone. Kate returned once more, and the couple moved into Fly's Boarding House together. They were on a vacation in Tucson when Morgan Earp found them and said Holliday was needed back in Tombstone.[164]

In 1880, Morgan was living in California with his parents and his wife, Louisa "Lou" Houston; his marriage was identified as being "probably of the common-law variety."[165] He had since moved to Tombstone, securing a job alongside Wyatt as a lawman in October 1881.[166] Although Wyatt, Virgil, and Morgan carried badges in Tombstone, their sometimes violent and questionable tactics to uphold the law had been questioned ever since their days in Dodge City. In Tombstone, Frank and Tom McLaury, Billy Claiborne, and Ike and Billy Clanton, all regarded as murdering thieves, challenged the Earps' authority. Thrown into the mix were prejudices against and favoritism for certain political stands and business concerns, as well as varied opinions regarding the robbery near Contention. Ike Clanton believed the Earps and Holliday had indeed taken part in the robbery, even after Wyatt tried to bribe Clanton into providing information on the killers.[167] Most interesting is the assertion by some historians that the gunfight at the O.K. Corral was in fact over control of the prostitution industry.[168] Wyatt's lease to madam Dutch Annie and his involvement with Josephine "Sadie Jo" Marcus are two indications that the deputy marshal condoned the prostitution industry in Tombstone. It was also no secret that Sheriff Behan, too, was involved in the industry, even if only as a customer, and his bitterness at losing Josie to Wyatt as well as the illegal activities perpetrated by all the parties involved certainly must have complicated the situation.

Kate and Doc Holliday returned to town on October 25. The next morning they heard that Ike Clanton was looking for Holliday. Kate later remembered that as Holliday left their boarding room, he told her, "I may not be back to take you to breakfast, so you better go alone." Kate never went to breakfast and witnessed the gunfight later that afternoon. With her was Mrs. Fly.[169] The McLaurys and Billy Clanton were killed, and Morgan, Virgil, and Holliday were injured. Kate said that when Holliday returned to the room, he sat on the bed and wept, saying, "That was awful. Just awful."[170] In the aftermath of the shoot-out, most of the Earp women were sent elsewhere. Kate was instructed to return to Globe "for her own protection."[171] Josie, who later claimed to have also witnessed the shoot-out, was sent to her family in San Francisco.[172] Where Louisa Earp was during the shoot-out is unknown, but Morgan sent her back to California to live with his parents in February 1882. He was murdered in Tombstone the following month. The rest of the Earp women—Allie, Bessie, and Mattie—stayed behind until the Earp clan set out for California following Morgan's death.[173]

Most of the Earp clan set out for California in 1882, but Wyatt went to Colorado. James and Bessie accompanied the others to Colton, California, before moving on to San Bernardino, where Bessie died in 1887.[174] James later lived for a short time in Idaho but eventually returned to California, where he died in 1926.[175] Mattie Blaylock also accompanied the Earps to California and waited for Wyatt to send for her. When he spurned her attentions, she eventually left the Earp household and began drifting from town to town.[176] Wyatt, meanwhile, retrieved Josie in the spring of 1882. For the next several years, Wyatt and Josie, sometimes in the company of Doc Holliday, lived or traveled through Colorado, Idaho, Texas, and California.[177]

Big Nose Kate also began traveling. For the next several years, she made the circuit through Arizona, including Bisbee, Cochise, Courtland, and Dos Cabezas.[178] At Bisbee, she was injured during a shooting incident in Brewery Gulch.[179] She also owned or worked at the Globe restaurant or hotel or ran a boardinghouse in Globe until 1887. It was then that she heard that Holliday was in Glenwood Springs, Colorado, and very ill. Kate traveled to Colorado and stayed at her brother Alexander's ranch at Redstone, some thirty miles away, while she tended to Holliday.[180] He was staying at the Hotel Glenwood when he died November 8, 1887.[181] Whether Kate was with him when he died has never been substantiated.

Two events in 1888 brought at least part of the Earp women's saga to a close. One was the sad death of Mattie Blaylock in Pinal, Arizona, on

July 3.[182] Established southwest of Globe in 1878, Pinal was a silver-mining town that once had a population of more than two thousand. By the time Mattie got there, however, the silver had played out, and Pinal was in its own death throes.[183] It mattered little to Mattie, who had told others that Wyatt Earp "had wrecked her life by deserting her and she didn't want to live." The *Arizona Enterprise* mentioned Mattie's death only in passing: "Mattie Earp, a frail denizen of Pinal, culminated a big spree by taking a big dose of laudanum, on Tuesday, and died from its effects. She was buried on the 4th." Likewise, the *Silver Belt* in Globe stated that Mattie had committed suicide. An inquisition into her death shed further light on the matter. Laborer S. E. Damon testified that Mattie had been drinking heavily over the past three months and that he had taken whiskey away from her on numerous occasions. About three days prior to her death, he said, Mattie had expressed an intent "to make away with herself as she said she was tired of life."[184]

Sixty-five-year-old Frank Bueler, who did chores for Mattie, also testified as to her condition in the days before she died. "The woman felt sick," he said, "and I knew pretty well what the sickness was as I had waited on her once before when she was the same way." Bueler stated that he visited Mattie's room on July 2 and found her lying in bed with a man. Bueler left, and when he returned the next morning, Mattie asked him to sit down. The two shared some whiskey, and Mattie asked him to go get some more, as well as some laudanum, because she couldn't sleep. Bueler did as Mattie asked and doled out fifteen drops of laudanum for her, but upon returning later discovered she had taken the whole bottle. Bueler supposed Mattie was asleep when another laborer, T. J. Flannery, stopped by and "saw by the position that she was lying in that something was wrong." Lighting a lamp, Flannery saw black spots on Mattie's face and arms and summoned a doctor. Nothing could be done, however, and Mattie succumbed to an overdose.[185] She was buried in the Pinal Cemetery near Superior.[186] The Pinal County sheriff sent Mattie's personal things to her mother in Iowa, including letters, a scrapbook documenting her travels with Wyatt, and a round-topped trunk.[187] Interestingly, Mattie's relationship with Wyatt Earp did not come into the public eye until Frank Waters's book *The Earp Brothers of Tombstone* was published in 1960. Historians speculate that although Earp biographer Stuart Lake knew of the affair, he chose not to go into detail when he wrote *Wyatt Earp: Frontier Marshal* some years prior to Waters's book.[188]

If Big Nose Kate had been in Globe, she probably would have heard of Mattie's suicide. She was most likely in Hot Springs or Aspen, Colorado, however, where she married blacksmith George Cummings between 1888 and 1890.[189] She may have married him under the name "Mary Horoney."[190] The marriage did not last long, and soon Kate was on the road again. Between 1890 and 1900, she was documented at Rock Creek, Bisbee, and Cochise, Arizona, in the latter working for John and Lulu Rath at the Cochise Hotel.[191] She eventually went to work as a housekeeper for John Howard near Dos Cabezas.[192] The 1910 census lists her as "Mary C. Cummings, servant," residing at Willcox, Arizona. The census also notes she was married and lived with Howard. Ten years later she was still with Howard at Dos Cabezas.[193] The 1930 census lists Kate as living alone as a widow in Dos Cabezas, indicating that Howard had probably died. Shortly after the census was taken, Kate took a trip to see her brother at Redstone before moving to the Arizona Pioneers Home in Prescott in 1931. Although she was not a U.S. citizen, she claimed she was born in Davenport, Iowa, in order to gain entry to the home.[194] She died November 2, 1940, and was buried under the name "Mary K. Cummings."[195]

Whether Kate maintained contact with Wyatt and Josie is unknown, but it is possible. The twosome was in California in the early 1890s, living with Josie's mother, allegedly spending a short time in Cripple Creek, Colorado, and attending the World's Fair in Chicago in 1893 before relocating to Alaska in 1901. The couple also tried ranching in Nevada before settling permanently in California around 1910. They lived in a series of small apartments, hotels, and tourist camps until Wyatt's death in 1929. Josie continued living in Los Angeles, fiercely defending Wyatt's questionable reputation and dispelling ugly rumors about him. She even wrote her own memoirs about her time with him. Glenn G. Boyer's book *I Married Wyatt Earp* gives a lively account of Josie's autobiography plus several additional notes. "I've learned to live alone," she wrote in 1940, "but I still painfully miss my husband." Josephine Earp died in 1944 and is buried beside Wyatt's ashes in the Jewish section at Hills of Eternity Memorial Park in San Mateo, California.[196]

There is no question that Tombstone's raucous reputation in history might not be so interesting without the Earps. Nevertheless, the town was equally famous for its nightclubs, including the Bird Cage Theatre, which opened as the Elite Theater on December 26, 1881.[197] The place was described as one and a half stories tall with two main rooms. A saloon was located in front, and the theater section was in the back. Fourteen secluded balconies ran down each side of the room, divided by partitions on each side and a curtain in the front.[198] Owner Billy Hutchinson originally intended the place to cater to respectable families in town and even offered a free ladies' night to the wives of Tombstone, none of whom cared to make an appearance.[199] Audiences at the Elite wanted—and got—more risqué shows. The balcony boxes came to be referred to as "birdcages," and the theater's name was soon changed to the "Bird Cage Theatre."[200]

By 1882, even the *New York Times* touted the Bird Cage as "the wildest, wickedest night spot between Basin Street [New Orleans] and the Barbary Coast."[201] Tombstone's red light ladies included Little Gertie, also known as "Gold Dollar." In 1882, Gold Dollar stabbed a fellow dance hall girl named Margarita over a man. Gold Dollar had apparently for some time been seeing gambler Billy Milgreen. When Margarita blew into town, she set her sights on Milgreen, who in turn promised Gold Dollar he would have nothing to do with the sultry newcomer. One evening Milgreen was engaged in a poker game at the Bird Cage, where Margarita worked. Overcome with jealousy, Gold Dollar left her job at the Crystal Palace and posted herself outside the door at the Bird Cage, where she could see in. Sure enough Margarita was flirting with Milgreen, who, true to his word, was trying to keep his mind on the game. But when Margarita plopped herself into Milgreen's lap and began kissing him, Gold Dollar had enough. Leaping through the door, Gold Dollar screamed, "Get away from my man, you Mexican chippy! I warned you before!"[202]

Gold Dollar dragged Margarita off Milgreen by her hair, pulled a knife from her own garter, and stabbed Margarita in the side. A doctor was called to the scene, but upon examining Margarita, he said, "You don't need me. This girl is dead."[203] Margarita was buried at Boothill Cemetery. Charges were never brought against Gold Dollar, but she left town anyway, without Milgreen, who departed a short time later. Whether the two hooked up after their departure is unknown.[204] Local rumor was that Gold Dollar was never charged because the murder weapon could not be located. It was not until about 1982 that an old stiletto found behind the Bird Cage was thought to be the one Gold Dollar used.[205]

Despite incidents such as the stabbing of Margarita, the Bird Cage and other dens of vice were largely supported by city officials. In March 1882, the Tombstone City Council voted to remove restrictions on the locations of their brothels, which were located primarily on Allen and Fremont streets. The decision was encouraged by Mayor John Clum, who was also editor of the *Tombstone Epitaph* and publicly declared that in order for the town to survive, it must support all businesses. The *Epitaph*, incidentally, tended to ignore any bad news regarding gamblers or naughty women.[206] In 1883, Billy Hutchinson sold the Bird Cage to Hugh McCrum and John Stroufe. The theater was sold again in 1886 to Joe and Minnie Bignon, and it was during their ownership that the Bird Cage experienced its greatest success. In fact, "Big Minnie's" duties as owner of the Bird Cage included serving as prostitute, madam, performer, and bouncer. Joe billed her as "two hundred and thirty pounds of loveliness in pink tights."[207]

Business at the Bird Cage involved rental of the balconies at $25 per evening.[208] The price probably did not include personal services because between performances, the girls from the stage and other girls worked as waitresses. Called "Percentage Girls," the waitresses sang as they served libations. If a customer wanted more than drinks, the girl need only pull the curtain. The evening's entertainment consisted primarily of burlesque shows.[209] Some of them were quite racy and included belly dancing. The costumes for such dancers consisted of Turkish silk pantaloons that left very little to the imagination and a brocaded vest that allowed the dancers' breasts to be exposed. Sex could clearly be had for sale.[210]

During the reign of the Bird Cage, some of the other fancy parlor houses of Tombstone towered as high as three stories with a saloon on the first floor, parlor rooms on the second, and bedrooms on the third. Most of these plush houses charged up to $10 for a visit or $30 for all night. They stayed open from noon to daybreak, resulting in high profits for the madams, and it was said that the most ambitious prostitutes could make up to $150 per week. In other areas, the habit seems to have been to charge according to race: twenty-five cents for a Chinese, African American, or Native American girl; fifty cents for a Mexican girl; and seventy-five cents for a French girl. Only white women rated on top and were able to charge a dollar for their services. Prices also varied depending on age, beauty, and skills, but an average payday at the mine yielded some women as many as seventy customers in a day.[211]

French girls especially did quite well in Tombstone. One of them was Blonde Marie, who, it was said, worked under some sort of French syndicate.

Marie conducted business in a large white house on Sixth Street, and it is notable that her position was strictly that of a love broker, not a working girl. Marie ran a straight house with no gambling or alcohol. She did not tolerate fighting and catered only to the wealthiest men. She was also able to trade her girls out from other places so that her customers had an endless variety of new girls at any given time. Blonde Marie and the other French women were ruled by a mysterious man called the Count, who appeared periodically, checked on business, brought new girls, and collected money from the madams before departing. Marie eventually saved enough money to retire and return to Paris.[212]

Tombstone also had its share of Chinagirls, who worked in "Hoptown." This area of town, blocked in by Third and First, Fremont and Toughnut, was so designated for its large population of Chinese. Because they tended to import and grow their own food and spent little of their hard-earned cash downtown, most Chinese were considered a public nuisance. One of the most popular girls was China Mary, who in fact appears to have ruled over Hoptown and its denizens. Chinese maids, laundresses, handymen, and prostitutes were in demand around town, but none could be hired without going through Mary. Her guarantee was "them steal—me pay!" and she offered up employees with her word that they would do the work assigned to them correctly. Mary also oversaw a bordello next to her own house, which came complete with opium dens, underground tunnels, and rooms in which to stash illegal Chinese immigrants. She even had a grip on the opium market, supplying the white prostitutes in town, and ran a shop that carried Chinese art and other "delicacies." Any pay, whether it was for servants, prostitutes, or drugs, went directly to Mary. Not incidentally, Mary was a part of the Six Companies, a Chinese mafia.[213] But she was also known to lend money to others and attend to the sick and the injured. One time when a cowboy broke his leg, she paid his boarding bill until he recovered. When Mary died, she was buried at Boothill Cemetery. The services followed Chinese custom.[214]

May Davenport was another infamous Tombstone trollop. May arrived in town with a traveling show but soon turned to prostitution because it was more lucrative. She saved a great deal of money, and when there was a copper boom at Cananea in Mexico, she moved there and opened her own house. Some of the girls from Tombstone ended up moving to Mexico and working for her, including Pearl O'Shea.

Lizette the Flying Nymph also came to town with a traveling show. Her performance consisted of floating over the audience from the stage, supported by tiny invisible wires. After the show, Lizette could be found drinking at any number of Tombstone's bars. Alcohol eventually got the best of her, and she suddenly left town. There was also Mrs. Mary or Marce DuPont, who was in Tombstone from at least 1886 to at least 1893.[215]

One of the most notorious prostitutes of Tombstone was Crazy Horse Lil. She was described as big, tough, mean, and foul-mouthed. That mouth was allegedly credited with the infamous saying, "The wages of sin are a damn sight higher than the wages of virtue."[216] When Lil went on an alcohol tear, she had no problems taking on anyone who offended her. Lil's actions often landed her in jail. On one occasion, upon discovering she would be sharing a stagecoach with a newlywed couple and that the groom was a former client, she teased the man mercilessly by offering him a nip from her bottle and telling racy stories. At the end of each story, she would turn to the uncomfortable bridegroom and say, "Ain't that so, Jake?" or "Wasn't that the way it was, Jake?" Lil eventually moved to Bisbee and did quite well. But when she and her man of the moment, Con O'Shea, began staging local robberies, authorities had had enough. Threatened with arrest, Lil and O'Shea departed Arizona for parts unknown.[217]

There was also Nosey Kate, who operated out of a tent and served whiskey, enough that she was soon able to buy a house. "She served the worst whiskey in the Territory and her prices were determined by how drunk the customer was," said author Ben Traywick. Unfortunately, Kate was not above robbing her inebriated customers; upon being notified that the sheriff was coming to see her the next day, she left town that night under cover of a buckboard. Emma Blair succeeded Nosey Kate, walking into the newly purchased brothel to find it fully furnished with a staff of girls.[218]

The year 1887 appears to have been especially violent in Tombstone. In June, prostitute Diamond Annie Watson pressed charges against Pete Rude for threatening to kill her. Rude was arrested, and subsequent news on the incident revealed that not only was the man enamored of Annie, but had spent all of his money on her. "The justice notified him that he really thought the better plan would be to send him before a lunacy committee for examination," said the *Tombstone Epitaph*. Rude couldn't make his bond of $500, but was released when Annie left town. The next month, a prostitute was charged with using foul language. She pleaded not guilty in court, but used so many expletives in defending herself that she was still fined $20. And the month after that, Irish Nellie filed a complaint against one "John Doe," proprietor of a saloon on Allen Street, for assault. The man was found guilty and fined a total of $13, at which point he then had Nellie arrested for using obscene language.[219]

The debauchery in Tombstone continued. In February 1888, a black man named Louis Robinson was charged with attempted robbery at the house of prostitute Charlotte Lopez on Sixth Street. When Charlotte heard the man breaking into her back room, she summoned help, and Robinson was arrested. In court, Robinson testified that the break-in was not a robbery attempt, but part of an agreement to meet with one of Charlotte's girls. The girl herself testified, however, that Robinson had once accosted her in the dark and made an indecent proposal to her, which she declined and then threatened to call the police. Robinson was released the next day, but the *Tombstone Prospector* did not take the matter lightly. The newspaper boldly suggested "to this colored Lothario that in the future it would inure to his benefit to confine his amours to those of his own color. The last attempt is not the only one he had made to obtrude his attentions on white women. He got out of a very ugly scrape this time by the skin of his teeth and should take warning by it."[220] Then in July the *Tombstone Epitaph* reported that "[a] Sixth Street Cyprian, was fined $20 and costs in the City Recorders court yesterday, for soliciting prostitution. The complaining witness was a next door neighbor, in the same line of business."[221]

Such antics began getting on people's nerves. In December 1888, a man knocked on the door of a brothel above Pasquale Nigro's saloon on Allen Street. When the working girl inside answered, he knocked her to the floor. The same man went through similar actions the next night at the place of a woman named "Jesefa." This time, however, Jesefa took after the man and received a serious knife cut on the bridge of her nose. The assailant was arrested while the newspaper speculated on why he committed the crimes. It is possible that the man was using his own means to rid Tombstone of its soiled doves. Interestingly, Nigro himself had been arrested in 1887 for slapping a working girl known as "Cuckoo" and knocking her to the floor.[222] Worst of all was Sheriff Johnny Behan, who came under fire in 1889 when it was discovered he had allowed twenty-one-year-old Manuela Fimbres to roam the jail freely during her several years' sentence after she and her pimp were convicted of killing a Chinese man. Manuela's wanderings led to the birth of two children one right after another.[223] Newspapers in 1890 reported on Carmelita Jimenez, a performer who lived in an adobe dwelling next to the Elite Theater. In a fit of jealousy, Carmelita had swallowed two tablespoons of rat poison. A Dr. Willis was able to save her, but a short time later the paper noted that the Elite had closed for the night out of respect for Carmelita, who had indeed this time succeeded in ending her own life. A Mexican woodcutter got into a brawl with bartender Charley Keene over the price of whiskey at the Bird Cage. Keene asked Big Minnie Bignon to get the marshal, but Minnie retorted, "You don't need Bob Hatch, I'll put him out myself!" and did just that.[224]

Although citizens were often shocked and enraged by their red light denizens' antics, Tombstone profited well from the fines and fees levied because of them. Money was generated not just from business licenses, but also from the monthly health exams. The bad girls of Tombstone also contributed to charities. The Episcopal church in town was built from donations by gamblers, saloon keepers, and the bawdy women of the town. These donations did not make the givers certified angels, however. One employee of the Bird Cage explained how she exacted a little revenge against the snobby women of Tombstone: "Them women always looked down their noses at us—excepting when they needed some money for a charity. Then they'd come down and ask us girls. Well, I always donated, but I got my licks in doing it. I had found out from a old lady that if you used a certain size coin and placed it just right—then you wouldn't get pregnant. Well, when I used them coins I laid them on the table in my room. Then, when them society ladies come down for a donation, I give them the coins on my table."[225]

Like so many other towns, Tombstone eventually began to decline during the early 1890s. The Bird Cage closed in 1892. The Bignons next tried their luck by buying the Crystal Palace, but it too failed.[226] Citizens began moving to nearby Pearce, which was undergoing a new gold boom. In fact, some of Tombstone's buildings went as well. The Bignons purchased another bar in Pearce and called it "Joe Bignon's Palace." It proudly advertised itself as "the only second-class saloon in the territory."[227] Minnie and Joe lived the remainder of their lives at Pearce and are buried there. Pearce itself has become a ghost town.[228]

For years, the soiled doves of Tombstone tended to alternate their time at Bisbee, just a short distance south. The first signs of prostitution appeared in Bisbee in about 1879, along with some of the earliest female

FIGURE 21 ❦ *The Bird Cage Theater appears to have been boarded up when the author's great-grandmother Frances Hennessey and her friend had their photograph taken in front of it in the early 1930s; when the theater was opened up in 1934, nearly the whole place remained intact from its closure in 1892. From the author's collection.*

bartenders in the West.[229] The first dance hall in Bisbee is thought to have opened in 1881, but it was soon overshadowed, at least in history, by one opened by Johnny Heith in 1883. Heith's grand opening was actually a decoy to cover the robbery of Castaneda & Goldwater's Store. The ploy failed, however, and the robbery resulted in what historians now refer to as the Bisbee Massacre because the five robbers left four dead victims in their wake. Johnny's mistress was Emma Mortimer, a well-known dance hall girl of Bisbee. When Johnny was lynched following the massacre, it was Emma who came forward and lovingly tied a handkerchief around his eyes before he was hanged.[230]

Despite Emma Mortimer's heroic act, it is a dance hall girl named Little Irish Mag who is credited with being the first gal of her profession in Bisbee.[231] Like all of Bisbee's prostitutes, Mag lived in a green-roofed house on Mule Pass, now known as Main Street. She also had a green parrot who emulated the rough speech of the local miners and mule skinners. Mag and her coworkers also walked the streets of Bisbee freely, ducking into the near-est saloon at the sight of a respectable woman. After the woman passed by, the girls would peek after her to see what the latest dress style was.[232] Mag also had a mining claim named for her that made millions. The story goes that a man named Jim Daley named the mine. If this story is true, Mag likely saw little money from it. Daley went on to try to sell the Irish Mag to the Copper Queen Mine. When the owners refused his offer, Daley took out his temper on a Mexican he caught trespassing. A deputy sheriff who tried to intervene was shot in the foot. When Sheriff Bill Lowther went to serve Daley a warrant for assault, he too was shot, this time fatally. Daley took off up Sacramento Mountain behind his house and disappeared, and his heirs ended up fighting over the Irish Mag for at least a decade.[233] Mag was still in Bisbee in 1885 when her neighbor, Sheriff Bill Daniels, was shot by Apaches. Joe Chisolm, who grew up in Brewery Gulch, recalled that Mag took tender care of Daniels while he recuperated.[234]

Also in 1881, at least one "promiscuous shooting affray" was reported in local papers. Two saloon owners, after arguing most of the night, finally shot it out with each other near the post office. It was seven in the morn-ing, and some thirty people had gathered to pick up their mail. One of the casualties was Black Jack, a visiting madam who received a glancing wound in the hip.[235] Another historian claimed Black Jack dressed like a man and was suspected of robbing stagecoaches.[236] Various others have said Black Jack was a "queen of the red light district."[237] In 1907, a woman named Mrs. Josie Harcourt, whose nickname was "Black Jack," was reported to have died in a Los Angeles hospital. She had first come to Arizona during the 1870s with her husband, and they had lived at Mineral Park. When the marriage dissolved, she joined the prostitution industry and was known throughout numerous mining camps and along the Pacific Coast. The newspaper report said Black Jack had settled in Kingman, Arizona, in about 1887 and had remained there since. She also had "two or three children but their whereabouts is unknown."[238]

By 1884, city officials were attempting to move Bisbee's red light dis-trict to the back streets of town, but it wasn't successfully confined to an area south of Main Street and West of O.K. Street until around 1892.[239] Clara Allen is notable as one of the longest-operating madams in Bisbee. Clara originally opened for business in Bisbee Canyon on the road to Naco, Sonora. She later moved to Bisbee's notorious Brewery Gulch and opened

Club Forty-One.[240] By 1894, news of Clara was surfacing in the local newspapers. In March of that year, she and three other women—Frida and Hilda Miller and Birdie Russell—were arrested following a complaint by businessman G. P. Angius that they had violated Bisbee's "four hundred yard limit in regard to houses of prostitution." Frida and Hilda Miller demanded a jury trial and were found not guilty. Eight of the jurors worked for the Copper Queen Mine. They were fired the next day, and the mining company threatened to shut down for six months if Frida and Hilda did not leave town within forty-eight hours. Less than two weeks later, the newspaper announced that the Miller girls, "the two females who a short time ago were driven to the town limits by the vigilante committee of Bisbee," had indeed boarded a train and left town.[241]

As for Clara Allen, she remained in Bisbee. The 1900 census notes that the thirty-one-year-old madam was keeping a "lodging house" with four working girls and a black male cook named Moya House. In later years, Clara became more motherly, not just toward her working girls, but also toward the young men who frequented her establishment. One young mining engineer who returned to Michigan for a family reunion was accosted by family members who, worried about him working in the wicked mining camps of the West, encouraged him to attend services by a famous evangelist. The man declined, claming he had received enough preaching from Clara Allen before he left. Of course, the boy declined to explain who Clara was, leading his family to conclude she must be a prominent evangelist out West. Clara eventually moved to Globe.[242]

Even the luxurious Copper Queen, Bisbee's fanciest hotel, was not safe from the wiles of the red light ladies. Prostitute Julia Lowell was believed to have worked there in the early 1900s. In the years since Julia committed suicide after being spurned by her lover, male visitors have claimed to see her spirit performing a strip-tease at the end of their bed or standing at the head of the stairs on the third floor.[243] In 1900, another famous painted lady of Bisbee was Anita Romero. The twenty-five-year-old wild woman and two other girls emigrated from Mexico in 1899 and worked for saloonkeeper Frederico Gillas in his Brewery Gulch dance hall.[244] Anita had a limited grasp of the English language, but men were said to have killed each other over her. After a particularly bad gunfight at Anita's, the male witnesses were called to court. Their respective fiancées found out and broke off their engagements. Anita felt so badly about this outcome that she threw the men an enchilada banquet, withdrew her money from the bank, and left Bisbee with several bastard children she had given birth to. She moved to Cananea, Sonora, retired from the profession, and raised her children.[245]

Anita Romero's absence was hardly felt in Bisbee, which had roughly twenty brothels in 1900.[246] When Bisbee was finally incorporated in 1902, Mayor J. J. Muirhead was the first official to ban women from working or entertaining in saloons.[247] The ordinance made an exception, however, for the women of the red light district "above a certain line up Brewery Gulch."[248] Next "a chart was presented," according to the *Bisbee Daily Review*, "which had been carefully prepared . . . showing a line down 'across the upper end of Brewery Gulch eight feet south of Clara Allen's place' designating the point below which no woman can remain where liquor is sold in any form." Furthermore, women were prohibited from performing in proximity to or as part of a saloon. Fines for violating the ordinance ranged from $20 to $50 or ten to twenty-five days in jail, or both. Certain business owners objected to the new law, and their opinions were voiced in the *Review* the next day: "Those who employ girls in saloons, do so to increase their business and claim that this materially affects trade." The article went on to say that a similar law in Globe was met with much opposition and that attorneys had been hired to test the new law's validity. Other arguments against the ordinance included the question as to why women could be "shut out of one section of the city, but not the other?"[249]

In 1906, another new ordinance was passed making it unlawful for bordellos to operate within thirteen hundred feet of the city hall, any public school, or "any other public building within the corporate limits of the city of Bisbee."[250] In 1910, the city outlawed prostitution altogether, but, as in other cases around Arizona, the industry still managed to maintain a small faction of bawdy-house girls.[251] In 1917, officials discovered that the ladies confined to Bisbee's red light district were making clandestine visits to army camps at Douglas, Arizona, and Naco, Sonora. The discovery came with the fear that government authorities would soon be pressuring Bisbee's city council to shut down the town's red light district once and for all.[252] In fact, the district *was* eventually shut down, but for many years prostitutes were still accessible at Naco just across the Mexican border. It was said that in 1929, during a rebellion staged by Mexican guerrilla leader Pancho Villa, parties from both sides ceased fire at night so they could party in the bawdy houses and saloons in Naco. At daylight, the revelers would go back to fighting.[253]

Another community in close proximity to Tombstone and Bisbee was Charleston, which enjoyed a rough-and-tumble life with plenty of bad men running around. In fact, the town was so wicked, it was said that even the schoolboys carried guns. It is no surprise, then, that children were often seen peeking in the windows of the town's largest bordello, and nobody thought to make them stop. But when some local schoolgirls came home proclaiming they wanted to be one of those pretty ladies when they grew up, authorities ordered the house to move. The madam obliged by relocating nearer to Fort Huachuca.[254]

Farther north in Arizona, other communities on either side of Flagstaff sported their own unique prostitution history. Shortly after its founding in 1881, Holbrook—some ninety miles east of Flagstaff—had visions of competing with rougher towns such as nearby Canyon Diablo and Tombstone. In 1884, the legendary Hashknife Cattle Company purchased two million acres near Holbrook. On Saturday nights, the rowdy and thirsty cowboys would blaze into town, whooping and hollering as they shot up the local dance halls. Added to the handful of outlaws among the Hashknife boys were other local rustlers. Holbrook's most famous tavern originally began as its first restaurant, the Cottage Café. Then two Hashknife cowboys got into a fight with two Mexican men over a poker game. The cowboys managed to kill the Mexicans. The dead men's blood pooled on the floor, looking like "a bucket of blood had spilled." Thereafter, the "Bucket of Blood" moniker stuck.[255] By the time Hashknife cowboy George Hennessey owned the infamous bar following Prohibition, prostitution was all but nonexistent in Holbrook. Hennessey's grandson, George Wallace Smith, recalled that when he was a child in Holbrook during the 1940s, citizens felt free to walk the streets at any time of the day or night without fear of crime or violence.[256]

To the west of Flagstaff was Williams, established in 1881.[257] Although Williams's red light district was originally spread throughout town, it eventually came to be located in the first block of Railroad Avenue at Second Street directly east of the railroad tracks and well within site of the depot. Nearby was Saloon Row with at least three combination saloons, brothels, gambling halls, and opium dens. The earliest was the Cabinet Saloon, built at the corner of Second Street and Railroad Avenue in 1893 or 1895.[258] The

FIGURE 22 Hashknife cowboys, including the author's great-grandfather
George Hennessey, pose in front of the Bucket of Blood saloon in Holbrook,
Arizona, circa 1900. The tavern saw many owners, but Saturday nights were all the
same—with poker, drinking, and a bevy of pretty girls. From the author's collection.

story of Georgie Clifford, also known as "Georgia Redmond" and "Stella
Campbell," is Williams's best—and saddest—claim to prostitute fame.
Born in South Carolina, Georgie had come to Arizona from Missouri with
a husband and child.[259] When she became addicted to opium, her husband
divorced her and took their child.[260] By 1893, twenty-year-old Georgie had
turned to prostitution in Williams and was charged with intentionally giving customer Peter Perry an overdose of morphine.[261]

    During Georgie's trial, madam Amy Powell testified that one of her
other employees, Lillie Taylor, had been the only one to serve any drinks
to Perry. Evidence also showed that Lottie Williams, another inmate who
had in fact been addicted to morphine for the past ten years, had given an
injection to Perry. But Lottie had fled the area, and a search for her turned
up nothing. Georgie testified that Lottie had shown her where she had
injected Perry, and upon checking on the couple a short time later Georgie
had found Lottie trying to revive the man. It was in fact Georgie who had

woken up everyone in the house and summoned a doctor. Despite the overwhelming evidence against Lottie Williams, Georgie Clifford was found guilty of murder and sentenced to three and a half years at the Arizona State Penitentiary in Yuma. A review of her case in February 1895 resulted in her release, and Georgie moved to Tucson. There, she reestablished herself as "Georgia Redmond," but her troubles continued. In August 1896, she filed charges against one Frank Serrano for stealing $100 in gold from her. Other skirmishes involved fighting with police officers and being sent for a short time to the insane asylum in Phoenix. In the days before drug rehabilitation and halfway houses, there seemed no better solution than to send Georgie to an asylum to cure her addictions. Georgie ran away from the asylum a few times ("I didn't run away," she later claimed, "I just walked off and came to town"), but was eventually released.[262]

In May 1897, the *Arizona Republican* identified Georgie as a "morphine fiend" and reported that she had tried to kill her current paramour, Henry Rubenstein or Rosenstein, in Phoenix. Newspapers noted that although Georgie had been in good physical health when released from prison, she was now thin and emaciated. She was committed to the insane asylum again, although she asked repeatedly not to be sent back there. "At the asylum all those crazy women are afraid of me but I wouldn't hurt them," she explained. "I never hurt anything immolate [sic], and never wanted to. But they'll put me in handcuffs again." Both the judge and the doctor in attendance assured Georgie she would be treated kindly and released as soon as she was cured. Rubenstein, meanwhile, was convicted of running a disorderly house. In court, he testified that he had a wife and seven children in Florida, but had been trying to cure Georgie of her dope habits. When he failed at this effort, he had turned to drink. Rubenstein was convicted and fined $20.[263]

Georgie ran away from the asylum once again in late May 1897, but was caught in Tempe. She was released again in June. Then in August, Rubenstein heard she had taken another lover. Overcome with jealousy, he threatened to kill the man. He was fined $90, but managed to talk Georgie into marrying him on September 30. At the time, she was going by the name "Stella Campbell," possibly her real name. All seemed well until October 24, when the *Arizona Republican* reported the sad news: Georgie's addiction to morphine and cocaine had caught up with her, and she had died from an overdose.[264]

In 1897, another saloon was constructed in Williams next to the Cabinet at 137 West Railroad Avenue, with libations downstairs and prostitutes upstairs.[265] August Tetzlaff, a German tailor, constructed the building to house a parlor and eight cribs on the second floor. A steep set of stairs, nicknamed the "Cowboy's Endurance Test" led upstairs to the ladies, who advertised their wares by calling to men from the windows. Out back was a two-story outhouse, constructed to prevent the inmates from having to negotiate the steep stairs. Whiskey flasks, medicine bottles, opium bottles, pipe parts, and morphine ampoules have been excavated from the outhouse over time, attesting to a wild and rowdy past.[266] In the back of the saloon were two other rooms housing Chinese railroad workers who ran a "chophouse" and opium den. The only woman identified as working there was known as "Big Bertha."[267]

Tetzlaff's saloon was often the scene of disturbances, and the sheriff was frequently summoned to investigate reported murders. But when he arrived, he would find nothing out of place. Once, convinced there were bodies in the cesspool below the outhouse, the sheriff ordered a local garbage collector to be lifted into the cesspool to have a look. Nothing was found. In later years, the saloon was operated by Longino Mora, a former U.S. Cavalry scout from New Mexico. During his long-term ownership of the bar, Mora became notable for having five wives and twenty-five children in a span of sixty years.[268] In the 1930s, he also sold bootleg liquor from the back door of the old saloon. In the 1940s, one of the upstairs girls stabbed a customer in the back. The victim fell down the front stairs and through the front door, dying on the sidewalk out front. Today this saloon is known as the Red Garter Bed & Bakery.[269]

In 1903, a third combination saloon and brothel was built next to the Cabinet and its 1897 counterpart.[270] The new place was still not large enough to satisfy the growing prostitute population in Williams, however, and in 1905 a local newspaper editor complained that prostitutes were infiltrating respectable parts of town.[271] By 1912, a saloon at the southwest corner of Route 66 and Third Street also housed prostitutes, from whom the town marshal collected "voluntary contributions" to aid the territory in forming the state of Arizona. During the 1920s, Mora's saloon contained a speakeasy in the basement.[272] Speakeasies became even more common during the 1930s Prohibition era, with poker tables hidden behind dividers and prostitution continuing to flourish upstairs, notably at 137 Railroad

FIGURE 23 🙢 *Longino Mora, with cane, poses alongside one of his madams in front of his combination saloon and brothel during the 1930s or 1940s. Even Mora claimed his building was haunted. Courtesy of J. Holst and the Mora family, Red Garter Bed & Bakery, Williams, Arizona.*

Avenue. By then, the place was said to be haunted, as illustrated in a 1934 photograph of the Mora family with the ghostly apparition of a woman where none was supposed to be standing. A murder on the stairs of the building during the mid-1940s, however, drew too much attention to the place, and the business was closed for good.[273]

As Arizona stepped into the twentieth century, prostitution continued to flourish there. In 1909, new copper discoveries facilitated the founding of Miami in close proximity to Globe. Because Miami was founded so late, the town ideally knew what to do in order to prevent places of vice from encroaching on the town. Among the first ordinances were laws against gambling and dance girls working in saloons, even though the first business in town was John Fitzpatrick's saloon. Recognition of the need for female companionship among hundreds of bachelor miners may have been why prostitution was never outlawed. A sizeable red light district soon sprawled up a small canyon behind the railroad station. And although the district saw plenty of action, its brazen hussies had few run-ins with the law. The biggest news of note was when the district, containing some eight houses of ill repute, burned early in 1909.[274]

Unlike in most other mining camps, a handful of women also worked within the town's boundaries. One of these women was known only as "Molly." Described as "an attractive, shapely woman who had long blond hair and was often seen wearing expensive kimonos," Molly operated discreetly over the town drugstore. She was also known for her generous contributions to the Red Cross and the purchase of a thousand dollars' worth of Liberty bonds during World War I.[275] Other women worked at the Keystone Hotel, Miami's largest house of ill repute. The Keystone was a rowdy place and often temporarily shut down, but gambling and prostitution continued in Miami for many years. In 1913, some thirteen gamblers were arrested for conducting illegal games and fined $100 apiece. Prostitution was still visible in Miami as late as 1962, when an advertisement in the yellow pages gave directions to the Keystone Hotel Massage Salon, along with the promise of "woman attendants from noon to 4 A.M. daily." Public outcry over the risqué ad closed the hotel for good. The Keystone was the last brothel in Miami and was torn down in the 1970s.[276]

The State of Arizona had officially outlawed prostitution in 1907, but the law was loosely enforced.[277] Only by enforcing laws against prostitution during World War I did the military have any real effect on prostitution in Arizona. After the war, however, as evidenced in many towns, prostitution did a reprise. During World War II, the community of Fry was nicknamed "Hook" by black soldiers from nearby Fort Huachuca because of the large number of hookers working there. Today Fry is known as Sierra Vista.[278] The big mama of them all, however, was the Top of the World Guest Ranch between Miami and Superior, which featured prostitution in the 1950s. The working girls there were reputedly the prettiest in Gila County and known around the state and beyond.[279] Top of the World also featured a Coke machine and a jukebox, but alcohol apparently was not available. When the place boldly placed an advertisement in a 1960 Phoenix phone book, the moral majority of the town voiced their objection and Top of the World closed for good.[280]

3

COURTESANS OF COLORADO

COLORADO RATES AMONG THE MOST BEAUTIFUL STATES IN THE union. Here, high mountain peaks can tower more than fourteen thousand feet, with beautiful prairies sprawled below them. The Rocky Mountains literally divide the state in half. Their ranges can appear anywhere from picturesque and welcoming to jagged and unforgiving. South and east, the mountains give way to rolling hills, high country prairies, and fertile grasslands.

Because the southern portion of the state was inhabited by Mexicans and Spanish as early as the 1600s, Colorado's heritage goes back a long way. When the state entered the union in 1874, many of its towns—Boulder, Colorado City, Denver, Pueblo, and many others—were well established. One of the very earliest cases of prostitution, however, occurred at the southern settlement of Greenhorn in 1841. Fur trapper John Brown fought a duel with an Indian called "Seesome" over a Mexican flirt known as Nicolasa.[1] Some of the earliest cases of prostitution in Colorado also took place at Bent's Fort, established in 1849 northeast of Greenhorn. Although builder William Bent kept a close eye on his men, it was commonly known that sex was for sale in a "raucous and unruly" community located outside the fort's walls.[2]

Another area fort, Fort Pueblo, eventually developed its own reputation not only with Mexican and Indian prostitutes, but also with white women.

94

Fort Pueblo's beginnings date to the 1840s. The population at the fort no doubt included a few Mexican and Indian prostitutes up to and after 1860, when the city was officially founded. Pueblo's earliest brothels in the new era were not confined to one red light district, but to several. Some of the more notorious bordellos in Pueblo included the Stranger's Home, which was the scene of numerous suicides and fights, including the 1872 death of prostitute Kitty Austin. Thirty-three-year-old Esther Baldwin, born in Canada and also known as "Sarah Fox," reigned as madam at the Hotel de Omaha. Like the Stranger's Home, the Hotel de Omaha also saw its share of fights, including an 1872 scuffle between Esther, her girls, and gambler Sam Mickey. In 1874, Esther also opened the European Dance Hall. Another woman, Mrs. Gropp, ran her Railroad House opposite the South Pueblo Depot.[3]

Pueblo did not pass its first ordinances against prostitution and gambling until 1875. Women such as Esther Baldwin and Mrs. Gropp occasionally moved to avoid authorities, so by 1877 prostitution seemed to be everywhere, both inside Pueblo and on its outskirts. Throughout the 1880s, a number of prostitute arrests were recorded, including those of madams Nellie Moon, Lizzie Dunkard, and Jennie King, along with a collective nine employees. Other prostitutes of Pueblo included Belle O'Neil, Mattie White (alias Mattie Fields), Clara Wilson (alias Clara Trott), Belle Bunnelson, and Lydia White. The girls and their coworkers were finding gainful employment in such notorious resorts as Tammany Hall, the Bagnio, and the Bucket of Blood. By 1885, Pueblo's official red light district was located on First Street between Santa Fe and what is now Albany Avenue. Cribs on the north side of the street measured approximately 180 square feet. On the south side, they were roomier, about 240 square feet. Many were owned by women who rented them to prostitutes; they were allegedly the best brothels in town and came complete with private entrances in the back.[4]

Reigning madams in Pueblo in 1895 and 1896 included Emma Brace and Nellie White, who employed prostitutes Mabel Miller, Stella Fisher, Nellie Marcus, Minnie Cumming, Jennie Holmes, and May Rivers. On occasion, Em Brace paid fines for her prostitutes, including Lillian Clark, Myrtle King, and Pearl Young. Authorities struggled to close the bordellos in central Pueblo, but even newcomers such as Etta "Spuds" Murphy of Leadville were undaunted. The 1900 census shows only five brothels in the red light district, with five prostitutes per site on average. The largest brothel

had ten residents—eight girls, a cook, and a musician. Altogether that year, there were thirty-six prostitutes in Pueblo, averaging twenty-eight years of age. The oldest was sixty-one, the youngest eighteen. There were eight children among them. Two were married. Fifteen were foreign born.[5]

Pueblo's red light district was temporarily closed down in 1910 following a series of raids. During January, raids resulted in seventy-five arrests. In the wake of the arrests, however, it was revealed that four police officers—including Police Chief Sullivan—had recently gotten drunk and spent the night at a brothel. All were demoted or dismissed, and the busts continued. In August 1911, Pueblo County pursued another means of ridding the city of whorehouses by allowing roadhouses in the county outside the city limits. Six years later, the city built its new city hall practically right on top of the old red light district. Prostitution continued both in and out of Pueblo, however, well into the late 1930s. Not until the 1950s did the old bordellos begin seeing other uses.[6]

East of Pueblo along today's Highway 50 was Florence, founded in 1873 as a coal-mining, cattle, oil, and agriculture town.[7] Lillian Powers was Florence's most famous madam. She was born in Wisconsin in 1873 or 1884 (census records vary) to parents of German descent.[8] According to Lil, "my father had this farm, you see, and nobody to work it but him and us two girls. I was fourteen, two years older than my sister, and he forgot most of the time that we wasn't horses. Got so I couldn't take it anymore." Whether Lil really worked as a schoolteacher as some say remains a mystery, but she did later verify that her first job was in a laundry. Such work was grueling. "It was almost as bad as the farm and my pay was one dollar a week. A room cost fifty cents a week. . . . I took up with a girl who worked next to me. We got to talking one day and I asked her how she made out on such a piddling wage. 'I don't,' she said. 'None of us girls do on what they pay us. Every last one of us has had to get ourselves a pimp. The quicker you do this the better off you'll be.'"[9] Before long, Lillian made her way to South Dakota, where she heard about the money prostitutes were making in Denver.[10]

From about 1903 to 1907, Lil ran the Cupola in Denver, but she didn't like the way prostitutes were being treated or the low wages they received. Around 1907, Lillian moved first to Victor for four years and then to Cripple Creek, where she rented a crib, which gave her more freedom. Her landlady was Leola "Leo the Lion" Ahrens, an alcoholic Frenchwoman whose bad temper was well known around town. Leo had once run a sporting house in

Cripple Creek, but eventually lost it to drink and became a working madam in her own cribs. She soon grew envious of Lil's business profits. One day, in a drunken rage and with gun in hand, she began pounding on Lil's door, threatening to kill her.[11] Lil fled out the back door to the telephone office, called madam Laura Evens in Salida, Colorado, asking for a job and took the earliest train there. The following day Lil cleaned up and paid Laura a visit, giving her rent in advance. The two became good friends, and Lil eventually managed the cribs for Laura in return for a percentage of the profits.[12]

With Laura's help, Lil also moved to Florence and opened her own brothel, Lil's Place. The two women continued doing business together and visited each other often. Lil spent $30,000 on her house, which featured a ballroom with a player piano and a walled-in beer garden complete with a dance floor. At first, she employed only two to three girls, and so was most likely a working madam.[13] By the 1940s, Tiger Lil, as she became known, could afford ten girls and was no longer a working madam. She was eventually closed down for good and simply retired, passing away at a local nursing home in 1960. Today, Lil's house is a private home, and her treasured Brunswick Record Player is on display at the Price Museum in Florence.[14]

Canon City, just nine miles from Florence, appears never to have had a red light district—possibly because Canon is home to the Colorado State Penitentiary. Notably, however, Fannie Burnett, a thirty-year-old prostitute, died from typhoid F in March 1880 in Canon City. She was listed outright as a "whore." Fannie may have worked at nearby Prospect Heights, a suburb of Canon City that did feature at least one bordello.[15]

Southwest of Florence was Silver Cliff, founded in 1878.[16] Silver Cliff's nightlife soon became legendary. The first women in town were prostitutes Belle McLain and Jennie Creek, and the first saloons were small shacks with long bars.[17] Within a few years, Silver Cliff's nightlife was well known. A parade was often held at 6:00 P.M. in the rowdier part of town to entice revelers to come party. Participants usually included a brass band, saloon advertisers, and a wagon of shady ladies.[18] The wayward women had no qualms about listing themselves in the 1880 census as "sporting women." They were twenty-one-year-old Emma Brown of Canada; twenty-one-year-old Mollie Colburn, who resided with one Burt Colburn (listed as a "sporting man"); and twenty-year-old Jennie Staples, a young widow who lived with a bartender and miner.[19]

Although Denver and Colorado City can lay claim to being the earliest

Anglo cities in Colorado, it was actually the city of Boulder that provided the earliest sporting houses in 1858.[20] The city was not incorporated until 1871, however, and the town fathers adopted their first ordinance against prostitution in 1873. At the start, Boulder's houses of ill repute were scattered throughout town. Soon, however, most of the houses were congregating at the end of Railroad Street or Waters Street (now Canyon Boulevard) between the 1900 and 2100 blocks. Reigning madams in 1877 included Julie "Frenchy" Nealis, who sued saloon keeper James Nevin to reclaim her furniture from an apartment above his bar in 1877.[21] Another famed madam was Susan Brown, who owned two brothels. Susan was often at war with madam Mary Day, and the two were in the habit of setting fire to one another's bordellos. When Susan's house burned in 1878, the *Colorado Banner* noted that this was the seventh time she had suffered a fire.[22]

By 1880, Boulder had five bawdy houses in operation run by Susan Brown, Bessie Pound, Alice Thomas, and Frances Vale.[23] Shortly after Susan opened, the *Boulder News and Courier* commented on a scuffle at her place. The fight "resulted in the complete demolition of one of the ladies, whose head came in contact with an empty beer bottle."[24] Knife fights at madam Mary Etta Kingsley's were common. In 1888, the marshal was called to Etta's house, where he found the large black madam thrusting a ten-inch carving knife at another working girl and arrested both women. The divine Ms. Kingsley did have a soft side, however, and even purchased a burial plot for employee Mamie Price after Mamie overdosed on cocaine in 1888. Etta died in 1902.[25]

By 1886, local papers were voicing their discontent regarding the red light district. "The first thing a person sees on lighting from the cars in Boulder," complained the *Boulder County Herald*, "and the last seen on getting on the train are these institutions of infamy." In fact, the situation grew worse each year. When eighteen-year-old Trixie Lee was murdered by a jealous wife in 1894, officials had just about had enough. The wife, Maud Hawks, was found not guilty. "[T]he life of a scarlet woman weighs nothing in the balance against the avenging right of a woman wronged," observed the *Boulder Daily Camera*. The Citizen's Reform League set about cleaning up Boulder in 1897. The plan appears to have worked more than any other employed in Colorado, although prostitutes were still paying fines in 1901. As of 1909, however, Boulder's red light district had been closed down for good.[26]

Boulder was founded very nearly at the same time as Colorado City, which was made the territorial capital in 1861. A short time later the capital was moved to Denver, and in 1873 the new, elite, and ostentatious city of Colorado Springs managed to win the county seat away from Colorado City. Colorado Springs strictly forbade gambling, alcohol, and prostitution, so Colorado City, just a few miles away, prospered where Colorado Springs did not. Customers to the saloons and sporting houses included residents of both places.[27] Colorado City was initially just a supply town, and its reputation as a saloon town was slow to grow. Records of Colorado City's early years are scant, largely due to its small population. The presence of at least a few soiled doves is implied in an 1877 letter to the editor in the *Colorado Mountaineer*, criticizing the former First National Bank president in Colorado Springs for expressing his belief that "female prostitution and houses of ill fame" were less evil than saloons.[28] But the 1879 city directory lists a mere 99 citizens, and the 1880 census records only 327 people. About half were women, and none exhibited tell-tale traits of the typical working girl.[29]

By the time madam Laura Bell McDaniel arrived in 1888, Colorado City's red light district was just beginning to bud. Laura Bell's strength, courage, and acute business sense are notable. She also proved to be an exception to so many thousands of such women who were ostracized from their families, suffered at the hands of authorities, forced to give up their children, and failed to win respect among their peers. To the contrary, Laura Bell achieved success that most women in her line of work only dreamed about. Born Laura Bell Horton in Missouri in 1860, she married, had a daughter, migrated to Colorado, then found herself alone in Salida in about 1882. She worked as a clerk until her paramour, liquor dealer Thomas McDaniel, apparently talked her into prostitution. Laura Bell set out on her own, though, after Thomas killed a man in her mother's living room less than a month after he married her. By 1888, she was living in Colorado City and soon went into business as a madam.[30]

Laura Bell was unique for several reasons. Her mother, Anna Warmouth, followed her not only to Salida, but also to Colorado City, where she lived around the corner from Laura Bell's parlor house. Laura Bell's younger sister, Birdie, as well as her daughter, Pearl, lived with Anna. Birdie, Pearl, and Laura Bell remained close throughout their lives, traveling to Denver often and spending time together. Anna's new husband also joined the intimate family group and not only knew about, but seemingly supported

Laura Bell's profession. Laura Bell was also good friends with a respectable citizen, John "Prairie Dog" O'Byrne, who ran a hack service between Colorado Springs and Colorado City. Laura Bell was extremely loyal to her family and contributed heavily to the family bank account. Her bordello during this time sported a ballroom, costly furniture, and even livery servants. It is highly unusual that her family not only accepted her for what she was, but was also willing to live in proximity to her place of business.[31]

In 1893, Laura Bell successfully filed for divorce from Tom McDaniel on grounds of failure to support. The rest of her family continued to grow when Birdie married and had a child. All continued living with Anna. When Birdie divorced, remarried, and moved to Cripple Creek, Laura Bell followed her and set up other bordellos. Laura Bell's niece, seventeen-year-old "Little Laura" Horton, moved to Colorado City in 1906. Laura Bell returned to Colorado City in 1908 and soon afterward, Little Laura moved in with her. By then, the red light district had grown considerably and included such competing madams as Mamie Majors, whose bordello was next to Laura Bell's. When Mayor Ira Foote repeated his warning to the prostitutes of Colorado City to get out of town in 1908, the point was emphasized by two mysterious fires that burned down most of the red light district. Laura Bell's brothel was one of the casualties. As always, however, she was heavily insured and immediately rebuilt a $10,000 parlor house of brick with fancy red lamps out front.[32] By 1910, twenty-one-year-old Laura Horton was listed as a "servant," as were her aunt's female boarders.[33] She is probably the same Anna Laurie Horton who married a Robert W. Pearson of Colorado City that summer.[34]

Laura Bell also married Herbert Berg, the financial editor of the *Colorado Springs Gazette Telegraph* in 1911. The union possibly gained Laura Bell some political power. When Colorado City authorities tried to shut down the red light district in 1913, some of its citizens moved a few blocks north and established their own "whiskey town" called "Ramona." Laura Bell refused to move out of her old digs in Colorado City, however, discreetly listing herself as the "keeper of furnished rooms" in city directories. But the power she gained by marrying Berg diminished somewhat upon his death in 1916. When Colorado City was annexed to Colorado Springs in 1917 and Laura Bell still refused to budge, authorities had enough. In November, she was arrested for harboring liquor stolen from the mansion of Charles Baldwin in the Broadmoor, Colorado Springs' most elite neighborhood.[35]

FIGURE 25 ❧ *For years, historians at the Old Colorado City Historical Society in Colorado Springs believed this portrait to be madam Laura Bell McDaniel. In 2008, however, historian Martha Lee discovered that the portrait is actually silent film star Maxine Elliott as the character of Portia in* The Merchant of Venice. *It is on display at the Old Colorado City Historical Society. Courtesy of the Old Colorado City Historical Society, Colorado Springs, Colorado.*

Laura Bell was acquitted in January 1918. The next day she, along with Little Laura and her blind friend Dusty McCarty, set out for Denver. Little Laura was now living in Denver near her cousins Pearl Kitto, Cecil Moats, Harry Hooyer Jr., and her sister Buelah. As Little Laura drove her aunt's Mitchell Touring Car near Castle Rock, however, the automobile left the road at forty miles per hour—an amazing speed for 1918—and rolled three times. Little Laura was killed instantly, and Dusty was knocked unconscious. Laura Bell died later that night in Colorado Springs from massive injuries to her ribs, chest, and lungs.[36] It soon came to light that the only witnesses to the accident were Colorado Springs deputy district attorney Jack Caruthers and two other men. Historians have since speculated that the men purposely ran the McDaniel car off the road.[37]

While Laura Bell was alive, she witnessed a number of skirmishes, both legal and illegal, between authorities and Colorado City's red light district. In 1890, a new city hall was built quite literally around the corner from the district, but that hardly stopped women such as Minnie Smith, who also went by "Lou Eaton," "Dirty Alice," and "Minnie the Gambler" and was well known throughout Colorado and the West. In 1890, Minnie was living in Colorado City.[38] She was described as "a dark slim brunette with traces of lingering beauty."[39] Alternately, Minnie was also described as being in her midthirties, "a slender little woman, not good looking and a vixen when aroused."[40] She was also well known for her terrible temper and was in trouble a great deal during her short stay in Colorado City. She was once brought in on charges of nearly beating a lawyer to death with the butt of a gun, and early magazines sported engravings of her horsewhipping a man she had caught cheating at cards. Minnie also got in trouble in Denver before going to Creede and opening her own sporting house.[41] When that didn't work, she tried her luck in Cripple Creek in 1893, opening a parlor house over the Anaconda Saloon on Bennett Avenue.[42]

Unfortunately, the competition proved too tough for Minnie in Cripple Creek. Following an argument with her husband, Charles Eaton, she spent the night getting liquored up and taking morphine, from which she finally died. It was noted that she had just recently willed her entire estate to a grown son and daughter, and reporters calling at her home were met by a "florid, meek-looking man, most likely her husband, who refused to give any information."[43] Her body was taken to Colorado City for burial. Minnie was buried in Evergreen Cemetery beside her first husband, Royster Smith. Her grave mate on her other side was allegedly Bruce Younger of the Younger Gang. When Bruce sickened and died "an ugly death" in 1890, the underworld of Colorado City paid for his funeral and gave him the plot near Smith's. Unfortunately, no records of these burials appear to exist.[44] Minnie left a considerable estate, including property in Creede, Buena Vista, Pitkin, Colorado Springs, and Oklahoma.[45] What became of her property is unknown.

The 1891 directory for Colorado City lists six bordellos, discreetly called "boardinghouses." The next year, the Sanborn Fire Insurance map shows "female boarding" in two buildings each on the north and south sides of Washington Avenue (now Cucharras Street).[46] In 1894, the Women's Christian Temperance Union submitted a petition to the city that would impose hours of operation on all dens of vice. A raid in 1896 was followed by a series of new ordinances: "Keepers of disorderly houses shall not refuse to admit officers. Officers may break doors and arrest with or without warrant." Getting caught in the act of prostitution was a $300 fine, with additional punishments for frequenting opium joints, houses of prostitution, or dance halls. Furthermore, music was not even permitted at houses of ill fame or saloons.[47]

Despite the ordinances, the scarlet ladies came. Mamie Majors first appeared in city directories in 1901 and initially worked for madam Nellie White. She opened her own brothel in 1902, but continued working off and on with Nellie. By 1903, her business was blooming and she purchased another brothel from madam Laura White. In 1905, Mamie was the target of a raid, along with Anna Wilson and Mamie Swift. Two saloon men posted bond for the three women, but Mamie's case especially caused quite a stir in Colorado City. Reporters fairly frothed at the mouth as various city employees and even Mamie's girls testified against her. Although she pled "not guilty" to running a house of prostitution, her house remained open during her trial. When she was found guilty, she appealed, eventually using her more influential friends to secure a governor's pardon. Following heated newspaper debates between Governor Henry Buchtel, who was accused of pardoning Mamie, and Reverend Frank Hullinger, who lambasted him for it, Mamie ultimately received thirty days in jail. She remained in business through at least 1916, when Colorado City succeeded in declaring liquor unlawful within city limits. After that, she disappeared from Colorado City without a trace.[48]

The war against gambling, saloons, and prostitution raged on in Colorado City for many years. Newspapers reported on such vices being outlawed in 1901, 1906, 1908, 1909, 1911, 1913, and, finally, 1916. The crackdowns were sometimes a result of certain events, such as Tucker Holland's suicide at Dolly Worling's brothel in 1908. In 1902, 1907, and 1909, mysterious fires broke out along Saloon Row and the red light district, destroying a number of businesses each time. The fires of 1909 numbered three, the last of which actually began in a nearby livery stable. Blamed on a vagrant, the fire killed forty-three horses, including Mayor Ira Foote's own steed. As always, the red light district simply began reconstruction even as reformers objected and the city looked the other way. "So far as I am personally concerned, I am unaware of the existence of [a red light district] such at the present writing," retorted Alderman Kelly in response to several angry letters. "I naturally presumed that the fire of last December [sic] had forever wiped from existence this so called 'Necessary Evil.'" Kelly also explained that "I, like Senator John Stephen, believe that, if we are to be cursed with this evil, the best way is to confine it to certain quarters of the community, and there control it."[49]

Prominent madams who weathered such storms during these years included not just Laura Bell McDaniel and Mamie Majors, but also Sadie Stewart, Bessie Paxton, Eula Hames, and Blanche Burton. It was in fact Blanche's mysterious and tragic death that drew a more sympathetic eye to the red light district. An Irish immigrant who came to America in 1881, Blanche was once married to a prominent Kansas man who later moved back east. The couple had a son and a daughter. The boy died in an explosion, and the girl was placed in a convent. Blanche moved to Colorado City in 1889, but went to Cripple Creek in 1891, where she was hailed as the city's first madam. She thereafter returned to Colorado City, where, on the night of December 20, 1909, two police officers found her engulfed in flames and running into the middle of Colorado Avenue. The men used their overcoats and snow to extinguish the flames, carried Blanche into her home, and found a broken oil lamp to be the cause of the fire. Blanche refused to give her real name before she died, but said her daughter lived in Illinois. Neither the daughter nor any of Blanche's money was ever found, and her death was treated as suspicious. Madam Mamie Majors paid for her funeral. During services for Blanche on Christmas Eve, it was pointed out that she had just recently purchased a ton of coal for needy families. Even the public and the press felt sympathy for her.[50]

In 1913, the Women's Christian Temperance Union successfully campaigned to vote Colorado City dry as a means of stopping prostitution once and for all. As noted earlier, in response the red light ladies and their liquor-selling counterparts simply established their own town, Ramona, outside the city limits. Nearby residents complained of the noise and traffic, and both cities refused to supply water to the new town. Until 1916, when the whole state outlawed liquor, attempts were made to arrest residents of Ramona for anything from operating illegal liquor houses to prostitution to child molestation. Saloon owners who had prospered for decades in Colorado City suddenly went broke, and the majority of soiled doves flocked elsewhere.[51]

The end of such activities in Colorado City was similar to that in Denver, but not before the latter city enjoyed more than fifty years of illicit fun. Denver's first Anglo prostitute was Ada LaMont, a nineteen-year-old beauty who married a young minister and came west with him in about 1858. Midway through the trip, the minister disappeared with a young lady of questionable character. Ada arrived in Denver alone, but with a whole new outlook on her situation. "As of tomorrow," she said, "I start the first brothel in this settlement. In the future my name will be Addie LaMont."[52] Addie had her work cut out for her. By 1860, she was in competition with such toughs as Charley Harrison, who not only owned the Criterion bar, but also ran two bordellos. Harrison once smuggled a thug named James Gordon out of town after the latter killed Addie's bartender and a German settler at her place. But he also ran around with Addie, and when he was banished from Denver in 1869, she mourned his loss as though he had died. Harrison did die later at the hands of some Osage Indians. By then, Addie's business had fallen off, and a visit from an old friend revealed that her minister husband had been murdered by Indians on the Kansas prairie. Addie lapsed into an alcoholic haze for a few months before closing her bordello and heading to Georgetown, Colorado. She was never able to reclaim her wealth and died in poverty there.[53]

A female visitor to Denver in 1868 was mortified at the number of prostitutes running amuck in the town. "Such a collection of fiends in human shape I hope never to see again," she declared in a letter home. "I did not meet more than two of my own sex who made the most distant claims to even common decency or self-respect."[54] The authorities felt the same way, and in 1870 ordinances were passed in the City of Denver prohibiting prostitution.[55] Denver's brothels eventually formed a neighborhood of their own along McGaa Street, a block away from the main drag, Larimer Street. Shortly after the railroad made it to Denver, a four-block-long series of brothels, gambling dens, and opium joints popped up in the area. Hop Alley between Larimer and McGaa was home to some eight hundred Chinese, including about fifty "slave girls" at any given time. In time, the McGaa Street "tenderloin district" had upwards of more than a thousand working girls, most of whom conducted their business out of cribs. The ladies paid $25 a week in rent. There does not appear to have been much racial segregation, except that white girls made about a dollar per trick, whereas their African American counterparts made half as much. There was also other segregation between the crib girls and the ladies of the parlor houses; the latter were not permitted to associate with the former. In time, McGaa Street was renamed Holladay Street after Ben Holladay as revenge after the livery owner scrapped a favored stage line.[56]

Denver's most notorious madam arrived in 1876. Her name was Mattie Silks, and for the next fifty-four years she was a force to be reckoned with. Mattie's birthplace has been identified by various sources as New York, Pennsylvania, Indiana, and Kansas.[57] Similarly, it is unclear whether she first worked as a freighter between Missouri and Colorado before beginning her prostitution career in the Kansas towns of Abilene, Dodge City, or Hays City, or possibly in Springfield, Illinois, in about 1865.[58] Most historians do agree that a sign on her parlor house read "Men taken in and done for," and that she was run out of Olathe, Kansas, before working the cattle town circuit out of Kansas City during the summer months.[59]

Mattie eventually took a wagon with four girls from Kansas to the Pikes Peak region in Colorado, visiting a number of mining camps. Her vehicle contained a "portable boardinghouse for young ladies," which was actually no more than a canvas tent attached to a wagon. The bordello did, however, include a canvas bathtub.[60] By 1873, she was in Georgetown, where she operated one of five brothels on Brownell Street. Her girls were touted as the "fairest frails in town." Mattie herself claimed she was very particular about her girls. "I never took a girl into my house who had had no previous experience of life and men," she stated in her later years. "That was a rule of mine. . . . No innocent, young girl was ever hired by me. Those with experience came to me for the same reasons that I hired them. Because there was money in it for all of us." Money, indeed: by 1875, Mattie was one of the wealthiest women in her profession.[61]

In Georgetown, Mattie allegedly met and married Casey or George Silks, a faro dealer from Pueblo. The couple may have had a child together. The two eventually separated, perhaps because Mattie's lover, Cortez Thomson, was also living in Mattie's brothel.[62] Author Harry Drago claims that the truth about this possible love triangle is that Mattie never married George, although he did accompany the madam and Thomson to Denver in 1876.[63] Thomson had left his wife and daughter behind in Georgetown or in Texas.[64]

After first renting a bordello, Mattie eventually bought the property at 501 McGaa. There was room enough for twelve boarders.[65] She later bought a new parlor house, a three-story brick affair with twenty-seven rooms and elegant furnishings. Gentlemen (and they were required to be so) coming to the house were greeted by Mattie herself, who showed them to a parlor where an orchestra played and her entertaining ladies awaited. Mattie kept a list of her regular customers, crossing off anyone who broke house rules.[66]

Mattie's love for Thomson was deep. She was willing to put up with his drinking and gambling habits, both of which he often financed with her money. On those rare occasions when Thomson won at the tables, he would buy small gifts for Mattie. One of them was a diamond-encrusted cross that she always wore on a chain around her neck.[67] Mattie didn't mind that the gifts were bought with money she had given Thomson, and it was said that despite two terrible beatings Thomson gave her, she loved him too much to leave him. Mattie Silks was certainly not the angel she aspired to be, however. The March 28, 1877, issue of the *Rocky Mountain News* reported that she was fined $12 for drunkenness, which she paid. Then in August, Mattie challenged madam Katie Fulton to a duel over Thomson.[68] Both women survived, and Mattie continued gaining success in Denver. Over the years, she traveled with Thomson, purchased a racing stable (only one of her horses, Jim Blaine, ever won a race), and bought several brothels. She also provided food and shelter to those who were down and out.[69]

In 1884, Thomson married Mattie in Indiana.[70] Soon thereafter, Mattie purchased three Denver bordellos and rented them to other madams, all of whom were successful.[71] When Thomson's daughter died during childbirth

FIGURE 26 ⚭ *One of the last known photographs of Mattie Silks at her ranch in Wray, Colorado, circa 1920s. Mattie is on the left; the girl on the right is thought to be either one of her employees or Cort Thomson's granddaughter, but her resemblance to Mattie has led to speculation that she is Mattie's daughter. Courtesy of the Colorado Historical Society, Denver, F-41, 400.*

in 1886, Mattie convinced him to adopt his granddaughter and purchased a ranch on the eastern plains at Wray as a suitable place to raise the girl.[72] She also continued to bask in Denver's limelight. During the 1880s, in an agreement with the Chamber of Commerce and Thomson, Mattie romanced the president of the St. Louis Railroad to convince him to extend the tracks to Denver (he didn't). She also purchased other real estate around Denver and extended her services to include call girls in uptown Denver hotels.[73]

Mattie's troubles with Thomson escalated in 1891, when she caught him with prostitute Lillie Dab of Leadville.[74] Mattie fired a shot, clipping two curls off of Lillie's coiffured head. Lillie scrambled out of the room while Thomson wrestled the pistol from Mattie's hand, clubbed her on the head, and gave her an "unmerciful beating."[75] Mattie sued for divorce, but soon forgave Thomson and withdrew the suit. In 1897, the couple took excursions to Great Britain and Alaska, where Mattie opened a temporary brothel in Dawson City. She netted $38,000 after only three months and returned to Colorado. In April 1900, Thomson died at the Commercial Hotel in Wray. Mattie was by his side and paid for his funeral costs.[76]

In 1910 or 1911, Mattie purchased the infamous House of Mirrors from the estate of rival madam Jennie Rogers and commissioned a local tile worker to inlay her name, "M. Silks," on the front step.[77] By 1922, however, she was seemingly retired and living with her beau, John Dillon Ready, also known as "Handsome Jack Kelley" and "Jack Ready," whom she had originally hired as a bouncer.[78] Some maintain the two married when Mattie was in her seventies, as illustrated by their sharing the same address between 1922 and Mattie's death in 1929. She was eighty-three, and her final estate amounted to only $1,922. The money was left to Jack Ready and Cort Thomson's granddaughter. Mattie is buried in Denver's Fairmount Cemetery under the name "Martha A. Ready," allegedly next to the unmarked grave of Cort Thomson.[79]

Mattie's biggest competitor was Jennie Rogers, also known as "Leeah J. Tehme" and "Leeah Fries" or "Friess." Jennie also once told police her maiden name was "Calvington." She was born in 1843 in Pittsburgh or Allegheny, Pennsylvania.[80] After growing up selling the family produce on the streets, Jennie was lucky enough to marry Dr. G. Friess.[81] The union proved too dull for Jennie, and she allegedly ran away with a steamboat captain named Rogers. The man named his ship the *Jennie Rogers* and traveled with Jennie throughout Pennsylvania and Ohio.[82] After a few years, Jennie tired of life on the river and took a job as a housekeeper. Her job landed her at the home of the mayor of Pittsburgh, but in time stories of her previous affairs and her divorces from Friess and possibly Rogers surfaced. The mayor was forced to fire her to save his image, but gave her enough money to start a business in St. Louis. Jennie chose prostitution as her new career.[83]

After a few years, Jennie decided to follow the gold rush to Colorado. She arrived in Denver just two years after Mattie Silks in 1879. Jennie purchased her first house from Mattie Silks in 1880. There, it was said, the chief of police from St. Louis would come to visit, and Jennie even had a portrait of him hanging in her brothel.[84] Jennie has been described as a raven-haired beauty who favored velvet dresses and emerald earrings. Her two-story brick bordello was suited to her taste, with brass beds, hand-carved furniture, and imported rugs.[85] Despite her lavish lifestyle, however, Jennie was arrested in 1880 along with madam Eva Lewis for racing

FIGURE 27 ❧ *Jennie Rogers's famous House of Mirrors in Denver, sometime after 1948. The four unidentified faces were affixed at the apex, with a bust of Jennie reigning above them all. Courtesy of the Colorado Historical Society, Denver, F-37, 953.*

their horses through town. She was arrested again in 1883 for vagrancy and for taking morphine.[86] But these arrests did little to quell her appetite for the finer things in life. In time, she was successful enough to buy a bordello next door to hers and constructed a passageway between the two. A year later she purchased a third house.[87]

Jennie paid her fines regularly and weathered several arrests. During an 1886 raid, she and fourteen other madams were fined $75 each. In about 1887, she married hack driver John "Jack" Wood, formerly a bartender at the Brown Palace Hotel, and soon purchased a saloon in Salt Lake City, Utah, for him to run.[88] When a few months later Jennie surprised Wood in Salt Lake City, she found him in the arms of another woman and shot him. When police asked why she did it, she exclaimed, "I shot him because I love him, damn him!"[89] Jack persuaded authorities to release Jennie. In 1889, she built another brothel, the infamous House of Mirrors at 1942 Market Street.[90] The architect was William Quayle, who also designed the First Congregational Church and later West High School.[91]

Although Jennie was quite wealthy when she built the House of Mirrors, a wonderful story surrounding her financing was widely circulated in later years. The police chief from St. Louis decided to assist Jennie in opening her Denver house of ill fame by blackmailing one of Denver's leading citizens. This man's first wife had apparently pulled a disappearing act, and the gentleman had since married into a wealthy Denver family. Jennie's St. Louis friend and other political adversaries began circulating the rumor that the first wife had been murdered, and they even buried the skull of an Indian woman found on the plains in the man's backyard. The St. Louis officer and two other men then called at the man's home posing as investigators, conducted a search, and dug up the skull. The surprised tycoon was innocent and knew he was so. Nevertheless, such a scandal could ruin his political career. Accordingly, the man "donated" $17,780 to Jennie for a new house. Jennie's St. Louis friend disappeared, and the matter was forgotten until it was related years later by someone who remembered the story.[92]

In time, the House of Mirrors became one of the most prominent structures in Denver's red light district. It had twenty-seven rooms in all, including a kitchen, ballroom, four parlors, a wine room, and sixteen bedrooms upstairs (given the square footage of the building, the sixteen bedrooms likely functioned as small, partitioned cribs). The front parlor was furbished in mirrors from ceiling to floor. A single bathroom, luxurious

FIGURE 28 ✢ *Jennie Rogers when she was still quite young. Note her
star-shaped emerald earrings, which she was fond of and wore often.
Courtesy of the Colorado Historical Society, Denver, F-37, 395.*

for the time, also serviced the house. The bedrooms were said to be well stocked with fancy furniture, commodes, slop jars, rockers, lace curtains, and even writing desks. Jennie also had five stone faces adhered to the facade of the building, including a bust of herself at the top. There has been never-ending speculation about who the other faces represent, including a story that they were the faces of those involved in the blackmailing of the rich man who gave Jennie the money for her house. But the truth about them will likely never be known. The exterior decor also came complete with fancy scroll work in a variety of mysterious designs.[93]

Jennie commanded only the best in female employees, among whom style, good looks, and excellent manners were a must. She also demanded the best in dress, selecting costumes from local dressmakers for her girls to wear and charging her employees for the cost. Jennie's success in 1889 was also marked by the finding of Jack Wood, whom she hadn't seen for two years and who was running a bar in Omaha, Nebraska. Jennie wrote to him asking him to come back to her, and the two were remarried in August. By 1890, even the newspapers knew that local lawmakers met regularly at Jennie's. Jennie also maintained a friendship with Mattie Silks. Despite their friendship, the two must have had at least some competitive feelings toward each other. Jennie called herself the "Queen of the Colorado Underworld," which surely irked Mattie.[94]

In 1891, Jennie sold the House of Mirrors to madam Ella Wellington. When the madams and bar owners of Denver cooperated to produce the *Denver Red Book* in 1892 (discussed more fully later), Ella was a prominent advertiser.[95] The former wife of Fred Bouse (or Bowse) of Omaha, Ella had forsaken her confining life as a wife and mother of two adopted children and had run off with one Sam Cross. After Cross apparently left her in Salt Lake City, Ella made her way to Denver. One evening in 1894 some old friends of the Bouses' unexpectedly paid Ella a visit. Fred was remarried, they said, and the new family was doing just fine. The news was too much for Ella, who abruptly started upstairs, exclaiming, "O I am so happy! So happy that I'll just blow my goddam brains out!" Upon reaching her bedroom, Ella did just that. At the time, Arapahoe County clerk William R. Prinn was lying in Ella's bed and later gave his statement to the coroner. Following a funeral procession that took every available carriage in town, Ella was buried at Riverside Cemetery. Her most loyal admirer, Frederick Sturges, spent the next three weeks sleeping on top of her grave; he eventually purchased a plot next to hers before overdosing on morphine. In his pocket was a picture of Ella with a note written on the back: "Bury this picture of my own dear Ella beside me."[96]

Following Ella Wellington's suicide, the House of Mirrors came back into Jennie Rogers's hands.[97] About a year later, Jack Wood died of unknown causes at the young age of thirty-eight. Jennie had him buried in Evergreen Cemetery with a headstone reading, "He is not dead, but sleeping."[98] The year 1902 proved to be even more stressful: Jennie's beloved dog died, and she was diagnosed with Bright's disease. She moved to Chicago, opened another brothel, and met a politician named Archibald Fitzgerald. The man was twenty years her junior, but Jennie married him anyway at Hot Springs, Arkansas, in 1904.[99] Following a brief trip to Denver for the funeral of prostitute Lizzie Preston, Jennie returned to Chicago only to find out that Fitzgerald was still married to two other women. Jennie left him and returned to Denver in 1907. Although she eventually forgave Fitzgerald and took some trips with him to Arkansas, her health continued to suffer. Fitzgerald also managed to squander almost all of her fortune. Jennie died in October 1909 after willing everything to her sister, a niece, and a nephew. She was buried in Denver's Fairmont Cemetery under the name "Leah J. Wood" next to Jack. Fitzgerald contested her will and claimed half of her estate. He eventually settled for $5,000 in cash, jewelry, and some property in Illinois.[100]

Other prominent Denver madams in 1880 included Belle Barnard, Lizzie Barton, and Nellie Bisco.[101] The women ruled over their girls with iron fists, but the red light ladies of Denver had their share of mishaps. In 1880, Josephine "Negro" Yates died of extensive burns. Records indicate that Josephine was twenty-three, married, and born in Michigan, but the circumstances of her injuries remain unknown.[102] Also drifting around at this time was Lizzie Greer, a long-time Denver madam whose end was near. By 1881, Lizzie had lost all of her money and admirers and had turned to alcohol. The newspaper noted she had been living for years in back alleys and along riverfronts, purchasing liquor when she could and eating out of the garbage bins of local restaurants. She was last noted as being found sleeping in a lumber yard and taken to the county hospital. Following her death, which probably occurred in January 1881, the sight of Lizzie's ghost lingering near the undertaker's parlor was the subject of *Rocky Mountain News* stories for several years, until 1885.[103] Three other women of the 1880s,

Daisy Smith, Belle Jones, and Annie Griffin, were charged with "naughty capers" when they were seen dancing nude on a Larimer Street corner.[104] Yet another woman, Blanche Farley, was arrested after she followed her paramour and another working girl to the Tabor Grand Opera House. Blanche waited outside for the pair to emerge following a performance. When they did, she belted her rival, knocking her unconscious. Blanche was fined $5 for the incident; she commented, "It was worth it."[105]

In 1882, there were approximately 480 prostitutes in Denver.[106] Open soliciting was legal at the time, with prostitutes participating in horse races, water fights to show off their wares, and public pillow fights. When soliciting was outlawed and curtains were required on all red light windows, "accidental" holes were ripped in the curtains, allowing passersby their own private peep show. In answer, officers raided the red light district regularly during a six-month period in 1886. Then in 1889, Denver authorities changed the name of Holladay Street to Market Street after a descendant of Ben Holladay complained about the name.[107] A short time later, authorities went on another tear. Newspapers statewide reported that authorities in Denver had rounded up two hundred "depraved women" and locked them in the courthouse overnight. "There seems to be a determination to rid the city of these creatures," reported the *Castle Rock Journal* on May 8, 1889. "The prosecuting attorney says there are 125 bawdy houses in town." The *Rocky Mountain News* joined the fight, commenting in July 1889 that saloons were "the most fruitful source for breeding and feeding prostitution."[108]

Unfazed, the wicked women of Denver collaborated on the *Denver Red Book* in 1892. Inside were ads for local saloons and a number of prostitutes, including Blanche Brown, Belle Birnard, Jennie Holmes, and Minnie Hall. Other women were equally undaunted by the authorities' actions, such as Verona (a.k.a. "Fannie") Baldwin. In 1883 in San Francisco, the British beauty had made headlines after she shot her millionaire cousin, Elias Jackson "Lucky" Baldwin, in the arm. Verona claimed Baldwin had sexually assaulted her while she was teaching school at his ranch. Baldwin survived, to which Verona commented, "I ought to have killed him. Yes, I ought to have killed him at the ranch."[109] Three years after she was acquitted due to Baldwin's refusal to testify, Verona sued her cousin for child support. He in turn committed her to an insane asylum. She fought him, along with the general public, and was released.[110] In the late 1890s, Verona arrived in Denver and purchased a house at 2020 Market Street. Her life in

Denver appeared to be much calmer than her earlier days, and she was in business for nearly twelve years.[111]

In 1908, District Attorney George Stidger became determined to overthrow police and shut down the red light district. Using an upcoming election as his tool, Stidger claimed that the red light district "rolls up ten thousand illegal votes for the police machine every election through the agency of its padded rooming houses and willing repeaters." He also gave notice to Denver's prostitutes that they had twenty-four hours to secure decent employment or leave town.[112] Authorities did finally shut down Market Street in 1915, but the following year twenty-nine prostitutes were arrested.[113] Only Charles "Big Time Charlie" Allen dared to challenge authorities. Allen blew into Denver in 1916 and was soon running a large ring of prostitutes. He allegedly used "a variety of underhanded tactics," including drug addiction, to lure women into his business. Over four years, Allen made more than a million dollars off the trade. He was arrested in about 1919 and sent to prison at Leavenworth.[114] In the meantime, Mattie Silks converted one of her houses into the Silks Hotel. Likewise, Verona Baldwin opened a discreet tavern called the Baldwin Inn. Whether Mattie and Verona's services included prostitution is unknown, but eighty-two women were charged with prostitution in Denver in 1917. A year later Mattie sold the House of Mirrors to the Buddhists, who used it as a temple until 1948.[115]

Throughout the early 1920s, Denver arrests continued to escalate: thirty-five in 1920, fifty-seven in 1921, and ninety-five in 1922. A few old-timers were still present, including Annie Ryan and Sadie Doyle. Sadie had once worked at the Circus, a three-story bordello across from Jennie Rogers's place that included Jim Ryan's Saloon. She later recalled a night in 1901 when she was thrown in jail. Later that night, after her release, the jail caught fire. In the late 1920s, Sadie and Anna, who had once run family-owned brothels in Cripple Creek and Denver with her daughters, moved to an area outside of the old red light district. There, on August 8, 1930, Anna shot and killed former police officer Maurice Lyons. Sadie, who was by then blind, was the only witness, and Anna was ultimately released by authorities due to lack of evidence. A short time later she died, and Blind Sadie moved to new quarters. Despite her loss of sight, Blind Sadie continued running a brothel known as the Lucky Strike Rooms. In 1949, it was discovered that her caretaker, Frank "Toughy" Keith, had been renting Sadie's bed to one Anne O'Neil for prostitution. The court put an end to Sadie's bed renting and ordered the eighty-six-year-old woman committed to a convalescent home. Sadie died in 1950. Even then, fifty friends and acquaintances attended her funeral services.[116]

During its early years, Denver was immediately surrounded by a series of mining camps in the mountains west of town. One of them was Central City. Founded in 1859, Central City already had at least one brothel within a year. The place was described as "a sort of hurdy gurdy saloon, built of rough logs and containing the usual primitive accessories of a dance house, viz: a bar well stocked with Taos Lightening, a few benches and tables, and three or four girls educated in the business of passing drinks and bandying coarse epithets with whomsoever pleased to call them out. There was music whiskey, cards, etc., and an occasional shooting match inside to vary the monotony of things. Women of any kind were scarce in those days, and the saloon was therefore well patronized."[117] By 1864, at least one prostitute, Madam Wright, was operating on Eureka Street. Newspapers took note when she was arrested for larceny. "It is high time she were routed out from the place she occupies on one of the most public and respectable streets in our city," lectured the *Miner's Register*. "Perhaps such creatures should be permitted to live in a community, but they certainly ought to be severely treated for their offenses against morality and law, and compelled to remove to some remote locality where their presence will not be so annoying."[118]

Citizens continued voicing their discontent in 1866, when an anonymous writer, identified only as "The Quincunx," pointed out that although the *Central City Register* openly complained about certain brothels, it failed to mention one operating right across the street from its own office on Eureka Street. The Quincunx noted that upon observation, five of the women and their customers appeared to be the best behaved of the group. About a month later, the special committee assigned to take a hard look at Central City's bordellos reported on "the impracticality of the removal of said houses." Finally, in October, the city council passed a motion to remove the place called the Hurdy Gurdy. Nevertheless, improvements in the situation remained at a standstill. In 1867, papers reported on the arrest of Moll Green and Elmer Hines for the murder of a man at Moll's crib. It was noted that the woman in question had previously been jailed for assault on another man. A few months later the inmates of a bawdy house on Lawrence Avenue were accused of throwing rocks through the windows of the nearby Episcopal parsonage. When the girls of the house explained that their own windows had also been broken, they were dismissed but with much suspicion. They were later fined for keeping a disorderly house and fined $10 each.[119]

Central City continued fighting against prostitution, warning the general public in 1868 that some women trying to inhabit Washington Hall were due to be chased out shortly. The warning may have been because a new "brothel dance house" had been started at the head of Dry Gulch just a month earlier. The *Daily Central City Register* was absolutely vehement over these "vampires and ghouls" taking root in the city, particularly Misters Barnaby and Keys, who were running the Dry Gulch operation. "It were better for the community that they should starve to death or die by their own hands."[120] In answer, the Shoo Fly Dance Hall was opened right downtown in 1870. The female bartenders doubled as singing waitresses and burlesque dancers. When journalist James Thomson visited a Central City bawdy house two years later, he wrote in his diary about seeing three men and women in some attic beds, as well as a woman who stripped to her stockings and danced on the bar.[121]

Central City's naughty girls eventually migrated to Gunnell Hill above town at the end of Pine Street just a few blocks from St. Mary's Catholic Church.[122] The red light district eventually became known as "Quality Row," with girls such as May Martin, Jane Gordon, and Della (or Lizzie) Warwick offering services.[123] A popular madam was Ruby Lee, who functioned as "an elegant courtesan." Likewise, the fond memory of Mae Temple was etched on a downtown warehouse wall, and regarding another girl, Myrtle, a customer wrote, "Myrtle. 13. Wow."[124] Another famous madam was Ada Branch, also known as "Big Swede," who dressed nicely and ran a respectable parlor house. In 1880, the *Rocky Mountain News* reported on a fight on Big Swede Avenue in Central City, illustrating that Pine Street had been temporarily renamed in honor of Ada.[125] A year later Ada boldly rented the Alhambra Theater downtown. Her advertisement in the *Central City Daily Register Call* stated, "I have taken a lease of the Alhambra Varieties for one year, and will open there on Friday evening, the 13th of May with a grand ball. A cordial invitation is extended to all. Free to all. Ada Branch."[126] But Central City's best-remembered madam is Lou Bunch, a three-hundred-pound delight whose presence in town surely could not be missed.[127]

Instantaneous Art Portraits,
New Studios
3136 Cottage Grove Avenue,

FIGURE 29 Madam Lou Bunch. Lou was a queen of Gunnell Hill for many years. Today the hefty woman is honored in Central City, Colorado, each year during Lou Bunch Days. Courtesy of the Colorado Historical Society, Denver.

Up on Gunnell Hill, a local child, about age twelve, once ventured up Pine Street on a Sunday morning shortly after attending church services. The girl witnessed a prostitute standing over the front rail of her porch, dangling a silver crucifix. In the yard below, a man was kneeling, begging the woman to give it back.[128] In 1886, one of Central City's fallen women, Daisy Starr, was found dead along a creek outside of town. The paper only noted that "near five o'clock she passed through Black Hawk and attracted considerable attention from the loose manner in which her clothing clung to her, and the style in which she was dressed." Daisy was last seen with an unidentified man from Black Hawk around 8:30 P.M. before she met her end, but authorities ruled her death accidental.[129]

Prostitution continued to infiltrate the downtown Central City area on occasion. In 1897, Ignatz Meyer bought a formerly respectable business building and converted it into a saloon. Across the street was the Gold Coin Saloon, also constructed in 1897. Girls were available at either place. Prostitution ceased in Central City around 1910, but the city has never lost its fondness for the shady ladies who once worked there. As late as 1947, Emma C. "Emmy" Wilson bought Meyer's old place and opened it as the Glory Hole Saloon. Emmy acquired a bar, back bar, and cabinet from the ghost town of Baltimore and brought them to her new building.[130] She is best remembered for hanging through a hole in the ceiling, thus allowing her patrons to gaze up her skirt. The Glory Hole still exists today.[131]

Literally one mile down the road from Central City was Black Hawk, founded in 1860. By June 1865, madams such as Moll Greer had settled up North Clear Creek near the Bobtail Mine. Moll's place was described as "a two-story log house situated on the bluff within sight of the mill."[132] In 1868, a local newspaper writer expressed alarm at a new brothel in Central City in 1868, as well as one St. Mark's Chapel at Black Hawk. Two days later, in a letter to the editor, a local resident dispelled that myth, stating, "Neither such institution . . . or any other will be permitted in Black Hawk this day or any future time whilst the present officials have control of the city."[133] Despite the bold statement, it was no secret that by 1871 weekends in Black Hawk featured dances for local miners and included entertainment by area prostitutes.[134]

Other nearby towns and camps with red light ladies included Nevadaville, Idaho Springs, Jamestown, Caribou, Eldora, and Arrow. Founded in 1860 and practically abandoned by 1864, Jamestown experienced one of its many booms in 1875 and again in 1882. Prostitutes lived in an area alternately known as Lower Jimtown or Bummerville. The women occasionally grew weary of their confinement and ventured to the town proper. One resident recalled a day when the ladies of Breckenridge's red light resort, some hundred miles away, stopped off at Jamestown in their travels: "they hired a fancy rig from the livery stable and went for a wild ride up and down the streets. They stopped at saloons for fresh inspiration and descended upon the stores whence respectable shoppers fled. They were finally routed and returned to their domain by the sheriff and some hardy aides." During this time, there were some thirty saloons and many dance halls and parlor houses in Jamestown.[135]

Founded in 1870 and located at nearly ten thousand feet, Caribou was cold, subject to one-hundred-mile-an-hour winds and terrible snowstorms with twenty-five-foot drifts. Despite such inconveniences, roughly sixty businesses—including a few brothels—managed to survive. When a new church was erected in 1881, citizens voted to outlaw gamblers and loose women from their community. In answer, the shady ladies and their counterparts moved to nearby Cardinal City, an 1870 mining camp that was already dwindling anyway. For a time, the scarlet ladies and barkeeps of Cardinal City hoped to overtake both towns, but by 1883 the new city had lost its appeal, largely due to the railroad's failure to reach town. A few residents moved to the nearby new gold-mining town of Eldora.[136] Founded in about 1875, Eldora soon had a fair-size red light district, including a place called the Bon Ton, located across the creek from town. The nearby town of Arrow also sported some fancy ladies, as evidenced by their attempt one evening to crash a family dance; they were immediately thrown out. Other soiled doves included a woman known as Mary Jane, after whom a local ski area is now named. Like Caribou and Cardinal, Arrow eventually declined due to the lack of railroad service.[137]

Just who those fancy ladies from Breckenridge were remains unknown, but plenty like them graced the town's history. Founded in 1860, Breckenridge was notable by 1880 for its numerous saloons and three "honky-tonks." Two were located in "a narrow passage" between French Street and Lincoln Avenue.[138] Later, those wishing to visit the Blue Goose, the Columbine Rest, the Pines, or any other house of prostitution need only cross the Blue River west of town. Breckenridge was one of only a handful of towns whose red light district respectfully flourished outside the city limits (another was Hahn's Peak, whose Poverty Flats above town contained both saloons and brothels). Prostitutes at Breckenridge in 1880 included Frankie Brace, Jessica Burns, Nellie Clark, Georgia Dowel, Allice Perry, and Ida Simmons.[139] By 1907, madam Minnie Cowles was leading the pack when she was robbed at gunpoint by a masked man. Minnie's house had closed for the night, but two customers upstairs were staying over. From her downstairs room, Minnie was awakened by the sound of a breaking window. The robber knew where Minnie kept her money, commanding, "Up with your hands—dig up that trunk key or I'll blow the top of your head off!" The thief absconded with $340. Minnie told police she recognized the man's voice and that in fact he had been there earlier that night.[140] Minnie remained in Breckenridge through at least 1920, but by then employed only one girl in her house.[141]

Buckskin Joe, a short distance from Breckenridge, is also notable for its early prostitutes. Founded in 1861, Buckskin soon claimed a red light district of fifty women located on one end of town. The town is best remembered for Silver Heels, the legendary dance hall girl who won many admirers, nursed the sick through a smallpox epidemic, was infected and became scarred for life, and left town suddenly, but occasionally and mysteriously appeared in the cemetery to visit the graves of her dead friends. Down the road from Buckskin was Fairplay, also established in 1861.[142] A travel writer noted in 1873 that "the time to see Fairplay is Sunday night. Then it is that all the miners come to town from the hills, and a jolly time they have. The dance and bawdy houses are then in their element, and money and wine (sometimes blood) flows [sic] freely." The Alma dance house and variety theaters were noted as being next door to the Methodist church, the only house of worship in town.[143] The goings-on at Fairplay were mighty exciting compared to those at more remote camps such as Leavick, which featured only a single bordello.[144]

From Fairplay and Buckskin Joe, travelers could maneuver Mosquito Pass over to Leadville. Founded in 1878, Leadville sported one of the wildest red light districts in Colorado. A local newspaper once called Leadville's dance halls "breathing holes of hell, where customers imbibe torchlight whiskey and indulge in the quadrille and the whirling sinuosity's [sic] of the waltz."[145] Leadville was actually an extension of the original town Oro City, which had sprung up in 1874. Almost immediately, miners, gamblers, and prostitutes had flocked to the town, the latter two conducting business in wagons and tents before buildings were constructed.[146] In fact, some historians maintain that all the first women in Oro City were prostitutes. At one time, when Augusta Tabor and her husband, Horace, were running a boardinghouse in Oro City, Augusta was classified as the only "family-type woman" in the gulch.[147]

Leadville had six dance halls by the end of its first year. The price of a dance then was only twenty-five cents, but some girls such as Maude Deuel of the Pioneer Dance Hall later remembered making as much as $200 a week. Other dance halls included the Bucket of Blood and the Carbonate Concert Hall, which advertised, "Wine, Women and Song. These three are supposed to make life palatial and while nothing of an improper character is permitted we can furnish all three any night." Leadville's red light district was scattered along Harrison Avenue, State Street, West Third and West Fifth streets, and Chestnut Street. "I seldom go down that street," wrote Princeton graduate George Elder to his family in those early days, "but when I do I always notice [the dance halls] full and lots of music and noise."[148]

State Street, in the older section of town, was especially noted for having everything from fancy houses of ill repute to lowly cribs housing a mixture of ethnicities. Crib girls could be as young as twelve or thirteen years of age, and violence was commonplace. Some historians claim that more than two hundred girls worked on State Street alone. French Row, Coon Row, and Tiger Alley were also located along State Street. French Row in its very early days was actually much more respectable than even some of the more elite brothels in Denver. The ladies there, most of whom did not speak English, were much cleaner and classier than their counterparts in Denver. They rarely served liquor, generally found profanity offensive, and kept tidy two-room cribs. They were also disgusted with American prostitutes, whom they regarded as drunken, disrespectful slobs.[149] Other parts of State Street, however, housed girls as young as fourteen or fifteen years of age who had arrived in town only to be "raped and forced to work in a bawdy house."[150]

By 1879, such notorious women as Carrie Linnel, Frankie Paige, Molly Price, and Minnie Purdy were making the papers often. And there was Mollie May, sometimes known as Jennie or Maggie Mickey. Mollie was said to have lost her virginity—sans marriage—as a young girl. She soon wandered west and was working as a prostitute–theater performer in Cheyenne, Wyoming. In 1876, at her house of ill repute in the Black Hills of South

Dakota, Mollie allegedly became the subject of a brief gun battle between two brothers. In fact, Mollie herself was shot, but the metal in her corset deflected the bullet, saving her life. Part of Mollie's ear was also bit off by prostitute Fanny Garretson when the two tangled over a man. Mollie next migrated to Colorado, where she gained a notorious reputation in Silver Cliff, Bonanza, and Pueblo. She arrived in Leadville in about 1879, and the 1880 census notes that Mollie had ten boarders and two male employees living at her house.[151]

Mollie also had adversaries—namely, fellow madam Sally Purple, whose brothel was next door. The two often engaged in battles, even shooting at one another's houses on at least one occasion. Most unusual was Mollie's friendship with a respectable woman named Mindy Lamb. Mindy's husband, Lewis, was shot to death in front of Winnie Purdy's bordello one night in 1880. The culprit was former marshal Martin Duggan, who had been bullying Lewis since they were children. The killing was written off as a suicide, but Mindy knew better and promised Duggan that she would "wear black and mourn this killing until the very day of your death and then, Goddam you, I will dance upon your grave."[152] A few days later, Mollie May stopped Mindy on the street. "You don't know me," she told Mindy, "but I wanted to tell you that what happened to a decent man like your husband was a dirty rotten shame and I'm really sorry for you."[153] A friendship was formed, which was not publicly announced until Mindy insisted on attending Mollie's funeral services in 1887.[154] Mollie's obituary noted she had adopted a local child in 1882 (which the newspapers had scandalized at the time), stating "she was a woman who, with all her bad qualities, was much given to charity and was always willing to help the poor and unfortunate." Unfortunately, Mollie's grave marker, which was probably wood, has long since disappeared.[155]

During Mollie's life in Leadville, newspapers continuously had fun with the antics in the red light district. In 1880, the *Leadville Weekly Chronicle* gave a detailed account on an old-fashioned sparring match between two men over a woman named Cora. After both men tried to win her affections at the parlor house where she worked, it was decided that the only way to pick a winner was for the men to duke it out. Coats and pistols were removed as a rug was moved into the center of the room. Another man stationed himself as a referee at the piano while Cora hopped up on a sofa to "give the word." Upon her command, the men commenced to fistfighting, which lasted several minutes. When the winner was declared, both men washed the blood off their faces and shook hands. The victor retired with Cora, and the loser left the house for greener pastures. "It was a novel to say the least," commented the paper, "and is thought to be the first of like nature on record."[156] One of Leadville's most "respectably kept and managed houses" was the Red Light Saloon on State Street. A visitor described the place: "The decorum of the place is remarkable—to be sure it is a sporting house in all that the term implies. . . . The girls are rounder, rosier and more beautiful than elsewhere and will take you through the mazy waltz in refreshing movements that will make you feel that you don't care a cent whether school keeps or not. So the girls are all there."[157]

Old-timers remembered the wicked women of State Street who drove their carriages around town in the early evenings, after most respectable women had retreated to their own homes for the night. The women were described as "usually intoxicated and smoking long black cigars, with a grand ability to hold the ribbons over the flanks of their fine, high-stepping animals."[158] The partying lasted all night, with incidents ranging from sad to silly. In September 1892, one Thomas O'Rourke cashed a $200 paycheck and wound up at the brothel of Ella Randall. There, O'Rourke bought a round of drinks, left, and shortly afterward reported that he had been robbed of a $20 gold piece. Officers accompanied O'Rourke back to Ella's, but declined to press charges, a decision that turned out for the best because O'Rourke, upon waking the next morning, found the gold piece where he had stashed it—in his own boot.[159]

Madam Laura Evens also remembered causing some trouble, including the night she and Etta "Spuds" Murphy drove a sleigh into the Leadville Ice Palace in 1896. The horse "got scared at the music and kicked the hell out of our sleigh and broke the shafts and ran away and kicked one of the 4 × 4' ice pillars all to pieces and ruined the exhibits before he ran home to his stable." On another occasion, Laura and Etta rented two chariots from the Ringling Brothers Circus for an "elephant bucket" of beer and went racing down Harrison Avenue. Laura wrecked the chariot on a telephone pole, and one of her customers saved her from arrest.[160] Laura and Etta parted ways in about 1896—Laura went to Salida, and Etta to Pueblo. For a time, Etta did well in Pueblo. In 1910, she was employing eight girls, though she often had to move to avoid authorities. In 1912, after several raids, Etta gave up and moved to Casper, Wyoming. There, she spent her retirement washing clothes for other prostitutes. Laura went to visit Etta at Casper to offer her a home in Salida, "but [Etta] was ashamed and wouldn't even see me. Poor little Spuddy." Etta died in 1929.[161]

Even after Etta Murphy and Laura Evens departed Leadville, the red light district there quickly grew again. In a sermon in February 1900, Reverend M. A. Rader lectured on the evils of the district. "I counted sixty four bawdy houses on the ground floor where the curtains were raised and where solicitations were made to passerby," he claimed.[162] A reigning madam in 1910 was Della Sullivan.[163] Another bawdy woman of Leadville was Grace Berkey or Egner. Little is known about Grace except that she was born in 1872 in Colorado. Her maiden name is thought to have been "Hodges," but her death certificate states it was "Betzold." Various sources indicate that Grace possibly grew up in Iowa and married one Fred Egner at Fort Collins in 1903. But the strong suspicion that she was once a working girl lies primarily in the notes she scribbled and items she saved in her own cookbook. Two receipts, for instance, reflect a rent of $20 paid by prostitute Gussie Smith of Alma to J. C. Spighton for June and July 1910. Also included is a recipe for orange cookies from Gussie. Perhaps most telling is a magazine clipping with a poem titled "Just Tell Them That You Saw Me":

> While strolling down the street one day,
> I was on pleasure bent—
> T'was after business worries of the day—
> I saw a girl who shrank from me in whom I recognized
> A schoolmate in a village far away;
> "Is that you, Madge?" I said to her; she quickly turned away;
> "Don't turn away, Madge, I am still your friend;
> Next week I'm going home to see the old folks, and I thought
> Perhaps a message you would like to send."
> Refrain—
> "Just tell them that you saw me, and they will know the rest,
> Just tell them I was looking well, you know,
> And whisper, if you get a chance, to mother dear, and say,
> I love her as I did long, long ago."
> "Your eyes are dim, your cheeks are pale. Come, tell me, are you ill?
> When I last saw you, your eyes shown clear and bright;

Come home with me when I go, Madge,
The change will do you good,
Your mother wonders where you are tonight."
"I long to see the folks at home, but not just yet," she said,
"'Tis pride alone that's keeping me away.
Tell them not to worry—I'm all right,
Don't you know—
Tell mother I'm coming home some day."[164]

In 1914, Grace married Johann Hoffman, and the two lived on a ranch near Alma. Others of the Hoffman clan lived nearby, but whenever family members visited, Grace would sprint from the house and hide in the woods until they left. She also wore a brown veil over her face on her trips to town. On occasion, however, she secretly left baked goods for other family members on their back porches. The Hoffmans never had children, but Grace's cookbook reveals a four-leaf clover pressed into a section on children, which may indicate that she hoped to have her own one day. The cookbook also has some cryptic notes regarding sex, such as "Sin . . . would seem a virtue if it was only shared by you." When Grace died in 1922, certain female family members burned up much of her fancy clothing, calling her "an old whore." Only a few items, including a photographic card illustrating several bawdy girls, some perfume bottles, and the cookbook give any indication of Grace's mysterious past life.[165]

Prostitution in Leadville was officially closed down in 1915, but some bawdy girls still remained for several more decades. During those years, the red light district was called "Springtown."[166] Among the city's last prostitutes was Emma "Pony" Nelson, who died in May 1918. Pony came upon her playful nickname during a time when Leadville's bordellos were jokingly called "riding academies." Three years before her death, the *Leadville Herald-Democrat* wrote a story about Pony. The elderly woman was living in poor conditions, although it was noted that she incessantly took in stray cats and dogs. When Pony died, she was buried with respect in Evergreen Cemetery. An anonymous friend donated her tombstone, which reads, "Friend of the Friendless." Pony's friend, Mrs. Clyde Robertson, also left some lasting impressions about her. "I can only say, if all that was told me was true, it never changed my feeling for her," said Mrs. Robertson. "I do not believe in double standards and the men, with whom she was reported to have been too friendly, were, some of them, now leading citizens of Leadville. I wager she is in heaven . . . God rest her soul."[167]

By the late 1920s, times were hard for the girls, noted Mamie G. of Leadville in a 1928 letter to Betty "Big Billie" Wagner in Silverton, who was looking for work. From all appearances, only Hazel Gillette "Ma" Brown was able to continue operating successfully. Hazel ran the Pioneer Bar, originally built in 1882.[168] The wild early days were marked by "a blood curdling number of bullet holes spattered about the walls," observed author and artist Muriel Sibell Wolle when she visited in the 1950s.[169] At least one former Pioneer prostitute had little use for contemporary working girls. "These modern girls are a bunch of ninnies," she commented, "and the modern man is worse—a sissy of the first water. . . . In my day, you were either good or bad. These ninnies do everything that branded us bad—and get away with it." Hazel may have ceased business by then, although she continued acting as proprietress of the bar until her death in 1970.[170]

West of Leadville was the short-lived shanty settlement of Douglass City. The community was home primarily to workers extending the Colorado Midland Railroad over Hagerman Pass in 1887. The majority of them were Italians, and Douglass City soon hosted eight saloons and a dance hall, all clustered together on one main street. There were no schools, churches, police, or firemen. Soiled doves who were too jaded to work in Leadville made their way to Douglass City, and shoot-outs and knife fights were common. According to author Marshall Sprague, the community met its end when the tunnel's dynamite powder house blew up by accident.[171]

Fifty or so miles from Leadville over precarious Independence Pass, Aspen—founded in 1879 and incorporated in 1881—sported a more subdued red light district. Because most of Aspen's new prospectors hailed from Leadville, it can be assumed that their soiled doves did too. As in other mining camps, ordinances in Aspen were almost at once formed to prevent prostitution from rearing its ugly head in the town. Aspen, however, soon saw the necessity of fallen women and saloons as a means to keep their miners happy. In August 1884, a $5 "tax" was imposed on prostitutes, resulting in a win-win deal for Aspen's economy and the girls who worked in town. When prostitute Fanny Chambers died that fall, her funeral was noted by local papers as elaborate and bearing an expensive coffin. The girls were indeed prosperous; in 1885, a dance hall and fifteen brothels were located within two blocks on Durant Avenue.[172]

As part of a relatively crime-free town, Aspen's red light district was discreet and largely ignored—at least until the Colorado Midland Railroad built its depot on Deane Street, one block south of Durant Avenue, and disembarking passengers had to pass through "the jungles of Durant Street" to access the town.[173] The prostitutes of Aspen were politely asked to move to a different locale, which they willingly did, or almost. An 1888 article told of twenty-four bad girls who were brought before a grand jury to discuss the matter. "The nymphs put on their best clothes and endeavored to make as much capital as they could out of the event, parading into the courtroom four abreast, swishing their skirts and tossing their heads in the most approved fashion," commented the *Aspen Evening Chronicle*.[174] But law enforcement appears to have been nothing to fool with in Aspen; the red light district isn't even detectable in the 1900 census.[175] Today Durant Avenue faces Aspen's ski slopes and is lined with luxury hotels and fancy restaurants.

North of Aspen was Glenwood Springs, which sprang to life in 1884. In November 1898, Mrs. Mollie Clark was tried for stealing a $20 gold ladies' watch. Her accuser was fellow prostitute Georgie Scott. Mollie was found guilty but stated her intent to appeal. By 1900, eighteen women plied their trade in East Glenwood, and, much to the authorities' alarm, the prostitute population continued to grow. Things got so bad that in 1909 Garfield County school officials refused to build a high school in Glenwood Springs until the red light district was cleaned up. Newspapers cited the presence of sixteen saloons, six bordellos, and an average of twenty to thirty men jailed each night for drunkenness and petty theft. Newspapers also pointed a finger at Johnny Richardson, who owned three saloons in Grand Junction and two in Glenwood, for claiming that Glenwood Springs made an ideal town for a new school. In 1911, the situation became even worse when prostitute Katharyn Taylor spurned twenty-seven-year-old Edwin Woolfolk, a member of a prominent and wealthy Virginia family, and he committed suicide. He drank chloral hydrate and died in the rear of the Silver Club Saloon.[176]

Colorado's camps and towns were not just limited to the mountains. Southeast of Denver was Petersburg, founded as a suburban farming community in 1876. Petersburg took on its wild reputation when Pap Wyman remodeled the Petersburg Inn into a saloon and restaurant. Wyman had first operated a very respectable saloon in Leadville, forbidding the use of cuss words, cutting off drunks, and encouraging married men to go home to their families. The face of a clock in the saloon read "Don't Swear," and a Bible was chained to a desk. Nevertheless, renowned writer Oscar Wilde allegedly drank six miners under the table at Wyman's in about 1882. Wyman apparently had changed his tune by the time he moved to Petersburg. As one of six roadhouses in town, the Petersburg Inn in particular had constant scrapes with the law through 1912. After 1916, Petersburg made some feeble attempts to keep its illegal gambling, bootlegging, and prostitution alive before succumbing to Prohibition altogether.

The nearby community of Boston also sported a wild nightlife. Cattle rustlers, outlaws, and prostitutes were responsible for a number of mysterious murders and other shootings. Owing to the lack of a railroad and to competition from nearby upstanding towns, Boston's wild and wooly residents eventually moved on.[177]

At the southern border of Colorado was Trinidad. Some of the earliest notes on prostitution there include the 1874 murder of a former Las Animas prostitute named Moll Howard. Although her killer claimed self-defense as his motive, a visiting party of prostitutes from Las Animas formed a mob and hanged him. In fact, Trinidad does not appear to have started enforcing laws against prostitution until about 1891. One reason why it began to do so may have been that too many young girls were appearing in the profession. An example was Katie Vidall of Albuquerque whose sister Alice tried to lure her into a bawdy house. Following the death of Katie and Alice's mother, the sisters had taken respectable jobs at Albuquerque's San Felipe Hotel. Alice left town suddenly, then contacted Katie a few weeks later from a fancy hotel in Trinidad and announced she was dying. Katie rushed to Trinidad, only to find Alice was fine and working at a local brothel. Alice tried to talk Katie into prostitution, but "I refused, and she called me a fool and left me." Destitute, Katie contacted the town marshal. Donations from some local people netted $20 so Katie could return to Albuquerque and resume respectable employment.[178]

The best-known prostitute in Trinidad at the turn of the century was Mae Phelps. The illustrious madam was unique not just in Trinidad, but also in the West, for several reasons. In 1910, she worked with other madams to establish the Madam's Trolley system into the red light district to keep drunken customers out of the downtown area. Around this time, the Madam's Association was also formed to provide protection and care for the girls. This respected organization followed guidelines resembling a union

© Colorado Historical Society

FIGURE 30 ❦ *Mae Phelps, Trinidad's reigning madam and one*
of the most innovative businesswomen in Colorado, circa early 1900s.
Mae enjoyed having her portrait taken often by photographer O. E. Aultman.
Courtesy of the Colorado Historical Society, Denver, Aultman #20158.

and included a convalescent home for those who became ill. Mae also may have had a hand in procuring the Madam's Rest Home in 1927 at a quaint, four-square ranch house outside of town. Because she does not appear in census records after 1910, however, she may have moved on shortly after the trolley system was implemented.[179]

In 1902, there were seven brothels within Trinidad's city limits. Eight years later, eight madams employed a total of thirty-six women. Madam Sarah Cunningham had the most girls, with nine employees. Madam Margarita Carillo had the least, with three. Three of the madams were widowed, and two were married. Madams Edith Crosland and Mattie Swain also had children living in their bordellos. From April 1911 to March 1912, the city of Trinidad took in nearly $6,000 in fines from prostitutes. Sooner or later, however, Trinidad's red light district began the typical slow decline. When the city opted to cease using the Madam's Trolley in 1922, eight months before its contract was up, the madams sued but settled out of court. The Madam's Rest Home functioned for only about seven years before being closed. During World War II, nearby military camps apparently caused authorities to bring even more pressure on Trinidad's red light district, and the district closed down for good.[180]

During this district's reign, prostitution worked its way through other southern towns, including Conejos, located somewhat west, where at least four prostitutes worked in 1880. At Alamosa, harder feelings were established against the red light girls. "There is considerable agitation of the question of removing the bawdy houses from Hunt Avenue to a more retired portion of town," reported the *San Luis Valley Courier* in 1889. "If this is a necessary evil then such restrictions should be placed upon it as to prevent the contamination of young children by its more or less injurious influences. By far the better way would be the suppression of such dens entirely, but if this cannot be done, then by all means let them be moved to less conspicuous quarters."[181]

More mountain towns sprung up during the 1860s. In Georgetown, founded in about 1864, free lots were offered to the first ten "respectable" women to come to town, but within a short time several brothels were flourishing. Shortly after Georgetown was incorporated in 1868, the women of the town succeeded in turning Barnes Saloon Hall into a Women's Christian Temperance Union hall, but questionable characters continued making the new town their home. The 1870 census lists at least one prominent madam, Martha "Mattie" Estes. Mattie was running a brothel with three employees and owned her house. In 1873, authorities charged her for keeping a bawdy house. The *Daily Colorado Miner* noted that the case, which had been pending for some time, had "caused quite a ripple in the gossip of the town." Martha and her attorney had apparently claimed that the jury was unfair, which resulted in a new trial. This time, the paper assured its readers, the marshal's assistant "certainly showed a commendable desire to select none but the very best men to try the case justly and sternly." It was also noted at the time that there were five other houses of ill repute in Georgetown. Mattie was found guilty and fined $60.90.[182] Later, she met her death at the hands of a jealous lover after being seen with another man.[183]

Madam Jennie Aiken was also killed when her house of ill repute burned to the ground shortly after a miner was shot to death in her brothel. Another madam of Georgetown, Mollie Dean, was murdered by her lover for going out with another man. Despite these mishaps, Georgetown held its own during the 1870s. Belle London was one of the better-known madams.[184] There is little doubt that Georgetown's ladies of the night were a feisty bunch, considering all the problems associated with them. In 1880, Mrs. Sallie Little, a local prostitute, died of heart disease although she was only thirty-five. In August 1906, John Eckman of Michigan and lately of Telluride was doped at a Georgetown bawdy house and robbed. A well-known mining man, Eckman was allegedly given "knockout drops" at Mattie Allen's Brownell Street bordello. Eckman was last seen visiting Mattie's house before he was found, two days later, wandering the streets of Georgetown in a dazed condition. A friend found him and took him to a room at the Barton Hotel, but when his condition worsened, he was checked into St. Joseph's Hospital. There was a large bruise on his side running from hip to shoulder, and $500 was missing from his person. Doctors held little hope for his recovery and notified his wife in Michigan, asking her to come to Colorado as soon as she could. As late as 1908, Georgetown continued its crusade against its fallen women by prohibiting them from entering bars.[185]

Unlike Georgetown and a large percentage of other towns, Fort Collins actually repealed its own ordinances against saloons in 1875. City fathers soon saw the error of their decision, though, when ordinary businesses became flanked by numerous gambling dens and taverns. In 1883, city authorities finally upped the price of their liquor licenses from $300 to $1,000 dollars. The plan worked. The number of saloons was soon back down to just six. As in other towns, however, Fort Collins's Cyprians did not completely disappear. In January 1912, a complaint was made about a two-woman bawdy house near Peterson and Elizabeth streets. Police cased the house for some time before raiding it one night. Prostitutes Maggie Yost and Lee-Eva Webber were arrested along with their customers, Silvert Higgins and Jesse Stewart. Higgins and Stewart were released the next day after claiming they had come to the house only to clean out an ash pit, despite the fact that the raid took place at ten o'clock at night. Judge Brewster fined the ladies $100 each, however, but took $75 off each fine for good behavior.[186]

Things were much wilder in the mining camps of Colorado's Western Slope. There, the town of Lake City offered one of the earliest red light districts in the region beginning in 1875. The district, dubbed Hell's Acre, was frequented by some of the roughest thieves and murderers around. The San Juan Central dance house was in fact owned by two men who were eventually lynched for killing the sheriff. The prostitutes in Lake City in 1880 included Belle Howard, Minnie Lee, Belle McLean, Hattie Mitchell, Gertrude Slocum, Mattie Timberlake, Mollie Tipton, and Ada Wilson. North of Lake City was Gunnison, whose best-known law officer in 1884 was Cyrus "Doc" Shores. Shores maintained law and order among the red light districts, but also maintained friendships with certain red light women. North of Gunnison was Crested Butte, which sported "One Eye" Ruby's Forest Queen brothel, and Irwin, which hosted balls with prostitutes during the 1870s. Farther on was Gothic, where the girls in one of the two dance halls daringly wore their skirts up to their knees.[187]

South of Lake City was Creede, founded in 1890. Originally called Jimtown, the settlement was soon jokingly referred to as "Gin Town" for the large quantities of alcohol served there. "I can hear the sound of saws and hammers, the tinkle of pianos, the scrape of violins, the scurry of flying feet in dance-halls," wrote a reporter for the *Saguache Crescent*, "the clink of silver on gambling tables, the sharp bark of six-shooters as some life was snuffed out in the smoke and the maudlin laughter of a dance hall girl as she swung in the arms of some human form." One Creede brothel proprietor was Bob Ford, killer of outlaw Jesse James. Ford was shot to death by Ed O'Kelley in June 1892, and his murder coincided with the death of a prostitute known as "Creede Lily." Hugh Thomason, a reporter for the *Creede Daily Chronicle*, spoke over Lily's grave before everyone turned their attentions to Bob Ford's raucous wake.[188]

Silver Plume Kate, Georgetown Jenny, Leadville Lucy, Slanting Annie, and Lulu Slain also met their end in Creede. Lulu and her housemate, known as the Mormon Queen, actually decided to commit suicide together. Only the Mormon Queen survived. Likewise, doctors revived Rose Vastine, also known as "Timberline," after an intended overdose. Another time, Timberline allegedly climbed a hill and shot herself six times in the chest— but still didn't die. She made yet another attempt to shoot herself in the chest in 1893. "Medical attendants were at once summoned and the would-be suicide is in a fair way to recovery," said the newspaper. Reports on such antics were occasionally peppered with stories of acts of kindness; when Creede suffered one of its notorious fires, a local madam and her girls saved the contents of a local respectable woman's rented room. Afterward, they carefully replaced the salvaged items. Just up the road from Creede were Spar City and Bachelor. The former had a two-story saloon and dance hall; the latter featured two saloons and a parlor house.[189]

Ouray was also accessible from Lake City via Engineer or Cimarron Pass. During the 1880s and 1890s, Ouray's red light houses included the Temple of Music, the Bon Ton, the Bird Cage, the Monte Carlo, the Clipper, the Morning Star, and the Club. About a hundred girls worked in Ouray's bawdy houses, which were ruled by large Italian families who also owned saloons, gambling dens, and dance halls. The best known of these families was the Vanoli clan, which managed operations in Ouray as well as in the nearby towns of Red Mountain and Telluride. John Vanoli first built property in Ouray's red light district in 1884. Despite occasional shooting frays and other arrests, he did well. In 1895, however, he shot himself after learning he was terminally ill. Prostitution, meanwhile, remained a viable industry in Ouray as late as 1908.[190]

Near Ouray was Silverton, which by 1875 was notable for its itinerant prostitutes, probably because during the harsh winter months many women migrated to warmer climates and then sometimes returned in the spring. Silverton's first permanent madam was Jane Bowen, also known as "the Sage Hen," who first appeared in Silverton with her husband, William Bowen. William invested in mining while Jane ran Silverton's first variety theater. Within a year, the Bowens constructed a combination saloon, dance hall, and bordello called Westminster Hall. The place soon became known as the Sage Hen's Dance Hall after Jane's colorful nickname. In 1880, the Bowens built a new residence behind the dance hall and adopted an eleven-year-old girl. City officials barely batted an eye; as in Ouray, many early brothel landlords in Silverton were respectable citizens with families.

In 1884, the Bowens moved their business out of the glare of the main street to their residence in back of the dance hall. William Bowen died in 1891. Shortly afterward, Jane bought the Palace Hall and threw a grand opening ball that was widely attended. Two years later Jane's newly arrived nephew died at the dance hall, leaving a wife and nine children back home in England. Then in 1895 another nephew, following an argument with Jane, was caught putting carbolic acid in food being served to her and her girls. And in 1898, Jane's adopted daughter, Emily, committed suicide in Denver. Following this last tragedy, Jane went to England. She returned in 1902, but finally retired from the profession in 1905.[191]

During the 1880s, Silverton's red light ladies were more brazen than ever, with newspapers regularly reporting fights, robberies, and other indecencies. Then in 1884, the Italian underworld stepped in and took control over the dens of Blair Street. Vigilante groups were formed in an attempt to restore order as city authorities sent for none other than Bat Masterson of Dodge City. Masterson was duly hired as police chief and at least managed to calm things down.[192]

Other prominent women of Silverton during the late 1890s and into the twentieth century included Matilda Wenden "Big Tilly" Fattor, Louisa and Marie Maurell, Dorothy "Tar Baby" Brown, Black Minnie, Sheeny Pearl, Kate Starr, and Mayme Murphy. During the 1918 flu epidemic, six prostitutes died between the last week of October and the first week of November, indicating that a number of girls were still in town then. In fact, Blair Street remained very much active throughout the 1920s. As late as 1923, Silverton continued seeing an influx of prostitutes, such as Leona "Diamond Tooth" Wallace, who was in business as late as 1928. Another notable Silverton prostitute was Pearl "21" Thompson, who operated the Mikado with Frances Belmont and kept a small dog whom she treated like a child. Pearl died in 1928. The 1930 census shows only one house of ill repute in Silverton, run by Josephine Daniels with three women and a male servant. But the census taker apparently missed Lola Daggett, a Silverton madam since about 1904 who first arrived with her sister Freda. After Freda died in 1912, "Nigger Lola," as she was known, continued working. Lola died a wealthy woman in 1939. Silverton's last brothel, operated by Jew Fanny, closed in 1948.[193]

Telluride, another town in the hub between Silverton and Ouray, was founded in 1878. Very quickly after its founding, the town supported a dozen dance halls and eight bordellos. At some point, a fire destroyed the red light district, including the popular Pick and Gad. Only a scattering of cribs survived the flames. When the district rebuilt, the Senate Saloon, among others, was used by prostitutes to solicit customers for their cribs around the corner on Pacific Avenue, also known as Popcorn Alley. The Silver Bell Saloon and Dance Hall, built in 1890, housed a brothel upstairs. In time, twenty-eight prostitutes worked at the Silver Bell alone, charging $4 per client. The girls of the cribs in Popcorn Alley charged $2. It is estimated that some 170 girls worked in Telluride at any given time. Some of them were brought to town by professional female recruiters who traveled the country and preyed on young girls, promising them legitimate jobs.[194] The amount of fines and license fees in Telluride was so great that citizens enjoyed several years of no tax levies.

Telluride's red light district could certainly be gritty and sad. Distraught by his girlfriend's attentions to another man, Duffy Cochran shot himself in the head at the White House dance hall in November 1901. Cochran, whose parents lived in Leadville, had apparently been living with the woman for some years in Silverton. He had followed her when she lit out for Telluride, and several arguments had ensued over the other man. The woman handed Cochran a pistol she had recently purchased, and he turned it on himself. "It is a pure case of self-murder prompted by jealousy of his consort, who supported both from her earnings in the bawdy house," the local paper concluded. Then in June 1903, the *Telluride Daily Journal* callously reported on a woman of the half-world who had attempted suicide: "One of the fairies of the half-world tried to commit suicide Saturday afternoon by the morphine route, but either took too much or not enough, and still lives to tell her playmates how it happened."[195]

In February 1906, the local paper reported on Viola Peterson, a habitué of the Gold Belt Dance Hall who had died at a local boardinghouse. Viola was only sixteen years old, but had run away from Sweden and come to New

York City as a very young girl. She then went West with a performing troupe called the Liberty Bells. At Denver, Viola left the group and made her way to Telluride, where she began work at the Gold Belt and subsequently contracted venereal disease. Viola told her doctor before she died that she had had no idea what the dance hall really was, but had been told it was simply a place of amusement. Having arrived in town with no money or friends, she had to take work at the Gold Belt because it was the only way to make a living. "How a man born in the image of his maker could seduce a mere girl and have her take up a life of this kind is a mystery," scolded the paper. "It's a wonder he was not stricken dead for the act." The paper nevertheless neglected to mention who the man was. Viola's friends took up a collection, and she was buried at Lone Tree Cemetery.[196]

A heated city council meeting in July 1915 saw angry citizens lodging complaints against Telluride's red light district. After a shouting match between the mayor and the chief of police, it was decided to put the matter into the hands of the fire and police board. The *Telluride Daily Journal* predicted that in doing so, "this said vicious character will no doubt pack her duds and leave for other parts within a very short time."[197] Just three days later, prostitute Jessie Clare was brought to court for violating city ordinances. An incensed Jessie refused to plead guilty or innocent. Jessie's attorney, L. W. Allen, pointed out that his client was "improperly before the court and therefore the court had no jurisdiction and further that there was no issue." Allen's objection was overruled, and two police officers testified anyway. Jessie was fined $50.[198] The prosecutors weren't finished. In April 1916, an action was made to close Telluride's six houses in the red light district, as well as some houses outside the district.[199] Lena Tafini, Pete Silva, T. B. McMahon, B. Perino, and Matt Mattivi were served with papers. Minnie Vanoli, who was at her bordello in Ouray, was also served.[200] Despite such proceedings, Telluride's red light district did not close down until 1923. Even then, prostitute Ollie Kelly managed to keep working throughout the 1930s.[201]

South of Silverton and Telluride was Durango, founded in 1880. Durango's best-known madam was Bessie Rivers, who in 1900 employed four girls. Next door was Jane Moss, who employed three women, a porter, and a musician. Durango's houses of ill repute later included the third floor of the distinguished Strater Hotel, which was built in 1887.[202] An ad for the Strater's saloon promised,

FIGURE 31 ❧ *The notorious Silver Bell Dance Hall had seen better days by the time the author visited it in the late 1980s. The building has since found new life as a school for the arts. From the author's collection.*

Best house in town!
Come all you boys who've been around,
Chambermaids you'll find at hand!
Best damn girlies in the land!
Press the annunciator and you get
All you want, and more, you bet![203]

For years, the third floor at the Strater was known as "Monkey Hall." Even today, some historians say that the "racy" pictures in the Strater's dining room reveal even more provocative pictures on the back side. Girls also worked in other parts of the city; in 1902, Anna Van Camp, also known as "Swede Anna," committed suicide in Room Three above the Office Saloon in the First National Bank building on Main Avenue. After using a pocket-knife to stab herself five times under the left breast, Anna had apparently slashed her own jugular vein. She was survived by her mother and two children in Glenwood Springs.[204]

Meanwhile, Bessie Rivers continued to prevail as the reigning madam in town. Both Bessie and madam Jennie Moss paid periodic fines of $150 apiece in 1901. In 1904, Bessie was the victim of a robbery during which $3,000 and some jewelry were stolen from her. Police were reluctant to believe her until some of the gems were recovered. Jennie Moss was still in Durango when she and Bessie were granted business licenses in 1905. Other clues about Bessie are revealed in newspaper tidbits, such as her fondness for her horse, George, and that she was an avid photographer.[205] The local papers often put a humorous, good-natured slant on news about Bessie. When she canceled her subscription to the *Durango Democrat* in 1908, the paper ended a long, complimentary description of her by saying, "She is yet in the flesh, tender, confiding and adored."[206] When Bessie put her house up for sale in May 1908, she was initially denied a license for her new property, but the decision was appealed two months later. In about 1910, she appears to have taken over operations at Monkey Hall with four new girls. The last mention of her was in 1911, when she was granted a new liquor license.[207] After that, she disappeared from Durango, and what became of her is unknown.

In the northern part of Colorado, a number of small camps sprouted up during the 1870s. Teller City in North Park once hosted a race between two horses named Sharp and Montgomery. Sharp was a known winner, and thousands of dollars were bet on the race. The event took place along the main street, and, much to everyone's amazement, Montgomery won. Sharp's rider, however, spurred the horse on and rode straight off into the woods. There, the jockey's favorite parlor house girl awaited him. The two rode off, welshing on all bets, and were never seen again. A more notorious camp was Oak Creek, founded in 1907. Because of its rural locale south of Steamboat Springs, the town was able to conduct itself in a free manner. Gambling, bootlegging, and prostitution were rampant. In 1911, the red light district was known as "Hickory Flats" and included both white and black prostitutes as well as some Italian families.[208]

Belle Reidy was a reigning madam in Oak Creek in 1915. She built what is now the Oak Creek Inn and ran it as a sporting house. Belle was married to a man named D. J., who distributed tokens that were good for twelve and a half cents. Belle's rate was a quarter, and all of her girls came from Leadville. Two of them, Violet May Mock and Mary Aline Ray, were married in a double ceremony in 1915. Mary wed bartender James Ray from the Big Six Saloon in Oak Creek, who also happened to be a constable. The couple pulled Mary's eleven-year-old daughter, Alta May Oswald, from her Minnesota boarding school and sought to settle into family life, but Mary refused to give up socializing with her former friends at Belle's. One night just eight months into their marriage, Ray once again retrieved Mary from the Doyle Saloon, where she had spent the day drinking and attending a dance, and escorted her home. A short time later two men who were staying the night at their house heard two shots. One of them heard Mary call out, "My god, what have I done? I've killed Jim." Both men ran to the kitchen to find Ray unconscious. Mary held his head in her lap, crying, "I'd give my life if I hadn't done it." As Ray died, Mary made a grab for the gun to shoot herself but was prevented from doing so.[209]

Mary later said that she had shot her husband because he had struck her twice and was going to beat her.[210] Questions were raised, however, over the fact that Mary had once threatened "to blow her husband's head off if he ever tried to beat her."[211] The night of the killing, Mary had also stated to another woman that "she would feed [her husband] bullets for supper, that that was all the supper he would get." Violet May Mock-Creek testified that Mary had shown her the gun and "said she was going to fill her husband full of lead." Other witnesses claimed Mary had threatened her husband's life if he ever struck her again, but also said "she was going to try and make him strike her."[212] Mary hardly helped matters, initially refusing to testify and often entering the courtroom smiling. During her mother's trial, Alta expressed a desire "to lead a Christian life."[213]

Mary Ray was ultimately sentenced to ten to twelve years at the state penitentiary.[214] She appealed, requesting an all-woman jury because "[m]en do not understand how a man can be like my husband was when he was with his friends away from home and then can go home, suddenly turn into a vicious brute and beat his wife into unconsciousness."[215] Despite her plea, Mary was again found guilty. Alta was sent to Washington State to live with relatives. As for Mary, she was paroled in 1919. Today folks around Oak Creek claim her ghost wanders the halls of her former place of employment.[216]

Bootlegging flourished in Hickory Flats during the 1920s, 1930s, and 1940s, and Oak Creek's lone police officer seldom ventured into the neighborhood. Peter Yurich, who grew up in Oak Creek, described one of the cribs: "The kitchen and sitting area was one long room. In the kitchen was a table and a couple of chairs, the water was just a pipe and tap which had a small stool and bucket, kitchen stove which heated the house, one of those coal wood stoves that had a warming oven above the stove top and baking oven. It also had a water reservoir for hot water. The most interesting room was the bedroom, a very small room with a double bed and the old fashion springs with a mattress, the whole thing had a big sag in the middle." Yurich also noted the walls and ceiling were covered with calendars from Steve's Liquor Store, and it was guessed there was a calendar for each year the store had been in business.[217] Yurich was most fortunate in that he knew Oak Creek's last two madams, Louise "Pee Wee" Piercen and Lee Wilson. According to him, Pee Wee had previously worked in Denver and Leadville. She had three sisters in California, Washington State, and Colorado. She also had three sons, who used the last name "Tartar." One had died in 1936, and another lived in New Jersey, but the third son, Paul, remained in Oak Creek. Pee Wee first worked for Tom Piercen, who had moved his Northwestern Saloon from Cripple Creek to Oak Creek. A brothel functioned upstairs. Late in their relationship, when Piercen got sick, Pee Wee married him. In the late 1930s, however, Piercen threw Pee Wee over for her own sister, Mary. When Piercen finally died, he left everything to Mary. Despite taking her case to the Colorado Supreme Court, Pee Wee was never able to claim any of the estate.[218]

Upon losing her case, Pee Wee moved to the site of Hugginsville between Oak Creek and Phippsburg. Yurich remembered her house. "She had two small bedrooms and a long narrow room where she placed a counter-like bar and had a table with chairs. She hung a lantern on the side of the house, facing the road."[219] Pee Wee still had to obtain her liquor license at Oak Creek, where the town board refused her request on several occasions. In one such instance, Pee Wee became so angry at being turned down again that she told the board, "You sons of bitches, if I was ten years younger I would give you all a dose of clap." Even without a license, Pee Wee's brothel did include a bar.[220] She was also in the habit of recording her thoughts on any scrap of paper available, "sometimes typing them on odd scraps of paper and sometimes sewing the pieces together." Most of Pee Wee's recordings date to 1936 and 1937, when she jotted down events she witnessed and the people involved.[221] Pee Wee's correspondence included a number of letters written to her by other women looking for work in post-Depression Colorado. When she was in her seventies, she raised goats, who had free run of her house. During the winter, she rented an entire box car to ship all of her belongings, including her goats, to Texas. She would also drive her "Hupmobile" to Leadville to see her old friends. Yurich saw Pee Wee several times at the drugstore where he worked. She once told him, "Honey, you could work yourself to death here, let me take you to Texas and I will set you up with those rich women who want a young man but are so old they have one foot on a banana peel and the other in the grave."[222]

Lee Wilson, also known as "Olivia Wilson" or "Olivia Washington" or "Nigger Lee," was another working girl of Oak Creek. According to Yurich, Lee was a "heavy set negro, but she had the slimmest legs and could really dance up a storm."[223] Surprisingly, she also sang in the choir at the "colored church" at Oak Creek that began in 1937. Yurich remembered that Lee's largest purchases from the drugstore were pomade, skin-bleaching cream, whiskey, and cigarettes. Lee resold the "whiskey by the shot and the cigarettes by the pack or one by one." When on one occasion Lee ordered a carton of plain-tipped Raleigh cigarettes, but the store was out of them, Yurich sent her filter-tipped instead. Lee called about the change and, after listening to Yurich's explanation, asked, "Sonny, do you know the difference between a plain-tipped Raleigh and a filter-tipped? Smoking a filter-tipped is like sucking a preacher's prick." Yurich was speechless, but "I could hear her strong, humorous laugh." In her later years, Lee married a Polish divorcée whose ex-wife and nine children lived out of state. The man paid Lee's property taxes, but when he died, the property was left to his heirs, and Lee had to move. Even into her seventies, Lee was still entertaining the elderly bachelors in town. Yurich remembered hearing her record player as she laughed and danced with the men. "They would go and spend the afternoon, visiting, I suppose talking about the old days and buying their drink by the shot and enjoying her company." Both Pee Wee and Lee Wilson remained in Oak Creek until their deaths.[224]

Salida, another new town in 1880, encapsulated several surrounding and earlier mining camps. One of the earliest of these camps was

FIGURE 32 ✥ *A combination saloon, hotel, and bordello in Arbourville, Colorado. The building today is in an advanced state of decay, but is still visible from Highway 50. From the author's collection.*

Arbourville, located along Monarch Pass in 1879. Arbourville is most unique because its social activities appear to have revolved solely around its single dance hall. The brothel, which is said to have also served as the site of a stage coach stop, saloon, and hotel, replaced a smaller log brothel that had operated in the town years earlier. The new bordello is thought to have been constructed in the late 1800s or early 1900s. The fact that Arbourville's brothel was the only one in the area made the place very popular on Saturday nights. There was little question that the brothel was the biggest business in town, leading more upstanding observers to note that Arbourville might have grown larger if its life had not revolved around the parlor house.[225]

Just down the road, Maysville had also sprouted in 1879 as the last stop before the Monarch Pass Toll Road into the Colorado goldfields. Alternately called "Crazy Camp" and "Marysville," Maysville was said to have an inordinately large number of saloons, dance halls, and gambling dens. Likewise, Monarch, founded very close to Maysville in 1879, was a bustling town with at least two bordellos, the Eureka Dance Hall and the Palace of Pleasure. Garfield, founded as Junction City in 1879, was the site of a suicide attempt by prostitute Lu Morrison in 1881. When the town suffered a fire in 1883, only the town hall and the red light district survived. In 1880, at the community of Shavano, some ten miles from Maysville, the population of 110 people included two women: one respectable wife and one prostitute.[226]

Most notable of Salida's satellite towns were Tin Cup, Bonanza, Sedgwick, and Buena Vista. At Tin Cup, the red light district was originally on the south end of Grand Avenue but moved to an alley behind Washington Avenue as the mining era played out. In 1900, the decent women of the town succeeded in running Tin Cup's "Alley Girls" out of town. Bonanza did feature at least a few brothels later, but often received visiting prostitutes from other camps.[227] At Sedgwick, there were two dance halls where "the giddy mazes of the dance can be enjoyed with giddier girls from Silver Cliff and adjoining towns." The cost of a dance was a dollar, fifty cents higher than in most other camps. "But the freights you know," said one local paper, "are high in this country."[228]

Last in league with Salida was Buena Vista, which by 1880 was a notorious town with four dance halls. One early bawdy house was called the Mule Skinner's Retreat. In 1882, the *Maysville Miner* noted that Molly Ledford, formerly of Maysville, had made a brief stop in Salida before traveling on and settling in Buena Vista. Shady ladies in 1886 included Lizzie Marshall, who advertised in the statewide *Traveler's Night Guide of Colorado*. But the town's most famous prostitute was Elizabeth "Cockeyed Liz" Spurgen. Born in 1857, Liz began her career in Denver in 1870. At age thirteen she married a man old enough to be her father, who forced her into prostitution. "I used to run away, but he would always find me and bring me back. He would beat me so badly, that I finally gave up." In fact, Liz once attributed her "cockeyed" look to a particularly bad beating. Some historians maintain, however, that Liz injured her eye in a fight at her brothel. In 1886, Liz purchased the Palace Manor in Buena Vista, nicknamed the "Palace of Joy." She retired in 1897 with her marriage to Alphonse "Foozy" Enderlin. Foozy expanded the former Palace of Joy to make an apartment for extra rental income, and the couple lived there many years. Liz died of a heart attack at age seventy-two in 1929. Even then, churches in town refused to hold services for her. Foozy resorted to having her funeral services in the couple's front yard.[229]

By the time Salida was founded in 1880, many of its surrounding communities were experienced in the skin trade. When the first passenger train pulled into town in May, a generous handful of shady ladies were waiting at the station for its male riders to disembark. The ladies initially took up quarters near the railroad tracks, and the houses of ill fame extended into the residential area. Respectable women of the town were not very comfortable with this arrangement, even if they couldn't always tell who was a prostitute and who wasn't. No matter, the bad girls of Salida soon made themselves known through drug overdoses, public drunkenness, and fighting. When the wild and woolly Lady Gay Dance Hall on Front Street was reported to be closing, it was noted that some of the gals there showed their bare wares in public, often during daylight hours. The Lady Gay did not close, however, and Salida citizens continued putting up with its inmates' antics.[230]

The first tragedy in the district struck in 1882 when madam Lizzie Landon's bordello suffered a fire. The flames were so quick that Lizzie's girls got out only with their bare essentials, and a customer lost $200 he had left in his pants pocket. Lizzie's loss, including her $500 piano, was estimated at about $800. A few months later, newspapers reported on the lawsuit *Lillian Browne vs. the Knights of Pythias*. Lillian had made an attempt to attend a ball held by the lodge but was ejected by three men "on the grounds that she was not a decent nor respectable person and therefore unfit to associate with guests at the party." Lillian sued for $20,000, leading the *Salida Mountain Mail* to speculate that this settlement, "if recovered, may deprive some of the defendants of their cigar money for a brief period." The result of the suit is unknown.[231]

Not until 1883 did authorities decide to initiate monthly fines and to regulate prostitution to an area on Front Street (today's Sackett Avenue). Marshal Stingley had already warned the ladies at least once that they were "getting entirely too loud in their conduct, and that they will have to go slow or skip." Although the women likely settled down for a while after such warnings, new city ordinances guaranteed that the revelry would break out less often. By July, the ordinances were in place, and the city was taking in more than $100 per month. Unlike many towns where corrupt police officers quietly upped the fines and kept some of the money for themselves, Salida's town council made sure their officers played it straight. Those who didn't turn in enough money or were discovered to be doubling fines and taking a cut were duly dismissed.[232]

In December 1886, another fire broke out in a "colored" brothel located, of all places, next to a Presbyterian church. The occupants, "Picnic Jim" and "Oscar Buck," were servicing white men. The building was a total loss, and only one of the girls' trunks was saved. The women lost $100 in cash between them, as well as a pile of blankets they were planning to take to Monarch. Firemen put the fire out without its spreading, but the *Salida Mountain Mail*'s report brought to light that not all bordellos were operating in the restricted area as they should. In 1888, yet another fire at a local hotel caused the loss of several business structures. Among them was Santa Fe Moll's place, an "establishment for the manufacture of 'checkered careers,'" at a loss of $750 dollars.[233]

Salida seems to have been an exception to the general rule of not accepting prostitution within the city limits. Long-term prostitutes such as Laura Evens remained as faithful to the city as the city was to them. In fact, Laura established herself as a very prominent madam, a position she enjoyed for more than five decades. She was thought to have been born in the South and married at the age of seventeen. Life as a wife and possibly mother did not suit her, however, and she soon made her way to St. Louis with a new career. Laura next spent time in Denver, but had little use for the likes of Mattie Silks and Jennie Rogers and their "Old Ladies Roost." She departed Denver in 1894, working for a short time at Park City near Fairplay before migrating to Leadville, where she remained to 1895.[234]

Laura's male friends in Leadville were many. During labor strikes as union men blocked entrance to a mine, Laura, with the payroll for the non-union miners hidden under her skirts, showed up under the guide of visiting a friend. She also claimed that Mayor Samuel Nicholson once bit her on the thigh, and she belted him for it. In 1896, after Leadville authorities set about chasing the lewd women out of town, Laura departed with a suitcase of champagne—a parting gift from the saloon keepers of Leadville. She remembered sharing the champagne with the train crew on the way to Salida, using the remaining five bottles to bribe local officers into letting her set up shop. By 1900, she had purchased her own parlor house. She commanded truth, respect, and good manners from her girls at all times, and everyone called her "Miss Laura." Her love for rolling her own cigarettes, throwing wild parties, collecting dolls, and swearing even when she wouldn't allow her employees to do it soon became well known. When she built a new set of cribs on Front Street, the building quickly evolved into

FIGURE 33 ⌘ *The only known photograph of Laura Evens's luxurious bedroom displays her lavish furnishings as well as her doll collection, circa 1940s. The girl on the bed is identified as Anne Patterson. Courtesy of the Colorado Historical Society, Denver, F51,400.*

the main part of Salida's red light district. A total of about twelve prostitutes plied their trade in the district, most of them employed by Laura.[235]

In 1914, authorities finally decided to wage a war against the red light district. "Without noise, ostentation or the usual 'raid' features associated with such movements, the greater number of resorts in Salida's Red Light District were closed last Saturday," the *Salida Record* reported in July 1914. Laura Evens was excepted, however, and her "large 'parlor house' is to remain open several months longer." Authorities obviously trusted Laura to maintain better control over her ladies, even though Mayor I. C. Alexander declared her place was to be closed by April 1 of the following year.[236] Laura never did close, and she bought even more property in 1915. When the deadly influenza epidemic hit in 1918 and the local hospital ran out of beds, Laura closed her house to make a temporary shelter for the sick. Her girls willingly worked as nurses.[237]

During the 1920s, Laura hit some hard times and was forced to sell some of her property. By 1922, all she had left was her Front Street parlor house, where she would remain the rest of her life. There were about fourteen prostitutes in Salida that year. Within another five years, Laura and Margaret Weber were the only madams left, but Laura's giving spirit continued to match her wealth. During the Great Depression, hundreds of food baskets were found on the doorsteps of families with children. Coal was mysteriously delivered free of charge. A church in town received a new roof. Railroad men who were injured on the job would suddenly receive offers for less-strenuous employment while they recuperated. One man recalled that shortly after suffering a severe hand injury, he was offered a job selling newspapers in a local store. The pay was unusually high. "I didn't learn until long after Laura died that she paid the storekeeper for my salary for more than a year while I got over my pain and learned to use what was left of my hand," the man later recalled.[238]

Miss Laura and her girls performed such good deeds anonymously. Young boys who ran errands for Laura after school were invited in no farther than the kitchen for hot chocolate or a warm meal during cold weather before being paid, usually $10, for their work. Miss Laura would instruct them to take the money home to their mothers, telling them, "You earned the money in honest work for a stranger." Respectable wives who suffered abuse often sought help from Laura, who gave them shelter and refused to let them work for her. "I doubt if anybody will ever know how many people Laura helped," said a Salida politician in later years. "She was an entire Department of Social Services long before there was such a thing." When Chaffee County authorities arrived to shut Laura down for good in 1950, they sincerely apologized for doing so. In an interesting twist, the closure resulted in an immediate upswing in sex crimes, to the extent that authorities asked Laura to reopen. She declined, explaining she had rented her rooms to railroad men who were "all settled in, and she didn't want to evict them." Laura passed away in 1953 at the age of ninety.[239]

One of Colorado's last notorious red light districts was formed at Cripple Creek in 1891. Seasoned soiled doves from around the state and beyond immediately flew into town, initially setting up for business along the main drag of Bennett Avenue before moving one block south to Myers Avenue in 1893. In those early days, the girls paid only a dollar apiece in fines. Although the original red light district of Myers Avenue consisted

FIGURE 34 ⊗ *An early photograph of Poverty Gulch, circa 1892.*
The place was home not only to the Cripple Creek District's poorer families,
but also to prostitutes, outlaws, gamblers, and rough types. Courtesy
of the Cripple Creek District Museum, Cripple Creek, Colorado.

of primitive wood shanties with muslin-lined interiors, class and ethnicity soon divided the neighborhood, with fancy parlor houses, cribs, and French houses staking their separate pieces of ground. Poverty Gulch, located just outside of town on the very east end of Myers featured black, Greek, Japanese, and Mexican prostitutes.[240]

Cripple Creek's red light district soon featured eleven parlor houses, twenty-six cribs, and four dance halls. Working girls there included Jessie Armstrong, Mary Davis, Nellie Marcus, Mary Marshall, Kitty Maxie, Bell Ricker, Anna and Emma Smith, Lou Thompson, and Marie Williams. Georgia Hayden was a professional mistress. Although she lived on Myers and took her meals at Crapper Jack's dance hall, she did not work from a crib or a parlor house. Rather, she spent her time circulating between Leadville, Creede, and Cripple Creek catering to the growing number of new millionaires. She was a particular favorite of miner Jimmy Doyle, who would soon rank among Cripple Creek's elite list of millionaires. Doyle even asked Georgia to marry him, but she declined on the basis that his mine had yet to strike it rich. What Georgia didn't know was that Doyle was already on his way to making millions.[241]

The first arrest for prostitution on record in Cripple Creek occurred in 1894. M. Vogie and Pearl Webster pleaded "not guilty" and were released without fine. Martha Petersen was not so lucky. In August, she paid $75 for a violation at her saloon. In October, she paid another $173. But Myers Avenue property owners in 1895 included several prominent men as well as madam Maggie Coyle. The red light district continued to grow, but authorities could do little about it because these prominent men had vested interests there between 1895 and 1897. There were also a number of female property owners—Louise Bohm, Marie Brown, Jennie Buck, Maggie Coyle, Julia Glenn, Isabelle Martin, Eva Prince, Lucy Drexel, Phebe Carrington, Mary Cross, Clara Simmons, and Mrs. W. H. Strom. Poverty Gulch, located on East Myers just outside the city limits, was also home to several black prostitutes. Most notable were millionaires Spencer Penrose and Charles Tutt, who owned madam Lola Livingston's parlor house and the Topic Theater.[242]

Tutt and Penrose also had a racetrack and casino at the Cripple Creek District town of Gillett, and Penrose had at least one scandalous affair with Sarah Elizabeth "Sally" Halthusen, a local equestrian and gold digger.[243] Another well-known millionaire, Winfield Scott Stratton, was sued by call girl Candace Root for $200,000. Candace, a sometime employee of madam Hazel Vernon, had been seeing Stratton on and off for some time. Stratton helped procure a home for Candace during their affair and even built a table for her sewing machine. On one occasion, upon finding the girl dead drunk and passed out under a pile of snow outside the Central Dance Hall, Stratton carried her home and took care of her. He left Candace $200 on that occasion and urged her to seek treatment for her alcoholism. Candace took the cure in Denver, but began drinking again upon returning to Cripple Creek.[244]

Another time, the budding millionaire paid Candace $2,500 to keep a business associate "busy for three weeks" so he would not exercise his option on Stratton's Independence Mine. By doing so, Stratton was able to keep the Independence and made his millions. Candace not only threw the option papers in the fire herself, but also accompanied the man to San Francisco for a while before returning to Stratton. That she had earned her $2,500 is unquestionable, but she also made Stratton her beau, illustrated at least once by an invitation she extended to him for dinner at Hazel Vernon's bordello on Christmas Day, which Stratton accepted. Other prominent men and their mistresses attended the dinner—Jimmy Burns and Georgia Hayden, millionaire Sam Strong and Nellie Lewis, gambler Grant Crumley and Grace Carlyle, and mining magnate Charlie MacNeill and Sally Halthusen—as did nine of Hazel's employees. A reporter from the *Colorado Springs Gazette*, Hiram Rogers, was also a guest. The house was set up for a banquet, with fancy linens, a fully set table, a punch bowl of champagne, and a set of "tiny nude maidens with exuberant breasts which propped up the place cards."[245]

It was Rogers who later revealed in a news story that Stratton had just become a millionaire. What he didn't mention was Candace Root's part in Stratton's achieving his newfound wealth. Other Myers Avenue ladies soon began appearing at Stratton's home at the Independence. His watchmen were instructed to give such women $5 and send them away. By the time Candace sued Stratton, her beauty had decreased as her alcoholism increased. She claimed Stratton had lured her to his bed, gotten her pregnant, and promised to marry her. In court, Stratton testified that Candace had worked as a prostitute since 1892 and that subsequently it was quite easy for any man to get her into bed. The case was dismissed. As Stratton left the courtroom, Candance accosted him a final time, throwing her arms around him and sobbing. Stratton merely gave her some money and asked her "not to betray him again." Presumably they never saw each other again. Candace's suit inspired other women to do the same. When mining millionaire Sam Strong married a respectable woman, prostitutes Nellie Lewis and Luella Vance sued him for leaving them. Each settled out of court for $50,000. Stratton also continued to be sued and pursued many times by women wanting or claiming to be his lover.[246]

As of 1896, some 350 soiled doves were plying their trade in Cripple Creek. The first of two devastating fires in 1896 began in the red light district when dance hall girl Jennie LaRue and her paramour Otto Floto (later a writer for the *Denver Post*) kicked over a gasoline stove. A second fire four days later was thought to have been inspired by an insurance scam. Myers Avenue casualties during the fires included the entire red light district as well as the business district. As Cripple Creek rebuilt, the *Colorado Springs Gazette* assured its readers that "[e]ntertainment and dance halls, grog shops and nameless places of vice are down below the business level. Myers Avenue is still given over to buildings of questionable purpose." In fact, the fires of 1896 gave officials the chance to initiate better ordinances with specific rules pertaining to prostitution, thereby allowing bigger and better houses of the demimonde to build and function within the limits of the law.[247]

Even as authorities cracked down on both prostitutes and dance hall girls, they paid little attention to the abuse and neglect of the girls themselves. The death of madam Pearl DeVere in 1897, however, overshadowed both the media's and citizens' disdain for the red light ladies. Pearl was the proud owner and operator of the Old Homestead parlor house, which in its time became one of the most notable bordellos in the West. Pearl, originally known as Mrs. Isabelle Martin, was a native of Indiana. Her first foray into the underworld began when she lived with a well-known gambler named Dietz.[248] Dietz may have been Billy Duetsch, a famous sporting man who once broke the bank at the Monte Carlo casino in Paris. One day in 1893, Duetsch arrived in Denver, ill and flat broke. It was also noted that "the woman for whom he made his plunge at Monte Carlo and into whose lap his gold was poured is gone too. Once he showered money upon her and she lived as a princess enough . . . [now] he is broke and she is singing in a New York concert hall." Deutsch was checked into the Brown Palace Hotel, where he promised to "live not frugally but not extravagantly."[249]

By October, following another "spree," Duetsch was "lying very ill in a hospital" in Denver. The paper noncommittally ended its article with, "He may die within a few hours or may temporarily recover."[250] What became of him is unknown, but newspapers later stated that Pearl DeVere had traveled the world with the said Dietz—possibly her husband—before he "blew his brains out after breaking the bank" at Monte Carlo.[251] Soon after the papers reported on Deutsch's dire illness in Denver, Pearl appeared in Gillett.[252] A year after purchasing property at Gillett with prostitute Eva Prince, Pearl moved to Cripple Creek. She may have taken her new pseudonym from a Madam Vida DeVere, clairvoyant, who was locating mines with her crystal ball out of the Cabinet Saloon in 1894. In May, Pearl and Eva purchased property on Myers Avenue. In July 1895, she sold her interest to Eva. The following February she purchased her own brothel right next door for $800 from saloon owner James Hanley. In about 1895, she married Charles B. Flynn, who had a small mill in the district.[253]

Life was not always cheery at Pearl DeVere's. In March 1896, Bessie LeClair made the papers after she "filled up with absinthe Friday night and after breaking half the furniture in the Old Homestead landed in jail. She kept the other prisoners awake all night by her screaming, but the 'molly' turned up in the morning and got her out. Her trial will come up Monday."[254] Despite the negative press, Pearl was a prominent advertiser in the *Traveler's Night Guide of Colorado*. Following the fires of 1896, she borrowed money from Orinda Straile of New York to rebuild her palatial parlor house based on the ones she had seen in France. Electric lights, running water, a bathroom, and a telephone assured maximum comfort for both residents and visitors. Wallpaper was imported from Europe. Brass fixtures on the inside doors were imported from London.[255] Each of Pearl's employees was a beautiful and gifted woman in her late teens or early twenties. Medical bills listed in her probate record illustrate that Pearl took extra good care of her girls, who received two nourishing meals per day.[256]

According to legend, a rich admirer from Denver sent Pearl an $800 dress from Paris prior to attending one of her famous Saturday night soirees in June 1897. During the party, the two argued over whether the gent should leave his wife, and Pearl lost. Whether this incident really took place is questionable, but when Pearl went to bed around seven o'clock the next morning, she complained that her nerves were unstrung and took some morphine to help her sleep. One of her girls, Maude Stone, had retired with her, and a few hours later the girl awoke to the sound of Pearl breathing heavily. Dr. J. A. Hereford was summoned, but Pearl died later that afternoon.[257] The *Cripple Creek Times* concluded that "[t]here is no evidence that the act was intentional."[258] Charles Flynn apparently saw no need to return to Colorado. His apathy was countered by Pearl's mother and sister in her home state of Indiana, who thought she was working as a successful hat maker or perhaps the designer of "DeVere Gowns." Pearl's brother-in-law initially telegraphed to have the body embalmed and sent home, but for some reason Pearl's sister then appeared in town and subsequently learned Pearl's true profession. Shocked and disheartened, she ordered police to burn Pearl's possessions and left town.[259]

FIGURE 35 ❧ *In its time, the Old Homestead parlor house catered exclusively to the rich and elite men from Denver and far beyond. For at least a short time, the house was among the best-known brothels in the West. From the author's collection.*

Pearl's Denver admirer supposedly sent $1,000 for her funeral, but the total cost was actually only a little more than $200. Following an elaborate funeral procession, Pearl was buried at Mt. Pisgah Cemetery. Her estate totaled more than $9,000. Her personal belongings were auctioned off, and Orinda Straile received the Old Homestead in lieu of repayment for her loan. In 1899, Straile sold the house to madam Hazel Vernon for $5,000. Hazel's father was said to be a photographer in Minot, North Dakota, and a portrait of her hangs in the Homestead today. During 1900, Hazel employed eight different girls, as well as domestics. Her servants in 1902 included a butler, a chambermaid, a musician, and a porter. Later that year Hazel moved either to Montana, where she died of pneumonia, or to California, where she succumbed to syphilis. An alleged descendant who visited the Homestead during the 1990s claimed Hazel actually moved to Pasadena, California, to care for her sick mother and that she had a daughter, also named Hazel Vernon, who lived in Montana. Either way, Hazel next sold the Homestead to one Phil DeWilde in 1905, and a former housekeeper, Inda Allen, was made proprietress. Inda employed five girls throughout 1907, but she had left the Homestead by 1911 when Pauline Russell was madam. Pauline departed a year later, leaving Nellie Johnson as the last documented working girl at the Homestead. As for Pearl DeVere, she was remembered even in the late 1910s when "the gold-digging Pearl DeVere" appeared as a character in a silent film called *The Busher*.[260]

The saga of the Myers Avenue girls continued. When twenty-year-old Maud Cotton died at the Sisters' Hospital of Bright's disease in 1898, the newspaper quickly established that her name was a pseudonym. Although the girl promised to reveal her real name, she died before confessing. It was noted that Maud had been living with a miner for the past year and a half in Poverty Gulch. Her parents were thought to reside in Dallas, Texas, and it was speculated that her real name was "Lizzie Breen." Nothing ever came of a search for people by that name. Just a month later, prostitute Claude Buckley suffered a severe beating by a former boyfriend, Tom Flaherty. It wasn't the first time Flaherty had beaten Claude, and a few months earlier he had also pummeled the girl, "but her injuries then were not serious." This time Flaherty broke into the back of Claude's crib and found a man named McNeal asleep with her. Flaherty made good use of a slop pail to beat McNeal's face to a pulp before the hapless man escaped. Flaherty then turned on Claude and beat her so badly she was spitting up blood and not expected to live. Flaherty was later apprehended, but no outcome of the case was reported.[261]

Pearl DeVere's former business partner Eva Prince remained in Cripple Creek through at least 1900 with four employees, including Gladys Carlyle, probably Grace Carlyle, an "angel faced platinum blonde" with an ornery disposition. As a girl, Grace had sung in the church choir in her hometown of Coffeyville, Kansas, but one night the choirmaster seduced her in a back pew. His wife caught the couple together, ending Grace's career as a choir singer. She ended up leaving Coffeyville with Grant Crumley, who brought her West to Cripple Creek. There, she started out working at Pearl Sevan's Old Faithful on Myers Avenue but retained a longtime relationship with Crumley. She was fond of performing strip teases on top of Crumley's bar at the Newport Saloon, but publicly reprimanded him once for scratching his fanny in front of a proper lady. After Grace attempted suicide with laudanum, she tried to beat up the doctor summoned to her aid. In 1901, she was implicated in the attempted suicide of Edward Sexton.[262]

Between 1900 and 1906, the city of Cripple Creek began various efforts either to control or to outlaw gambling and prostitution. The casino proprietors and madams acquiesced by either moving upstairs or establishing private membership clubs, but sometimes they refused to budge at all. In 1904, world traveler and author Lowell Thomas, who grew up in nearby Victor, guessed there were still about three hundred prostitutes on Myers Avenue. The crusades continued throughout 1905, and in 1906 the axe-wielding prohibitionist Carrie Nation gave a thundering lecture on temperance and smashed a few windows. Efforts by authorities finally appeared to be doing the trick, and the number of prostitute arrests during 1906 was much smaller than in prior years. But it is also probable that the decline in arrests coincided with residents' exodus as district mines played out. Authorities continued with their battle against prostitution. New ordinances included letting the girls do their shopping on Bennett one day a week, allowing them to raise their skirts no more than six inches above their ankles, and tightening up on monthly health exams and fines. City officials kept a careful register of each girl, stating her name, known aliases, description, physical condition, where she was born, where she last came from, where she currently lived, and where she was going upon leaving town. Every scar and birthmark were also recorded.[263]

Women of Myers Avenue in 1911 and 1912 included Louisa Davis, Grace Howard, Belle Butler (who was denied her health certificate), Bessie Blondell (a.k.a. "Bessie McSean" and "Dorothy McCleave"), and "Mexican Jennie" Wenner, who was chased to Mexico and brought back for the murder of her abusive lover. The city register also noted that prostitute Viola Sellers had "quit rustling." Things had slowed considerably by the time *Colliers Magazine* writer Julian Street visited Cripple Creek in 1914, but his impression of the town unfortunately centered solely around the aging madam Leo the Lion (Leola Ahrens). Street noted Leo's outdated way of dress and her stringy hair, although her crib appeared tidy enough. City hall did not find Street's article at all humorous. Mayor Jimmie Hanley and a number of citizens sent telegrams and angry letters to *Colliers,* and editor Mark Sullivan promised to publish a letter from Cripple Creek as long as it fit the magazine's editorial standards. A contest was held in town for the best essay, and it was submitted to *Colliers,* but Sullivan never published it. For years, the joke around town was that in revenge the city council changed the name of Myers Avenue to "Julian Street."[264]

One last effort to do away with the red light district was made in 1916 by a Sheriff Kingston, but he was gone by the 1920 census. Cripple Creek's goodtime gals eventually died, moved away, married, and faded into obscurity on their own. "Nigger Mollie" and "Liverlip" found employment as a cleaning woman and a bootlegger, respectively. Another dance hall girl, Lelia Loveless, had worked in Fairplay or Alma before moving to Cripple Creek in 1896. At some point, she was a dancer at the Mikado, a rival brothel one door down from the Old Homestead. Although her playful-sounding name seemed to have been made up, Lelia really had married one Earl Loveless in 1909. Throughout the years, Lelia invested in properties around the red light district but always appeared to be running a boardinghouse. She divorced Loveless in 1923 and next married Frank Wicks, a widower with six children.[265]

Lelia's stepgrandson, Art Tremayne, remembered having to cross Myers Avenue as a child with his mother whenever they went to visit Lelia. On at least one occasion, some girls at a second-story window waved at him, and he waved back, at which point his mother immediately whisked him up the street. The Tremaynes may have loved Lelia, but they had little use for the Myers Avenue girls. Art's wife Loretta also remembered Lelia from the time when Lelia ran a restaurant. While the men ate breakfast, Lelia would prepare their lunch pails before they went to work. "She was a very good cook," Loretta remembered. "Man alive, she always had something on the stove: stew, or ham and beans." Art and Loretta regularly escorted Lelia to the local bars. "She was fun-loving," said Loretta. "She lived life to the fullest as long as she could." Lelia's house was cozy and cute, and she hauled her own water. Her prized possessions included some garnets, a kewpie doll, and an ornate clock dating back to the 1840s. She also "liked her beer and her cigarettes," according to Loretta. "She could roll her own cigarettes with one hand." Lelia's friends also included a few former Myers Avenue women. On her downtown excursions, however, she "dressed like a lady. Gloves, hat, scarf, her hair all done." At the tavern, Lelia could sit for hours with friends. "She never over-indulged but she had fun," Loretta emphasized. One morning in 1954 a friend came to visit Lelia in her home, but found her dead. She was buried in Denver's Fairmount Cemetery near family members.[266]

The Cripple Creek District was home not just to Cripple Creek, but also to roughly two dozen other towns and camps. Most sported a handful of prostitutes, but only Victor, the second-largest city in the district, had any real wicked women of substance. As the district's blue-collar town,

Victor was home to thousands of miners and, subsequently, to hundreds of working girls. One of the first prostitutes there, Haillie Miller, was hired by mine owners during strikes in 1893 to bed and filch information from striking miners. Another woman of note was Hook and Ladder Kate, so named because of her dazzling height. In the early days when Kate worked in Cripple Creek's Poverty Gulch, budding millionaire Jimmy Doyle brought her and some other girls to the shack he shared with his partner, Jimmy Burns. When Burns tried to make Kate leave, the Amazon "took him in her arms, removed his nightgown and spanked his bottom," while Doyle laughed.[267]

The large male population in Victor is probably why the brothels seemed welcome to coexist with other businesses throughout the town. But Victor's prostitutes were a rough bunch. Pioneer wife Anne Ellis recalled renting a house from a madam whom she described as the "hardest-boiled" in the district. The woman controlled her crib employees by "placing the Indian sign" on them and beating them. Victor sported three separate red light districts between 1894 and 1918. The first was located on Third Street south of Victor Avenue and along Portland Avenue. Like Cripple Creek, Victor's infamous fire of 1899 began in a local bordello. The district then relocated along a portion of First Street north of Victor Avenue.[268]

In about 1913, the city began cracking down on prostitution. Five years later it was announced that the old bawdy houses along First Street were to be demolished. Mrs. Emma Hopkins of Fourth Street Real Estate arranged a purchase of the buildings with the understanding that the structures were to be torn down. The girls of the row consented to the deal but quietly moved to the west side of town on a rocky hill above the west entrance to town, largely out of the general public's sight. Old-timers maintain that prostitutes remained in Victor as late as the 1930s. Victor's last resident from the old demimonde was "French Blanche" LeCoq or La Croix, who migrated to America from France at the age of eighteen. She was hired by saloon owner Morris Durant, but when she became pregnant by him in 1918, Durant's wife threw acid in her face. The baby, identified as Katherine Wilcock and fathered by one William Chuckman, was ultimately taken away by authorities in 1923.[269] Blanche moved to the faded district camp of Midway, where she worked and lived until the 1950s, when she moved to Victor. She died in 1959 and was buried in Victor's Sunnyside Cemetery.[270] Blanche's Midway cabin has since been dismantled and moved to Cripple Creek, and her former home in Victor is currently undergoing extensive renovations.

In 1915, Senator Helen Ring Robinson successfully passed a law in Colorado making houses of prostitution illegal on the basis that they were a nuisance. Such places would be raided, their furnishings sold off, and the houses locked up for one year. Only a bond by the property owner with a statement that the structure would not be used for prostitution again would allow the locks to come off. Robinson's decree was followed by statewide prohibition as of January 1, 1916. For the most part, Colorado's shady ladies eventually went away altogether, save for such clandestine businesses as Lillian Kneisser's place near the elite Broadmoor Hotel in Colorado Springs. Named the "Cheyenne Cañon Inn," this place was built in 1920 to cater to what was left of Cripple Creek's millionaires and other wealthy men. When the brothel failed, Kneisser sold to Grace Casey, who reopened the inn as an illegal casino. The building was abandoned in the 1930s, but was renovated into a bed and breakfast in 2001.[271]

During the 1970s and 1980s, the profession was still operating along South Nevada Avenue extending south to Cheyenne Boulevard, along South Tejon Street at Moreno near a cluster of adult bookstores, on North Nevada Avenue at Fillmore, and along East Platte Avenue from Union to Circle Drive. Prostitutes could also be had near the Golden Bee Tavern in the elite Broadmoor area and on B Street outside the gate at Fort Carson. A sporting house at North Nevada and Fillmore was known as "Oscar's."[272] On Colorado's Western Slope, prostitution continued during the 1970s and 1980s around smaller towns such as Parachute. The oil boom made a brief reprise during this period, and longtime residents took the increase in prostitution as a sign of prosperity. One local newspaper editor, noting the girls working out of Volkswagen buses, commented, "Well, hell! That's big time. Parachute came of age! It meant that the boom was real."[273]

4

ILLICIT LADIES OF IDAHO

FROM THEIR BEGINNINGS IN CANADA, THE ROCKY MOUNTAINS extend south into the United States through Idaho. There, they cut along the eastern border, comprising parts of the Salmon River, Bitterroot, and Clearwater mountain ranges. During the Civil War, Idaho experienced a great influx of prospectors. Gold seemed to be everywhere they looked, and men from all over the country were soon flocking in to seek their fortunes in Idaho's spectacular mountain ranges. The Boise River provided plenty of water, and hunting was abundant. Even today the Sawtooth Mountain Range is particularly enticing, with nine-thousand-foot Bald Mountain providing a spectacular backdrop.[1]

The beginnings of prostitution in Idaho can likely be traced back to the area near Boise, which attracted fur trappers as early as 1820. When Fort Boise was erected in the 1830s, the goods most certainly included Indian girls for trade or sale. By the time Boise City was incorporated in 1864, there is little doubt that a few white women began plying their trade as well.[2] Chinese girls were also present, as illustrated by the trial of China Annie, a brothel slave who escaped and married her lover, Ah Guan. Legal charges accused Annie of "stealing her own self," but she was acquitted.[3] By 1908, Boise's red light district was referred to as the "restricted district." Locals knew it as "the Alley."[4] About ninety women composed this somewhat shabby district at the time. One unusual advocate in their favor was Reverend P. Monroe Smock. Without houses of vice, he reasoned, Boise's crime rate against women might rise.[5] Monthly expenses for Boise prostitutes included a $30 fine to the city, plus $75 to $100 to their landlord. To meet these and other bills, most madams supplemented their income with liquor sales and charged their girls $9 to $15 dollars per week for their rooms. Most madams averaged between four and fourteen employees.[6]

At Boise in 1910, madams Nona Dee and May Bradbury had three girls each.[7] By 1920, Honora Ornstein, also known as "Evelyn Hildegard" and "Diamond Tooth Lil," had easily usurped the others' place. If all the myths about this enigmatic woman are true, she also entertained in Alaska; Tombstone, Arizona; Death Valley, California; Denver, Colorado; as well as Montana, Nevada, Oregon, and Washington. To make matters more confusing, several women of the West called themselves "Diamond Tooth," "Diamond Tooth Lil," or "Diamond Lil." Depending on the story, the Lil in Boise is credited with being a dance hall girl, gambler, prostitute, or madam who smoked cigars and carried a gun. In all stories, she has a sizeable diamond imbedded in her front tooth. She was also married and divorced an alleged thirteen times, once sang and played piano at the 1903 World's Fair, and ran several successful brothels throughout the West, including in Denver.[8]

The Diamond Tooth Lil of Boise was born Honora Ornstein in 1882 in Austria.[9] She later apparently became known as "Evelyn Hildegard." Lil herself claimed, "I dance [sic] my way from Youngstown Ohio to San Francisco when I was thirteen years old."[10] It was while working in the dance halls of Alaska in about 1908 that she had the infamous diamond set in her tooth. Also, "from one of her rather plump bare shoulders to her wrist she wore a fascinating white gold snake bracelet that was studded with one hundred twenty five real diamonds."[11] Lil's escapades included several marriages, and one of her ex-husbands once shot her in El Paso, Texas. She also maintained a longtime friendship, or possibly romance, with one Diamond Field Jack, whom she met during a nine-month stint in Goldfield, Nevada.[12] In 1920, Lil's place in Boise was called the "Star Rooms" and offered steam heat, plus hot and cold water.[13] Idaho marriage records indicate that Lil, as Evelyn Hildegard, married three times during this era: to L. Carl Houk at Emmett in 1920, to Albert Ford Gambil in Nampa in 1925, and finally to Andrew Marker in Mountain Home in 1928.[14]

© Colorado Historical Society

FIGURE 36 ❦ *Fred and Jo Mazzulla identified the woman in this photograph as Diamond Tooth Lil. Many historians have speculated, however, that this woman is a different Diamond Lil and not the one who lived in Boise, Idaho. Courtesy of the Mazzulla Collection, Box 22, FF 1275, Colorado Historical Society, Denver.*

When Lil became ill and checked into a Seattle "insane asylum" as Mrs. George Miller in 1936 at the age of fifty-four, the news made papers across the country.[15] In 1944, she announced she was willing her famous diamond to the Idaho Children's Home.[16] She began selling off her jewelry in the 1950s, but found it difficult because some of the buyers did not wish to be associated with her. In 1960, she moved to a rest home in Yakima, Washington, but granted an extensive interview to historians Fred and Jo Mazzulla in 1963.[17] Lil died in Yakima in 1975 at the age of ninety-two, and it was noted she had spent the last forty years of her life in "institutions and nursing homes."[18] The 1933 film *She Done Him Wrong*, starring Mae West, was loosely based on this Diamond Tooth Lil.[19]

In the northern part of Idaho near the Wyoming state line, Pierre's Hole also housed some very early prostitution. An impressively large mountain man rendezvous comprised hundreds of trappers and fur traders in 1832. On the outskirts of the rendezvous camped Nez Perce and Flatheads, who had limited supplies to trade, but more women, so as might be expected, the Indians "cleaned up." Trader Joe Meek was required to purchase his bride-to-be's horse, saddle, bridle, and "musk-a-boots," plus her clothing. The total fee was more than $550. Men who were not so wealthy had to make do with the temporary company the maidens had to offer.[20]

The lingo for prostitution tends to change depending on the region. In Idaho, "whores" were prostitutes, and "chippies" were dance hall girls. Plenty of both types of ladies were found at Ruby City, just southwest of Boise near the Oregon border. At least "one hurdy house" was present in 1864, although one visitor claimed there were no prostitutes at Ruby City. Surely the hurdy-gurdy house contained a few women of the night. A year after gold was discovered in the region, Silver City was established nearby and soon excelled because it was less windy and better promoted than Ruby City. Soon afterward, most of Ruby City's buildings were moved to Silver City. In 1865, newspapers reported on a Mr. Hanson who was beat up in a hurdy-gurdy house and faced the loss of sight in one eye. Between 1865 and 1874, Silver City boasted a number of saloons and as many as eighteen bordellos.[21]

Unlike the Chinagirls who were brought to America by force, some saloon owners in Silver City actually made a trip to Germany to hire dancing girls to come to America and work for them in payment for their passage. Among these hurdy-gurdy girls was Katerine Spese, who earned fifty cents a dance to pay off her passage and married William Gabriel in 1869. Other hurdy-gurdy girls turned wives included Mary Dewey, the wife of Silver City promoter Colonel William Dewey.[22] The 1870 census has a curiously low count of prostitutes in Silver City. Of more than twenty-six unmarried Chinese women documented, seventeen of them have no listed occupation, leading to the suspicion that they were prostitutes. Most of these women resided in the Chinese area on the outskirts of town along Jordan Street. One set of these women resided at Charley Owe's house. Three other women were listed as mulattos and appear to have been servants. Of the white women counted in the census, twenty-eight-year-old housekeeper Molly Cloud is a probable suspect as a madam because her house contained three other women, all listed as housekeepers. There was also a one-year-old child in the house.[23]

Of seven Caucasian women who were possible prostitutes in Silver City in 1870, only one is possibly identifiable as Mormon Ann. In May 1870, the *Owyhee Avalanche* reported on a disturbance at her brothel: "One night this week a party of roughs made an attack on the house of a Cyprian named 'Mormon Ann.' They broke in the windows, threw Greek fire, China stinkpots and all sorts of ugly projectiles in her room." Two weeks later, Ann and another "gay and festive blonde" borrowed some horses from a man named Springer and neglected to return them. Springer and another man, Jack Stoddard, set out after the women and "found the equines all soft and well cared for about thirty miles from here. All hands returned to town where the little Miss-understanding was satisfactorily arranged, and now, everything is lovely and goose hangs high."[24]

Historians have noted that Silver City tended to have a larger population of Chinese, both women and men, than most other mining towns.[25] The purchase of Chinese prostitutes in Silver City was documented as early as October 1870, when the local newspaper complained about the brothel license policy already in effect. It seems that Congress had recently passed an act prohibiting discrimination against the Chinese. "If license can be collected from white brothel keepers, it can be collected from Chinese," said the paper. In November 1870, the *Owyhee Avalanche* confirmed the presence of at least one Chinese wife who had been purchased by a local Chinaman for $1,400. The woman had died. "The widower," quipped the *Avalanche*, "is disconsolate and says that he would not invest so much money in female flesh anymore."[26] The same issue reported on the anticipated arrival of more "hurdies" in Silver City.[27]

By 1874, Silver City was on a decline, but it took some time for the population to dwindle. In the next year, the town's bad girls made headlines on several occasions, including reports of a young lady who solicited a reporter from the *Avalanche*, a "music teacher" who "discharged a revolver and appeared on the street en dishabille," and a "nymph of the pave" who "came to town disguised as a man."[28] The last item is of special note because for many years Silver City unknowingly boasted its own transgender cowboy. Her name was Johanna Monahan, and she was born in New York in 1850. When she first appeared in Silver City in about 1867, however, she was in men's clothing and using the masculine name "Joe Monahan." Unbeknownst to the general public, Joe decided to disguise her gender when she came West. She lived a quiet and private life among them for years as a prospector, bronco buster, sawmill operator, sheepherder, cowboy, and rancher. People who knew Joe, however, described her as "a small, beardless little man with the hands, feet, stature and voice of a woman." Longtime cowboy W. F. Schnabel also verified that although Joe "fought his way through with many of us [and] suffered hardship and hunger in early days and never whimpered," it was also "surmised that Joe was a woman."[29] In spite of the respect she earned among her peers, it would not be so unusual for paparazzi to take a stab at Joe Monahan by calling her a "nymph of the pave," if only to see how she would react. It was only upon her death in 1904 that her sex was ascertained once and for all.[30]

During the late 1870s, many of Silver City's frail sisters made a circuit, returning only long enough to entertain cowboys attending roundups on the ranches of nearby Jordan Valley.[31] The 1880 census for Silver City records seventeen Chinese women and three white women—Maria Clapper, Mattie Lewis, and Mary McIntosh—as prostitutes. Their average age was thirty-two years old, however, leading to the speculation that they were seeing out the mining boom in town. Some of them had been there for at least ten years, and it is possible that some of the Chinese women were still working as indentured sex servants. Furthermore, the red light district as a whole was growing roots in Chinatown.[32] One woman who missed the census, possibly because she had not yet arrived in town, was Sally Snyder or Schneider. In October, Sally was fined $50 and costs for "using abusive language to Sheriff Jones who was at the time escorting a party of ladies in a carriage to War Eagle Mountain." Sally married Richard Thomas in 1881. Although theirs was a long union, it was not necessarily a happy one. In

April 1896, the couple inexplicably disappeared, leaving behind not only their livestock, but also their saddle horses, clothing, and a half-eaten meal. Whether they were ever found is unknown.[33]

Regarding the fate of the three white women recorded in the census, only that of Maria Clapper is known. When Maria died in 1883, she left a probate will. She apparently had been sick for some ten days, and upon realizing she was dying, she made out the will to be signed by saloon owner B. F. Hastings and Dr. D. H. Belknap, who was attending her. Maria decreed that $500 from her estate should be set aside for her burial in a cemetery near San Francisco. This request was fulfilled in October, although Maria was initially buried in Silver City. She also stipulated that another $500 and all of her clothing be left to her twenty-two-year-old daughter Saddie Payne or Paine, who resided in New York State. Her remaining property, including her house, investments, jewelry, and money were left to saloon keeper William Williams, whom she named as executor of her estate. Although she would have been considered wealthy at the time, her estate unfortunately amounted to only about $775, and it is not known if her daughter ever received her portion of the money.[34]

In 1891, the prostitutes of Silver City were either working out of the second floor of saloons or in nearby cribs that they rented or owned. Some girls lived elsewhere, using the cribs only for business. In this way, they may have been able to share the rent with other women. Most of the cribs were one- or two-room cabins. The front room was the "parlor room" with a bed, dresser, washbasin, and stove. Back rooms were generally reserved for cooking and storage. At the height of Silver City's red light district, there were about a dozen bordellos operating with fifty to one hundred soiled doves.[35] It eventually came to be located on Main Street north of Riverside Avenue.[36] By 1895, it actually overlapped old Chinatown.[37] The majority of the houses of ill repute were on Jordan Street between Avalanche Street and Chinatown. The upper-echelon brothels were located nearer the commercial district, but the cribs and lower-end girls remained on the south end of the red light district nearest Chinatown.[38]

In 1900, for the first time since Silver City was founded, white prostitutes actually outnumbered Chinagirls. Nine Anglo women versus two Japanese prostitutes—Kate Tarna and Ki Ah—were identified as working near old Chinatown.[39] The white women were located near a large boardinghouse for men. They were identified as madam Lottie Young, who employed Otta Harrington and Edna Campbell, and madam Lea Perry, who employed Blance Talbot, Bernice Davenport, Bonnie Earl, and May Black.[40] May Black and May Davenport were arrested in August 1900 for using opium and were fined $30 each. There was also "Fanny," identified by old-timers as a Chinese prostitute. It is speculative whether there were actually more prostitutes in Silver City than listed on the census, but for unknown reasons were overlooked.[41]

Silver City resident Ned Williams recalled that in 1901, at about the age of six, he and his friends would station themselves on the porch of the Idaho Hotel. Because by social decree the red light ladies were not allowed to leave their district on Jordan Street, they were in the habit of calling the boys over from the porch of the hotel to run errands for them. Ned became a favorite of at least one girl, Josephine Lavender, whom he once heard say, "I love that little guy." Josephine had at one time worked for madam Lea Perry before moving to a crib near Long Gulch Creek on Jordan Street. "Old Joe," as she was known, had attended the University of Virginia. One time, Ned recalled, a former classmate showed up as an employee of a geographic survey team. "There was a ruckus," Ned said, "the carrying on she went through, making him promise not to tell what she was doing."[42] Ned and his friends made good tips by carrying out the working girls' wishes, and Ned later increased his take by peddling newspapers to the girls for fifty cents each. Ned's mother ultimately found out about his activities and "put an end to my paper route."[43] Ned also recalled several African American prostitutes who worked south along Jordan Creek outside of town at "the pink house." But the fancier bordellos remained close to the commercial district. In fact, one house butted up so close to the post office that one could listen at the post office walls and hear what was going on next door.[44]

The 1903 Sanborn Insurance map shows that most houses of prostitution in Silver City gave access to back alleys and discreet pathways, whereby girls of the night and their clients could access saloons, a cigar factory, and the livery stable. In some cases, the brothels shared a common wall with saloons to provide even more discreet access.[45] Although the girls of Silver City appear not to have suffered fines for prostitution, Lola Browner was arrested in November 1903 for disturbing the peace. Integration was likewise not a problem. In about 1908, old-timers of Silver City recalled, a Japanese soiled dove worked in a house of white prostitutes. Thirteen-year-old Ned Williams was working in a cow camp when the Japanese cook for the camp heard about the woman and was so anxious to meet her that he set out on snowshoes. When the cook hadn't returned by the next day, a party was sent out and eventually found the lost man freezing to death under a bush. Williams also remembered that many of the dance hall girls around Silver City eventually married local residents. One woman married a stage driver named Thompson, and a woman named Margaret married "Shorty" Hawes.[46]

Lea Perry's employees in 1910 included Casey the Irish Queen, Dotty "Miss Dot" Reynold, and Lola Evans. Other loose women in Silver City at the time included Big Dick, Mother Max, Zeda "Toots" Meyers, and Long-toed Liz, who had formerly worked for Jennie Mitchell in DeLamar, Idaho. In Silver City, Liz's place was called the War Eagle Hotel, and she had the most unique way of exercising discretion with a customer whose store was located some "twenty five to thirty steps" away from hers. The man would tie a string to his toe, and when Liz was open for business, she would jerk the string. One time Ned Williams and his friends decided to play a joke. "Well we kids jerked that string and old Charlie came down in his night shirt and sandals."[47] Lola Evans was still working for madam Lea Perry in Silver City in about 1912. Lea had in fact been in business since the early 1900s, and her house was located directly next to the post office. "Lea was a good manager," Williams noted. "She split revenues, if a girl wasn't producing to what she thought they should, they went out." As evidenced by the ledger of a local merchant, Lola often acted as assistant manager for Lea, purchasing cigars for the brothel and taking over business when Lea died in 1912 or 1913. Like so many before her, Lea was remembered as a kind-hearted woman who helped those in need, purchased coats for poor children, and grubstaked miners. All the male pallbearers at her funeral were married and, although prevented from burying her inside the old Ruby City cemetery, laid her to rest as close to the gate as possible.[48]

Other houses of prostitution were run by two women known as "Georgie" and "Stella." Williams noted that a popular pastime for the young men of the town was to visit each prostitute along the row for either sex or simply a drink.[49] By 1914, Silver City was once more in the midst of an economic slump, and the ladies of the lamplight duplicated the actions of the generation of prostitutes before them by moving on.[50] Lola Evans married and moved to Boise in about 1915. Likewise, Casey the Irish Queen married a sheep rancher and probably moved to the Jordan Valley, but returned to Silver City's red light district to both visit and work for extra cash.[51]

Northwest of Silver City some 140 miles away was Rocky Bar, whose prostitute history is equally interesting. Rocky Bar's most famous lady of the evening was "Peg Leg" Annie McIntyre, who first came to Idaho in 1864 as a child. Annie was only four when she arrived in a pack on the back of her father, Steve McIntyre. Shortly after Annie's mother died in Mountain Home, McIntyre brought Annie to Rocky Bar. There he bought a cabin and employed an Indian woman to take care of the house and little Annie.[52] McIntyre also partnered with an old friend, George Jackson, on the Golden Star Mine. The endeavor was a success, but Rocky Bar was a rough place, full of bar flies and prostitutes. In 1872, when McIntyre was killed in a street fight, twelve-year-old Annie found herself orphaned in a rough mountain mining town. Four years later, at the age of sixteen, she married one Thomas Morrow.[53] She bore five children, but three of them died. When Morrow himself died in about 1895, Annie dealt with her grief by drinking so much that her husband's relatives took her two surviving sons away from her. Then her father's Gold Star Mine hit a large pocket of gold, but Annie received nothing. Penniless and determined to make her way, she went to Atlanta, fourteen miles from Rocky Bar across Bald Mountain, and went to work as a prostitute.[54]

By 1898, Annie was secure enough in her new profession to feel she could show up in her old hometown. In March, she donned some snow shoes for a trek across Bald Mountain with a fellow prostitute, Emma "Dutch Em" Von Losch. The two women meant to attend a spring dance at Rocky Bar but got caught in a deadly blizzard instead. Two mail carriers who met at the summit of Bald Mountain every other day to exchange mail bags knew Annie and Em were somewhere on the mountain but failed to find them. It took three days for the storm to subside, and a search party of twelve men set out to find the pair. When one of the men checked a side canyon and spied Annie, her condition rendered him speechless. The help-less woman was crawling around wearing nothing more than a thin dress, babbling incoherently and failing to acknowledge the presence of her res-cue party. The men forced some whiskey down her, wrapped her in blan-kets and strapped her to a sled for the trek back to Atlanta. The next day, when she had regained her senses, Annie explained that she had given her warm wool underskirts and coats to Dutch Em, who had not survived the storm. "I remember we saw a big black rock that for a minute we thought was the cabin the mail carriers use. We got in close, trying to get out of the wind. Em lay down in the snow and refused to move. If I had gone on, I might have made it. But I couldn't leave her." Annie stayed with Em until the woman died, and then she went on. True to Annie's story, Em's body was found the next day. The searchers brought her back to Atlanta and buried her.[55]

Annie's refusal to leave her friend and the fact that she had risked her own life in doing so struck the hard hearts of the mountain men. In the meantime, Annie's rescuers realized that her badly frostbitten feet needed to be amputated. The doctor they sent for might not get to Atlanta in time to perform the operation and save Annie's life, so a man named Tug Wilson performed the procedure with a hunting knife and a meat saw while the other men held down a whiskey-anesthetized Annie. The surgery was a success, and Annie recovered amazingly fast. A friend of Annie's, saloon keeper Henry Longheme, took up a collection to supply her with artificial limbs, and Annie eventually was able to open a combination rooming house and restaurant.[56] She also allegedly lived with Longheme for twenty-two years, although he is not listed as living with her in the 1920 census.[57] In 1924, when Longheme made a trip back to Italy, Annie gave him some $12,000 to deposit in a San Francisco bank for her. The deposit was apparently never made, although Longheme did write from New York before disappearing from Annie's life forever. Unwilling to believe her long-time lover could have robbed her, Annie maintained throughout the rest of her life that Longheme must have been murdered or met with an accident. When she grew too old to take care of herself, her friends in Mountain Home provided a house for her. She died in 1935.[58]

The next town meriting mention in Idaho's prostitution history is Warren, founded in 1872. Warren's outstanding soiled dove was Polly Bemis. Among the thousands of Chinagirls who were brought to Idaho, Polly's tale was truly a Cinderella story among prostitutes. Born Lalu Nathoy in Shanghai, China, in 1853, Polly was first traded for a bag of seeds to feed her starving family when she was eighteen.[59] "My folks had no glub [sic]," she later told a friend. "They sellee me to buy glub."[60] Her new owner, a Chinese man known as "Big Jim," shipped Polly and several other girls to San Francisco. There, the girls were auctioned off. Polly, an attractive young girl, later said she was sold for $2,500 and smuggled to Portland, Oregon, by an old woman. From there, another Chinese man took her to Warren.[61] Big Jim, Polly, and four other girls arrived in Warren in July 1870 or 1872.[62]

Their arrival constituted the first brothel in the young mining camp, which had been founded just a few years earlier and was now home to three thousand people. One-third of them were Chinese.[63] In fact, the number of Chinese was so great that they merited their own saloon and gambling house.[64] When Big Jim died unexpectedly, four of his girls were claimed by another Chinese businessman and put back to work. Polly, however, managed to break free and open a restaurant.[65]

Several authors claim that Polly, who was already a slave to prostitution, was won in a poker game by Charley Bemis, the owner of a saloon next to the dance hall where she worked. The tiny Chinagirl took a liking to Bemis, who offered limited protection but never tried to corrupt her. Sometimes she would quietly sneak into the back rooms of his saloon and clean them. It was Polly's owner of the moment, Hong King, whom Bemis allegedly challenged to a poker game. Hong King was losing heavily when he bet one of his best assets: Polly.[66] Others, however, maintain that Charlie was one of Polly's customers at the restaurant. When an enemy shot Bemis in the face outside Polly's restaurant, a local doctor pronounced the wound terminal. Undaunted, Polly painstakingly dressed and took care of the wound. Bemis fell in love with her, and the two spent the rest of their lives together.[67]

The 1880 census shows Polly and thirty-two-year-old Charles Bemis living near the town of Washington in Idaho County. Charlie is listed as running a saloon.[68] It was probably around this time that the couple decided to homestead along the Salmon River. Polly became a model wife, cooking, cleaning, and performing chores at the ranch. She also weathered a few incidents, including one in which Bemis and a half-breed Indian got into a gunfight over her, and the man shot out Bemis's eye.[69] The couple finally married in 1894.[70] They may have finally married because anti-Chinese sentiments were on the rise, and the marriage would prevent Polly's deportation.[71] Countess Gizicka, who interviewed Polly for *Field and Stream* magazine in 1921, described the petite Chinese woman: "She stands not much over four feet, neat as a pin, wrinkled as a walnut, and at sixty-nine is full of dash and charm."[72]

In 1922, the Bemis home caught fire and burned to the ground, and two months later Charlie died. The combination of the two losses was enough to break Polly's heart, and she rarely left the ranch after that.[73] She did take a trip to Grangeville to see a doctor about her failing eyesight. When she returned, she strengthened her longtime friendship with her

FIGURE 37 ❧ *The last known photograph of Polly Bemis, circa 1921. Sold into sexual slavery as a teenager, Polly was fortunately able to marry relatively early in her career and thereafter live a respectable life. Courtesy of the Idaho State Historical Society, Boise, 62-44.1.*

closest neighbors, Charles Shepp and Peter Klinkhammer. The men ran a telephone line from her ranch to theirs and talked with Polly every day.[74] Interestingly, the 1930 census identifies Polly three times: as working as a "farm operator" on an "improved district road" near Warren on April 11; as living in the South Fork Valley in the Idaho National Forest on April 25; and, finally, as living in Dixon with no occupation listed. In all instances, she lived by herself.[75] Polly died in 1933 at the age of eighty and was buried near Charlie on Bemis Point, close to the homestead.[76] She left her homestead to Shepp and Klinkhammer in return for their faithful friendship.[77]

Polly's early plight as a Chinese slave girl did not draw the authorities' attention, but that of Native Americans did. In November 1873, a special report was generated concerning the condition of Indians in Idaho and adjacent territories. Commissioners J. P. C. Sharks, T. W. Bennet, and H. W. Reed reported that the Indians were complaining that "worthless white men associated with bad Indian women, prostituting them, and leaving such women and their children a burden upon the Indians."[78] The trade and sale of Chinese slaves did not seem to bother government officials, however. The purchase of Chinese women as wives or courtesans was still going on in 1874, as indicated by a report about Louis, a Chinese man who had run off with another Chinese man's woman in Fairview. "The injured owner of the runaway woman was at Fairview and did not become aware of his loss until the next morning," reported the *Owyhee Avalanche*. "He had recently bought her for $500 and is now in a very disconsolate mood."[79]

Chinese women were certainly present in the middle of Idaho at Bonanza when it was founded in 1876, but it was a white woman known as Amanda who drew public attention to that town.[80] Amanda first appeared in 1879. Rumor had it she was from Council Bluffs, Iowa, and had spent her time in a refined convent school until the age of eight. She had begun her career at Vienna, Idaho, and had also worked for a time at Sawtooth City. Amanda's downfall, however, was that she tended to move in with her favorite customer, which always ended in turmoil. At Bonanza, she set up shop in a cabin on the lower end of town and tried to do better. It soon became apparent that she had picked up nursing skills, and she became known as a "soiled angel of mercy." If an ill or injured miner couldn't come to her, Amanda would load up her saddle bags with medicine and go to him. Unfortunately, alcohol started getting the best of her, and within a few years she was known as a woman of extremely easy virtue because she often failed to charge her customers and needed to make money somehow. One such patron was John Bee, who became Amanda's friend. How good a friend is questionable considering that one night, as Amanda slept beside him in a local saloon, Bee offered her up in a game of poker.[81] The other gambler, a man named Pete, won the hand and carried Amanda off to his cabin. A jealous Bee reclaimed her the next day, but as he went for a pail of water, Pete fired a couple of shots in his direction. The disgruntled Bee had to surrender Amanda a second time. What became of their relationship can only be ascertained by the fact that in her later years Amanda began drifting from town to town and was admitted to the Custer County Poorhouse in Challis. She died at the home when she was about sixty, still retaining her beautiful chestnut hair, and was buried in a pauper's grave.[82]

In 1880, there were fifteen hundred people in Bonanza.[83] A mere seven of them were Chinese girls born between 1837 and 1850 in China.[84] Local papers paid less attention to them than they did to Anna King. When she died in a bawdy house fight, the townsfolk refused to let her be buried in the cemetery, so admirers carried her body to a place in the woods and buried her there. The grave was naturally marked by four pine trees at each corner. In later years, the area was made into a park.[85]

The 1880 census identifies women of easy virtue all across the small mining camps of Idaho. There were no less than three in Challis; one apiece at Blackfoot, Pioneer, and Washington; two Chinagirls each at Centerville and Mt. Idaho; eleven Chinagirls at Placerville; and seven girls at Lewiston.[86] In 1898, newspapers reported that W. M. Redding, lately of John Day Creek, was found dead in a brothel at Lewiston.[87] Although the notable Mabel Harris was a proprietress of the Luna House on Main Street in Lewiston, she was not above traveling to surrounding camps to drum up business.[88] At Bellevue in 1882, sisters Emma and Alvie DeMarr (real names "Matilda Turnross" and "Christina Elvitina Turnross") were operating a brothel. When the girls had saved $3,000 by autumn of that year, they moved to Salt Lake City and continued in the profession.[89]

Most notable among Idaho's red light districts was Wallace, founded as Cedar Swamp in about 1883. A year later the fledgling town was renamed Placer Center for the large amount of placer mining that occurred there. In 1888, when the town was incorporated, city fathers settled on the name "Wallace."[90] Jack Mayfield, owner of the famous Oasis Bordello Museum in Wallace, maintains that Shoshone County, where Wallace is located, "has

FIGURE 38 ❦ *The Oasis bordello in Wallace, Idaho. It is now*
a museum and remains one of the most perfectly preserved
specimens of its kind in the West. From the author's collection.

always sort of run by its own rules" and that prostitution was always largely overlooked. In fact, one woman dared to muse that "Wallace was founded by brothels."[91]

Wallace was certainly not without its share of troubles. One of the earliest records of prostitution there is less than happy. In 1889, an anonymous person wrote a letter to the editor. The stranger had recently broken through a group of laughing men to see that they were observing a woman he had known years ago. Back then "she was handsome; beauty and loveliness shown forth from every feature of her innocent countenance and grace accompanied every movement." The woman was also the mother of two children. Now, the stranger reported, she was drunkenly reeling around to the men's amusement. The writer lambasted the observers. "How any man or set of men could witness depths of degradation to the extent which was here pictured, and forget, even for a moment, that this . . . sore, bruised and withered flower had changed from a fresh, blooming plant . . . to the poor, unfortunate and miserable piece of humanity that she was." The writer further appealed to the general public for a place "to hide away from public view such unfortunate and helpless creatures."[92]

Such pleas for public sentiment largely went unnoticed. In December 1890, Gracie Edwards of the Star at the corner of Fifth and Pine streets gaily announced her grand opening ball, sporting an unusual boldness by advertising in the local paper. But the Star was hardly open a year before a knife fight broke out among Gracie's girls. At two o'clock in the morning, Lulu Dumont stabbed Frankie Dunbar seven times. Frankie's screams awakened night watchman Fred Brewer and bartender John Davis, who ran to the scene. Upon their arrival, Lulu disappeared into the darkness. Search parties looked for her throughout the next day, and rumors abounded about where she had gone, but Lulu was never found. Frankie, meanwhile, was carried into the Star, her wounds were dressed, and she survived.[93]

Leading madams in Wallace included Effie Rogan and Miss Huff on Pine Street. Effie's place was called the Reliance and ran from 1895 to 1912.[94] In 1906, the Idaho Press noted that two young men had been arrested for vagrancy. The men had shown up the previous week with two women who were described as "ragged and penniless" and who went to work for Effie at the Reliance. When the young men then raised a ruckus at Effie's, the police were called, and they were arrested. The men had since been warned to leave town, but declined to do so. A few days later one of them, again on a drunk, was so bold as to stride into the police station and "made boasts about who he was and what he would do with the police." The drunk and his partner were arrested again and this time were given until 2:00 P.M. that day to leave Wallace. They left.[95] Later, Wallace's red light district relocated to the area near Sixth and Cedar streets near the railroad depot.[96] Effie Rogan appears in the 1900 census with four girls. Ten years later she was down to only one employee and seems to have disappeared from Wallace sometime after that.[97]

In 1905, another notorious place in Wallace was the Coliseum Theater. Prostitute Gussie Snow was attending the theater there when she inexplicably dropped into a coma. She died a few days later, and the local doctor diagnosed a blood clot as the cause of death.[98] Gussie's unusual death was overshadowed just a few months later by the antics of Irene Thornton, "the hard working colored lady who was convicted a few weeks ago of conducting a disorderly house on Residence Street." Following the conviction, Irene moved to a house above the Bank Street bridge, where she continued to alternate taking in laundry with entertaining gentlemen. A can of beer was negotiated in the price for services, often resulting in Irene and her customers' getting into "a beastly state of intoxication" and "scandalizing the neighborhood." On one such night, Irene and two men were arrested for making a ruckus. A third man, Tom Bowers, was arrested when he mistakenly walked into an allegedly respectable home thinking it was Irene's. In court, Irene pleaded to Judge Featherstone, "Why, judge, I didn't do anything bad. We just had fifteen cents worth of beer, and there wasn't no beer there when Mr. [Police Chief] Beck came, was there, Mr. Beck? I wasn't making no disturbance and God knows I wasn't drunk." Featherstone gave Irene a couple of days to leave town or else spend six months in jail.[99] Whether she left remains unrecorded.

The Sanborn Fire Insurance map of 1908 shows a large number of bordellos in operation in Wallace. In all, twelve houses of prostitution operated along or near the banks of the Coeur D'Alene River. One place consisted of ten cribs. Another combination saloon and brothel at 307½ Pine Street was quite large and featured multiple skylights.[100] Meanwhile, Mrs. M. Vinas and her mother, Della Mount, were fined for running a disorderly house on Bank Street. Mrs. Vinas told the judge that her husband had recently divorced her on grounds of infidelity. Despite this information and the fact that the women were apparently embarking on a career in prostitution, the judge fined them only $5 each. Later that year Reverends MacCaughey and Neilan professed a plan to force Mayor Hugh Toole to run the red light ladies of Wallace out of town. Nothing came of the threat.[101]

But Wallace's bordello owners soon came under fire again when it was discovered that Jennie Girard and her "alleged" husband, Emil Vaucamp or Van Camp, kept one of their employees virtually enslaved. The girl, Lillian Dubois, had arrived in America from France just eleven months earlier. While at Jennie's, Lillian testified, she was forced to turn over all of her earnings. Her clothes had been taken from her, and she was not allowed to leave the house unless she was "under some sort of guardianship or unless accompanied by one or other of the defendants or their satellites." It was only by being arrested that Lillian was finally rescued from Jennie and Van Camp's clutches. Two months later, Louis Maraninchi was arrested for assisting Jennie and Van Camp to import more would-be prostitutes to the United States. During the proceedings, Jennie admitted she was not married to Van Camp. It was also noted that Maraninchi's wife, Louise "Blondie" Maraninchi, was in jail awaiting deportment to France, and that the husband had lived off her earnings for the past seven years. In the case of Jennie Girard and Emil Van Camp, Jennie testified she had met Van Camp at his saloon in New York. After traveling as far as British Columbia, the two had landed in Wallace, where Van Camp proposed building seventeen cribs for Jennie to rent from him at $250 per month. Jennie in turn rented the cribs out at $2 per day. The trial lasted throughout December. Van Camp was busted again in May 1909 for running a theater without a license. At least one prominent businessman was also arrested, along with the theater manager, the bartender, and three performers, including Jennie Girard and another woman named Ladonna Ridgway. Ten other women employed by Van Camp escaped arrest.[102]

The perils recounted by Lillian Dubois were accented by the attempted suicide of Leo Williams in Wallace in December 1908. Leo had in fact tried to do herself in three other times but had failed. In her fourth attempt, she drank half a bottle of laudanum as well as "a large quantity of carbolic acid." She was only twenty, and it was believed she would again recover from her attempt. The dangers of living as a red light lady were made even more obvious in late December when Peter Lindahl gave prostitute Freedna Carlson a black eye. Lindahl had apparently broken a chair and punched Freedna when she demanded payment for the damage. Violence and suicides continued to plague Wallace through the spring of 1909. In March, Georgia Ross took some poison and was found lying half dead in the snow. The *Daily Idaho Press* noted that Georgia had three children and her mother in Seattle to look after, but was in ill health herself. The previous summer she had tried to kill herself at Wardner, an attempt that had landed her in the hospital for four months and had put her even further in debt. Following some sort of emergency surgery, Georgia had fallen into a deep depression before making this last attempt. It was thought she would recover, but the newspaper declined to speculate whether anyone might help the girl.[103]

It was not until June 1909 that Wallace authorities considered submitting their prostitutes to health exams. Whether the mayor officially approved the monthly health exam idea is unknown.[104] Following a gigantic fire in 1910 that burned down Wallace along with three million acres between Idaho and Washington State, the town rebuilt. New brothels in Wallace included the Arment, and business continued just the same. Unlike other states, Idaho was fairly permissive with regards to its prostitution industry, which it regarded as being the same as any other business. City authorities tended to look the other way when incidents of an illegal or suspicious nature occurred, even if the local papers did not. "Not one man died in any of the brothels of Wallace," maintained Jack Mayfield in 2006, "but plenty of dead men were found in the hotel across the street." Mayfield explained that if a man "stopped breathing," the ladies would dress him and clandestinely put him in his own wagon or, later, his car. If the vehicle couldn't be located, special arrangements were made with the Ryan Hotel across the way to rent a room in which to put the body.[105]

In 1895, the Bi-Metallic block was built at 605 Cedar Street as a three-story hotel and saloon. Such fancy decor as mosaic floor tiles from China attest to the Bi-Metallic's one-time luxurious surroundings. Following the fire of 1910, the building downsized to two stories, becoming a brothel in about 1913.[106] The Arment, the Jade, the Lux, and the U & I were joined by the Oasis, which became one of the fancy parlor houses near the main street.[107] In all, a bar was set up downstairs, and entertainment was provided upstairs. Prostitution flourished in these buildings for literally decades. In time, the Oasis featured a downstairs buzzer so the girls were aware of customers coming up. There were two waiting rooms, the Green Room and the Gray Room, to cut down on the risk that customers would run into each other.[108] Wallace madams and independent women during 1910 included

FIGURE 39 ⚬ *One room at the Oasis illustrates what a brothel bedroom looked like during the Victorian era. The Oasis weathered a number of decades and changes in both fashion and social norms. From the author's collection.*

Daisy Brown, Foos Cormie with three girls, Laura Butler and Clara Murphy, Emma Clayton with two girls, and Mary Bessette with six employees.[109]

During the 1950s, madams Loma Delmonte and Lee Martin carried on in Wallace, but the Oasis still reigned supreme. By the 1960s and 1970s, color-coded waiting rooms there were furnished with couches, chairs, and tables with magazines. Five bedrooms were also color coded. Interestingly, a peek hole in each door let a girl look in before entering to assure no troubles with her customer. The rooms were typically furnished with a dresser and a twin bed, with foam rubber installed behind the headboard to cut down on the noise factor. Some rooms also had armoires because there were few closets when the building was constructed. The madam's room was a large suite with a locking dresser and desk to prevent theft. A large linen closet in the upstairs hall included towels, sheets, bedspreads, mattress covers, blankets, and a large stack of small rugs to place on the ends of the beds so customers wouldn't have to remove their shoes. At the end of the hall was a large tub for giving bubble baths, plus individual medicine cabinets for each employee.[110]

In 1973, the houses of prostitution in Wallace closed, but then later reopened.[111] Delores Arnold, who had first set up shop after World War II, remained a famous madam in Wallace for nearly fifty years and in this later period still had the Lux as well as the Plaza in the Kellogg building.[112] When prostitution was officially outlawed in Wallace in 1983, the girls at the Oasis simply took to hiding in the basement when they heard "state men" were coming to close them down. By then, the trade was well established at the Oasis. The girls of the house typically worked "two weeks on and two weeks off." In the kitchen was a list of important phone numbers and a drawer filled with timers because the girls charged by the minute. Liquor was also kept in the kitchen after the old back bar downstairs was sold. Because the house lacked a liquor license, customers were asked to donate $2 per drink to the jukebox. Outside the kitchen window was an adjoining roof where the girls could sunbathe between customer sessions.[113]

The last price list at the Oasis reflected fees between $15 for eight minutes and $70 per hour. Bubble baths were offered at $50 for a half-hour or $80 for a full hour. The prices also included additional fees for using various positions, vibrators, and double parties.[114] If a customer hadn't finished by the time the timer went off, a maid was instructed to tap on the door and call out, "Time's up!" Discounts were given to college students older than eighteen. Following each transaction, the girls would drop their money into a safe, write down in code the amount of money they made, and go to their next customer. They also went to the doctor once a week and paid a fee of $35 to $50, depending on the year.[115] Similar customs were likely present at the Lux and Luxette, which closed in 1986. The U & I and the Oasis closed in 1988. In 1991, the federal government got fed up with Wallace's bad girls, and agents raided the whole area with 150 men from the FBI. The Oasis's last madam was eighty-six years old in 2006 and still lived near Coeur d'Alene.[116]

Near Wallace were Mullan, Murray, Kellogg, Burke, and Wardner. In Mullan, the leading madam was Ada View, who ran the Michigan Lodging House. The red light district was along Hunter Avenue.[117] In 1907, a fray broke out when one Gus Jones threatened the life of dance hall girl Marie Hansen. Jones had done so before, but this time he pulled a gun. Marie ran behind the bar, and the bartender, owner William Lawrence, assured her she wouldn't be hurt. Then he gallantly faced Jones and joked with him, whereupon Jones left the bar. Enter Barney Ford, the chief of police, on his rounds. Lawrence told Ford what had transpired, whereupon the policeman went looking for Jones. At the corner near the Cromwell Hardware store, Ford commanded Jones to give up his gun. Instead, Jones pushed his revolver into Ford's face. Ford reacted by shooting Jones to death. To his utter surprise, Ford was arrested pending an investigation. Meanwhile, Marie Hansen revealed she had been traveling with Jones for some time and had been victim to his threats and abuse on several occasions. There had been other incidents in which Jones had pulled his gun. It turns out that Marie had taken up dancing only in the previous six months and had in fact moved out of her and Jones's house in Mullan after a recent quarrel, but Jones had come to her room and taken her clothes before threatening her at Lawrence's dance hall. Marie further stated that she was only eighteen years old and that her parents in Portland did not know what she was doing. Despite the ill treatment Jones had shown her, Marie lamented she was "sorry the poor fellow is dead." As for Barney Ford, he was acquitted.[118]

When the mining town of Murray was founded in close proximity to Wallace in 1885, the number of shady ladies far outstripped the number in the other town.[119] Maggie Hall, also known as "Molly b'Damn," was the most popular soiled dove in Murray during the 1880s. Molly was born in Dublin in 1853 to a caring home with plenty of love and education. Despite several proposals of marriage, the bright young lady found Ireland boring, and she made the trek to America in 1873. Upon her arrival in New York, she almost immediately fell on hard times and began working as a barmaid under the name "Molly Hall." There, she was won over by a young wealthy man named Burden and married him. The marriage was less than ideal. Although she lived in a plush apartment, her husband insisted on keeping the marriage a secret from his influential father, who soon found out anyway. The father cut off his son, and the couple began moving from apartment to apartment, just one step ahead of their unpaid landlords. Burden had never worked in his life and lacked the skills to do so. Before long, he asked Molly the unthinkable: to become a prostitute. Molly was shocked at the request, but could see no other way out and gave in to her husband. The act resulted in heartbreak for Molly as well as excommunication from the Catholic Church when she went to confession.[120]

In about 1877, feeling her soul was damned forever, Molly left her husband and struck out on her own.[121] She traveled as far as Virginia City, Nevada, San Francisco, and Portland, honing her skills and charging more money as she went. At one time, she was purported to work as the mistress to a millionaire.[122] In 1884, after reading about the gold strikes in the Coeur d'Alene Mountains, Molly went to Idaho to try her luck.[123] On her way there, she met Calamity Jane on a Northern Pacific train. Calamity, however, turned back at Thompson Falls, Montana, and headed for Deadwood, South Dakota.[124]

Molly, meanwhile, purchased a horse and joined a pack train headed for Murray.[125] The town was only two years old and looked to be an opportune place to set up shop.[126] Along the way, the party was besieged by a blizzard, and Molly noticed a woman and her child struggling through the snow. Realizing the two couldn't go on, Molly found shelter where the three of them could stay the night while the train moved on. When the pack train reached Murray, word spread about Molly's heroic efforts. It was a great surprise and relief when everyone saw Molly and her new charges come into the town the next day. Molly put the woman and her child up in a cabin and paid for their board, thus winning the town residents' hearts.[127] Before long, she met Phil O'Rourke, and the two formed a longtime friendship. When she told O'Rourke her name was "Molly Burden," he misunderstood her, thinking she said "Molly b'Damn." Thus, Molly's colorful nickname was born. She next asked for "Cabin Number One," a code throughout the West meaning she wanted the madam's cabin in the red light district. She was soon running her own popular bordello in Paradise Alley.[128]

One of Molly's ploys to make money was her "bath time," which coincided with the miner's payday. She would fill a tub in the alley behind her house with water, then beckon the miners to throw gold dust in the tub. When enough of the stuff covered the bottom of the tub, Molly would shed her clothes and have her bath. For a little extra dust, she would even let the miners scrub her a bit.[129] But Molly b'Damn was also known for her kindness and charity. The new Florence Nightingale of Murray fed the hungry, housed the homeless, and nursed many a sick prospector. Soon after her arrival, a miner known as Lightenin' came to town, got drunk, slept with several of Molly's girls, and awoke in the morning to find his pouch of gold missing. Lightenin' confronted Molly, who stubbornly refused to return the gold. Admitting to his own drunkenness, Lightenin' bought some supplies on credit and headed once more for the hills. A few months later Lightenin's partner came to Murray with the news that Lightenin' was dying. When Molly heard about it, she called a meeting with her girls and pleaded with them to return the miner's pouch of gold. The pouch mysteriously reappeared on Molly's dresser, and the madam lost no time in gathering supplies and trekking to Lightenin's cabin. After several days, the man came out of his fever to see Molly sitting before him. When he asked what she was doing there, she gave him back his pouch.[130]

Molly indeed earned the respect and admiration of the people of Murray. "She was a sight to behold, riding around Murray on her spirited horse," gushed one of her admirers. "She decked herself out in silks and velvets like a queen and could quote Shakespeare with the best of them. But she wasn't one of them cultured society women, not by a long shot. Molly b' Damn was both good and bad. She could let loose a string o' oaths that would curl a mule skinner's hair. But she was gentle with the sick, and that made up for a lot of things." One story about Molly has her riding her horse into saloons and up to the bar for a drink, but she also attended church regularly, although it was not the Catholic house of worship.[131]

In 1886, the town of Murray suffered a smallpox epidemic but had only one doctor and no hospital. Citizens were in a panic, fearing the sick and hoping that if they confined themselves to their homes, they wouldn't catch the dreaded illness. Molly called a town meeting and inspired everyone to work together. Soon there were makeshift hospitals all over town as Molly and her fellow citizens toiled to see the epidemic through. Molly worked herself to exhaustion and contracted consumption in October 1887. She

FIGURE 40 ❧ *Maggie Hall is buried at the Murray, Idaho, cemetery. Her wooden grave marker has been replaced several times, and the most recent one has in fact deteriorated badly since this photograph was taken. Courtesy of the Special Collections and Archives, University of Idaho, Moscow.*

died on January 17, 1888, at the age of thirty-five. Phil O'Rourke was at her side.[132] Murray and its surrounding mines closed down for Molly's funeral. A Methodist minister conducted services when the Catholic priest refused to do so, and, per Molly's request, she was buried under the name "Maggie Hall." Someone even wrote a moving eulogy for her, remembering her as "a ministering angel to the sick and suffering when exposure of illness laid men low. Neither snow nor heat kept her from an unfortunate's bedside, and these kind acts have been recorded in the Book of books to her credit, overbalancing the debt side."[133]

Murray went on without Molly b'Damn. In 1909, it was noted that Frank Monroe and Henry Lawrence's famous dance hall closed after county commissioners denied their business license.[134]

Kellogg, west of Wallace, was so named in 1887.[135] As in all the surrounding mining camps and towns, there was soon a raging red light district in the town. News of the district reared its ugly head in 1893 when a young girl in Opera House Alley committed suicide. The girl drank almost an ounce of carbolic acid and forty grains of morphine—enough, she probably thought, to knock her out while the poison did its job. Instead, the poor girl was left in agony. "The presiding physician applied all the usual antidotes, but the girl died at midnight." A relative newcomer to Kellogg, she "was of fine appearance and education." A search of her belongings came up with the name "Sage" and a clue that the girl might have friends in Iowa. For some reason, her untimely death struck the hearts of the red light ladies. When she was buried in the Kellogg Cemetery, "a large number of people attended."[136] Although other areas around Wallace suffered serious slowdowns during the early 1900s, Kellogg did not. The 1915 Sanborn Fire Insurance map shows a still-active red light district in an alley. No less than sixteen brothels flourished. One of them was located just off the dressing rooms of a vaudeville theater. Interestingly, the local jail was conveniently located right next door to one of the brothels.[137]

In July 1888, the *Wallace Free Press* reported on Little Allie, a young prostitute at Burke who was addicted to morphine. A friend found Allie "lying on a pile of straw with nothing over her but some gunny sacks." The friend, Carry Young, quickly and successfully appealed to the camp for clothing and money to send Allie to the county hospital.[138] In 1896, prostitute Georgie Ryan was acquitted in the shooting death of Albert Paquin, her sometime pimp and a saloon owner. Georgie and several others testified that Paquin had beat and harassed Georgie throughout the afternoon and evening despite her attempts to get him to leave her alone. Even the townspeople were on Georgie's side, and when the judge dismissed the case, the crowd applauded and shook the girl's hand."139

DeLamar was another town into which prostitution found its way quickly. Shortly after it was established in about 1888, nearby Toughtown was designated the saloon and red light district. DeLamar's founder, Captain Joseph De Lamar, immediately decided the town's amenities should include a naughty girl or two. Accordingly, he lured madam Jeanie Mitchel and some other madams from the nearby failing town of Hailey.140

In 1906 in Wardner, also located near Wallace, prostitute Lily Thompson, alias "Thelma," died from an intentional overdose of "antiseptic tablets." Lily decided to do herself in when she saw her paramour dancing with other women. She got drunk before committing the deed; if she had been sober, she might have realized that the tablets she took would produce torturous pain with an agonizingly slow death. It took nearly two weeks for her to die. In December, police, fed up with the goings on in the red light district, raided a few resorts and arrested eight men. In a rare act of fairness, the *Idaho Press* had no qualms about publishing the men's names. "The arrest of these men caused a great sensation here yesterday when it became known who were caught in the raid," noted the paper, "and the trials will prove an interesting affair." Poor Lily Thompson's suicide was among the undesirable incidents that prompted officials to crack down. The same day the article appeared, it was also reported that one Al Mason was wanted for clubbing Grace Wilson with his revolver after she rejected his attentions. The force of the blow crushed the bridge of Grace's nose, disfiguring her for life. That life was short; due to her troubles with Mason and probably depression over her nose, Grace committed suicide with carbolic acid a few weeks later. Mason was never caught.141

Just a week later, Wardner began a serious crusade against the "questionable characters" of the town. Among them was A. L. Florette, charged with vagrancy. Unfortunately, Jack Parsons's efforts on Florette's behalf did more harm than good, not only for Florette but also for the town in its efforts against the town roustabouts. When an objection made by the state's attorney was sustained, Parsons, who had appointed himself Florette's attorney, yelled, "You can't stop me from explaining; you just leave me alone." The judge tried to clarify that Parsons was riding over the court's decision, but the witness retorted, "I ain't ridin' over no court's decisions, I'm testi-fyin'." The courtroom could hardly contain its laughter when Parsons fur-ther decided to testify as his own witness, jumped on the witness stand, and "proceeded to question himself and answer in the same breath his own questions." During the proceedings, it was also brought to light that Parsons himself had once been convicted of vagrancy. Florette was duly found guilty.[142]

By 1909, dance halls in the Coeur d'Alenes were beginning to close, one by one. The *Daily Idaho Press* noted in August that Monroe and Lawrence's dance hall and the North Side resort in Murray were closed. In fact, the paper stated, only two dance halls remained in the area: the Owl in Burke and the Arcade in Wallace. It was also noted that the owner of the Arcade, Dan McInnis, had his place up for sale. Dance halls at Wardner, Mullan, and Kellogg, according to the paper, had closed some time ago. The Sanborn Fire Insurance map for 1909 shows several vacant buildings along Hunter Avenue in Mullan, although one place, a saloon with several rooms for girls in back, was still occupied.[143]

Farther northwest, on the east side of the White Cloud Mountains was Mackay, founded in about 1900. The town initially forbade saloons and bawdy houses to be built in the city limits. Accordingly, the gamblers and red light ladies flocking over from Montana simply built their own shanty towns north and south of town. Both were located about a mile from Mackay and serviced by a "horse drawn bus" from Mackay that ran on the hour. The town, upon realizing it was losing money to such places, gave up in about 1902, and before long a red light district was operating within the city limits.[144] Prostitution was still present there in 1912, when it was noted that harlot Sophia Green of Mackay had gone to Cripple Creek, Colorado. Sophia sometimes used the last name of her husband, Brockey Jones.[145]

Although Idaho's silver production began a slow decline beginning in 1902, prostitution obviously prospered for several more decades.[146] Various tragedies also continued to occur. In 1905, a Mrs. Wilford of North Dakota traced her runaway daughter, Mrs. Edward Rusk, to Coeur d'Alene. The girl had apparently been working her way through the West by finding employ-ment in various brothels and had obviously married at one point. In 1904, Mr. Rusk had been arrested for larceny along with a "Negro" prizefighter called "Jolly Rogers." Tragically, by the time her mother caught up with her daughter, the girl had already hung herself.[147]

MADAMS AND OTHER WOMEN
OF MONTANA

᠅ MONTANA IS MOUNTAINOUS ON THE WEST AND PRAIRIELIKE TO the east, making it somewhat an alternate version of Colorado. Like Colorado, it sports notable scenic wonders and such historic sites as Glacier National Park and Little Big Horn Battlefield. Also like Colorado, it has vast mountain ranges, deep canyons, rocky crags, and high country prairies that proved to be a life-threatening challenge to the pioneers who struggled and strived to conquer unknown and dangerous territory. Today, Montana residents, at least in the western portion of the state, remain both proud of and amused by the sordid history of their "hurdy-gurdy girls."

As early as 1850, Fort Sarpy, located in Rosebud County, was reported by American Fur Company trader Samuel Chambers as being home to an amazing number of Crow prostitutes. "Fort full of loafers," Chambers wrote in his journal, "feasting and lounging in the houses. Every pan, plate and cup is brought in requisition three or four times a day to feast brats and whores . . . the women are all whores. . . . I find this morning that Murrell, not being satisfied with one whorehouse, has converted the Store into another."[1] Ten years later, Montana's prostitute population had expanded to include the Anglo women who were working hurdy-gurdy houses in Virginia City. Newspaper editor Thomas Dimsdale gave a description of those early houses: "One institute, offering a showy and dangerous substitute for more legitimate female association, deserves a more peculiar notice. This is the hurdy gurdy house . . . let the reader picture himself a large room, furnished with a bar at one end—where champagne at $12 per bottle, and drinks at 25 to 50 cents are wholesales, correctly speaking—and divided at the end of this bar, by a railing running from side to side." Dimsdale also offered his opinion on the hurdy-gurdy girls of the West: "If a woman be lewd let her take her place with her fellows; but if she be virtuous, let her dress decently and act modestly."[2]

One of the first hurdy-gurdy women in Virginia City, Ranche Belle, arrived in 1860. In about 1865, she was accused of stealing three silver half-dollars from a customer but was released. A month later she was arrested again for "using indelicate and disgusting language" and fined $5.[3] Virginia City's most notable prostitute, however, was probably Marie Virginia Slade. Virginia, as she was known, came to Virginia City in about 1863 with her notorious husband, Jack. Scandalous rumors followed the couple, the most prominent being that Virginia was once a lady of easy virtue, a good shot, and a marvelous equestrienne. She retired when she met Jack during the Mexican-American War of the 1840s and professed to love him with all her heart. But Slade was a hard-working freighter with a nasty temperament when drunk.[4]

In Colorado, Slade had already had his share of skirmishes, but he did name a stagecoach stop, Virginia Dale, for his wife. In all, it was said Slade killed twenty-six men before he and Virginia made their way to Montana. Once there, Slade bought Virginia a nice rock house in Meadow Valley some eight miles from Virginia City and allowed her to purchase beautiful furniture shipped from Salt Lake City. Virginia led a respectable life and was admired for her handmade silk gowns. The Slade's peaceful existence, however, was peppered with Jack's drunken episodes.[5] He often bragged about Virginia but had only distaste for other women. On at least one occasion, he pointed his six-gun at a local dance hall girl, telling her, "Pull up your skirts, let's see your legs . . . we paid our money. . . . Let's see your legs. Hell, there's a couple of dozen girls here probably got better. Pull 'em up . . . take off that skirt."[6]

One night in 1864 a group of vigilantes sized up Jack's murderous past and his refusal to straighten up, and decided that a good hanging would teach him a lesson and at the same time rid Virginia City of the town's most notorious drunk. As Jack pleaded for his life, a message was sent to

FIGURE 41 ❧ *During the 1890s, madams Myrtle Butler and Pearl McGinnis operated out of these small houses in Virginia City, one of which was called the Green Front Boarding House. These structures are lucky in that they remain on their original site today. From the author's collection.*

Virginia. The helpless wife saddled up her horse and rode into town, but she was too late. The sight of her husband's body, surrounded by those who did him in, was too much for her. From that day forward, she harbored a hate for the people of Montana in general. Jack was buried across from the rock house, and Virginia eventually had his body moved and buried at the Old Mormon Cemetery in Salt Lake City, Utah. Although a friend of the couple, Jim Kiskadden, later married Virginia, it was for naught. Kiskadden could not replace Jack. Virginia finally left her husband and Montana, taking up prostitution and dying in an unknown location.[7]

Around the time of Slade's hastened departure from this world, prostitution made the local newspapers. An October 1864 mention in the *Montana Post* merely announced that lewd houses "were all the go." Subsequent articles mentioned how the houses were full nightly, but by December the number of men attending such places merited the editorial comment that they were spending their time at the "dancing resorts with which our city is cursed." Just two weeks later came another editorial asking the inevitable question, "In Oregon the dance houses have to pay a license of $100 per month. Why not in Virginia City?" Sure enough, a short time later the hurdy-gurdy houses of Virginia City were paying $400 per year for a license. By 1866, the paper announced, "There is no hurdy-gurdy house in this city," but the truth of this statement is doubtful.[8] Virginia City's population in 1870 numbered at 2,555 and included "whites, Chinese and negroes."[9] Ten years later, according to the 1880 census, there were at least four Chinese prostitutes in the city. Among the white women was a dancer known as Lieli. Virginia City's red light district was located along Idaho Street. Today a structure known as Bonanza House is one of three remaining brothels where actors from the local theater now stay. The other two brothels are now the Virginia City visitor center.[10]

Bannack (as "Bannock" was spelled at the time), some eighty miles from Virginia City, was the next Montana town to take on a notorious night life. Founded by gold prospectors in 1862, it was quite the wild town. As Virginia City was ruled by Jack Slade, Bannack was run by an outlaw named Henry Plummer. Upon getting himself elected sheriff, Plummer and his cohorts masterminded the robbing of stagecoaches regularly from nearby Skinner's Saloon and Robbers Roost. Murders and shoot-outs were common. In fact, despite building the town jail, Plummer was estimated to have killed more than one hundred men during his short tenure as sheriff. Disgruntled citizens eventually formed a vigilante committee from both Bannack and Virginia City, and they hanged their thieving sheriff and two of his cronies in January 1864. The following May, due to the efforts of Oregon Territory's chief justice Sidney Edgerton, Montana Territory was formed. Edgerton had in fact settled in Bannack while Plummer was still running amuck and was eventually appointed governor of the territory in 1864 following Plummer's death. Thus, Bannack was Montana's first capital. When Virginia City outgrew Bannack, the meetings were moved to that town. Despite the growing legislature, Virginia City and such surrounding towns as Adobe, Centerville, Junction, Nevada City, and Ruby continued supporting their red light districts.[11]

One of the early madams at Bannack was the French-born Simone Jules, also known as "Eleanore Dumont" and "Madam Moustache." Stories about her are numerous, involving everything from staving off disease-ridden steamboats in Montana to horsewhipping card cheaters in Colorado. The French bombshell claimed to have been born in Paris in 1829 and first became known at the Kootenai mines in British Columbia. She began a gambling career at San Francisco in 1850 and relocated to Nevada City, California, in 1854, where she opened a combination saloon and gambling hall. Hers was a straight house, with no profanity or violence allowed. She also served free food and champagne to gamblers around the clock and kept a bevy of girls upstairs. Eleanore herself resided alone in a suite at the National Hotel. Although she spurned the advances of most men, she did carry a torch for editor E. G. Waite of the *Nevada Journal*. Alas, although Waite occasionally called on her for sexual favors, he was not interested in pursuing a relationship. When he married a "respectable" woman, the marriage broke Eleanore's heart.[12]

Eleanore's business began struggling, so she took on a business partner and sometime lover named "Lucky" David Tobin. The union was a good one, and Tobin's improvements to Eleanore's place soon had the business back on top. Despite her new success, however, Eleanore continued to pine for Waite. She and Tobin eventually split when the latter began demanding more and more of the profits. Eleanore sold out in 1856 and left Nevada City. Thus began an extensive traveling stint that lasted for years. Over time, Eleanore was documented as being in California, Idaho, Nevada, New Mexico, and Colorado. In the latter state, she took a new lover named Charlie Utter and once horsewhipped a fellow she caught cheating at cards at Colorado City's Hoffman House. Indeed, Eleanore was now an itinerant gambler, staying in one place just long enough to win big at the tables before moving on.[13]

By 1864, Eleanore had amassed enough money to buy a two-story combination saloon, gambling hall, and brothel in Bannack. There she took on yet another new paramour, Mac McHarney. She also enhanced her gambling house with some upstairs girls and even found a madam to run the brothel for 10 percent of the take. A short time later, however, McHarney was killed in the gambling room. The culprit was a man named MacFarlane, and Eleanore must have been fond of him, for she bailed him out of jail and even made him her partner. One of Eleanore's employees in 1867 was fifteen-year-old Martha Canary, soon to be known as "Calamity Jane." By then, however, MacFarlane had become abusive and threatening. When Eleanore sold out and decided to take to the road once more, neither MacFarlane nor Martha Canary followed her. Along the way, Eleanore earned her first real nickname, "the Angel of Sin."[14] She spent about a year in Wyoming and Nevada, then time in Bozeman and Fort Benton. At the latter place, she opened a new gambling house with a dozen prostitutes in her employ. When a steamboat captain along the Missouri River attempted to unload some passengers with smallpox, Eleanore outsmarted him by presenting a friend of hers who had recently been horribly mangled by a grizzly. "We have a bear pox outbreak here," she told the captain. "If your people come ashore, they'll all be infected like this and no cure in sight." The captain acquiesced, and Eleanore's friend received a bottle of whiskey for his trouble.[15]

In about 1868, Eleanore temporarily tired of the gypsy life and purchased a ranch near Carson City, Nevada. There she met and married Colonel Reginald Carruthers, a refined gentleman gambler. After a mere month of courtship, the two married. All would have been well if it hadn't turned out that Carruthers was already married and had five children in Montana. The diamonds and fancy gowns he bestowed upon Eleanore were merely a ruse; within a year, all of Eleanore's savings had been wiped out. When Carruthers forged her signature to gain ownership of her ranch, Eleanore shot him and fled to Salt Lake City.[16] Author Emma Green says that Eleanore then married a saloon owner named McKnight in Pioche, Nevada, in 1861. The new groom stole Eleanore's cash and disappeared.[17] Now beyond reach of the law, Eleanore took out a fresh ad for sporting girls and received several applications, again including one from Calamity Jane. The madam gave the girls a quick lesson in cards and set out with her five new employees for Wyoming. On their first night of business, however, the group was attacked by Indians, and their driver was killed. Calamity Jane allegedly played hero in this instance, killing the leader of the band before leaping into a wagon and making fast for Fort Bridger.[18]

Eleanore returned to San Francisco in the fall of 1869. This time she opened the fanciest of posh parlor houses. All went well until one evening when she recognized one of her customers as a police officer from Carson City, Nevada, where she was still wanted for the killing of Carruthers. That very night, Eleanore packed her bags and left town once again.[19] A local stage magician learned of her departure. "I was told that early this morning carriages took the ladies and their baggage," he reported, "and shortly after dinner the proprietress was seen departing, without a word to anyone, as perhaps fitting. A man came later this afternoon and took those two loads of chairs, but not the beds."[20] It was probably around this time that Eleanore next surfaced in Tombstone, Arizona, where she reigned over a house on Sixth Street. Although she enjoyed advertising her girls by riding them around town in a fancy carriage, competition from another madam, Blonde Marie, proved too much for her.[21]

To make matters worse, Eleanore's drinking was beginning to affect her skills at cards. Her beautiful face began showing signs of her grief, and a small moustache appeared above her upper lip, earning her the name "Madam Moustache." There was little to do but keep traveling, playing cards, and plying her trade, wandering to Montana, then Idaho, South Dakota, Wyoming, and finally Bodie, California. In 1879, after losing all of her money at poker, Eleanore took a long walk and swallowed a vial of poison outside of town. A suicide note clutched in her hand requested she be buried next to her fantasy man, E. G. Waite. Unfortunately, there was no money to do so. All her friends could do was take up local donations and have her buried in Bodie's cemetery.[22] Her obituary circulated all the way to Butte, Montana, which poignantly stated, "Those who remember the madam will agree that she commanded a degree of respect very rarely accorded to one of her class, respect due to traits of character."[23]

In the years following Eleanore Dumont's departure, Bannack's mines played out. By 1870, only a couple hundred people were left in town, with only two saloons and nary a prostitute working in the city.[24] The town remained nearly abandoned and all but forgotten until 1918, when newspapers reported the story of Nellie Paget, a twenty-two-year-old prostitute who had been shot to death in 1864. Nellie, whose real name was Helen Patterson, had left Illinois for a trip West in 1862. She also left behind her fiancé of two years, Howard Humphrey, promising to return within a year. "Wait for me," she told him. Humphrey waited out the year, then another and another. Four years after his sweetheart had departed, a returning prospector told Humphrey that Helen was working in a hurdy-gurdy house at Bannack. An unbelieving Humphrey thumped the prospector on the head for his trouble, but he did write to Bannack inquiring about Helen Patterson. Word came back that she was not known there. Years later a boyhood friend reiterated to Humphrey what the old prospector had said: Helen Patterson had become enticed by all the gold flowing around Bannack, worked in a hurdy-gurdy, and was shot to death in 1864 by a jealous lover. Newspapers followed as Humphrey finally made the trip to Bannack some forty-four years later and visited Nellie's grave. "When he left for Chicago he

FIGURE 42 ❧ *Eleanore Dumont, unfortunately better known as "Madam Moustache." Although it is true Eleanore sported some hair on her upper lip, most historians agree this early photograph of her was obviously touched up. Courtesy of the Mazzulla Collection, Colorado Historical Society, Denver.*

returned broken in spirit," one paper reported, "and convinced that Nellie was Helen."[25]

The goings-on at Bannack were largely overshadowed by new diggings at Last Chance Gulch, some 150 miles northeast, in 1864. At first, the men of the gulch outnumbered women twenty to one.[26] By the time the official name "Helena" was established for the town in 1865, red light ladies were already lined up along Main Street. Early on, however, Helena's red light district was removed from Main Street to a less conspicuous area between Wood, Bridge, and Clore streets.[27] Reeder's Alley has also been identified as a place where the red lantern hung.[28] Author Volney Steele speculates that the decent members of society who banished the red light women to their new quarters appeared to care little about them, save for alderman R. H. Howrey. "All sin and fault is [sic] laid at the doors of the women; no charity is expressed for them," Howrey said during one of his frequent speeches. "Some mercy should be shown them. . . . It is an evil arising from the vile passions of men that made them what they are."[29] It was also probably during these early years that many prostitutes were called "sum-mer women," so named because they left town during the cold and slower winter months.[30]

Steele also points out that "between 1865 and 1886, prostitution provided the largest source of paid employment for women" in Helena.[31] But the sur-roundings were quite primitive. The *Montana Post* reported on August 26, 1865: "One of the dancers in the Gayety Saloon, being a new hand and not well posted as to the surroundings of the hurdy-gurdy house, on stepping out the back door, made a sudden and unexpected descent of ten feet, fall-ing on the bed rock, unfitting herself for business for a short time, but not sustaining serious injury. The house has been undermined, and is sup-ported by stilts at the rear and on one side." The presence of more perma-nent brothels was more obvious in 1866, when Frances "Fannie Spencer" Fordonski borrowed money from madam Louisa Couselle to invest in her own brothel. Louisa moved on to Bozeman, but Frances's new bordello announced the official birth of Helena's permanent red light district.[32]

Helena's best-known prostitute by far was Chicago Joe, who first arrived in Helena in 1867.[33] Mary Welch had left Ireland just nine years earlier at the tender age of fourteen and had traveled from New York to Chicago, changing her name to "Josephine Airey" and eventually going to work in Chicago's red light district. When she had saved enough money

FIGURE 43 ❦ *Mary "Chicago Joe" Welch, probably at the height of her career during the 1870s. Joe was one of the most astute businesswomen of her time. An emigrant from Ireland, she ran her first brothel in Helena, Montana, just nine years after coming to America. Courtesy of the Montana Historical Society, Helena, 944-615.*

following the Civil War, she moved to Helena and allegedly opened the first female-run hurdy-gurdy house in town. That first house was a one-story log structure on Wood Avenue. Josephine had been in town only a short time when she married Chicago gambler Al Hankins on Valentine's Day in 1869. Two months later, the first of several devastating fires in Helena's history hit the town.[34] Josephine's house of ill repute escaped harm, but the Hankinses decided to do some traveling anyway. They settled in White Pine, Nevada, for a time, but the marriage didn't suit Josephine. She eventually left Hankins and returned to Helena.[35]

When Josephine wanted to expand in about 1870, she "mortgaged everything, including her underwear—three dozen pair of underclothes" and borrowed money from Alex Lavenberg, a leader of Helena. Josephine's efforts paid off, and she was able to repay the loan six months before it was due in full.[36] She also, no doubt, was able to reclaim her undergarments. She clearly was determined to make it in Helena. When the legislature passed an ordinance against "dancing saloons or hurdy-gurdy houses" in 1873, she skated around the law by offering dances for free, but her customers were required to buy a drink afterward. In this way, she was still able to make a profit.[37]

Unfortunately, Josephine lost everything in another fire in 1874. The new man in her life, gambler James T. "Black Hawk" Hensley, had been on a winning streak, though, and helped her build a new house out of brick. She named her new endeavor the "Red Light Saloon."[38] She also built a two-story building next door, renting out the downstairs and using the upstairs as a home for herself, Hensley, and some of her girls. With her profits and Hensley's winnings, Josephine also invested in several properties around town. In the wake of the fire, many property owners were uninsured and had no means to rebuild—a fact Josephine coolly took advantage of. Between her two businesses, her rental properties, and her newly acquired land, she was soon among the largest landowners and wealthiest women in Helena. She also at this time acquired her colorful nickname, "Chicago Joe."[39]

By 1880, the Hensleys were still living in their plush quarters with their two favorite working girls, twenty-four-year-old Nellie Reynolds and twenty-two-year-old Elizabeth Lynch. No occupation is listed for either girl or for Chicago Joe in the 1880 census. Their neighbors included many men with various occupations, but also some women—notably Rose Diamond, Fannie Spencer, Elizabeth Kimball, Mary Waters, Annie M. Fisher, and Mary Young. Nearly all of these women were living alone and most likely working as prostitutes. Josephine's brothel continued to prosper throughout the 1880s, and by 1886 she had purchased a new home on Water Street.[40]

The year 1886 appears to be the first time Helena attempted to outlaw prostitution. Among those brought into court was Josephine, whose attorney successfully argued that the term *hurdy-gurdy* as applied to her place meant a hand organ, not the three-piece band that played regularly at the Red Light Saloon. The case was dismissed. Two years later Josephine built the Coliseum at 15 Wood, an elite and elaborate theater and variety house with beautiful decor, expensive furniture, and the best in female entertainment. Many of her girls were solicited from the East, and a special bell system at the bar allowed gentlemen to summon the woman they wanted. Josephine's property values soon exceeded $200,000, an impressive figure for that time. Joe naturally enjoyed the best in jewelry and gowns. Her typical wardrobe consisted of "a flowing robe of heavy velvet, generally green or purple, with a pink-lined Elizabethan collar of enormous size, a wide golden, jewel-studded girdle around the immense expanse where her waist once was and jewels on every part of her dress where it was possible to place them. Thus attired and carefully painted and powdered she presented an imposing appearance as she swept along."[41]

Chicago Joe's wealth also provided for sizeable donations to both charities and politicians around Helena. Such benevolence was well known. Less known was the fact that Josephine also anonymously paid for schooling for her two younger sisters, two nieces, a nephew, and a half-brother. She also reportedly had a son named "Joe Eary" in Missouri. It is notable that she also made several business loans, a number of which were never repaid. When Josephine threw a grand Valentine's Day masquerade ball in 1889, the event even caught the attention of the newspaper's society editors: "Frail coquettes in silken tights and decollated bodices, their symmetrical limbs and snow white arms revealed to public gaze, glided to the enchanting numbers of melodic music over the glassy floor, forming a picture pleasing to behold." Shortly after the party, however, a new law prohibited sales of liquor in bawdy houses. In answer, Josephine simply cut a hole in the wall between her saloon and the Coliseum so that she could serve liquor in the saloon but deliver it to the Coliseum without breaking the law. City authorities were stumped again.[42]

The Hensleys and their employees were residing at the Coliseum by 1890, but their wealth suffered with the financial panic of 1893 and its subsequent depression. Despite efforts to save her businesses, Josephine lost the Coliseum and all of her property except the Red Light Saloon. The Hensleys moved into an apartment above the saloon and appear to have retired. Josephine caught pneumonia and died on October 25, 1899, at the age of fifty-five. Her friends conducted a large funeral service extolling her many virtues.[43] The *Helena Daily Independent* hailed her as "a woman of extraordinary strength of character." Following an elaborate funeral complete with speeches upholding her accomplishments, Joe was buried in the Catholic cemetery.[44]

Another famous madam of Helena was Lillie McGraw, alias "Bridget Ryan," who arrived in 1875 from Portland, Oregon. By 1880, Lillie owned much property on Wood Street. Her brothel on Joliet Street was connected to her other houses via an overhead walkway. Lillie rented out most of her properties to other madams, taking a short business excursion to Butte in 1891.[45] In 1896, a visiting prostitute, Dora Forrest of Butte, was found dead in bed at Lillie's brothel. "Her companion, Madge V. Dawe, who was in bed with her, was found to be at the point of death from an overdose of morphine," reported the *Butte Miner.* "She is now out of danger and will recover. The two women went on a spree last night and came home drunk early this morning. The Dawe woman was in the habit of taking morphine and it is supposed she induced her companion to take some with her. They probably took an overdose, Miss Forrest died because she was not used to the drug. The inquest will be held tomorrow. The Forrest girl came from Portland several days ago."[46] As for Lillie McGraw, she died of cirrhosis of the liver at the age of sixty-one in 1898.[47]

In 1880, Mollie Byrnes, also known as "Belle Crafton," from New Orleans, was the newest investor in Wood Street properties. In 1886, she built the Castle, an elegant bordello across from Lillie McGraw's on Joliet Street. Mollie died of alcoholism at the age of forty-two in 1900. Some believed her husband was responsible, for he married less than a year later and lived at the Castle until his death in 1951. The place has since been torn down.[48] The year 1880 was also the first time Chinese women officially put in an appearance in Helena. The 1880 census lists twenty-four Chinese girls. Their birth years ranged from 1841 to 1864, the youngest girl being Woon Hay, who was actually born in California. The youngest white prostitute was seventeen-year-old Caroline Schneider.[49]

By 1884, the antics of the Wood Street ladies were increasing. When the gaudily dressed working girls were banished to the back rows at Ming's

Opera House, five of them managed to acquire some habits from the nearby Sisters of Charity and attended a show dressed as nuns. The manager was obligated to seat them in a more respectable section of the theater, much to the chagrin of those respectable audience members who had lodged the original complaint. In 1886, there were no less than fifty-two prostitutes in Helena. The women who controlled the red light district were referred to as "proprietor madams" who actually rented out their bordellos for management by other women. But life was not necessarily all fun and games; during the late 1880s, no less than three women killed themselves. Blanche Mitchell shot herself, Kitty Williams intentionally overdosed on morphine, and Nellie Summers poisoned herself.[50]

Wood Street addresses in 1890 included those of the city Health Office, Nancy Prince, Peter Wilson's saloon, Chicago Joe's Coliseum and Coliseum bartender William King, Lottie O'Neil, Goldie Du Chene, Bella Orando, Pearl Howard and Sadie Davis, Cora Milton, and Hattie Johnson.[51] The women's various plights were typical of the era, as illustrated by an 1891 letter from Helena prostitute Gussie Raymond to a Mr. Holladay requesting the return of a small diamond ring belonging to her. During a visit to the town of Dillon, a Mr. R. B. Sullivan had pawned Gussie's ring to Holladay for $10. The couple had since split up, Gussie claiming that Sullivan "abused me all the two years I was with him." Gussie's letter expressed the hardships of earning the money for the ring "in the very hard way which all sporting women have to make their money" and requested that "if I send you the money you will let me have the ring." Gussie also explained that she had not written previously because she was "in very hard luck and have had the blues too badly to attend to anything." She had traveled to Hecla, Butte, and even Boulder in Jefferson County looking for work with no luck and had been in Helena for only three weeks. She also implored Holladay to find her watch "with the initials of my right name on it L.V.," which Sullivan had also pawned. Gussie even enclosed a stamped envelope for Holladay's reply, but whether she ever recovered her jewelry is unknown.[52]

Helena's nightlife continued flourishing with a vengeance. Old-timers recalled the girls of the line staggering down Main Street on Sunday mornings in the early 1900s, "their stockings so full of silver dollars that they had to use both hands to hold them up." The bawdiest prostitutes were called "blisters," and their pimping counterparts were referred to as "McGoofers."[53] But the early part of the twentieth century also saw at least some cracking down by authorities. In 1911, Arthur "Curly" Darrah, owner of the Windsor bordello in Helena, was arrested along with partner Floyd "Slim" Robinson under charges of white slavery. The men had apparently "imported" prostitute Glenn Parker and another girl from Chicago. At least one of the girls was prepared to testify against the men. Despite the crackdown, Helena's prostitution industry saw a resurgence in 1917 when San Francisco's Barbary Coast was shut down. A number of girls shuffled back and forth between Helena and Butte as the law and money dictated.[54]

Interestingly, unlike hundreds of other towns across the West, Helena does not appear to have suffered a shutdown at the hands of the military during World War I. To the contrary, upwards of a thousand women plied their trade between Helena and Butte at the time.[55] Ida Levy, also known as "Jew Ida," first appeared in Helena in about 1918 and was still operating her brothel as late as 1947. In the latter year, when Ida boldly tried to attend a meeting of state business and professional women, a businessman named Robbie Robinson turned her away at the door, explaining, "You can't come in here. This is a meeting for professional women, not whores." Not missing a beat, Ida retorted, "But Robbie, I'm the most professional woman here."[56]

Dorothy Josephine "Big Dorothy" Baker took over Ida's business in about 1953.[57] Indeed, the skin trade remained "wide open" in Helena. "Whether it's gambling, a girl or that 'happy mud' [opium] you hanker for, you can get it in Helena," explained writer Stephen Hull. An old-timer at that time said that Helena's prostitutes, who amazingly still numbered around three hundred, were just about as good looking as the ones in town some fifty years earlier. The red light district was now located in a two block area near the intersection of Main and State streets. It was also noted that the red light districts in Helena, Butte, and even Great Falls were larger than those in Las Vegas and Reno, Nevada. Prostitution was evident not just in local brothels, but also anywhere from upscale hotels to downtown flophouses. The Helena Ministerial Association and similar groups did try to shut down Helena's houses of vice now and then, but as in the old days the girls would simply disappear for a few days or weeks before opening up for business once again.[58]

The folks of Helena still exercised caution at celebrating their prostitution history as late as 1963, when writer Charles D. Greenfield pointed out that the Vigilante Pageant of Helena High School, with nearly three hundred floats, would not be including any exhibits from Helena's bawdy past. Today hardly anything exists to attest to Helena's wicked women. For some years, only a bar called Big Dorothy's functioned as a tribute to the city's last notorious woman. Docents at the Montana State Historical Society say, however, that two photographs at the bar allegedly depicting Dorothy are not her, as verified by family members on a recent visit. Big Dorothy's had recently changed ownership and was known as "The Windbag" in 2006. The Montana Historical Society keeps a file on Dorothy. It contains old receipts dated 1953 and 1954, including a license from the Montana Liquor Control Board and receipts from H. F. Sheehan and Bros. for Coca-Cola, Earl Tucker's Beer & Bar Supplies, 7Up Bottling Co., and Capital Laundry.[59]

North of Helena were a slew of small mining towns, including Marysville. According to a woman there in the 1950s, much commotion was once made over Lily Jones, a soiled dove who decided to drown herself in a pond by the Drumlummon Mill at shift change. "Right away the bets were on," recalled the woman. "Five hundred dollars she would drown. Six to one she wouldn't. One of the miners jumped in to save her. They bet on him, too. Oh, those were the days." The woman neglected to say whether Lily survived the incident or what became of her.[60] It is little wonder that a miner tried to save Lily; women were scarce in that town. The 1886–87 Marysville directory lists only three women besides the local assistant school teacher: Miss Annie Dillon, proprietress of the Drum Lummon Hotel, and the Misses Sophia and Lizzie Schafer, who ran the Marysville Hotel.[61]

Although Helena's bad girls and the prostitutes of Montana in general gained much notoriety in history, none can ever surpass the reputation of Martha "Calamity Jane" Canary. Jane's great-great-niece, Norma Slack, probably put it best when she pointed out that "the historical renditions of Calamity Jane's life are in conflict." Indeed, many historians searching for the truth have muddled the facts, resulting in a number of contradictions about Jane's life.[62] But even Jane herself exploited the contradictory facts about herself to create an even more colorful legend. If all that has been said about her is true, Jane was at one time or another an alcoholic, an army scout, a Florence Nightingale, a gold miner, a stagecoach driver, an Indian fighter, a Pony Express rider, a bull-whacker (teamster-freighter), a mother, and, last but not least, a prostitute.[63]

Jane's autobiography, *Life and Adventures of Calamity Jane*, says she was born "Martha Jane Canary" in Princeton, Missouri, on May 1, 1852.[64] Her

FIGURE 44 ⊛ *An abandoned business house on the main street in Marysville, Montana, circa 2006. The ruins of the Drumlummon Mill still stand, but the pond where Lily Jones tried to drown herself has long been dried up. From the author's collection.*

parents were Charlotte and Robert Canary, the latter allegedly a Mormon minister.[65] According to one of Charlotte's descendants, however, Jane's parents met at Charlotte's place of employment in an Ohio bawdy house. Also, census records and other documents do not show Robert Canary as ever being anything other than a farmer. In 1864, the family, consisting of Calamity's parents and six children, set out for Salt Lake City but eventually ended up in Virginia City, Montana. Jane's mother, Charlotte, loved alcohol and men, and it is speculated that an affair is what prompted the family to leave Missouri.[66]

Jane's father appears to have been almost afraid of Charlotte and despite his Mormon beliefs was spending much of his time in bars as the family traveled between Washington State and Kansas. In Virginia City, Charlotte took in washing for extra money, but it did little good. An 1864 article in the *Montana Post* told of the little Canary girls, who came begging at a city official's door, cold and hungry. "The father it seems was a gambler. The mother is a woman of the lowest grade." The newspaper explained that two local women gave the children food and some clothing before the girls set off for Nevada City, Montana, a five-mile walk. The paper also had something to say about their parents, calling them "inhuman brutes who have deserted their poor, unfortunate children" and appealing for law to be "applied to their case, and stern justice meted out to the offenders."[67]

Neglected and unsupervised much of the time, Jane ran freely with the boys of Virginia City and Nevada City, who enticed her to drink whiskey and taught her dirty jokes. By the age of twelve, she was a frequenter of local saloons, standing outside the door in boys' clothing and watching the gamblers, harlots, and drinkers within.[68] When the family couldn't make it in Virginia City, they relocated again, this time to Blackfoot, Montana. Charlotte died, and Jane's father took the children to Salt Lake City. Soon after their arrival, in about 1867, he too died. Orphans now, the Canary children were forced to make it on their own. Jane, who was fifteen, had learned to drive a team, was handy with a bullwhip, and preferred the open prairies to the stifling cities where people stared at her way of dress and harsh manners. Upon leaving Salt Lake, she returned to Montana and applied for a job at Madam Eleanor Dumont's brothel in Bannack. Later she moved on to Fort Bridger and South Pass, Wyoming, making her way by working as a teamster and dishwasher. She also began chewing and smoking tobacco while learning a slew of cuss words that would add to her infamousness.[69]

By 1868, Jane was working as a dance hall girl in Virginia City, but is also documented as being in Cheyenne, Wyoming, and Salt Lake City, where she once again applied to work for Eleanore Dumont.[70] In Cheyenne, she may have worked for James McDaniels, whose hurdy-gurdy house included a museum, live theater, and zoo. If we go by her other stated birth year of 1856, Jane would have been twelve during any or all of these incidents. But the presence of so many accounts suggests that at least some of these events really happened and that perhaps Jane really was born in 1852. It can at least be surmised that Jane was at Cheyenne during its infancy. "When I first came to Cheyenne there was not a respectable shelter in the place," she said during an 1887 interview, "and the proprietor of a tent was a lucky person indeed."[71]

By her own account, Jane did not remain in Cheyenne very long. By 1870, she said, she was working as a scout for General George Armstrong Custer out of Fort Russell, Wyoming. If her presence among Custer's troops was at all possible, Jane may have in fact served as a camp follower. By dabbling in the prostitution trade, she eventually earned a reputation as a friendly woman of easy virtue who may or may not have charged for her services. For Jane, both male companionship and alcohol became staples of life. By the age of twenty-four, she had become known as an alcoholic freighter who worked wherever and however she could.[72] Even Jane joked that she was once thrown out of a brothel in Bozeman "for being a low influence on the inmates."[73] A low influence she might have been, but her female friends were limited mostly to the red light ladies in the various towns through which she passed. One of them was a tall, breathtaking blonde named "Cotton Tail."[74] Another was Dora DuFran, whose friendship with Jane was immortalized in Larry McMurtry's book and screenplay *Buffalo Girls*. Whether Jane had lasting friendships with the women she encountered is uncertain, but men were another matter.

Of all the men Jane loved, no one stirred her heart as Wild Bill Hickok did. Some say the two met in Laramie when the newly married gambler was working to save enough money to bring his new bride West. Jane later claimed that she joined an expedition Hickok was leading into South Dakota in about 1870.[75] Any romance between them, implied or otherwise, has largely been disputed by Hickok's friends and biographers, however. "Wild Bill would have died rather than share a bed with Jane," stated Hickok's longtime friend Charlie Utter.[76] Nevertheless, Jane later claimed she bore a baby by Bill in 1873. She also claimed that after the child was born (in a cave) and Wild Bill had taken to the hills, Captain James O'Neil mysteriously appeared out of nowhere to assist her. O'Neil later adopted the child and took her to England with his wife.[77]

In 1875, Jane was said to have worked at Wyoming's Three Mile Hog Ranch, located three miles east of Fort Laramie and operated by Adolph Cuny and Julius "Jules" Ecoffey (numerous sources have spelled the name either "Ecoffey" or "Coffey"). Although Jane was in Wyoming only a brief time during her life, she worked at the ranch at least twice.[78] She is also documented as unofficially accompanying a government survey to the Black Hills in 1875. Upon being discovered and expelled from the troop, she appealed to a couple of teamsters to take her in, in exchange for cooking their meals. At the time, she was described as "about fifteen years of age, quite good looking, dark complexioned, black eyes and black hair, which she wore short."[79] She had moved to Fort Laramie by 1876, where, according to Hickok's friends and historians, she and Hickok really first met. Hickok, however, was already married.[80]

Charlie Utter remembered he first met Jane when he was requested to take her in his wagon train in 1876. The officer who asked this favor said Jane "had been on a big drunk with the soldiers and had been having a hell of a time of it." She was in fact being kept in the guard house following her spree.[81] "White-Eye" Jack Anderson also remembered the event. "She was nearly naked," he said of Jane. "Charley and Steve Utter outfitted her with a buckskin shirt, buckskin pants and a wide-brimmed hat."[82] Although Hickok appeared to have no use for her, White-Eye Anderson noted she could drive a team of mules, was good with a rifle and six-shooter, was a good cook, and could tell rough and tough stories to a large audience of men.[83] Others later remembered that during the day Jane worked hard alongside other freighters. At night, "if any of the boys wanted to go to the brush, she was always willin' to pull off a pants leg."[84]

Around the same time that Jane was spotted at Ecoffey and Cuny's in 1876, she was also supposedly signed on with Professor Walter Jenny's expedition into the Black Hills, according to her own claim. She was hired under the guise of a man, but later said that her sex was discovered and she was dismissed. Other historians speculate that after the discovery, Jane became one of the camp's prostitutes. She later hooked up with General George Crook's expedition to Montana, and while she was bathing in her long johns at a river with other officers, someone noticed her telltale breasts. She was again dismissed, but may have hung on once more as a camp follower. The most complete fact about Jane's whereabouts at this time comes from the *Cheyenne Daily Leader*. On June 20, 1876, the paper ran a story about "Jane's Jamboree." Some ten days earlier, Jane had procured a wagon from a man named Abney to drive to Fort Russell, but was so drunk by the time she reached it that she forgot to turn off and subsequently arrived in the town of Chug, located fifty miles beyond her original destination. After several more drinks, she traveled another ninety miles to Fort Laramie and continued on her spree. One Joe Rankin eventually caught up with her and, after listening to her pleas not to be arrested, returned the rig to Cheyenne. While in Laramie, Jane was next arrested for stealing a dress from a local store. Rancher John Hunton also remembered a day in 1876 when he encountered a wagonload of prostitutes headed from Fort Laramie, Wyoming, to Deadwood, South Dakota. One of the girls was Jane.[85]

By 1878, Jane was in Deadwood when a smallpox epidemic swept through town. Jane had already suffered through the disease and was therefore immune to it, so she worked as a nurse. The *Black Hills Pioneer* called her an "Angel of Mercy."[86] In spite of her good qualities, Jane was a confirmed alcoholic by 1880. Four years later she overcame her whiskey-induced haze long enough to take a trip to California, stopping in Ogden, Utah, on the way to try and find two of her sisters and a brother. And despite her love for Wild Bill, she married someone else in 1885. This person may have been Clinton Burke, whom she wed in El Paso, Texas, but historians are definitely confused about who this Clinton Burke was, when he met Jane, where and when they married, and whether they had children. Author Michael Rutter maintains that although Jane said she had a daughter by Wild Bill Hickok, she later claimed that the baby, born October 28, 1887, was Burke's child.[87] Author Harry Drago says that Jane stated she met Burke in Yuma, Arizona, in 1884 on her return trip from California. According to Drago, Jane later lived and ran a restaurant with a Clinton "Charley" Burke for several years in Boulder, Colorado, and the two married in 1891 at Deadwood. Burke was a Civil War veteran who was missing a leg and had a ten-year-old daughter.[88]

However her relationship with Burke unfolded, Jane did make an appearance in Cheyenne in 1887. The *Democratic Leader* reported it was her first visit to Cheyenne in ten years, that she was "in a very dilapidated condition" and that she was lying low.[89] By then, Jane had gained much notoriety throughout America as the heroine in a number of dime novels, which she did not necessarily enjoy. But if she did not enjoy people's spinning yarns about her, she certainly did have fun telling tales on herself. Once, during a brief stint in Texas, she passed herself off as the daughter of well-known gambler Allegheny Dick and even donned fancy women's clothes for a time. The folks of the town nicknamed her the "Prairie Queen" before she cast off her fine clothes for her old freighter's outfit and took to the hills once more.[90]

The year 1893 found Jane running a restaurant in Castle City, Montana, bringing with her the daughter of one of her soldier friends in Texas. Jane was determined to go straight, but couldn't help soliciting a little side business with a man in the nearby camp Gilt Edge one evening. Alas, the man's wife saw the pair heading for the barn and ran them off with a pitchfork. Jane ended up drunk in a saloon, was subsequently arrested, and was imprisoned in a nearby barn to keep her from cavorting with the male prisoners of

FIGURE 45 ᴥ *Calamity Jane and her friend E. C. "Teddy Blue" Abbott traded hats while sharing cocktails in 1897 or 1898. The two longtime friends had just met up for a reunion in Utica or Gilt Edge, Montana. Courtesy of the Montana Historical Society, Helena, 941-409.*

the jail. While there, Jane bribed a small boy to get her a bottle of whiskey. When she was let out, she returned to Castle City, picked up the little girl, and made her way to Deadwood. Along the way, she was forced to give the child to the Sisters of St. Martin's Academy in Sturgis, South Dakota.[91]

During the mid-1890s or possibly as late as 1901, Jane was next invited to join *Buffalo Bill's Wild West Show.* Around this time, she also procured some unknown assistance to write and publish *Life and Adventures of Calamity Jane, by Herself.* The pamphlet was rife with fibs and tall tales, and Jane confused even the most often stated facts. Although she traveled with Buffalo Bill's show for a time, she was eventually let go because of her drinking.[92] In 1901, she was working for the Pan American Exposition in New York City and selling her autobiography, but was once again fired for drinking.[93] Upon returning to Deadwood, she discovered Charley Burke had left town.[94]

After that, Jane took up sporting and drinking once more. She also made her way once again to Livingston, Montana, with intentions to open a new bordello, but the plan never came to fruition, and she left there in 1901. A story also surfaced about Jane and madam Kitty O'Leary, also known as "Madam Bulldog," getting into a tousle in Livingston. Kitty threw Jane in the street, and for once Jane didn't resist.[95] Jane next surfaced in Billings, where she moved into Yee Sam's seedy hotel under the name "Mrs. R. S. Dorsett" and probably opened for business. Before long, she and Yee Sam were in court, he claiming she owed him rent and she saying he was holding her trunk with her dresses and bedding. The trunk was found to contain "only three dresses that would not bring very much at even a secondhand store." Jane got it back.[96] She was next seen, sick and drunk, at the mining town of Horr before she moved on to Terry, South Dakota. She arrived there on July 31, 1903, with an ore train and was so ill she had to be carried to her lodgings at the Calloway Hotel. The next day she died at the age of fifty-one. Her body was returned to Deadwood, where she was buried near Wild Bill. Some maintain that Jane had not purchased the plot, but that it was donated by a friend and just happened to be near Bill's. For many years, Livingston, Montana, laid claim to being a sometime home to Jane. Resident Billy Miles even put a sign on his cabin along Main Street that said it had been her home. The cabin was torn down for firewood in the 1930s.[97]

Jane's legacy has lived on: at least two women said they were her daughter. Jean Hickok McCormick showed up in Billings, Montana, in 1941 claiming to be the daughter of Jane and Wild Bill.[98] McCormick said she was born in a cave at Benson's Landing near Livingston in 1870. She also showed a page torn from a Bible that documented that her parents were married "en route to Abilene, Kansas" just a few days before she was born.[99] McCormick also said that it was she who had been adopted by Captain O'Neil and his wife and raised in England. She eventually married Lieutenant Edward McCormick, who died in action during World War I. Jean McCormick enjoyed national recognition for a short time as her story was proved and then disproved. When White-Eye Anderson came to Billings to see the letters McCormick offered as proof, he concluded that Jane had not met Hickok until 1876 and that at that time she had merely "slept with Steve Utter, ate her meals with us, and helped drink up Bill's whiskey."[100] McCormick was never able to prove definitively that she was Jane's daughter. She died in 1951.[101]

The most convincing story about Jane's supposed offspring comes from Ruth Shadley, who claims her mother, Maude Weir, was Jane's child. In her 1996 book *Calamity Jane's Daughter: The Story of Maude Weir*, Shadley says that her mother was adopted by Joe and Mary Weir from Sadie Beck, an unwed mother. Sadie, according to Shadley, was Jane's sister, but it was Jane who was really Maude's mother, Jane who took little Maude to attend St. Martin's Catholic academy in South Dakota, and Jane who often visited her there. Maude didn't know Jane was her mother and so was also puzzled by her visits and embarrassed by her drunkenness. After Maude came "home" to Pierre, North Dakota, in 1895, Mary Weir died, but Jane continued visiting the family ranch. Word eventually got out that Jane was really Maude's mother, a fact that was terribly embarrassing to the girl. She persevered, however, and did not see Jane again until after she had married and given birth to her own daughter. The year was 1901, and Maude clearly remembered Jane's coming to see the new baby. When Maude told her to go away and not come back, a tearful Jane flipped a gold ring onto the baby's blanket and left, never again returning. After Joe Weir died in 1902, Sadie Beck reappeared in Maude's life. The two bought a farm in South Dakota and ran it with their husbands. Sadie died under the name "Sarah Parker" in 1915. Besides Sadie Beck and Joe Weir, Ruth Shadley's uncle Frank and her father confirmed to her that Maude was Jane's daughter. Ruth's sister Elsie also claimed to have found Maude's birth certificate, which listed Jane as her mother, but did away with it. Photographs of Jane and Maude certainly appear to show similar features between the two, but the only real "proof" was that both women could make an identical howling sound from the backs of their throats.[102]

In death, Calamity Jane is every bit as famous as she ever hoped to be. No less than seven movies, one starring Doris Day, have been made about her life, and her character has been featured in dozens of other films. She has also been the subject of a number of books, including fictionalized accounts and, of course, her own autobiography. Today dozens of women, including Jane's great-great-niece Norma Slack, continue to emulate the infamous lady who brought the West alive and made it truly wilder than it had ever intended to be.

Bozeman, where Calamity Jane was thrown out "for being a low influence on the inmates," had a sizeable red light district for a town of six hundred in 1870. Nearby cattle ranches and Fort Ellis three miles away made for many single men. The red light district in town could be found a half-block north of Main Street between North Rouse and North Bozeman avenues. Ten years later there were still two houses of prostitution in town.[103] According to the 1880 census, one was home to a twenty-five-year-old Chinagirl named Leene, who resided with two male Chinese laborers. Next door was English madam Louisa Canselle or Couselle, who employed Ella Loraine and Kittie Warren.

Louisa had begun her career in 1866 in Helena. When she learned that Bozeman's red light district consisted mainly of a couple of Chinese houses, the enterprising woman decided to take advantage of the situation. Almost immediately she impressed and appalled the good people in town by buying fifteen lots in the vicinity of Main Street. By 1875, her success enabled her to buy two farms outside of the city limits and to extend loans to other women so the red light district could grow. Within three years, Louisa was wealthier than 95 percent of the rest of the town. When she died at the age of fifty-four in 1886, her estate was worth $20,000. "It is not necessary for us to describe her calling, or occupation," said the *Avant Courier*, "but that she was a remarkable woman in many respects cannot and will not be gainsaid by anyone who knew her."[104]

One of Louisa's protégés was Kittie "Roberta Warn" Warren, who borrowed money from Louisa to get her own place on Mendenhall Street in 1875. Kittie's new house contained seven bedrooms, each with its own stove, mirror, and brass bed. Kittie also invested in several pieces of property and was soon very successful. In 1885, however, she dropped a lighted match on her dress and burned herself severely. She died from her injuries a month later and was buried beside her sister, Louise Buttner, who had committed suicide in the same house just a year and a half earlier. Another famous madam of Bozeman was Frances Jackson, also known as "Lizzie Woods," born 1860 in Missouri. Lizzie's bordello was on Mendenhall Street, and she ran the eighteen-room Maxwell Rooming House in Livingston. Lizzie was in business for more than thirty years. In about 1900, she adopted an infant boy whom she named "Baby." When Baby was ten years old, though, he was "farmed out" to another family. Unlike Louisa Canselle's obituary, which touted her as a decent woman, Lizzie's obituary in 1918 called her a "social derelict." In her day, Lizzie had paid $10 in monthly fines.[105]

In 1889, there were still five houses of ill repute on Mendenhall Street. Six other places were noted as "Chinese" and were possible bordellos as well. By 1892, however, some of the houses had relocated to Minnesota

Avenue. Within twelve years, the number of bordellos in the town was up to nine. Probably hoping to reform the neighborhood, the city built the Carnegie Library directly across the street from them and immediately set about complaining about library patrons being exposed to the red light district. Monthly $5 fines were imposed on the eighteen or so bad girls, with their madams paying twice as much. A year later police began cracking down harder on the prostitutes of Bozeman, but there were still seven houses of ill repute in the city in 1912. City authorities kept up the battle, however, and prostitution was shut down for good in about 1917.[106]

Another early site of prostitution in Montana was Beartown, originally founded in 1865 near what was to become Missoula. Beartown soon had several saloons, and Chicago Joe of Helena kept a dance hall there. The camp was one of the roughest in Montana, being made up primarily of stores, saloons, hotels, and brothels.[107] By the time Fort Missoula was established in 1877, Beartown's population was already shrinking. Little by little, the bad girls of Beartown migrated to Missoula, which was considered an official city within three years.[108] Front Street, located two blocks from the main drag of Broadway, constituted the red light district and was interspersed with a number of saloons.

By far, Missoula's most imposing figure was Mary "Mother" Gleim, a three-hundred-pound delight who had long sported a reputation for acting as her own bouncer and declaring war on anyone who did her wrong. Among her escapades was the early-morning dynamiting of Bobby Burns's place in 1894, which was located in the "segregated" area of the red light district. Despite her rowdy behavior, Mother Gleim prided herself on being quite educated and very private about her past, but stories circulated about her smuggling diamonds. She also invested in many of Missoula's red light properties. Mother Gleim died in 1914, leaving an estate of $148,000.[109] She is still paid tribute with plaques on both of her buildings, the Gleim Building I and the Gleim Building II. The other buildings on that side of the street are similar in architecture, although Mother Gleim is credited with "building" both of her brothels. Front Street is now a fashionable shopping district.

Northwest of Missoula was Wickes, also founded in 1877. By the time the Northern Pacific Railroad rolled through in 1886, fifteen hundred people lived there, serviced by twenty-two saloons and five dance halls. Alberton, another town west of Missoula, appears to have been founded

FIGURE 46 ❧ *An early Missoula, Montana, prostitute, circa late 1800s. Although Mary Gleim is best known among the city's madams, many other women also worked in Missoula, but unfortunately left little information about themselves behind. Courtesy of Jay Moynahan.*

solely by saloon owners in 1894. As a railroad town, Alberton was no doubt a friendly sight to railroad workers disembarking there. At the even smaller community of DeBorgia, a working girl was still allegedly plying her trade as late as 2006.[110] Taft, located seventy miles west of Alberton, developed as a railroad town beginning in 1906. Its population varied between thirty and two thousand, and the number of its soiled doves varied according to the population. With the Chicago, Milwaukee & St. Paul Railroad coming through, it was easy enough to ply their trade. By 1907, roughly five thousand men lived in the area, most of them single.[111] A year later the red light population consisted of sixty-two soiled doves.[112]

Early on, Taft took on a reputation as the toughest mining camp in America. Newspapers from as far away as Butte, Montana, spewed forth tales of men being robbed for as little as $10 in 1908. Guests at the Hotel St. Joe were advised not to step out after dark, and a fire that swept through the town was thought to be the work of looters. Open gambling was conducted night and day, and one Edward Murphy reported he was robbed and severely beaten along the railroad tracks. Sixteen unmarked graves along the road gave evidence of murders that had taken place there.[113] By February 1909, even the *Chicago Tribune* was calling Taft "the wickedest city in America." During the winter of 1906–1907 alone, eighteen men were murdered. Because the ground was too frozen to dig graves, their bodies were packed in snow. At the time, there were twenty-two prostitutes in town. The only other woman was the minister's wife. By 1909, the railroad had been completed, and the men moved elsewhere, as did the soiled doves. In 1914, only twenty-four people were left in Taft.[114]

Even more towns lay north of Missoula, notably Kalispell, which was founded in 1896. Early on, the red light district there was quite sizeable and conveniently located next to Chinatown along Second Avenue West. Of particular interest is the fact that much of Chinatown had underground dwellings beneath the business houses. It will thus likely never be possible to find out how many Chinese prostitute slaves were held prisoner under Chinatown. Among the Anglos, there was still only one woman for every three men in Kalispell by 1900. In desperation, Mayor W. H. Griffin took out advertisements in eastern newspapers soliciting residency by young ladies. A number of women replied with various directives, from asking for more information to requesting that someone meet them when they arrived. One respondent was a widow with five children and a mother-in-law. For the most part, Kalispell's red light ladies laid low. They weathered busts for smuggling opium from Canada during 1902 and a fire and brimstone speech by Carrie Nation in 1910. The following year, however, the Women's Christian Temperance Union asked for the abolishment of the red light district anyway—but were refused. In about 1916, there were still twenty-six prostitutes in Kalispell, all of whom worked out of four houses on First Avenue West. The Women's Christian Temperance Union prevailed that year, however, and all twenty-six girls were made to leave town.[115]

Of all of Montana's red light districts, the one in Butte surely served as the big mama. The area was originally discovered by gold seekers, but silver and copper deposits had Butte on the rise by the time it was incorporated in 1879. Miners flocked into town from all over the world, necessitating plenty of female entertainment. Today the city's architecture is absolutely amazing, with ornately detailed Victorian business buildings as well as blocks and blocks of big houses reflecting fine period designs. In its day, however, Butte also featured seedy back alleys, hidden passageways, and underground tunnels that formed a network of its numerous and large red light districts.[116]

Madeleine Blair, a former prostitute who later wrote a book outlining the evils of the industry, remembered her first view of Butte's red light district after she ran into a male acquaintance she had known in Chicago:

We did not tarry long in either of the two first-class houses. They were interesting only because I had not expected to see girls so well dressed nor houses so elaborately furnished in this out-of-the-way place. But the variety shows and the dancehalls were a source of wonder, and the "cribs" were a source of horror to me. I had never seen the seamy side of the underworld in all the five years that I had belonged to it. I had never had any desire to see it, but in Butte it was underfoot at every step and there was no avoiding it even if we had not gone for the express purpose of sizing it up. Despite my shuddering horror, the sight fascinated even while it repelled me. It gripped me by the throat and forced me to examine it, even though I was sickened and faint at the horror of it. It filled me with many sad forebodings. I drew my skirts back from contact with the poor creatures who represented this seamy side of prostitution; I could not help it. I wanted to take them by the hand and tell them that I was one of them, but I could not touch them. I could barely touch my lips to the glasses of beer which they served.[117]

In one place, Madeleine was so filled with pity for the forty-year-old barmaid that she and her consort spent almost all of their money on her to make sure "she should have at least one profitable night." Upon leaving, however, the woman followed Madeleine to the door and called her a "stuck up parlor house tart." That same evening Madeleine ran into another girl, Norma, that she remembered from a high-class parlor house back in Chicago. The girl's beautiful face was now "so lined with marks of dissipation and care that she looked ten years older."[118]

The women Madeleine encountered in Butte were excellent representatives of the way prostitutes in that city lived. By 1880, there were at least forty working girls in Butte, about half of whom were Chinese. The number of Chinese girls located in Butte's red light district is not so unusual. Between 1880 and 1930, Chinatown was located directly west of the red light district and included a handful of physicians practicing ancient medicine from their homeland. Its convenient location allowed girls from the row to seek herbs and other remedies for birth control and venereal disease, as well as healthy and tasty Chinese cooking. Upwards of a thousand Chinese may have lived in Butte at its peak, although their numbers are hard to pinpoint. Most of their Anglo counterparts worked on Park Street, with a few girls scattered on West Main Street. Some of the women had children residing in their homes. And, just as would be expected, many experienced troubles of a violent nature. In February 1880, Florence Bentley intentionally overdosed on morphine. She was only twenty-eight years old. In May, a woman known only as "Big Lil" also tried to kill herself with morphine.[119]

Prostitute Mollie Forrest was murdered in Butte in 1880. At the tender age of twenty-two, Mollie was killed by her husband, Joe Scott. The couple had only recently arrived in Butte after Scott was arrested in Helena for assaulting a night clerk at the Cosmopolitan Hotel. Upon arriving in Butte, Mollie gained immediate employment at the Union dancing saloon. One night when she got into an argument with Scott over whether she should visit another dance hall, he dragged her off the dance floor and up to her room, shooting her and blowing off half her face. Scott later claimed that Mollie had shot herself and that the only reason he had run was that he was afraid of being lynched. But the newspaper noted that Scott "did not invoke

FIGURE 47 ❧ *A typical young prostitute of Butte, Montana, circa late 1800s. All around the red light districts, photographers, grocers, laundresses, seamstresses, and drugstores profited from the earnings of literally thousands of girls. Courtesy of Jay Moynahan.*

the protection of the armed officer of the law who confronted him when he emerged from the room where his wife was lying in the agonies of death" and that he had failed even to stick around in the room long enough to see if she had died. He also made the "most obscene" remarks as Mollie's body was removed to a hearse.[120] Despite the newspaper's fear that Scott's testimony would be accepted as the truth, the murdering husband was found guilty in October and sentenced to life imprisonment.[121]

By the time Butte was established as the seat of Silver Bow County in 1881, the incidents along the red light district had already grown quite notorious. In September 1881, two Park Street girls got in a terrible row and were arrested. In court, both women expressed remorse, promised not to skirmish again, paid their fines, and left. The peace was short-lived; a month later Anna Parker, after being arrested for grand larceny, attempted suicide while under watch by city constables at her home. Upon discovering Anna had swallowed a lethal dose of laudanum, Constable Owens summoned a doctor, who induced her to throw up the stuff. Anna duly appeared in court and even managed to come up with $700 in bail money. Then in November a Chinese prostitute, Yow Kum, appeared in court after her former master, Gong Sim, stabbed her in the back with a hatchet. Gong had apparently sold Yow to another man for $1,100. When the new owner didn't pay, Gong sought revenge by damaging the merchandise.[122] The year's antics ended two weeks later when Inez Maybert went on a drinking spree before committing suicide with morphine. Inez was depressed after a man she loved refused her advances. She left behind a note for a coworker named Gussie with instructions to dress her in black for burial and to tell the man she loved that "he may thank himself for this. If there is any such thing as haunting I will haunt him to his death bed."[123]

Indeed, suicides were frightfully common in Butte. Lottie Ables Pickett deserves the prize for the most attempts to do herself in. Born in California, twenty-two-year-old Lottie had traveled much of the state before trying to settle in Helena. There, despite being an attractive dancer with auburn hair, she was dubbed "Sorrel Mike" after a local racehorse. Although Lottie appeared gay and friendly in social circles, she was in actuality deeply depressed. She eventually moved to Butte and attempted suicide several times. One of her attempts was in 1879, just two weeks after marrying a virtual stranger named "Picket" who kept a saloon and, it turned out, made it clear that Lottie was to continue in her profession after the marriage.

Dr. C. P. Hough saved Lottie, but she made another attempt in July 1880. By this time, though, the press had had enough of her antics and openly ridiculed her, stating, "Sorrel Mike made up her mind the other day to go and be an angel, and with that intent, swallowed an overdose of morphine."[124]

Lottie was saved again and moved in with her sister Dolly, only to suffer further problems. Arguments with a new lover resulted in her attempting suicide a final time in 1881. Her sister came home to find her with a bullet in her abdomen. It was noted that this was the second time in a week that Lottie had tried to do herself in.[125] The ashamed harlot tried to blame an anonymous man, and Dolly recalled that an argument with a customer who refused to pay for wine might have resulted in a struggle during which Lottie accidentally shot herself. Still, Dolly admonished her sister when she tried to blame the customer. "Lottie, you know that is not so; you did it yourself. Some innocent man may suffer from your talk; and you know you did it yourself." Lottie never officially admitted to shooting herself, but her refusal to deny her sister's accusations was taken as a confession. Lottie languished under heavy sedation while the man she allegedly tangled with before shooting herself was summoned. Whether he returned before Lottie died is unknown.[126] The Coroner's Jury concluded that Lottie had indeed been shot by a unknown person.[127]

During the mid- to late 1880s, Butte's growing business district necessitated moving the red light district. Accordingly, Park Street's women of the night relocated one block over to Galena Street, which was soon overflowing with dance halls, saloons, gambling houses, and brothels. Things were not much better in the new location; Butte journalist George Wesley Davis described Galena as "a street leading into hell."[128] Later, as the downtown district expanded even more, the ladies would move one more block to Mercury Street. In fact, Butte's red light population seemed welcome on the whole. Local mine owners knew their men were happy, the monthly fines made the city coffers fat, and real estate investors made a haul from renting out cribs and parlor houses. Even some of the city's respectable women approved of prostitution because it kept Butte's rowdy male population busy.[129]

Among Butte's notable prostitutes was Lou Harpell, who arrived in about 1889 and originally operated on Park Street. By 1891, she had relocated to a place on East Mercury, where she would remain throughout her career. The amenities Lou offered were no secret; in fact, the fallen woman openly advertised her house in theater and racetrack programs.[130] In 1900, Lou's house was known as the "Hotel Victoria." Her four girls were said to be "among the most beautiful girls in the world," quite an achievement for a blue-collar boom town such as Butte.[131] By 1903, she was in such good graces with authorities that when a raid was staged on local brothels, Lou was allowed to post bond from her bordello without her girls being taken to jail. Lou appears to have retired around 1905, when she was in her sixties.[132]

Lou Harpell's biggest competition was the Richelieu, which first made the papers in about 1895 and was located directly next door to the Hotel Victoria. Lillie Reid (or Reed) was its first madam, followed by Bertha Leslie. Historic photographs of the building reveal a three-story mansion with rounded two-story oriel bay windows, a central Palladian window, elegant stone trim, and twenty-four lavish rooms. The decor included satin-covered sofas and chairs, gilded mirrors, and red drapes in two bottom-floor parlors. There was a fancy dining room and an ample kitchen with sleeping rooms for a Chinese cook and two servants. Bedrooms were located on the upstairs floors with fine oak and mahogany bedroom sets. The opening night included engraved RSVP cards and uniformed butlers. Eight women were initially employed at the Richelieu under Bertha, the twenty-nine-year-old madam.[133] But even Bertha's plush parlor house suffered such incidents as the 1896 suicide of Blanch McGarvin in room number eight. "The evidence of Mamie Stephens," reported the Coroner's Docket, "who was called to see the deceased at bout six o'clock in the morning, settles all doubt on the subject of what drug had been used and for what purpose." Witnesses to the incident consisted of the seven other women of the house.[134]

By 1900, Bertha had changed the name of the Richelieu to "the Windsor Hotel." There was likely some conflict over the change because one James Hamilton was operating a legitimate hotel under the same name on East Broadway. By 1903, Bertha had changed the name again, this time to "Irish World." After Lou Harpell left the Hotel Victoria next door, Irish World expanded into that building, and a telephone was installed.[135] When Bertha left, madam Ruth Clifford took over operations. In 1907, Ruth hosted a grand dinner party with her twelve girls in attendance. "Miss Ruth" dressed to the nines for the affair and greeted her guests "in the ivory and gold room, which has a rich carpet of bottle green moquet with yellow flowers and Japanese silk portieres in parti-colors producing an effect which on clear nights can be heard as far as Anaconda."[136]

It is speculation that Ruth's party was so successful that it necessitated hiring a partnering madam, May Maloy.[137] Ruth appears to have run Irish World, while May ran the place next door under the now-resurrected name "the Windsor." Throughout 1910, Ruth Clifford employed at least seven prostitutes and five Chinese male servants. Next door, May employed another three girls. During that year, the infamous Carrie Nation decided to visit Butte and a neighboring city, Anaconda. Despite signs in Butte and Anaconda that read "All Nations Are Welcome Except Carrie," Nation entered Ruth and May's places with the intention to smash up a painting of a nude woman with her signature hatchet. May saw her coming and socked her in the mouth, sending her sprawling out into the street.[138] May then swished back into her brothel, where she and her patrons downed a round of drinks to celebrate Nation's defeat.[139]

The bad girls of Butte continued operations for several more decades, heeding or hiding from new laws and attempts by city authorities to keep the district quiet and low key. By 1920, most of the working girls of Butte were hiding their profession from authorities. Madam Irene Robinson was listed in the 1920 census as the "landlady" of the Windsor House (as the Windsor Hotel was called by then), even though she does not appear in the Butte city directory for that year. One of her girls, Marie/Mary Demonstrand or Demontrond, listed herself in the census as a manicurist for a barbershop. A third woman, Bertha LeClair, said she was a cook in a restaurant. Other girls on the row, such as Alice Spanny and May Reel, claimed to be dressmakers. By now, nearly all of women listed on Mercury Street were older than thirty, and many were in their forties. Irish World was once again named the Victoria Hotel and, with the Windsor Hotel, continued serving as a brothel for literally decades longer. Beginning in 1929, both places were occasionally listed under "furnished rooms" in the city directory. In 1930, Marie Demonstrand, who had formerly worked for Irene Robinson, was madam of the Windsor. Madams at the Victoria included Hillia Blixt in 1942, Mrs. Julie Hindley in 1952, and Mrs. Ole Rod in 1954.[140]

By 1961, Butte's red light district was still active, although it had downsized considerably. Madam Beverly Snodgrass was running a "boardinghouse" at 14 S. Wyoming, which she had probably acquired from another madam of the era, Ruby Garrett.[141] The old Victoria Hotel was now called the "Missoula Hotel" and run by Julie Hindley. Later that year, Beverly purchased the old Windsor House and continued operations there. In 1968, a fire of suspicious origins broke out at the Windsor House, resulting in its closure. Beverly lost little time in complaining to the Internal Revenue Service and Montana state senators Mike Mansfield and Lee Metcalf that she had been paying $700 per month in "protection money" to local police since 1963. The deal included free services to Butte's uniformed officers. Beverly claimed the fire was set when she didn't pay up. Mansfield concluded the case wasn't within federal jurisdiction, but Mayor Tom Powers openly admitted to newspapers that prostitution was alive and well in Butte. It was ultimately assessed that three police officers had taken it upon themselves to try and close down the city's three brothels. Whether they were held responsible for their actions is unclear.[142]

Aside from the Hotel Victoria and the Windsor, literally hundreds of cribs, bordellos, dance halls, and burlesque theaters were present in Butte throughout the 1800s. One such place was the Theatre Comique, which premiered on Main Street in 1886 directly between the old district on Park and the new district on Galena. So bawdy was the entertainment that although common miners and laborers were free to enter the theater from the front, respectable men typically came in through a discreet back door. The back stairs led to upstairs theater boxes, each with a door bolting from the inside and enclosed by mesh screens. From the audience's side, the screens were painted, allowing prominent men of the town total privacy while viewing the show. A slot in the door allowed drinks to be slipped into the boxes while they were in use. Downstairs, the floor was covered in sawdust and filled with tables. Early performers at the Theatre Comique included Eddy Foy, Bobby Gaylord, Bill Mack, and Charles Murray. The waitresses doubled as entertainers between shows, singing and dancing for tips and making several hundred dollars a week.[143]

In 1890, a "fairy" of the Comique named Mabel Hale attempted suicide at her room 26 in the Iron Block. The cause of her discontent was her inability to secure a lasting relationship with a man named Waller who owned a large store in Helena. Mabel was saved, and despite her declaration that she was "born for better things and couldn't bear the life," she had no choice but to go back to serving beer at the Comique.[144] Indeed, the Comique itself soon began experiencing hard times. In 1894, theater owner Fiskey Barnett recruited a group of girls from San Francisco, whom he hoped "would cause the average Butte man to loosen up his purse strings and put the theater on a paying basis." Two of Barnett's recruits, Lulu and

Josie Baldwin, worked only three weeks before they found employment with madam Lillie Reed. It came to light soon thereafter that the girls, whose real last name was Mahoney, were runaways and were wanted back home. Nineteen-year-old Josie agreed to go, but her younger sister refused, resulting in her arrest.[145] Theatre Comique eventually closed and was converted to other uses. The building was razed in the late 1980s to make way for the new Metals Bank building.[146]

The Theatre Comique actually may have set a precedence for the rest of Butte's red light district. During the late 1880s and the 1890s, several underground passages were constructed so customers could enter respectable business houses and access hidden doors into saloons. By 1893, there were 212 drinking houses in town, and most bordellos also served liquor. The moving of the red light district to three locations in such a short period of time merely resulted in houses of vice remaining on Park, Galena, and Mercury. In 1888, East Park Street still had at least one brothel nestled between a Chinese grocery and a cigar factory. East Galena Street between Main and Wyoming was literally filled with houses of prostitution. The Casino Theater, at the west end of Galena, functioned as a brothel, dance hall, saloon, and theater, and hosted prizefights.[147] In 1905, Reverend William Biederwolf called Butte the "lowest sinkhole of vice in the west" and even gave a resounding revival sermon at the Casino. The *Butte Miner* did note that nearly a thousand gamblers, drinkers, and bawdy women attended.[148] Biederwolf's sermon may have had at least some lingering effect because five years later the Casino was noted as a "distinguished ill-looking landmark" and was torn down to make room for, of all things, a parking garage. Local papers encouraged everyone to come take a souvenir of the old building for old times sake.[149]

During the Casino's reign, cribs were also still present on Wyoming Street and in the back alleys between streets. Journalist Wesley Davis described a typical crib room with "a bed in one corner, in another a stove, a coal hod and bundle of kindling. A small dresser with a wash basin against the wall. Permeating everything a mixed odor of disinfectant, hair oil and cheap perfume. On the walls, a few art pictures, oddly enough, usually of some pastoral or equally innocent scene, never a picture of a pornographic nature. A photograph or two, usually of other prostitutes or the favorite pimp of the moment."[150] One pioneer remembered Galena Street and its prostitutes: "There were some sprightly lookin' lasses down there, too. A lot of them prettier by far than the theater and society ladies with their pictures in the paper. But there was some tough lookin' blisters too. A man could have got hydrophobia from even lookin' at them."[151]

Butte's best-remembered parlor house was the Dumas, built in 1890 at 45 Mercury Street on the site of an old barn. The house was constructed by brothers Joseph and Arthur Nadeau, and original property records show the owner as Joseph's wife, Delia. The Nadeaus had previously owned the respectable Windsor Hotel and Restaurant, but were also known to have associated with Butte's less-respectable residents. Whether the mysterious "No. 2" on the top cornice of the building illustrates that this building was the Nadeaus' second brothel or second business is unknown.[152]

The Dumas measured two floors with a cellar. Today there are forty-three rooms in the place, but there were less when the building first opened. The interior featured an indoor wrap-around balcony from the second floor. The first floor included formal parlors and a dining room, with pocket doors that could open up to accommodate larger parties.[153] Beyond the parlors, a hallway was been built to emulate the bordello alleys of Amsterdam, with long hallways opening onto crib rooms, each with its own door and window.[154] Most historians speculate that many of the original rooms in the cellar and on the first floor were later partitioned off. Only the second-floor rooms retain their original design today. Each bedroom sported a corner sink, and each door had a transom with a number painted on it. A central skylight provided light, with the second-floor balcony affording a view of the first floor. Front rooms on the second floor were reserved for the various madams who ran the Dumas, and a bathroom was also available there. Clients were free to cruise the hallways, literally window-shopping in front of each room before making their selection. Early prices ranged from fifty cents to a dollar. The girls typically made about 40 percent plus tips, which sometimes came in the form of jewelry, furs, and other gifts.[155]

Curiously, much of the Dumas's early history—including when it became known as "the Dumas"—is unknown. Early census records reveal several boarders, including men with such occupations as "gambler" and "saloon man." When the Nadeau Investment Company built the Copper Block at the corner of Galena and Wyoming in 1892, the new structure became home not only to a saloon, but also to gamblers and prostitutes, the latter of whom may have been working girls from the Dumas. Madam Grace McGinnis and four girls, plus a Chinese cook and another servant,

FIGURE 48 ❧ *The imposing Dumas brothel on East Mercury in Butte, Montana. It eventually had forty-three rooms, from cribs to suites. Today the old building holds a fascinating slew of secrets and stories about its women. From the author's collection.*

were living at the brothel in 1900. Although Grace merited a listing in the city directory, her employees did not—possibly because Grace was experiencing a high turnover. In 1902, she still had only five girls and a musician, a small number of employees for such a big place.[156]

To conform to new laws in 1903, the Dumas was largely accessible by a back door opening into Pleasant Alley, the busiest section of the red light district. In fact, the district was so in demand that the Dumas and other places expanded their basements to create more cribs. The quarters were not necessarily comfortable; the smallest crib at the Dumas was actually stuck underneath a stairway and was less than half the size of the other teeny basement cribs. The basement cribs could also be accessed by a stairway from the front sidewalk. Despite the increase in the number of rooms, only two women were documented as living at the Dumas in 1910. It is more than likely that prostitutes lived elsewhere and worked the brothel in shifts, thereby affording a much better profit for the madam and the Nadeaus. In fact, from all appearances, the Dumas and other red light properties in Butte did well by the Nadeau family. Profits allowed the family to take a trip around the world in 1908. Joseph Nadeau's son, Albert, attended Harvard University, receiving his law degree in 1911. Joseph's two daughters, Phedora and Rosalba, married prominent doctors who were brothers. When Joseph died in 1925, he left a sizable estate that was managed by another son, Ovila.[157]

More cribs were added to the Dumas in 1913. The one-story addition included eight rooms, four of which opened onto Pleasant Alley, which was now called Venus Alley. Three years later an upswing in Butte's economy merited building even more cribs. For the first time, the Dumas's elegant main-floor parlors were partitioned off into small rooms. A total of five partitions and a stairway were added.[158] In addition, even more rooms were installed in the basement. The changes toned down the Dumas into a simpler brothel rather than the grand parlor house it had been. The furnishings included radiators in each room.[159] New girls to the house began their career in the basement and gradually worked their way to the upper floors with the fanciest and largest rooms. The "party suite" on the second floor contained the best bed in the house. The plushest room, of course, was the madam's bedroom, which looked out over Mercury Street and featured built-in shelves and French hand-painted wallpaper. No matter which room customers accessed, they typically bought paper scrip before entering, and a ten-minute timer was used for their purchase.[160]

Anna Vallet was proprietress of the Dumas by 1925. Following the traditions established before her time, Anna lived off the premises and employed women who worked in shifts. In 1928, she listed herself as the keeper of furnished rooms. Under the direction of madam Rose Davis during the 1930s, a shower was installed at the end of the upstairs hallway. The bathroom retained its original claw-foot tub and pull-chain toilet. In 1940, Lillian Walden and her husband, Dick, took over operations. It was in this year that the brothel first appeared as "the Dumas" in city directories. Lillian's girls charged about $2 per trick. Between customers, the girls socialized and even made an "Exercycle" from an old bicycle.[161]

In 1943, in answer to the federal government's crackdown on red light districts, a new back door was installed over the old arched doorway in back of the Dumas, along with a buzzer. Additional buzzers were added to the bedrooms, and a code system was used to call for alcohol or for help in case of trouble with a customer. In addition, cribs in the back of the building included doors, some of them hidden, for quick escape into the alley or into the tunnels that ran alongside and below it. The window-shopping was discarded in favor of the waiting-room method, wherein customers were led to a room full of girls from which to choose. Some improvements were also made; each of the eight-by-twelve-foot basement cribs featured a bed, a dresser, and a corkscrew mounted on the wall. There was also a basement ballroom where customers could be entertained well out of sight from authorities.[162]

By 1945, Dick Walden had died, and Lillian, now listed as "Mrs. Gabrielle Walden," ran the Dumas by herself. Despite raids by authorities, the Dumas continued employing women under the guise of being a boardinghouse. By 1953, a new system was employed wherein customers entered through a heavy steel door in the back, knocking first and waiting for a small sliding window to open before gaining admittance. The price for services was around $5. Lillian retired in about 1950, and the Dumas was next run by Elinore Knott. It was probably also around this time that the Dumas finally passed from the hands of the Nadeau family after sixty years of ownership.[163] Elinore's time at the Dumas was short-lived but notable. In 1954, the madam became distraught after her boyfriend died of a heart attack. She packed her bags to leave town, but then ended up committing suicide with an overdose of sleeping pills instead. Today her ghost is said to wander the Dumas.[164] The Dumas's next madam, Bonita Ferran, died of cancer after running the brothel from 1955 to 1969.[165]

The Dumas's last madam was Ruby Garrett, who purchased the building in 1971. A resident of Butte for some thirty years, Ruby had dabbled in the industry for several years prior to buying the Dumas. In 1959, she served nine months at the state prison in Deer Lodge for killing her abusive husband in a local bar. At the time, she was pregnant and running another brothel on Wyoming Street. She also owned a parlor house on Arizona Street at one time. At the Dumas, Ruby's office was located on the bottom floor, next to the "Peekaboo" room. This room featured a two-way mirror through which Ruby could watch new girls perform to make sure they were worthy of employment. Male voyeurs also enjoyed the benefits of the mirror. Ruby later said that during her time at the Dumas, she paid the police $200 to $300 a month in hush money and charged $20 for services. She was a most astute businesswoman, living at a different address, listing herself as "retired," and being careful not to link herself directly to the Dumas. She did, however, oversee the process by which the historic bordello was added to the National Register of Historic Places.[166]

Despite the Dumas's new lease on life, business sometimes simulated the rowdy days of old. Four bullet holes in the front door attest to the time one of Ruby's girls panicked when she thought she saw her husband's car out front and apparently fired shots at him. One of the bullets barely missed Ruby and a customer. Ruby was also robbed three times. During the last robbery, which took place in 1981, two men broke in at gunpoint, tied up Ruby and three of her girls, beat them, and stole $4,500.[167] "They kicked the black girl so bad, she couldn't walk the next day," Ruby recalled of the robbery. The men then taped the women's mouths shut and left. Jo Jo Walker, an employee who had been hiding upstairs, untied the girls. Most of the women left town the next day, possibly because they feared the robbers would return. Ruby was hesitant to call the police because of her murder conviction in 1959, but eventually she did file a report.[168]

Those girls who remained with Ruby apparently did so out of loyalty to her, even though some of them had their own issues to deal with. A small refrigerator in the back hallway was fitted up as a hiding place for Sandra, a small French prostitute who feared the police. The refrigerator had an inside lock and air holes, but appeared from the outside to be an old broken appliance. Sandra worked at the Dumas until she was sixty-one years old. Women like Sandra often had real fears; even at that late date, certain police officers still pressured the local madams for "protection" money.[169] Nevertheless, Ruby was generally outspoken about the prostitution industry, comparing her employees to so-called respectable girls. "These little chippies will do it for a burger and a beer. I say they might as well sell it," she said.[170] The last robbery at Ruby's was the undoing of prostitution in Butte. The attention the holdup brought eventually focused on Ruby, who was consequently convicted of tax evasion and sentenced to six months at a maximum security prison in California. She also had to agree to close the Dumas and pay $10,000 in back taxes. Before her departure in 1982, Ruby's friends threw a good-bye bash for her at a local tavern.[171]

Businessman Rudy Giecek bought the Dumas in Butte in 1990 on the promise to Ruby that he would restore the building to its former glory. Upon taking over, Giecek was amazed at the number of artifacts left behind during the brothel's near-century run. The basement cribs, some of them boarded up since 1943, had long been abandoned and contained liquor bottles, Vaseline jars, medicine bottles, bedding, clothing, photographs, and even a glass globe fire extinguisher. Of particular interest was one room

FIGURE 49 ❧ *A hidden bedroom. When Rudy Giecek purchased the Dumas, this bedroom had long been boarded up. Inside it were a bed, dresser, chair, stove, and sink, as well as cigarette butts and matches on the windowsill and other personal effects. From the author's collection.*

whose condition told of a violent skirmish. The room, which contained a bullwhip, had its door kicked in. Even today, eerie-looking bloodstains are still spattered along the walls and a bloody set of fingerprints smeared along the doorjamb give evidence that someone did not leave the room willingly.[172] Giecek even found a hidden bedroom that had been walled off for quite some time. The room had been left in its original state, with a dresser, standing ashtray, stove, sink, chair, and a brass bed. A well-worn path in the linoleum floor mapped out where the girls walked from the window to the door to the bed, and the bed legs had literally worn holes in the floor.[173]

Although the Dumas and other fancy houses of shame tended to employ classy girls, literally thousands of lesser women also worked in Butte. Pleasant Alley, also known as "Venus Alley," was home to an amazing behind-the-scenes neighborhood of cribs occupied by poorer, older, and washed-up girls. Girls also continued to be available along East Mercury, East Galena, South Wyoming, and Arizona streets.[174] The city's population in 1890 was about thirty-five thousand, and prostitutes were free to adjust their prices to the rise and fall of miner's wages.[175] A visiting reporter from Anaconda who toured the red light district at this time noted piles of food waste, including fruits, vegetables, and meat, around the shacks in the alleys. There were also outhouses built as high as three stories and "banked to a height of six feet to confine the excrement, which sometimes leaked, and the foul liquid sluggishly worked its way down through the ground."[176]

The filth paralleled a lifestyle featuring suicides and acts of violence, but the district continued to be a favorite sporting area for men.[177] During the 1890s, another visiting journalist gave his impression of the red light district: "Young men, boys, old men, hundreds of them wandering about. Girls in the doors and windows soliciting in honeyed words. Young girls, some looking as though they should be in school. Beauty, withered hags, Indian squaws, mulattoes, Japanese, Chinese. Every race and color. Here and there a Chinaman with a wash basket. Indians with gay colored blankets. Noise. Ribaldry. The shrill shrieks of a police whistle. The clang of the patrol wagon. Drunken cries. Maudlin tears. Bodies for sale."[178] Certain businesses, such as the Paumie Parisian Dye House and Cleaners, knew that by relocating to places near the district, they too could prosper.[179]

It certainly seemed to matter little that many of the women providing sexual services were ill, sick, old, poor, or chronically depressed. Between April 1894 and October 1895, Butte's Coroner's Docket kept a list of unusual or suspicious deaths. Of these deaths, only six women were listed, and three of them were prostitutes. Among them was Clara Norton, a thirty-year-old woman who drank herself to death in White Chapel Alley. Witnesses at the inquest of her death included madam Lizzie Hall and prostitutes Annie Whitemore and Pauline Foster. When Francis A. "Rita Rodgers" Evos, a twenty-two-year-old Spanish girl, did herself in with laudanum at the Garrison Building, it was noted that Francis had attempted suicide many times previously. Witnesses at her inquest included Grace LaRue, Hattie Show, Bessie Cornin, Ella Wallace, and Mrs. Jennie Dohl.[180]

In fact, other prostitutes were often the only witnesses to crime. Madam Lizzie "Nigger Liz" Hall was hailed as one of the first prostitutes in Butte. She had previously worked in Bannack and Virginia City. Court documents show that she went before the judge often and fined regularly for prostituting herself and stealing customers' wallets. But she was also compliant in assisting officers during cases of death or crime.[181] On September 27, 1896, the *Butte Miner* reported on fourteen-year-old Celia Decker, who was committed to the state reform school. The girl had apparently learned of her mother's plan to send her to an orphan asylum in Helena and had run away. A man named John Angove had taken her to Lizzie's brothel. The county attorney's office, learning of her whereabouts, charged her with incorrigibility. In court, Celia stated that she was merely hiding from her mother by renting a room at Nigger Liz's. Celia's mother offered to send Celia to live with her father in Denver as soon as she could raise funds, but the judge committed her to the reform school anyway. Both mother and daughter cried at the verdict, and Celia demanded to know how the court could carry out such an action without her parents' consent. Her arguments were for naught, however, and she was duly sent away.[182]

Lizzie appears to have lived in her own crib while renting cribs to other women. She was probably one of many women working out of cribs owned by male businessmen. Cribs were regarded as good investments because they rented for $2 to $5 per night. The more respectable businessmen employed agents to collect the rent for them. One such landlord was Anton Holter of Helena, whose Montana Loan and Realty Company kept a branch office in Butte. A devout Lutheran, Holter was well known in Helena as a mason in the Knights of Templar, was president of the Society of Montana Pioneers and of the Helena Board of Trade, and was in Montana's first House of Representatives in 1889. He also owned several parcels of real estate, including a large number of cribs in Butte from which he extracted rents regularly. Holter's properties in the red light district went through at least twenty other owners between 1896 and 1902 as he traded with other wealthy investors. Another prominent bawdy house owner of Butte, Frank Stephens, built the Silver Queen block on Galena Street. The structure rose three stories and was located at the corner of Montana and Park streets. Brothel business was conducted on the first and second stories, and Stephens resided on the third. When he died of appendicitis in 1898, his son Thomas took over the Silver Queen. The younger Stephens transferred ownership of the building to the Stephens Investment Company in 1901, which also owned some low-end cribs in a blind alley known as Little Terrace.[183]

Coroner's Dockets dating between 1895 and 1901 recorded the deaths of a great number of prostitutes, listing them as "natural causes" even though the girls' young ages made this judgment suspect. In March 1900, twenty-year-old Violet Russell was arrested and taken to the county jail. When it was apparent that Violet was ill, she was taken to the county hospital, where she died. "The coroner was notified that the woman had been assaulted and kicked brutally several days before and made an investigation," reported the recorder in the docket. "He decided the woman had not been injured as alleged and that death was due to natural causes." Likewise, when Georgia Steward "died suddenly" later that year, the coroner was notified, "but learning that a physician had been in attendance decided death was due to natural causes and an inquest was not necessary."[184]

Detailed information, when it was available, accompanied the coroner's notes on many women. Recorded deaths of prostitutes in 1897 include Fanny Gillette, alias "Nellie Collette"; May Sherman, whose trunk was shipped to Nebraska after her suicide; Jessie Kelley, real name unknown, who died of a morphine overdose; and Caroline Covan, alias "Perring," who also died from morphine. In 1900, Dollie Lee died from alcoholism, and Carrie Largess committed suicide with poison. In most cases, the girls' personal effects were turned over to the judge or sometimes kept by landlords in lieu of rent. Caroline Covan's things were given to Pete Harbec, with whom Caroline had been living as his wife for more than a year. All of the women were buried in local cemeteries.[185]

By 1900, Butte's red light district along Mercury Street consisted of six parlor houses. The smallest belonged to Willie Lindell, who lived with a saloon man and employed two women. Willie was in her late thirties. Butte's youngest madam was twenty-six-year-old Yola Graham, who ran a brothel near Galena Street with five boarders. Another madam of note in the city was Dolly Copeland, who migrated to Butte following a tough childhood in Idaho. Upon taking up prostitution, Dolly worked hard to own and work alone in her own house. She kept her place clean and made more money selling liquor than sex. She also never drank or smoked and kept detailed records of her finances. Another madam, Nellie Burns, may

FIGURE 50 ⚶ *Looking at the Blue Range building today, one can easily discern the brothel's numerous cribs. Contrary to the usual practice, the new women here began on the top floor and worked their way down to more accessible first-floor cribs. From the author's collection.*

have lived in Anaconda before migrating to Butte. Nellie's house on South Wyoming Street had three girls. Across from the Dumas was another large brothel, known today as the Blue Range building. In 1900, the Blue Range was owned by Lee Mantle, who was formerly a U.S. senator, mayor of Butte, one-time speaker for the Montana territorial House of Representatives, and owner of a Butte newspaper. On the first floor, the building originally housed cribs measuring about twelve feet in width, each with a closet and tiny bathroom. The second floor contained rooms with less-expensive girls who shared a common bathroom. The building had also no less than seven entrance doors.[186]

Down the class scale, several saloons offered low-rent cribs. One of these saloons was the Royal Rooms, built in about 1900 by Joseph Williams. By 1910, the Royal Rooms were alternately known as the "Casino Lodging House," and the building was functioning as a brothel.[187] R. Blaustein, proprietor, advertised "strictly clean beds" and "respectable" rooms for fifteen cents. Other rooms, however, cost twenty-five or thirty-five cents, with no explanation as to the difference in price.[188] During the 1920s and 1930s, the Royal was operated by Mrs. Mary Verite and Mrs. Frances Scott in turn and remained listed in city directories through 1940.[189]

A new alley off Mercury Street in 1900 was aptly named "Little Terrace." Over time, cribs were built onto the backs of the buildings, one on top of another as high as three stories, until at one point no daylight showed through at street level. Little Terrace was not the gentlest of neighborhoods, as evidenced by the behavior of Trixy and Eveline Evans, who broke a window in Elsie Ritter's crib and shouted epithets at her. Trixy and Eveline went to jail for the incident.[190] But the darkest place in Butte's red light district continued to be Pleasant Alley. Here were the retired and washed-up girls of the town, including French, African American, and Japanese prostitutes. A man—or woman—could fear for their lives in such a place because pickpockets and robbers lurked constantly in darkened doorways. Of Pleasant Alley, the *Butte Miner* said, "It is a disreputable place during both day and night and sightseers from other cities marvel that such a place is allowed to exist at all, to say nothing of its close proximity to the business houses. Many robberies and stabbing affrays have taken place in the alley and at one time the police were instructed to run out every woman in it. For some reason, this was never carried out."[191]

The crib women of Pleasant Alley, Little Terrance, and other places in Butte do not appear to have been divided by race or background. Even the Chinese girls of the red light district were free to live among other women. The 1900 census notes no less than nine black women in Butte, but there were likely many more than that. French and Belgian women were included in the Galena Street prostitutes. Although only fifty-one bad girls are documented as being in Butte during 1900, this number represents only a fraction of the actual total. City directories, for instance, did not bother to list every single girl in the cribs of Galena Street. Also, the girls simply moved too quickly for the census taker, who was more than likely too frightened to walk down the back alleys and take the time to gather accurate information. Of the number known, eleven women were single, seven were married, six were widowed, and four were divorced. The marital status of the other twenty-three women remains unknown. Nine others were foreign born, and only two had children.[192]

During 1900, Butte had a total of 355 saloons. That amazing number included several taverns in the red light district, which was now reaching an all-time high of debaucherous proportions. In 1901, a campaign to do something about Butte's worst cribs was published in the *Butte Miner*. Photographs of some of the cribs along Galena Street and Pleasant Alley appeared in the article, revealing the sinful goings-on in certain parts of the district.[193] City officials, however, knew the economic dangers of closing down the district. Rather, they issued orders for the girls of the row to lengthen their skirts, heighten their necklines, and "refrain from any indecent exposures." The girls adhered to the new laws, although the *Miner* reported on the number of "long dresses and long faces" gracing the row the morning after the new laws were decreed. But the authorities had just begun and soon issued new orders to the women of the district to lower their window curtains. This time the girls were outraged, responding by tearing face-size holes in the shades and tapping incessantly on their windows with thimbles and rings to attract passersby. Ten percent of their $5 monthly fines went to the police chief. Those against the system often complained that some of the money also went into the pockets of city councilmen.[194] The girls were also paying $2 per night or $14 per week for their rooms. Most of the bad girls of Butte, however, maintained a willingness to pay if it meant they could stay in business.[195]

The city directory of 1902 gave a much more accurate number of women in the red light district, listing ninety-two, although there were likely many more.[196] Officials continued their rampage against the red light district in January 1903 by confining its boundaries to the alleys between Mercury and Galena streets. Cribs facing the streets were no longer tolerated, although two-story brothels and parlor houses were allowed to continue functioning. Accordingly, doors were cut into the backs of the cribs, but the poorer women occupying the alleys were soon run out of their own places. A virtual maze of pathways sprang up in the district's obscure and hidden alleys. More cribs were added, one on top of another, to create such terraces as the Copper King, the Model, the New, and the Old-Fashioned. In this manner, hundreds of prostitutes were able to continue working even if it meant crowded, unsanitary, and dangerous conditions. Similar conditions were present at the Copper Block, where numerous tiny cells occupied the basement. In some places, underground tunnels and passageways were created. Many were already in existence, built by the city when an underground steam heating system was installed under most of the downtown area. Authorities also took matters a little further by segregating the races in the red light district for the first time. The black women of the district were made to move to an alley a half-block south of Pleasant Alley. That alley soon became known as "Four-Bit Alley."[197]

The *Butte Miner* frantically tried to keep up with the forced changes. In August 1903, the paper reported on how Minnie Pasco, Nellie Hazleton, and their friends Frank Cashe and Frank "Doc" Chiero had been arrested as "dope fiends." That same evening, two other prostitutes were taken to the city jail for threatening to fight one another. They were released after promising to calm down.[198] Arrests of Butte's bad girls continued into December, with one raid netting sixty women, who were fined $10 apiece. The reason they had been arrested, however, was that some policemen who had been threatened with exposure for taking protection money had promised in turn to reveal that the local judge and police chief were doing the same thing. Newspapers noted that only the crib girls were arrested during the raid, but parlor house girls were left alone.[199]

Arrests, some comical but many serious, continued being reported through 1907. One night, for instance, prostitute Gussie Clark was given a dollar by one Teodosio Campanelli. The two stood outside Gussie's crib for a while before Campanelli inexplicably asked for his dollar back. Gussie, who had just moved from Seattle two weeks earlier, called to her neighbor Mollie Quinn for advice. Mollie said not to return the dollar, at which point Campanelli pulled a knife. Gussie escaped, but Campanelli succeeded in stabbing Mollie in the stomach. Mollie's husband arrived just as she was being put on a stretcher, only to be accosted by an elderly woman who shook her fist at him. "You have disgraced your dead father in the bone yard," she admonished. "You told me years ago that you had quit her. Yet here you are. . . . May you die the death that woman is dying."[200] Others voiced similar sentiments. A writer for a publication titled *Butte and Montana Beneath the X-Ray* put out this poetic comment on Butte's red light district in 1907:

> Vulgar manner, overfed, overdressed and underbred
> Heathen godless hell's delight, rude by day and lewd by night
> Dwarfed the man, enlarged the brute, ruled by roui and prostitute.
> Purple robed and pauper clad, raving, rotting, money-mad.
> Squirming herd in Mammon's mesh, wilderness of human flesh.
> Crazed by Avarice, lust and rum, Butte, thy name is Delirium.[201]

Despite public sentiment, scores of women continued working in Butte through 1910, when the census recorded an amazing 250 prostitutes. In January 1911, one hundred businessmen presented a petition to Mayor Charles Nevin demanding that the red light district be moved. Although the mayor complied by gathering a "blue army" that was meant to close the bawdy houses as of midnight on January 31, some of the businessmen changed their minds. They realized that even with the district swept clean of its soiled doves, nobody would want to move into the empty cribs. Plus, the business generated by the red light population and their customers would be a blight to the legitimate businesses nearby. A second petition, this one asking the mayor to reconsider the sweep, was generated. In the end, it was the shady ladies of Butte who got the goods on everyone involved by closing the district themselves. They rightfully reckoned that if they disappeared for a few weeks, the squabbling would subside, and they could eventually resume business. Among the voluntary closures were the Castle, the Nadeaus' Copper Block, Beulah Frawley's, Little Terrace, Mercury Street, Pleasant Alley, Ruth Clifford's, Willie Crawford's, and the Windsor. The mass exodus was an incredible sight as women packed, loaded their belongings into express wagons, brought out their pets, and left the district on February 1. By eleven o'clock that night, some two thousand men and boys were milling around the district, calling out their goodbyes to their favorite shady ladies. The ladies had done the right thing; the red light district was back up and running within a few weeks, and because the city was taking in an average of $2,000 in fines per month, the matter was put to rest.[202]

The temporary closing did little to divert the red light ladies' antics. Shortly after the district reopened, seventeen-year-old Blanch Desseau was arrested for taking her fifteen-year-old sister to Great Falls, Montana. Blanch intended to put both herself and her sister to work in a brothel there. The two were discovered by authorities and returned to Butte, only to have a girl from the red light district accuse Blanch of stealing her clothes. Blanch's parents lived in a respectable neighborhood, and it was noted that "they have tried to cure her waywardness with but little success. It is said she ran the streets and attended cheap dances prior to the time she took up her life of shame." Blanch's mother, the paper announced, was working with Mrs. C. H. Bucher "of the Florence Crittenden circle" to get the girl into the Home of the Good Shepherd.[203]

Just a year earlier, a Mr. and Mrs. W. W. Wall had been arrested in Great Falls for attempting to seduce fourteen-year-old Elsie Burch of Butte into prostitution. Mrs. Wall was formerly a prostitute in Missoula, but the couple had told Elsie's mother that they were taking the girl to work on a ranch near Melrose. Upon investigating, however, Mrs. Burch learned not only that was there no ranch, but also that Mrs. Wall had told others numerous stories of seducing young girls into the prostitution industry. It was further learned the Walls weren't previously married and that they had only done so upon learning the authorities were looking for them. Elsie was returned home, and the Walls were arrested. In another such case, one town leader, Max Fried, was accused of importing twenty-three-year-old Grace Beal, a married woman from Spokane, for the purposes of prostitution. The case was dismissed, although Fried's partner in crime, Sigmund Suslack, was found guilty.[204]

Butte officials weren't to be outdone. Many brothels, including Irish World, had saloons in or attached to the buildings, and they were attacked next. A new ordinance prohibited saloons and liquor in the city limits. Police had a hard time enforcing the ordinance, however, largely due to the underground tunnel system that allowed for transporting both illegal liquor and prostitutes without being seen. But the resulting arrests were enough to encourage some women, such as Florence McCoy, to try their luck elsewhere. In 1912, Florence ended up moving to Denver and then to Cripple Creek, Colorado. Arrests continued. In 1915, a white prostitute was apprehended for consorting with a black customer and instructed to leave town. The woman refused and continued her relationship with the man, resulting in another arrest and ultimately jail. With the onslaught of World War I and rumors of nationwide prohibition on the horizon, Butte officials made another serious attempt to close the red light district in January 1917. The effort was a failure, although it did bring drastic changes to the district. Some bordellos, such as that in the Blue Range building, became boardinghouses. Other brothels simply masqueraded as boardinghouses and even took in a male boarder or two, but inside the business was the same. Still other women moved into respectable lodging houses, discreetly operating out of their rooms or soliciting on the streets.[205]

When Butte reached its peak population of 41,611 in 1920, the skin trade once more blew out of control. In his 1964 biography, actor Charlie Chaplin recalled that "Butte boasted of having the prettiest women of any red light

FIGURE 51   *A couple of Butte harlots sport their best evening coats, circa 1920. The girls were just two among hundreds, perhaps thousands, of girls working in the city's red light district. Courtesy of the Dumas Brothel Museum, Butte, Montana.*

district in the West, and it was true. If one saw a pretty girl smartly dressed, one could rest assured she was from the red light quarter, doing her shopping." Residents of East Mercury Street during 1928 and 1929 included Marie Demonstrand, Mary Verite, Julia Verite, Martha Schoblitz, Chris and Rhoda Sedaris, Anna Vallet, and Peggy Woods. Most were working out of the old bordellos and likely employed women who lived in other parts of the city.[206] Authorities quietly accepted their presence, although they did take extra measures to suppress the red light district. Venus Alley was blocked off at either end by a green fence with a sign reading "Men Under 21 Keep Out." New laws prohibited women of the night from working until after 5:00 P.M. But the cribs remained "dingy, crude offices for a revolting 'business' that even in Butte was a little furtive."[207]

Between 1930 and 1940, only a handful of girls remained on East Mercury.[208] Even so, newspaper boys from the *Montana Post* just around the corner used to race each other to sell papers in the red light district because "the women there gave us good tips." If it was cold out, the women sometimes also gave the boys a cup of hot chocolate.[209] Ruby Garrett, the former landlady of the Dumas, recalled that prostitutes were charged $2.50 for rent and that the gates at Venus Alley were guarded by policemen. New girls in town were also fingerprinted and photographed for police files.[210] In January 1943, the federal government ordered all brothels closed in an effort to prevent venereal disease from spreading during World War II. Prostitution persevered on a smaller level, but by 1953 Venus Alley had degraded to a miserable and dank place that locals referred to as "Piss Alley." When the entire city of Butte was designated a National Historic Landmark in 1962, some attempts were made to preserve what was left of the red light district.[211] Today only the Dumas Brothel Museum, the Blue Range Building (now serving as offices), and the Victoria Rooms (now a garage) exist as testimony to Butte's bawdy past.

North of Butte was Deer Lodge, which at least aspired to compete with Butte's sizeable red light district. A letter written to twenty-two-year-old Lee Williams in 1904 from Deer Lodge illustrates the bad behavior many men exhibited. "A few days after you left I heard some very bad reports of your conduct last winter," wrote C. H. Williams, adding that two-thirds of the population of Deer Lodge verified Lee had conducted himself as a "whorehouse pimp" while running around with a fallen woman. "The object of your affections openly boasts of the influence she has over you."

FIGURE 52 ⚜ *A 1930s portrait of a working girl from the Dumas. The photograph was found in the old brothel in 1990, leading to the suspicion that the girl probably worked there at one time. Courtesy of the Dumas Brothel Museum, Butte, Montana.*

Williams ended by advising Lee that "I can name a half dozen men of my acquaintance who are in their graves, placed there by the influence of a lewd woman." In particular, Williams cited four men he knew of who "fell under the hypnotic influence of one Effie Worthington" and met their ends. He also warned Lee against the dangers of morphine and encouraged him to return to Deer Lodge to "show the people that you can be a man both physically and mentally."[212]

Nearly all of Montana's smaller camps and towns also supported the prostitution industry to some extent. At Philipsburg, northwest of Butte, old-timers remembered longtime prostitute Nellie Talbott. She was remembered as "a good woman [who] did many charitable acts, and always took care of the sick and helpless." Nellie later developed what was thought to be tuberculosis, and her gambler husband deserted her. She lived out her life as a scrubwoman until she died.[213] No less than one prostitute, but sometimes at least four were present at the tiny camps "Elk and Bear" and "First Chance and Bear" in Deer Lodge County during 1880, as well as at Glendale in Beaverhead County. When Mary Kelly died of pneumonia at Fort Assinniboin in 1880, it was noted she was living at the home of Fannie Gallagher. With Mary were her six children, whose ages ranged from four months to fifteen years. Mary is listed as a "wife," although no husband seems to have been present. It is possible that Mary had recently been left on her own and had turned to prostitution to support her children. At Mondak, located on the border of Montana and North Dakota, things were so rough that local gunmen sold "protection" to the ladies.[214]

The size of any given red light district naturally was proportionate to the size of the town. When Billings was platted in 1882, the original red light district lined both sides of First Avenue South between the 2500 and 2700 blocks, with a number of two-room cribs built to resemble rowhouses. The red light district later relocated to a place conveniently near the railroad depot on Minnesota Avenue. Kirk's Grocery, located in the heart of the red light district, likely sold groceries to Minnesota Avenue girls. Mattie "Kit" Rumley was Billings's first madam of note in 1883. By the time city officials were first elected in 1885, at least a handful of soiled doves had a firm foot in the red light district.[215] Those early authorities apparently had little to say about red light ladies being in their midst so long as the girls behaved themselves.

The city officials' easy-going attitude likely encouraged other ladies to move to Billings. The next madam of note was Ollie Warren, who arrived in 1897. Ollie had graduated from a convent school in Denver and initially went to work at Yegen Brothers' general store. Before long, however, she was having an affair with a young but wealthy lawyer. Whose idea it was to open a bordello is unknown, but Ollie used her attorney friend's money to open the Lucky Diamond on Minnesota Avenue between Twenty-fifth and Twenty-sixth streets. She later ran the Virginia Hotel as well. In time, Ollie was also a notable cattlewoman, and old-timers recalled seeing her fancy four-horse carriage. She was enough of a lady to use a sidesaddle when riding horseback, but her wardrobe was always quite flashy.[216] Billings Brewery worker Red Welsh remembered Ollie as "a handsome, demanding woman who usually got what she wanted, although she occasionally made a few people angry along the way." But Ollie's staunch business tactics spelled success, and for several years she did quite well. She became fond of donning her green velvet riding habit with a plumed hat and lots of jewelry as she paraded around town on a fine black horse.[217]

In October 1917, following a raid that netted $385 in fines, Ollie's place was shut down. She and her girls moved to a second-floor parlor house on Montana Avenue between Twenty-seventh and Twenty-eighth streets. An alley access was constructed for carrying out business more discreetly. "Got to have a private entry for these stuffed shirts who patronize their churches once a week and my business every night," she told the local lumberman. Ollie was married for a time to one Jay McDaniels and for a time was known as "Olive Dewey McDaniels." The two later divorced. Ollie also had a nephew she talked of often in Wyoming who turned out to be her son. When she began suffering kidney problems at the age of seventy, she traveled to Rochester, Minnesota, for treatment. The treatments failed, and Ollie died in 1943. Per the instructions of a young man who many thought must be her son, Ollie's body was returned to Billings and entombed in a mausoleum at Mountview Cemetery. In 1996, the Sheraton Hotel in Billings paid homage to Ollie by naming their dining room the "Lucky Diamond." A portrait of Ollie once hung on the wall but was removed after it was defaced.[218]

As late as 1913, Billings police were still pulling in about $25,000 a year in fines. The federal government, however, forced city officials to shut down the red light district for good during World War I. "Our health tests have proven that if a potential recruit spends twelve hours in Billings, he's unfit for military service," said a visiting military officer. "I am talking about your line of cribs where naked women lean over window sills and entice young boys in for fifty cents or a dollar. Close that south-side line in twenty four hours or the military will move in and do it for you." The city did as it was instructed, but following the war the cribs opened up again immediately and remained that way before being permanently closed in 1972.[219]

Farther west of Billings were Castle City and, later, Livingston. Founded in about 1875, Castle City is memorable for a young prostitute named Mabel. Early one morning Mabel showed up at the post office demanding to know which of her customers from the night before had stolen her false teeth. By 1888, the town still boasted seven bordellos, one of which was located over a saloon. There was also a dance hall called the Badago. The bawdy houses of Castle City were still in full swing as late as 1893. When the town began downsizing in 1893, several soiled doves simply flocked south to Livingston. As of 1971, only one brothel was still standing in the abandoned town.

Those women who did go to Livingston in 1893 found a seasoned town with an established red light district. Platted in 1882, Livingston already had a population of three thousand, plus thirty-three saloons within a year.[220] One of the saloons was the Bucket of Blood, run by madam Kitty O'Leary. Kitty was described as a "190-pound woman who was built like an elephant."[221] It was probably after the Bucket of Blood days that the red light district in Livingston moved to South B Street, where it was in existence in 1898. At least four houses built between 1896 and 1907 served as bordellos. Chinatown was erected nearby.[222] In about 1915, old-timers recalled young boys selling fresh trout to the girls on the line. The prostitutes of B Street made the best customers, often paying more than local restaurants and markets.[223]

When Don Fraser of a local pioneer family was appointed to the police force in 1946, he remembered about a dozen brothels were still operating in Livingston. Each was run by a madam with up to four employees. Although the businesses were illegal, the police department "tolerated" them but enforced such rules as getting the girls' fingerprints, performing background checks on them, and requiring periodic health exams. In addition, "No boy friends were allowed in town or in the district. No drinking in public bars or places, and no parties outside the district. They were not allowed up town or in the residential area after the hours of darkness. There was no soliciting in town or on the streets or outside their residence at any

FIGURE 53 ❧ *A few of the B Street bawdy houses survive in Livingston, Montana. All of them, including the two shown here, are today private homes in a peaceful residential neighborhood. From the author's collection.*

time." Fraser said there were other rules as well, but the ones listed here were the most "strictly enforced." When in 1948 a new madam appeared in town and began disregarding the rules, the red light district was ultimately shut down. A few houses continued operations outside of town but were eventually closed as well.[224]

Northeast of Billings was Miles City, which sported a good-size red light district as early as 1881. That year Miles City had at least six whorehouses: Annie Turner's Coon Row, Mag Burns's 44, Connie Hoffman's, Frankie Blair's, Cowboy Annie's, and Fanny French's Negro House. In January 1894, a grand jury was "making it interesting" for gamblers and prostitutes. Mary Coakley and Grace Powell were arrested for running brothels, and Grace was also charged with selling liquor without a license. W. F. Schmasle and a man named Bullman were arrested for leasing property for immoral purposes. It was said that the largest deposit ever made in the bank at Miles City was $50,000. The depositor was Mag Burns.[225]

In 1904 in Lewistown, located roughly a hundred miles north of Billings, Benjamin Wills appeared at the bordello of Carrie Atkins, a black madam. Wills had apparently become infatuated with one of Carrie's girls, Lulu Littlejohn. When Lulu spurned his requests to marry him, Wills announced his intent to kill her. Carrie persuaded the man to leave, and he was arrested but subsequently released because he did not have a gun on him. He later visited the house again, this time with a pistol. In the ensuing skirmish with Lulu, the gun went off, and the bullet lodged in a wall. Wills went out back to the chicken house at that point and blew out his brains.[226]

6

Nubians of New Mexico

As early as 1598, Spanish colonist leader Don Juan de Oñate led settlers through what is now New Mexico. Throughout the 1600s, four missions were established within the region, but the Pueblo Revolt of 1680 drove most of the Spanish settlers out. After 1821, when Mexico won its independence from Spain, it took several years for new pioneers to rediscover New Mexico. It was not until 1841, when General Stephen Watts Kearny arrived in Santa Fe and declared New Mexico to be a territory of the United States that white settlers began arriving en masse.[1] Gold and other mineral discoveries in the 1860s led to a number of mining camps. Nearly all of them—with the exception of only a few, such as Tyrone outside of Silver City—featured a red light district.[2]

New Mexico's earliest city was Santa Fe, established as the capital of New Mexico in 1609.[3] Santa Fe's most celebrated courtesan was Gertrude or Gertrudis Barcelo, alias "La Tules" and "Doña Tules."[4] She was also known, through time, as "Tula," "Tulas," "Tia Barcelona," "Lona Barcelona," "La Barcelona," "Madam Barcelo," "Señora Toulous," "Doña Lona," "Doña Julia," and, simplest of all, "Madam T." Gertrude is thought to have been born in the Mexican state of Sonora.[5] In 1815, her family moved to Valencia, south of Albuquerque. Seven years later Gertrude married Manuel Antonio Sisneros. True to the customs of her homeland, Gertrude retained all of her personal rights after marriage. Her maiden name, property, legal rights, money, and control over her own body remained hers alone, a benefit that probably largely contributed to her independence throughout her life. At the time of her marriage, however, Gertrude was already pregnant. The child, a son, died after a month. A second son died at four months. The couple finally succeeded in adopting a daughter, who lived with them until she married in 1841. Gertrude later adopted another daughter.[6]

Gertrude alternated her time as a mother with honing her gambling skills, and she began playing professionally in about 1825 and traveling to outlying camps around Santa Fe. She paid her first fine for gambling at Real del Oro in 1826. Likewise, her husband, too, paid fines. By 1833, Gertrude and her husband, adopted daughter, and mother lived in Santa Fe proper. She was soon making money left and right, some of her earnings coming from mining endeavors. When her husband inexplicably disappeared in 1841, she began taking on a series of lovers, most of them powerful and intelligent men who could assist in her career.[7]

Most historians have established that Gertrude was running a house of prostitution by the early 1840s. Her gambling house was in fact located in Burro Alley, Santa Fe's red light district between San Francisco Street and Palace Avenue. She also gambled in other parts of Santa Fe.[8] In either profession, Gertrude was known as "rich and stately, wearing diamonds and rubies on every finger, a massive cross of gold on her ample bosom, a servant used as a human footstool beneath her brocaded slippers." Her customers included churchmen, army officers, and politicians.[9] By 1846, however, it was also noted by those who encountered Gertrude that her looks had faded considerably. Pioneer wife Susan Magoffin noted on a visit to Santa Fe that Gertrude was an "old woman with false hair and teeth . . . a stately dame of a certain age, the possessor of a portion of that shrewd sense and fascinating manner necessary to allure the wayward, inexperienced youth to the hall of final ruin."[10] Such descriptions were in constant conflict regarding Gertrude, however. In December 1847, the *Santa Fe Republican* reported on a local ball that Gertrude attended. "Madame T was there, as young and blooming as we ever saw her, and seemed to enjoy it." Two weeks later at another ball, the *Republican* noted that "[t]he social life in Santa Fe surely required enormous stamina by the gambler called La Tules, who, after dancing away the evening, played Monte the remainder of the night."[11] Beauty was, indeed, in the eye of the beholder.

FIGURE 54 ❧ *One of only two known portraits of Doña Tules, circa 1825, shows her as a young professional gambler. The other depiction, created years later, shows a much more haggard and careworn figure. Courtesy of the Photo Archives, #50816, Palace of the Governors, Santa Fe, New Mexico.*

Gertrude's independence, daring behavior, and staunch pride unnerved American traders even as it intrigued them. In 1847, a Dr. J. M. Dunlap took note of "Madam Toolay" and also of the fact that women, some of them pregnant, participated in fandangos and other goings-on at such places as the madam's.[12] Throughout her career, Gertrude made many loans, and others became indebted to her through games of chance. Those who failed to pay her in a timely manner were often hauled into court. Such legal action, combined with her wild behavior, caused public sentiment to turn against her. It mattered little to Gertrude, however, who managed her business dealings as well or better than any man. She died of heart disease in 1852. Even on her death bed, she conducted business, instructing the executors of her estate to make sure they collected all debts owed to her. Although some of Gertrude's properties still stood in the twentieth century, most have since been demolished. One house owned by her in 1844 is now the site of the Santa Fe County Courthouse. The last known rendering of Madam T was published in *Harper's Monthly Magazine* in April 1854. Given her reputation as a beautiful mistress, the drawing hardly seems to do her justice.[13]

Santa Fe received protection from Fort Marcy on the northeast side of the plaza from 1846 to 1867. In 1850, Lieutenant Colonel E. V. Sumner noted that the soldiers of Santa Fe were spending too much time in the bars, gambling dens, and bagnios nearby. Under the lieutenant's direction, subsequent military posts tended to be established only in remote regions, including another post that was in place at Santa Fe until 1894.[14] Burro Alley, however, continued catering to men. There was also allegedly a house of prostitution on Apodaca Hill during the 1920s.[15] Burro Alley was paved in 1923, and by 1926 normal businesses were moving in. Just south of Santa Fe was Real del Oro, where two prostitutes were once incarcerated in 1835. In court, one of them explained that she had escaped from her husband in Mexico. The judge decided she should either return to Mexico on her own accord or be kept in a respectable house until her mother could come get her.[16]

Like Santa Fe, Albuquerque also received military protection. Although the town was founded in 1706, many historians assert that Albuquerque had no red light district until the coming of the railroad in 1880. The presence of Fort Marcy west of Old Town Plaza between 1846 and 1867, however, strongly suggests that ladies of the evening were on hand to entertain the soldiers.[17] Very early on, the red light district could be found along the west and south sides of the plaza in what is today called "Old Town."[18] During the 1800s, the original red light district was located on Railroad Avenue west of Fourth Street.[19] North of town was Martineztown, where Pasqual Cutinola's dance hall was open to rougher types.

The two largest bordellos in Old Town were owned by Mariano Martin and Sim Ovelin, the latter of whom ran the Old Town Music Hall. In a friendly effort to share the wealth, both men agreed to alternate their hours of operation. The arrangement was a limited success because employees of both houses refused to adhere to it. On a November night in 1881, Martin entered Ovelin's establishment only to find his own girls soliciting inside. Martin commanded the women to leave, but "they did not feel inclined to go, and he, as a persuader, thumped them over the head with a six shooter. A general row was threatened, but it was averted, and there was no damage done except to the thick skulls of the giddy girls." In fact, Martin was well known for beating and kicking his employees. Although he was married, his two-year affair with Santa Fe Mary was well known. Mary in fact gave Martin a serious stab wound in 1881; he in turn pistol-whipped and kicked her during an incident in 1883. This incident resulted in a $10 fine and enough public outcry that Martin left Old Town a month later.[20]

Such violence was commonplace around Albuquerque. Just a few months before Martin clubbed his "giddy girls," two men had a shoot-out over the proprietress of a wine room near the Exchange Hotel. Then, in October 1881, two women known only as "Marinda" and "Minnie" stabbed customer John Connors in the back after he refused to treat them to a drink at Mariano Martin's. Connors's wounds were severe, but a full recovery was expected. Meanwhile, the girls, who were "known and feared as two of the worst lost souls in the business" in Santa Fe, Rincon, and El Paso, Texas, were arrested. They could not pay their $500 bonds, and Martin seemed disinclined to pay, so they were sent to jail. In December, two other women, Georgie Smith and Maud Eddie, got into a fight at Sim Ovelin's. Georgie pulled a small pistol and shot at Maud, but the bullet glanced off the girl's corset steel resulting in only a small flesh wound. Georgie "skipped out and the matter was hushed up without any arrests being made." Next, the Gem on Fourth Street was robbed in June 1882. At the time, the place was run by "two gay French women and their solid men." Two men suddenly stormed in, broke up the furniture, and threw it into the street, "whipped and robbed" the girls of the house, and left. They got away with $120, plus two watches and chains. The newspaper noted that this was not the first time the Gem had been robbed. The robbers were never caught.[21]

For the next few years, bordellos, dance halls, gambling joints, saloons, and wine rooms supported the prostitution industry in Old Town. An alley running south of the plaza provided discreet access to such places. Madam Maggie Morris, also known as "Maggie Clemmons," opened a wine room in 1882 and became known for having the largest bordello in Albuquerque's early years. In 1885, Maggie's employees were Anna Burke, Jennie Morgan, Gertie Oliver, Jessie Hortan, Belle Springer, and Ada Mann. She also employed a servant and three cooks. Grace Bernard, Mary Doane, Cassie Schroeder, and Allie St. Clair were also in Albuquerque in 1882. But madam Rumalda Griego operated the most notorious bagnio. In 1882 and 1883, she was hauled into court on numerous occasions, most often on charges of being a public nuisance. Deputy Sheriff Cornelius Murphy recalled that Rumalda's place contained two to three rooms, each with several beds in the same room. Murphy also testified that he had seen men sharing these beds with the women who lived in the house.[22]

Another notorious Albuquerque bad girl was known as "Madam Henry." She worked part time as a milliner, but her reputation as a prostitute was also known about town. One day in 1883, Madam Henry "got drunk and raised a row" on a streetcar and was jailed. The next evening she appeared at one of the fancier saloons on Harrison Avenue and began singing in "screeching" tones. Two men, one of whom wished the madam would shut up and the other who did not, got in a fight. The proprietor threw out Madam Henry and her number one fan. The two retired to Madam Henry's house across from the saloon, where the drunken madam pulled a revolver on the very man who had fought for her honor. He succeeded in disarming her and threw the gun into the street, whereupon it discharged. No injuries resulted, but the incident drew a large crowd.[23]

More violence followed in 1884. The *Albuquerque Evening Democrat* gave a lengthy account of two black men, Allen Smith and Dick Williams, who got in a jealous argument over the "dusky harlot" of a Railroad Avenue bordello. After several attempts to procure a gun, Smith succeeded in stealing the rifle of a local judge who had lent it to a local dance hall owner for a hunt. Smith returned to the bagnio, resumed the argument with Williams, lured him onto the avenue, and shot his arm nearly off. Williams died within twenty minutes, and there is no record of Smith's arrest. What the female occupants of the house, known as "Tennie" and "Carrie," thought of the incident is unknown. Things became even more complicated around the same time when a mysterious mischief maker began blowing up sections of sidewalk in New Town before throwing a stick of dynamite onto the roof of Nora Moore's Copper Avenue wine room. A hole one foot in diameter was blown in the roof, but nobody was hurt. Chief of Police Harry Richmond offered a $100 reward to anyone who could identify the assailant. Nobody was caught, but the dynamite incidents ceased. Nora continued operations in Albuquerque for at least two more years. Her employees in 1885 included Lilly Ashton, Nellie Driscoll, Mattie Fitzgerald, and Anna McGee, the latter having a three-year-old daughter named Emma.[24]

Interestingly, city officials and local newspapers tended to express their sympathies toward the soiled doves, more so than others in similar towns across the West. When a local brick maker complained he had been robbed in a house of ill fame in 1884, the newspaper merely lectured the victim. "Anyone who frequents these places, carrying large amounts of money with him, deserves to lose it and cannot get any sympathy from any citizen," admonished the *Albuquerque Evening Democrat*. "This event may teach him a lesson." When city officials decided they had had enough of the debauchery at Old Town, they imposed a $10 daily tax on the dance halls and insisted they remain closed on Sundays.[25]

Even as the red light district of Old Town was giving authorities fits, a new and more official red light district was springing up in the heart of downtown on Copper Avenue and Third Street. The earliest bordellos in the new district were started in about 1882 by both existing madams and prostitutes who were new to town.[26] One of them was Lizzie McGrath, who ran the Vine Cottage at 312 West Copper for many years. Born in Kentucky in about 1862, Lizzie was only twenty-one years old when she ran off from her Topeka, Kansas, finishing school with a contractor for the Santa Fe Railroad. When the man abandoned her in Albuquerque in 1880, Lizzie turned to prostitution to make her way. Within three years, she was able to open the Vine Cottage and was soon known as the "Lily of Copper Avenue."[27] The Vine was actually just a clapboard house with only two girls, Jennie Adams and Minnie Hall. Two male boarders, including a Chinese laundryman, also lived there.[28]

Around the corner from the Vine were, ironically, fancy Victorian homes belonging to the city's most respected citizens. These upstanding residents

FIGURE 55 *Lizzie McGrath, circa 1880s. Lizzie was Albuquerque's best-known madam and among the longest-lasting bordello operators, in business from about 1882 until her death in 1921. Courtesy of the Albuquerque Museum, Albuquerque, New Mexico, 1984.014.001.*

somehow managed to coexist with the red light district around the corner, and the agreement not to get in one another's way appears mutual. After all, Lizzie put much of her wealth back into the community and was well liked by everyone, including her girls. Both her employees and at least one gentleman admirer sent her postcards as they traveled the West. Despite her profession, Lizzie was an astute businesswomen. Unlike other madams who preferred to keep their clients' identity a secret, Lizzie openly sued those who neglected to pay their debts to her, including prominent men. In about 1883, she had a baby, but very little else is known about it. Newspapers happened to mention the child while reporting that her room was robbed of $140. As for the thief, he was only described as wearing eyeglasses.[29]

Lizzie's attempts to run a clean house were thwarted on occasion. Newspapers reported in 1885 that a local businessman had become inebriated and passed out at her place. Two hours later the gentleman awoke to the strong smell of chloroform and escaped the room. Lizzie, asleep at the time, was awakened and conducted a search, whereupon it was discovered that a hole had been cut in the window screen of the room that the man had occupied. "It is evident that an attempt was made by persons outside of the house to render the gentleman insensible and rob him." Lizzie's employees at the time were Gertie Oliver, who had at one time operated her own wine room, Mattie Mitchell, Lulu Malley, Jennie Adams, and Lilly Dale. When Lilly had a daughter she named Malvina, she apparently had no means to leave the profession.[30] Lizzie apparently hadn't the means to assist Lilly, although she usually did extend compassion toward others who were down on their luck. When her own cook and handyman Joe Kee absconded with a bank deposit and went on a gambling spree in 1887, Lizzie tried to drop the charges against him. Because anti-Chinese sentiments were running strong at the time, though, Kee, who obviously had a limited grasp of the English language during his trial and no interpreter, was sentenced to two years in prison. He was pardoned after fifteen months.[31]

In 1900, Lizzie's employees numbered four: Lillian Williams, Lola Sullivan, Lottie Turner, and a black porter. When the city passed an ordinance in 1901 prohibiting brothels to operate near a church, Lizzie and two other madams simply bought the nearby Lutheran church on Third Street and tore it down. Locals protested this act, but the church administrators, who had been paid a hefty $3,000 for the church building, were only too happy to relocate. When similar circumstances threatened her newest bordello for being too close to the Masonic Lodge in 1910, Lizzie didn't hesitate to take her case all they way to the New Mexico Supreme Court. She lost the case, but made news as the first New Mexico madam to take a lawsuit that high. Lizzie and her four employees at the time, Bessie Wilcox, Blanche Stern, Josephine Brooks, and Midget Wolfe, gave in and moved elsewhere in the red light district.[32]

Lizzie operated until 1914, when the city officially closed the red light district. She left for a couple of years, possibly visiting Washington Territory, where she had property. By the time she returned to Albuquerque in 1917, her Vine Cottage had been converted to a boardinghouse. In 1921, while standing in line to make a deposit at the First National Bank, Lizzie collapsed and died. She was buried in her hometown, Topeka, Kansas. During the 1960s, a trunk belonging to her was opened for the first time, revealing emeralds, rubies, and diamonds, as well as small bags full of gold coins. Today McGrath's Bar & Grill, located in the Hyatt Hotel near the site of her old house, pays tribute to this unique madam.[33]

Other madams in Albuquerque during Lizzie's time included Minnie Carroll, Nellie Driscoll, and Kate Fulton. All were prominent, as illustrated by the birthday presentation of a beautiful silver loving cup to one of them. It was engraved with the names of several prominent customers on it and was lovingly placed on the mantel. When the woman died, the cup disappeared and was never seen again. Despite their notoriety, all three women were also susceptible to domestic violence and thievery. In 1883, Kate Fulton's house was robbed of a $30 watch and chain and a $10 Colt revolver from employee Minnie Baldwin. A customer, identified only as John Doe, also had a $10 gold piece stolen. In this case, one Frank Edwards was arrested for the crime and served three months of hard labor.[34]

By 1885, when Albuquerque was incorporated, the old district had been completely abandoned. Gone, too, were the Hispanic and African American women who had previously worked at Old Town. Five brothels and five wine rooms were functioning in the new district. Women of the row in 1885 included at least two madams and several girls. For the most part, the parlor houses appeared respectable, clean, and classy. Some featured bay windows and long porches from which the girls could solicit. Who chose the location is unknown, but it was probably not the prominent men of the town; only a few blocks from the district was a well-respected neighborhood that was home to Mayor Henry Jaffa and a number of well-known businessmen. In

November 1886, officials did, however, pass an ordinance prohibiting prostitution. Like the ordinances in other towns, this one merely guaranteed
regulation of the red light district, which from most appearances conducted
business in a manner pleasing to the city council. Unlike other towns, however, Albuquerque lacked the police manpower, not to mention the inclina-
tion, to enforce the ordinance on a regular basis. Within six months, the
ordinance had been quietly repealed. In its place came a revised ordinance
that simply prohibited the girls of the row from appearing in public, soliciting on the street, using foul language, or being seen in the company of
men. The floosies and flossies of Albuquerque were in essence accepted as
part of society. Former Territorial Fair manager Roy Stamm later remembered that the ladies of the row contributed heavily to the annual fair, "and
you should have seen them in full bloom sitting in the boxes along the front
of our grandstand." In time, the ladies were banished to more discreet seat-
ing underneath the grandstand.[35]

Most of Albuquerque's shady ladies were indeed gentlewomen, but
another section of the new district was alternately known as Hell's Half
Acre.[36] Still, nobody seemed to object to the district's unmistakable prominent location, although certain citizens were not too quick to point it out to
tourists. A streetcar driver outright lied to one woman during a tour of the
town in 1883. "You may have noticed that we do not number houses here
in the regular manner," he told her. "There is 444, and then 222, and to be
more irregular, there is 101 and so on." The numbers were actually names
of various bordellos, and the further explanation was given that "[i]n regard
for their daughters [our people] place their names in large golden letters
over the door. There is, for instance, Maud and Lillie and Nellie and Maggie
conspicuous on the transoms." Although the woman appeared to buy the
story, the three men also on the trip were hardly fooled and could barely
contain their laughter.[37]

In 1891, Albuquerque's red light district supported seven parlor houses
but, surprisingly, no cribs. By 1893, the number had changed; only four
parlor houses competed against ten privately operated cribs. It is also notable that the presence of cooks in Albuquerque's parlor houses was nearly
nonexistent after 1900. But a number of new madams in the area indicates
that the red light district was still functioning quite well. Among them was
twenty-three-year-old Victoria Kirk, who employed Clyda Hall, Cora Miller,
Irene Colleson, and Cleo Raymond. Minnie Carroll had also arrived by 1900

and employed Grace Howard, Minnie McCall, and Nona Leslie. Both madams also kept other boarders, and in 1910 Minnie bought Victoria's brothel. Her employees there were Allie Rhodes, Theresa Roberts, Eron Rosenstiel, and Pearl Henderson.[38] During 1908, the city took in more than $9,000 in liquor licenses from local saloons, parlor houses, and cribs. Altogether, seventeen cribs were operating in Albuquerque at this time. Things were thus looking shadier; in 1910, at least two women, Anna Dunlap and S. Gutierrez, were plying their trade on the second floor of the Sturges Hotel, once applauded as one of the top two hotels in town.[39] Although crib girls were known to push aside the law, madams Minnie Carroll and Lizzie McGrath—Albuquerque's only madams between 1910 and 1914—upheld it to the letter.

It was in fact the mayoral election of 1914 that decided the fate of Albuquerque's red light industry. Democrat D. K. B. Sellers argued that it was more sensible to have a legal red light district in one spot rather than watching the ladies scatter all over town to sell their wares. Republican D. H. Boatright wanted the district closed altogether. After years of seemingly supporting the red light ladies, the *Albuquerque Morning Journal* turned tail and campaigned for Boatright, who won. It took several months to draft an ordinance outlawing the red light district, but once it was in place, the city marshal was instructed to close the ladies down. Mayor Boatright received a few threatening letters demanding he reopen the district, but he stood his ground. Some of the girls moved back to Old Town, which still lacked laws against prostitution. Lizzie McGrath took a long vacation, and Minnie Carroll opened a boardinghouse. Today absolutely nothing of Albuquerque's red light districts remain. Haunted Hill, however, located at the northeast end of Menaul Boulevard, is said to be rife with the ghosts of shady ladies. For years, residents have claimed to hear screaming, footsteps, and the sounds of bodies being dragged. People have seen a lantern swinging in the dark of night. Local legend has it that an old man used to live in some caves at the top of the hill and would lure prostitutes to his den before killing them.[40]

Aside from Santa Fe and Albuquerque, several other military forts were stationed throughout New Mexico, especially during the early 1800s. One of them was Fort Conrad, established near Socorro in 1816.[41] The "laundresses" of the fort were situated in the secluded northwest corner, near the stables.[42] Their placement in a remote section of the fort suggests that such women might have doubled as prostitutes. This theory is backed up by Fort Union army wife Anna Maria Morris, who referred to the domestics of the fort as "so-called laundresses." There is little doubt that Mrs. Morris was aware that such women provided other services to the soldiers as well.[43]

In fact, the layouts of several forts throughout New Mexico give clues, depending on where the laundresses were situated, as to whether the fort commanders tolerated prostitution. Certainly, prostitution was prevalent around these military forts, evidenced by the fact that with the onset of the Civil War, outbreaks of venereal disease among New Mexican soldiers grew to epic proportions. Incidents of venereal disease in New Mexico were in fact three times higher than the national military average. At Fort McRae in 1870, the laundresses were in a remote section at the north end of the fort and across a small creek. Fort Bascom's laundry ladies worked directly across from the barracks in 1874. Also in 1874, Fort Tularosa's laundresses were living right alongside married soldiers, with the barracks located just across from them. At Fort Wingate in 1875, the laundresses were located in a series of buildings comprising stables and shops directly across from the barracks.[44]

Officer's wives rarely interacted with either laundresses or prostitutes and recorded such occasions even less. Only minute evidence exists that army wives may have accepted prostitution as part of frontier army life. Anna Maria Morris referred to working girls in three instances in her memoirs. On one occasion, Mrs. Morris and her friends gathered to hand sew garments for the baby of a Mrs. Murphy, identified as a "camp woman." The other two entries concern Sarah Bowman, a war hero and near-famous prostitute from El Paso, Texas. Sarah was nicknamed "the Great Western" after a famous steamship, the largest of its kind, that was put to sea in 1837. Exactly when Anna Marie Morris saw Sarah Bowman is not clear, but during an excursion to Fort Webster the Morris wagon was behind that of the Great Western. Anna appears to have mentioned this connection more in passing than because it bothered her. She also sewed a skirt for an orphan girl whom Sarah had adopted after the mother died on the trail. Sarah and her new child were headed to California, the original destination of the girl's parents.[45]

Born in 1812, 1813, or 1817 in Tennessee, Sarah stood out as quite the Amazon, towering more than six feet tall and weighing around two hundred pounds. She was illiterate, but spoke fluent Spanish. During her life, Sarah alternately went by the surnames "Borginnis," "Bouget," "Bowdette," "Davis," and "Knight." A few of these names were associated with various men, some of whom Sarah had married or lived with.[46] During her first marriage, Sarah joined her husband in the army at St. Louis just before the Mexican-American War of 1846. As a means to travel with her husband, she served as a laundress and cook. By August, however, the *Niles National Register*, a nationwide newspaper, was referring to her as a "camp follower." Indeed, Sarah liked men, and she adored the soldiers she lived among, as well as their leader, President Zachary Taylor. Even after she and her husband separated in about 1846, she continued traveling with the troops. Her kind heart, combined with her unwavering courage, soon endeared her to the men. She would willingly fight any man, and stories about her included killings and other daring acts. During battles, she never failed to administer to the injured or to provide food for the soldiers, even when a stray bullet pierced her bonnet. After the war, Sarah opened her own brothel in Mexico, sometimes working solo and sometimes hiring girls.[47]

While in Mexico, Sarah also took up with two men—one so she could once again legally follow the army troops, and the other because she fell in love with him while on the trail. She later opened the very first bordello in El Paso, Texas. By 1850, Sarah had relocated to Socorro, New Mexico, and was running a house of Mexican prostitutes. She also fell in love with Danish soldier Albert Bowman, who was in fact fifteen years her junior. Even so, the couple lived together for the next sixteen years. The Bowmans alternated their time between Socorro and Yuma, Arizona, where Sarah was again the first woman to open a business. This time, she ran a combination restaurant, bar, boardinghouse, and brothel. She also recruited call girls for men upon request, and Lieutenant Mowry of Fort Union supposedly meant it as a compliment when he called her "an admirable pimp." Sarah and Albert next purchased property in Tucson, Arizona, moving there in 1857 and opening a saloon at Patagonia. It was a rough place with frequent shoot-outs and at least two deaths.[48]

The 1860 census found the Bowmans at Arizona City. Albert worked as an upholsterer. Sarah's occupation was not listed, although she was still running her brothel.[49] When Fort Buchanan was abandoned in 1861, the majority of Sarah's customer base left the area, so she closed her Patagonia

FIGURE 56 ⊛ *The Capitol Bar was opened in Socorro, New Mexico, in 1896. The building may initially have served as a courthouse and jail before being converted to a tavern. It is directly across from the plaza. From the author's collection.*

operation and returned to Yuma for good. She died after she was bit by a tarantula in 1863. Sarah Bowman was the first and only woman to be buried at the Fort Yuma Cemetery. In 1890, her body was exhumed, along with the rest of the cemetery occupants, and reinterred at the Presidio of San Francisco cemetery.[50]

Although Sarah Bowman's time in Socorro was short, she left a memorable impression there. In 1854, Fort Conrad was abandoned in favor of Fort Craig. Some twenty-five years later "Colorado Charlie" Utter, the well-known saloon man and gambler of the West, arrived in Socorro and opened a tavern. He hired two women, Minnie Fowler and another gal named Maude, to deal faro at his Monarch Saloon. Both women, who also served as working girls, were quite adept at the game, and their beauty drew gamblers from all over. Other easy women of Socorro included Diamond Molly, Dutch Min, Hop Fiend Kit, and Rocky-faced Kate.[51] Socorro was, at that time, a rough-and-tumble town of seedy-looking adobe buildings situated on dirt streets with lots of blowing dust and scorching heat. In his book *Tacey Cromwell*, author Conrad Richter wrote a heartfelt fictionalized account of a madam trying to go straight. Basing the story on his own experiences and real places, Richter described a Socorro parlor house through the eyes of his main character, Nugget Oldaker: "Since then I have been back and seen it by day, a dingy, one-story mud building half washed away by rains and standing in an alley. But that night it awed me to my bones. When the door opened, it was like peeping into Ali Baba's cave with brass lamps swinging through rich tobacco smoke. The shining bar was loaded with glittering glasses and veritable haycocks of things to eat, while small tables stood stacked with gold and silver and red, white, and blue chips."[52] The picture was probably little different during the 1930s when a woman known only as "Doobie E." ran a bordello in Socorro. Doobie and her husband unfortunately tended to drink the house profits.[53] Judging by its appearance today, Socorro's red light district was likely situated along Becker Street near First and Second Streets, just around the corner from the railroad and the Harvey House restaurant that served meals to train passengers.

Socorro, Santa Fe, Albuquerque—all sported noteworthy red light districts with some memorable women within their realms. By far, however, Loma Parda's wild and raucous night life surpassed that of all these places. The settlement never had more than five hundred people, but "catered to all the vices of lonely men."[54] Founded in the 1830s or 1840s east of Santa Fe, Loma Parda originally survived quite nicely as a farming and ranch community until Fort Union was constructed some five miles away in about 1851. The laundresses, who appear to have been nothing more than that, lived in the east section of the fort across from company barracks and in between the married men's quarters. Soon, however, a bevy of buxom girls, who were not allowed in the fort, cleverly set up shop in some nearby caves. When one Captain Sykes found out about them, he ordered two of the women captured and shaved their heads to teach them a lesson.[55] In a letter home, Fort Union army wife Katie Bowen mentioned the burning of the shanties in the caves, commenting that "Mexican women scattered like sheep from all the places." If Katie was aware of how the two imprisoned prostitutes were treated, she chose not to mention it.[56]

Thus, new prostitutes to the area were directed to Loma Parda. There, the girls could service Fort Union's soldiers without interference. The community soon became known as "Little Sodom" and "Sodom on the Mora," an allegorical tongue-in-cheek reference to the town's location on the Mora River and the biblical phrase "Sodom and Gomorrah."[57] Whiskey called "Loma Lightening" was always available to loosen inhibitions.[58] In 1861, soldier O. J. Hollister wrote of the goings-on at Loma Parda: "drinking, fighting, and carousing with the whores at Loma . . . was [sic] the favorite pastime of our regiment."[59] Following the Civil War, the place just got wilder. In 1866, Major John Thompson actually declared the place off limits to his soldiers. The effort was only a limited success, though, as evidenced by the frequent trips made by Samuel and Martin McMartin's wagon taxi, which ran between Loma Parda and the fort for a dollar per round trip. In addition, several prostitutes set up shop around McMartin's store.[60] More gamblers and prostitutes could be found at some buildings that had been abandoned by Fort Union. The army ordered these buildings torn down in 1867, once it recognized that "there are always a lot of Mexicans and unknown Americans harbored around these buildings. Gambling, drink and prostitution seem to be the principle use to which many of these rooms are appropriated, and soldiers of the Garrison are enticed and harbored there to carouse all night."[61]

Back at Loma Parda, Julian Baca's dance hall was open twenty-four hours a day. Fort Union leaders were at a loss what to do. At one point, they even considered leasing the entire town in order to tear it down. By 1872, however, of the four hundred people at Loma Parda, none expressed much interest in leaving. When the older town of Watrous was officially platted in 1879, some soldiers tried their luck there. A series of mishaps, however, including one soldier's loss of an eye in a fight and another's loss of his life in the Mora River, convinced the men that Loma Parda was preferable for partying. The incidents at Watrous may have just been bad timing because Loma Parda itself was well known as a rough and rowdy town. One story tells about James Lafer, who rode into town on a night in 1888. Lafer grabbed a woman and dragged her across his saddle before riding his horse right into a saloon. When the animal refused to drink a shot of whiskey offered to it, Lafer shot it in the head, snatched up his newly kidnapped companion, and marched out, leaving the horse dead on the floor. The occupation of Fort Union became more sporadic beginning in about 1881. By the time the fort was officially abandoned in 1891, Loma Parda's bad girls had gone to seek greener pastures. In later years, one of the dance halls was made into a church. Julian Baca's dance hall still stood as of 1987.[62]

At least one of Loma Parda's wanton women, Pablita Martin, also known as "Paula Angel," suffered for her actions. Pablita grew up around Las Vegas, New Mexico. In 1850, Las Vegas had already made history as home to the state's youngest prostitute, an eleven-year-old girl. In 1861, its women made history again when Pablita became the first female to be hanged in the territory. Pablita was accused of being not only a prostitute, but a witch and murderess as well.[63] She was in her twenties when she was accused of stabbing Juan Miguelito Martin (no relation). The wounded man rode his horse into Las Vegas before collapsing on the steps of the jail. His last words were, "Pablita Martin me mato" ("Pablita Martin killed me"). Miguelito Martin's good friend happened to be Sheriff Antonio Herrera, who immediately rode to the village of Sapiro, kicked in Pablita's door, and forced her to walk behind his horse as he took the long way back to Las Vegas. Rumors about her included one that she frequented the bordellos and gambling houses at Loma Parda roughly twenty-five miles to the northeast. Pablita's husband, Domingo, hardly helped matters, claiming that his wife often disappeared during the night and that he never knew where she went.[64]

As the case unraveled, it came to light that Miguelito was Pablita's lover and that she stabbed him when he tried to end their affair. No matter that Miguelito was already married with five children. In a swift trial just five days into her jail time, Pablita was declared guilty. She was sentenced to hang a month later. Sheriff Herrera enjoyed taunting Pablita while she awaited execution, but rumors that she was also a witch allegedly frightened him. As a precaution, the sheriff was said to have sprinkled graveyard dirt across the entrance to the woman's cell and posted a cross in the doorframe. He even wore a Cachana root around his neck to ward off any evil. Part of Herrera's paranoia was caused by a red candle some stranger had supposedly placed at the door of the jail. The candle was always burning, and when it got low, a new one mysteriously reappeared.[65]

Pablita's forthcoming execution drew crowds from Fort Union and as far away as Santa Fe. When Herrera came to the jail the next morning, Pablita was forced to sit on—or in—her own coffin for the trip to the gallows.[66] Amidst the crowd of locals yelling obscenities and "hang the stinkin' whore," Pablita was taken to a nearby cottonwood tree where a noose awaited. Once it was placed around her neck, she was supposed to have bitterly placed a curse on the crowd, which caused considerable unease. Either Pablita's curse unnerved Herrera even more or he was just plain inept; either way, he forgot to tie Pablita's hands. When the wagon was removed from under her, she was able to grasp the noose. Even Pablita's enemies were appalled when the sheriff ran to the woman's struggling body and tried to hang from her waist in an effort to strangle her. Pablita was subsequently cut down, only to be hanged again—this time with her hands securely bound. Her sentence to hang "until dead" was finally carried out.[67]

Ninety miles north of Las Vegas was Cimarron, founded in 1857. Seven years later the most impressive place at Cimarron was the estate of land baron Lucien B. Maxwell. Spanning the space of a city block, Maxwell's house was not only big enough to accommodate himself, but also gambling rooms, a saloon, dance hall, billiard parlor, and boarding for ladies of easy virtue. The rooms were lavishly furnished, and the girls were allowed to stay on one condition: if they left, they were not allowed back. More entertainment could be found just across the road at the St. James Hotel. Built in 1872, the St. James housed a saloon, a restaurant, and forty-three rooms. The saloon in particular was the scene of a number of shoot-outs, including twenty-six murders. One of them may have been committed by gunslinger Clay Allison, who killed a man for abusing a Native American woman and forcing her into prostitution: the offender's head was cut off and posted on a spike in front of a Cimarron bar for several days.[68]

By the 1860s, hundreds of Indian women were plying their trade in New Mexico either by design or by force. In 1865, James Carleton of the U.S. Army Department of New Mexico reported that, among Indians, "Prostitution prevails to a great extent amongst the Navajos, the Maricopas, and the Yuma Indians, and its attendant diseases . . . have more or less tainted the blood of the adults, and by inheritance the blood of the children, who from diseased parents become possessed of but feeble energies, feeble vitality; in short become emasculated in body and mind." Carleton further encouraged Senator John R. Doolittle, to whom the report was sent, to allow government interference for the good of the women in the profession.[69] But new mine discoveries across the state were bringing a slew of new settlers, including hundreds of pioneer prostitutes.

Over the next thirty years, New Mexico was home to many boom-and-bust mining towns. In the northern Rockies, Elizabethtown's first bagnio opened with two women in the winter of 1868. Just a year later there were already seven saloons and three dance halls in town. Near Socorro, the town of Kelly, founded in 1870, once had a population of three thousand and no less than two dance halls and seven saloons.[70]

And in the southern portion of the state, there was Pinos Altos. Rich minerals had previously been discovered as early as 1803, but the town itself, originally christened "Birchville," grew up around new mining discoveries in 1860. One of the earliest taverns was built by George Harrington—a log house one hundred feet long and twenty feet wide, big enough to hold a barroom and fifteen or twenty gambling tables, with a brass band and twenty-five "fast Mexican women."[71] By 1889, there was a roaring little red light district located on what is now Spring Street, a block off Main Street.[72] Spring Street was also livened by Sing Lee's laundry, complete with an opium den. If the "hop joint" had not been located in such close proximity to the town's school, there would have been fewer problems, but local papers tended to comment heavily on the arrests made of men and women at Sing's. At the same time, newspapers complained about laws prohibiting women from entering saloons. "Since [the law] has gone into effect," noted the *Pinos Altos Miner*, "disreputable women stand on the streets and have their drinks brought to them and flaunt their shame in the face of women and children." Furthermore, saloon owners had simply added on a back room to their places so women could discreetly gain access. The paper went on to suggest it might have been better to prohibit the selling of liquor to such women and the men who accompanied them.[73] In fact, the presence of naughty girls at Pinos Altos had grown to such proportions that many folks felt compelled to move their families away from the camp. In one instance, "three saddle colored wenches on horseback" were seen galloping up and down the main drag.[74]

Rather than rely on local laws, Pinos Altos officials tended to fall on more stringent state laws for their efforts against prostitution. At least one woman, Edna de Ray, was arrested under such a law. She was fined $51 and promised to leave town within two days. For every Edna de Ray who left town, however, another such woman took her place. In 1889, a Miss Cordelia was arrested after "shooting up" the house of a Miss Williams.[75] In about 1890, Lucy Small shot Edward Fountain to death, claiming that after a night of drinking, Fountain had called her names. As Fountain left, Lucy fired a shot after him, "wishing to scare him," but the bullet struck him, and he died hours later. Lucy's real name was Luciana Baldonado, and she was the daughter of Mexican family in nearby Central City.[76] She was about twenty-six years old at the time of the shooting; the paper neglected to mention if she went to prison for her crime.[77]

FIGURE 57 ⚘ *A former dance hall at Pinos Altos, New Mexico. Unfortunately, nothing at all is left of the Pinos Altos red light district, located one block south of the main drag. From the author's collection.*

Down the road from Pinos Altos was Silver City, founded in 1870. In 1873, the town was most notable as the home of future outlaw Billy the Kid, whose ramblings took him all over southwestern New Mexico. It may have taken some time for the rowdies at Pinos Altos to realize there were better pickings nearby. Silver City's first notes on prostitution did not appear until 1884, but the town's red light district was already by that time known as scandalous. That February, Verdie Bell and Miss Ollie Barbee were noted as being "registered at Hudson's."[78] The new announcement may have signified that the ladies were new to Silver City. Within months of Verdie's arrival, her girls were already stirring up trouble. In May, it was reported that two harlots had dressed up as Sisters of Charity one evening and "made a tour of the town soliciting aid for the hospital." The newspaper added its opinion that "[a] charge of obtaining money under false pretenses should have been filed against them."[79] If authorities thought they could quell Verdie and her girls with fines, however, they were wrong. In June 1884, Verdie inherited $10,000 from her wealthy family in New Jersey.[80] Most unfortunately, however, she failed to live the usual colorful life of women in her position. She died from a "hemorrhage of the lungs" in January 1885 at her house and was buried at a local cemetery.[81]

Verdie's time in Silver City was cut short, but the lady just may have set precedents for other naughty women. John Fleming, future mayor of Silver City, was credited with rescuing a young girl from the Centennial, a brothel owned by a procuress named Collins, shortly after the girl arrived in town. That same night, Pete Zimmerman broke in the door of a bagnio called "No. 11." Upon finding his wife snuggling with one Harry McLean on a couch, Zimmerman took a gun from the man and beat the couple. He was arrested. Then there was Kate Stewart. Born in 1855 in New York, Kate bought her first place on Texas Street in Silver City. She saved her cash until January 1885, when she made excursions to New Orleans and Georgia. Upon her return, it was discovered that she had been on a recruiting mission and had brought back two new girls with her.[82] A few months later she sold all of her furnishings, a sign that she may have been redecorating. "Kate Stewart has made an assignment," announced the *Silver City Enterprise*, "Captain M. G. Hardee has been appointed to dispose of her effects. This is a rare opportunity to secure some good furniture."[83]

A third sign of Kate's wealth came in June when she pledged $10 during a fund-raising effort for a new wagon road to nearby Fort Bayard and Georgetown.[84] Despite this sign of civic-mindedness, Kate had enemies. In 1893, local papers reported on the attempted dynamiting of Kate Stewart's place. In her defense, one article expressed the opinion that "[n]o matter how aggravated the cause, such acts amount to willful murder and a necktie reception should be immediately tendered the perpetrators of such fiendish crimes as soon as their arrest and conviction can be secured."[85] Kate persevered, employing five girls in 1900. By 1910, the fifty-five-year-old madam lived alone in the red light district, either freelancing or retired.[86]

Kate's girls were apparently not as naughty as Verdie Bell's, but there were plenty of crib women around town. In August 1884, the *Silver City Enterprise* reported on two girls from the demimonde who were shamelessly smoking cigarettes while riding their horses. One of them, Ada, managed to ignite her clothing and was "frightfully burned."[87] A few months later, two fast women were hauled in from the nearby town of Fleming on charges of prostitution, but were let go. Then, in March 1885, another young girl cried to the *Silver City Enterprise* about her brush with the prostitution industry. The girl was from St. Louis, where a procuress had enticed her to come to Silver City. The girl told a number of persons how she had been deceived by this woman, who held her trunk and clothing as security for her fare from St. Louis. The girl's story was corroborated by a gentlemen who knew her from her hometown and said she was a respectable young girl.[88]

If the bad girls of Silver City were getting a bad rap, they were redeemed at least briefly by the actions of madam Bessie Harper. During the summer of 1885, a group of Apaches attacked and killed some Mexican settlers only three miles from Silver City. The site was horrifying; witness Wayne Whitehill recalled that at least one small child died after being pierced and hanged from a meat hook and that fifteen others, mostly women and children, had been killed. Men from Silver City loaded the dead into wagons and brought them to an adobe house, where they were laid out. Bessie's actions were indeed memorable, according to Whitehill. "Bessie Harper, ya," he said, "well, she went in there and dressed all these bodies and bought clothes and fixed them all up and paid the whole funeral expenses to bury these people."[89] Bessie remained a heroine until 1888, when she was arrested for knocking out Ruby Fowler with a stone wrapped in a towel and then beating the unconscious woman. Ruby suffered several cuts, and Bessie got out on bail.[90] In 1889, Bessie and Millie Forest were arrested after threatening to do each other in. The newspaper noted the number of local harlots who appeared for the hearing, including a few who "flirted out of the windows with the boys" during the proceedings.[91]

Despite her faults, Bessie Harper became one of the best-known madams of Silver City. Her care for the massacred Mexican family was not soon forgotten, and she was known to pay for food and coal for poorer families at Christmas. She also married at some point, but nothing is known about her husband. Bessie's employees in 1900 were Lillie Breen, Blanch Earle, and bartender John Peas. Ten years later Bessie employed three girls, Inez Bell, Mary Handa, and Dova King. By 1920, she was apparently retired at her stated age of fifty and living alone.[92]

Silver City also saw its share of European and African American women. One of the French madams, aptly named "French Nettie," was known "for her irascibility and miserly ways." French Nettie was eventually run out of town.[93] In 1888, the *Silver City Enterprise* expressed its dismay at two "colored girls, of the soiled variety" who were seen on Broadway dressed in scanty "Mother Hubbards"—the Victorian version of a mumu—while smoking cigarettes. "If there is no ordinance to prohibit such vulgarity," lectured the *Enterprise,* "one should be passed immediately."[94] By 1889, Sheriff H. H. Whitehill had had enough and issued a proclamation that anyone without visible means of support had to leave Silver City. Furthermore, any lewd women found drunk on a public street would be arrested. Prostitute Claudie Lewis was arrested almost immediately.[95]

Then in 1890, Edna de Ray, who had only recently been ousted from Pinos Altos, was involved in a shooting. Edna apparently had had some words with a black prostitute named Lucy Washington and fired a shot at her. When Lucy defied her to do it again, Edna accidentally shot another giddy girl, Mollie Forest, in the foot. The wound was found to be quite serious, and there was talk of amputating Mollie's foot. Lucy testified that the shooting was indeed accidental, and Edna does not appear to have suffered any jail time over the incident. Lucy, meanwhile, paid a $3 fine. By then, such goings on were commonplace in Silver City. When certain members of the lost sisterhood took to sitting on their doorsteps along Eaton's Row (the main portion of the red light district) and cussing at passersby, the *Silver City Enterprise* gave an empty promise that the city council would look into the matter if such behavior continued. In October, Antoinette "Nettie" Simone of Chicago was arrested for operating as a procuress.[96]

There were also further tragedies, including the shooting of Mrs. Victor Croenne at El Paso, Texas. Mrs. Croenne was in fact married and had a daughter, but also ran Nettie's Place on Hudson Street. She had apparently taken a trip to El Paso with one Charles "Frenchy" Baine. At a respectable boardinghouse, Baine shot Mrs. Croenne in the head while the couple lay in bed and then turned the gun on himself. A full day lapsed before the landlady discovered the deed. No note was found, only a number of empty champagne bottles. Mrs. Croenne's husband traveled to El Paso and had his wife buried.[97] When Dottie Lorraine died in Silver City in April 1892, Reverend W. T. Topham willingly gave services for the twenty-year-old Italian native. He also took the opportunity to tell Dottie's friends that they could still be forgiven for their sins if they would forsake their evil ways.[98] Few of the girls listened.

Silver City citizens drew the line when it was discovered that a house of ill fame was opened on Main Street, right next door to the primary school, in 1893. Things had settled down only slightly by 1900, when fifteen prostitutes were recorded in the census. Of them, three were foreign born, six were single, four were widowed, three were divorced, and one, B. Grace Caulton, had been married for six years and had three children. There were four other children among the women as well. Grace worked for madam Bertha Conness with fellow working girl Dona McNeill.[99]

Ten years later, the number of Silver City's soiled doves remained at just fourteen. Madam Camille James employed three women, and madam Myrtle Howard had nine girls working for her. As with prostitution throughout the West, the military commanded that Silver City's red light houses be closed during World War I. The alluring ladies of Silver City were too close to Camp Cody for comfort, as were those in nearby Deming.[100] Several years after the war, in 1930, at least three prostitutes were in Silver City, but they were quickly overshadowed by the town's most illustrious businesswoman, madam "Silver City" Millie. Today Millie remains an icon in Silver City, even though her last house has long been torn down. Millie preserved her own history by willingly confiding her life stories to friend and author Max Evans. Through Millie's willingness to tell of her good times as well as her hardships and struggles through poverty, violent marriages, and even rape, Evans was able to give an extremely well-rounded view of the life of a prostitute through Millie's eyes. Evans's book *Madam Millie* was published in 2002 and remains an open-minded and candid memoir sought after by history buffs.

Mildred Cusey was born Willette Angela Fantetti in 1912 to Italian immigrants in Paducah, Kentucky. When her parents died during the 1918 flu epidemic, Millie found herself orphaned at age six. Millie and her older sister, Florence, lived for short periods of time in hellish foster homes, then ran away to Kansas City and lived in an abandoned tenement. Millie went to work plucking chickens and came near to being sexually assaulted by her boss. The incident, combined with her rough home life and other threats such as being beat up by the local "toughs," made Millie strong and independent. The girls were soon discovered by authorities and again sent to foster homes. Millie lived with a police officer's family who mistreated and starved her. She saw her first prostitutes when she was twelve and was soon running their errands for money.[101]

Millie was eventually sent to live with Florence and her foster family. Florence, unfortunately, contracted tuberculosis and was sent to a Catholic home in Deming, New Mexico. Millie went along, working as a Harvey

House girl before learning that prostitution was a much more viable way to make money.[102] Early on in her career, Millie learned how dangerous her new profession could be when she was kidnapped, beaten, raped, beaten again, and left for dead by a seemingly polite and classy trick. When she was sixteen, she went to work for madam Billie at Carrizozo, New Mexico, for a time. While there she met her first love, Sheriff Tom Masters. She was soon temporarily retired, courting Masters and receiving expensive gifts from him. He even sent gifts to the sickly Florence, but life as somebody's girl didn't suit Millie, and they eventually broke up.[103]

By the time Millie was seventeen, she knew that the best way to make money was to run her own house.[104] She moved to Silver City in 1929 and went to work for the most promising madam there, Margie Dell.[105] "The town marshal threw me out of a house because I was under age," Millie later reminisced. "I told him I would come back and buy the whole block and run it to suit myself. And, p.s., I did."[106] After stints at Roswell, Tucumcari, Socorro, Lordsburg, and Alamogordo, Millie returned to Silver City and purchased bordellos from Margie Dell and Mildred Thomas.[107] In fact, Millie owned three houses on Hudson Street over time. Her main house was known as the "McComas house," named for the judge who built it. The judge and his wife had been killed by Apaches in 1883. Her other houses were the Bronstein mansion and the Swift estate. Because all three were in the 500 block of Hudson, Millie's places became known as "the 500 Club."[108]

Millie later also owned brothels in Lordsburg, Deming, and Hurley, as well as a ranch in Arenas Valley, property in El Paso, Texas, a bordello in Laramie, Wyoming, and cathouses, bars, and restaurants in other areas.[109] Like most madams, Millie was extremely generous. Over the years, she gave thousands of dollars worth of donations to charities, the Catholic Church, the poor, the uneducated, and families.[110] She and her girls put together Christmas packages that they would personally hand out to the needy, and Millie once purchased peanut butter and milk for the school children during a local strike. Even on Easter morning, Millie's girls dressed in their best "trick suits" to hide colored eggs for the local kids. In the 1970s, a retired cowboy recalled that during the 1930s and 1940s Millie willingly lent him $30 or so until the end of the month, admonishing him, "Don't you spend this in my place, now."[111] Millie even had a special room for those customers who overimbibed, preferring to keep them overnight than risk their being robbed upon leaving.[112]

FIGURE 58 ❧ *Millie Cusey, circa 1930s or 1940s. Millie was quite young when she joined the prostitute profession. Fortunately, she figured out quickly that becoming a madam was the best way to make a profit. Courtesy of Max Evans.*

Millie was also a kind but firm madam to her girls, whom she called her "little cats." Girls wishing to apply for a job had to provide references. Once hired, they were required to take a physical exam before coming to work and regular weekly exams during their employment. "I wasn't running a finishing school for whores," Millie said later. "If they didn't want to make money, I didn't want them around." And although the girls were not allowed to frequent local bars, eat in local restaurants, or be seen with their customers in public, Millie did encourage them to do their shopping in town. "I believe you should support the community that you are doing business in," she explained.[113] For the convenience of her girls, Millie employed full-time cooks and housekeepers; the latter were especially useful, encouraging customers to play the jukebox, timing their sessions with the girls, and collecting their money. She also strictly forbade her girls to do drugs or drink on the job. "If a girl tried to rob a man, Millie would arrest her before the police could," remembered an admirer. In fact, the one time Millie was robbed, she quickly deduced it was an inside job.[114]

Those who were allowed to stay at Millie's soon learned the routine there. New girls were sent to walk Millie's poodle, Lula. If Lula was sporting a miniature straw hat, fondly called her "whoring" hat, customers knew the woman walking her was new to town. These new employees began in rooms at the farthest end of the hall, gradually working their way closer to the bathroom and kitchen. One such girl, Birdie, once set a house record with ninety-seven tricks in one night and, when done, complained only that her feet were tired. The girls were kept on a six-week circuit, moving from house to house to keep customers happy. Millie's houses employed an amazing twelve to eighteen women at a time.[115]

During her career, Millie weathered several marriages and affairs. Her first husband, Howard Shapiro, was very wealthy but contracted tuberculosis. As Millie made her business trips throughout the Southwest, Shapiro began drinking more and seeing other women. While visiting her own bar, the Mint, in El Paso in 1933, Millie beat one of Shapiro's floozies unconscious. Charges were filed, but the case was dismissed. Shapiro died in 1936, five days after the death of Millie's sister, Florence.[116]

Millie's second husband, Ben Harker, eventually turned into an abusive drunk who beat her. Millie later admitted she had intended to kill Ben on several occasions. The first time was when he came home drunk with three dead chickens and ultimately "just beat the hell out of me with the chickens."

When Ben was arrested for the incident and subsequently released, Millie made him eat the same, half-cooked chickens at gunpoint. On another occasion, she pushed Ben into a septic tank. "I intended to drown him in that shit, pour the lime over him and let the honey wagon suck him up and haul him to the dump," she later explained. Ben survived and exacted revenge by breaking Millie's arm. He also stabbed Millie in the leg as she napped. Millie removed the knife and managed to stab Ben in the back as he ran out the back door. As she chased Ben down the street, the knife still in his back, she spied a neighbor working in his garden across the street. "Mr. Trujillo! Mr. Trujillo!" Millie hollered. "Catch that thieving son-of-a-bitch! He stole my knife!" When asked why she didn't leave Ben, Millie replied, "I loved his family. I loved his mother. I just didn't want to hurt them . . . they were the only family I had." Millie eventually got rid of Ben, but not before he gave her one more terrible beating in her own bar. This time the bone above her nose was exposed, an eye was knocked out of its socket, and her jaw was fractured. In the end, Millie required extensive plastic surgery and had to pay Ben $50,000 in the divorce.[117]

During a trip to Alaska during the 1940s, Millie learned that the mayor of Silver City was trying to close down her houses. She returned via Seattle, where she heard former First Lady Eleanor Roosevelt talking about the lack of orphanages for black children. Millie immediately contacted Mrs. Roosevelt on the phone and decided to make her Silver City houses available on a temporary basis. When the all-white city council heard that Millie planned to move 250 black children to Silver City, they changed their minds about letting her keep her houses open for the sex trade. She paid all the expenses for the people visiting on behalf of the children and made a large donation, but also got back to business.[118] In 1948, Millie and three other women were arrested on the complaint of Grant County health officer Dr. John C. Mitchell. The good doctor just may have been new in town; old-timers interviewed at the time of the arrests verified "that they cannot remember when Silver City has not had a pretty well defined red light district," the exception being during World War I. Nevertheless, Millie, along with Norma Miers, Roberta "Bobby" Alexander, and Dorothy Smith were charged with prostitution. Millie received the heaviest fines because she owned two brothels. She was also charged with hiring Dorothy for prostitution purposes.[119]

Officers staged raids again in November 1949 and arrested four women. Millie, out of town at the time, was served upon her return. The ladies had apparently weathered the raid of 1948 and were again operating quietly, their customers using the password phrase "I'm looking for Mickey" to gain access. This time, police also arrested three customers and padlocked the houses as the girls left.[120] But the push and shove between the girls and the authorities continued. The police would close a house, then the madams would pay their fines and discreetly reopen. When Bert Bowker shot Fred Runkle at Millie's in January 1951 and kidnapped a nude prostitute named Marie Mansicalco as he made his escape, however, the law could no longer officially turn its head. Word around town was that Bowker had actually wanted to shoot Millie because she was doing her best to prevent him and his wife from opening their own whorehouse.[121]

Bowker's wife, Marlene Joyce Bowker, alias "Dolly," was arrested along with her husband. Troy Winchester and his wife, Rose Irene Winchester, alias "Jackie Noorham," were arrested for stealing a watch. Mabel Brake and Gertrude Murrell were charged with vagrancy. Although the latter was too ill to attend court, Mabel pleaded not guilty and was held for trial. Even Marie Mansicalco, the kidnap victim, was fined $500. Added to the fiasco was Millie's charge that Dolly had reneged on a deal to buy some furniture. Dolly went to jail, but Millie paid a $500 fine and was closed down for a year as punishment. Bert Bowker got off the kidnapping charge but was sentenced to three years in jail for the shooting.[122]

Millie couldn't resist disobeying the judge's order to close for a year. Two months after the Bowker case was settled, a new girl in Millie's employ, Mary Nicholas, alias "Mary Valencia," bounced a check at a local grocery store. An investigation revealed that the girl was paying Millie half her earnings, the traditional deal Millie struck with her girls. Millie was charged with contempt of court and sentenced to ninety days in the county jail, then released without bond prior to serving her time. In fact, Millie had still not served her time by the time yet another raid took place in August 1951. This time, Millie had leased her house to Norma Myers, but she was present, along with Norma, two employees, and fourteen male customers when police knocked on the door that August night. Millie hid in a closet, claimed she was just there getting clothes when she was found, and pointed fingers at another madam in town. For all of her fuss, she and Norma were fined only $100 each. The police department's trust and even fondness for Millie were illustrated when she was again released on her own recognizance.[123]

Even the general public was fond of Millie, and in 1954 *Good House-keeping* magazine featured a story about her.[124] When New Mexico finally outlawed prostitution in the late 1960s, Millie was closed for good in 1968. Although she never forgave Police Chief Thomas Ryan for closing her down, she did admit that by then she was losing business anyway. "How can we charge for the same thing the college girls give away for free?" she asked.[125] Even in retirement, Millie remained very much in the public eye. She became a favorite pet of various newspapers who appreciated her candor about what it was like to be a New Mexico madam. When it was announced in 1978 that she intended to sell a warehouse full of memorabilia from her bordellos, the story was even picked up by the *Albuquerque Journal*.[126]

Millie married James Wendell Cusey in the 1960s and lived peaceably with him until he died in 1991. "I look across at his chair where he once laid his head," Millie wrote in a sad little memorial to him a year later, "and think of all the happy days that we shared together but now his chair is empty and those happy days are gone. But we will share more happy days in the Great Beyond. Always in my heart, your loving wife, Mildred."[127] Millie met James in the Great Beyond a little more than a year later. She died November 8, 1993, at Pinos Altos and is buried at Fort Bayard National Cemetery.[128] Her legendary places on Hudson Street had been torn down while she was still alive, replaced by the Silver City post office. Their passing made her sad. "A man once told me," she confided in 1978, "he didn't need the mail half as much as he needed me."[129]

North of Silver City was Hillsboro, founded as a gold-mining town in 1877. But the town's greatest claim to fame was madam Sadie Orchard. Born Sarah Jane Creech in England, Sadie first came to America in 1870, where she married and had two children. Her daughter eventually pursued a career as an actress but died at a young age. Her son lived out his life in and around Hillsboro and is buried there.[130] Sadie got her start in New Mexico at Kingston between 1882 and 1884.[131] She was described as short and weighing only about a hundred pounds, with tiny feet, blue eyes, a "creamy English complexion," and black hair. But she also had a "wicked chuckle" and "could swear with the best of them." Sadie once took a bet that she would not ride naked down Main Street on her horse. She won the bet, but she also helped collect money to build a church.[132]

In about 1886, Sadie moved to Hillsboro. She first ran a "hotel" on the west side of town but ultimately settled on the east side, where her place was known as the Ocean Grove Hotel. Built sometime before 1893, the hotel featured fine linens, real silver, and fancy furnishings. A specially designed dining room guaranteed privacy to diners, and Sadie hired a Chinese cook, Tom Ying, to prepare the meals. Ying lived next door to Sadie and remained a loyal employee for many years. Sadie later opened a second hotel around the corner called the Orchard.[133]

Despite moving to a rough mountain town, Sadie still enjoyed wearing clothing representative of the British upper class, especially when she was out shopping or riding her horse around town. With her husband, James, she purchased the Kingston–Lake Valley stage line in 1888 and soon became quite adept at driving for her husband's line.[134] "We had sixty five hand-picked horses, also an express wagon and two yellow and red concord stages," she later recalled. "I could handle the four-horse team and the heavy stage from the high driver's seat on top of the front of the stage, and I could kick the foot brake with the very best of them."[135] Sadie also boasted that her stages had never been robbed even when Indian bandits lurked in the area.[136]

Following the famous Hillsboro case of the disappearance of Colonel Albert J. Fountain and his son in 1896, Sadie took part in the festivities when several men were acquitted of any wrongdoing. On the night of the trial's conclusion, the stage line filled to a record twenty-three people. Sadie decided to throw a "proper English garden party" and sent engraved invitations to every prominent citizen in town. Many of the people invited were reluctant to attend a soiree hosted by the prominent madam, but the turnout was still good. James eventually lost the mail contract on his stage line and sold out to Fred Mister. A short time later the couple divorced.[137]

In 1910, Sadie was listed in the census as a hotel keeper. She won accolades again in 1918 when she tended flu epidemic victims and helped dig their graves. In fact, she was the only one the local doctor would allow into quarantined homes.[138] According to historian Jacqueline Meketa, "She cut up her silk and velvet gowns for cloth to line children's coffins, and, when needed, used her own buggy to transport them up the steep hill to the cemetery. . . . [She also] found homes for orphans created by the epidemic."[139] After the epidemic had run its course, the folks in town resumed their habit of not speaking to her and of crossing the street to avoid her.[140]

During Prohibition, Sadie kept a not-so-secret wine cellar and made her own beer. When two tax agents appeared at the Ocean Grove, she slipped

FIGURE 59 ⟶ *Sadie Orchard, circa 1880s. With her fancy dress, beautiful jewelry, and British accent, Sadie made quite an impression on Hillsboro, New Mexico. Sadie's Place was located at the very entrance to town, even though certain citizens tried to pretend it wasn't there. Courtesy of the Photo Archives, #58824, Palace of the Governors, Santa Fe, New Mexico.*

each of them a "mickey" and called some miner friends to come have a laugh at them after they passed out. When the men awoke, they left without pressing charges. On another occasion when Sadie was caught with the liquor, she followed a letter to a high-ranking official she knew in Santa Fe with a visit to him and his wife. She was acquitted. The 1930 census found sixty-eight-year-old Sadie living alone, possibly on her five thousand acres, and running a rooming house. She was also listed as a widow.[141] When she grew old enough to need assistance, her friends hired a man to take care of her for $50 a month. It eventually became apparent that the man left Sadie alone much of the time, checking on her only when he heard people were coming to see her. One friend remembered visiting Sadie and finding her "sprawled across the bed, too sick to even drink the small bottle of milk left there for her."[142] Sadie died in 1943 or 1945 at her Hillsboro house.[143] Only $45 dollars remained of Sadie's fortune. She was survived by a sister and a brother, neither of whom attended her funeral. Because nobody in Hillsboro could blast a grave from the rocky terrain, she was buried in style at the nearby Hot Springs Cemetery instead.[144]

Despite her sad ending, Sadie did well by Hillsboro. There were four saloons there in 1880. Thirteen years later the small town had an amazing sixteen saloons. Tom Murphy's Parlor Saloon was still doing well in 1898. Other notorious places included a combination general store, pool hall, and dance hall on a Main Street corner, the Union Hotel, which burned in 1904, and the S-Bar-X, originally a dance hall and later a bar. When Hillsboro lost the county seat in 1938, its population dwindled to just a very few people.[145]

West of Hillsboro was Kingston, founded in 1882. The area's mining boom began with Jack Sheddon, who had only recently been "evicted" from nearby Lake Valley due to his fondness for "dizzy dames and John Barleycorn."[146] Sheddon next found rich deposits in the area around Kingston, and the boom was on. Early on, Kingston was beset by a small-pox epidemic. When the local doctor was at a loss to employ respectable male nurses, he turned to three prostitutes who worked in the red light district, and they proved to be of much help. Soon there were seven thousand people in Kingston, their thirst quenched by twenty-two saloons, a number of gambling halls, and even a brewery, plus Sadie Orchard's first brothel on Virtue Avenue.[147]

Indeed, the folks of Kingston enjoyed nothing better than a rowdy Saturday night with crowds so thick it took half an hour to push ahead a mere ninety feet. The premiere of Pretty Sam's casino and dance hall was particularly memorable. The grand opening was held on Christmas Eve. Although the front of the new casino was level with the street, the back of the structure was built on stilts over a stream. Because there was no bridge leading over the stream, Sam simply nailed the back door shut to avoid a mishap. Brothel girls from all over town attended the gathering, including Big Annie and her girls from the Orpheum. Unfortunately, one of Big Annie's customers got drunk and forgot about the party. After banging on the door of the darkened Orpheum for some time, the miner finally remembered the party at Pretty Sam's and burst through the door, guns a-blazing. Big Annie led the rush for the back door in an effort to get away from the shooting. If she realized the door was nailed shut by the time she got to it, it was already too late. With the crowd pushing from behind, the door gave way, and Annie and several of her party friends fell headlong into the creek.[148]

Shakespeare, another Silver City satellite town, was founded in 1882 but was lacking many amenities, such as a church, a school, a fraternal lodge, and a bank. Even the red light ladies were brought by carriage from Deming or Lordsburg and returned to their homes at the end of the evening. During the late 1800s, at least one clever saloon owner found a way around the law prohibiting women from entering his place: he simply pushed the piano up to the window, whereby his female musician could reach through it and play while standing outside. In time, however, at least a few bad girls moved to Shakespeare. By 1917, when the nearby town of Valedon opened its post office for the first time, it was well known that those wanting to kick up their heels could do so at Shakespeare. Mining men from Valedon and Lordsburg who walked the railroad right of way to and from work could easily stop and partake of the libations and shady ladies there. During the 1930s, when a woman known only as "Mamie" who ran a bordello in Lordsburg was dying and the only girls she had left were a mother and daughter, Silver City Millie took over the management of the bordello and got it in good running order. When Mamie died, Millie bought the house.[149]

Yet another town associated with Silver City was Mogollon, founded in 1891. The high-mountain road to this town squirrels precariously along cliffs above amazing valleys, preventing any railroads from ever making it to town. Hauling supplies must have been extremely difficult, but almost right away after its founding the town had seven saloons. A miner from

Mogollon noted that, at first, three or four women would arrive in town on payday, conduct business, and leave after a few days. Where these mobile ladies came from or where they went remains unknown.[150] Two red light districts later developed in the town. On one end of town, one district housed white girls; on the other end was a separate district for Spanish girls. Because of the two districts and the town's difficult-to-reach locale, Mogollon quickly gained a wild and woolly reputation. Fire and floods wiped out the early town in 1894, but it was quickly rebuilt. More floods rushed through in 1896 and 1899, and more fires plagued the town in 1904.[151] Mogollon's residents, however, seemed to have a knack for persevering.

Even as late as 1909 Mogollon still boasted two red light districts and five saloons. When the Little Fanny Mine was staked in 1909, the population was about two thousand people. Two years later there were fourteen saloons and a number of brothels. More fires wiped out the town in 1910, 1915, and 1942, and the town was flooded again in 1914. But in 1915 Mogollon's two red light districts were still active. "Little Italy," located on the west end of town, was occupied by eighteen white girls. Fifteen years later the population had dropped to only two hundred people. The closing of the Little Fanny Mine in 1952 spelled the end for Mogollon.[152]

Boomtowns continued sprouting throughout New Mexico during the late 1870s and the 1880s. Engle, founded east of Truth or Consequences in 1879, hosted the Blue Goose brothel through at least 1917. Also established in 1879 was Otero, south of Raton, where the town's red light claim to fame was Dolores "Steamboat" Martinez. Dolores was a 350-pound madam who ran a popular dance hall. Another 1879 town was White Oaks, located northeast of Las Cruces. Certain historians claim White Oaks never had a red light district, but author Ralph Looney says that a place there called "Hogtown" catered to prostitutes. Author Philip Varney substantiates this claim, stating that Hogtown contained bars, casinos, dance halls, and brothels. Most others agree that White Oaks was never without at least one saloon. The Starr Saloon hosted stag shows and performances by traveling female troupes. Even today, the White Oaks Saloon and Dance Hall attests to the town's at least mildly bawdy past.[153]

The greatest evidence of prostitution in White Oaks is Madam Varnish, who appeared one day with three lovely daughters in tow. She was soon dealing faro at Hogtown. When the treasurer for the next county came to town, he fell in love with the madam, who promised to marry him in

FIGURE 60 ❧ *The ghost town of Mogollon, New Mexico, is somewhat lucky that when a movie was filmed there in 1973, some buildings were shored up and repaired. New buildings were also constructed, however, which today are hard to distinguish from the originals. Nothing remains of either red light district in the town. From the author's collection.*

return for support of her family. The deal was sealed, and the couple were married at Roswell. Two days later Madam Varnish and her girls returned to White Oaks alone. The new husband arrived by stage a day later, hotter than a pistol because his new wife had stolen the $3,500 he had stashed under his pillow on their wedding night. Madam Varnish was arrested and released on her own recognizance, at which point she made a beeline for the bridegroom's hotel. There, she promised that if she went to trial, she would reveal that the money had been stolen from the county. The charges were dropped, the husband left town, and the madam and her girls set up shop at the Little Casino, White Oaks's newest bordello.[154]

There was also Chloride, founded northwest of Truth or Consequences in 1881 as a mining town.[155] Shortly after its founding, Apaches attacked the general store, killing two. The incident may have kept any soiled doves or any woman for that matter from flocking to Chloride right away. When the

FIGURE 61 🙐 *Chloride remains one of the most complete ghost towns in New Mexico, with several homes and buildings attesting to a wilder day. This is one of the three saloons still standing. From the author's collection.*

all-male population offered a free town lot to the first woman settler, they hardly cared what her character was so long as a member of the gentler sex showed up. Their sentiment was illustrated by the additional offer of a city council seat to the father of the first child born in Chloride, "if it is known who he is."[156] The number of men and women checking into the Chloride Hotel in 1888 merited an announcement in the *Black Range* newspaper: "That assignation office on upper Wall Street is a nuisance and a disgrace to the respectable inhabitants of the west end. Such an institution should not be allowed to exist in the midst of a respectable community." Furthermore, the innkeeper had to declare a new rule. "From now on all gentlemen boarders who make application for sleeping apartments for female 'friends' must flash up their marriage credentials."[157] Today, a dance hall and three saloons, including the Monte Cristo, remain standing in Chloride.[158]

During the 1880s, railroad towns were also flourishing. One such town was Raton, founded as a railroad town in northeastern New Mexico in 1880. Bordellos were soon flourishing along Garcia Street across the tracks from the city's main drag, First Street. Well-known bad women of that time included La Josie, who had a peg leg but could dance up a storm, and La Suave, who was Josie's partner. When the business district relocated to Second Street, Garcia Street's bawdy women crossed the tracks and set up shop along First Street. The district soon spanned a two-block area on First Street between Rio Grande and Park streets. The district was conveniently located near the railroad tracks, with brothels also running up side streets just one block from the downtown area. Raton's red light district was most active during the late 1880s and into the early 1900s. In fact, a fire in 1888 originated in a brothel when a woman threw a lamp at a man. The red light district burned, but so did much of the business district.[159]

Very little is known about Raton's red light ladies aside from speculation about where they worked. Working girls probably plied their trade at the Gem Saloon at the corner of Park and First streets, built during the 1890s. The Palace Hotel at the same corner was built in 1896 by three brothers named Smith who had migrated from Scotland. When the building was run as Tinnie's Palace restaurant during the 1980s, the manager claimed the Palace was once a posh parlor house with private partitioned dining areas and a stained-glass likeness of the madam adorning one wall. In the same area, the Raton Hotel and Corner Bar was constructed in about 1910 and offered entertainment plus "lodging." The Coors Building, now home to the Raton Museum, also had rooms for girls upstairs.[160]

During February 1908, thirty-two women paid a total of $272 in fines in Raton. When a local deputy was caught embezzling part of the fines, he was found guilty after several prostitutes testified against him. The women were also unfortunately fined, $25 apiece, for admitting to being prostitutes. The incident caused a small uproar because the ladies had just recently paid their customary monthly fine of $8.50. Nobody is sure exactly when prostitutes ceased doing business in Raton. The industry probably met its demise during World War I, when the government cracked down on towns across the state and forced the brothels out of business.

Near Raton was Dawson. In 1907, the *Raton Range* reported on Lizzie Zeller, an inmate at Dawson's sizeable red light district. Lizzie had apparently been "in friendly dispute" with one John Jenkins over a gun when it

FIGURE 62 ❧ *The Palace in Raton, New Mexico, sits across from the depot but also in the heart of the old red light district. As a former owner claimed, the dining room on the first floor features a beautiful stained-glass entrance dome and private, partitioned dining areas. From the author's collection.*

went off, wounding Jenkins. Tom Jenkins, John's brother, was so incensed he went to the brothel where Lizzie worked. Upon seeing Lizzie, Tom called her vile names and promptly shot her to death. He was arrested, and Lizzie's body was taken to Las Vegas for burial.[161]

Although most shady ladies of Raton remain unidentified, plenty of New Mexicans knew about Bronco Sue Yonkers during the 1880s. Born in Wales in 1855, Sue was living with her parents in Nevada when she became known, at age fifteen, as a "daring horsewoman and a deadly shot with a six-gun." Sue's first husband was Thomas Raper, with whom she moved to California. Sue's devotion to her husband was evident when he was wounded during an Indian raid and she bravely rescued him. But her greed overshadowed her love for him, and when his Downieville mine played out, she left him for a "gallant scout." After spending a year or so in Nevada, where she was tried unsuccessfully on several occasions for cattle rustling, she moved to Colorado. There, under the name "Sue Stone," she briefly lived in Pueblo and owned a stage line between Conejos and San Antonio.[162]

Following her marriage to Jack Yonkers in about 1882, Sue and her new husband moved to Rio Arriba County in New Mexico. Sue ran a tavern in Wallace for a short time before the couple relocated to a place near La Luz in Lincoln County. The Yonkers settled in a cabin and lived quietly until Jack died of smallpox. Sue told her neighbors she buried her husband in a grave near the cabin and almost immediately set herself up as a mistress and prostitute for area cattlemen. She also began circulating among cow camps, offering her services during round-up time. During one of these excursions, she met and married Robert Black. She convinced Black to sell off his cattle and sign over his property to her. She used the money to run a boardinghouse in Socorro, and Black opened a saloon. When Black lost his tavern in about August 1884, however, a drunken argument with Sue resulted in his being taken from his own house.[163]

The spurned husband vowed revenge and turned up drunk at Sue's a day later. Sue shot him to death, then hastened to the sheriff's office, where she claimed her husband had come at her with an axe. The public in general didn't buy the story, so the sheriff was eventually sent to arrest Sue, but the sly woman was one step ahead of him and managed to escape. Sue's stepson, William Raper, and a son, Joseph, were arrested (exactly why is unknown). Only William, it appears, plea-bargained his way out of the situation and later joined his mother at her new location in Doña Ana. There, Sue met cowboy Charles Dawson and soon had him in the clutches of matrimony. In 1885, Dawson had a falling out with one John Good, and they decided that a duel at La Luz would settle the matter. Sue, her stepson, and two other people attended the shoot-out, during which Dawson was killed. Good was arrested and subsequently acquitted, but Sue's attendance at the event reminded authorities that she had been a suspect in the Robert Black case. She was at last tried for Robert Black's murder in 1886. During her trial, newspapers referred to her as the "Lucretia Borgia of the West," but she was found not guilty. The day after her release Sue departed for Arizona, never to be seen in New Mexico again.[164]

New Mexico's red light history continued expanding into the 1890s. When Gallup was founded in 1891 as a railhead for the Atlantic & Pacific Railroad, the old red light district was located along Coal Avenue. The Rex Hotel on U.S. Highway 66 also served as a bordello during the 1930s. At Cabezon, located near Gallup, the post office opened in 1891, and by 1920 the town was home to a number of dance halls and bars.[165] When

FIGURE 63 🌿 *Girls were known to work out of the second-floor rooms at the Rex Hotel in Gallup, New Mexico, as well as along Coal Avenue behind the hotel. Today the Rex Museum tells Gallup's history, but little is known about its shady ladies from the past. From the author's collection.*

Amizette first materialized north of Taos in 1893, it was called the "Cripple Creek [Colorado] of New Mexico." Cripple Creek's wild reputation no doubt influenced the settlers at Amizette, and before long there were scores of saloons and dance halls to choose from.[166] Likewise, the town of Bland near Santa Fe was also christened the "new Cripple Creek" in 1894. True to its Colorado sister city, Bland was soon a rip-roaring town. The best-known woman of Bland's red light district, "Diamond Queen," paid for the altar and a Bible for the Methodist Episcopal church.[167]

Also near Taos and Santa Fe was La Belle, founded in 1894 and, with six hundred people by 1895, large enough to support six saloons. The town was becoming a ghost by 1910, but in those fifteen years prostitution flourished openly. Certain cabins made up a small red light district, and other girls worked out of the second floors of saloons. Drinks were conveyed upstairs via a dumbwaiter. In July 1895, two brothers named Hagen brought several girls from Colorado Springs and opened a high-class sporting house complete with a piano. Although the outlaw Black Jack Ketchum and his bandits frequented town dances, the townsfolk never learned their true identity until after their capture, and the jail was said never to have held even one prisoner.

In contrast to La Belle's open-minded attitude toward the world's oldest profession, the town of Phenix, located near Socorro, soon found its bad girls to be intolerable. In the spring of 1895 the new sheriff in town declared that the Edmunds Law, which prohibited cohabitation without the sanctity of marriage, was being violated in Phenix. Within a few months, it was noted that sixteen ladies of easy virtue had departed, leaving only six or seven women to ply their trade at one of the town's two saloons.[168]

Northwest of the mining towns around Taos was Farmington, long used as a gateway for prostitutes wishing to access both Colorado and New Mexico. In 1905, the *Durango Democrat* published a letter addressed to the authorities of Durango, Colorado, commenting that since the city had ousted its gambling element, some of the members of that "fraternity" had been looking to open for business in Farmington. "Only a few weeks ago some ladies of the half-world made an incursion into our midst and settled down to stay," the writer stated. "But a number of contrary minded citizens firmly but kindly effected their speedy removal." The writer also admitted that doing so had created a public outcry among Farmington saloon owners. The only result, however, was that the citizens of Farmington organized an antisaloon league. The fifty-two members decided that the best plan of action was to refuse to renew liquor licenses as they expired, resulting in an eventual prohibition of liquor—and red light ladies—altogether.[169]

The authorities' actions in Farmington may have encouraged others who wished to abolish prostitution in their midst, including General John "Black Jack" Pershing. In 1916, as the military wrestled with the presence of brothel camps and U.S. involvement in World War I approached, Pershing opted to legalize prostitution in Columbus, New Mexico. The wild and woolly days were over, however, because now Columbus had strict rules regarding houses of prostitution. The established district featured segregated houses. Alcohol and firearms were forbidden. All other brothels in town were closed, and prostitutes who did not pass their health exams were run out of town. The women were examined once a week by two doctors, one of which was Mayor T. H. Dabney. The physicians received $50 a week for performing the exams. As a result of Pershing's actions, the incidence of venereal disease fell, although some infected women still freelanced in the saloons and managed to elude the law. Following the war, of course, houses of prostitution in Columbus and other places did open up again. One of them was at the village of Central, near Silver City. As late as the 1930s, Central had at least one African American bordello operating, George Washington's, which was run by a madam they called "Mama Della."[170]

THE UNDOING OF
UTAH'S SOILED DOVES

⁂ THE ROCKY MOUNTAINS INCLUDE MUCH OF THE EASTERN PORTION of Utah, particularly the northern section. As early as 1776, Catholic fathers Francisco Atanasio Dominguez and Silvestre Velez de Escalante first viewed what was to become Utah. Next came the trappers and fur traders, followed by the first Mormon emigrants in 1847. During the 1860s, especially after the establishment of Fort Douglas at Salt Lake City, prospectors discovered minerals in the canyons southeast of the city. Conflicts dividing the Mormons and "Gentiles" (non-Mormons) were immediate. The Mormon religion was deeply based on the discovery of "new scripture" promoted by Joseph Smith Jr. that promoted hierarchy, political rule, and multiple marriages. Thus, the Mormons proceeded to build their own private exile, a "Kingdom of God" in the Salt Lake Valley. Around them, Gentiles promoted such patriotic beliefs as free enterprise, independence, and equality. But the two belief systems often clashed.[1]

Prostitutes in general exercised no prejudices against either side of the Mormon/Gentile conflicts. During the Utah War of the 1850s, as Mormons battled the U.S. government over their autonomy, camp followers apathetically serviced Union soldiers stationed south of Salt Lake City and at Fort Douglas. Their presence was no doubt reviled by both the Mormons and the Gentiles, although the latter arguably felt that any man sporting multiple wives put those women in the position of prostitute as well. This feeling was even shared by many Mormon women. Many were of the opinion that plural marriage was comparable to enslavement, even though the Mormon Church maintained that women could not be forced into multiple marriages. Furthermore, the first wife of any marriage had final say as to whether her husband could take on additional wives. Although Mormon women may not have been forced into polygamy, many were heavily pressured into it by the church, their husbands, and their neighbors.[2]

In spite of Mormon president Heber Kimball's threat to abolish any prostitutes or their cohorts who infiltrated Salt Lake City in 1854, the sordid ones did come. Some of those early harlots may have even stood trial before William Drummond, the thirty-year-old associate justice of the Supreme Court of Utah. Drummond had secured his position from his home in Oquawka, Illinois, before traveling west to take his post in Salt Lake City. With him was his wife, whom he introduced as Mrs. Justice Drummond. She often accompanied her husband to court and sat right beside him. Sometimes, locals said, she would nudge him on the knee to indicate the number of years in prison he should give convicts. She also had the mouth of a sailor, and Drummond's new associates were soon whispering about the strange, ill-bred wife who liked to bang her husband's gavel.[3]

What folks didn't know was that Mrs. Drummond was actually Ada Carroll, a working girl from Washington State. Drummond had abandoned his legal wife and his children in Oquawka. When letters surfaced from the abandoned wife and were made public, Drummond and his mistress lit out for Carson City, Nevada, and later for San Francisco, where they were last seen boarding a ship. The 1860 census shows a "William W. Drummond" who was working as an attorney back in Chicago. It is possible that Drummond came to his senses and returned home to his wife and children. Ada Carroll, however, is nowhere to be found in the records.[4]

As early as 1856, Mayor Jedediah Grant admitted that prostitution had reared its ugly head in Salt Lake City. Mormon sentiments against prostitution were strong; police captain Hosea Stout recorded in 1858 that some men had gone to the house of one male resident "and dragged him out of bed with a whore and castrated him by a square and close amputation." Not even such a brutal attack, however, remained long in the memories of men seeking female companionship. Although initial visitors to Salt Lake City noted a smaller number of brothels and saloons within its suburbs, the coming of the railroad in 1869 caused that number to grow. By the early 1870s, Salt Lake City's red light district was well established on Commercial Street (now known as Regent Street). Even Brigham Young was forced to notice the number of taverns along Main Street in 1871.[5]

In 1872, several ladies of the lamplight were hauled into court, including Cora Conway, Kate Flint, Sady Hulbert, and Nettie Hutchison. Both Nettie and Sady testified that since they had been fined a few days earlier, they had since quit the business, so their cases were dismissed. As for Kate and Cora, per the judge's ruling, police officers were sent to their respective houses of ill repute to demolish all the furniture while a large crowd of spectators watched.[6] Among the spectators was Brigham Young, identified by the *Corinne Daily Reporter* as "the chief manager of prostitution."[7] Mormon newspapers went over the affair with a vengeance. "Now for these women, the low, nasty street-walkers . . . the low, nasty, dirty, filthy, stinking bitches—they stink—that will invite strange men into their houses and introduce them into the family circles . . . they ought to be shot with a double-barreled shot-gun."[8] Despite such insults and the loss of their houses, furnishings, and money, Kate and Cora and their coworkers refused to leave Salt Lake.[9]

Already in 1873, fines from prostitutes were so great that general business taxes were not charged to local merchants. In 1876, Salt Lake City saw the arrival of Matilda Turnross, alias "Emma DeMarr." Born in Sweden in about 1860, Emma worked for madam Emma Davis. Then DeMarr and her sister Alvie ran a brothel together, which they had previously done in Idaho. When Alvie married in 1883, she left the business to Emma. In 1886, however, she sued Emma, claiming that she had been defrauded. Emma won and two years later married saloon and restaurant owner Charles Whiting. The couple resided at one of Emma's brothels at 243 South Main but began investing in real estate while Emma leased most of her property to other madams. She took over her main house again in the 1890s, but in 1900 leased it again to Ida Walker, who successfully ran three other places of ill repute between 1891 and 1906. Emma and Charles also moved from the house and continued investing. In 1909, Emma sold all of her property for $120,000 to William Ferry, who became mayor of Salt Lake in 1915. When she died in 1919, she left most of her estate to Charles, about $145,000. The rest of her money went to her two sisters, a brother, and his three children.[10]

In 1880, Salt Lake City had five houses of prostitution. The 1880 census lists eighteen prostitutes, all of whom likely worked in these houses. Among them was Sadie Noble, born in 1854 in Boston. By 1880, Sadie was working for a madam in Salt Lake. Two years later she was running her own house, but closed it after a raid in 1886. Her employees were believed to have left for Butte, Montana. As for Sadie, she decided to get some muscle behind her. Upon traveling east, she married saloon keeper and former Mormon John Finley Free and had a daughter in Iowa. By 1887, Sadie and her new family were back in Salt Lake, where they sold her brothel and invested in new properties beginning in 1889. Sadie now called herself "Susie Free" and used her financial holdings to purchase bordellos for other madams to run. Her leasers included Jessie Blake in 1892, who fled town owing everyone money a few months later. During the financial panic of 1893, Susie had to sell some of her lots and mortgaged her furniture several times before losing most of her money altogether in 1895.[11]

By the 1880s, Salt Lake's red light district was located mostly along Commercial Street and Franklin Avenue. The predominantly white authorities raised few objections because the neighborhood was populated largely by racial minorities. Chinatown was located in Plum Alley paralleling Commercial Street. Other houses of vice were operating on West Temple Street between First and Second and on Second South Street. These houses existed in these areas for only a short time, but later popped up again during the 1890s.[12] In 1885, the Mormons decided "to expose the moral hypocrisy of the people who are hammering us" by pointing fingers at federal officials who were known to solicit prostitutes. Brigham Young Hampton, an adopted son of Mormon leader Brigham Young, set up a pseudobrothel on West Temple Street and hired two women "detectives" to entrap officials. Police watched through holes in the walls and netted upwards of one hundred guilty men. In a most humorous turn of events, however, the men who were convicted in Mormon court were acquitted by a non-Mormon judge in a higher court, and Hampton was sentenced to a year in jail for running a brothel![13] Nevertheless, authorities continued their campaign against the red light district. A bust in March 1885 netted fines of $99 dollars each for madams Flint, Davis, DeMarr, Lawrence, Noble, and Grey. Twenty-four girls in all were arrested, though only fifteen of them were fined $15 each. In August, Mrs. A. J. Field was also arrested for prostitution.[14]

In 1886, Salt Lake City had six brothels, forty bars, and numerous gambling houses. None was being run by Mormons.[15] In an effort to control the vice, officials made several arrests for prostitution that year. During one of the raids, it was noted that authorities thought "there wasn't much money" in the industry and so had waited for the women "to lay up boodle enough to make it worthwhile to effect a capture."[16] The girls were arrested, paid a fine, subjected to a health exam, and released. In between arrests, the women were "allowed to go along without fear of molestation as long as they did not ply their trade so openly and brazenly as to offend the public eye."[17] Salt Lake City was up to thirty-five bordellos by the 1890s. Like most other houses of prostitution across the West, the bordellos of Salt Lake were occasionally raided to keep the girls under control while raising revenue for the city. Madams were fined $50 per month, and their girls paid $8.50. The fines were accompanied by required health exams.[18]

In 1892, Martha Turner of Chicago was accused of attempting to defraud Minnie Barton. Minnie had leased a house from Emma DeMarr in November 1891 but then fell deathly ill. Martha came to Minnie's side in her last minutes in February 1892 and later claimed that the sick woman had turned everything over to her. The administrator of Minnie's estate, however, argued that the madam had been much too ill to sign anything. In the end, the Utah Supreme Court found that Martha Barton and Helen Smith (a.k.a. "Helen Blazes") had coerced Minnie into signing. Helen Blazes in fact survived the prosecution and remained in Salt Lake for many years. After successfully borrowing $1,500 from Martha Turner, Helen ran her own place at 243 South Main until at least 1894. Helen and three other madams were arrested again that year, according to the *Ogden Standard Examiner*. Following news of the arrest was a lengthy editorial against prostitution encouraging the city to abolish the industry in town. The writer of the article was no match for Helen Blazes. Beginning in 1895, the enterprising madam succeeded in running a house of ill fame at Sadie Noble's old place. In 1897, she moved to a house on Victoria Place.[19]

Indeed, during 1900 twenty-eight-year-old Helen employed no less than ten girls, all in their early to midtwenties. She was also regularly arrested throughout that year and may have taken a brief reprieve in Glenwood Springs, Colorado. By 1902, however, Helen's place catered to the wealthiest of men and served only wine. Lesser parlor houses and brothels served beer at a dollar a bottle. In 1903, Helen built a new parlor house on Seven South Street.[20] She did well in her profession: the *Salt Lake*

Herald reported in 1909 that she "has departed for Europe. Her establishment here has been sold. Miss Blazes will probably never return to Salt Lake."[21] Helen in fact did retain at least some of her property, leasing it to Harry Robinson. In her absence, Robinson leased it to Edna Prescott, who opened a new parlor house. Upon her return from Europe, Helen sued Edna for using the property for immoral purposes. The outcome of the case is unknown, and it is the last time Helen was mentioned in local newspapers. From all appearances, Helen Blazes retired from and even spurned her former profession; in her time, however, she was so notorious that in 1922 she was included in a Union Pacific Railroad poem.[22]

Essie Watkins, who was arrested with Helen Blazes in 1894, fared less well. A veteran of Dallas, Texas, Essie had been in Salt Lake only a short time before one of her girls killed a customer. Essie also violated certain social norms by employing two black prostitutes and boldly attempting to establish herself in the *Salt Lake Times* building. She was ousted almost immediately and next tried her luck at Kate Flint's former brothel on East Second South. Her circumstances did not improve; she mortgaged her belongings seven different times during a two-year span and was forced to borrow $800 from her mother. The year 1897 was her undoing when she was convicted of stealing another prostitute's property and again for not paying her fines. Essie left her furnishings and bills in Salt Lake and disappeared.[23]

Essie, of course, was not Salt Lake City's only bad girl. In 1894, a black madam named Nellie Davis was found guilty of abducting a woman for purposes of prostitution, but was released because the woman was "not of previously chaste character." Madeline Mortimer, another madam, was also arrested for grand larceny and keeping a house of prostitution.[24]

Authorities were up in arms over their wicked women by 1895. "I think the best plan is to put them [prostitutes] in one locality as much as possible," commented Salt Lake police chief Arthur Pratt, "and keep them under surveillance. The evil cannot be suppressed, but it must be restrained and kept under strict police control. It is a more difficult problem to handle when the women are scattered out than when they are kept together."[25] While officials debated over Pratt's statement, the red light ladies stubbornly continued business, as did several businessmen who had started investing in bordello properties. When Stephen Hayes financed the building of a brothel on Commercial Street in 1899, the building was designed by renowned architect Walter Ware.[26]

At last in 1903, city officials began seriously considering ways to restrict prostitution to one district. Houses of ill fame were beginning to spread beyond Commercial Street and included several brothels on Main Street and Helen Blazes's new parlor house at number 7 on South Street. At issue was how and where to move the district from the public eye.[27] John J. Held, who became a sports illustrator and cartoonist for the *Salt Lake Tribune* in 1905, recalled the red light district in Salt Lake City as it was when he was a child and it was located on Commercial Street. "Within the street were saloons, cafes, parlor houses, and cribs that were rented nightly to the itinerant Ladies of the Calling. Soliciting was taboo, so these ladies sat at the top of the stairs and called their invitation to 'C'mon up, kid.'"[28] Held's uncle earned money installing electric bells in the parlor houses of Salt Lake City, and there is little doubt the boy became more familiar with the red light district than most fifteen-year-olds would have.[29] Held recalled that solicitations were not allowed in the fancy parlor houses. One simply rang the bell and "was admitted by a uniformed maid or an attendant. The luxury of these houses always included a 'Professor' at the piano. There was none of the brashness of the mechanical piano; those were heard in the saloons and shooting galleries of the street."[30]

Held also remembered two prominent madams, Miss Ada Wilson with a lavish house on Commercial Street and Miss Helen Blazes.[31] Held's father, a printer, printed business cards for the two madams. "They demanded the finest and most expensive engraving, and the cards were of the finest stock, pure rag vellum."[32] From 1897 to 1908, Ada actually operated on the upper floor of the Brigham Young Trust Company building. Her place was called "the Palace." Other women, however, continued finding it hard to stay away from the eye of the law. In 1906, newspapers commented on Minerva Reeves, who had formerly been committed to the "industrial school" and was subsequently accused of trying to burn it down. In 1906, she was convicted of trying to kill her sister and another woman at a house on South Main Street. In 1907, Tillie Williams, also known as "English Laura," was convicted of petty larceny. Tillie had worked in Victoria Alley since 1897 and had only recently finished serving five years for robbery.[33]

John Bransford, a non-Mormon, was elected mayor of Salt Lake City in 1907.[34] Almost immediately new discussion began regarding what to do about the red light district. In his 1907 report, official Thomas Pitt came up with an idea. "Let the city set aside a piece of ground of sufficient size to accommodate several hundred of these prostitutes. Enclose same carefully with high fences; build cottages or houses to accommodate these inmates; charge them rent; license them and place them under control of the Police Department as to their safety and confinement, and to the Board of Health as to their cleanliness and sanitary conditions."[35] Bransford and others discussed this idea and many others throughout 1907 and into 1908, including an agreement that the red light district should move from its now prominent spot along Commercial to a more ethnically diverse neighborhood. By then, Salt Lake City's fining system had been simplified, with madams simply turning in a list of their girls with a $10 fine for each one. It was estimated that around 148 girls paid fines each month throughout the year.[36]

Despite these attempts at organization, Salt Lake City's red light district was now coming under fire by local citizens. Not only were brothels thriving on Commercial Street, but there was also one on South Temple and two others on East Third South. Citizens were becoming more and more enraged by the antics in the district, including the July suicide attempt of Myrtle Densmore. Not only was the attempt Myrtle's sixth, but all of her attempts apparently were in an effort to score attention from a lover who had spurned her.[37] Mayor Bransford, who had decided to act on Pitt's idea, announced to the public his intention "to take these women from the business section of the city, and put them in a district which will be one of the best, if not the very best, regulated districts in the country."[38] For some reason, however, Thomas Pitt changed his mind. Even as city officials moved forward on the plan, Pitt refused to follow up on it and was subsequently fired. He never publicly made known the reason behind his reverse decision, but it is notable that his wife was heavily involved in the Women's Christian Temperance Union.[39]

With Pitt out of the way, Mayor Bransford next set precedence by doing the unthinkable for 1900s prostitution reform: he hired Mrs. Dora B. Topham, better known as "Madam Belle London," to oversee the new red light district. Dora was an obvious choice, reasoned the officials. Not only was she a diplomatic businesswomen, but she also had a proven track record in Ogden and was Utah's best-known madam.[40] The only other prospects were Salt Lake's more notorious madams who had been dealing with authorities for years. It is safe to assume that authorities wanted a fresh start with a different madam whose antics were not known to the city's police or public. The appointment of Dora Topham in fact made history as

FIGURE 64 🙢 *Dora Topham, circa early 1900s. Dora's studious appearance echoed the way she conducted herself. A self-proclaimed reformer of prostitution, she hired only women who were hell-bent on entering the profession, but also discouraged a great many others from doing so. Courtesy of the Utah State Historical Society, Salt Lake City, 921 17253.*

the first time a city government actually approached a known madam to run a place of prostitution for the city.

Dora's early life is somewhat sketchy, identified only through guesswork and a few known facts. She is thought to have been born Adora Long in Kentucky. Alternately, she may have been born around 1865 in Illinois. Under her pseudonym "Belle London," she may also have worked in Georgetown, Colorado, during the 1870s.[41] Despite her marriage to Thomas Topham in Salt Lake City in 1890, she was soon known as the "Queen of Ogden's Underworld." In about 1896, Dora gave birth to her daughter Ethel, in Nebraska.[42]

Three years later Thomas Topham was accused of murdering one Charles L. Wessler. He was acquitted, but his involvement in the incident may have been the beginning of the end of his marriage to Dora. By 1900, Dora was apparently alone and running a house of ill repute in Ogden. Her employees included Dawn Frost, Leslie St. Elmo, May Rich, Pearl Mack, Jennie Anderson, and Annie Borg. It is certain that only Jennie Anderson's occupation as a housemaid is legitimate. Dawn Frost listed herself as a music teacher, and Leslie St. Elmo said she was a dressmaker. The other three girls put their occupation as "sewing." Also living in the house was three-year-old Ethel. Dora listed herself as having been married for ten years.[43] In 1901, she opened a new business on Twenty-fifth Street in Ogden. She also made a deal with the London Ice Cream Parlor next door to construct a three-foot-wide walkway between their building and hers so that men could access Electric Alley—the red light district's main thoroughfare—in back.[44] In 1902, she filed for a divorce from Thomas Topham for willful neglect. During the proceedings, she requested that her maiden name, "Dora Bella Hughes," be restored and that she be given $75 to $100 per month in alimony. Oddly, newspaper accounts of the divorce noted that Dora and Thomas had no children. It was also rumored that Dora had recently inherited a large sum of money from relatives back east.[45]

Dora's newfound wealth enabled her to take over the bordello on the second and third floors of the Livingston Confectionary in 1903. She also purchased three other buildings—the Gasberg Building, the Palace Billiard Hall, and another building on Twenty-fifth Street—in 1906. By 1908, when Salt Lake City authorities approached her about running the city's red light district, Dora's holdings were said to be worth about half a million dollars. Ever on the lookout for more prospects, Dora agreed to the deal. She immediately established the Citizens' Investment Company and began looking for land in Salt Lake City. She found some in a prime area close to downtown. Upper-class citizens were already vacating the area due to the recent influx of Italians and Greek immigrants who did not meet Salt Lake's predominantly white citizens' approval.[46] "I know, and you know, that prostitution has existed since the earliest ages," Dora explained later on, "and if you are honest with yourselves, you will admit that it will continue to exist, no matter what may be said or done from the pulpit or through the exertions of women's clubs. I believed that I could segregate the evil, that I could control it, and that I could decrease disease by an intelligent management, and while profiting financially myself, do some good."[47] Indeed, Dora not only truly believed herself to be a reformer of sorts, but also felt she could make the best of a bad situation by keeping firm control over those women who chose to follow a profession in prostitution. To Bransford, Dora's reasoning sounded solid enough.

In addition to being an ethnically diverse neighborhood, the city block Dora chose was far from schools and surrounded by railroad tracks. It was bordered by First and Second South and by Fifth and Sixth West. The new district, called the Stockade, was constructed at a cost of $200,000 to $300,000. Interestingly, the plans included every type of house of prostitution rather than a simple uniform code of just cribs or just parlor houses. Part of the reason for this setup may have been that some buildings were already in existence, although others were demolished to make way for the new district. Architect L. D. Martin, who was also on city council, was chiefly in charge of design. There is little doubt that Martin worked closely with Dora because the design closely resembled Ogden's Electric Avenue and Electric Alley. In fact, although the main drag was officially called "Boyd Avenue," census records referred to it as "Electric Avenue."[48]

The finished product included six parlor houses, each large enough to accommodate six women. A number of cribs were also constructed of brick. Each measured ten feet square with a door and window. Each was also partitioned into two rooms by a wooden wall or curtain, with a chair and washstand in the front and a fresh white-enameled iron bedstead in the back. There was also a dance hall, some saloons, and a cigar store. Dora had her own office, and there was even a small jail cell for anyone who got out of hand. In all, between 100 and 150 women could work in the Stockade at any one time. Later, restaurants and even opium dens were added. The

FIGURE 65 ❧ *The Stockade is shown here under construction in Salt Lake City, 1908. In this row, the cribs were built neatly and in an organized fashion. Courtesy of the Utah State Historical Society, Salt Lake City, 979.21 22357.*

entire complex was surrounded by a ten-foot-high cement wall. Outside of the Stockade, shops and storage areas completed the surroundings. Not so ironically, it turned out that Mayor Bransford owned property directly across the street and lost little time constructing housing for prostitutes as well as a saloon, a barbershop, and a coffeehouse.[49]

The city wisely opted not to reveal their plans until December 1908, just before the Stockade opened for business. Of course, by then word had gotten out, resulting in protests from various citizens. Bransford held a press conference, explaining that prostitution was here to stay whether citizens approved or not and that his best recommendation was that it be regulated, minimized, and therefore controlled. Bransford was backed by no less than fifty local residents who agreed that the Stockade would prevent prostitution from spreading throughout the city and "add to the safety and respectability of that portion of the city known as W. Second South."[50] Ten days after the press conference, Mayor Bransford officially ordered all prostitutes on Commercial Street and Victoria Alley to vacate their premises. He strongly encouraged them (but never directly told them) to take up their professions inside the confines of the Stockade, and their alternatives were limited because anyone choosing to remain outside the Stockade could leave town or be arrested.[51]

Dora Topham followed up Bransford's orders by personally contacting the local madams and offering them free room and board for a week if they would give the Stockade a try. "There is no danger," Dora assured the women. "I will protect you with my life, if need be. I know what I am talking about and want you women to show the others in Salt Lake that this place will not be molested."[52] Madams Cleo Starr, Madge Daniels, Irene McDonald, and Rose Bartlett accepted Dora's offer; only madam Lou Sheppard declined. Other independent operators also refused to vacate their old premises. "I own property here," declared one, "and neither the chief of police, the mayor nor anyone else will drive me away. I'll not go into any district or stockade and any woman who does, that is one who owns a house, is a fool. They can't bluff me. I'll stay where I am."[53] Edna Prescott, who leased Helen Blazes's old place, managed to stay put, as did Bee Bartlett, who stoutly refused to listen to Dora or to authorities. Dora ultimately advertised for women from other towns to make up the difference.[54]

In the end, it is estimated that roughly one hundred women chose to relocate to the Stockade. Dora welcomed them in, renting cribs to individual girls, procuring madams for each of the parlor houses, and laying down the rules. The parlor houses rented for $175 per month. The women of each house would receive 50 percent of what they made, and the madams would get the rest. Cribs rented for $1 to $4 a day. All profits were split with Dora. In keeping with a uniform code, all employees of the Stockade wore short red dresses and were subjected to regular health exams.[55] The girls were not required to live on the premises, but were warned that if they were caught conducting business anywhere else in town, "things would be made most unpleasant for them."[56] Police kept a register listing each madam, who was in turn expected to supply an up-to-date list of her employees. All girls were to pay a monthly $10 fine to the city. Furthermore, customers entering the Stockade were to be advised that an elaborate alarm system would periodically let them know that the police were patrolling the place and staging "raids." By doing so, the police were in compliance with other state and federal laws. Furthermore, the city posted policemen at each of the two entrances. With the laws and rules set in place, a grand opening was held on December 18, 1908, as the red lights on Commercial were extinguished and the new lights at the Stockade were turned on.[57]

Although the Stockade initially did well for Dora and the city, it wasn't long before issues developed. Customers wishing to avoid being seen entering the Stockade began knocking clandestine holes in the cement wall surrounding the place. When police grew suspicious, a second secret alarm system was installed to warn of any sudden raids to give violators extra time to vacate the premises. Added to the mix were complaints by the girls. Aside from being subject to stringent health exams every ten days, Stockade employees had to have permission from their "landlady" if they wished to change houses or to leave the grounds. Crib girls living in rooming houses outside the Stockade were strongly encouraged to pay the $5 per week at Mayor Bransford's place, the Plumas. All girls were required to shop only at places owned by the Stockade.[58]

To some women, the strict rules were a fair payoff for being able to conduct business unmolested by authorities. To others, the financial burden seemed to outweigh the financial freedom and independence they had on the outside. Plus, nobody appeared willing to play by all the rules all of the time. Dora Topham had initially issued passes for certain women to solicit on the streets directly in front of the Stockade. When it came to her attention that the passes were making the circuit among all the girls, she changed them to a nontransferable patch sewn onto the girls' skirts. In contrast, at least one woman claimed to have paid police some protection money even though the girls were supposed to be immune to arrests. In fact, in an effort to stay on top of county, state, and federal laws, authorities did stage raids periodically, and a few women were even brought to court. Sometimes the arrests were made by the county sheriff, adding to the girls' confusion and anguish. When such raids happened too often, Dora would announce the Stockade's closure. Most cases against the girls, however, were dismissed, and the Stockade would reopen.[59]

The tug-of-war between authorities, reformers, and Dora Topham continued throughout 1909. Reformers would visit the Stockade for the purpose of being solicited just so they could press charges against the girls. In an effort to make good, Dora also invited social workers from the Church of Latter Day Saints and other women of Salt Lake City to tour her luxurious bordello in Ogden and attend a fancy dinner. During the event, she proclaimed to be a reformer herself, promising to keep girls under eighteen out of her brothels and to explain to each applicant to the profession "the awful shame, degradation, and misery that is invariably the final result of seamy life in the underworld." If the prospective prostitute was still bent on life as a working girl after hearing such a lecture, "then I [will] receive her into my district."[60]

Dora's story proved to be a hard sell. To make matters worse, officials in Salt Lake were still dealing with madams who had been in business before the Stockade was built and who refused to give up their houses on Commercial Street. Citizens also pointed out that Dora's advertisements for girls throughout the West increased the prostitute population in Salt Lake rather than keeping it at a minimum. It was guessed that between ninety and two hundred women worked at the Stockade and that in Salt Lake City at large there were between two and three hundred prostitutes in all. Enraged citizens also noted that whereas Dora received police protection, brothels outside the Stockade did not. Then in May 1909, possibly in an effort to turn the pointing fingers away from themselves, Salt Lake officials proclaimed that Dora was the actual owner and manager of the Stockade and a member of the Citizens' Investment Company. What was not mentioned was the fact that Dora had been fined for owning a building used for "lewdness."[61]

Dora's only real defense was that during 1910 her house in Ogden was occupied by herself, thirteen-year-old Ethel, and a servant, but no working girls. Authorities did continue supporting Dora as best as they could without incriminating themselves. In 1910, 453 warrants were issued for women working at the Stockade, yet not one was served; police claimed that the entire block was deserted when they went to arrest their would-be convicts.[62] Dora, however, must have felt compelled to make a statement to the public about the Stockade. "I am the greatest woman reformer in the world," she told the *Ogden Standard Examiner* in March 1910. "When you know me and the grand work of reform that I am doing, you will hold me high in your esteem."[63]

The 1910 census offers much speculation as to the Stockade's success. During the census taker's first round, twenty-four women were listed as residing there. Of those, four women were married, and three were divorced. Two had children who did not reside with them. The occupations listed for the three women in the parlor house of L. B. West were "housekeeper," "chambermaid," and "hair-dresser." The recording of one of these women as African American indicates that all three may have been legitimately employed under their listed occupations rather than residing in a mixed-race house. The rest of the women were in houses with three to four women. Also listed was Madge Daniels, who was among those madams who had accept Dora's original offer to move to the Stockade. Madge was operating alongside several other women on Electric Avenue and had the largest parlor house, with ten girls. Only two men were listed in the Stockade, a Chinese saloon porter and a blacksmith named Edward Hardin. Because Hardin resided at the parlor house of Margaret Sanford, and because both listed themselves as being married for eight years, chances are they were husband and wife. Later, a supplemental record to the census indicated another sixteen women at the Stockade, but no more than their names are listed. One parlor house was run by Cora Walker. Two other women, Pauline Gostey and Adelaide Langlett, shared a house. The rest of the women occupied cribs. Furthermore, Japanese women said to work out of the westside cribs were left out of the census altogether, having no choice whether to provide information about themselves.[64]

Much to the authorities and Dora Topham's chagrin, prostitution continued to flourish in other parts of Salt Lake during 1910. Gustave Holmes's place on Commercial Street was home to French prostitutes, who probably were not allowed within the confines of the Stockade. Bee Bartlett was still employing seven women in Victoria Alley. Likewise, Cleo Starr was also no longer at the Stockade, but operating on State Street. Longtime madam Ada Wilson employed three girls at her bordello on South West Temple. The presence of women both inside and outside the Stockade continued to outrage citizens. One group, the West Side Citizens' League, had formed as soon as the Stockade opened and had immediately begun a barrage of petitions to the city council. Only two out of five newspapers supported the Stockade, and exposés constantly revealed the crimes committed within the block. Dora and her many employees were regularly harassed. Even though they usually ended with a dismissal of charges, the continued arrests became quite annoying.[65]

Then in May 1911, Bee Bartlett accused Dora Topham of using authorities to monopolize the prostitution industry in Salt Lake City.[66] Bee's accusation was followed by another charge, this one filed by Helen Lofstrom, that Dora was guilty of "inducing Dogney Grey, aged sixteen years, to enter the Stockade for immoral purposes."[67] The accusations in fact came two weeks after the ladies of the town appeared at a town council meeting, pointed out that elections were coming up, and voiced their opinions that the Stockade was shameful to the city and should be closed. Helen Lofstrom, who claimed to be the girl's mother, said that Dogney was drinking coffee at a local restaurant when a strange woman poisoned the beverage. The unconscious girl was taken to the Stockade, where she awoke to find herself a prisoner at the brothel of Ethel Clifford. Dogney also found that she had been dressed in the Stockade uniform and that her face had been painted. Dora allegedly refused to call the girl's mother, and when she finally did, the woman arrived at the Stockade with a loaded revolver and a young man to assist her. The daughter was rescued and, according to witnesses, married the heroic young man who helped save her.[68]

Helen Lofstrom's credibility slipped, however, when she let it be known that years earlier in Ogden, Dora had allegedly broken up Helen's marriage to a tailor who made costumes for Dora's girls. Helen said that Dora had sworn revenge, although if the story were true, Dora had nothing to get even for. Then Dogney Grey née Lofstrom testified that she had entered the Stockade because she had lost her job during a strike at the local laundry. Dogney furthermore apparently revealed that she had entertained some men she knew from Helen Lofstrom's rooming house and that her own sister was working at the Stockade as well. The charges against Dora were dropped, but considerable damage had been inflicted. Dora was next accused of permitting a house of ill fame on the premises. Despite several references and testimony on her behalf, she was ultimately accused of working as a madam by the same city officials who had in fact hired her to be one.[69]

The hypocrisy was too much, and at noon on September 28 Dora turned out the red lights at the Stockade.[70] "The Stockade will be closed on Thursday and the same will not be opened again," she stated to the papers. "So soon as I can arrange my business I shall advertise the property for sale."[71] Most of the newspapers, even those who were initially against the Stockade, immediately voiced their discontent at turning hundreds of women loose onto the streets of Salt Lake City. Their whining meant little to Dora, who meanwhile was convicted of pandering and initially sentenced to eighteen years of hard labor. The brazen businesswoman appealed her case to the state supreme court, however, where it was finally revealed that Dogney Grey had been in a Stockade parlor house a full day before Dora even knew she was there.[72]

The case was eventually thrown out in 1912, but both Dora and city authorities had had enough. Dora discreetly leased out one last brothel at the Stockade just long enough to get her business affairs in order. She sold all of her holdings, including her remaining bordellos in Ogden, and quietly disappeared. By 1920, she was living in San Francisco under the name "Maxine Rose," with Ethel, an eighteen-year-old adopted daughter named "Charlotte Hill," and several boarders. One of them was lawyer Thomas Matthews, who in fact had been Dora's police lieutenant during her Stockade days. What became of Dora for sure is unknown; in 1926, Ethel appeared to be living alone in Mayfield, south of San Francisco, and in 1930 was definitely living alone in Santa Clara and working as a teacher at the public school. She died in 1986.[73]

In the wake of Dora Topham's departure from Salt Lake, the local Women's League quickly organized a rescue mission for those prostitutes who suddenly found themselves unemployed. The effort was a very limited success. Rather than go to work as a domestic, most of the girls either left town or continued in the profession elsewhere in the city. Quite a few of them simply returned to Commercial Street. Ever anxious for the monthly fines the prostitutes might pay, the city obligingly looked the other way. It is guessed that only a dozen or so women sought the services of the Women's League. In time, the Stockade was torn down. Within a few years, Salt Lake City's red light district was once again considered a major public nuisance.[74]

In March 1914, Chief of Police H. H. Grant addressed the issue, reminding a large crowd at the Methodist church of his part in closing the Stockade and that "today there is not a public house of prostitution or a public gambling house in Salt Lake." He had also continued raiding houses in the old district. At present, Grant had police officers stationed in front of suspected houses with instructions to take down the names of every man entering the houses, no matter what the reason. As a result, most men were shying away from the new makeshift brothels. Grant further dispelled the myth that gambling houses and prostitutes still paid most of the city taxes. He was backed by local newspapers, which commented, "Evil is not necessary, but, on the contrary, it is undesirable from every point of view."[75] Despite the authorities' efforts, however, not all of Salt Lake's shady ladies were likely known. Newspapers also claimed that most of the city's prostitutes were foreign born, increasing the unlikelihood of such women being known to authorities.[76]

Salt Lake City's prostitution on Commercial Street ceased in the 1930s. The industry made a brief reprise as late as 1967, however, when it was noted that venereal disease had risen 100 percent and that homosexual prostitutes were in vogue. Mayor Joseph Bracken Lee employed a number of ways to crack down on prostitution, including through a loose interpretation of vagrancy laws and a campaign of haranguing businesses who catered to the profession. In 1971, he began using female police officers to work undercover to arrest men seeking services. The ploy worked somewhat, especially in 1976 when a Utah congressman was caught soliciting sex for hire following a Democratic Party campaign. In 1998, only one building remained from Salt Lake City's sordid past, the Felt Electric Building on Regent Street.[77]

Even as Salt Lake City launched into its historic campaigns against prostitution during the 1850s, other places around Utah sported red light districts as well. As early as 1858, Camp Ford in Utah County saw an influx of soiled doves. Frogtown was also settled in 1858 by recruits from Fort Leavenworth in the Cedar Valley. By summer that year, the new camp had a population of a thousand, consisting mostly of a motley band of soldiers, gamblers, laundresses, and prostitutes who often practiced more than one occupation. Murders occurred frequently. The soldiers were relatively safe due to fears of army retaliation, but risked catching venereal disease and being cheated or robbed of their monthly $12 salary.[78] Frogtown was alternately known as "Dobeytown" and at one point was said to have "a thousand or more inhabitants all gamblers or whores."[79]

When Camp Douglas was established in 1862, the usual camp followers arrived soon afterward. One day a soldier named McCoy who had landed himself in the territorial penitentiary received a visit from a woman claiming to be his wife. When it was brought to General Connor's attention and the woman was described to him, Connor replied, "It's that old strumpet, Mrs. Hall, that keeps at the mouth of Dry Canon." The warden approached McCoy about the matter, who answered tongue in cheek, "Mr. Warden, you introduced her as my wife, and I understand that you Mormons have a way of marrying by proxy, and I accepted the ceremony."[80] In fact, battles between the Gentiles and the Mormons over the morality of prostitution were frequent. Writer Orson Whitley discussed the idea of prostitution versus polygamy as early as 1870. "I am challenged again to prove that polygamy is no prevention of prostitution," he wrote. "It has been affirmed time and time again, not only in this discussion, but in the written works of these distinguished gentlemen around me, that in monogamic [sic] countries prostitution, or what is known as the social evil, is almost universally prevalent."[81]

Although larger cities tended to better support the Mormon culture, many of Utah's mining towns did not. Park City, just thirty miles east of Salt Lake City, gleefully made much money from saloon licenses and prostitution fines.[82] Only one initial complaint is recorded, when the *Park City Record* reported that respectable citizens were complaining about the "shirt-tail factory" in the residential section of town. The madam, reported the paper, was given thirty days to move. She relocated near the "green house." Periodic fines of $40 per madam and $20 per prostitute were made in lieu of a license being issued. The raids were most often made when city coffers were low.[83]

A 1907 ordinance banished Park City's red light district from its blatant location along Main Street to the nearby community of Deer Valley. Everyone, from the girls to the law, seemed to like it that way. The streets of Park City remained safe, and the red light district was discreetly located away from the general public. By 1910, the district at Deer Valley spanned sixteen houses along Heber Avenue. Customers there and other places typically paid $2.50 for a visit or $10 if they wanted to stay all night. At either location, the red light occupants paid regular fines to the city. In 1899, madam Francis Foster paid $10. Her girls—Bessie Scott, May Mitchell, Louise Wilson, Hilda Richardson, Hazel Morris, and Margaret Henderson—paid $5 each.[84]

Deer Valley could be wild; tales are told of the madam whose unruly customer poked a revolver into her breast. The gun misfired, and both escaped injury, but the man was arrested. On another occasion, a young customer tried to leave without paying and was held at gunpoint while his lady of the evening demanded not one but two timepieces he had on his person. The boy complained to police, but no action was taken. Gambler Fred Flint told of informing his long-time prostitute lover it was time to part company. The girl suggested a final drink together, only to collapse on the floor and die. Further investigation revealed the girl had tainted Flint's cocktail with a heavy dose of arsenic and drank it by mistake.[85]

Park City's biggest madam, quite literally, was Rachel Beulah Urban, also known as "Mother Urban."[86] Rachel was born around 1864 in Ohio to Irish immigrants. During her life, she married twice and gave birth to six children, only one of whom survived. Her last marriage was to miner George Urban in 1898 in Utah. By then, Rachel had been in the state since at least 1889. The couple settled down with Rachel's surviving daughter, nine-year-old Florence. In 1900, the threesome were living in Park City, where George was mining. Rachel's occupation is not listed in the census for that year, but she was probably in business. Her purple house at 346 Heber Avenue became known as the "Purple Palace." It turns out that Rachel actually managed all of Heber Avenue's houses of ill repute, which has led some to speculate that George, who also worked as a carpenter, built them.[87] Rachel also had a wooden leg and was known for wearing a striped dress. In such a dress, she was hard to miss because she weighed in at two hundred pounds. For those who might miss her, however, the brazen madam caught their attention with the black uniformed chauffeur who drove her around town and her well-known parrot, which from its perch on the porch delighted in cussing at passersby. In 1910, Rachel and George had several female boarders living with them at the house on Heber.[88]

Rachel's girls adhered to strict rules. They were not allowed to walk the streets, and to make sure they didn't, Rachel paid a disabled neighbor named Mr. Reynolds to run their errands. Girls caught breaking the rule were bought a ticket for the next bus out of town. The girls were also expected to be on hand for the annual Christmas party Rachel threw for the single miners in town. Mine owners appreciated this and her other services. They knew that if their employees could not find sex for sale in Park City, they might travel to other places, resulting in absences and delays in getting to work. Mother Urban, as her employees affectionately called her, also dutifully paid her girls' monthly fines, usually all at once. She was also known to take exceptional care of her girls, and her generosity spread beyond the red light district. One old-timer recalled that if there was a death

in the family, Mother Urban would discreetly visit in the night and give money to the family.[89]

Rachel herself tended to keep to herself for the most part, but there were exceptions. When the mayor decided to close down the district, Rachel appealed to a local mine superintendent who happened to be single. The man had a long talk with Park City's council, and the matter was resolved by changing the official occupation of Deer Valley's twenty-five naughty girls to "seamstresses."[90] On at least one occasion, Rachel managed to ingratiate herself with two of Park City's respectable ladies who were strolling past her bordello. The madam recognized one of them, Blanche Fletcher, as a local piano player and invited the ladies in for tea with the promise that the house was empty. After an enjoyable hour or so, the ladies made their leave, and Rachel asked the woman who was a stranger to her what her name was. When the woman told her, Rachel smiled and said, "Oh yes, I know your husband well." Whether her comment was a slip of the tongue or tongue in cheek is unknown.[91]

Rachel's efforts to be a part of her community are further evidenced by an editorial she wrote to the *Park Record* in 1913. The letter was submitted in defense of physician E. P. LeCompte. "Never in the history of the camp has a doctor been more attentive than Dr. E. P. LeCompte," she wrote, "and if he had just one-fourth of what is owed him he could undoubtedly move into Salt Lake with his family and live on Easy Street. I have called him hundreds of times to come over and see some unfortunate woman of the underworld and, unlike some of the other doctors, he did not ask me who was going to pay him . . . but he would come immediately and render all assistance possible."[92]

George Urban died in 1924 and was buried in Park City's cemetery. In 1933, Rachel died following complications from stomach cancer. She is probably buried in Park City Cemetery, but by then there was nobody left to pay for her headstone.[93]

In 1870, Alta, located just west of Park City, had twenty-six saloons and six breweries. Within a year, Alta had a population of five thousand that included two breweries and twenty-six saloons. Alta Nell and Kate Hayes were the reigning madams, the latter having a mine claim named for her in 1878. Likewise, the town Corinne was settled in about 1870 near the confluence of the Union Pacific and Central Pacific railroads in Box Elder County. By the time Corinne was a mere few months old, it already had nineteen

FIGURE 67 ❧ *Alta Nell (left) was the best-known madam
at Alta. Little else is known about the shady ladies of Alta, Utah;
today nothing is left of the original town, and the area is a ski resort.
Courtesy of the Alta Historical Society, Alta, Utah.*

saloons, two dance halls, and an amazing eighty prostitutes. Notably, it was a "Gentile" city and strongly discouraged Mormons from settling there.[94]

Prostitute Kate Flint is credited as being Utah's first official madam. Kate first settled in Corinne.[95] In 1870, she employed three girls and worked next door to two other women whose listed occupations are questionable. Two years later Kate moved to Ogden for a short time, where she was better known as "Gentile Kate." It is said that following the death of Brigham Young, she purchased his carriage, complete with Mormon symbols emblazoned on the doors. She would drive the carriage up and down the streets. Of Kate, author Bernard De Voto said, "She was a respected part of the business life of town, a speculator in real estate, the most liberal customer of the stores . . . and an unofficial great lady."[96] Like Dora Topham, Kate alternated her time in Ogden by opening Salt Lake City's first brothel on Commercial Street in the middle of downtown. Almost immediately she was arrested for prostitution. In no time, the notorious lady became a hot topic for local newspapers. Kate's name appeared in the papers four times in 1872, twice in 1873, four times again in 1874, and a whopping six times in 1875. In September 1872, her house was among those whose furnishings were destroyed in a public raid. Undaunted, she refused to leave Salt Lake and was back in business by December. One of her employees was Cora Conway, who had suffered losses in the same raid and could not afford to reopen her own house.[97]

In 1875, Salt Lake City authorities exhibited their rage against Kate Flint's newest brothel by raiding it. Incensed, Kate sued. She claimed they not only tore her silk underwear, but also stole some of it along with $1,000 in cash. Other madams sued as well, and authorities were in the end held responsible for "destruction of non-business-related property." Kate was awarded $6,000 to replace her damaged and stolen goods.[98] The court reasoned that Kate was no more in violation of the law than were Mormon polygamists. The *Deseret News* agreed. "If Kate Flint kept a house and it was proved that fifty men frequented it for purposes of illicit intercourse, and process could be issued and her furniture and household goods be broken up therefore, the same could be done with say John Smith, who might have in his house twelve women with whom he had illicit sexual intercourse."[99] The *Salt Lake Tribune*, which enjoyed taking a stance against Mormons, also agreed with Kate. "What is the difference?" the newspaper asked. Mormons had an answer: prostitution is lechery, whereas polygamy is an act commanded by

God.[100] Kate's victory was echoed by Cora Conway's successful suit in court in which she was awarded $2,600. When Cora was arrested nine days after the award, however, she apparently left town.[101]

By 1880, Kate was married to D. Frank Connelly, who invested in red light property for her. But she was apparently a widow by 1887 when a fire at her place caused $150 worth of damage. Kate sold her property a year later for $25,000 and moved, at least for a time, to respectable Social Hall Avenue. In 1890, Kate's property at the corner of Fifth South and Fourth East streets was valued at more than $17,000. One morning in January 1896, Kate opened the door to her house to find a box sitting on the porch. Inside were a diamond necklace and two bracelets belonging to her, worth thousands of dollars. Two diamonds, valued at $800 to $1,000, were missing from the necklace. Up until they appeared on her porch, she had had no idea that the items had been stolen. A well-known sporting man who had been down on his luck was suspected, but the culprit does not appear to have been caught.[102] The last mention of Kate in the papers was in 1898, when a *Salt Lake Tribune* reporter interviewed someone who remembered when a mortuary opened next door to Kate's. A passing policeman asked her how she liked it, and she replied, "Oh, that's allright; sin and the wages of sin ought to go together."[103] Kate apparently left Ogden and Salt Lake in the early 1900s, and what became of her is unknown.[104]

In fact, soon after Ogden's red light district experienced its first boom in 1870, the city's soiled doves practically became interchangeable with those at Salt Lake City just forty miles away. City authorities appear to have largely been disinterested in Ogden's red light district until February 1904, when revenue officers announced their plans to go after it with a vengeance. The district on Twenty-fifth Street, better known as Electric Avenue, contained thirty-three houses (the alley behind the street was called "Electric Alley"). A new law decreed that the proprietors of such houses would now be required to buy liquor licenses that would be good until the end of the fiscal year on July 1. The *Ogden Standard Examiner* reported that all thirty-three houses paid. The paper also addressed the Hudson Avenue district, which had been taxed "some time ago." Following the part-time departure of Dora Topham—Ogden's primary red light landowner—in 1908, authorities cracked down harder. In January 1912, reformers of Ogden's red light district decreed that no more liquor would be sold in the district. But prostitution flourished well into the 1920s on Twenty-fifth Street, and mafia boss

FIGURE 68 ❧ *When Dora Topham left Ogden to open the Stockade at Salt Lake City in 1908, she also retained ownership of some of her brothels in Ogden. This building is just one of many she owned, all of which now operate as legitimate businesses. From the author's collection.*

THE UNDOING OF UTAH'S SOILED DOVES   321

Al Capone even commented that Ogden's vice district was too rough even for him. During the 1930s, much of the city's illicit businesses literally went underground during Prohibition.[105]

Historian John Costello theorized that World War II expanded the sexual boundaries for soldiers and women. The prospect of dying at any time unleashed inspiration to live life as if there were no tomorrow. Unfortunately, this approach to life created a "love 'em and leave 'em" attitude among servicemen, who fell in love for a night or even got married, only to go to war and forget the girls they left behind. Thus, it was suggested that prostitution be condoned so the servicemen could have a last hurrah before being shipped out with fewer strings attached. In Ogden, Two-Bit Street (a play on words— the red light district was located on Twenty-fifth Street) actually expanded during the war, its prostitutes called "Victory Girls."[106] During 1942–43, when Mayor Harman Peery was in office, eleven houses of prostitution were still operating in Ogden. Four of them were owned by Rosette Duccinni Davie and Bill Davie: the Rose Rooms, the Denver Hotel, the Wilcox Hotel, and La Siesta Hotel. Rosette was particularly flamboyant, publicly expressing her opinions about prostitution in general while walking her pet ocelot (a small leopard) or driving her rose-colored Cadillac convertible along the city streets. The situation seemed agreeable enough to Mayor Peery, who, like others before him, felt it was better to control the vice and make money off of it at the same time. He remained in office through 1949.[107]

When Peery was succeeded by W. Rulon White in about 1949, however, the latter did much to clean up the red light district. Of particular interest to the public was the arrest and conviction of Rosette and Bill Davie, who were sentenced to two and a half years and five years, respectively, for prostitution. Another notable police bust was that of Eddie Doherty, tagged as "a big-time gambler, pimp, dope peddler and junkey [sic]." Several brothels that included the Parkway Hotel, the Rose Rooms, the Wilcox Rooms, the Wilson Rooms, and the Wyoming Rooms were closed down. By 1955, prostitution was nonexistent on Twenty-fifth Street, although it was still prevalent in the back alleys and remote parts of Weber County.[108] Today, Ogden's shady ladies are just a memory; in a 2003 interview, resident Tom Reese remembered that his grandmother was once a Twenty-fifth Street madam. "But I was so young I didn't know," he said. "All these women around, I just thought she was popular. We used to watch people coming out of the bus station, drunk. It was a wonderful childhood."[109]

Like every other state in the Rocky Mountains, Utah authorities battled the ups and downs of prostitution as their cities boomed and busted. Perhaps the most unique facet of the industry in Utah, therefore, was "the Strip," a section of land that was literally hands off to all law enforcement. The beginnings of the Strip date to 1886, when Fort Duchesne was established in a northeastern section of Utah. Coincidental to the fort's opening was the discovery of "gilsonite," a mineral that could be processed for water proofing. The trouble was that the initial mines staked by Samuel Gilson, Bert Seaboldt, and other miners were located on Ute land. In order to carry on their business, Seaboldt and Gilson successfully appealed to Congress to purchase the land and decree it as public lands so they could continue mining in 1888. More than seven thousand acres became U.S. government property and therefore not subject to any county or state law. Almost immediately, the Strip, as this property became known, was a lawless place where towns could openly sport prostitution, gambling, and liquor without any law interfering. By its own decree, the place was also not subject to Indian or county law aside from requiring all businesses to be licensed. Federal laws still applied, but because laws against vice were in general local, the occupants of the Strip literally lived law free.[110]

The Strip soon drew an amazing variety of ne'er-do-wells, from outlaws to gamblers to prostitutes. The first hotel, built by J. F. Colberth, doubled as a bordello. A dance hall was next door.[111] Elza Lay, a member of Butch Cassidy's notorious Wild Bunch, was among the first to establish a saloon. Lay alternated his time at the saloon with counterfeiting silver dollars, and before long his place was known as the Strip's "worst gambling-hell saloon."[112] Lay's cohorts often found shelter from the law within the Strip's boundaries. In a time when the Wild Bunch boys spent much of their time holed up in cabins and camps along the Outlaw Trail in Utah, Colorado, and Wyoming, a visit to the Strip was a welcome relief from the constant fear of arrest in any other law-abiding city. Other outlaws and their gangs, namely Red Bob and his notorious Red Sash Gang, also found temporary shelter there.[113]

Things were soon so out of control on the Strip that in December 1888 Major Chaffee of Fort Duchesne requested the Strip be made part of the fort to "exclude whiskey ranches, which are now a nuisance." For unknown reasons, Chaffee was turned down. Major James F. Randlett, commanding officer in 1892, sent a similar request, but was again denied. During this time, the *Vernal Express* jokingly called the Strip "Sobertown" and "Sober City." Both officers had issued their pleas on the basis that their soldiers were visiting the Strip too often. Randlett's solution was to post guards at the Duchesne River Bridge, but the men simply walked beyond the bridge and swam across the river. Because liquor was forbidden at the fort, the men would drink their purchased whiskey on the way back to the post and throw the empties in a ravine that came to be known as "Bottle Hollow." As a boy, Clarence Dean Powell would gather the discarded bottles in a gunny sack and drag them to saloon owner Tom Nichols, who paid three to five cents per bottle. Any soldier caught at the saloons or bawdy houses at the Strip was arrested and fined a month's pay.[114]

Given that the Strip was so close to Vernal and the hideouts of the Wild Bunch, there is no doubt that members of the gang, along with their outlaw ladies, visited there often. Among them would have been Etta Place, who remains the most intriguing of the Wild Bunch women. Maude Davis Lay, Ann and Josie Bassett, Laura Bullion, Lillie Davis Carver, Della Moore, Annie Rogers Logan, Dora Lamorreaux, and Mary Calvert, among many other women, deserve recognition for daring to date members of Butch Cassidy's notorious gang. But Etta stands out as the most sophisticated, beautiful, and mysterious, and her story has fascinated historians for decades.[115]

The simplest facts are these. Etta Place ultimately became the girl-friend of Wild Bunch member Harry Longabaugh, alias the "Sundance Kid." She accompanied Sundance and fellow Wild Bunch member Robert Leroy Parker, alias "Butch Cassidy," to Bolivia for a few years. She eventually returned to the United States and disappeared into obscurity. The rest of Etta's story is a true mystery, though, that has been speculated on by hundreds of researchers, historians, writers, and even the Pinkerton Detective Agency, who tracked the Wild Bunch all over the West and beyond. Three burning questions about Etta remain to this day: Where did she come from? What was her real name? And what became of her?

The only real clue to Etta Place's physical identity is a 1901 photograph taken with Sundance in New York shortly before the couple, along with Butch, embarked on their fateful journey to Bolivia.[116] The photograph matches Pinkerton Detective Agency's description of Etta, who stood about five feet four inches tall, weighed around one hundred pounds, and wore her hair "on top of her head in a roll from the forehead."[117] Marvel Lay Murdock, daughter of Maude Davis and Elzy Lay, remembered her mother

FIGURE 69 The Sundance Kid and Etta Place were having a fine time as New York tourists when a local photographer took their portrait in 1901. Etta may be wearing the fancy watch they recently purchased at Tiffany's. Courtesy of the Library of Congress, Washington, D.C.

saying that Etta was beautiful, tall, and stately and that she admired her very much.[118]

There are also some random descriptions of Etta by people who knew her, including Butch Cassidy himself. According to historian Kerry Ross Boren, Butch once spent the better part of an hour talking to Boren's grandfather, Willard Schofield, about Etta as he sat in a saloon in Linwood. Butch spoke fondly of Etta that night. "He didn't come right out and say anything," Schofield related, "but I could tell that he was anxious to tell someone about it and he spent nearly an hour just telling about things she did."[119] According to Percy Seibert, who worked with Butch Cassidy in Bolivia before returning to the United States in 1906, Butch once described Etta as "a great housekeeper with the heart of a whore." Given Butch's fondness for and tenderness toward wayward women, the remark can be considered a compliment.[120] Beyond these scant descriptions, statements about where Etta came from are rife with speculation. Pinkerton's estimated her birth year to be 1874, but she is also thought to have been born between 1875 and 1880.[121] Sundance Kid biographer Ed Kirby claims Etta was the daughter of Emily Jane Place of Oswego, New York, a distant cousin of Sundance's mother, Annie G. Place. If that is true, Etta probably knew Sundance in Pennsylvania long before coming West. Others say Etta was born in Pennsylvania.[122]

Other historians give the very confusing explanation that Etta was Laura Etta Place Capel, daughter of George Capel, who was the seventh earl of Essex in England.[123] In this explanation, Etta's mother is identified as American actress Emily Jane Place or one Anna Louisa Morton. When the unwed Emily became pregnant, George fled to Wyoming (some say in 1871) and began using the alias "George Ingerfield." Etta was allegedly born to Emily in New York in 1877 (making the 1871 date inconsistent) or possibly in Innishannon, County Cork, Ireland. Ten years later, either Etta's father took her to Wyoming, or she ran away from Ireland at age thirteen and went to America to find her father. Father and daughter sometimes stayed at the fancy and lavish "76" Ranch along the Powder River near Kaycee, Wyoming. The 76 was owned by Morton and Richard Frewen, who were either George's cousins or his childhood friends.[124] Another version of Etta's story claims that Ingerfield fathered Etta by a Mexican prostitute in Arizona. It should also be noted that Butch Cassidy used the alias "George Ingerfield" while in Bolivia with Sundance and Etta. If father and daughter did indeed hook up, Capel/Ingerfield was thriving as a cattle rustler, and Etta allegedly learned the trade from him. When he was killed in Arizona around 1892, Etta was raised by her father's outlaw friends, who paid for her education.[125]

The claim of Etta's relationship to the Capels appears to be almost entirely based on an alleged autobiography she supposedly penned herself under a pseudonym in 1928. Her story asserts that she was born November 25, 1876, near Dublin, Ireland. In this newly surfaced document, Etta says she was christened "Beatrice Desmond" after her grandmother. She also says that only one man, a British police official, knew of her true identity. Interestingly, historians have noted that the names "Capel" and "Place" are anagrams. Another theory suggests that Etta may have been Butch Cassidy's cousin Ann Parker. Ann was born in 1879 at Kanosh, Utah, and grew up in Joseph. Similar birth years and looks link the two women, but nothing has ever been proven. Authors Donna Ernst (a niece of Sundance) and Dan Buck say that Etta's real name was "Ethel," which is also supported by Pinkerton documents. Pinkerton's also used "Eva," "Rita," and "Etta" as possible names for Etta, but must have thought the latter was the most likely choice because it used that name in its wanted posters.[126]

Pinkerton's also believed Etta's parents might have resided in Texas. Circumstantial evidence included testimony from people who later knew Etta in Argentina in which they said she spoke some Spanish and knew how to cook Mexican dishes. Because so many believed Etta may have worked for madam Fannie Porter in Texas, including Pinkerton detective Frank DiMaio, Ernst and Buck researched women fitting Etta's description in Texas census records. They located an Ethel Bishop, prostitute, who lived with four other prostitutes near Fannie Porter's in San Antonio in 1900.[127] The census lists Ethel as working for madam Jessie Sewall at 212 S. Concho Street in San Antonio. She was born in West Virginia in September 1876, to parents who were also natives of that state. Ethel was single with no children, she could read and write, and her occupation was listed as "music teacher." Unfortunately, as interesting as this information is, it is inconclusive whether Ethel Bishop was in fact Etta Place.[128]

Alternative theories place Etta in Monticello, Utah, after the death of her supposed father. There, she lived with another relative known as Lord Carlisle. It was also at Monticello that Etta may have first met Butch Cassidy, or Butch may have brought her there after he rescued her from Fannie

Porter's. In another version, Butch took sixteen-year-old Etta from Fannie's, where she was working under the name "Laura," and took her to Price or Wellington, Utah, where she lived with a Mormon family named Thayne. Butch then returned to Wyoming.[129] There, Etta took the name "Hazel" or "Ethel" and taught school for a short time before meeting the Sundance Kid. In 1970, a man named Harry Thayne Longabaugh, also known as "Harry Longabaugh II" and "Robert Harvey Longabaugh," claimed to be the son of Harry Longabaugh. He also said Etta Place's real name was "Hazel Tryon" or "Tryone." Thayne-Longabaugh claimed that Hazel (Etta) was a half-sister of his mother, Anna Marie Thayne. Census records from Wellington and Price show the "Thayn" family, but nobody named Anna Marie is among them. Author Kerry Ross Boren claims that Sundance dated Annie Thayne before Laura Etta Place Capel-Ingerfield stole him away. Etta, Thayne-Longabaugh said, married twice and had two children, abandoning her family to run off with Sundance after Thayne-Longabaugh was born in 1901. There is also speculation regarding Etta's last name. The Sundance Kid sometimes used the alias "Harry A. Place," and some believe Etta did not use that surname until she met Sundance. Later, in Argentina, Etta was also known to go by "Anna Marie Place." Interestingly, the first two names in Etta's alias match "Anna Marie Thayne," who is speculated to have been Etta's half-sister.[130]

Equally numerous are theories about how Etta Place met Butch Cassidy and the Sundance Kid. At least one author maintains that the outlaw pair first met Etta in 1893, when they used money from one of their robberies to pay for her schooling at the State Normal and Training School in Buffalo, New York. Etta received her teacher's certificate and went to work in Telluride, Colorado, but soon found the life of a teacher boring.[131] Mrs. Jane Fish came forward in 1990 and said she "was pretty sure" Etta was her father's second cousin from Door County, Wisconsin. Etta's father, according to Mrs. Fish, was thought to have been murdered by Sundance in 1894.[132] Some say Etta received her schooling before she rejoined her outlaw friends at Robbers Roost, located near Horseshoe Canyon in northern Wayne County about twenty-five miles east of Hanksville, in 1895. In his romanticized history of the Wild Bunch, author James Horan claims Sundance did not meet Etta until 1901 at Fannie Porter's.[133]

Overall, most historians agree that in 1896 Butch Cassidy and Elzy Lay were living in a cabin rented to them by rancher Jim Jones. The cabin was located near Maesar north of Vernal, close to the home of the parents of Lay's companion, Maude Davis. That fall, Elzy and Maude supposedly married and moved in with Butch, dividing the cabin with blankets strung across a wire down the middle of the room.[134] Butch's youngest sister, Lula Parker Betenson, stated in her book *Butch Cassidy, My Brother*, that Pearl Baker, author of *The Wild Bunch at Robbers Roost*, had mistakenly said Etta was living with Butch, not Sundance. "Butch had more sense than to play around with Sundance's girlfriend," Lula explained.[135] Even so, the woman sharing the cabin with Butch and the Lays is thought to have been Etta Place, or perhaps Ann Bassett or Sadie Moran, both daughters of nearby ranchers. Baker theorized that the woman could also have been named Rose Maguire or Nancy Ingalls. Although Ann Bassett was the daughter of a prominent rancher at Brown's Park (also known as Brown's Hole) along the Green River who was good friends with Butch, it is suspected she may have also worked from time to time as a prostitute.[136]

Butch and his outlaw friends spent Thanksgiving Day of 1896 at the Bassett Ranch, during which Butch and Sundance playfully served as waiters. Some writers believe Etta Place was present during the festivities and that this was when Etta first began her relationship with the Sundance Kid. Others say Etta was at the Bassett Ranch as Butch's companion, although Ann Bassett was also present.[137] It is also interesting to note that despite theories that Ann was a Wild Bunch prostitute, her sister, Josie, "who it is known escorted both Butch and Elzy Lay to dances and may have dated them," is cleared of the same charge for some reason, even though she was also once the girlfriend of Wild Bunch member Will Carver.[138] Friends of the Wild Bunch noted that Josie was actually Butch's favorite Bassett sister. A neighboring rancher named Meacham once claimed he saw Josie and Ann get into a "knock-down-drag-out fight" over Butch.[139] One also wonders if Ann's respectable father would permit her to run off and live with Butch Cassidy in an outlaw cabin.

Following the holiday, the men rode off to Robbers Roost. They were later joined by Ann Bassett or Etta Place, depending on the source. The mystery lady, along with Maude Lay, remained at the cabin until March 1897, when Wild Bunch member Blue John Griffith took them to town.[140] In the summer of 1897, Butch Cassidy and his cohorts, fresh from the robbery of the Pleasant Valley Coal Company's payroll office at Castle Gate, moved from their hideout at Robbers Roost to a spot under the Orange Cliffs some twelve miles east of Horseshoe Canyon. New tents were purchased, and three women who were new to the Bunch came to stay—Maggie Blackburn, Ella Butler, and Millie Nelson. Whether these women were prostitutes is unknown. Author Charles Kelly maintains that Millie and Maggie were from the town of Loa and that on at least two occasions, two of the women were sent to buy supplies. The girls were spotted first in Green River and later in Price buying, among other items, plenty of ammunition.[141]

Who the three mysterious dames were at the hideout remains a mystery, but by 1900 the speculated romance between Sundance and Etta Place had become fact. By December that year, the couple were on their way to New York to catch a ship to Bolivia.[142] They spent New Year's Eve and early January 1901 in New Orleans before boarding a train for Pennsylvania to visit Sundance's sisters and brother.[143] In mid-January, they traveled to New York. Some think they may have married during this time, but all that is known for sure is that Sundance and Etta checked into Dr. Pierce's Invalids Hotel in Buffalo. The place was a spa of sorts offering Turkish baths and holistic medicine for healing "chronic diseases, specifically those of a delicate, obscure, complicated or obstinate character." Thus, many historians theorize the couple were being treated for venereal disease, although others have pointed out that Sundance was suffering from an old gunshot wound to his left leg and might have had tuberculosis.[144] Whatever their ailments, the couple were well enough upon checking out to visit Niagara Falls before joining up with Butch in New York City.[145]

Some historians say that Butch initially objected to Etta's going to Bolivia, but that Sundance convinced him she would be a good hand and cook and provide a good cover for them. The threesome checked into Catherine Taylor's boardinghouse at 234 West Twelfth Street in New York as "Mr. and Mrs. Harry A. Place" and "Jim Ryan." Etta signed her named "Ethel Place" in the register, and the trio claimed to be cattle buyers from out west. For the next three weeks, the outlaws played tourist in New York City. During this time, the famous portrait of Sundance and Etta was taken, shortly after the three had visited Tiffany's and purchased a $150 gold lapel watch for Etta. Sundance also bought a diamond stickpin.[146] On February 20, 1901, Etta, Sundance, and Butch boarded the SS *Herminius* for Buenos Aires.[147] Others claim that only Sundance and Etta, posing as Mr. and Mrs. Harry Place, sailed for Argentina and that Butch joined them later.[148] The threesome then made their way to Bolivia.

Although her time in Bolivia was sporadic, Etta appears to have influenced how the outlaws lived there. At a ranch house operated by the three in Cholila, where they went by the names "Anna Marie and Harry Place" and "Santiago Ryan," a burgundy-and-gold brocade wallpaper adorned the walls. Primo Caparo, an Italian immigrant who spent a night at the ranch in 1904, later recalled that "the house was simply furnished and exhibited a certain painstaking tidiness, a geometric arrangement of things, pictures with cane frames, wallpaper made of clippings from North American magazines, and many beautiful weapons and lassos braided from horsehair." Caparo also noted that Etta was well dressed and reading when he arrived, but that she made dinner later.[149] There was also a white picket fence in front of the cabin and curtains in the window. The occupants also kept a springer spaniel. In contrast to this testament to Etta's feminine influence, descriptions of her in Cholila noted that although she was an elegant woman, she "never wore dresses, just pants and boots." She was also described as "good-looking, a good rider, and an expert with a rifle, though not with a revolver." Contrary to her romance with Sundance, some suspected Etta may have had an affair with an English neighbor, John Gardiner. According to Frank O'Grady, who knew Gardiner in Britain in 1907, Etta and her neighbor were drawn together by the fact they both were educated and often shared books and magazines from England. Gardiner naturally had little use for Sundance, whom he called "a mean, low cur."[150] It is not likely, though, that Etta would dare take up with another man while living with two outlaws, and she probably used her friendship with Gardiner merely as a means to pass the time.

While traveling, working, assisting in at least one robbery, and living in various parts of Argentina, Chile, and Bolivia, Etta returned to the United States as many as four times. The first time was in March or April 1902 with Sundance for another visit to the hospital in New York and to see relatives. A second trip was taken in 1903 possibly to see Etta's family in Fort Worth, Texas. In 1904, it is believed the couple attended the World's Fair at St. Louis. Pinkerton's in fact traced the couple to Fort Worth, but they eluded capture and returned to Argentina.[151] Etta's final trip to America was in 1905. In June that year, Sundance, under the alias "H. A. Place," wrote to his friend Dan Gibbon from Valpariso, Chile. "We arrived here today," he wrote, "and the day after tomorrow my wife and I leave for San Francisco."[152] In December, however, Bolivian authorities asserted that Etta was with the "*banditos Yankee*" (as the description was given on wanted posters) when they committed another robbery. Newspapers identified "Miss Place" as Sundance's wife and described her as "an interesting woman, very masculine, who wears male clothing with total correctness, and who is dedicated more to the occupations of men than to those of women." The paper also noted Etta was a "fine rider, handles with precision all classes of firearms, and has an admirable male temperament."[153]

Most unfortunately, the mystery of what happened to Etta Place once she returned to America remains irreparably jumbled. Authorities on the matter have ranged from self-glorifying thrill seekers to admirers who so badly want to believe they know what happened that they have accepted fiction as fact. Thus, the end to Etta's story may never be known, although several intriguing tales exist as to what finally became of her. Butch later allegedly said that she was stricken with appendicitis and that Sundance had taken her back to Denver.[154] Butch's friend Percy Seibert said Butch told him that after Sundance checked Etta into a Denver hospital, he went on a "roaring drunk." The next morning, Sundance expressed his irritation at the lack of room service in his boardinghouse by firing two shots into the ceiling. The landlord threatened to call the police, so Sundance left Denver and went back to South America without Etta. Neither he nor Butch ever saw her again.[155] Other historians have asserted Etta returned to Denver to have a baby or an abortion. Lula Betenson said that Butch accompanied the couple and that the three of them stayed in Wyoming from 1906 to 1908. Betenson's proof lay in a 1972 letter from a man named "Cowboy Joe," who said he worked for the threesome as a young boy.[156]

In 1908, Butch and Sundance were shot and supposedly killed in Bolivia by South American soldiers. Whether they survived instead has been the bane of historians for decades, but one thing is clear: Etta was not with them by then. One early report about their deaths, however, claimed that Etta's infamous gold watch was found on one of the bodies. What became of Etta after 1908 is equally mystifying. When a still alive Butch allegedly returned to his family at Circleville in the 1920s, he said that Etta and Sundance ended up living in Mexico City and he ran into Etta in a bar when he was visiting there. He spent several days with the couple before leaving the city and did not know what became of them. Others claimed that Etta later left Sundance and hooked up with American boxing promoter Tex Rickard. But Tex and his wife, Edith Mae, are said to have migrated to Mexico after marrying in America some years earlier. Pinkerton detective Frank DiMaio thought Etta may have lived in Arizona under the name "Laura Etta Place." Others have claimed Etta became a teacher in Denver or returned to prostitution in California, New York, or Texas.[157]

Theories about Etta's final years are numerous and largely without substantial proof. She may have died sometime between 1907 and 1910 during a battle at Chubut, Argentina. In 1909, however, Frank Aller, the U.S. vice consul in Chile, was approached by a pretty woman inquiring about obtaining a death certificate for the Sundance Kid. The woman apparently disappeared after making the request, and no documentation has surfaced to support who she was. Etta is also said to have spent six years fighting in the Mexican Revolution beginning in 1910. Author Ed Kirby claims Etta went to Mexico in about 1916 and spent time with Pancho Villa's army.[158]

Perhaps the most telling indication of Etta's fate comes from a newspaper of the time. In January 1918, the *Millard County Progress* in Utah published a sensational article from New York. "Woman Eludes All But Death" read the headline to the story, which went on to detail the alleged final death of one "Etta Longabaugh" in Argentina. The article chronicled Etta's life, claiming she did not know Sundance was a bandit until after they were married. After that, the article said, she became a willing participant and even led Butch Cassidy's gang. During various times, she was credited with holding the getaway horses during robberies and even holding back a posse in Nevada while the rest of the gang escaped. Much of the article was the stuff of dime novels, but the last sentence probably rang truest: "With the authorities of four continents on her trail, Etta might wish to be officially 'dead' and then come back to live quietly in the West that she loved so well in younger days."[159] Despite such an early confirmation that Etta was still alive at the time, a snippet from the *Fur News* of September 1920 gives a rather muddled report to the contrary. "They say Mrs. Longbow [*sic*], or Etta Place, has ridden more miles on horseback than any other woman in the United States," the writer explained. "She shoots, or used to shoot—one man says she is dead—birds flying with a rifle." The writer also praised Etta for her adeptness at trapping wolves.[160]

More outlandish stories of Etta's ultimate fate have her marrying an Irish adventurer and killing Sundance; marrying Elzy Lay and living out her life in La Paz, Bolivia; marrying Sundance, alias "Hiram BeBee," and retiring to Wyoming; marrying Sundance and retiring to Chile; wedding a Paraguayan government official; running an Arizona sanitarium under the name "Janette Magor"; getting shot during Butch and Sundance's infamous shoot-out with Bolivian soldiers; being killed in Buenos Aires by a *fronteriza*; or returning to America to bear several children. One of these children, a daughter named Betty Weaver, apparently led her own gang of bank robbers during the 1920s and 1930s. Still others claim Etta died in a shoot-out in Chubut, Argentina, in 1922 or committed suicide there in 1924 or ended up in Denver, where she lived as late as 1924.[161]

Harry Thayne-Longabaugh claimed that after Etta was unsuccessful at locating her two children by one of her marriages, she moved to Marian, Oregon, taught school, and died in 1935. Another historian, Art Davidson, agreed with Thayne-Longabaugh's claim that Etta died in Oregon, but he also claimed Etta had an older sister, Marion Bennion, and a brother named "Hiram" who was really the Sundance Kid. Marion, said Davidson, eventually married Butch Cassidy and gave birth to a daughter who later became a silent film star. Hiram was also known as "Hiram BeBee" and "George Hanlon." As BeBee, he was given a life sentence for murdering an off-duty town marshal in Utah in 1945 and died in prison in 1952 at the age of eighty-eight. Historian Ed Kirby agreed that BeBee was indeed Sundance, but further research revealed it was not so.[162]

Another researcher speculates that Etta taught school in Utah before marrying into the Parker clan through a man named Harris and that she died in Leeds in 1959.[163] A more logical alternative of this story is that it was Ann Bassett who married Frank Willis in 1923 and settled with him in Leeds before dying in 1956. In fact, in 1992 Doris Karren Burton of the Outlaw History Center at the Uintah County Library in Vernal published her assertions that Ann and Etta were one and the same. Both women shared several characteristics, including being born in about the same year, standing at five foot three or four, weighing one hundred ten to one hundred fifteen pounds, having medium dark complexions and blue or gray eyes, and wearing their hair the same way. Despite being a prominent cattle woman, Ann was also once tried for cattle rustling in Colorado and was known around Brown's Park as having "loose morals." She also maintained a friendship with Madam Baker of the Baker House Hotel in Colorado. Both women were excellent equestrians and could shoot.[164] Burton's strongest evidence, however, is in a computer analysis of photographs of Etta and Ann. Burton worked with Bill Webb of the Outlaw Trail History

Association and Dr. Thomas G. Kyle of the Computer Research Group at Los Alamos National Laboratory to compare the portraits. Kyle initially concluded there was only a one in five thousand chance that the two were the same woman, but changed his mind when he found an identical scar or cowlick on each of their foreheads.[165]

A simple scar notwithstanding, Burton noted other similarities between Ann and Etta. Ann Bassett was born in 1878, and Etta is thought to have been born between 1875 and 1880. Both ladies attended eastern finishing schools: Etta is thought to have attended the State Normal and Training School in New York in 1893, and Ann went to a Salt Lake City Catholic school in 1895 or Miss Potter's School for Girls in Boston in 1897. To Burton, further similarity can be found in the alleged story that both women got in trouble for cussing and performing tricks with their fancy horses and the fact that Etta first surfaced in Brown's Park shortly after Ann left school.[166]

Burton also tried to match Ann's occasional disappearances from Brown's Park with sightings of Etta. In November 1900, for instance, Ann's outlaw friend Matt Rash was murdered by persons unknown after being warned to leave the county and refusing to do so. When Ann secured some cattle from his estate, she too received a note of warning to leave town. Her brother received a similar note, and three months later the family dog was strangled by a prowler who took a shot at Ann. The cattle queen relocated to Vernal in January 1901.[167] On February 2, 1901, the *Vernal Express* noted that "Miss Annie Bassett left on this morning's stage for Texas." Ann's departure occurred shortly before Etta met up with Butch and Sundance for their trip to New York.[168] According to author Richard Patterson, however, Etta was already with Butch and Sundance by January 1901. Anne Meadows backs up Patterson's claim, saying that Ann left Utah the day after Etta signed the guest register at as Ethel Place at Catherine Taylor's New York boardinghouse.[169]

According to Pinkerton files, Etta and Sundance arrived back in the United States on July 29, 1902. Six months later Ann Bassett resurfaced in Brown's Park, and the newspaper noted she had been traveling the past two years. Ann was also in Mexico from about 1912 to 1916, the same years Etta was also supposedly there.[170] Next, Ann spent the winter of 1916 in El Paso, Texas, established a homestead near Vernal in 1918, and married Frank Willis in 1923. The couple eventually moved to Leeds, where Ann later claimed Etta visited her at the McMullins house (the McMullins were cousins to Butch Cassidy). Ann died in 1956.[171]

Unfortunately, the first snag in the Ann/Etta theory is the fact that Ann Bassett was still in Colorado when Etta first surfaced in New York in December 1900. Ann was also known to be in Utah during 1903, when Etta was documented in South America. There is also a serious lack of evidence from those who knew the two women. Ann Bassett eventually recorded her memoirs, but never once did she claim to be Etta Place. Neither did Ann's sister Josie, who it was also speculated might have been Etta. Maude Davis Lay retained a friendship with Ann and also knew Etta. But nobody ever seems to have claimed or questioned her as to whether Ann and Etta were the same person. In addition, it has never been established whether Ann and Etta ever truly met.[172]

Yet another theory came from Fort Worth newspaper editor Delbert Willis, who claimed Etta was actually named "Eunice Gray." Born in Missouri, Eunice had formerly worked as a prostitute in Fort Worth as early as 1914 and ultimately died in a Waco hotel fire in 1962. Willis based his claim solely on several interviews he had conducted with Gray, including her admission that she once went to South America to avoid the law, but he had no solid evidence to prove her real identity. Furthermore, research by historian Richard Selcer failed to turn up Etta at any time in Fort Worth. Even Eunice Gray never claimed to be Etta, although it is notable that she avoided such questions during her interviews with Delbert Willis.[173]

It is next to impossible to document just when Etta Place and her cohorts may have visited the Strip. By 1903, activity in the area slowed as new laws controlled the sale of liquor to Indians and the town of Moffatt was established nearby. By 1910, however, bootlegging was extremely common within the Strip's boundaries. Only the ultimate abandonment of Fort Duchesne in 1911 affected business at the Strip enough to shut it down. Some of the more daring harlots may have moved to Vernal. In 1919, a madam known as Mrs. Canady was tried for soliciting and prostitution there. Canady had only recently opened a brothel in the back of the Hub Building. Witnesses testified that an average of seven to fourteen men visited there daily. After the trial, Canady moved to the house of Mrs. Rock Labrum in Maeser and continued business, which became brazen enough to merit a complaint, and one of her own nineteen-year-old customers testified against her. Mrs. Canady apparently was shut down for good. Other bordellos in the county included a

FIGURE 70 ❧ *"Queen Ann" Bassett. Although Ann Bassett and Etta Place shared many characteristics in both looks and manners, historians have for the most part concluded that they were not the same person. Even if they never met, the two women probably knew about each other. Courtesy of the Western History Collection, Z-153, Denver Public Library.*

place associated with the Babcock Saloon. Prostitution continued in Vernal in a building near the Thirst Parlor as late as the 1940s.[174]

Utah officially became a state in 1894. Then, in 1906, it became public that Latter Day Saints Church president Joseph Smith had continued to live with plural wives despite an 1890 ban on doing so. Gentiles continued using prostitution as an argument against polygamy until 1913, when respectable women from all religions began putting their foot down. In 1913, the female members of the Progressive Party organized to clear Carbon County of its soiled doves. Dozens of prostitutes vacated the county during the fall, but the endeavor remained a limited success. In March 1914, a page one article in the *Carbon County News* told of the death of Mrs. J. R. Mattingly, a prostitute of Carbon whose Oak Bar and brothel were south of the Continental oil tanks. She apparently had been kicked and beaten by a patron at her brothel the previous Saturday. An autopsy revealed bruises and even a "cystic tumor," but no internal injuries. The coroner concluded that she must have died of poisoning or perhaps heart disease because she had been taken ill some thirty-six hours earlier. The body was shipped to Salt Lake City. Carbon County never completely shed itself of its soiled doves; during the 1930s, prostitutes joined bootleggers and gamblers by offering their services in remote parts of the county.[175]

In fact, throughout the 1910s and 1920s, Carbon and other remote towns of Utah remained somewhat lawless. In April 1914, waiter Carl Small was accused of stealing diamonds and jewelry from prostitute Ruby Garnetti at Bingham. The goods were found hidden under a bridge on the way to Copperfield. Then, in December that year, Bingham prostitutes Peggy Dean, Norma Dean, and Lola Kendall were arrested along with Burt Heaton, former St. Joseph roadhouse owner Scott Cunningham, Ed Turner, and Frank Welch for participating in the holdup of the Bingham State Bank. The robbery had netted more than $16,000, which was duly returned to the bank. Bingham was a virtual sea of crime and violence during 1917. The *Carbon News Advocate* announced in January that, following the murder of miner Tom Park in a brothel in Bingham's red light district, the sheriff was planning to close down the district once and for all. Six months later a man known as "Mike Morris" was convicted of voluntary manslaughter for the killing of prostitute Connie Mack in Bingham's red light district the previous December 24.[176]

By 1917, Utah had several dry counties.[177] Bootlegging became a

FIGURE 71 ❧ *Despite her disfigurement, "No-Nose Maggie" lived the hearty life of a pioneer prostitute. This is the only known photograph of her, circa 1950. Courtesy of the Frank A. Beckwith Digitization Collection, J. Willard Marriott Library, University of Utah, Salt Lake City.*

national pastime, especially after nationwide prohibition was enacted in 1919. It was only natural that gambling and prostitution accompanied the illicit vice. During the 1930s, when bootlegging and prostitution ran rampant in remote places such as Carbon County, attorney Reva Beck Bosone recalled meeting her first prostitute. The woman was an attractive blonde who "was pretty and well dressed, but looked hard as nails. This was the first time in my life I had met a prostitute. My heart was pounding for I was really nervous." As late as 1951, raids in Price and Helper resulted in the arrests of twelve women practicing prostitution.[178]

One of Utah's last notable prostitutes was Mrs. Mary Alice Ann Devitt Laird, who lived in Joy.[179] Born in Minnesota, Mary, also known as Maggie, was living in the Dakota Territory with her large family by 1875.[180] By 1880, she was living with some of her siblings at Fargo, North Dakota. At some point, she turned to prostitution, traveling the West and living in Washington State, San Francisco, and finally Virginia City and Pioche, Nevada. Maggie was married at some point and had a child who died. She was ultimately disfigured when a beer bottle was thrown at her and broke the bridge of her nose. She eventually settled in the dwindling mining town of Joy as postmistress and lived out her life there. She died at Payson in 1934.[181]

WICKED WOMEN OF WYOMING

WYOMING PROSTITUTES WERE A TOUGH BUNCH. GIVEN THEIR geographic opportunities at mountain man rendezvous, remote "hog ranches," and budding boom camps, most women had few places with nice amenities to choose from, at least in the early days. The first known rendezvous took place at Henry's Fork in 1825, and it can be assumed that the women selling their wares there were Native Americans.[1] Several "hog ranches"—a most slovenly term for a brothel—flourished outside of Wyoming's numerous military posts. Writers Willah Weddon and Marion Huseas speculated that back when hog ranches actually sold hogs, they were located a safe, odor-free distance from the forts. But then prostitutes, whom the army wives strongly disapproved of, began staying at the hog ranches, too. Teamster Harry Young gave his own reasons why this name was used. "Why so called, I could not say," he remembered of his visits to hog ranches as a young man, "as I never saw any hogs around . . . but think perhaps it had reference to the girls as they were a very low, tough set."[2]

The rendezvous at Henry's Fork was followed by another one at Riverton in 1838.[3] Increases in the number of trappers passing through the state ultimately enticed mountain man Jim Bridger to build a trading post at what was later called Fort Bridger in 1842.[4] In all cases, Indian maidens likely sold or traded their bodies, but it was at Fort Laramie, circa 1849, that real commercial sex in Wyoming first came into being. In fact, an early trading post built by trappers was probably the state's oldest bagnio.[5] The chaplain of Fort Phil, after visiting Fort Laramie in 1867, declared the latter post "a perfect whorehouse."[6] Probably to the chaplain's relief, soldiers moving in kicked the shady ladies out, and both the white and Indian women moved six miles away from the post and reopened for business. The nickname of their new district was "Openly Lewd."[7] In time, the place became known as "Six Mile."

Six Mile is first mentioned in Fort Laramie post records in February 1867. Two months later the records noted that Sargent Kesner, who lost his stripes and $10 of his pay for stealing an ambulance wagon, had visited Six Mile and returned to the fort drunk. Meals, liquor, cigars, and the attentions of six girls were available there, and in time the ranch also was noted as having lots of children's graves around it. For more than forty years, however, Six Mile prospered under a number of different owners.[8] The ladies of Six Mile were certainly not always content or bound to stay within their quarters. Colorado marshal "Doc" Cyrus Shores wrote of a scene he witnessed in 1868: "We stopped at Laramie, still camping across the river. The weather was warm and I remember one day dance house women of all kinds came across the river on the bridge, all stripped, and two rough men with them, and they all went swimming together in front of our camp. Some of the women were big old fat women. I thought at the time it was the worst sight I had ever seen."[9]

Six Mile's ladies of the lamplight were not necessarily the cleanest, either. When Fort Laramie suffered an outbreak of venereal disease in 1869, it was really no surprise. In fact, for several years officers at Fort Laramie were at a loss as to how to control their men and keep them from visiting the hog ranch. In April 1876, Private William McCormick disappeared overnight and returned to the fort inebriated. McCormick was fined $12 and served twenty days of hard labor.[10] By then, some of the painted ladies from Six Mile and other places had drifted back to Fort Laramie, the outskirts of which were becoming home to more civilian residents. Adolph Cuny and Julius "Jules" Ecoffey built the Three Mile Hog Ranch near Fort Laramie in 1872 as a trading post, saloon, and hotel. The men hired prostitutes to boost business after a particularly slow summer. There were six two-room cottages at the ranch, with one cottage per girl. John Hutton, who visited Ecoffey and Cuny's trading post in the 1870s, recalled several years later that the traders "sent to Omaha, Kansas City, and other places and in a short time had their houses occupied by ten or more young women all of whom were known as sporting characters. Among this bunch was 'Calamity Jane' her name generally given her by magazine writers and newspaper correspondents."[11]

Lieutenant John G. Bourke visited Fort Laramie in 1877 and recorded that "[t]hree miles [from Fort Laramie] there was a nest of ranches . . . tenanted by as hardened and depraved set of witches as could be found on the face of the globe." The ranches Bourke referred to were Cuny and Ecoffey's Three Mile Hog Ranch and another place belonging to a man named Wright.[12] To Bourke, the ranches were the lowest of the low. "Each set of these establishments was equipped with a run of the worst kind and each contained from three to half dozen Cyprians, virgins whose lamps were always burning brightly in expectancy of the coming of the bridegroom, and who lured to destruction soldiers of the garrisons. In all my experience I have never seen a lower, more beastly set of people of both sexes."[13] Sometime around Bourke's visit, Cuny, who had once served as a deputy sheriff, was shot to death at Six Mile. He was the last known gunfight victim there.[14]

The girls' antics in what was now called "Laramie City" were typical during the 1870s. A young girl named "Belle Vernon" trained in Laramie City with an older prostitute named "Nellie Wright." Belle, who probably began working at the age of fifteen, showed up frequently in court documents as being arrested for getting drunk and working as a prostitute.[15] Between August and November 1877, prostitutes Annie Hamilton and Nellie Davis were arrested in Laramie five times, paying $7 for each offense. Another woman, Sophie Rickard, suffered through an amazing thirty-five arrests between 1877 and 1883.[16]

The "beastly" girls of Laramie County in 1880 included twenty-eight-year-old Minnie Kessler, thirty-four-year-old Sarah Petite, who ran a hog ranch outside of Chugwater, and thirty-eight-year-old Josephine Whalen.[17] Their ages indicate these "girls" were past their prime in the industry. But *beastly* was not a word used to describe the fairer Cyprians at Laramie City; the girls there proved quite profitable to the young city. Between 1878 and 1880, Laramie officials took in $1,179.50 in fines at $7 per prostitute.[18] Wicked women of Laramie City in 1880 included thirty-seven-year-old Loesa Burton, twenty-six-year-old Josephine Demar of Denmark, twenty-five-year-old Kate Hart, thirty-year-old Kate Frost, twenty-nine-year-old

FIGURE 72 ❧ *The hog ranch at Fort Laramie, Wyoming. Hardly the equal of the fancy city brothels, the hog ranch was situated in squalid conditions in the middle of nowhere. Courtesy of the Mazzulla Collection, Colorado Historical Society, Denver.*

Fannie McManus, twenty-four-year-old Maria Summers, and thirty-year-old Sallie Thixon.[19] In 1881, Sallie Thixon died of alcoholism and exposure in Laramie. She had worked there for at least the past seven years and had been before the court on many occasions.[20]

In fact, the courts of Laramie City were less than lenient on their shady ladies. In 1884, Bessie Summers of Laramie came close to losing her rental house of ill repute. The rent of $22.46 had gone unpaid, along with another bill for $30. When an agent was sent to take Bessie's furnishings as payment, a Mrs. Mary Ash stepped up and paid the $30 debt. Bessie obtained a continuation of her case regarding the unpaid rent, but left town before her court date the following January. In 1885, Sue Bannon of Laramie lost all of her possessions when the court took them for unpaid rent. Sue's belongings were sold, and the money paid to her landlord.[21] Then, in 1887, Private John Collins was found dead a short distance from Fort Laramie, his death caused by alcohol poisoning.[22] Laramie's bad girls were undoubtedly blamed for the tragedy, but prostitution nevertheless survived in Laramie for another sixty years or more. During the 1940s, a lady called "Mother Watson" had a place in Laramie, and prostitution continued to be legal through the 1950s.[23]

Between Laramie and Rawlins lay Arlington Stage Station. One building there housed a blacksmith shop but also a combination dance hall, saloon, and gambling den.[24] The stop was representative of several like it that served as way stations along Wyoming's early trails. It should also be noted that not all hog ranches served military forts, though many did. Moreover, women were not always banned from such forts, although officers sooner or later wished they were. One of the women at Fort Phil Kearney in 1866 was Colored Susan, who was given a warning that November for causing disruptions. Susan, it appeared, had for some time been selling alcohol and fruit pies that were in fact made from fort provisions. She was also accused of encouraging officer's servants to abandon their posts, using profanity, and being abusive. It was also noted, however, that by her wicked ways Susan was able to make more money than the average army post prostitute.[25]

One of Wyoming's most notorious red light districts was in Cheyenne. Shortly after the city was first founded in 1867 on the Union Pacific Railroad line, it took on a life of its own as home to cowboys, railroaders, outlaws, and hundreds of shady ladies.[26] Soon the "Bob-Tail District," as it was known, was home to a number of cribs and bordellos.[27] During one month in the summer of 1868, Cheyenne authorities recorded an amazing $943 in fines taken from prostitutes. City officials attempted a reform effort in 1873, which failed.[28]

Authorities couldn't close the district, so they chose instead to keep a very close eye on it. They also exercised strong prejudice against their soiled doves. In February 1877, a man named Joseph Lucas was tried for raping prostitute Susie Bennett in Cheyenne, a most unusual act for the justice system to carry out on behalf of a fallen woman. No one in the courtroom, however, knew Susie was a soiled dove. It appeared that the jury who convicted Lucas and the judge who sentenced him to two and a half years in the state pen were unaware that Susie was a prostitute until after the verdict was rendered. Upon the discovery, Governor John Thayer immediately pardoned Lucas on the recommendation of several citizens, the prosecuting attorney, and even the jury who had convicted him.[29]

Other women continued making their mark on Cheyenne. Annie Ferguson died in 1877 and was buried in an unmarked grave. Prostitute

FIGURE 73 🙣 *A Cheyenne, Wyoming, whorehouse, probably in the late 1800s. The madam is most likely the woman on the floor, and house entertainment included a male piano player. Courtesy of the Mazzulla Collection, Colorado Historical Society, Denver.*

Frankie Lester shot at two Fort Russell soldiers for disturbing the peace in her saloon in 1878. That same year, Cheyenne authorities once again tried a reform movement. This time their attack was solely against black prostitutes. Like the effort in 1873, however, the movement was a failure. Some of the girls, tired of being picked on by authorities, began to protest in their own way. When Mollie Russell left Cheyenne in June 1879, she outright refused in court to abide by a ruling that she must reveal her new destination when she left town.[30]

Things took a more serious turn in 1879 when violence erupted at Ida Hamilton's brothel. Twenty-eight-year-old Ida Snow was threatened with a knife and beaten by her longtime lover Edward Malone.[31] In fact, the couple had relocated to Cheyenne from Bodie, California, only a month earlier.[32] Ida Hamilton, who was only twenty-nine herself, testified that when she heard screams for help from Snow's room, she assisted customer Charles Boulter in breaking down the door. Boulter pulled Malone off Ida Snow.

The enraged Malone left the house but returned moments later with a pistol. Both men ended up back in the street, where Boulter pulled his own pistol and ordered Malone to drop his. When Malone refused, Boulter fired a fatal shot at him. Both Ida Snow and Ida Hamilton, along with fellow prostitutes Ida Moore, Florence Vaughn, and Mary West, testified as to what they had seen.[33] Women from Jennie Mortimer's brothel next door, including Bessie Laurence, also testified.[34] Boulter was acquitted.[35] There is little doubt that the ladies felt somewhat vindicated by having the courts accept their testimonies as truth for a change. Ida Snow and Florence Vaughn were still working in Cheyenne in 1880, but Ida Hamilton had relocated to La Porele (La Prele) Creek.[36] In August, however, Ida Snow died of apoplexy. Because she had no family in town, she was buried beside Malone.[37]

The 1880 census presents interesting and varied clues as to the Cheyenne girls' backgrounds and situations, as well as to the social situation in Cheyenne. There was, for instance, only one large white bordello run by Ida Hamilton, but two operated by black madams Octavia Reeves and Pauline Alexander. In all, there were fifteen white and twelve black prostitutes in Cheyenne, a very surprising statistic for the time. It is interesting to note that the girls in the black houses were listed as "mulatto," but servants were listed as "black." The smaller houses, all operated by white women, included one two-girl crib, one house with four girls working independently and alone, and one house with three women who lived with others unrelated to the prostitution industry. Fourteen women were single, eleven were married, three were widowed, and one, Puss Newport from Ida Hamilton's place, was divorced. Two children were found. One was Charlie Woods, the five-year-old son of Lillie Woods, who was twenty-nine and living with twenty-three-year-old Pauline Todd, listed as a housekeeper, and a male clerk named John Mills. The other child was William Reeves, who had just been born to Octavia Reeves a month before the census was taken. Octavia may not have been back to work yet, which is why she listed herself as a housekeeper. Ida Hamilton also employed a sixteen-year-old Chinese boy, John Crow, as a servant. Also of note is Louisa Harris, age forty-five. Louisa, black and married, was residing in a boardinghouse with mostly male occupants. Thirty-year-old Nellie Smith, single, was living with forty-four-year-old Flora Clifford, who does not appear to have been a madam.[38]

The ladies of Cheyenne were not without their own troubles, including that of personal health. In June 1882, black prostitute Hattie Anderson was found dead in bed by her fellow prostitutes. Though only thirty-five years old, Hattie died of constitutional syphilis. Fellow prostitute Maud Brooks paid for Hattie's funeral.[39] In Cheyenne in 1883, a Dr. W.A. Wyan tried in vain to save painted lady Sallie Talbot. His notes simply recorded that the girl was twenty-one years old and was found at 8:15 P.M. with a bottle of laudanum nearby. The girl died a little after midnight.[40]

One Cheyenne prostitute who did survive the dangers of her profession was Belle Barnard (also spelled "Bernard" and "Birnard"). Born in Pennsylvania in about 1842, Belle had previously lived in Iowa, where she gave birth to a daughter in 1871. Belle was in Cheyenne by the time of the 1880 census. She is listed as a dressmaker, as is her only female lodger, Susie McCarthy. Clerk J. C. Vandyke was also a lodger and the only male in the house. Most intriguing is Grace Barnard, who is listed as Belle's niece. Grace was in fact Belle's daughter from Iowa.[41] By 1884, Belle was working as a prostitute when she left Cheyenne for Denver. Within a year, she had a stately, two-story brick brothel in Denver's red light district.[42] There she flourished for several years, and her advertisement in the 1892 *Denver Red Book* boasted fourteen rooms, five parlors, a music and dance hall, plus twelve boarders. What became of her was unknown for sure. She may have retired in 1900 to Florence, just east of Canon City, to live with her brother, E. Bernard.[43]

Cheyenne hardly missed the likes of Belle Barnard. In 1887, the Wyoming State capitol building was constructed in Cheyenne.[44] The capitol put new emphasis on Cheyenne, but also pressure. Between March 1887 and January 1890, authorities logged eighty-seven women into its jail system. The fines imposed upon these women varied between $10 and $116, and authorities collected $1,028.50 between March and December. The standard fine for prostitutes appears to have been $18. Overall, however, only thirteen inmates are noted as having paid their fines. The majority waited out their time in jail, although a few paid partial fines and negotiated other ways to come up with the balance.[45]

Cheyenne's red light district continued to be plagued with violence. In March 1888, Cheyenne prostitute Jennie Howard came across the dead body of Mrs. Annie St. Clair (or Forbes). All Jennie knew about the dead woman was that she was a former inmate of the Colorado State Penitentiary. Even so, Jennie was instructed by officers to go into Annie's house, look at the body for signs of violence and ascertain whether there were any valuables inside. Why the officers did not perform this duty themselves is a puzzle. Jennie reported back that she found nothing unusual and did not see any valuables. Because she was illiterate, she signed a report to that effect with an "X. The attending physician noted that Annie had a large tumor on her neck, but that her death was the result of natural causes.[46]

Then in 1891 two Cheyenne doves, Alice Pleasants and Florence Gains, got in a fight on the street. Alice was at the time being accompanied by two men, who left immediately when Florence pulled a pistol. After shooting at Alice but missing, Florence next grabbed a knife from her pimp and stabbed Alice six times. Nineteen at the time of her crime, she was sentenced to two years of hard labor in prison and was released a month early. Another notable criminal was Annie Curley Johnson, who opened a wild and raucous bagnio in Cheyenne in 1892. Annie, who stood five foot nine and weighed 217 pounds, was a match for any toughs in her place. In 1893, she married one Ed Johnson. Eight months after the marriage, she was arrested for neglecting to pay tax on the liquor she sold. She was fined $100 and sentenced to a year and a day in prison.[47]

The courts were equally unsympathetic to Emma Lenore Nash. In September 1903, Emma provided sexual services to a sheepherder named Perfecto Macs for the price of $4. Macs simply gave his $4 paycheck to Emma as payment. All would have been fine had her husband, Joe, not decided to add some zeros to the amount on the check. Moreover, both he and Emma forged Macs's signature on the check. When the girl presented the altered check for $400 to a Cheyenne secondhand store, the storekeeper caught on and turned her in. Emma and her husband served time in prison for the deed.[48] In 1906, Cheyenne prostitute Dolly Brady had just finished entertaining a wealthy Japanese man, Tohichi Watanabe, at her brothel for the price of $5. Knowing the man had more on him, Dolly employed the help of Fort Russell soldiers Art Cordieu and William Bond to relieve Watanabe of his entire wallet. Dolly and Cordieu were sentenced to two years in the state pen, and Bond, who was caught with the goods, got three and a half years. Six months later, Gerty Brown joined Dolly in prison. A young widow with a small boy to care for, Gerty had been engaged in prostitution and its accompanying habits for some time. In 1907, she was convicted of stealing a silk kimono and jewelry box from one of her coworkers in the red light district.[49]

It would appear that city officials began a cleanup campaign in Cheyenne during the late 1910s. Their shady ladies began drifting to other parts

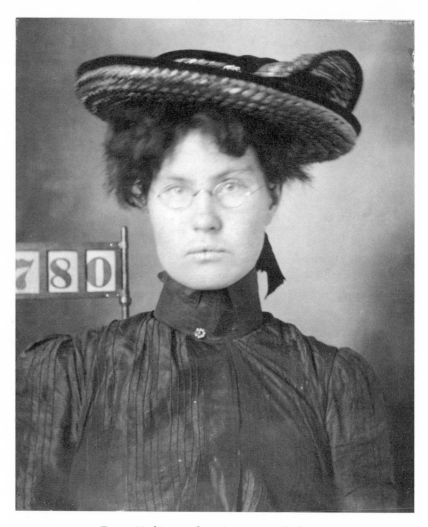

FIGURE 74 ⌘ *Emma Nash's mug shot, circa 1903. Whether the hapless girl had engaged in prostitution before her arrest is unknown. Courtesy of the Department of State Parks and Cultural Resources, Wyoming State Archives, Cheyenne.*

of the West. Ruth Rice and Grace Rubby left Cheyenne for Cripple Creek, Colorado, in 1911 and 1913, respectively.[50] Sure enough, in 1917, news of the city's intent to clean out the bawdy houses of Cheyenne made regional newspapers. A new federal law made it illegal to operate such a place within five miles of an army post, a fact that city authorities had apparently overlooked. Accordingly, Deputy Marshal Richard Coyle and Cheyenne police officers raided two bordellos. Four women and three men were arrested.[51]

Like Cheyenne, Fort Fetterman was also established in 1867.[52] Intended as a supply post, the fort was abandoned in May 1882 but was one of only a few forts to evolve into a city. Rechristened "Fetterman City," the old fort was transformed into a new wild frontier town with saloons, dance halls, and brothels. The former military hospital was turned into a dance hall by John "Jack" Sanders and John D. Lawrence. Sanders also undertook a solo operation at the One Mile hog ranch located a mile north on the Bozeman Trail. In time, One Mile offered whiskey, poker, dancing, and between six and eight prostitutes. Most of the women were seasoned in the profession, averaging in age between twenty-five and forty-five years.[53]

Jack and his wife, Viola, better known as Vi, resided on one side of the brothel. Seven crib stalls were provided for the girls. The bar was twenty feet long, and the room included a big wood-burning stove and a poker table. Spanish monte was the game. A small stage could accommodate a fiddler. The Sanderses also maintained a kitchen and dining room in a separate building with special chairs for themselves; everyone else sat on benches during meals. Vi was remembered as pretty, but she wouldn't drink with customers until they bought a drink for themselves and for her. Like other seasoned madams, Vi's secret was to drink a shot and then spit it into a brown bottle under the guise of drinking a chaser. After all, being sober meant being in control.[54]

Customer George Cross recalled that business boomed at One Mile, perhaps because in order to reach the bar one had to cross in front of the stalls where Jack and Vi's girls operated. As the cowboys walked by, the girls would snatch their hats in order to lure them into the crib.[55] The stalls may have been crude to more refined working girls, but things were rough at One Mile. Indeed, the place certainly had a reputation for its filth and violence. At times, the girls working there were well past their prime, with some being almost fifty years old. Many declined to wear dresses or other feminine costumes—some because they had no such thing and others because they had traded parts of soldiers' uniforms in exchange for their wares. There was also often a lack of soap around the place.[56] Shootings were not unusual; in August 1884, a prostitute named Ella Wilson was wounded in the shoulder during a gunfight. Late in 1884 Sanders partnered with William "Billy" Bacon to build an all new hog ranch outside of Fetterman City. The partnership was doomed. One night in 1885 Sanders and Bacon got into an argument over the books, and Vi accused Bacon of not getting enough girls. Bacon slapped Jack Sanders, then the two wrestled and ultimately each shot the other to death.[57] What became of Viola Sanders is a mystery.

Another new city in 1867 was Rawlins, originally named Rawlins Springs. The town quickly became known as a gateway for stages and wagons to access the goldfields in the northwest.[58] The red light district probably originated along Front Street directly across from the Union Pacific Railroad tracks, or possibly along Railroad Street south of the tracks. Rawlins's largest bordello in 1880 was run by two men, John Curtis and J. A. Gordon. They employed seven women, all in their twenties except for eighteen-year-old Anna Nelson. All were single, including Mollie Morton, who was divorced. One girl, twenty-five-year-old Annie Bloom, had a two-year-old daughter named Lillie. There were also two male boarders, listed as a teamster and a laborer. Because Curtis and Gordon openly listed themselves as keeping a house of prostitution, the men's occupations are probably correct. There was no cook or chambermaid listed, so the girls probably kept house themselves and provided meals for the men.[59]

Prostitution likely slowed down with the announcement of construction on the Wyoming State Penitentiary at Rawlins in 1888.[60] It was another ten years, however, before the prison was completed in its entirety.[61] In the interim, lawmen had to settle for jailing prisoners at Laramie. Once the new prison opened in about 1901, however, it quickly filled up. Trouble began almost immediately as prison officials coped with a major glitch in their new system. In 1902, Pearl Smith and Gertie Miller were convicted of shoplifting at Rawlins. The girls were imprisoned in the Female Prison on the third floor of the new prison, but their close proximity—and in fact their availability—to male prisoners soon created a problem. The women were removed to the old prison at Laramie, but the damage was done. Within a few months, it was obvious that Gertie was pregnant. She was released early, only to die during childbirth that December. Pearl was released about a week after Gertie on the promise that her husband would take her back to their home in Kansas City and she would forever stay out of Wyoming.[62]

Perhaps because of the state prison, little else is available regarding Rawlins's prostitution history. It is known that as late as the 1940s, the Midway bordello still functioned in Rawlins. The male owner of the Midway, Manny Stevens, also owned another place called "the Green Lantern." The Green Lantern's "landlady" was a four-hundred-pound woman known as "Big Alma." The madam had in fact formerly worked as the "fat lady" in a circus. Later, Madam Millie of Silver City, New Mexico, bought a place in Laramie, fixed it up, and hired Alma to run it. Millie also opened a gambling parlor downstairs, all with advice from Police Chief Sal Veitreie, who knew the loopholes. Millie later recalled her clientele in Laramie. "We didn't have any dancing," she said, "but the customers were really well trained up there. They knew to come into the little parlors, buy the landlady and whatever girl they were interested in those nice drinks of colored water, along with their own real drink . . . everybody knew the rules and went by them. Seemed like they truly appreciated a clean, well-run whorehouse." When Millie sold the place to another woman named Dutch Marie, Sal Veitreie threw her a big going-away party.[63]

Additional forts—Fort Fred Steele and Camp Auger—were established in the late 1860s. Even at that late date women in Wyoming were still scarce. By 1870, the ratio of white men to white women was still six to one throughout the state. Pioneer George McClellan of Washakie County once claimed he went six whole years without seeing a white woman.[64] Despite these statistics, plenty of women were available at the hog ranches. In 1870, Mary and Ed Brady were running a saloon and brothel near Fort Sanders, just north of Laramie along the Union Pacific Railroad near the Big Laramie River.[65] Two years later, in an unusual brush with the law, Mary was charged with keeping a disorderly house "to the encouragement of idleness, drinking and fornication." She in fact suffered troubles with the law through 1875 and was once charged with threatening the life of a man named Thomas Dillon.[66] The Bradys were still in business as late as 1875, when Mary paid personal taxes in the amount of $62.72.[67] By 1880, however, they were gone.[68]

In 1875, Camp Auger was renamed "Lander" and became known as the town "where the rails end and the trails begin."[69] The Den of Vixen was located on the south side of the Popo Agie River, across the street from a

FIGURE 75 ❧ *Etta Feeley and some of her girls. Etta is believed to be the woman on the right in this undated photograph and appears to have enjoyed having her picture taken often. Park County Archives, Cody, Wyoming, PO2-15-05.*

stage stop. There was also a house called "Crimson Way" run by Etta Feeley. Etta once paid more than $300 in fines in one month.[70] She eventually moved to Montana and established herself at Billings.[71]

The fines paid by the Bradys and Etta Feeley were signs of things to come. As more women began following their soldier husbands to Wyoming's frontier posts, the presence of both white "laundresses" and Indian prostitutes became an increasing problem. The army wives' discontent led to the Banning Committee in 1876, which began investigating immorality at such posts. The investigation concluded that officials should give up their Indian prostitutes in order to conduct themselves as American soldiers. The idea was a limited success: white wives were still repelled by the Indians even as they attempted to extend their Christian charity toward them. And at least one man, Colonel Albert Brackett, found the Indian courtesans to be "unquestionably happier than the do-nothing, thankless, dyspeptic life led by a majority of American women."[72] Nevertheless, hog ranches such as the one just a few hundred yards from Fort Fred Steele were still flourishing in 1877.[73]

Wyoming's most famous madam was a woman initially known only as

"Mother Featherlegs." The middle-aged madam was rumored to have come from Louisiana.[74] Little else was known about her when she arrived in 1876 and set up shop near Lusk. Her brothel was really no more than a dugout located along the Cheyenne–Black Hills Trail between the Running Water and Rawhide Buttes stations. But the woman was indeed memorable for the mess of red hair piled on her head. Her colorful nickname came from her red "pantalettes [sic] that were tied at her ankles." The underwear was especially noticeable when she rode horseback.[75] "Them ruffled drawers make the old girl look like a feather-legged chicken in a high wind," said one observer.[76]

Whiskey, gambling, and sex aside, Featherlegs was also known to harbor stolen jewelry and money for her outlaw friends.[77] She also employed robbers to relieve wealthy travelers of their money. The madam would look for those with full pockets and point them out to her accomplices, who would then rob the customers after they left her place.[78] Beginning in about 1878, Featherlegs took in a desperado known as "Dangerous Dick the Terrapin," whom she appeared to have known for quite some time. One day in 1879, Mrs. O. J. Demmon, whose husband owned the Silver Springs Road ranch between Rawhide Buttes and Lusk, decided to visit Featherlegs. She found the unfortunate woman shot to death at the spring close to her dugout.[79] Featherlegs appeared to have been dead at least two or three days.[80] Fifteen hundred dollars known to be in Featherlegs's possession was missing. Likewise, Dangerous Dick was nowhere to be found.[81]

Featherlegs was buried near her bordello, and Dangerous Dick remained a suspect in her death. Nothing came of the matter until sometime later, when the outlaw was apprehended for some other crimes in Louisiana. Only then was it ascertained that Dangerous Dick's real name was "Davis," and that he had indeed murdered Mother Featherlegs. Before Davis was hanged, he confessed to the killing. He also revealed that Featherlegs's rightful name was "Charlotte Shepard." During the Civil War, according to Davis, he, Charlotte, and Charlotte's sons Bill and Tom had comprised a small group of robbers and murderers in Louisiana. When Bill and Tom were hanged, Charlotte had headed West to elude the law. No other information was given before Davis, too, was hanged, very close to the spot where Charlotte's sons had met their fates years earlier.[82]

Russell Thorp Jr., who grew up in the same area as Featherlegs's bordello, recalled a day in 1893 when, as a boy, he and some friends decided to dig up the old madam. The boys camped near the grave in order to make

FIGURE 76 ❧ *The only known depiction of Madam Featherlegs is this undated, uncomplimentary sketch of her. Featherlegs not only ran with outlaws, but died at the hands of one of them. Courtesy of the Wyoming Recreation Commission, Cheyenne.*

a midnight raid. "When we removed the lid of the home-made pine coffin," he said, "her features were clearly recognizable with a great mass of red hair." Thorp was on hand in 1964 when Wyoming State auditor Jim Griffith and his friend, Bob Arrow, decided to reenact a stagecoach run from Denver to Deadwood. The journey would include passing by Featherlegs's grave, and Griffith decided to solicit donations for a proper memorial to the madam. Donors included madam Del Burke, who was still running the Yellow Hotel bordello in Lusk at the time. With a 3,500-pound red granite marker in tow, the stagecoach came through on May 17, and the monument was delivered, Thorpe pointing out the appropriate spot.[83] Located down ten miles of rough road from Lusk on the Old Cheyenne Trail, the monument reads:

Here lies Mother Featherlegs.
So called, as in her ruffled pantalettes she looked like
a feather-legged chicken in a high wind.
She was roadhouse ma'am.
An outlaw confederate, she was murdered by
"Dangerous Dick Davis the Terrapin" in 1879.[84]

Although there were surely more Chinese sex slaves in Wyoming than recorded, the 1880 census documents a total of nineteen Chinese women living throughout the state. Most of them are listed as servants, residing in houses filled with Chinese men. Sixteen of them were at Evanston, where four Chinagirls—Hoon Kom, Gee Snug, Com Yung, and Fun Ye—were listed as prostitutes. All of them were noted as being born between 1847 and 1858, indicating that they were seasoned in the business.[85] Little else is known about Evanston's prostitution history aside from the fact that during the 1930s the town supported three brothels. All were located upstairs, simply because they were easier to keep warm from the stoves down below.[86]

More is known about La Prele Creek outside of Douglas. There, William "Billie" Brown and his wife, Ella or Ellie, ran the Brown Ranch during the 1880s.[87] In 1880, the couple were listed as innkeepers but employed three prostitutes, Lydia O'Brien, Ida Hamilton, and Alice Bean. Alice had a four-year-old daughter with her, Hattie Hatter, who was (we hope) mistakenly listed as a prostitute. Also living at the inn were two teamsters and a ranch hand.[88] Ellie was remembered as good looking and friendly, advising her customers to "always take your drinks standing up" so they would know when they'd had enough. In the summer of 1880, a young man died by gunshot at Brown's. Whether he was murdered, committed suicide, or met with an accident was never ascertained. The Browns claimed his gun went off as he was cleaning it.[89]

Douglas's best-known madam was Angie La Fontaine, who operated a successful bordello from at least 1887 through 1899. Her employees were May Arms and Jennie Smith. It is notable that the court records of Douglas between 1887 and 1890 dealt primarily with prostitution. Many of the women named therein were repeat offenders. Charges against them ranged from operating bawdy houses and intoxication to public disturbances and waving guns around in public. In 1890, the monthly fine for prostitution was $4 plus a court fee of $1.[90]

Prostitutes in general continued surfacing throughout the state during the 1880s. Two of them merited mention in the *Cheyenne Democratic Leader* when they arrived at Pine Bluffs. "Both wore yellow hair and store complexions," the paper described. "The garments they wore weren't very costly but they were rather variegated and colors bordering on crimson predominated. Each had on a Leghorn hat, which was only less elevated than a steeple, and wore bangle bracelets and jewelry until you couldn't rest. The jewelry was of that character which is euphoniously termed 'snide' but it shone like a tin pan on a milk house." The women's apparent wealth stood out in primitive Pine Bluffs. Even citizens of that community were appalled, however, when the giddy ladies voted to camp out on the depot platform. Before long a cowboy named Pete recognized one of the girls, whom he called "Maude." "Other cowboys soon appeared, and without the formality of an introduction, immediately became intimately friendly," the paper jeered. "Then followed beer. This was succeeded by more beer, which was succeeded by quite a lot of beer. Then came beer." Before long, the party was in full swing on the platform, lasting a full eight hours. "It was a scene of the wildest and most extravagant carousel set down in the quiet midst of the bleak prairie," the *Leader* concluded of the festivities, "and one which would give life and reality to an early-day border romance."[91]

Things were not always so rosy; in June 1882, it was noted that a man named Mattison Hall had shot black prostitute Georgie Cox to death near Fort Russell. Even though the judge warned the jury to be just during Hall's trial, the killer was acquitted. Hall later commented he would rather be convicted for killing a prostitute than for stealing a horse because the latter carried much more severe punishment.[92] More violence erupted during the late 1880s and 1890s at Thermopolis, where "Bad Land Charlie" Anderson ran a hog ranch with his brother Lyman a half-mile east of town. The hog ranch's biggest claim to fame occurred in June 1899, when several members of Butch Cassidy's Wild Bunch hid there after their infamous train robbery at Wilcox.[93] Things turned ugly in 1905, however, when Thermopolis prostitute Hattie LaPierre shot her abusive lover Frank McKinney, alias "Harry Black." The authorities, who were familiar with McKinney's constant physical and mental abuse of Hattie, initially sentenced her to three years in prison for the killing. A short time later Governor Bryant B. Brooks kindly cut her sentence to fifteen months, and she was paroled in 1907.[94]

Another famous shady lady of Wyoming was Ella Watson. A native of Lebanon, Kansas, Ella first made a name for herself in the Sweetwater Valley. She had previously worked in Dodge City, Ogallala, and Cheyenne before moving to Rawlins.[95] She was soon known not just for her sexual prowess, but also for her talents with guns and a branding iron. At one of Rawlins's six bordellos, Ella fell in with Jim Averill.[96] Soon after the meeting, Averill began running a combination saloon, grocery store, and post office in the Sweetwater Valley near Independence Rock. In the spring of 1887, Averill proposed that Ella come do business with some of his female-hungry cow-hands, and the twenty-seven-year-old madam agreed.[97] In 1888, Ella set up shop at her own place about a mile from Jim's store. Her hog ranch consisted of a one-room cabin on a small pasture along Horse Creek.[98] Some of Ella's customers paid her in cattle, sometimes trading her an unbranded calf that may or may not have been stolen.[99]

Ella soon earned the nickname "Cattle Kate."[100] When rumors abounded about Averill running stolen cattle, Ella remained steadfast in her defense of him.[101] Added to the rumors was the fact that some of the cattle were branded "EW," Ella's brand, which had in fact been rejected by the Carbon County brand committee. Likewise, although Averill had also applied for a brand for five years straight, he, too, had been shot down.[102] The rumors grew uglier, and for a few months Averill and the larger stockgrowers, including Albert John Bothwell, hurled insults at each other via the local papers. In the meantime, Averill continued acquiring the cattle from Ella and sending them to market. Most of the cattle were branded with Ella's own brand, but it was still suspected that some weren't branded until they found their way into her corral.[103]

Following a harsh winter, local cattlemen caught Ella red-handed with some unbranded cattle. Then in June 1888, Averill and partner Frank Buchanan were accused of shooting cows belonging to someone else to prevent them from following their unbranded calves.[104] Following a meeting at Bothwell's late that month, a posse formed and rode out to Ella's under the guise of arresting her.[105] Fourteen-year-old Gene Crowder, who had made friends with Averill, later testified what happened next. "I was at Ella's trying to catch up a pony when they rode up. John Durbin took down the wire fence and drove the cattle out, while McLain and Connors kept Ella from going to the house. After a while they told her to get into the wagon and she asked them where they were going. They told her to Rawlins. She wanted to go to

FIGURE 77 ❧ *Artist Herndon Davis rendered this portrait of Ella "Cattle Kate" Watson, probably during the 1930s and years after her death. Davis is also known for his famous* Face on the Barroom Floor *at the Teller House in Central City, Colorado. Courtesy of the Mazzulla Collection, Colorado Historical Society, Denver.*

the house and change her clothes, but they would not let her and made her get into the wagon. Bothwell told her he would rope and drag her if she did not get in. She got in then and we all started toward Jim's. I tried to ride around the cattle and get ahead, but Bothwell took hold of my pony's bridle and made me stay with them."[106]

The posse next appeared at Averill's place, where the cattleman was preparing to depart for Casper to buy supplies. The men commanded Averill to throw up his hands and said they had a warrant, which he asked to see. According to Crowder, the men patted their rifles and "told him that was warrant enough." Averill was forced into the wagon at gunpoint, and the group moved toward Independence Rock. Averill's associate John DeCorey testified he tried to follow but was held off at gunpoint by Bothwell.[107] Crowder and DeCorey rode off to find help. The men at Averill's store, save for one Frank Buchanan, were afraid to act. When Buchanan located the posse, they had Ella and Averill in a canyon with ropes around their necks. Buchanan fired some shots but was outnumbered and forced to go look for more help. In the meantime, Averill and Ella were pushed off of the rocks they stood on. The fall wasn't enough to snap their necks, so the couple slowly strangled to death. Upon ascertaining they were dead, the posse rode off, leaving their bodies to swing from the tree.[108] Ella Watson made history as the first woman to be lynched in Wyoming.[109]

Even as Ella and Averill died, efforts were still being made to save them. The nearest sheriff was in Casper, some fifty miles away. Buchanan headed there but lost his way and was able only to reach the ranch of Tex Healy, about halfway to Casper. Healy rode on, and Buchanan returned to Sweetwater. Undersheriff Phil Watson at Casper soon set out with his men to see what the fuss was about, but it took three days for a legal posse to arrive from Carson City. The party found the bodies, buried them, and issued arrest warrants for the killers. The culprits were named as Bothwell, Tom Sun, John Durbin, R. M. Gailbraithe, Bob Connors, E. McLain, and an unknown man.[110]

The accused men, mostly powerful cattlemen, were allowed to bond out at $5,000 each. The trial was set for October, but in the meantime Frank Buchanan disappeared, and Gene Crowder succumbed to possible poisoning while in protective custody. Thus, there were no witnesses to testify at the trial, and the killers went free. Only one of the murderers was shot to death some months later, and his killer, too, went free.[111] Ella's surviving murderers continued to portray her as an evil bandit who had killed at least one husband and several men.[112] Her house of ill repute was eventually purchased by one of her killers, who moved it to his ranch and made an ice house out of it. Averill's store was torn down.[113]

Camp followers were also among Wyoming's harlots. At a place called the Flats near Wheatland in 1894, where the Wyoming Development Company was constructing an irrigation ditch, a Denver madam and four of her girls set up shop. One of the girls, known only as Babe, committed suicide there via carbolic acid. A Mr. and Mrs. McCallum assisted with her funeral services. Babe was buried in back of the camp.[114] At the rural settlement of Encampment west of Laramie, one of the saddest cases to come before Wyoming courts was that of nineteen-year-old Anna Groves in 1907. Anna had the misfortune of contracting venereal disease from a prominent local businessman. When he refused to help with her doctor bills, Anna tried to shoot him. She missed, but was still sentenced to a year of hard labor at the state pen. During her trial, however, it was painfully obvious that much of Anna's lower lip had been eaten away from the disease. Public sympathy was generated in local newspapers, and Governor Bryant B. Brooks pardoned her after five months.[115] What became of her is unknown, but she likely succumbed to her illness at an early age.

Among the more notorious women of Wyoming were Laura Bullion (alias "Laura Casey," "Clara Hays," "Della Rose," "Nellie Rose," "Cock-eyed Rose," "Freda Arnold," and "Freda Bullion Lincoln").[116] Laura's claim to fame was her association with the Wild Bunch—namely, her relationships with outlaws Will Carver and Ben Kilpatrick. Born in Arkansas or Texas in October 1876, Laura learned at least some of her outlaw ways from her father, Henry Bullion.[117] She first met Carver and Kilpatrick at the age of about thirteen. At the time, Carver was married to Laura's aunt, Viana Byler. He was also riding with the Tom "Black Jack" Ketchum Gang. When Viana died in 1891, Laura took up with Carver.[118] Others say Laura met Carver when he was with the Wild Bunch and she was working at a Sheridan dance hall.[119] She was also rumored to have worked for madam Fannie Porter in San Antonio, Texas, whose bordello was a popular hangout for the Wild Bunch.[120]

Records are unclear as to whether Laura worked in Sheridan and San Antonio before or after she spent some time with her grandparents in 1900. The census that year finds Laura living with E. R. and Serena Byler

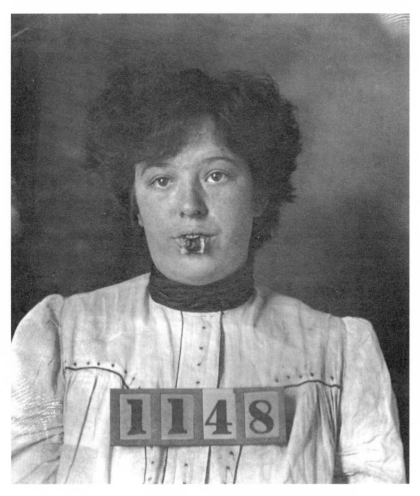

FIGURE 78 ❧ *Anna Groves's mug shot made for a pitiful sight,
her bottom lip showing the effects of venereal disease, 1907.
Upon her release from prison, the unfortunate girl disappeared, and
what became of her is unknown. Courtesy of the Department of State
Parks and Cultural Resources, Wyoming State Archives, Cheyenne.*

in Tom Green County, Texas. She is listed as single, literate, and working as a housekeeper.[121] Once she joined up with the Wild Bunch, however, she became a willing participant in their robberies.[122] The outlaws' acceptance of her is evidenced only by snippets of information about her. The men fondly referred to her as the "Rose of the Wild Bunch," but also as the "Thorny Rose" due to her tough demeanor. The unkindest remark about her was that she "could not think on her feet, she could only think on her back!"[123] Author Charles Kelly asserts that Laura was "passed along to other members of the gang."[124] On their behalf, Laura often sold the stolen goods acquired during various robberies.[125] Such references certainly imply that Laura also functioned as a prostitute among the Wild Bunch. When Will Carver died after a shootout with authorities in 1901, however, in his pocket was the wedding ring from his marriage to Viana as well as a photograph of Laura.[126]

The same train robbery that cost Carver his life, that of the Great Northern near Wagner, Montana, in 1900 also cost Laura in a substantial way. Laura was thought to have participated in the robbery, escaping with Ben "the Tall Texan" Kilpatrick to St. Louis, Missouri. The couple were masquerading as "Mr. and Mrs. John Arnold" when Laura was caught passing forged banknotes from the robbery. Kilpatrick was arrested a short time later.[127] Laura's occupation was listed as a prostitute.[128] "I wouldn't think helping to hold up a train was too much for her," noted St. Louis chief of detectives W. Desmond. "She is cool, shows absolutely no fear, and in male attire would readily pass for a boy. She has a masculine face, and that would give her assurance in her disguise."[129] Other notes about Laura include her nervous habit of chewing gum and the fact that she talked "like a machine gun."[130] She was sentenced to five years in prison but was released in 1905.[131]

From prison, Kilpatrick exchanged letters with Laura for the next few years. She passed the time by working under the name "Freda Arnold" in Georgia and Alabama.[132] Kilpatrick was released in 1911, but was killed just a few months later during a Southern Pacific train robbery.[133] In 1918, Laura moved to Memphis, Tennessee, living under the name "Freda Bullion Lincoln" and passing herself off as the war widow of one Maurice Lincoln. She also changed her birth year to 1887. Her occupations over the years included that of a drapery maker, interior designer, and seamstress. From 1927 to 1948, she lived in a quaint cottage on Madison Avenue in Memphis.

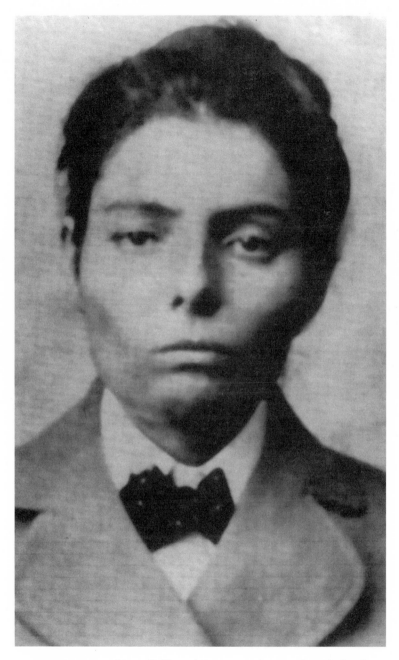

FIGURE 79 ❦ *Laura Bullion, circa 1901. Laura was the only female member of the Wild Bunch besides Etta Place to actively participate in robberies. She was said to have been descended from outlaws. Courtesy of the Library of Congress, Washington, D.C., LC-DIG-ppmsca-10777.*

The 1930 census lists Laura as "Freda Lincoln," a self-employed seamstress who was renting rooms to Luther and Pearl Butler. Laura died in 1961 and was buried in Memphis. Her great-niece purchased a headstone for her, which includes both her pseudonym and her real name, followed by the Wild Bunch's moniker for her, "The Thorny Rose."[134]

From the late 1910s through the 1940s, the prostitution industry kept a low but prominent profile in Wyoming. In 1912, former Pueblo, Colorado, madam Etta "Spuds" Murphy quietly moved to the Sandbar District of Casper. There, she spent her retirement washing clothes for other prostitutes. Fellow Colorado madam Laura Evens once went to visit Etta to offer her a home in Salida, "but she was ashamed and wouldn't even see me. Poor little Spuddy."[135] Departing women of Casper in 1912 included Kitty Hart and Marion Kent.[136] During the 1940s, when the town of Bon Rico was threatened with the demise of its coal mines, a dancehall with several girls still did a good business.[137] Violet Morgan owned a brothel in Rock Springs during the 1940s. At the time, there were seven whorehouses in town; the largest was the White House, which was noted for its excellence in both women and food.[138]

9

Where Did They All Go?

⚜ Between 1825 and 1988, the prostitution industry sprouted, flourished, and died within the Rocky Mountains. At its height, tens of thousands of women plied their trade in hundreds of mining camps, tent cities, towns, and metropolises. As one of the most enduring professions anywhere, prostitution was blatantly present in the region for more than 150 years. There is absolutely no question that even this most illicit of trades influenced and shaped the American West. Within that time span, the industry saw a number of changes as authorities first condoned it, then fined it, and ultimately outlawed it altogether. As disrespected and put upon as the madams and their working girls were, however, they managed to influence the way city, county, and state governments were formed. In their own way, they also brought comfort to an otherwise gritty world.

A business relationship between prostitution and government began when authorities figured out that they too could make money from the sex trade. Fines, fees, and licenses filled city hall safes, although authorities often wondered if this largesse was worth the violence, thievery, and tragedy that accompanied it. As more respectable women and wives began migrating West, the crackdowns grew harsher. During the 1890s and into the twentieth century, the Women's Christian Temperance Union and other female lodges came after the prostitution industry with a vengeance and ultimately were the main influence in getting it outlawed.

But the respectable women across the Rockies also instituted homes for women, hospitals, and counseling in their mission. They circulated petitions, appeared at city council meetings, and voiced their opinions in letters to high-ranking officials and local newspapers. Finally, in 1913, the American Federation for Sex Hygiene and the National Vigilance Association merged to form the American Social Hygiene Association. But even the new organization was divided between abolitionists looking to do away with prostitution and sanitariums hoping to promote health regulations among prostitutes.[1]

Other influences included the military, whose soldiers were inclined to overimbibe, become victims of violence, and contract venereal disease from the red light districts. Military officials personally closed down a number of red light districts throughout the West during World War I and again during World War II. As the large number of mining camps throughout the West dwindled into ghost towns, the harlots were forced to go elsewhere. They typically ended up in large cities, where the grungy alleys and back streets offered little in the way of sanitation or even police protection.

During the 1960s, America in general saw attitudes change regarding sex without marriage, cohabitation, and multiple partners. Although the profession managed to survive in the mountain towns, specifically in Montana, and Idaho, working girls in larger towns began seeing competition from college students and other young women who socially engaged in free love. "How can we charge for the same thing the college girls give away for free?" asked Silver City Millie.[2] Her thoughts in fact echoed the sentiments of Ruby Garrett, the famous Butte, Montana, madam who retired in 1982. "These little chippies will do it for a burger and a beer. I say they might as well sell it," she said.[3] A former working girl in Colorado felt the same way. "These modern girls are a bunch of ninnies. . . . These ninnies do everything that branded us bad—and get away with it."[4]

In the years since prostitution's confinement to the bad neighborhoods of large cities (the exception being Nevada, where the industry is legal in some counties), the profession has continued to intrigue certain historians and romantics. City governments, church officials, and many others have in fact done their part to do away with proof that prostitution ever existed. To make matters worse, Hollywood has enjoyed a long run as the primary

FIGURE 80 ❧ *A young prostitute from the 1920s or 1930s. Despite crackdowns by authorities and even the military, prostitution continued to flourish throughout the West for several decades. From the author's collection.*

peek into prostitution history. In a large majority of these instances, poetic license has marred the images of wanton women even more than when they were alive. It is only recently that historians have started searching for serious documentation, often having to piece it together in order to make up for large chunks of missing or incorrect history.

Another facet of prostitution's past has also suffered from both neglect and efforts to do away with it: the former brothels and red light districts themselves. For years, such neighborhoods remained abandoned or ignored due to their seedy pasts. They have gone from being warehouse districts to vacant lots. Some have been absorbed into commercial districts. Only a few remain somewhat in their original footprints, including brothel museums in Alaska, Colorado, Idaho, and Montana. These places especially deserve attention as the last authentic vestiges of Victorian prostitution in the Rocky Mountains.

Arizona

Throughout Arizona, much physical evidence remains of the state's prostitution history. Abandoned bordellos can still be seen in such remote places as Eden Hot Springs and Haynes. As late as 1963, a dance hall still stood at Mowry. Today one of the brothels at the ghost town of Chloride still survives just outside the city limits.[5]

Fortunately, there are still several "live" places that give a better sense of prostitution's vintage days. At Bisbee's elite Copper Queen Hotel, male visitors have spotted the ghost of prostitute Julia Lowell performing a striptease at the end of their bed or standing at the head of the stairs on the third floor. The Crown King Saloon at Crown King, Lulu's Bordello in Goldfield, and Yuma's Great Western Brothel Café pay homage to the wanton women of the past. Flagstaff's Hotel Monte Vista is said to be home to the ghosts of two prostitutes who were murdered on the third floor in the 1940s.[6]

Two other places are extremely worthy of mention: Jerome and Tombstone. Unfortunately, hardly anything is left of Jerome's red light district on Hull Avenue, including the celebrated cribs that survived long enough to be featured in more than one book about the town. Some of the houses of ill repute, including the Monte Carlo, eventually slid down the hill and were destroyed. More houses were torn down between 1948 and 1960. One of Jennie Bauters's places was torn down in 1972, and the remaining cribs were bulldozed during the 1980s. Only a few business houses remained in

Jerome as of 1999, including Lillian Douglas's brothel, which was serving as an apartment house, the Cuban Queen, and a small house used by two prostitutes during the 1920s and 30s.[7] The Sullivan Hotel, formerly Jennie Bauters's parlor house, remains on Jerome Avenue. Visitors can also go to the House of Joy gift shop which alleges to be a former brothel and Belgian Jennie's Bordello Bistro and Pizzeria. Jerome's museum includes displays on the fashion of Jerome's former naughty ladies.

Hull Avenue and Jerome in general still give a wonderful sense of place. Locals claim that a "phatom prostitute" is occasionally seen walking in front of the Community Center.[8]

Only a few success stories are known about Tombstone's red light ladies. One of them, Copperhead, was from the old South. Because her family's plantation had been destroyed by General Sherman and his troops, she claimed, she hated supporters of the Union and refused any customer wearing an army uniform. But she did eventually marry a rancher in the Sulpher Springs Valley and retired as a housewife.[9] Today nothing remains of the bawdy houses of Sixth Street in Tombstone. The only alleged remaining brothel is housed at the O.K. Corral, located near the site of the famous gunfight between Fremont (where the fight happened) and Allen streets. The Bird Cage Theatre, however, offers a marvelous view into the past. When it was reopened in 1934, the interior of the Bird Cage had been virtually untouched.[10] By some miracle, it survives today looking very much like it did during Big Minnie's reign and is now a museum. The theater is also allegedly haunted, and so attracts both history buffs and ghost hunters.

Tucson's Gay Alley no longer exists. The Leo Rich Music Hall, the Tucson Convention Center, and the police and fire stations now occupy the site. There is, however, rumored to be a boarded up brothel on the outskirts of town. The Sosa-Carillo-Fremont House Museum also remains as a remnant of the red light district. Ghost lovers lay claim to the spirit of a working girl who once worked at the Congress Hotel on East Broadway. The clicking of her high-heels can be heard across the lobby, and the ghost of her young son enjoys playing in the elevator.[11]

In 1979, the Mora saloon at 137 Railroad Avenue in Williams was purchased, converted into a bed and breakfast, and opened as the Red Garter Bed & Bakery. The upstairs rooms are Victorian in decor and named for some of the former working girls. Alleged ghosts include those of the people reportedly killed there in the early days, a murder victim from the 1940s, and the spirit of a young girl possibly named "Eva."[12] The old brothel saloons on either side of the Red Garter also contain some prostitute history.

Colorado

During the 1940s and 1950s, historians Fred and Jo Mazzulla specialized in visiting and interviewing former madams and prostitutes throughout Colorado. The endeavor was highly successful, most likely because the women were bona fide senior citizens who were willing to tell their stories in exchange for one more chance at fame and recognition. "In 1948," the Mazzullas later recalled, "a gentleman walked into the office with a shirt box bundle under his arm. He introduced himself and said, 'I was supposed to burn this box but I just can't do it. I hope you will accept it and preserve it.' In the box were fifty photographs which he identified in detail. Included were twenty five beautiful studio portraits of 'call' girls employed by Anna Gould [of Denver]. One girl became a Hollywood star, two had successful Broadway careers, and three married professional and influential husbands." As he left, the man confessed he was once married to Anna, which was how he came by the pictures.[13] In fact, the Mazzullas amassed an impressive collection of documents and photographs of Colorado's prostitutes. Most are on file with the Colorado Historical Society.

Countering the Mazzullas' success has been the occasional destruction of former brothels by people who care little for their history. At Matterhorn, located on the lake fork of the San Miguel River near Telluride, at least one dance hall with girls of ill repute survived for many years. But the population was only nine in 1940, and in the late 1970s the Forest Service ordered the remaining occupants of Matterhorn to tear down the dance hall.[14]

In other parts of the state, those on the trail of prostitution history can still see several worthy former red light districts. At Fraser's Crooked Creek Saloon, visitors can hear stories of Rosie, the lady of the evening said to haunt the place. Rosie and several of her friends are supposed to have died when her house caught fire during a bad blizzard in 1909. The Crooked Creek Saloon was built twenty-five years later on the site of Rosie's brothel, and a supposed painting of her was unearthed in the former house of one of her admirers. Similarly, another Fraser working girl known only as "Mary Jane" has a ski resort named for her.[15]

In what is now old Colorado City, admirers may view the tombstone of

Laura Bell McDaniel and her family at the entrance to Fairview Cemetery, where her family had her body moved in 1921. The red lamps from her last house are at the Old Colorado City Historical Society. Laura Bell's last brothel as well as those of Mamie Majors and a few others remain mostly intact on Cucharras Street (all are privately owned, and permission should be obtained before entering them). Blanche Burton is buried at Fairview as well, on a hill in the middle of the graveyard.

Likewise, Laura Evens's last brothel also survives in Salida. After Laura's death, her daughter, Lucille Sneddon, tried to give the building away, but no one wanted it. The Mon-Ark Shrine finally agreed to use the building as a lodge. The property did not include a wooden garage nearby, which contained five of Laura's cars. Lucille Sneddon removed the cars and rented out the garage for $75 per month. When she died in 1992, she left the garage to the Shriners, and they tore it down. Laura Evens's building has changed significantly over the years. It has been stuccoed, and several windows were covered over. Only the interior of the second floor remains similar to Laura's original decor. Likewise, Laura's cribs across the street have also been stuccoed and are now private apartments.[16]

Of Telluride's twenty-six houses of ill repute, only three cribs remain today, at 121, 123, and 125–27 East Pacific. Most of them were small two-room brothels, and the surviving buildings now serve as private homes. The Silver Bell Dance Hall also survives as the Ah Haa School for the Arts. A more authentic view of prostitution history can be found in Central City. In 1976, the campy film *The Duchess and the Dirtwater Fox*, starring Goldie Hawn and George Segal, was filmed in Central City and at the Gold Coin Saloon, which today sports photographs of the filming and other historic memorabilia.[17] Central City also holds its annual Lou Bunch Days each June with bed races, a parade, live music, and other activities honoring the three-hundred-pound madam. Visitors to the casino at Emmy Wilson's Glory Hole can still see the hole in the ceiling through which the lady dangled her legs for her customers' pleasure.

In Denver, Mattie Silks's old place is now a fancy restaurant adorned with photos from the red light district's past. Certain male employees of the restaurant claim that Mattie is still present and occasionally tickles the backs of their necks.[18] Just up the street, the Soiled Dove nightclub offers live music. Leadville's Pioneer Bar was converted to apartments in 1998, but the Pastime Bar next door retains traces of the town's bawdy past.

FIGURE 81 ⚜ *Historian and writer Melissa Trenary puts the finishing touches on some flowers at the grave of Pearl DeVere. Admirers from everywhere visit the grave often and leave Pearl tokens of love. From the author's collection.*

By far, the best example of Colorado's prostitution history is at the Old Homestead Parlour House Museum in Cripple Creek. Its furnishings reflect the way madam Pearl DeVere would have kept the Old Homestead. Among the period furnishings in the museum today is a gambling table from Johnny Nolon's Saloon, which in its time was one of the biggest casinos in town. A serving table in the dining room still has the mirror installed underneath, which the girls used to assure themselves that no petticoats protruded from under skirts. Other interesting features of the Old Homestead include a corset chair. The girls would straddle this chair and hang onto its back for dear life as another girl cinched them into their tight, waist-slimming corsets. Owned by the Wild Horse Casino next door, the Old Homestead came under management by the Cripple Creek District Museum during the summer of 2007 and celebrated its fiftieth year as a museum in 2008. Although the Wild Horse closed in October, the District museum hopes to continue running the Old Homestead in 2009. Another worthy site in Cripple Creek is the cabin of prostitute French Blanche LeCoq, which was formerly located at the nearby town of Midway. In 2005, Blanche's cabin was dismantled and moved to Cripple Creek. At this writing, it sits at the corner of Highway 67 and Golden Avenue at the entrance to the city.

Idaho

As in other states, Idaho's prostitution history can be found in the remotest of towns, such as at the Shady Lady Espresso Bar in Idaho City, and in the larger cities such as Boise, whose impressive Union Block downtown once housed a brothel in back for local businessmen. Other towns are even better about celebrating their prostitution history. In Murray, the folk song "The Legend of Molly b'Dam" is still heard throughout the town's local bars, and a two-day celebration each August, Molly b'Damn Days, pays tribute to the harlot with a heart of gold. Although Molly's original wooden headstone has been replaced, it can be viewed at the cemetery.[19] In 1961, St. Gertrude's convent in Cottonwood, Idaho, had many of Polly Bemis's personal effects on display. In 1987, her body was moved to the Bemis Ranch on the Salmon River. Both Polly's grave and her former home are accessible only by boat and are privately owned.[20]

In Wallace, several former bordellos remain standing. One of them is the 1313 Club, so named either because its bar ran thirteen feet long and thirteen feet wide (a real stretch for bartenders) or because when the club opened in the 1930s, twelve brothels and twelve saloons were already open in town. But Wallace's older prostitution history can also be found at the wonderful Oasis Bordello Museum, which is maintained by Jack and Michelle Mayfield. Nearly all the rooms are as they were left when the brothel closed in 1988, and a turn-of-the-twentieth-century room and several other antiques make for an informative and fun guided tour. Artifacts include the original sign from the Jade Rooms and other memorabilia. Some of the former working girls still occasionally pay a visit, including one woman who remembered she had stashed $5 under a small table statue![21]

Montana

Montana is still famous for its many intact ghost towns, some of which still have pieces of their red light history remaining. Intact brothels can be viewed in Virginia City and Nevada City's living history museums or in remote places such as the ghost towns Elkhorn and Garnet. Individuals on the prostitution trail can also stay at the prestigious Hotel Metlen in Dillon, once a brothel of the town, or see authentically furnished underground cribs in Havre, complete with sheets strung up between beds. Four houses of ill-repute remain, serving as private houses, in Livingston. In Missoula, two of "Mother Mary" Gleim's buildings still stand downtown and now function as businesses. At Halloween in 2007, local artists pooled their talents to create the Tainted Saints Old West Zombie Brothel in the back of the Badlander Bar. More than a thousand Missoulians turned out for the event.[22]

By far the best representative of Montana prostitution history, however, is the Dumas Brothel Museum in Butte. Unfortunately, the building is in dire need of structural repair, including a new roof. Because of its deteriorating condition, the museum was open only by appointment as of 2006, but reopened in 2007. Owner Rudy Giecek gives a most interesting and truly haunting history of the Dumas and its thousands of working girls. In April 2007, the museum received a sizeable donation and was seeking additional funds. Those seeking more information are encouraged to access the Dumas Web site at http://www.thedumasbrothel.com.

New Mexico

Pieces of New Mexico's brothel history are largely scattered in various ghost towns throughout the state. The ruins of a dance hall are visible in Elizabethtown. A dance hall and three saloons, including the Monte Cristo, remain standing in Chloride. The ghost town of Mogollon is most complete, and although no trace of the red light district is visible, it is an excellent representative of New Mexico's mining camps. In 1973, the movie *My Name Is Nobody* starring Henry Fonda was filmed there.[23]

At Pinos Altos, at least one dance hall remains standing as a private home. The same goes for a dance hall at the 1840s town of Placita, located two miles south of Monticello and twenty-five miles north of Truth or Consequences. The ghost town of Loma Parda, New Mexico's wickedest party town from 1851 to 1891, is still accessible and has a few buildings that may include the dance hall of Julian Baca. At Hillsboro, Sadie Orchard's house is now the Black Range Museum. In larger towns, the state's hooker heritage is not so visible. In Santa Fe, however, Burro Alley is still a local landmark. McGrath's Bar & Grill, located in the Hyatt Hotel in downtown Albuquerque, pays tribute to madam Lizzie McGrath.[24]

Utah

In Utah, remote places such as Alta, now a ski resort, still display information about their ladies of the evening. One house of ill repute can also still be seen at Deer Valley outside of Park City. But Utah's paths of prostitution can also be illusive. The Carbon Hotel in Carbon County, for instance, discreetly recognizes its racy history with only a cutout of a scantily clad woman in a second-floor window.[25]

In Salt Lake City, absolutely nothing is left of the old Stockade or its surroundings, save for the Citizens' Investment Company building. Indeed, only Ogden seems proud to show off its wicked past. Twenty-fifth Street, also known as "Two-Bit Street," offers an interesting walking tour that includes interpretive signage on most buildings. In more recent years, the City of Ogden has promoted the sordid history of its infamous street. A $30,000 grant from both the state and the city enabled historians to reconstruct Twenty-fifth Street's past and even put up a kiosk to tell about it.[26]

Wyoming

Wyoming's harsh winters and high winds have been most unkind to ghost towns all over the state. Most brothel history therefore actually lies in the downtown areas of the state's larger cities. At Cheyenne near the railroad tracks, for instance, several three-story brick buildings that served as former brothels remain, but without any signage identifying them. Such places typically had restaurants on the first floor, a tavern on the second, and bordellos on the third.[27] Former red light districts can also be found in Casper, Gillette, Green River, Laramie, and Rawlins, especially if one looks for the older portions of the business district one or two blocks off the main drags.

Wyoming's largest monument to prostitution, dedicated to Mother Featherlegs, lies down ten miles of rough road from Lusk on the Old Cheyenne Trail. When the monument was placed in 1964, a pair of red pantaloons were left draped over the monument but have long disappeared. Reenactors occasionally gather to honor the murdered madam. At least one of them made history in 1990 at Saloon No. 10 in Deadwood, South Dakota. Eva Lou Paris, portraying the spirit of Mother Featherlegs, waltzed into the saloon with a "proclamation from the governor," demanded her underwear back, and forcibly took them off the saloon girl who was wearing them. The historic pantaloons were put on display at the Stagecoach Museum in Lusk.[28]

Such antics are typical in towns all across the Rocky Mountains and the West, where hundreds of towns include the characters of bawdy house women in their annual celebrations today. Among these celebrations are Madam Lou Bunch Days in Central City, Colorado, Molly b'Damn Days in Murray, Idaho, and many others. These events are not only raucous fun, but also keep alive the spirit of the Rocky Mountain's wicked women. In truth, even though the hardiest of these women have passed into the great beyond, time is on their side. The larger the time gap between their illustrious lifetimes and the present, the greater the chance they will eventually be recognized—at least in a scholarly context—as an integral part of the Old West. At least, that is what we can hope.

APPENDIX I:

PROSTITUTES IN LEADVILLE, COLORADO, 1880

Mollie Alderson, born 1860 New York
Laura Ashton, born 1858 Ohio
Frankie Clark, born 1858 Illinois
Jamie Clark, born 1856 New York
M. Cunningham, born 1857 Missouri
Kitty Darby, born 1857 Vermont
Mamie Dolan, born 1847 Georgia
Mollie Edwards, born 1852 Missouri
Lillie Elmer, born 1855 Louisiana
Etta Farr, born 1855 Iowa
James Farr, born 1849 Illinois
Jenine Farr, born 1850 Iowa
Nettie Ferrel, born 1862 Kansas
Jessie Green, born 1860 Pennsylvania
Minnie Hall, born 1860 New York
Mollie Harris, born 1858 Kentucky
Nellie Harris, born 1853 Indiana
Hattie Jackson, born 1859 Missouri
Jennie Jones, born 1856 Colorado
Pearl Lake, born 1858 Missouri
Clara Lewis, born 1862 Missouri
Carrie Linnell, born 1849 Illinois
Mabel London, born 1857 England
Jennie Mahoney, born 1857 Ireland
Katie Marom, born 1861 Ireland
Eugene Mater, born 1846 Italy
Mollie May, born 1850 Virginia

Julia Nanton, born 1850 Ohio

Della Price, born 1855 Ireland

Frank Otaria, born 1860 Canada

Mollie Price, born 1858 Ireland

Sallie Purple, born 1860 Illinois

Sallie's employees:

> Josie Collins, born 1861 Colorado
>
> Birdie Meillar, born 1860 Virginia
>
> Maggie Fisher, born 1860 Indiana
>
> Della Ross, born 1858 Missouri
>
> Amie Arthur, born 1859 Indiana
>
> Blanch Terry, born 1852 Missouri
>
> Dot, born 1861 Missouri
>
> Ruby Thompson, born 1858 Texas

Gertrude Roe, born 1856 Canada

Lottie Sandels, born 1856 Missouri

Angelina Saxe, born 1855 Canada

H. E. Scott, born 1849 Illinois

Minnie Seane, born 1858 Massachusetts

N. Smith, born 1856 Kentucky

Mollie Stanton, born 1855 Maryland

Clora Stone, born 1855 Pennsylvania

Nettie Storms, born 1857 New York

Bella Williams, born 1846 Missouri

Source: U.S. Bureau of the Census, *Tenth Census of the United States, 1880* (Washington, D.C.: National Archives and Records Administration, 1880).

APPENDIX II
PROSTITUTES IN BUTTE, MONTANA, BY ADDRESS, 1902

East Galena

17 Palmer, Josie
21 Casey, Ophelia
Thomas, Bessie
22 DeBrias, Emma
23 Brown, Irene
26 Peters, Pauline
28 Nowlin, Inez
29 Miller, Gussie
30 Martin, Mollie
31 Love, Jennett
32 Smith, Freda
33 Ofzoald, Maguerite
34 Dykes, Daisy
36 Donohue, Bridget
39 Zantier, Blanche
42 Dorothy, Bridget
44 Hazelby, Alice
46 Cassidy, Clara
49 Laval, Louie
50 Peterson, Dora
51 Laval, Adrienne
52 Lavelle, Irene
53 Yancy, Mary
54 Hooligan, Mazie
55 Fouchet, Mignon
57 Luetgen, Jeanette

59 Ulmstrum, Mini
60 Waters, Sally
61 Kuse, Jennie
62 Smith, Millie
63 Reischsle, Lea
64 Winslow, Alice
65 Brum, Juana
67 Brum, Suzanne
68 Lamon, Lillie
69 Levy, Ulna
73 Elta, Marie
Jane, Blondinette
109 Lorn, Bessie

East Mercury

8 Rank, Ida
10 Franklin, Nellie
12 Anderson, Mattie
14 Mahoney, Biddy
18 Wilson, Emma
22 Blake, Della
25 Arnold, Sadie
26 Evans, Ollie
27 Lazy, Lucy
28 Jones, Alma
Maloney, Bridget
29 Miller, Gussie
30 Martin, Rose
Troy, Mildred
31 O'Dair, Marguerite
32 Stuart, Helen
33 Martin, Fannie P.
35 Remy, Alice
37 Winston, Belle
39 Haywood, Ella
40 Munro, Nellie
42 Mahoney, Nora

44 Proctor, Alice

46 Martin, Pearl

47 Howard, Cora

Inman, Vera

Sherman, Marie

Stephens, Jessie

48 Lee, Nellie

50 Russ, Tillie

51 Cramer, Carrie

Louis, Margaret

52 Brooks, May

54 Duval, Florence

55 Sayre, Julia

62 Lumeau, Louise

South Wyoming Alley

114 Wilbur, Hazel

Pleasant Alley

23 Foster, Jennie

27 Thomas, Jessie

29 Hall, Lizzie

30 Preston, Lou

32 Thompson, Edith

34 Japanese Lodging House

36 Dillon, Bertha

37 Bassett, Blanche

38 Parlow, Katrina

39 Johnson, Lillie

40 Wilson, Ida

44 Jones, Jennie

53 Florence, Kitty

57 Steward, Florence

59 Sona, Mamie

64 LeRoux, Anna

Source: Butte–Silver Bow County, Montana, Directory, 1902, http://www.ancestry.com.

Appendix III

Prostitutes in
Cheyenne, Wyoming, 1880

All-White House

Ida Hamilton, married, age 34
Florence Vaughn, married, age 30
Puss Newport, divorced, age 30
Ida Snow, widow, age 38
Mattie Lloyd, single, age 19
May West, single, age 29
Lillie Hughes, single, age 20
Emma Whitrow, single, age 28
John Crow, Chinese, male, servant

All-Mulatto House

Octavia Reeves, widow, keeping house, mulatto, age 29
William C. Reeves, son, mulatto, age one month
Fannie Reeves, born Missouri, married, mulatto, age 20
Mary Brooks, born 1846 Ohio, married, mulatto
Maggie Cartwell, born 1858 Missouri, married, mulatto
Laura Copeland, born 1855 Ohio, married, mulatto
Willie Young, mulatto, married, age 21
Sallie Barney, black, servant, age 23

All-Mulatto House

Pauline Alexander, married, black, keeping house, age 30
Cathine, Mollie, born 1847 Virginia, mulatto, single
Sarah Harris, born 1856 Arkansas, mulatto, widow
Libbie Jennings, mulatto, single, age 20
Bettie Montgomery, mulatto, single, age 20

Henry Alexander, black, barkeeper, age 24

William Alexander, black, waiter, age 21

Note: Neither of the Alexander boys appear related to
Pauline, and all three were born in different states.
Also note that the ladies of the house were delicately
referred to as "mulatto," whereas their servants are
called "black."

Cribs Girls

Lizzie Richmond, born Ohio, single, white, age 25,
resided with Mabel Smith, single, white, age 20

Addie C. Edwards, born 1854 Ohio, single, white

Ida Flora, born 1858 Michigan, married, white

Mary Hill, born 1855 Germany, single, white

Belle Ridge, born 1850 Ireland, single, white

Lillie Woods, born 1851 Virginia, single, white, resided
with Pauline Todd, housekeeper, age 23, and Lillie's
son, Charlie, five years old. A male clerk, John Mills,
also lived there.

Louisa Harris, born 1845 Virginia, black, married, residing in a boardinghouse of mostly male occupants

Nellie Smith, born 1852 Indiana, single, resided with
forty-four-year-old Flora Clifford, who does not
appear to have been a madam

Source: U.S. Bureau of the Census, *Tenth Census of the United States, 1880*
(Washington, D.C.: National Archives and Records Administration, 1880).

NOTES

Chapter One

1. Walter O'Meara, *Daughters of the Country: The Women of the Fur Traders and Mountain Men* (New York: Harcourt, Brace and World, 1968), 151.
2. Leslie Gourse, *Native American Courtship and Marriage* (Summertown, Tenn.: Native Voices, 2005), 70.
3. O'Meara, *Daughters of the Country*, 153, 159.
4. Ibid., 153–54, 170.
5. Ibid., 150.
6. Volney Steele, M.D., *Bleed, Blister, and Purge: A History of Medicine on the American Frontier* (Missoula, Mont.: Mountain Press, 2005), 59.
7. Ibid., 58.
8. O'Meara, *Daughters of the Country*, 159.
9. Steele, *Bleed, Blister, and Purge*, 60.
10. Jan MacKell, *Brothels, Bordellos, and Bad Girls: Prostitution in Colorado 1860–1930* (Albuquerque: University of New Mexico Press, 2004), 32.
11. Ibid., 33.
12. Ibid., 34.
13. Roman Malach, *Oatman: Gold Mining Center* (Kingman, Ariz.: H&H Printers for the Arizona Bicentennial Commission, 1975), 39.
14. Joan Swallow Reiter, ed., *The Women* (New York: Time-Life Books, 1978), 129.
15. Bennie Blake, "Women of the Back Streets: Jerome's Ladies of the Night," in *Experience Jerome and the Verde Valley: Legends and Legacies* (Sedona, Ariz.: Thorne Enterprises, 1990), 219.
16. Elliott West, *The Saloon on the Rocky Mountain Frontier* (Lincoln: University of Nebraska Press, 1979), 48.
17. MacKell, *Brothels, Bordellos, and Bad Girls*, 52.
18. Rosen cited in Jay Moynahan, *Ladies of Easy Virtue in the Bitterroot Mountains* (Spokane, Wash.: Chickadee, 1999), 23.
19. Byron A. Johnson and Sharon P. Johnson, *Gilded Palaces of Shame: Albuquerque's Redlight Districts 1880–1914* (Albuquerque, N.Mex.: Gilded Age Press, 1983), 30.
20. Miscellaneous news clipping, July 7, 1881, p. 2, Prostitution File, Silver Bow County Archives, Butte, Montana.
21. West, *The Saloon on the Rocky Mountain Frontier*, 22.

22. Ben T. Traywick, *Behind the Red Lights—History of Prostitution in Tombstone* (Tombstone, Ariz.: Red Marie's, 1993), 71–73.

23. Ibid., 32, 44.

24. West, *The Saloon on the Rocky Mountain Frontier*, 21.

25. Jeffrey Nichols, *Prostitution, Polygamy, and Power: Salt Lake City, 1847–1918* (Urbana: University of Illinois Press, 2002), 50.

26. U.S. Bureau of the Census, *Thirteenth Census of the United States, 1910* (Washington, D.C.: National Archives and Records Administration, 1910).

27. Alexy Simmons, *Red Light Ladies: Settlement Patterns and Material Culture on the Mining Frontier*, Anthropology Northwest no. 4 (Corvallis: Department of Anthropology, Oregon State University, 1989), 80.

28. MacKell, *Brothels, Bordellos, and Bad Girls*, 258.

29. Simmons, *Red Light Ladies*, 14.

30. Ibid., 15.

31. Ibid., 14.

32. Lawrence Powell, "Early California Society," *Westways Magazine* (August 1965), 17.

33. Jay Moynahan, *Photographs of the Red Light Ladies 1865–1920* (Spokane, Wash.: Chickadee, 2005), 101.

34. Herbert Asbury, *The Barbary Coast* (New York: Pocket Books, 1957), 130.

35. Ibid., 130–34.

36. Jay Moynahan, *Remedies from the Red Lights: Cures, Treatments, and Medicines from the Sportin' Ladies of the Frontier West* (Spokane, Wash.: Chickadee, 2000), 18.

37. Simmons, *Red Light Ladies*, 89, 16.

38. Asbury, *The Barbary Coast*, 158, 162.

39. Simmons, *Red Light Ladies*, 15.

40. Moynahan, *Remedies from the Red Lights*, 11.

41. Simmons, *Red Light Ladies*, 18.

42. Ibid., 19.

43. MacKell, *Brothels, Bordellos, and Bad Girls*, 195.

44. Asbury, *The Barbary Coast*, 171.

45. Simmons, *Red Light Ladies*, 89.

46. Asbury, *The Barbary Coast*, 137.

47. Simmons, *Red Light Ladies*, 17.

48. Ibid., 16, 17.

49. Ibid., 15.

50. Asbury, *The Barbary Coast*, 168.

51. Lambert Florin, *Ghost Towns of the West* (Superior, Neb.: Superior Publishing for Promontory Press, 1970), 119.

52. Asbury, *The Barbary Coast*, 166.

53. Simmons, *Red Light Ladies*, 17, 88.

54. John Astle, *Only in Butte: Stories off the Hill* (Butte, Mont.: Holt, 2004), 150.

55. MacKell, *Brothels, Bordellos, and Bad Girls*, 195.

56. Simmons, *Red Light Ladies*, 14.

57. MacKell, *Brothels, Bordellos, and Bad Girls*, 195.

58. Nichols, *Prostitution, Polygamy, and Power*, 96.

59. Jay Moynahan, *The Good Time Girls' Guide to Gold Rush Cuisine* (Spokane, Wash.: Chickadee, 2006), 71.
60. Correspondence with Jay Moynahan, Spokane, Washington, December 2007.
61. MacKell, *Brothels, Bordellos, and Bad Girls*, 184.
62. Correspondence with Dr. Thomas J. Noel, Denver, Colorado, December 2007.
63. Jimmy Harold Smith, "Prostitution in Arizona Mining Camps 1870–1917," thesis, Northern Arizona University, Flagstaff, May 1977, 4.
64. Simmons, *Red Light Ladies*, 137.
65. Ibid.
66. Johnson and Johnson, *Gilded Palaces of Shame*, 27.
67. Max Evans, *Madam Millie: Bordellos from Silver City to Ketchikan* (Albuquerque: University of New Mexico Press, 2002), 86–77.
68. MacKell, *Brothels, Bordellos, and Bad Girls*, 2.
69. Simmons, *Red Light Ladies*, 33.
70. MacKell, *Brothels, Bordellos, and Bad Girls*, 46.
71. *The Butte Miner*, September 10, 1896, Prostitution File, Silver Bow County Archives.
72. MacKell, *Brothels, Bordellos, and Bad Girls*, 171.
73. Evans, *Madam Millie*, 86–87.
74. MacKell, *Brothels, Bordellos, and Bad Girls*, 43, 30.
75. Traywick, *Behind the Red Lights*, 7–8.
76. MacKell, *Brothels, Bordellos, and Bad Girls*, 28.
77. Warren J. Brier, "Tilting Skirts and Hurdy-Gurdies: A Commentary on Gold Camp Women," *Montana Magazine* (Autumn 1969), 58.
78. Moynahan, *Remedies from the Red Lights*, 14.
79. Brier, "Tilting Skirts and Hurdy-Gurdies," 58.
80. *Montana News Association*, insert 2:93, December 23, 1918, p. 1, col. 3.
81. Richard Erdoes, *Saloons of the Old West* (Avenel, N.J.: Grammercy Books, a division of Random House Value, 1997), 199.
82. *Montana News Association*, insert 2:93, December 23, 1918, p. 1, col. 3.
83. MacKell, *Brothels, Bordellos, and Bad Girls*, 12.
84. Evans, *Madam Millie*, xiv.
85. Mary Murphy, "Women on the Line: Prostitution in Butte, Montana 1878–1917," master's thesis, University of North Carolina, Chapel Hill, 1983, in the archives of the Montana Historical Society, Helena.
86. Simmons, *Red Light Ladies*, 33.
87. Joanne West Dodds, *What's a Nice Girl Like You Doing in a Place Like This?* (Pueblo, Colo.: Focal Plain, 1996), 16.
88. Elliott West, "Scarlet West: The Oldest Profession in the Trans-Mississippi West," *Montana Magazine* (Spring 1981), 18.
89. Cathy Luchetti, *I Do! Courtship, Love, and Marriage of the American Frontier* (New York: Crown Trade Paperbacks, 1996), 206.
90. MacKell, *Brothels, Bordellos, and Bad Girls*, 6.
91. Parker got his. A few months later he accosted Albright and tried to shoot him, but Albright was quicker and killed Parker in self-defense. Nichols, *Prostitution, Polygamy, and Power*, 101–2.

92. Jay Moynahan, *Soiled Doves, Sportin' Women, and Other Fallen Flowers* (Spokane, Wash.: Chickadee, 2005), 68.

93. MacKell, *Brothels, Bordellos, and Bad Girls*, 131.

94. Simmons, *Red Light Ladies*, 92.

95. MacKell, *Brothels, Bordellos, and Bad Girls*, 46.

96. Blake, "Women of the Back Streets," 230.

97. Johnson and Johnson, *Gilded Palaces of Shame*, 27.

98. MacKell, *Brothels, Bordellos, and Bad Girls*, 3–5.

99. Maxine was once caught liberating a customer's diamond stud and was accordingly banished from her place of employment. Traywick, *Behind the Red Lights*, 11, 15.

100. Menu from the Red Onion Saloon, Skagway, Alaska, 2002, http://www.redonion1898.com.

101. West, "Scarlet West," 18.

102. Allen M. Jones, review of *Bleed, Blister, and Purge: A History of Medicine on the American Frontier* by Volney Steele, M.D., *New West Network*, July 14, 2005, http://www.newwest.net/index.php/main/article/2240/.

103. Simmons, *Red Light Ladies*, 34.

104. Beth Sagstetter and Bill Sagstetter, *The Mining Camps Speak* (Denver: Benchmark, 1998), 151.

105. Clark Secrest, *Hell's Belles: Denver's Brides of the Multitudes* (Denver: Hindsight Historical, 1996), 107.

106. Simmons, *Red Light Ladies*, 35.

107. Steele, *Bleed, Blister, and Purge*, 92.

108. Ron V. Jackson, Accelerated Indexing Systems, comp., *U.S. Federal Census Mortality Schedules Index* (online database) (Provo, Utah: Generations Network, 1999).

109. Lester Ward Ruffner, *All Hell Needs Is Water* (Tucson: University of Arizona Press, 1972), 53–54.

110. Jackson, *U.S. Federal Census Mortality Schedules Index*.

111. Dodds, *What's a Nice Girl Like You Doing in a Place Like This?*, 27.

112. Coroner's Docket, November 1895–December 1897, Silver Bow County Archives.

113. Traywick, *Behind the Red Lights*, 29.

114. Douglas D. Martin, *Silver, Sex, and Six Guns* (Tombstone, Ariz.: Tombstone Epitaph, 1962), 10–16.

115. Traywick, *Behind the Red Lights*, 29.

116. Martin, *Silver, Sex, and Six Guns*, 27.

117. "Gunfight at the O.K. Corral," *Wikipedia*, http://en.wikipedia.org/wiki/Gunfight_at_the_O.K._Corral.

118. Martin, *Silver, Sex, and Six Guns*, 27, 38.

119. Ibid., 44.

120. Traywick, *Behind the Red Lights*, 29.

121. Martin, *Silver, Sex, and Six Guns*, 47.

122. Traywick, *Behind the Red Lights*, 30.

123. Martin, *Silver, Sex, and Six Guns*, 47.

124. Ibid., 51.

125. Traywick, *Behind the Red Lights*, 10, 41.

126. Undated, untitled manuscript, author unknown, Prostitution File, Bisbee Historical Society, Bisbee, Arizona, 37.

127. Ben T. Traywick, ed., *Frail Prisoners in Yuma Territorial Prison* (Tombstone, Ariz.: Red Marie's, 1997), 149–54.

128. Jay Moynahan, *Red Light Revelations: The Sportin' Women of Wallace and the Silver Valley, 1888 to 1909* (Spokane, Wash.: Chickadee, 2001), 19–20.

129. Ibid., 14.

130. Traywick, *Frail Prisoners in Yuma Territorial Prison*, 165–67.

131. Sian Rees, *The Floating Brothel* (New York: An imprint of Hyperion, 2002), 91.

132. "Painted Ladies of the Old West," *Legends of America*, http://www.legendsofamerica.com/WE-PaintedLady2.html.

133. MacKell, *Brothels, Bordellos, and Bad Girls*, 41.

134. Johnson and Johnson, *Gilded Palaces of Shame*, 53.

135. Steele, *Bleed, Blister, and Purge*, 138.

136. Simmons, *Red Light Ladies*, 34.

137. Steele, *Bleed, Blister, and Purge*, 93.

138. Simmons, *Red Light Ladies*, 34.

139. Steele, *Bleed, Blister, and Purge*, 32.

140. Simmons, *Red Light Ladies*, 34.

141. Steele, *Bleed, Blister, and Purge*, 195.

142. MacKell, *Brothels, Bordellos, and Bad Girls*, 2.

143. Simmons, *Red Light Ladies*, 33.

144. Ibid.

145. MacKell, *Brothels, Bordellos, and Bad Girls*, 41.

146. Moynahan, *Remedies from the Red Lights*, 27.

147. MacKell, *Brothels, Bordellos, and Bad Girls*, 42–43.

148. "Victorian Prostitution," http://www.home.pacbell.net/tonyprey/burning/viceran/htm.

149. Anne M. Butler, *Daughters of Joy, Sisters of Misery* (Chicago: University of Illinois Press, 1985), 45 n. 35.

150. Coroner's Docket, November 1895–December 1897, Silver Bow County Archives.

151. MacKell, *Brothels, Bordellos, and Bad Girls*, 2, 42.

152. Traywick, *Behind the Red Lights*, 6.

153. MacKell, *Brothels, Bordellos, and Bad Girls*, 197.

154. Traywick, *Behind the Red Lights*, 74.

155. Johnson and Johnson, *Gilded Palaces of Shame*, 51.

156. Luchetti, *I Do!*, 209.

157. Herbert V. Young, *They Came to Jerome* (Jerome, Ariz.: Jerome Historical Society, 4th printing, 2000), 107.

158. Clark Secrest, *Hell's Belles: Prostitution, Vice, and Crime in Early Denver*, rev. ed. (Boulder: University of Colorado Press, 2002), 233.

159. West, *The Saloon on the Rocky Mountain Frontier*, 27.

160. Johnson and Johnson, *Gilded Palaces of Shame*, 43.

161. Ibid., 52.

162. Sanford C. Gladden, *Ladies of the Night*, Early Boulder Series no. 5 (Boulder, Colo.: Privately published, 1979), 34.

Chapter Two

1. James E. Sherman and Barbara H. Sherman, *Ghost Towns of Arizona* (Norman: University of Oklahoma Press, 1969), 3.
2. See "The Road Wanderer," http://www.theroadwanderer.net/railghosts. htm.
3. "Arizona Legends: Canyon Diablo—Meaner Than Tombstone," *Legends of America*, http://www.legendsofamerica.com/AZ-CanyonDiablo.html.
4. Gerald M. Knowles, *Route 66 Chronicles*, vol. 1 (Winfield, Kans.: Central Plains Book Manufacturing, 2002), 34.
5. "Arizona Legends: Canyon Diablo."
6. Knowles, *Route 66 Chronicles*, 1:42.
7. Gladwell Richardson, "A Drink for the Dead," *Arizona Highways* (June 1963): 34.
8. See "City of Tucson," http://www.ci.Tucson.az.us/about.html.
9. Roy P. Drachman, *this is not a book* Just Memories*, at *Parent's Eyes Arizona*, http://www.parentseyes.arizona.edu/drachman.html.
10. Joan Schuman, "Working Women," *Tucson Weekly*, June 1, 2003, http://www.tucsonweekly.com/gbase/CityWeek/Content?oid=47171.
11. It is unknown whether Jennie and Roy Drachman were related to one another. Drachman, *this is not a book* Just Memories*; Schuman, "Working Women."
12. Marshall Trimble, *Arizona: A Cavalcade of History* (Tucson, Ariz.: Treasure Chest, 1989), 229.
13. Debe Branning, *Sleeping with Ghosts! A Ghost Hunter's Guide to Arizona's Haunted Hotels and Inns* (Phoenix: Goldenwest, 3rd printing, 2007), 130.
14. Schuman, "Working Women."
15. Drachman, *this is not a book* Just Memories*.
16. Undated, untitled manuscript, author unknown, Prostitution File, Bisbee Historical Society, Bisbee, Arizona, 68.
17. Marshall Trimble, *Roadside History of Arizona* (Missoula, Mont.: Mountain Press, 2004), 434.
18. Undated, untitled manuscript, author unknown, Prostitution File, Bisbee Historical Society, 71–76.
19. Ibid.
20. Ibid., 74–75.
21. "Arizona's Saints and Shady Ladies," Arizona Memory Project, contributed by the Arizona Historical Foundation, http://www.azmemory. lib.az.us.
22. Undated, untitled manuscript, author unknown, Prostitution File, Bisbee Historical Society, 73, 80.
23. "Arizona's Saints and Shady Ladies."
24. Undated, untitled manuscript, author unknown, Prostitution File, Bisbee Historical Society, 80, 81.
25. "Phoenix," *Wikipedia*, http://en.wikipedia.org/wiki/Phoenix,_Arizona.
26. Bradford Luckingham, *Phoenix: The History of a Southwestern Metropolis* (Tucson: University of Arizona Press, 1989), 60–61.
27. *Akron Weekly Pioneer Press* (Colorado), July 21, 1899, p. 4, col. 3.

28. Luckingham, *Phoenix*, 94, 115.

29. Ibid., 115.

30. Ibid., 144–45.

31. Undated, untitled manuscript, author unknown, Prostitution File, Bisbee Historical Society, 32.

32. Writer's Program of the Work Projects Administration, *Arizona: A State Guide* (New York: Hastings House, 1940), 193.

33. W. A. Haak, *Copper Bottom Tales: Historic Sketches from Gila County* (Globe, Ariz.: Gila County Historical Society, 1991), 62.

34. Undated, untitled manuscript, author unknown, Prostitution File, Bisbee Historical Society, 34–35; Haak, *Copper Bottom Tales*, 63.

35. Undated, untitled manuscript, author unknown, Prostitution File, Bisbee Historical Society, 35.

36. Elliott West, *The Saloon on the Rocky Mountain Frontier* (Lincoln: University of Nebraska Press, 1979), 49.

37. Undated, untitled manuscript, author unknown, Prostitution File, Bisbee Historical Society, 36–39.

38. Ibid., 40.

39. Trimble, *Arizona*, 135.

40. Undated, untitled manuscript, author unknown, Prostitution File, Bisbee Historical Society, 40–41.

41. Haak, *Copper Bottom Tales*, 63; Trimble, *Roadside History of Arizona*, 126.

42. Trimble, *Roadside History of Arizona*, 72.

43. Platt Cline, *Mountain Town: Flagstaff's First Century* (Flagstaff, Ariz.: Northland Press, 1994), 1, 124, 176.

44. *Coconino Weekly*, July 27, 1893, p. 3, col. 2.

45. Cline, *Mountain Town*, 44–46.

46. Ibid., 47.

47. Ibid., 47–50.

48. Sanborn Fire Insurance maps, October 1901–1904, Arizona Historical Society, Northern Division, Flagstaff.

49. Cline, *Mountain Town*, 90, 97.

50. Sanborn Fire Insurance map, 1916, Arizona Historical Society, Northern Division.

51. *Coconino Sun*, September 5, 1916, p. 1, col. 2.

52. Maurice Kildare, "Dutch May's Shimmy Shakers," unpublished, undated manuscript, Gladwell Richardson Collection, archives of the Arizona Historical Society, Northern Division, 1–7.

53. Ibid.

54. Ibid., 8.

55. Ibid., 13.

56. *Coconino Sun*, September 1, 1916, p. 1, col. 2.

57. Ibid.

58. *Coconino Sun*, September 5, 1916, p. 1, col. 2.

59. *Coconino Sun*, September 1, 1916.

60. *Coconino Sun*, September 5, 1916.

61. *Coconino Sun*, September 1, 1916.

62. *Coconino Sun*, September 5, 1916.
63. "Prescott Case," undated photocopied document, Prostitute File, Arizona Historical Society, Northern Division.
64. Kildare, "Dutch May's Shimmy Shakers," 15.
65. *Coconino Sun*, September 5, 1916.
66. Branning, *Sleeping with Ghosts!* 49.
67. Author's interview with George Wallace Smith, Laughlin, Nevada, January 2008.
68. Author's interview with Barbara Espino, Laughlin, Nevada, January 2008.
69. Herbert V. Young, *They Came to Jerome* (Jerome, Ariz.: Jerome Historical Society, 4th printing, 2000), 5.
70. Bennie Blake, "Women of the Back Streets: Jerome's Ladies of the Night," in *Experience Jerome and the Verde Valley: Legends and Legacies* (Sedona, Ariz.: Thorne Enterprises, 1990), 219–23.
71. Ibid., 223.
72. Young, *They Came to Jerome*, 58–59.
73. The Fashion exhibit, Jerome Historical Society Museum, Jerome, Arizona.
74. Jim Smith, "Prostitution in Arizona, 1870–1935: A Brief History," thesis, Northern Arizona University, Flagstaff, 1975, in Special Collections and Archives, Jerome State Historic Park Collection, Cline Library, Jerome, Arizona, 2.
75. Young, *They Came to Jerome*, 59.
76. The Fashion exhibit.
77. Jerome Walking Tour, Jerome, Arizona.
78. Blake, "Women of the Back Streets," 220.
79. Young, *They Came to Jerome*, 106.
80. Blake, "Women of the Back Streets," 220.
81. Jennie Bauters exhibit, Jerome Historical Society.
82. Blake, "Women of the Back Streets," 222.
83. Young, *They Came to Jerome*, 107.
84. Blake, "Women of the Back Streets," 222.
85. Young, *They Came to Jerome*, 107.
86. Smith, "Prostitution in Arizona," 2.
87. Young, *They Came to Jerome*, 110, 69.
88. *Jerome Mining News*, February 15, 1904, p. 1, col. 1; Blake, "Women of the Back Streets," 226.
89. Smith, "Prostitution in Arizona," 2.
90. Blake, "Women of the Back Streets," 226.
91. Smith, "Prostitution in Arizona," 3.
92. Ibid.
93. Jerome Walking Tour.
94. Branning, *Sleeping with Ghosts!*, 61.
95. John Muretic, *To Heaven in the West* (Sedona, Ariz.: Oak Creek Press, 1970), 16.
96. Blake, "Women of the Back Streets," 227.
97. Ibid., 228.

98. Sherman and Sherman, *Ghost Towns of Arizona*, 82.

99. Blake, "Women of the Back Streets," 230.

100. Ibid.

101. Dr. Frank Brown exhibit, Jerome Historical Society Museum.

102. Blake, "Women of the Back Streets," 230.

103. The Fashion exhibit.

104. Blake, "Women of the Back Streets," 230.

105. Dr. Frank Brown exhibit.

106. *Boothill Grave Yard, a Descriptive List of More Than 250 Graves on Boothill,* informational pamphlet, Boothill Cemetery, Tombstone, Arizona, 2007, 13.

107. Ben T. Traywick, *Behind the Red Lights—History of Prostitution in Tombstone* (Tombstone, Ariz.: Red Marie's, 1993), 41.

108. West, *The Saloon on the Rocky Mountain Frontier*, 48.

109. Kalambaki [full name unknown], "The Busy Belles of Bisbee or There's More to Life Than Smelting Copper," undated manuscript, Prostitution File, Bisbee Historical Society, 5; Traywick, *Behind the Red Lights*, 43.

110. Sherry Monahan, *The Wicked West: Boozers, Cruisers, Gamblers, and More* (Tucson, Ariz.: Rio Nuevo, 2005), 144–45.

111. Traywick, *Behind the Red Lights*, 66.

112. Monahan, *The Wicked West*, 105.

113. Traywick, *Behind the Red Lights*, 80.

114. Ibid., 2.

115. Trimble, *Roadside History of Arizona*, 91.

116. Sherman and Sherman, *Ghost Towns of Arizona*, 153; Trimble, *Roadside History of Arizona*, 91.

117. Traywick, *Behind the Red Lights*, 19; "Big Nose Kate," *Wikipedia*, http://en.wikipedia.org/wiki/Big_Nose_Kate.

118. Other spellings of Kate's maiden name include "Harony," "Horony," "Haroney," and "Horoney." Letter from Pat Bowmaster to the Bisbee Historical Society, February 9, 2007.

119. "Big Nose Kate."

120. Chris Enss, *Pistol Packin' Madams: True Stories of Notorious Women of the Old West* (Helena, Mont.: Twodot, an imprint of the Globe Pequot Press, 2006), 50.

121. Letter from Pat Bowmaster. Author Chris Enss believes Kate may have come by her nickname later, when she was in Texas. Enss, *Pistol Packin' Madams*, 51.

122. Enss, *Pistol Packin' Madams*, 51.

123. Letter from Pat Bowmaster.

124. Some also say the marriage failed only after the baby died. JoAnn Chartier and Chris Enss, *Love Untamed: Romances of the Old West* (Guildord, Conn.: Twodot, an imprint of the Globe Pequot Press, 2002), 80; Enss, *Pistol Packin' Madams*, 50.

125. Fred Mazzulla and Jo Mazzulla, *Outlaw Album*, 12th ed. (Denver: A. B. Hirschfeld Press, 1979), 8.

126. Traywick, *Behind the Red Lights*, 19.

127. Chartier and Enss, *Love Untamed*, 82; "Doc Holliday," *Wikipedia*, http://en.wikipedia.org/wiki/Doc_Holliday.

128. Chartier and Enss, *Love Untamed*, 82.

129. Traywick, *Behind the Red Lights*, 19.

130. Enss, *Pistol Packin' Madams*, 53.

131. Earp family tree by Larry Crawford, http://www.ancestry.com.

132. Enss, *Pistol Packin' Madams*, 53.

133. The 1860 census spells Mattie's name "Cele A. Blylock" and shows she was born in Iowa to farmers Henry and Elizabeth Blylock. The family was living in Monroe, Johnson County, Iowa (U.S. Bureau of the Census, *Eighth Census of the United States, 1860* [Washington, D.C.: National Archives and Records Administration, 1860]). In the 1870 census, the family name is spelled "Blalock" (U.S. Bureau of the Census, *Ninth Census of the United States, 1870* [Washington, D.C.: National Archives and Records Administration, 1870]). The 1880 census lists Mattie as being born in Wisconsin. It should be noted, however, that her parents' birthplace was left blank in the census, as was Bessie Earp's, which seems to indicate that neither Mattie nor Bessie were present when the census was taken and that one of the other occupants of the house mistakenly gave Mattie's birthplace as Wisconsin (U.S. Bureau of the Census, *Tenth Census of the United States, 1880* [Washington, D.C.: National Archives and Records Administration, 1880]).

134. This information originally came from Mattie's descendants (Blaylock-L Archives, http://www.rootsweb.com; PoeForward, "Western Dead Girls—Earp Women," http://www.PoeForward.com). What is known for sure is that according to the 1870 census, Wyatt was living with his family in Missouri. Following the death of his first wife, Urilla Sutherland, he left Missouri. By 1872, he was in Peoria, Illinois, residing at Jane Haspel's bordello. In February of that year, Wyatt, his brother Morgan, and one George Randall were arrested in a raid on the house. Four women were arrested as well, leading to speculation that Mattie was one of the occupants ("Wyatt Earp," *Wikipedia*, http://en.wikipedia.org/wiki/Wyatt_Earp). According to other historians, however, Mattie was in Fort Scott in 1872, where she had one documented photograph taken of herself (http://www.genealogy.com/famous folks/Earp/notes.html). At least one historian claims Mattie and Wyatt married as early as 1873 in Illinois (Constance Staarmann Ancestry, http://www.ancestry.com). Another says they may have met in 1873 in Fort Scott or Dodge City, Kansas (PoeForward, "Western Dead Girls—Earp Women"). Yet another says they married in Rice or Scott County in 1874 (Avestwater family tree, http://www.ancestry.com). Others maintain Wyatt met Mattie as early as 1875, making Kate's statement about when Wyatt "went back to Mattie" applicable to Texas. For at least part of 1875, Wyatt and his brother James were in Wichita ("Wyatt Earp"). There, according to author Don Chaput, several fancy girls who were involved with the brothers at various times took the name "Earp" as their own ("Celia [Cely, Celie] Ann Blalock [Earp?]", http://www149.pair.com/marilynn/mattie.htm). Some biographies say Mattie was with Wyatt when he arrived in Dodge City, further illustrating that she may have met him previously ("Wyatt Earp"). Unfortunately, virtually no documentation exists to back up any of these statements.

135. Wyatt Earp first recounted this incident for Stuart Lake's whimsical biography, *Wyatt Earp: Frontier Marshal* (Boston: Houghton Mifflin, 1931), but the story has no documentation to back it up. Enss, *Pistol Packin' Madams*, 51–52; "Big Nose Kate."
136. Chartier and Enss, *Love Untamed*, 82–83.
137. The *Wikipedia* article "James Earp" (http://en.wikipedia.org/wiki/James_Earp) says the couple married in Kansas. Author Glenn Boyer says it was Illinois. Glenn G. Boyer, ed., *I Married Wyatt Earp: The Recollections of Josephine Sarah Marcus Earp* (Tucson: University of Arizona Press, 2d printing, 1979), 57 n. 6.
138. Other sources have placed Kate back at Fort Griffin, "Contonment" (as spelled), Sweetwater, or Hidetown, Texas. Letter from Pat Bowmaster.
139. "Mattie," http://www.milams.com.
140. Enss, *Pistol Packin' Madams*, 53.
141. Letter from Pat Bowmaster.
142. Chartier and Enss, *Love Untamed*, 84.
143. Enss, *Pistol Packin' Madams*, 53.
144. Chartier and Enss, *Love Untamed*, 84.
145. "Doc Holliday."
146. James's wife would have been Bessie Earp. Wyatt's wife may have been Mattie Blaylock, although Kate does not name her. Chartier and Enss, *Love Untamed*, 84.
147. "James Earp."
148. "Two More Old West Prostitutes and Their Men," in *The Life, Times, and Adventures of Rambling Bob*, http://www.ramblingbob.wordpress.com.
149. Chartier and Enss, *Love Untamed*, 85.
150. Author Ben Traywick maintains Annie first came to Tombstone in 1881, so there is a likelihood that Earp was her first landlord. In time, she became known as "Queen of the Red Light District." Annie was remembered as a kindly woman who staked many a miner's claim and frequently offered up her house as a temporary hospital during epidemics. When she died in 1883, according to Traywick, more than a thousand buggies and wagons accompanied her to Boothill Cemetery. U.S. Bureau of the Census, *Tenth Census of the United States, 1880* (Washington, D.C.: National Archives and Records Administration, 1880); Traywick, *Behind the Red Lights*, 32, 90; Lambert Florin, *Ghost Towns of the West* (Superior, Neb.: Superior Publishing for Promontory Press, 1970), 137; *Boothill Grave Yard*, 11.
151. Jan MacKell, "The True Love of Wyatt and Josie Earp," *Colorado Gambler* magazine (February 6–12, 2007), 23.
152. Anne M. Butler, *Daughters of Joy, Sisters of Misery: Prostitutes in the American West 1865–90* (Chicago: University of Illinois Press, 1985), 79.
153. Ibid.
154. Josie could not have been performing at the famous Bird Cage Theatre, however, as many claim, because it did not open until December 26, 1881. Traywick, *Behind the Red Lights*, 25.
155. Sadie Jo and Josephine Marcus exhibits, Bird Cage Theatre Museum, Tombstone, Arizona, September 2007.
156. PoeForward, "Western Dead Girls—Earp Women."

157. Waters cited in Casey Tefertiller, "What Was Not in Tombstone Travesty," http://www.home.EarthLink.net/~nuthcol/Travesty/notintravestysource. htm. It is notable that many scholars, Tefertiller among them, hotly disputed Waters's manuscript when an earlier version was discovered minus Allie's scathing testimony. Thus, historians continue to debate whether the Earp women knew of Wyatt's affair with Josie and how much it affected Mattie.

158. MacKell, "The True Love of Wyatt and Josie Earp," 23. These days, Terry and Wyatt continue to tour the West and perform in shows about Wyatt Earp and Big Nose Kate. Author's interview with Terry Earp, Cripple Creek, Colorado, 2005.

159. Chartier and Enss, *Love Untamed*, 85.

160. Traywick, *Behind the Red Lights*, 19.

161. Other historians claim that Behan and County Supervisor Milt Joyce, neither of whom liked Holliday, got Kate drunk and coerced her into signing the papers. Some say that the judge took it upon himself to dismiss the charges, having no evidence that Holliday did anything. Also, Kate sobered up to find she had herself been fined $12.50 on two counts of being drunk and disorderly. Chartier and Enss, *Love Untamed*, 85; Traywick, *Behind the Red Lights*, 20.

162. Chartier and Enss, *Love Untamed*, 86.

163. Traywick, *Behind the Red Lights*, 20.

164. Chartier and Enss, *Love Untamed*, 84.

165. Myra Vanderpool Gormley, "Wyatt Earp's Family," http://www.ancestry. com. Louisa is said to have been the granddaughter of Samuel Houston, founder of Texas (FamilyHart Database, http://www.ancestry.com). In 1880, she was living with Morgan, his brother Warren, and their parents, Nicholas and Virginia Earp, in Temescal, California ("Earp Family," http://www. ancestry.com). It should be noted that in the 1880 census, Louisa, like Mattie Blaylock, is listed as an Earp. Researchers have apparently failed to find any record of Louisa's marriage to Morgan, but the likelihood of her being allowed to live in Morgan's parents' house without sanctity of marriage is questionable. Noting Louisa as Morgan's common-law wife also stirs speculation that she, like Mattie, may have formerly been a prostitute.

166. "Morgan Earp," *Wikipedia*, http://en.wikipedia.org/wiki/Morgan_Earp.

167. "Gunfight at the O.K. Corral."

168. Rubén Sálaz Márquez, *New Mexico: A Brief Multi-history* (Albuquerque: Cosmic House, 2005), 344.

169. Chartier and Enss, *Love Untamed*, 86.

170. "Big Nose Kate."

171. Chartier and Enss, *Love Untamed*, 87.

172. MacKell, "The True Love of Wyatt and Josie Earp," 23.

173. "Morgan Earp." Louisa apparently left the Earp household in California sometime after Morgan's murder. She died in Long Beach in 1894. "Louisa Houston," *One World Tree*, http://www.ancestry.com.

174. Boyer, *I Married Wyatt Earp*, 57 n. 6; MacKell, "The True Love of Wyatt and Josie Earp," 23.

175. "James Earp."

176. Earp family tree by Larry Crawford.

177. "Doc Holliday"; MacKell, "The True Love of Wyatt and Josie Earp," 23.
178. Traywick, *Behind the Red Lights*, 21.
179. Richard Erdoes, *Saloons of the Old West* (Avenel, N.J.: Grammercy Books, a division of Random House Value, 1997), 198.
180. Letter from Pat Bowmaster.
181. Chartier and Enss, *Love Untamed*, 87.
182. Frank Waters, *The Earp Brothers of Tombstone: The Story of Mrs. Virgil Earp* (New York: Framhall House, 1960), 212.
183. Earp family tree by Larry Crawford.
184. Blaylock-L Archives.
185. Ibid.
186. Visitors to Mattie's lonely grave today have noted that her original tombstone has been stolen and a homemade marker identifies the site. "Gravesites," http://www.WesternOutlaw.com.
187. Blaylock-L Archives.
188. Waters and Lake cited in PoeForward, "Western Dead Girls—Earp Women."
189. Chartier and Enss, *Love Untamed*, 87.
190. "Big Nose Kate."
191. Enss, *Pistol Packin' Madams*, 54. Cummings committed suicide in 1915. "Big Nose Kate."
192. Letter from Pat Bowmaster.
193. U.S. Bureau of the Census, *Thirteenth Census of the United States, 1910* (Washington, D.C.: National Archives and Records Administration, 1910). The 1920 census lists the town as "Des Calegas." U.S. Bureau of the Census, *Fourteenth Census of the United States, 1920* (Washington, D.C.: National Archives and Records Administration, 1920).
194. Traywick, *Behind the Red Lights*, 21; U.S. Bureau of the Census, *Fifteenth Census of the United States, 1930* (Washington, D.C.: National Archives and Records Administration, 1930).
195. Letter from Pat Bowmaster.
196. MacKell, "The True Love of Wyatt and Josie Earp," 23.
197. Jay Moynahan, *Soiled Doves, Sportin' Women, and Other Fallen Flowers* (Spokane, Wash.: Chickadee, 2005), 34.
198. "Bird Cage Theatre," *Wikipedia*, http://en.wikipedia.org/wiki/Birdcage_Theater.
199. Moynahan, *Soiled Doves, Sportin' Women, and Other Fallen Flowers*, 35; Traywick, *Behind the Red Lights*, 25.
200. The Bird Cage allegedly inspired the song "She's Only a Bird in a Gilded Cage" by Arthur Lamb, although the tune was not written until about 1900. "Bird Cage Theatre"; "Arthur J. Lamb," Internet Movie Database, http://www.imdb.com.
201. "Bird Cage Theatre."
202. Traywick, *Behind the Red Lights*, 27–28.
203. Ibid.
204. Traywick, *Behind the Red Lights*, 28.
205. Moynahan, *Soiled Doves, Sportin' Women, and Other Fallen Flowers*, 39.
206. Butler, *Daughters of Joy*, 78.

207. Traywick, *Behind the Red Lights*, 25–26.

208. Florin, *Ghost Towns of the West*, 134.

209. Trimble, *Arizona*, 228; Traywick, *Behind the Red Lights*, 25.

210. One of the most vulgar dances at the Bird Cage was once executed by three men wearing tights with ladies' underwear over the top. When the dancers began emulating sexual moves, male audience members threw a rope around the manager and beat him up. Erdoes, *Saloons of the Old West*, 172.

211. Traywick, *Behind the Red Lights*, 6–7.

212. Ibid., 23–24.

213. Ibid., 14, 33–35.

214. In 1884, a new cemetery was opened in town, and the original cemetery literally fell to ruins. Both cemeteries, however, continued to fulfill a need for burial spots, given Tombstone's rowdy reputation. Ibid., 35; *Boothill Grave Yard*, 2.

215. Traywick, *Behind the Red Lights*, 22–23, 64–68.

216. Jay Moynahan, *The Prairie Prostitute's Own Cookbook* (Spokane, Wash.: Chickadee, 2000), 55.

217. Traywick, *Behind the Red Lights*, 24–25, 43–44.

218. Ibid., 21–22. Nosey Kate should not be confused with Big Nose Kate. Similar and identical-sounding nicknames ran rampant throughout the Old West, so it is no surprise that historians have confused Nosey Kate and Big Nose Kate. A similar circumstance occurred in 1887 when a local paper noted that Dutch Annie and Augustine Martinez were arrested for using foul language. The original Dutch Annie had died in 1883, though, so the woman in 1887 must have been a newcomer who knew nothing of the first Dutch Annie. The new Dutch Annie was in Tombstone through at least 1900 (ibid., 33). As for Augustine Martinez, city records note that she was down with rheumatism in April 1894 and did not pay for her license, but that she was doing so again by September 1897 (ibid., 94).

219. Ibid., 36–37, 42, 63.

220. Ibid., 37–39.

221. Jay Moynahan, *Photographs of the Red Light Ladies 1865–1920* (Spokane, Wash.: Chickadee, 2005), 19.

222. Traywick, *Behind the Red Lights*, 41–42, 63.

223. Butler, *Daughters of Joy*, 80.

224. Traywick, *Behind the Red Lights*, 26, 44.

225. Ibid., 18.

226. Traywick, *Behind the Red Lights*, 26.

227. Trimble, *Arizona*, 229.

228. Traywick, *Behind the Red Lights*, 26.

229. Muretic, *To Heaven in the West*, 25–26.

230. Bob Newman, "The Gulch's 'Soiled Doves' Were Part of History," undated newspaper article, Prostitution File, Bisbee Historical Society.

231. Ibid.

232. Muretic, *To Heaven in the West*, 30.

233. Governor Jack Williams, *From the Ground Up: Stories of Arizona's Mines and Early Mineral Discoveries* (Douglas, Ariz.: Phelps Dodge Corporation, 1981), 11.

234. Kalambaki, "The Busy Belles of Bisbee," 7. Irish Mag's story is also told in Tombstone, where it is claimed she lent money to a stranger to stake a claim. The stranger left without thanks, but came back several months later and handed her a bank receipt for half a million dollars. In this version of the tale, Mag got her money and retired to Belfast. Traywick, *Behind the Red Lights*, 29.

235. Kalambaki, "The Busy Belles of Bisbee," 6.

236. Newman, "The Gulch's 'Soiled Doves' Were Part of History."

237. Kalambaki, "The Busy Belles of Bisbee," 6.

238. *Mohave County Miner*, September 14, 1907, B2.

239. Kalambaki, "The Busy Belles of Bisbee," 6, 10.

240. Newman, "The Gulch's 'Soiled Doves' Were Part of History."

241. Kalambaki, "The Busy Belles of Bisbee," 9.

242. Newman, "The Gulch's 'Soiled Doves' Were Part of History"; Kalambaki, "The Busy Belles of Bisbee," 9.

243. Branning, *Sleeping with Ghosts!*, 20.

244. Kalambaki, "The Busy Belles of Bisbee," 8.

245. Newman, "The Gulch's 'Soiled Doves' Were Part of History."

246. Wes Patience, *Bune to Bisbee and Back: A Swedish Family's Pilgrimage 1883–2004* (Bisbee, Ariz.: Cowboy Miner Productions in cooperation with the Bisbee Mining and Historical Museum, 2005), 114.

247. Muretic, *To Heaven in the West*, 28.

248. Debra L. Mues, "Women Contributed to Bisbee's Past," *Bisbee People*, October 25, 1978, 4.

249. "By First Ordinance: Women Are Barred from Saloons," *Bisbee Daily Review*, undated news clipping, author unknown, Prostitution File, Bisbee Historical Society.

250. Patience, *Bune to Bisbee and Back*, 191.

251. Trimble, *Roadside History of Arizona*, 81.

252. Patience, *Bune to Bisbee and Back*, 198.

253. Trimble, *Roadside History of Arizona*, 81, 97.

254. Florin, *Ghost Towns of the West*, 81–84.

255. Knowles, *Route 66 Chronicles*, 1:61–64.

256. Author's interview with George Wallace Smith, Laughlin, Nevada, December 2007.

257. See "Williams, Arizona," http://www.williamschamber.com.

258. "The Red Garter," *Legends of America*, http://www.legendsofamerica. com/AZ-RedGarter; *The American West on America's Main Street, Williams Arizona, Historic Walking Tour*, pamphlet (Williams, Ariz.: City of Williams Historic Commission, 2007).

259. Ben T. Traywick, ed., *Frail Prisoners in Yuma Territorial Prison* (Tombstone, Ariz.: Red Marie's, 1997), 38.

260. See "Western History," *Horse Feathers*, http://www.64.233.167.104/ search?q=cache:tMguOupuhzgJ:www.cowboythings.com/store/ westernhistory.html+%22Georgie+Clifford%22+Arizona&hl=en&ct= clnk&cd=1&gl=us.

261. Traywick, *Frail Prisoners in Yuma Territorial Prison*, 33.

262. Ibid., 35–40.

263. Ibid.

264. Ibid., 38–44.

265. *The American West on America's Main Street.*

266. Cabinet Saloon display, Cabinet Saloon, Williams, Arizona, September 2007.

267. "The Red Garter."

268. Ibid.

269. Branning, *Sleeping with Ghosts!*, 133.

270. *The American West on America's Main Street.*

271. Jim Harvey, "Arizona History: Web of Time 28," *Web Newsroomer*, Arizona History, January 2002, http://www.66.218.69.11/search/cache?ei= UTF-8&p=prostitute+in+arizona+history.

272. *The American West on America's Main Street.*

273. "The Red Garter."

274. Undated, untitled manuscript, author unknown, Prostitution File, Bisbee Historical Society, 42–45.

275. Ibid.

276. Haak, *Copper Bottom Tales*, 65.

277. "The Red Garter."

278. Trimble, *Roadside History of Arizona*, 100.

279. Haak, *Copper Bottom Tales*, 66.

280. Trimble, *Roadside History of Arizona*, 165.

Chapter Three

1. Jan MacKell, *Brothels, Bordellos, and Bad Girls: Prostitution in Colorado 1860–1930* (Albuquerque: University of New Mexico Press, 2004), 107 (this printing cited unless otherwise noted).

2. Walter O'Meara, *Daughters of the Country: The Women of the Fur Traders and Mountain Men* (New York: Harcourt, Brace and World, 1968), 167.

3. MacKell, *Brothels, Bordellos, and Bad Girls*, 108–9.

4. Ibid., 110.

5. Ibid., 111, 210.

6. Ibid., 252–53.

7. Jan MacKell, *Cripple Creek District: Last of Colorado's Gold Booms* (Mount Pleasant, S.C.: Arcadia, 2003), 47.

8. U.S. Bureau of the Census, *Thirteenth Census of the United States, 1910* (Washington, D.C.: National Archives and Records Administration, 1910); U.S. Bureau of the Census, *Fifteenth Census of the United States, 1930* (Washington, D.C.: National Archives and Records Administration, 1930).

9. Elliott West, *The Saloon on the Rocky Mountain Frontier* (Lincoln: University of Nebraska Press, 1979), 23–24.

10. Jan MacKell, "Lillian Powers, Genteel Harlot of the West," unpublished manuscript, 2005, 1.

11. "Lillian Powers of Florence," miscellaneous clipping, Lillian Powers File, Canon City Public Library, Canon City, Colorado.

12. MacKell, *Brothels, Bordellos, and Bad Girls*, 119–20.

13. MacKell, "Lillian Powers," 2.

14. MacKell, *Brothels, Bordellos, and Bad Girls*, 260.

15. Linda La Rocca, "The Season of the Spirits at Leadville's Evergreen Cemetery," *Colorado Central Magazine*, http://www.cozine.com/archive/cc1995/00210102.html; U.S. Bureau of the Census, *Federal Mortality Census Schedules, 1850–1880 (Formerly in the Custody of the Daughters of the American Revolution), and Related Indexes, 1850–1880*, T655, 30 rolls (Washington, D.C.: National Archives and Records Administration, n.d.), available at http://www.ancestry.com; MacKell, *Brothels, Bordellos, and Bad Girls*, 120.

16. William H. Bauer, James L. Ozment, and John H. Willard, *Colorado Post Offices 1859–1989* (Golden: Colorado Railroad Museum, 1990), 132.

17. Perry Eberhart, *Guide to the Colorado Ghost Towns and Mining Camps*, 4th ed. (Columbus: Swallow Press, Ohio University Press, 1981), 427; Muriel Sibell Wolle, *Stampede to Timberline* (Boulder, Colo.: Muriel Sibelle Wolle, sponsored by the University of Colorado, 2d printing, 1949), 291.

18. Robert L. Brown, *Ghost Towns of the Colorado Rockies* (Caldwell, Idaho: Caxton Printers, 1977), 326.

19. U.S. Bureau of the Census, *Tenth Census of the United States, 1880* (Washington, D.C.: National Archives and Records Administration 1880).

20. The Colorado City referred to here is now the west side of Colorado Springs. Present-day Colorado City is located twenty-five miles south of Pueblo, close to the ghost settlement of Greenhorn.

21. MacKell, *Brothels, Bordellos, and Bad Girls*, 83.

22. Sanford C. Gladden, *Ladies of the Night*, Early Boulder Series no. 5 (Boulder, Colo.: Privately published, 1979), 5.

23. MacKell, *Brothels, Bordellos, and Bad Girls*, 83.

24. Jan MacKell, "Bad Girls of Northern Colorado," *American Western Magazine* (March 16, 2005), http://www.americanwesternmagazine.com.

25. MacKell, *Brothels, Bordellos, and Bad Girls*, 85.

26. Ibid., 84, 198, 233.

27. Ibid., 70.

28. *The Colorado Mountaineer*, March 14, 1877, 2.

29. MacKell, *Brothels, Bordellos, and Bad Girls*, 71; U.S. Bureau of the Census, *Tenth Census of the United States, 1880*.

30. Jan MacKell, "Laura Bell McDaniel, Queen of the Colorado City Tenderloin," paper presented at "Extraordinary Women of the Pikes Peak Region," 2007 Pikes Peak Regional History Symposium, Pikes Peak Library District, Colorado Springs, Colorado, June 9, 2007.

31. Ibid.

32. Ibid.

33. U.S. Bureau of the Census, *Thirteenth Census of the United States, 1910*.

34. *Colorado Springs Gazette Telegraph*, July 31, 1910, p. 15, col. 3.

35. In Baldwin's time, the estate was called Claremont. Today this home is known as "the Trianon," home of the elite Colorado Springs School. MacKell, "Laura Bell McDaniel"; Jim Easterbrook, *The Time Traveler in Old Colorado* (Colorado Springs, Colo.: Great Western Press, 1985), 23.

36. *Colorado Springs Independent*, January 31, 1918, p. 1, col. 2.

37. MacKell, "Laura Bell McDaniel."

38. MacKell, *Brothels, Bordellos, and Bad Girls*, 74.

39. *Cripple Creek Daily Advertiser*, February 21, 1894, p. 2, col. 2.

40. *Colorado Springs Gazette & Telegraph*, March 9, 1924, p. 4, col. 7.

41. MacKell, *Brothels, Bordellos, and Bad Girls*, 77.

42. *Cripple Creek Daily Advertiser*, February 21, 1894, p. 2, col. 2.

43. Ibid.

44. MacKell, *Brothels, Bordellos, and Bad Girls*, 79. A number of family trees claim that Younger was briefly married to Myra "Belle Starr" Shirley and that his mummified remains were found in a New Mexico cave in 1888. See http://www.ancestry.com.

45. *Cripple Creek Daily Advertiser*, February 21, 1894, p. 2, col. 2.

46. MacKell, *Brothels, Bordellos, and Bad Girls*, 76.

47. Colorado City Board of Trustees, *Ordinances of the Town of Colorado City*, compiled by John R. Watt, City Attorney (Colorado City, Colo.: W. P. Epperson, Iris Printers, 1896).

48. MacKell, *Brothels, Bordellos, and Bad Girls*, 135–38.

49. Ibid., 203–5.

50. In 1983, Bill Henderson, former mayor of Colorado Springs, told Blanche's story to the Garden of the Gods Rotary Club. The audience was so moved that they appealed to Richard Wilhelm of Wilhelm Monument Company to donate a proper gravestone for Blanche. Ibid., 207–8.

51. Ibid., 223, 245–47.

52. Clark Secrest, *Hell's Belles: Prostitution, Vice, and Crime in Early Denver*, rev. ed. (Boulder: University of Colorado Press, 2002), 75.

53. Gary Wiles and Delores Brown, *Femme Fatales, Gamblers, Yankees, and Rebels in the Gold Fields [1859–1869]* (Hemet, Calif.: Birth of America Books, 2005), 39–40, 213, 293–312.

54. Hillyer Best, *Julia Bulette and Other Red Light Ladies* (Sparks, Nev.: Western Printing, 1959), 9.

55. MacKell, *Brothels, Bordellos, and Bad Girls*, 53.

56. Harry Sinclair Drago, *Notorious Ladies of the Frontier* (New York: Dodd, Mead, 1969), 128–30.

57. For the 1900 census, Mattie said she was born in New York in about 1846, but changed her birthplace to Pennsylvania for the 1910 census. Authors Clark Secrest and Chris Enss have identified her as being born in Indiana or Kansas, respectively. U.S. Bureau of the Census, *Twelfth Census of the United States, 1900* (Washington, D.C.: National Archives and Records Administration, 1900); U.S. Bureau of the Census, *Thirteenth Census of the United States, 1910*; Secrest, *Hell's Belles*, 215; Chris Enss, *Pistol Packin' Madams: True Stories of Notorious Women of the Old West* (Helena, Mont.: Twodot, an imprint of Globe Pequot Press, 2006), 56.

58. *Fairmount Cemetery, Distinguished Women Walking Tour*, Denver, undated pamphlet; Enss, *Pistol Packin' Madams*, 57; MacKell, *Brothels, Bordellos, and Bad Girls*, 55.

59. *Fairmount Cemetery, Distinguished Women Walking Tour*.

60. Max Miller, *Holladay Street* (New York: Signet Books, 1962), 72.

61. Enss, *Pistol Packin' Madams*, 57.

62. MacKell, *Brothels, Bordellos, and Bad Girls*, 57.

63. Drago also maintains Mattie was using her last name long before she ever met George Silks. Drago, *Notorious Ladies of the Frontier*, 131.

64. MacKell, *Brothels, Bordellos, and Bad Girls*, 57; Enss, *Pistol Packin' Madams*, 58.

65. Drago, *Notorious Ladies of the Frontier*, 131.

66. Enss, *Pistol Packin' Madams*, 58.

67. Some sources say Mattie's famous necklace was once owned by prostitute Lizzie Preston of Denver. Madam Lil Powers of Florence owned it later. MacKell, *Brothels, Bordellos, and Bad Girls*, 120; Enss, *Pistol Packin' Madams*, 58.

68. MacKell, *Brothels, Bordellos, and Bad Girls*, 57. There are several versions of this incident. Author Chris Enss claims Kate showed up at an engagement party hosted by Mattie and Thomson at the Olympic Gardens and accused Mattie of "stealing her man" (Enss, *Pistol Packin' Madams*, 59). In his book *Holladay Street*, author Max Miller made the ridiculous claim that Mattie and Katie actually stripped to their waists before duking it out. The newspapers surely would have reported on such an outrageous incident, leaving historians to conclude that Miller's version is purely a figment of his own fantasy (see Clark Secrest, *Hell's Belles: Denver's Brides of the Multitudes* [Denver: Hindsight Historical, 1996], 232). During the duel, according to Henry Drago, the women took their shots but missed—save for Katie's stray bullet, which struck Thomson in the neck. He lived and even pledged to be faithful to Mattie (Drago, *Notorious Ladies of the Frontier*, 132). In the end, the best source for the fight comes from the *Rocky Mountain News*, which reported that Katie and Mattie had an argument following a footrace that Thomson won and for which Mattie collected $2,000. During the argument, Thomson punched Katie in the face and knocked her down. Next, Katie's friend Sam Thatcher was knocked down as well. Then Katie was knocked down again and kicked in the face, which broke her nose. After the fight broke up, Thomson took off toward town in his buggy. A carriage soon pulled up beside him, and a shot from said carriage hit him in the neck. Katie left town for a while, but returned to Denver in September, where she had another fight with Mattie. This time, Mattie punched Katie, knocking her down and injuring her nose again (MacKell, *Brothels, Bordellos, and Bad Girls*, 58).

69. MacKell, *Brothels, Bordellos, and Bad Girls*, 58; Enss, *Pistol Packin' Madams*, 59.

70. MacKell, *Brothels, Bordellos, and Bad Girls*, 60.

71. Enss, *Pistol Packin' Madams*, 59.

72. Several mysteries surround the child that Mattie and Thomson took in. Harry Drago claims the baby was adopted in 1889, and Chris Enss says Mattie placed the girl, whose name was Rita, in a boarding school. Once, when Mattie took in an abused little girl and police arrived to take the girl back to her mother, they discovered another five-year-old named Theresa Thompson. It was speculated that Theresa may have been a daughter of Mattie and Thomson or even perhaps a child by Casey Silks, who had been adopted by Thomson. Or she may have been Thomson's granddaughter, for whom Mattie purchased the ranch. Drago, *Notorious Ladies of the Frontier*, 137; Enss, *Pistol Packin' Madams*, 60; MacKell, *Brothels, Bordellos, and Bad Girls*, 61.

73. MacKell, *Brothels, Bordellos, and Bad Girls*, 61.

74. Ibid., 62.

75. Drago, *Notorious Ladies of the Frontier*, 137.

76. MacKell, *Brothels, Bordellos, and Bad Girls*, 62–69.

77. Ibid., 68–69.

78. Enss, *Pistol Packin' Madams*, 60.

79. MacKell, *Brothels, Bordellos, and Bad Girls*, 249.

80. See "Denver, Colorado History," http://www.denvergov./AboutDenver/ history_char_rogers.asp; Enss, *Pistol Packin' Madams*, 2; MacKell, *Brothels, Bordellos, and Bad Girls*, 58–59.

81. Enss, *Pistol Packin' Madams*, 2.

82. Joann Ditmer, "City's Last Bordello Now Glamorous Restaurant," *Denver Post*, April 5, 1999, E3.

83. Enss, *Pistol Packin' Madams*, 3.

84. MacKell, *Brothels, Bordellos, and Bad Girls*, 59–60; Ditmer, "City's Last Bordello Now Glamorous Restaurant."

85. Enss, *Pistol Packin' Madams*, 1–2.

86. MacKell, *Brothels, Bordellos, and Bad Girls*, 60.

87. Drago, *Notorious Ladies of the Frontier*, 135.

88. Enss, *Pistol Packin' Madams*, 4; Secrest, *Hell's Belles*, 235; Richard Erdoes, *Saloons of the Old West* (Avenel, N.J.: Grammercy Books, a division of Random House Value, 1997), 199; Enss, *Pistol Packin' Madams*, 5.

89. MacKell, *Brothels, Bordellos, and Bad Girls*, 60. An extremely similar story is told of Tessie Wall, a California madam who shot her ex-husband Frank Daroux in 1917 after seeing him with another woman. When police arrived, Tessie was kneeling beside Daroux, gun in hand. When asked why she shot him, she replied in distress, "I shot him because I love him, God-damn him!" Later Tessie also tried to kill Daroux's fiancée without success. Daroux successfully married his fiancée and moved to the East Coast. Enss, *Pistol Packin' Madams*, 66, 75.

90. Harry Drago claims that Jennie bought the house from Minnie Clifford (*Notorious Ladies of the Frontier*, 135). See also Enss, *Pistol Packin' Madams*, 5–6.

91. Ditmer, "City's Last Bordello Now Glamorous Restaurant."

92. An alternate version of this tale is that Jennie simply blackmailed the man by threatening to reveal he was one of her clients. Forbes Parkhill, *Wildest of the West* (New York: Holt, 1951), 72; Enss, *Pistol Packin' Madams*, 4.

93. MacKell, *Brothels, Bordellos, and Bad Girls*, 62.

94. Enss, *Pistol Packin' Madams*, 1–6.

95. MacKell, *Brothels, Bordellos, and Bad Girls*, 63.

96. Secrest, *Hell's Belles*, 232.

97. MacKell, *Brothels, Bordellos, and Bad Girls*, 67.

98. Enss, *Pistol Packin' Madams*, 7.

99. Enss says Fitzgerald was a contractor. Ibid.

100. MacKell, *Brothels, Bordellos, and Bad Girls*, 68.

101. U.S. Bureau of the Census, *Tenth Census of the United States, 1880*.

102. U.S. Bureau of the Census, *Federal Census Mortality Schedules, 1850–1880*.

103. MacKell, *Brothels, Bordellos, and Bad Girls,* 58.
104. Jay Moynahan, *Photographs of the Red Light Ladies 1865–1920* (Spokane, Wash.: Chickadee, 2005), 30.
105. Arlene J. Fitzgerald, "Bawdy Houses of the West," *Oldtimers Wild West Magazine* (August 1976), 33.
106. MacKell, "Bad Girls of Northern Colorado."
107. MacKell, *Brothels, Bordellos, and Bad Girls,* 5; Enss, *Pistol Packin' Madams,* 4; Drago, *Notorious Ladies of the Frontier,* 130.
108. MacKell, *Brothels, Bordellos, and Bad Girls,* 67.
109. Ronald Dean Miller, *Shady Ladies of the West* (Los Angeles: Westernlore Press, 1964), 96.
110. MacKell, *Brothels, Bordellos, and Bad Girls,* 67. Baldwin was shot one other time while on trial for seducing Lillian Ashley. The culprit was Lillian's sister. Also, Sarah Josephine Marcus claimed she and Wyatt Earp were married while aboard Baldwin's yacht. Glenn G. Boyer, ed., *I Married Wyatt Earp: The Recollections of Josephine Sarah Marcus Earp* (Tucson: University of Arizona Press, 2d printing, 1979), 148 n. 8, 149 n. 10.
111. MacKell, *Brothels, Bordellos, and Bad Girls,* 68.
112. *Durango Democrat,* March 27, 1908, 1.
113. MacKell, *Brothels, Bordellos, and Bad Girls,* 235.
114. "Old West Legends, Complete List of Old West Scoundrels," *Legends of America,* http://www.legendsofamerica.com/WE-ScoundrelList.html.
115. MacKell, *Brothels, Bordellos, and Bad Girls,* 249. Around this time, historian Fred Mazzulla, Denver bookstore owner Don Bloch, and others removed several items from the House of Mirrors during a midnight raid. At the time, according to Sam Morrison of Victor, Colorado, the event was more "an act of juvenile delinquency" than an effort to preserve the former brothel. Parts of the interior paneling were taken and later installed at the Denver Law Library (author's interview with Sam Morrison, Victor, Colorado, January 2008). More interesting, at least three of the five mysterious faces Jennie Rogers had adhered to the building, including a bust of herself, were chiseled off the front facade (author's interview with Sam Morrison, Victor, Colorado, September 2006). All of the heads ended up missing off and on for some fifty years (Ditmer, "City's Last Bordello Now Glamorous Restaurant"). In 1964, Bloch still owned at least two of them (Online Digitized Photograph Archive, Call X-27053, Denver Public Library). Historian Ed Bathke says he obtained the heads from Bloch in the early 1970s and stored them in his garage in Manitou Springs (correspondence with Ed Bathke, Denver Posse of the Westerners, January 2008). According to Morrison, one of the heads, supposed to be the bust of the Greek god Bacchus, was offered as a door prize during a Denver Posse of the Westerners meeting in about 1975 (Sam Morrison interview, September 2006).

Sometime between 1973 and 1975, Bob Akerley and David Hartman of the Denver Museum of Natural History did some restorative work on the heads, and then made a latex rubber mold. Bathke remembered that "one head was too far deteriorated, but the other was in pretty good condition, and several copies were cast. The copies and the originals then remained in Bob Staadt's residence in Aurora, in his garage. We sold several copies, and gave one to the Denver Public Library." According to Bathke, the Staadts got tired of storing one or both of the heads, but he didn't remember where they next went (correspondence with Ed Bathke, Denver Posse of the Westerners, January 2008). During the 1990s, another head was discovered in the basement of an elderly unidentified man in Denver, but what became of it is unknown (author's interview with Mark Rathgeber, Denver, 1995). When the House of Mirrors was restored in 1999, the Denver Posse of the Westerners still owned the remaining two original heads. What became of the others was unknown, so casts were made using historical photographs to re-create them (Ditmer, "City's Last Bordello Now Glamorous Restaurant").

116. MacKell, *Brothels, Bordellos, and Bad Girls*, 62, 250.
117. Alan Granruth, *A Guide to Downtown Central City, Colorado* (Black Hawk, Colo.: One Stop Printing and Graphics, 1989), 27. The saloon vacated in 1868.
118. Darlene Leslie, Kelle Rankin-Sunter, and Deborah Wightman, *Central City: "The Richest Square Mile on Earth" and the History of Gilpin County* (Black Hawk, Colo.: TB, 1990), 33.
119. Ibid., 35–36.
120. Ibid., 34; Caroline Bancroft, *Gulch of Gold: A History of Central City, Colorado* (Denver: Sage Books, 1958), 228.
121. "James Thomson's Colorado Diary 1872," with introduction and notes by K. J. Fielding, *Colorado Magazine* (July 1954), 113.
122. MacKell, *Brothels, Bordellos, and Bad Girls*, 54.
123. Granruth, *A Guide to Downtown Central City, Colorado*, 43; MacKell, *Brothels, Bordellos, and Bad Girls*, 54.
124. Leslie, Rankin-Sunter, and Wightman, *Central City*, 33.
125. Ibid.
126. Granruth, *A Guide to Downtown Central City, Colorado*, 44.
127. MacKell, *Brothels, Bordellos, and Bad Girls*, 54.
128. Leslie, Rankin-Sunter, and Wightman, *Central City*, 33.
129. Roger Baker, *Black Hawk: The Rise and Fall of a Colorado Mill Town* (Central City, Colo.: Black Hawk, 2004), 107.
130. Granruth, *A Guide to Downtown Central City, Colorado*, 43–47.
131. MacKell, *Brothels, Bordellos, and Bad Girls*, 151.
132. Baker, *Black Hawk*, 26. It should be noted that historically the city was first called "Black Hawk," but the name has alternately been spelled as one word, "Blackhawk," over time. Jan MacKell, "Blackhawk Sports Early Colorado History," *Colorado Gambler* magazine (February 2006), 22.
133. Leslie, Rankin-Sunter, and Wightman, *Central City*, 34.
134. MacKell, "Blackhawk Sports Early Colorado History," 22.
135. Mary Ellen Gilliland, *Summit: A Gold Rush History of Summit County, Colorado* (Silverthorn, Colo.: Alpenrose Press, 1980), 51; Eberhart, *Guide to the Colorado Ghost Towns*, 97.
136. The name "Cardinal," as in "cardinal sin," was purely coincidental. Robert L. Brown, *Colorado Ghost Towns Past and Present* (Caldwell, Idaho: Caxton Printers, 1981), 75–78; Jan MacKell, "From Gold and Tungsten to Rock and Roll: Nederland," *Colorado Gambler* magazine (June 2007), 23.

137. Brown, *Ghost Towns of the Colorado Rockies*, 140; Eberhart, *Guide to the Colorado Ghost Towns and Mining Camps*, 72; Brown, *Colorado Ghost Towns Past and Present*, 23; correspondence with David Pratt, Crooked Creek Saloon, Fraser, Colorado, April 22, 2006.

138. Brown, *Colorado Ghost Towns Past and Present*, 57.

139. Gilliland, *Summit*, 51; U.S. Bureau of the Census, *Tenth Census of the United States, 1880*.

140. *Breckenridge Bulletin*, May 25, 1907, p. 1, col. 2.

141. U.S. Bureau of the Census, *Fourteenth Census of the United States, 1920* (Washington, D.C.: National Archives and Records Administration, 1920).

142. Brown, *Ghost Towns of the Colorado Rockies*, 70; MacKell, *Brothels, Bordellos, and Bad Girls*, 46–50; Bauer, Ozment, and Willard, *Colorado Post Offices 1859–1989*, 53.

143. *Golden Weekly Globe*, August 16, 1873, p. 2, col. 2.

144. Brown, *Ghost Towns of the Colorado Rockies*, 206.

145. Rosemary Fetter, "Hurdy Gurdy Gals of the Old West," *Colorado Gambler* magazine (June 22–28, 2004), 30.

146. Brown, *Ghost Towns of the Colorado Rockies*, 250–54.

147. Eberhart, *Guide to the Colorado Ghost Towns and Mining Camps*, 192; Brown, *Ghost Towns of the Colorado Rockies*, 254.

148. Kay Reynolds Blair, *Ladies of the Lamplight* (Ouray, Colo.: Western Reflections, 2002), 91; Wolle, *Stampede to Timberline*, 50.

149. Kristen Iversen, *Molly Brown: Unraveling the Myth* (Boulder, Colo.: Johnson Books, 1999), 101; MacKell, *Brothels, Bordellos, and Bad Girls*, 91.

150. West, *The Saloon on the Rocky Mountain Frontier*, 22.

151. MacKell, *Brothels, Bordellos, and Bad Girls*, 92; Eberhart, *Guide to the Colorado Ghost Towns and Mining Camps*, 196; Linda La Rocca, "The Season of the Spirits at Leadville's Evergreen Cemetery," *Colorado Central Magazine*, http://www.cozine.com/archive/cc1995/00210102.html.

152. MacKell, *Brothels, Bordellos, and Bad Girls*, 93; Erdoes, *Saloons of the Old West*, 188. Duggan himself was shot to death in 1888 in front of the Texas House Gambling Hall. Whether Mindy did indeed dance on his grave is unrecorded. Eberhart, *Guide to the Colorado Ghost Towns and Mining Camps*, 195.

153. Eleanor Perry, *I Remember Tin Cup* (Littleton, Colo.: Privately published, 1986), 17.

154. MacKell, *Brothels, Bordellos, and Bad Girls*, 31.

155. Joanne West Dodds, *What's a Nice Girl Like You Doing in a Place Like This?* (Pueblo, Colo.: Focal Plain, 1996), 7; La Rocca, "The Season of the Spirits at Leadville's Evergreen Cemetery."

156. *Leadville Weekly Chronicle*, February 14, 1880, p. 6, col. 3.

157. Wolle, *Stampede to Timberline*, 50.

158. Iversen, *Molly Brown*, 101.

159. *Leadville Daily and Evening Chronicle*, September 8, 1892, 1:3.

160. Fred Mazzulla and Jo Mazzulla, *Brass Checks and Red Lights* (Denver: Privately published, 1966), 38; MacKell, *Brothels, Bordellos, and Bad Girls*, 32.

161. U.S. Bureau of the Census, *Thirteenth Census of the United States, 1910*; MacKell, *Brothels, Bordellos, and Bad Girls*, 255.

162. *Leadville Carbonate Chronicle*, February 5, 1900, p. 3, col. 3.

163. U.S. Bureau of the Census, *Thirteenth Census of the United States, 1910*.

164. Death certificate of Grace Hoffman, courtesy Erik Swanson, Alma, Colorado; author's interview with Erik Swanson, Cripple Creek, Colorado, 2006. In 1905, Fred Egner inexplicably disappeared, having been last seen setting out to repair a ditch. A month later he surfaced at the home of his mother in Shiloh, Ohio, with "no excuse for his conduct in deserting his family." U.S. Bureau of the Census, *Twelfth Census of the United States, 1900*; *Fort Collins Weekly Courier*, December 23, 1903, p. 8, col. 1, June 21 1905, p. 6, col. 3, and July 26, 1905, p. 6, col. 3; Grace Hoffman's cookbook, courtesy of Erik Swanson, Alma, Colorado, 2006.

165. MacKell, *Brothels, Bordellos, and Bad Girls*, 96–97; Erik Swanson interview; Grace Hoffman's cookbook.

166. MacKell, *Brothels, Bordellos, and Bad Girls*, 98; Peter Yurich, "Louise Piercen, 'Pee Wee,'" unpublished, undated manuscript, courtesy Peter Yurich, Oak Creek, Colorado, November 2007.

167. La Rocca, "The Season of the Spirits at Leadville's Evergreen Cemetery."

168. MacKell, *Brothels, Bordellos, and Bad Girls*, 254, 261.

169. Wolle, *Stampede to Timberline*, 451.

170. Erdoes, *Saloons of the Old West*, 202; MacKell, *Brothels, Bordellos, and Bad Girls*, 261.

171. Eberhart, *Guide to the Colorado Ghost Towns and Mining Camps*, 232; Jan MacKell, "Hagerman Pass Makes Great Fall Trek," *Colorado Gambler* magazine (September 2006), 19; Marshall Sprague, *The Great Gates: The Story of Rocky Mountain Passes* (Boston: Little, Brown, 1864), 278.

172. Malcolm Rohrbough, *Aspen: The History of a Silver Mining Town 1879–1893* (New York: Oxford University Press, 1986), 30–32; Sally Barlow-Perez, *A History of Aspen*, 2d ed. (Basalt, Colo.: Who Press, 2000), 5; Jan MacKell, *Brothels, Bordellos, and Bad Girls: Prostitution in Colorado 1860–1930* (Albuquerque: University of New Mexico Press, 1st paperback printing, 2007), 106.

173. Martha Whitcomb Sterling, *Oh Be Joyful! An Historic Tale of the Aspen Silver Camp* (Aspen, Colo.: Roaring Fork Valley Centennial/Bicentennial Committee, 1975), inside cover; Barlow-Perez, *A History of Aspen*, 26; Rohrbough, *Aspen*, 201.

174. Wolle, *Stampede to Timberline*, 240.

175. The absence of prostitutes as well as the low number of residents recorded in the 1900 census may have been because the Silver Crash of 1893 had caused the population to dwindle considerably. Barlow-Perez, *A History of Aspen*, 33; MacKell, *Brothels, Bordellos, and Bad Girls* (2007 print), 106.

176. Bauer, Ozment, and Willard, *Colorado Post Offices 1859–1989*, 63; *Glenwood Post*, November 19, 1898, p. 2, col. 2; U.S. Bureau of the Census, *Twelfth Census of the United States, 1900*; *Durango Wage Earner*, April 1, 1909, p. 4, col. 3; *Telluride Daily Journal*, March 15, 1911, p. 4, col. 3.

177. Bauer, Ozment, and Willard, *Colorado Post Offices 1859–1989*, 112; MacKell, *Brothels, Bordellos, and Bad Girls*, 117; Wolle, *Stampede to Timberline*, 48; Eberhart, *Guide to the Colorado Ghost Towns and Mining Camps*, 196.

178. MacKell, *Brothels, Bordellos, and Bad Girls*, 112–13; Byron A. Johnson and Sharon P. Johnson, *Gilded Palaces of Shame: Albuquerque's Redlight Districts 1880–1914* (Albuquerque: Gilded Age Press, 1983), 32.

179. MacKell, *Brothels, Bordellos, and Bad Girls*, 252.

180. U.S. Bureau of the Census, *Thirteenth Census of the United States, 1910*; MacKell, *Brothels, Bordellos, and Bad Girls*, 112, 252–53.

181. U.S. Bureau of the Census, *Tenth Census of the United States, 1880*; *San Luis Valley Courier*, February 20, 1889, p. 1, col. 1.

182. Jan MacKell, "Georgetown & Silver Plume," *Colorado Gambler* magazine (February 2006), 23; *Georgetown Daily Colorado Miner*, February 7, 1873, p. 4, col. 3.

183. MacKell, "Bad Girls of Northern Colorado."

184. Ibid.; Eberhart, *Guide to the Colorado Ghost Towns and Mining Camps*, 50. Belle London may have been the same madam whom Salt Lake City officials later hired to run the Stockade red light district in 1908, but this has not been verified. MacKell, *Brothels, Bordellos, and Bad Girls*, 98.

185. U.S. Bureau of the Census, *Federal Census Mortality Schedules, 1850–1880*; *Telluride Journal*, August 23, 1906, p. 7, col. 1; MacKell, *Brothels, Bordellos, and Bad Girls*, 98.

186. MacKell, *Brothels, Bordellos, and Bad Girls*, 199; *Fort Collins Weekly Courier*, January 12, 1912, p. 3, col. 4.

187. Bauer, Ozment, and Willard, *Colorado Post Offices 1859–1989*, 84; MacKell, *Brothels, Bordellos, and Bad Girls*, 86, 106; U.S. Bureau of the Census, *Tenth Census of the United States, 1880*; Wolle, *Stampede to Timberline*, 201.

188. Brown, *Colorado Ghost Towns Past and Present*, 84–85; Wolle, *Stampede to Timberline*, 322; MacKell, *Brothels, Bordellos, and Bad Girls*, 122.

189. MacKell, *Brothels, Bordellos, and Bad Girls*, 122; Wolle, *Stampede to Timberline*, 325, 334; Eberhart, *Guide to the Colorado Ghost Towns and Mining Camps*, 402, 405; West, *The Saloon on the Rocky Mountain Frontier*, 21.

190. MacKell, *Brothels, Bordellos, and Bad Girls*, 103–4.

191. Ibid., 86–89; Eberhart, *Guide to the Colorado Ghost Towns and Mining Camps*, 338.

192. Allan G. Bird, *Bordellos of Blair Street* (Pierson, Mich.: Advertising, Publications & Consultants, 1993), 17; MacKell, *Brothels, Bordellos, and Bad Girls*, 87; Brown, *Ghost Towns of the Colorado Rockies*, 340.

193. MacKell, *Brothels, Bordellos, and Bad Girls*, 89–90, 247–48; Max Evans, *Madam Millie: Bordellos from Silver City to Ketchikan* (Albuquerque: University of New Mexico Press, 2002), xxi n. 15; U.S. Bureau of the Census, *Fifteenth Census of the United States, 1930*.

194. Brown, *Ghost Towns of the Colorado Rockies*, 358; Eberhart, *Guide to the Colorado Ghost Towns and Mining Camps*, 323; Wolle, *Stampede to Timberline*, 389; Elizabeth Barbour and the Telluride Historical Museum, *Telluride* (Charleston, S.C.: Arcadia, 2006), 88–89.

195. Brown, *Ghost Towns of the Colorado Rockies*, 359; *Telluride Daily Journal*, November 20, 1901, p. 3, col. 2, and June 8, 1903, p. 3, col. 3.

196. *Telluride Journal*, February 1, 1906, p. 10, col. 3.

197. *Telluride Daily Journal*, July 7, 1915, p. 2, col. 2.

198. *Telluride Daily Journal*, July 10, 1915, p. 1, col. 3.

199. *Telluride Daily Journal*, April 8, 1916, p. 1, col. 3.

200. *Telluride Daily Journal*, April 10, 1916, p. 1, col. 3.

201. Barbour and Telluride Historical Museum, *Telluride*, 88; MacKell, *Brothels, Bordellos, and Bad Girls*, 248.

202. Bauer, Ozment, and Willard, *Colorado Post Offices 1859–1989*, 48; U.S. Bureau of the Census, *Twelfth Census of the United States, 1900*; MacKell, *Brothels, Bordellos, and Bad Girls*, 123.

203. Erdoes, *Saloons of the Old West*, 199.

204. MacKell, *Brothels, Bordellos, and Bad Girls*, 123; correspondence with Jan Pettit, Green Mountain Falls, Colorado, September 22, 2004; *Durango Democrat*, January 28, 1902, p. 1, col. 1.

205. *Durango Democrat*, April 17, 1902, p. 1, col. 1, November 6, 1906, p. 3, col. 3, and December 27, 1906, p. 3, col. 3; *Durango Daily Journal*, June 14, 1904, p. 3, col. 3; *Durango Wage Earner*, November 9, 1905, p. 3, col. 3.

206. *Durango Democrat*, February 2, 1908, p. 1, col. 1.

207. *Durango Wage Earner*, July 9, 1908, p. 4, col. 3, August 20, 1908, p. 4, col. 3, and April 6, 1911, p. 2, col. 3; U.S. Bureau of the Census, *Thirteenth Census of the United States, 1910*.

208. Eberhart, *Guide to the Colorado Ghost Towns and Mining Camps*, 110; correspondence with Mike Yurich, Oak Creek, Colorado, October 2007.

209. Correspondence with Mike Yurich; *Oak Creek Times*, October 21, 1915, transcribed by Mike Yurich, Oak Creek, Colorado.

210. *Oak Creek Times*, October 21, 1915; Autumn Phillips, undated, untitled news clipping, courtesy Mike Yurich, Oak Creek, Colorado.

211. *Oak Creek Times*, October 21, 1915.

212. *Oak Creek Times*, January 21, 1916, transcribed by Mike Yurich, Oak Creek, Colorado.

213. *Oak Creek Times*, October 21, 1915, and January 27, 1916, transcribed by Mike Yurich, Oak Creek, Colorado.

214. *Oak Creek Times*, February 3, 1916, transcribed by Mike Yurich, Oak Creek, Colorado.

215. *Oak Creek Times*, February 24, 1916, transcribed by Mike Yurich, Oak Creek, Colorado.

216. *Oak Creek Times*, October 3, 1919, and May 11, 1916, transcribed by Mike Yurich, Oak Creek, Colorado; correspondence with Mike Yurich.

217. Peter Yurich, "Hickory Flats," unpublished manuscript, April 2004.

218. Yurich, "Louise Piercen, 'Pee Wee'"; correspondence with Mike Yurich.

219. Yurich, "Louise Piercen, 'Pee Wee.'"

220. Correspondence with Mike Yurich.

221. Ibid. Mike Yurich gathered much of the material after Pee Wee died and her house had been ransacked. In 1992, the diaries were published, with the proceeds going toward a marker for Pee Wee in the cemetery.

222. Ibid.

223. Ibid.

224. P. Yurich, "Hickory Flats"; correspondence with Mike Yurich.

225. Jan MacKell, "A Ghost Town Endangered: Arbourville," *Colorado Gambler* magazine (May 2005), 23; Brown, *Colorado Ghost Towns Past and Present*, 6.

226. Eleanor Fry, *Salida: The Early Years* (Salida, Colo.: Arkansas Valley, 2001), 225–26, 228, 231; Wolle, *Stampede to Timberline*, 166; MacKell, *Brothels, Bordellos, and Bad Girls*, 98.

227. MacKell, *Brothels, Bordellos, and Bad Girls*, 123, 255.

228. Wolle, *Stampede to Timberline*, 298.

229. Fry, *Salida*, 116, 219; Lambert Florin, *Ghost Towns of the West* (Superior, Neb.: Superior Publishing for Promontory Press, 1970), 295; MacKell, *Brothels, Bordellos, and Bad Girls*, 105; Lisa Everitt, "Play Shows Bawdy Buena Vista Brothel History," *Denver Post*, June 22, 2007, http://www.denverpost.com/travel/ci_6198637.

230. Fry, *Salida*, 218–19.

231. Ibid., 67, 122.

232. Ibid., 218–19.

233. Ibid., 78, 219–20.

234. MacKell, *Brothels, Bordellos, and Bad Girls*, 99.

235. Mazzulla and Mazzulla, *Brass Checks and Red Lights*, 38; Everitt, "Play Shows Bawdy Buena Vista Brothel History"; MacKell, *Brothels, Bordellos, and Bad Girls*, 99–100; Fry, *Salida*, 220–21.

236. Fry, *Salida*, 220.

237. MacKell, *Brothels, Bordellos, and Bad Girls*, 101; Fry, *Salida*, 220.

238. MacKell, *Brothels, Bordellos, and Bad Girls*, 101–2; Fry, *Salida*, 220–21.

239. MacKell, *Brothels, Bordellos, and Bad Girls*, 252.

240. MacKell, *Brothels, Bordellos, and Bad Girls*, 155; Marshall Sprague, *The King of Cripple Creek* (Colorado Springs, Colo.: Magazine Associates, 1994), 26.

241. Sprague, *The King of Cripple Creek*, 1, 5, 9.

242. MacKell, *Brothels, Bordellos, and Bad Girls*, 157; Property Block Books, Teller County Assessor, Teller County Courthouse, Cripple Creek, Colorado; Marshall Sprague, *Money Mountain* (Lincoln: University of Nebraska Press, 1953), 202; Thomas J. Noel and Cathleen M. Norman, *A Pikes Peak Partnership: The Penroses and the Tutts* (Boulder: University Press of Colorado, 2000), 36.

243. Although Sally and Penrose never married, they did remain friends for many years. Sally is also unique for having one of her prized steeds buried in Cripple Creek's Mt. Pisgah Cemetery. MacKell, *Brothels, Bordellos, and Bad Girls*, 160.

244. Ibid., 161; Sprague, *The King of Cripple Creek*, 30, 78.

245. Sprague, *The King of Cripple Creek*, 30–41.

246. Ibid., 42–49, 78–81.

247. MacKell, *Brothels, Bordellos, and Bad Girls*, 165; Alexy Simmons, *Red Light Ladies: Settlement Patterns and Material Culture on the Mining Frontier*, Anthropology Northwest no. 4 (Corvallis: Department of Anthropology, Oregon State University, 1989), 136–37.

248. *Victor Daily Record*, June 5, 1897, p. 1, col. 2.

249. In April 1893, the *Aspen Weekly Times* gave a full report on the gambler Billy's doings, including an allegation by the *Denver Post* that he never really broke the bank. Deutsch, it was explained, was managing Booth's Theater in New York in 1877. It was when he went to Europe a year later with $125,000 in his pocket that the gambling bug bit him. *Aspen Weekly Times*, April 29, 1893, p. 1, col. 3.

250. *Greeley Tribune*, October 19, 1893, p. 9, col. 1.

251. *Victor Daily Record*, June 5, 1897, p. 1, col. 2.

252. Pearl's affair with Deitz or Duetsch is only one theory regarding her past. Other research has possibly placed her in Trinidad, Colorado, as early as 1880, and she allegedly married one Ed Martin sometime before or upon reaching Denver. Evidence that Pearl spent time in Denver comes from the fact that her other name, "Isabelle Martin," was scribbled on some panel doors that were shipped from there to the Old Homestead. MacKell, *Brothels, Bordellos, and Bad Girls*, 106; undated news clipping, Old Homestead Parlour House Museum, Cripple Creek, Colorado.

253. Jan MacKell, "The Old Homestead Parlour House, Cripple Creek, Colorado: A Complete History and Case Study," unpublished manuscript, 2007, 1–2. When the Old Homestead burned in 1896 along with much of the red light district, Flynn was ruined. It is said that he went south to Monterey, Mexico, where he took a job smelting iron and steel. MacKell, *Brothels, Bordellos, and Bad Girls*, 166.

254. *Cripple Creek Morning Times*, March 1, 1896, p. 1, col. 2.

255. MacKell, "The Old Homestead Parlour House," 3.

256. MacKell, *Brothels, Bordellos, and Bad Girls*, 167–70.

257. *Victor Daily Record*, June 5, 1897, p. 1, col. 2.

258. MacKell, *Brothels, Bordellos, and Bad Girls*, 171.

259. *Victor Daily Record*, June 5, 1897; MacKell, *Brothels, Bordellos, and Bad Girls*, 171.

260. MacKell, *Brothels, Bordellos, and Bad Girls*, 175–78, 215; author's interview with Charlotte Bumgarner, Cripple Creek, Colorado, 2004; see also "The Busher," http://www.silentsaregolden.com/featurefolder6/bushercommentary.html.

261. *Cripple Creek Morning Times*, November 12, 1898, p. 1, col. 1, and December 28, 1898, p. 6, col. 1.

262. U.S. Bureau of the Census, *Twelfth Census of the United States, 1900*; MacKell, *Brothels, Bordellos, and Bad Girls*, 184–85; Sprague, *The King of Cripple Creek*, 39–40.

263. "Every Gambling Den in the City Silent Last Night" and "Mayor Decides Myers Avenue Cribs Must Go," *Cripple Creek Gold Rush*, undated news clippings, Cripple Creek District Museum, Cripple Creek, Colorado; MacKell, *Brothels, Bordellos, and Bad Girls*, 185, 211; "Carrie Nation Promises to Visit Saloons," *Cripple Creek Gold Rush*, undated news clipping, Cripple Creek District Museum.

264. MacKell, *Brothels, Bordellos, and Bad Girls*, 216–19, 227–28.

265. "Sheriff Takes Steps to Abolish Red Light Districts," unidentified news clipping dated January 23, 1916, Cripple Creek District Museum; MacKell,

Brothels, Bordellos, and Bad Girls, 234; Jan MacKell, "She Rolled Her Own with One Hand," *Soiled Doves*, http://www.soiled-doves.com.

266. MacKell, "She Rolled Her Own with One Hand."
267. MacKell, *Brothels, Bordellos, and Bad Girls*, 157; Sprague, *The King of Cripple Creek*, 2.
268. Mary Murphy, "Women on the Line: Prostitution in Butte, Montana 1878–1917," master's thesis, University of North Carolina, Chapel Hill, 1983, copy at the Montana Historical Society, Helena, Montana; Sanborn Fire Insurance maps, 1896, 1900, and 1908, Cripple Creek District Museum.
269. Records indicate that Blanche's daughter was born December 21, 1918, in Cripple Creek. According to the Cripple Creek city directory for 1918, Blanche was living at the Idaho rooming house at 103 E. Masonic Avenue within half a block of the red light district. The 1920 census notes Blanche at the same address, working as a servant at a rooming house run by M. Tregonna. She is recorded as a widow, age thirty-eight, and born in France. The census also notes that her daughter's name was "Dora." The baby was admitted to the Teller County Hospital twice: once in May 1922 for an unspecified illness and again on October 2, 1923, for eczema. This last time, the child was discharged on October 22 "by order of the county judge," which may indicate the date she was taken from her mother. Cripple Creek city directory for 1918, Cripple Creek District Museum; U.S. Bureau of the Census, *Fourteenth Census of the United States, 1920*; Teller County Hospital Records, Cripple Creek Wellness and Rehab Center, Cripple Creek, Colorado.
270. MacKell, *Brothels, Bordellos, and Bad Girls*, 233–34, 257–60; "Victor Red Light District Houses Being Torn Down," undated news clipping, and Sanborn Fire Insurance map, 1919, Cripple Creek District Museum.
271. *Telluride Daily Journal*, April 8, 1916, p. 1, col. 1; *Cripple Creek Gold Rush*, January 4, 1980, 6:1; correspondence with John J. Potterat, Colorado Springs, Colorado, January 20, 2005.
272. Correspondence with John J. Potterat; "Did You Ever Wonder?" *Colorado Springs Gazette*, undated news clipping, author's collection.
273. Andrew Gulliford, *Boomtown Blues: Colorado Oil Shale, 1885–1985* (Boulder: University Press of Colorado, 1989), 147.

Chapter Four

1. *The New Encyclopedia Britannica* (Chicago: Encyclopedia Britannica, 1987), 29:158.
2. "Boise, Idaho," *Wikipedia*, http://en.wikipedia.org/wiki/Boise,_Idaho.
3. Cathy Luchetti, *I Do! Courtship, Love, and Marriage of the American Frontier* (New York: Crown Trade Paperbacks, 1996), 290.
4. Jay Moynahan, *The Prairie Prostitutes' Own Cookbook* (Spokane, Wash.: Chickadee, 2000), 7.
5. Anne M. Butler, *Daughters of Joy, Sisters of Misery* (Chicago: University of Illinois Press, 1985), 85.
6. Ibid., 60.
7. U.S. Bureau of the Census, *Thirteenth Census of the United States, 1910* (Washington, D.C.: National Archives and Records Administration, 1910).

8. Fred Mazzulla and Jo Mazzulla, *Brass Checks and Red Lights* (Denver: Self-published, 1966), 12.

9. Social Security Administration, *Social Security Death Index, Master File* (Washington, D.C.: Social Security Administration, 2007).

10. Vardis Fisher and Opal Laurel Holmes, *Gold Rushes and Mining Camps of the Early American West* (Caldwell, Idaho: Caxton Printers, 1968), 110. Although Fred and Jo Mazzulla maintain that Diamond Lil was also known as "Evelyn Hildegard," there is no hard documentation to confirm this assertion.

11. *Reno Evening Gazette* (Nevada), January 24, 1944, p. 1, col. 3; *Sheboygan Press* (Wisconsin), June 30, 1936, p. 3, col. 2; correspondence with Jay Moynahan, Spokane, Washington, January 2008.

12. Fisher and Holmes, *Gold Rushes and Mining Camps of the Early American West*, 110.

13. Mazzulla and Mazzulla, *Brass Checks and Red Lights*, 12. The 1920 census identifies Honora Ornstein as living in Seattle managing an apartment house and that she was born in France. U.S. Bureau of the Census, *Fourteenth Census of the United States, 1920* (Washington, D.C.: National Archives and Records Administration, 1920).

14. Upper Snake River Family History Center and Ricks College (Rexburg, Idaho), *Idaho Marriages, 1842–1996* (online database) (Provo, Utah: Generations Network, 2005).

15. *Sheboygan Press* (Wisconsin), June 30, 1936, p. 3, col. 2. Author Jay Moynahan says that the marriage did not last and that Lil divorced Miller a week before she learned she was to inherit $150,000 from her mother in Los Angeles. Correspondence with Jay Moynahan, 2008.

16. *Reno Evening Gazette*, January 24, 1944, p. 1, col. 3.

17. Correspondence with Jay Moynahan, 2008; Mazzulla and Mazzulla, *Brass Checks and Red Lights*, 13.

18. *Herald Times Reporter* (Manitowoc, Ohio), June 21, 1975, p. 3, col. 7.

19. *She Done Him Wrong*, Internet Movie Database, http://www.imdb.com/title/tt0024548/.

20. Walter O'Meara, *Daughters of the Country: The Women of the Fur Traders and Mountain Men* (New York: Harcourt, Brace and World, 1968), 169–70.

21. Alexy Simmons, *Red Light Ladies: Settlement Patterns and Material Culture on the Mining Frontier*, Anthropology Northwest no. 4 (Corvallis: Department of Anthropology, Oregon State University, 1989), 78–92.

22. Ibid., 80–81.

23. U.S. Bureau of the Census, *Ninth Census of the United States, 1870* (Washington, D.C.: National Archives and Records Administration, 1870).

24. Simmons, *Red Light Ladies*, 81.

25. Ibid., 89.

26. Ibid., 83.

27. Ibid., 81.

28. Ibid., 84.

29. Peter Boag, "Go West Young Man, Go East Young Woman: Searching for the Trans in Western Gender History," *Western Historical Quarterly* 36, no. 4 (Winter 2003), http://www.historycooperative.org. In the 1880

census, Joe was also identified as being of "doubtful sex." U.S. Bureau of the Census, *Tenth Census of the United States, 1880* (Washington, D.C.: National Archives and Records Administration, 1880).

30. The 1993 film *The Ballad of Little Jo* (see Internet Movie Database, http://www.imbd.com/title/tt0106350/) is based on Joe's life and speculates why she chose to masquerade as a man. See also Boag, "Go West Young Man, Go East Young Woman."

31. Simmons, *Red Light Ladies*, 88.

32. Ibid., 85.

33. Ibid., 88.

34. Ibid., 87.

35. Jay Moynahan, *Ladies of Easy Virtue in the Bitterroot Mountains* (Spokane, Wash.: Chickadee, 1999), 11–12.

36. Ibid.

37. Simmons, *Red Light Ladies*, 85.

38. Ibid., 92–93.

39. Ibid.

40. U.S. Bureau of the Census, *Twelfth Census of the United States, 1900* (Washington, D.C.: National Archives and Records Administration, 1900).

41. Simmons, *Red Light Ladies*, 90.

42. Josephine later moved to Cripple Creek, Colorado, where she was noted in the city directory of 1907. Ibid., 92–93; see also Jan MacKell, *Brothels, Bordellos, and Bad Girls: Prostitution in Colorado 1860–1930* (Albuquerque: University of New Mexico Press, 2004), 156 (this printing cited unless otherwise noted).

43. Simmons, *Red Light Ladies*, 90.

44. Ibid., 91–92.

45. Ibid., 93.

46. Ibid., 91–92.

47. Ibid., 92–93.

48. Ibid., 91.

49. Ibid., 93.

50. Ibid., 90.

51. Ibid., 93.

52. Harry Sinclair Drago, *Notorious Ladies of the Frontier* (New York: Dodd, Mead, 1969), 236–37.

53. Upper Snake River Family History Center and Ricks College, *Idaho Marriages, 1842–1996*.

54. Drago, *Notorious Ladies of the Frontier*, 237.

55. Ibid., 237–39.

56. Ibid., 240.

57. U.S. Bureau of the Census, *Fourteenth Census of the United States, 1920*.

58. Drago, *Notorious Ladies of the Frontier*, 240.

59. Jay Moynahan, *Soiled Doves, Sportin' Women, and Other Fallen Flowers* (Spokane, Wash.: Chickadee, 2005), 25.

60. Grace Roffey Pratt, "Charlie Bemis' Highest Prize," *Frontier Times* (Winter 1961), 26.

61. Moynahan, *Soiled Doves, Sportin' Women, and Other Fallen Flowers*, 25.

62. Pratt, "Charlie Bemis' Highest Prize," 26; Moynahan, *Soiled Doves, Sportin' Women, and Other Fallen Flowers*, 31.

63. Moynahan, *Soiled Doves, Sportin' Women, and Other Fallen Flowers*, 31.

64. Wayne Sparling, *Southern Idaho Ghost Towns* (Caldwell, Idaho: Caxton Printers, 1989), 51.

65. Moynahan, *Soiled Doves, Sportin' Women, and Other Fallen Flowers*, 31.

66. An alternative version of this story came from a friend of Polly's, Jake Czizek. In 1933, Czizek explained to a newspaper reporter from Portland, Oregon, that the subject of the "poker bride" story was actually a young American Indian named Molly. In 1879, he said, a group of Lapwai stole a horse belonging to one Pony Smead. When Smead and two of his friends reclaimed the horse, they also kidnapped Molly and brought her to Warren. All three of the men wanted Molly, so a poker game was decided upon to settle who should get her. Smead won the game, married Molly, and the couple lived happily ever after. Molly and Pony Smead's descendants remain in Idaho today. Pratt, "Charlie Bemis' Highest Prize," 27; Moynahan, *Soiled Doves, Sportin' Women, and Other Fallen Flowers*, 25.

67. Moynahan, *Soiled Doves, Sportin' Women, and Other Fallen Flowers*, 31.

68. U.S. Bureau of the Census, *Tenth Census of the United States, 1880*.

69. Pratt, "Charlie Bemis' Highest Prize," 28.

70. Moynahan, *Soiled Doves, Sportin' Women, and Other Fallen Flowers*, 32.

71. Pratt, "Charlie Bemis' Highest Prize," 28.

72. Lambert Florin, *Ghost Towns of the West* (Superior, Neb.: Superior Publishing for Promontory Press, 1970), 487.

73. Moynahan, *Soiled Doves, Sportin' Women, and Other Fallen Flowers*, 32.

74. Pratt, "Charlie Bemis' Highest Prize," 28.

75. U.S. Bureau of the Census, *Fifteenth Census of the United States, 1930* (Washington, D.C.: National Archives and Records Administration, 1930).

76. Pratt, "Charlie Bemis' Highest Prize," 38; Moynahan, *Soiled Doves, Sportin' Women, and Other Fallen Flowers*, 31.

77. Pratt, "Charlie Bemis' Highest Prize," 38.

78. University of Washington Libraries Digital Collections, http://content.lib/washington.edu.cig-bin/docviewer.exe.

79. Simmons, *Red Light Ladies*, 83.

80. Sparling, *Southern Idaho Ghost Towns*, 97; Florin, *Ghost Towns of the West*, 456.

81. Florin, *Ghost Towns of the West*, 456.

82. Ibid., 457.

83. Sparling, *Southern Idaho Ghost Towns*, 97.

84. U.S. Bureau of the Census, *Tenth Census of the United States, 1880*.

85. Arlene J. Fitzgerald, "Bawdy Houses of the West," *Oldtimers Wild West Magazine* (August 1976), 33.

86. U.S. Bureau of the Census, *Tenth Census of the United States, 1880*.

87. "Vital Records, 1886–1903," *Idaho County Free Press*, http://www.ancestry.com.

88. Moynahan, *The Prairie Prostitutes' Own Cookbook*, 14.

89. Jeffrey Nichols, *Prostitution, Polygamy, and Power: Salt Lake City, 1847–1918* (Chicago: University of Illinois Press, 2002), 55.

90. Jay Moynahan, *Red Light Revelations: The Sportin' Women of Wallace and the Silver Valley, 1888 to 1909* (Spokane, Wash.: Chickadee, 2001), 11.
91. Author's interview with Jack Mayfield, Oasis Bordello Museum, Wallace, Idaho, September 2006.
92. Moynahan, *Red Light Revelations*, 13.
93. Ibid., 15.
94. Moynahan, *Ladies of Easy Virtue in the Bitterroot Mountains*, 32–33.
95. Moynahan, *Red Light Revelations*, 29.
96. Jack Mayfield interview.
97. U.S. Bureau of the Census, *Thirteenth Census of the United States, 1910* (Washington, D.C.: National Archives and Records Administration, 1910).
98. Moynahan, *Red Light Revelations*, 24.
99. Ibid., 26.
100. Ibid., 54.
101. Moynahan, *Ladies of Easy Virtue in the Bitterroot Mountains*, 39–40.
102. Moynahan, *Red Light Revelations*, 42–49.
103. Ibid., 45–46.
104. Ibid., 51.
105. Jack Mayfield interview.
106. Ibid.
107. Oasis Bordello Museum pamphlet, Wallace, Idaho.
108. Jack Mayfield interview.
109. U.S. Bureau of the Census, *Thirteenth Census of the United States, 1910*.
110. Jack Mayfield interview.
111. Oasis Bordello Museum pamphlet.
112. Jack Mayfield interview.
113. Ibid.
114. Oasis Bordello Museum pamphlet.
115. Jack Mayfield interview.
116. Ibid.
117. Moynahan, *Ladies of Easy Virtue in the Bitterroot Mountains*, 32.
118. Moynahan, *Red Light Revelations*, 33–35.
119. Ibid., 12.
120. Anne Seagraves, *Soiled Doves: Prostitution in the Early West* (Hayden, Idaho: Wesanne, 1994), 103–5.
121. Ibid., 106.
122. Fitzgerald, "Bawdy Houses of the West," 38.
123. Seagraves, *Soiled Doves*, 106.
124. Jay Moynahan, *Culinary Delights from the Red Lights* (Spokane, Wash.: Chickadee, 1999), 20.
125. Seagraves, *Soiled Doves*, 106.
126. "Molly b'Dam and Murray," *True West Magazine* (April 1984), 53.
127. Seagraves, *Soiled Doves*, 106.
128. Ibid., 107–8.
129. Moynahan, *Culinary Delights from the Red Lights*, 20.
130. Seagraves, *Soiled Doves*, 107–8.
131. Fitzgerald, "Bawdy Houses of the West," 37.
132. Seagraves, *Soiled Doves*, 109.

133. In the interest of clarity, an alternative source says that according to cemetery records, "Neither wind nor weather kept her from the unfortunate's bedside." See Seagraves, *Soiled Doves*, 111; also Grace Ernestine Ray, *Wily Women of the West* (San Antonio, Tex.: Naylor, 1972), 78.
134. Moynahan, *Red Light Revelations*, 51.
135. Ibid., 11.
136. Ibid., 17–18.
137. Ibid., 56.
138. Ibid., 13.
139. Ibid., 23.
140. Florin, *Ghost Towns of the West*, 461–62.
141. Moynahan, *Red Light Revelations*, 28–31.
142. Ibid., 31.
143. Ibid., 52–55.
144. Sparling, *Southern Idaho Ghost Towns*, 89.
145. MacKell, *Brothels, Bordellos, and Bad Girls*, 26.
146. Simmons, *Red Light Ladies*, 90.
147. Moynahan, *Ladies of Easy Virtue in the Bitterroot Mountains*, 13–14.

Chapter Five

1. Walter O'Meara, *Daughters of the Country: The Women of the Fur Traders and Mountain Men* (New York: Harcourt, Brace and World, 1968), 166.
2. Warren J. Brier, "Tilting Skirts and Hurdy-Gurdies: A Commentary on Gold Camp Women," *Montana Magazine* (Autumn 1969), 59.
3. Ibid., 67.
4. Gary Wiles and Delores Brown, *Femme Fatales, Gamblers, Yankees, and Rebels in the Gold Fields [1859–1869]* (Hemet, Calif.: Birth of America Books, 2005), 28.
5. Robert L. Brown, *Ghost Towns of the Colorado Rockies* (Caldwell, Idaho: Caxton Printers, 1977), 384–86; Anne Seagraves, *Soiled Doves: Prostitution in the Early West* (Hayden, Idaho: Wesanne, 1994), 119–22.
6. Richard Erdoes, *Saloons of the Old West* (Avenel, N.J.: Grammercy Books, a division of Random House Value, 1997), 198.
7. Seagraves, *Soiled Doves*, 122–23.
8. Brier, "Tilting Skirts and Hurdy-Gurdies," 64–67.
9. Muriel Sibell Wolle, *The Bonanza Trail* (Chicago: Sage Books, 1953), 186.
10. Virginia City Visitor Center, Virginia City, Montana.
11. Wolle, *The Bonanza Trail*, 178–80; University of Montana, Western Homepage, "Hanging the Sheriff: A Biography of Henry Plummer," hypertext version at http://www.umwestern.edu/Academics/library/libroth/MHD/vigilantes/HTS/intro.htm; "Dillon Region," Montana's Gold West Country, http://www.goldwest.visitmt.com/communities/dillon.htm.
12. Wiles and Brown, *Femme Fatales*, 266; Chris Enss, *Pistol Packin' Madams: True Stories of Notorious Women of the Old West* (Helena, Mont.: Twodot, an imprint of the Globe Pequot Press, 2006), 9, 11–12; Jan MacKell, *Brothels, Bordellos, and Bad Girls: Prostitution in Colorado 1860–1930* (Albuquerque: University of New Mexico Press, 2004), 144 (this print cited unless otherwise noted); *Butte Daily Miner*, September 8, 1869, p. 4, col. 3.

13. Enss, *Pistol Packin' Madams*, 12–13; Erdoes, *Saloons of the Old West*, 156; MacKell, *Brothels, Bordellos, and Bad Girls*, 144.

14. Wiles and Brown, *Femme Fatales*, 174–77, 254–56.

15. Ibid., 270.

16. Ibid., 257, 270. Author Chris Enss offers an entirely different story, stating that Eleanore married cattleman Jack McKnight sometime between 1865 and 1868. The couple moved to the ranch near Carson City, Nevada, and appeared happy until McKnight suddenly absconded with all of their money. Enss, *Pistol Packin' Madams*, 14.

17. Emma Green, "Biography of Eleanore Dumont," http://www.64.233.167.104/search?q=cache:Sb9vwbUFUFAJ:www.luckyblackjack.com/eleanore-dumont.html+dumont+mcknight+nevada&hl=en&ct=clnk&cd=3&gl=us. In Eleanore's enigmatic timeline, this last story appears to be the most accurate.

18. Wiles and Brown, *Femme Fatales*, 266–68.

19. Ibid., 301–3.

20. Enss, *Pistol Packin' Madams*, 14.

21. Ben T. Traywick, *Behind the Red Lights—History of Prostitution in Tombstone* (Tombstone, Ariz.: Red Marie's, 1993), 24.

22. Enss, *Pistol Packin' Madams*, 14–16.

23. *Butte Daily Miner*, September 8, 1879, p. 4, col. 3.

24. U.S. Bureau of the Census, *Ninth Census of the United States, 1870* (Washington, D.C.: National Archives and Records Administration, 1870).

25. *Montana News Association*, insert 1:352, July 29, 1918, p. 4, col. 1.

26. Stephen Hull, "Helena: The Shame of Montana," *Stag Magazine* (February 1953), 17.

27. These streets are now Miller, State, and Park streets, respectively. Ellen Baumler, "Soiled Doves," *Helena Independent Record*, August 10, 1995, C1.

28. Arlene J. Fitzgerald, "Bawdy Houses of the West," *Oldtimers Wild West Magazine* (August 1976), 30.

29. Volney Steele, M.D., *Bleed, Blister, and Purge: A History of Medicine on the American Frontier* (Missoula, Mont.: Mountain Press, 2005), 94.

30. Jay Moynahan, *Photographs of the Red Light Ladies 1865–1920* (Spokane, Wash.: Chickadee, 2005), 46.

31. Steele quoted in Allen M. Jones, review of *Bleed, Blister and Purge: A History of Medicine on the American Frontier*, by Volney Steele, M.D., *New West Network*, July 14, 2005, http://www.newwest.net/index.php/main/article/2240/.

32. Wolle, *The Bonanza Trail*, 193; "The Notable Women of Bozeman's Red Light District," undated news clipping, Prostitute File, Pioneer Museum, Bozeman, Montana.

33. The actual date may have been 1868 or later because Chicago Joe is not listed in the 1868 Helena directory. Helena city directory, 1868, Montana Historical Society, Helena.

34. Seagraves, *Soiled Doves*, 88; Baumler, "Soiled Doves"; Rex C. Myers, "An Inning for Sin," *Montana Magazine* (Spring 1977), 27; "Helena, Montana," http://en.wikipedia.org/wiki/Helena,_Montana.

35. Myers, "An Inning for Sin," 27. Hankins's eventual demise is interesting, if only because he was somehow suffocated in a folding bed. *Helena Daily Independent*, October 26, 1899, p. 8, col. 2.

36. Shannon Field, "Bordellos Once Did Booming Business," unidentified news clipping dated July 1, 1996, Pioneer Museum; Seagraves, *Soiled Doves*, 88.

37. Myers, "An Inning for Sin," 27.

38. Rex Myers states that the new building was constructed in 1874. Author Anne Seagraves claims the couple married and built the Red Light in 1878. Myers, "An Inning for Sin," 27; Seagraves, *Soiled Doves*, 88.

39. Myers, "An Inning for Sin," 27; Seagraves, *Soiled Doves*, 88.

40. U.S. Bureau of the Census, *Tenth Census of the United States, 1880* (Washington, D.C.: National Archives and Records Administration, 1880); Helena city directory, 1886–87, Montana Historical Society.

41. Seagraves, *Soiled Doves*, 89, 95; Myers, "An Inning for Sin," 31.

42. Seagraves, *Soiled Doves*, 89; *Helena Daily Independent*, October 26, 1899, p. 8, col. 2; Myers, "An Inning for Sin," 33.

43. Helena city directory, 1890, Montana Historical Society; Seagraves, *Soiled Doves*, 89.

44. Field, "Bordellos Once Did Booming Business"; Seagraves, *Soiled Doves*, 95.

45. Baumler, "Soiled Doves"; Montana directories, 1889–91, http://www.ancestry.com.

46. Jay Moynahan, *Remedies from the Red Lights* (Spokane, Wash.: Chickadee), 2000, 5.

47. Baumler, "Soiled Doves."

48. It is interesting to note that Helena's three most prominent madams—Chicago Joe, Lillie McGraw, and Mollie Byrnes—networked together and with madams in other cities to trade or lend their girls to each other. It is also interesting that the women's properties lay within close proximity of the Catholic grammar school and that architect James Stranahan built a new home for his bride overlooking Lillie and Mollie's parlor houses. Most coincidentally, all three madams also died within two years of one another. Baumler, "Soiled Doves."

49. Jay Moynahan, *Soiled Doves, Sportin' Women, and Other Fallen Flowers* (Spokane, Wash.: Chickadee, 2005), 46.

50. Baumler, "Soiled Doves"; Steele, *Bleed, Blister, and Purge*, 93.

51. Helena city directory, 1890. In all likelihood, there were more women than those listed, but their identities have been muddled over time. A prime example is "Jackie," whose photograph has been published in a number of books. A photograph of her at the Montana Historical Society in Helena is all that exists, with no other information (Moynahan, *Soiled Doves, Sportin' Women, and Other Fallen Flowers*, 43). As late as the 1960s, someone published young Jackie's portrait—which was actually taken in Salt Lake City—and verified her as a Helena prostitute. Jackie and several historic photographs of other women, whose portraits were taken in such faraway places as New York, were apparently included in an exhibit displayed at the Loranz Gallery in Helena. Only Richard Lockey, formerly a prominent

Helena citizen, is identifiable as "the Duke." The photographs' donor, John Schroeder, gave copies of them to the Montana Historical Society in 1964 (Photograph Archives Division, Montana Historical Society).

52. Undated "Soiled Doves" calendar featuring photographs from the Timothy Gordon Collection, photocopy, Silver Bow County Archives, Butte, Montana.

53. Hull, "Helena," 17.

54. *Butte Miner*, February 21, 1911, news clipping, Prostitution File, Silver Bow County Archives.

55. Hull, "Helena," 17.

56. Max Evans, *Madam Millie: Brothels from Silver City to Ketchikan* (Albuquerque: University of New Mexico Press, 2002), xxi.

57. Dorothy Josephine Baker Papers, Montana Historical Society.

58. Hull, "Helena," 17, 47.

59. Charles D. Greenfield, "Hurdy-Gurdy Girls Earned Better Reputation Than They've Been Given," *Great Falls Tribune*, April 28, 1963, p. 13, col. 1; interview with Darren Oss, Helena, Montana, September 2006; Dorothy Josephine Baker Papers.

60. Wolle, *The Bonanza Trail*, 199.

61. Photograph Archives Division, Montana Historical Society.

62. Norma Slack, "Calamity Jane Presentation," undated manuscript, Laramie Historical Society, Laramie, Wyoming.

63. James D. McLaird, *Calamity Jane: The Woman and the Legend* (Norman: University of Oklahoma Press, 2005), 3.

64. Cited in Michael Rutter, *Upstairs Girls: Prostitution in the American West* (Helena, Mont.: Farcountry Press, 2005), 159.

65. Harry Sinclair Drago, *Notorious Ladies of the Frontier* (New York: Dodd, Mead, 1969), 212.

66. McLaird, *Calamity Jane*, 13; Drago, *Notorious Ladies of the Frontier*, 213; Rutter, *Upstairs Girls*, 160.

67. Seagraves, *Soiled Doves*, 124; McLaird, *Calamity Jane*, 22, 21; Rutter, *Upstairs Girls*, 160.

68. Seagraves, *Soiled Doves*, 124. Jane's early fondness for wearing men's clothing, which were surely more comfortable, became one of her trademarks.

69. Rutter, *Upstairs Girls*, 160; Seagraves, *Soiled Doves*, 125; Wiles and Brown, *Femme Fatales*, 254.

70. Drago, *Notorious Ladies of the Frontier*, 214; Wiles and Brown, *Femme Fatales*, 267.

71. McLaird, *Calamity Jane*, 29.

72. Rutter, *Upstairs Girls*, 161; Seagraves, *Soiled Doves*, 125.

73. Seagraves, *Soiled Doves*, 124.

74. Hillyer Best, *Julia Bulette and Other Red Light Ladies* (Sparks, Nev.: Western Printing, 1959), 17.

75. Rutter, *Upstairs Girls*, 165; Drago, *Notorious Ladies of the Frontier*, 214.

76. Drago, *Notorious Ladies of the Frontier*, 209.

77. Ibid., 218. If this incident happened at all, it was perhaps remembered euphemistically or even metaphorically by Jane.
78. Seagraves, *Soiled Doves*, 124.
79. McLaird, *Calamity Jane*, 37.
80. Drago, *Notorious Ladies of the Frontier*, 219.
81. McLaird, *Calamity Jane*, 57.
82. Drago, *Notorious Ladies of the Frontier*, 220. Other notable camp followers on the expedition were Eleanore Dumont and Dirty Em.
83. McLaird, *Calamity Jane*, 57.
84. Ibid., 161.
85. Rutter, *Upstairs Girls*, 162–64; Seagraves, *Soiled Doves*, 133; Drago, *Notorious Ladies of the Frontier*, 142.
86. Drago, *Notorious Ladies of the Frontier*, 220.
87. Ibid., 208, 221; Rutter, *Upstairs Girls*, 166–68.
88. Drago, *Notorious Ladies of the Frontier*, 211. Drago's source may have been Jane's supposed daughter, Jean McCormick, who said the same thing. McLaird, *Calamity Jane*, 246.
89. Seagraves, *Soiled Doves*, 133.
90. Rutter, *Upstairs Girls*, 166; Seagraves, *Soiled Doves*, 125.
91. Lambert Florin, *Ghost Towns of the West* (Superior, Neb.: Superior Publishing for Promontory Press, 1971), 405.
92. Drago, *Notorious Ladies of the Frontier*, 211, 218; Rutter, *Upstairs Girls*, 167.
93. Rutter, *Upstairs Girls*, 168. Henry Drago says Jane was working for Pan American before being hired by Buffalo Bill. Drago, *Notorious Ladies of the Frontier*, 211.
94. Drago, *Notorious Ladies of the Frontier*, 211.
95. Ibid., 222; McLaird, *Calamity Jane*, 124, 166, 169; *Livingston, Montana, Historic District Walking Tour*, pamphlet (Livingston, Mont.: Livingston Area Chamber of Commerce and Park County Friends of Historic Preservation, 2006); Moynahan, *Photographs of the Red Light Ladies*, 82.
96. McLaird, *Calamity Jane*, 169.
97. Drago, *Notorious Ladies of the Frontier*, 222; *Livingston Historic District Walking Tour*.
98. Drago, *Notorious Ladies of the Frontier*, 209.
99. Interestingly, the same minister who supposedly married Jane and Hickok is also recorded as marrying Agnes Lake and Hickok in 1876. Drago, *Notorious Ladies of the Frontier*, 215.
100. Ibid., 210, 218.
101. Ibid., 222.
102. Ruth Shadley, *Calamity Jane's Daughter: The Story of Maude Weir, a Story Never Before Told* (Caldwell, Idaho: Caxton Printers, 1996), 6, 9, 12–18, 31, 50.
103. "The Notable Women of Bozeman's Red Light District," *Avant Courier*, undated news clipping, Pioneer Museum.
104. Ibid.
105. Ibid.; untitled, undated manuscript, author unknown, Prostitution File, Pioneer Museum.
106. "The Notable Women of Bozeman's Red Light District"; Field, "Bordellos Once Did Booming Business"; B. Derek Strahn, "Tycoons

in Petticoats: Frontier Montana's Uncommon Red Light Madams," http://
www.distinctlymontana.com/index.aspx/issues/Summer2006/reside/
TYCOONS_IN_PETTYCOATS_FRONTIER_MONTANA_UNCOMMON_
RED_LIGHT_MADAMS.

107. Wolle, *The Bonanza Trail*, 209; Florin, *Ghost Towns of the West*, 399.

108. Although there were once seven thousand people in Beartown, by
1898 its population consisted of one soul. Nothing is left of Beartown
today except a sign. Photograph Archives Division, Montana Historical
Society; "Missoula, Montana," *Wikipedia*, http://en.wikipedia.org/wiki/
Missoula,_Montana.

109. Jay Moynahan, *Culinary Delights from the Red Lights* (Spokane, Wash.:
Chickadee, 1999), 12.

110. Wolle, *The Bonanza Trail*, 200; author's interview with Ray, Montana
Valley Bookstore, Alberton, Montana, September 2006.

111. Jay Moynahan, *Ladies of Easy Virtue in the Bitterroot Mountains* (Spokane,
Wash.: Chickadee, 1999), 16–17.

112. Jay Moynahan, *Red Light Revelations: The Sportin' Women of Wallace and
the Silver Valley, 1888 to 1909* (Spokane, Wash.: Chickadee, 2001), 37.

113. Ibid., 43.

114. Moynahan, *Ladies of Easy Virtue in the Bitterroot Mountains*, 17–19, 38.

115. Ellen Baumler, "Devil's Perch: Prostitution from Suite to Cellar in Butte,
Montana," Montana Historical Society, http://www.montanahistoricalsociety.
org/education/cirguides/buttearticbaumler.asp, 6; Henry Elwood, *Kalispell,
Montana, and the Upper Flathead Valley* (Kalispell, Mont.: Thomas Printing,
1980), 60–66; Kathryn L. McKay, *A Guide to Historic Kalispell* (Helena,
Mont.: Montana Historical Society Press, 2001), 31.

116. "Find History and You May Never Leave Butte," in *Butte Montana Visitor
Guide* (Butte: Butte–Silver Bow Chamber of Commerce, n.d.), 2; author's
interview with Jack Mayfield, Oasis Bordello Museum, Wallace, Idaho,
September 2006.

117. Madeleine Blair, *Madeleine, an Autobiography* (New York: Persea Press,
1986), 65.

118. Anne M. Butler, *Daughters of Joy, Sisters of Misery* (Chicago: University of
Illinois Press, 1985), 34.

119. Moynahan, *Remedies from the Red Lights*, 9, 19; Baumler, "Devil's Perch,"
6; U.S. Bureau of the Census, *Tenth Census of the United States, 1880*; Butler,
Daughters of Joy, 68; Ron V. Jackson, Accelerated Indexing Systems, comp.,
U.S. Federal Census Mortality Schedules Index (online database) (Provo, Utah:
Generations Network, 1999); Butler, *Daughters of Joy*, 68.

120. Seagraves, *Soiled Doves*, 117; *Butte Daily Miner*, August 5, 1880, p. 3, col.
2, and August 7, 1880, p. 3, col. 2.

121. Miscellaneous notes, Prostitution File, Silver Bow County Archives.

122. "Find History and You May Never Leave Butte," 7; Butler, *Daughters
of Joy*, 96; *Butte Daily Miner*, October 6, 1881, p. 8, col. 2; Mary Murphy,
"Women on the Line: Prostitution in Butte, Montana 1878–1917," master's
thesis, University of North Carolina, Chapel Hill, 1983, Montana Historical
Society.

123. *Butte Daily Miner*, November 11, 1881, p. 8, col. 2.

124. Seagraves, *Soiled Doves*, 117–19; Blair, *Madeleine*, 65.
125. *Butte Daily Miner*, December 16, 1881, p. 8, col. 2; Seagraves, *Soiled Doves*, 119; Blair, *Madeleine*, 65.
126. *Butte Daily Miner*, December 16, 1881, p. 8, col. 2.
127. Miscellaneous notes, Prostitution File, Silver Bow County Archives.
128. Baumler, "Devil's Perch," 2–6.
129. Ibid., 2–3.
130. Butte city directory, 1889, Silver Bow County Archives; Field, "Bordellos Once Did Booming Business"; Montana directory, 1891–92, http://www.ancestry.com; Murphy, "Women on the Line."
131. Baumler, "Devil's Perch," 4.
132. Murphy, "Women on the Line."
133. Baumler, "Devil's Perch," 4, 13.
134. Coroner's Docket, November 1895–December 1897, Silver Bow County Archives.
135. Baumler, "Devil's Perch," 7, 13; Butte city directory, 1907, Silver Bow County Archives.
136. Baumler, "Devil's Perch," 5.
137. Ibid., 4.
138. Ibid., 8; Rosemary Fetter, "Hurdy-Gurdy Gals of the Old West," *Colorado Gambler* magazine (June 22–28, 2004), 15. Very similar stories of Carrie Nation's antics and the painful results can be found in Cripple Creek, Colorado, and in Kansas.
139. Baumler, "Devil's Perch," 8.
140. U.S. Bureau of the Census, *Fourteenth Census of the United States, 1920* (Washington, D.C.: National Archives and Records Administration, 1920); Butte city directories, 1928–54, Silver Bow County Archives.
141. Butte city directory, 1961, Silver Bow County Archives; International Sex Worker Foundation for Art, Culture, and Education (ISWFACE), *Tales of the Dumas Parlor House, Butte Montana: The Mining City's Last Brothel 1890–1982* (N.p.: ISWFACE, 1998), 14.
142. Baumler, "Devil's Perch," 10.
143. Ibid., 2.
144. *Anaconda Standard*, May 27, 1890, p. 5, col. 4.
145. *Anaconda Standard*, April 28, 1894, p. 1, col. 1.
146. Baumler, "Devil's Perch," 2.
147. *Butte Montana Visitor Guide*, 14, 15; Murphy, "Women on the Line"; Baumler, "Devil's Perch," 3.
148. Baumler, "Devil's Perch," 8.
149. Ibid., 7.
150. Murphy, "Women on the Line."
151. Baumler, "Devil's Perch," 5.
152. Ibid., 1, 4; ISWFACE, *Tales of the Dumas Parlor House*, 9. It is believed that "Dumas" was Delia's maiden name. Author's interview with Rudy Giecek, Dumas Brothel Museum, Butte Montana, September 15, 2006.
153. Baumler, "Devil's Perch," 5.
154. Rudy Giecek interview. It was probably later that a kitchen was added on the bottom floor.

155. Baumler, "Devil's Perch," 4–5; ISWFACE, *Tales of the Dumas Parlor House*, 4.
156. Baumler, "Devil's Perch," 4, 14; ISWFACE, *Tales of the Dumas Parlor House*, 3; Butte City Directories, 1900 and 1902, Silver Bow County Archives.
157. Baumler, "Devil's Perch," 4, 7–8; ISWFACE, *Tales of the Dumas Parlor House*, 3.
158. ISWFACE, *Tales of the Dumas Parlor House*, 3; Baumler, "Devil's Perch," 9.
159. When Rudy Giecek bought the Dumas in 1990, he found such personal effects as a vibrator patented in 1911, opium vials, and lipsticks that were produced in paper tubes during World War I. Rudy Giecek interview.
160. Howling Wolf Productions, *Dumas Brothel: The Tour*, DVD (Dumas Brothel, 2006).
161. Baumler, "Devil's Perch," 10; Butte City Directories, 1925–40, Silver Bow County Archives; Howling Wolf Productions, *Dumas Brothel*; ISWFACE, *Tales of the Dumas Parlor House*, 4, 13; Rudy Giecek interview.
162. ISWFACE, *Tales of the Dumas Parlor House*, 4; Howling Wolf Productions, *Dumas Brothel*; interview with Rudy Giecek.
163. ISWFACE, *Tales of the Dumas Parlor House*, 4, 13; Baumler, "Devil's Perch," 10.
164. ISWFACE, *Tales of the Dumas Parlor House*, 14. Rudy Giecek maintains that Elinore was murdered. He claims that her ghost appeared to him as he sat in a basement crib one day. The meeting inspired him to write "Venus Alley," a fictional account of Elinore's life at the Dumas. Rudy Giecek interview.
165. Butte City Directories, 1955–69, Silver Bow County Archives; ISWFACE, *Tales of the Dumas Parlor House*, 14.
166. ISWFACE, *Tales of the Dumas Parlor House*, 2, 13–14; interview with Rudy Giecek; Baumler, "Devil's Perch," 10; Butte city directory, 1972, Silver Bow County Archives.
167. ISWFACE, *Tales of the Dumas Parlor House*, 7, 15.
168. Murphy, "Women on the Line."
169. ISWFACE, *Tales of the Dumas Parlor House*, 8, 13.
170. Ibid., 16.
171. Baumler, "Devil's Perch," 10. Ruby is now in her eighties and lives at an undisclosed location to protect her privacy. Rudy Giecek interview.
172. ISWFACE, *Tales of the Dumas Parlor House*, 12; Rudy Giecek interview; Baumler, "Devil's Perch," 11; Giecek interview, September 2006.
173. Howling Wolf Productions, *Dumas Brothel*. Due to financial difficulties in 1998, Giecek put the Dumas up for sale. Norma Jean Almodovar, president of ISWFACE, arranged the purchase and hired Giecek as curator-manager. In 2000, the business relationship fell apart. Giecek subsequently sued ISWFACE for back wages and won his case, although to date he has not been paid (Decision 524–2001, *Giecek vs. ISWFACE*, State of Montana Department of Labor and Industry Hearings Bureau, http://dli.mt.gov/hearings/decisions/2002/whdec524_2001.htm). A substantial donation made to the museum in the spring of 2008 enabled it to open for summer tours ("The Dumas Brothel," http://www.thedumasbrothel.com).

174. Baumler, "Devil's Perch," 1, 3; Moynahan, *Remedies from the Red Lights*, 10.

175. John Astle, *Only in Butte: Stories off the Hill* (Butte, Mont.: Holt, 2004), 32; Evans, *Madam Millie*, xiv.

176. Astle, *Only in Butte*, 33.

177. Coroner's Docket, April 1894–October 1895, Silver Bow County Archives.

178. Murphy, "Women on the Line."

179. Baumler, "Devil's Perch," 6.

180. Coroner's Docket, April 1894–October 1895, Silver Bow County Archives.

181. Murphy, "Women on the Line."

182. Moynahan, *Soiled Doves, Sportin' Women, and Other Fallen Flowers*, 43.

183. Baumler, "Devil's Perch," 3.

184. Coroner's Docket, January 1900–November 1901, Silver Bow County Archives.

185. Coroner's Dockets, November 1895–December 1897, January 1900–November 1901, Silver Bow County Archives.

186. Baumler, "Devil's Perch," 1, 3, 6, 13; Murphy, "Women on the Line"; Deer Lodge County, Montana, Anaconda city directory, 1896, http://www.ancestry.com; U.S. Bureau of the Census, *Twelfth Census of the United States, 1900* (Washington, D.C.: National Archives and Records Administration, 1900).

187. Baumler, "Devil's Perch," 13.

188. Butte city directory, 1910, Silver Bow County Archives.

189. Butte city directories, 1929–40, Silver Bow County Archives.

190. Murphy, "Women on the Line"; *Butte Miner*, June 14, 1901, p. 3, col. 3.

191. Baumler, "Devil's Perch," 5.

192. Ibid., 3; Murphy, "Women on the Line"; *Butte Miner*, December 6, 1901, p. 2, col. 2; U.S. Bureau of the Census, *Twelfth Census of the United States, 1900*; Butte city directory, 1900, Silver Bow County Archives.

193. Butte city directory, 1900; *Butte Miner*, December 6, 1901, 2.

194. Baumler, "Devil's Perch," 7.

195. *Butte Miner*, December 6, 1901, 2; Baumler, "Devil's Perch," 7.

196. The women included Mazie Hooligan, whose silly pseudonym surely represented her lust for fun. Butte, Silver Bow County, Montana, directory, 1902, http://www.ancestry.com.

197. Baumler, "Devil's Perch," 8; Murphy, "Women on the Line."

198. Moynahan, *Soiled Doves, Sportin' Women, and Other Fallen Flowers*, 48.

199. *Anaconda Standard*, December 31, 1903, p. 2, col. 1.

200. Murphy, "Women on the Line."

201. Baumler, "Devil's Perch," 1.

202. Ibid., 8; Astle, *Only in Butte*, 240.

203. *Butte Miner*, February 21, 1911, Prostitution File, Silver Bow County Archives.

204. *Butte Miner*, June 25, 1910, p. 5, col. 2, and June 1, 1911, p. 1, col. 3.

205. Baumler, "Devil's Perch," 9; MacKell, *Brothels, Bordellos, and Bad Girls*, 213; Murphy, "Women on the Line."

206. *Butte Montana Visitor Guide*, 27; Chaplin quoted in Baumler, "Devil's Perch," 10, 12; Butte city directories, 1928 and 1929, Silver Bow County Archives.

207. Baumler, "Devil's Perch," 10.

208. Butte city directories, 1930–40, Silver Bow county Archives.

209. ISWFACE, *Tales of the Dumas Parlor House*, 5.

210. Ibid., 13. Police were unable to fingerprint every single girl. Descendants are still looking for Lillian Apley Knutson, who was last seen in Butte when she was in her forties in 1942. Lillian was a prostitute earlier in her life and had apparently migrated to Butte to work. Later, according to her family, she married a Mr. Knutson, who may have been a minister (http://www.ancestry.com, http://www.boards.ancestry.com/mbexec/message/an/localities.northam.usa.states.montana.counties.silverbow).

211. ISWFACE, *Tales of the Dumas Parlor House*, 4; Baumler, "Devil's Perch," 1, 10.

212. Prostitution File, Silver Bow County Archives.

213. Steele, *Bleed, Blister, and Purge*, 94.

214. U.S. Bureau of the Census, *Tenth Census of the United States, 1880*; Jackson, *U.S. Federal Census Mortality Schedules Index*; Moynahan, *Photographs of the Red Light Ladies*, 75.

215. Montana city directory, July 1894, Montana Historical Society; Field, "Bordellos Once Did Booming Business"; http://www.billings.com/billings.html; Billings city directory, 1883 and 1884, Montana Historical Society.

216. Field, "Bordellos Once Did Booming Business"; "Billings, Montana," http://www.billings.com/billings.html.

217. Field, "Bordellos Once Did Booming Business."

218. Ibid.

219. Ibid.

220. *Livingston Historic District Walking Tour*; Moynahan, *Remedies from the Red Lights*, 15.

221. Moynahan, *Culinary Delights from the Red Lights*, 15.

222. *Livingston Historic District Walking Tour*.

223. *Livingston Historic District Walking Tour*; Park County Historical Society, *History of Park County, Montana* (Dallas: Taylor, 1984), 503.

224. Park County Historical Society, *History of Park County, Montana*, 503.

225. Steele, *Bleed, Blister, and Purge*, 91; *Anaconda Standard*, January 7, 1894, p. 1, col. 2; Raymond Schuesller, "Bawdy Houses of the Old West," *True West* magazine (May 1984), 29.

226. Florin, *Ghost Towns of the West*, 404–7; Sherry Monahan, *The Wicked West: Boozers, Cruisers, Gamblers, and More* (Tucson, Ariz.: Rio Nuevo, 2005), 106; *Butte Miner*, May 22, 1904, p. 1, col. 4.

Chapter Six

1. See Desert, USA, "Socorro, New Mexico," http://www.desertusa.com/Cities/nm/Socorro.html.

2. Philip Varney, *New Mexico's Best Ghost Towns* (Albuquerque: University of New Mexico Press, 1987), 121.

3. "History at a Glance," in *Santa Fe Official 2007 Visitors Guide* (Santa Fe: n.p., n.d.), 11.
4. Mary J. Straw Cook, *Doña Tules: Santa Fe's Courtesan Gambler* (Albuquerque: University of New Mexico Press, 2007), 1; Richard Erdoes, *Saloons of the Old West* (Avenel, N.J.: Grammercy Books, a division of Random House Value, 1997), 155.
5. Cook, *Doña Tules*, 1.
6. Ibid.
7. Ibid., 10–20.
8. Erdoes, *Saloons of the Old West*, 155; "A Living History," in *Santa Fe Official 2007 Visitors Guide*, 15; Cook, *Doña Tules*, 50.
9. Erdoes, *Saloons of the Old West*, 155.
10. Cook, *Doña Tules*, 42.
11. Ibid., 47.
12. Ibid., 31.
13. Erdoes, *Saloons of the Old West*, 155; Cook, *Doña Tules*, 2, 34, 55–58.
14. See "American Forts: New Mexico," http://www.northamericanforts.com/West/nm.html#marcy; Southwest Ghost Hunters Association, "Ghost Hunt of Loma Parda, NM," http://www.sgha.net/nm/lasvetas/lomaparda.html.
15. Antonio R. Garcez, *Adobe Angels: Ghost Stories of O'Keefe Country* (Truth or Consequences, N.Mex.: Red Rabbit Press, 1998), 27.
16. Cook, *Doña Tules*, 61.
17. "Historic Old Town Albuquerque," map published by the City of Albuquerque in conjunction with New Mexico Land of Enchantment Tourism Department, 2005; see also http://www.northamericanforts.com/West/nm.html#marcy.
18. Byron A. Johnson and Sharon P. Johnson, *Gilded Palaces of Shame: Albuquerque's Redlight Districts 1880–1914* (Albuquerque: Gilded Age Press, 1983), 9.
19. Howard Bryan, *Albuquerque Remembered* (Albuquerque: University of New Mexico Press, 2006), 143, 154.
20. Johnson and Johnson, *Gilded Palaces of Shame*, 14, 76.
21. Ibid., 15, 38–39, 43.
22. Ibid., 17, 79–82.
23. Ibid., 38.
24. Ibid., 40–44, 78.
25. Ibid., 16, 45.
26. Lizzie McGrath display, McGrath's Bar & Grill, Albuquerque, New Mexico; Johnson and Johnson, *Gilded Palaces of Shame*, 19.
27. Bryan, *Albuquerque Remembered*, 154; U.S. Bureau of the Census, *Twelfth Census of the United States, 1900* (Washington, D.C.: National Archives and Records Administration, 1900); Lizzie McGrath display.
28. Johnson and Johnson, *Gilded Palaces of Shame*, 80.
29. Mo Palmer, "Of Churches and Brothels, Homes and Firehouses." *Albuquerque Tribune*, http://web.abqtrib.com/archives/opinions02/090902_opinions_mo.shtml; Lizzie McGrath display; Johnson and Johnson, *Gilded Palaces of Shame*, 46.

30. Johnson and Johnson, *Gilded Palaces of Shame*, 46, 79.
31. Charles H. Gildersleeve, reporter, "Territory of New Mexico v. Joe Kee," in *Reports of Cases Determined in the Supreme Court of the Territory of New Mexico from February 4 1888 to July 24 1891* (Columbia, Mo.: E. W. Stephens, 1896), 511–14.
32. U.S. Bureau of the Census, *Twelfth Census of the United States, 1900*; Lizzie McGrath display; U.S. Bureau of the Census, *Thirteenth Census of the United States, 1910* (Washington, D.C.: National Archives and Records Administration, 1910).
33. Lizzie McGrath display; Johnson and Johnson, *Gilded Palaces of Shame*, 72–80.
34. Bryan, *Albuquerque Remembered*, 155; Johnson and Johnson, *Gilded Palaces of Shame*, 46.
35. Johnson and Johnson, *Gilded Palaces of Shame*, 19, 21, 61–62, 66, 79–82.
36. Bryan, *Albuquerque Remembered*, 154.
37. Johnson and Johnson, *Gilded Palaces of Shame*, 8.
38. Ibid., 26–27, 81; U.S. Bureau of the Census, *Thirteenth Census of the United States, 1910*.
39. Johnson and Johnson, *Gilded Palaces of Shame*, 27, 62, 81.
40. Ibid., 69–72; see also "New Mexico Legends: Ghosts of Albuquerque," *Legends of America*, http://www.legendsofamerica.com/ HC-AlbuquerqueGhosts.html.
41. Desert, USA, "Socorro, New Mexico."
42. Daniel C. B. Rathbun and David V. Alexander, *New Mexico Frontier Military Place Names* (Las Cruces, N.Mex.: Yucca Tree Press, 2003), 213.
43. Cheryl J. Foote, *Women of the New Mexico Frontier 1846–1912* (Niwot: University Press of Colorado, 1990), 45.
44. Volney Steele, M.D., *Bleed, Blister, and Purge: A History of Medicine on the American Frontier* (Missoula, Mont.: Mountain Press, 2005), 116; Rathbun and Alexander, *New Mexico Frontier Military Place Names*, 228–39.
45. Foote, *Women of the New Mexico Frontier 1846–1912*, 45–46.
46. U.S. Bureau of the Census, *Eighth Census of the United States, 1860* (Washington, D.C.: National Archives and Records Administration, 1860); Jay Moynahan, *Sarah Bowman: Pioneer Madam* (Spokane, Wash.: Chickadee, 2004), 11–13.
47. Moynahan, *Sarah Bowman*, 14, 16, 24.
48. Ibid., 31–38, 45–47; U.S. Bureau of the Census, *Seventh Census of the United States, 1850* (Washington, D.C.: National Archives and Records Administration, 1850).
49. Albert's real estate was valued at $600, whereas Sarah's was appraised at $2,000. U.S. Bureau of the Census, *Eighth Census of the United States, 1860*.
50. Moynahan, *Sarah Bowman*, 49–50.
51. James Abarr, "Desolate Outpost," *Albuquerque Journal*, August 30, 1998, C4; see also "Old West Legends: Charlie Utter, Bill Hickock's Best Pard," *Legends of America*, http://www.legendsofamerica.com/WE-CharlieUtter. html; Chester D. Potter, "Socorro Vigilantes," *New Mexico Historical Review* 40 (1965), 32–33.

52. Conrad Richter, *Tacey Cromwell* (Albuquerque: University of New Mexico Press, 1974), 13. Richter's book was later the basis for the movie *One Desire*, which premiered in 1955 (Internet Movie Database, http://www.imdb.com).

53. Max Evans, *Madam Millie: Bordellos from Silver City to Ketchikan* (Albuquerque: University of New Mexico Press, 2002), 72.

54. Ralph Looney, *Haunted Highways: The Ghost Towns of New Mexico* (New York: Hastings House, 1968), 31.

55. Rathbun and Alexander, *New Mexico Frontier Military Place Names*, 215; "Ghost Hunt of Loma Parda, NM."

56. Foote, *Women of the New Mexico Frontier*, 46.

57. Looney, *Haunted Highways*, 32; "Ghost Hunt of Loma Parda, NM."

58. Cy Martin, "Loma Lightening and Wicked Women," *Golden West* magazine (August 1972), 15.

59. Ibid., 16.

60. Looney, *Haunted Highways*, 33–34; Martin, "Loma Lightening and Wicked Women," 16.

61. See David Sedivy, "Fort Union," *Colorado History*, http://members.tripod.com/~mr_sedivy/colorado11.html.

62. Looney, *Haunted Highways*, 34; "Ghost Hunt of Loma Parda, NM"; Florin, *Ghost Towns of the West*, 657; T. J. Sperry and Harry C. Myers, "A History of Fort Union," http://www.kansasheritage.org/research/sft/ft-union.htm; Martin, "Loma Lightening and Wicked Women," 16; Varney, *New Mexico's Best Ghost Towns*, 22.

63. "Women and the Death Penalty in New Mexico, an Historical Review: The Twice-Hanged Angel," CLEWS, the Historic True Crime Blog, http://laurajames.typepad.com/clews/2005/11/women_and_the_d.html; Armando De Aguero, *The Curse of Pablita Martin* (Clovis, N.Mex.: Guadalupe County Communicator, 2004), 8; Cook, *Doña Tules*, 42.

64. De Aguero, *The Curse of Pablita Martin*, 3. It is interesting to note that Paula and Domingo Martin are inexplicably listed twice in the 1860 census. In the first listing, they are recorded as ages thirty-six and twenty-nine, respectively, and as having a five-year-old child named Carpia Angel Martin. The second listing identifies them one address away. In this instance, Paula's age is recorded as thirty-four, and the couple are listed as having two children, six-year-old Carpia and one-year-old Paulina. In both listings, the Martins are recorded as being illiterate. U.S. Bureau of the Census, *Eighth Census of the United States, 1860*.

65. "Women and the Death Penalty in New Mexico"; Don Bullis, "Observations on the Demise of Paula Angel," *Rio Rancho Observer*, August 4, 2005, http://www.observer-online.com/articles/2005/08/04/news/don_bullis/bullis.txt; De Aguero, *The Curse of Pablita Martin*, 3.

66. De Aguero, *The Curse of Pablita Martin*, 4, 25; Bullis, "Observations on the Demise of Paula Angel."

67. De Aguero, *The Curse of Pablita Martin*, 26–27.

68. Florin, *Ghost Towns of the West*, 609; *A Walking Tour of Old Town, Cimarron, New Mexico in the 1800's*, pamphlet (Cimarron, N.Mex.: Cimarron Historical Society, n.d.); see also "Cimarron," *New Mexico Magazine*, http://www.nmmagazine.com/regions/northeast/Cimarron.php.

69. Butler, *Daughters of Joy*, 9.

70. Looney, *Haunted Highways*, 92; James E. Sherman and Barbara H. Sherman, *Ghost Towns and Mining Camps of New Mexico* (Norman: University of Oklahoma Press, 1975), 73E; "Surrounding Communities," in *Discover Socorro 2007 Visitors Guide* (Socorro, N.Mex.: El Defensor Chieftain, 2007), 14.

71. Bob Alexander, *Six-Guns and Single-Jacks: A History of Silver City and Southwestern New Mexico* (Silver City, N.Mex.: Gila Books, 2005), 29.

72. "Pinos Altos Notes," undated, untitled news clipping, Prostitution File, Silver City Museum, Silver City, New Mexico; interview with George Schafer, Pinos Altos Museum, Pinos Altos, New Mexico, November 2007.

73. *Silver City Enterprise*, June 21, 1889, Prostitution File, Silver City Museum.

74. Miscellaneous undated news clipping, Prostitution File, Silver City Museum.

75. Ibid.

76. Ibid.

77. U.S. Bureau of the Census, *Tenth Census of the United States, 1880* (Washington, D.C.: National Archives and Records Administration, 1880).

78. *Silver City Enterprise*, February 1, 1884, Clippings Index, Silver City Museum.

79. *Silver City Enterprise*, May 23, 1884, Clippings Index, Silver City Museum.

80. *Silver City Enterprise*, June 20, 1884, Clippings Index, Silver City Museum.

81. *Silver City Enterprise*, January 16, 1885, Clippings Index, Silver City Museum.

82. *Silver City Enterprise*, February 22, 1884, Clippings Index, Silver City Museum; U.S. Bureau of the Census, *Twelfth Census of the United States, 1900; Silver City Enterprise*, February 29, 1884, and January 23, 1885, Clippings Index, Silver City Museum.

83. *Silver City Enterprise*, May 30, 1885, Clippings Index, Silver City Museum.

84. *Silver City Enterprise*, June 19, 1885, Clippings Index, Silver City Museum. The road would be useful in expanding Kate's business.

85. Miscellaneous newspaper clipping, Prostitution File, Silver City Museum.

86. U.S. Bureau of the Census, *Twelfth Census of the United States, 1900*, and *Thirteenth Census of the United States, 1910*.

87. *Silver City Enterprise*, August 14, 1884, Clippings Index, Silver City Museum.

88. *Southwest Sentinel*, November 1, 1884, and *Silver City Enterprise*, March 13, 1885, Clippings Index, Silver City Museum.

89. Alexander, *Six-Guns and Single-Jacks*, 217.

90. *Silver City Enterprise*, June 1, 1888, Prostitution File, Silver City Museum.

91. *Silver City Enterprise*, September 27, 1889, Prostitution File, Silver City Museum.

92. Elliott West, *The Saloon on the Rocky Mountain Frontier* (Lincoln: University of Nebraska Press, 1979), 21; U.S. Bureau of the Census, *Fourteenth Census of the United States, 1920* (Washington, D.C.: National Archives and Records Administration, 1920); U.S. Bureau of the Census, *Twelfth Census of the United States, 1900*, and *Thirteenth Census of the United States, 1910*.

93. West, *The Saloon on the Rocky Mountain Frontier*, 21.

94. *Silver City Enterprise*, June 1, 1888, Prostitution File, Silver City Museum.

95. Miscellaneous news clipping dated 1889, Prostitution File, Silver City Museum.

96. *Silver City Enterprise*, January 10, 1890, July 18, 1890, and October 31, 1880, Prostitution File, Silver City Museum.

97. See http://www.roots web.com/~trespass/1800s.html; U.S. Bureau of the Census, *Twelfth Census of the United States, 1900*.

98. *Silver City Enterprise*, April 22, 1892, Clippings Index, Silver City Museum.

99. *Silver City Enterprise*, March 31, 1893, Clippings Index, Silver City Museum; U.S. Bureau of the Census, *Twelfth Census of the United States, 1900*.

100. *Silver City Enterprise*, January 29, 1948, p. 1, col. 1.

101. Evans, *Madam Millie*, 5, 9–11, 15; Social Security Administration, *Social Security Death Index, Master File* (Washington, D.C.: Social Security Administration, 2008); "Millie—The Madam of the '500 Club,'" *Wilderness Outlook* (July 15–July 30, 1988), 5; *Albuquerque Journal*, August 11, 1978, B1, col. 1.

102. Evans, *Madam Millie*, 16, ix–x. So much for Harvey House girls, the majority of whom were well trained as highly respected waitresses, having reputations as respectable young women! Even so, it should be noted that Millie left her position as a Harvey House girl and does not appear to have pursued the prostitution profession while still employed.

103. Evans, *Madam Millie*, 25, 35–42.

104. *Albuquerque Journal*, August 11, 1978, B1, col. 1.

105. Two other madams were unsuitable: Merle Belmont sold more bootleg whiskey than sex, and Birdie Abbott was too old. Evans, *Madam Millie*, 46.

106. Miscellaneous news clipping dated June 25, 1978, Clippings File, Silver City Museum.

107. At the time, Merle Belmont and Birdie Abbott were still Millie's competitors. Evans, *Madam Millie*, 53, 62–65, 71.

108. Miscellaneous news clipping dated June 25, 1978, Clippings File, Silver City Museum; "Millie—The Madam of the '500 Club.'"

109. The bordello in Deming was reputedly haunted. Owner Thelma Austin asked Millie to take it over because she couldn't keep madams and girls there. Millie agreed that the place was indeed haunted, but she still did a booming business there. Miscellaneous news clipping dated June 25, 1978, Clippings File, Silver City Museum; "Millie—The Madam of the '500 Club'"; Evans, *Madam Millie*, 85.

110. Evans, *Madam Millie*, xvi.

111. Miscellaneous news clipping, June 25, 1978, Clippings File, Silver City Museum.

112. "Millie—The Madam of the '500 Club.'"

113. Miscellaneous news clipping, June 25, 1978.

114. "Millie—The Madam of the '500 Club.'"

115. Ibid.

116. Evans, *Madam Millie*, 101–5.

117. Ibid., 3, 161, 164–67, 195.

118. Ibid., 178–82.

119. *Silver City Enterprise*, January 29, 1948, p. 1, col. 1.

120. *Silver City Enterprise*, November 10, 1949, p. 1, col. 4.

121. Miscellaneous news clipping, March 22, 1951, Silver City Museum.

122. Undated news clipping, Clippings File, Silver City Museum. The closing of Millie's house for a year certainly indicates that authorities were willing to continue permitting her to operate (miscellaneous news clipping dated March 22, 1951). In later years, Millie claimed that the authorities told her she could no longer lease out her bordellos, but had to run them herself (miscellaneous news clipping dated March 29, 1951, Clippings File, Silver City Museum).

123. *Silver City Enterprise*, June 1951 and August 23, 1951, Clippings File, Silver City Museum.

124. *Albuquerque Journal*, August 11, 1978, B1, col. 1; Evans, *Madam Millie*, x; miscellaneous news clipping dated June 25, 1978, Clippings File, Silver City Museum.

125. Miscellaneous news clipping dated June 25, 1978; Evans, *Madam Millie*, xvi.

126. *Albuquerque Journal*, August 11, 1978.

127. *Silver City Press*, February 21, 1992, Clippings File, Silver City Museum.

128. *Silver City Daily Press*, November 9, 1993, Clippings File, Silver City Museum; National Cemetery Administration, *U.S. Veterans Gravesites, ca. 1775–2006* (online database) (Provo, Utah: Generations Network, 2006).

129. *Albuquerque Journal*, August 11, 1978, B1, col. 1.

130. Dave Cushman, "The Fabulous Sadie Orchard," *Sierra County Sentinel*, July 6, 1967, 7; Jay Moynahan, *Soiled Doves, Sportin' Women, and Other Fallen Flowers* (Spokane, Wash.: Chickadee, 2005), 77; U.S. Bureau of the Census, *Fifteenth Census of the United States, 1930* (Washington, D.C.: National Archives and Records Administration, 1930).

131. Although some resources place Sadie at the nearby town of Kingston in 1880, the town was not surveyed until 1882. The latter date, therefore, is likely more accurate. Moynahan, *Soiled Doves, Sportin' Women, and Other Fallen Flowers*, 62–64.

132. Ibid., 67–68.

133. Cushman, "The Fabulous Sadie Orchard"; *Historic Hillsboro, a Walking Tour Guide*, pamphlet (Las Cruces: Rural Economic Development Through Tourism Project, New Mexico State University Cooperative Extension Service, n.d.); Moynahan, *Soiled Doves, Sportin' Women, and Other Fallen Flowers*, 73.

134. Others say James W. Orchard already owned the Lake Valley, Hillsboro & Kingston Stage Line when he married Sadie. Moynahan, *Soiled Doves, Sportin' Women, and Other Fallen Flowers*, 68–70; Sherman and Sherman, *Ghost Towns and Mining Camps of New Mexico*, 133.

135. Moynahan, *Soiled Doves, Sportin' Women, and Other Fallen Flowers*, 70–71.

136. Florin, *Ghost Towns of the West*, 635.

137. Moynahan, *Soiled Doves, Sportin' Women, and Other Fallen Flowers*, 75–76.

138. U.S. Bureau of the Census, *Thirteenth Census of the United States, 1910*; Cushman, "The Fabulous Sadie Orchard."

139. Meketa quoted in Moynahan, *Soiled Doves, Sportin' Women, and Other Fallen Flowers*, 77.

140. Cushman, "The Fabulous Sadie Orchard."

141. Ibid.; U.S. Bureau of the Census, *Fifteenth Census of the United States, 1930*.

142. Cushman, "The Fabulous Sadie Orchard."

143. Moynahan, *Soiled Doves, Sportin' Women, and Other Fallen Flowers*, 62. Writer Dave Cushman maintained that Sadie died of a broken neck in 1945. Most of her jewelry had been stolen, and her money was gone. Cushman, "The Fabulous Sadie Orchard."

144. Moynahan, *Soiled Doves, Sportin' Women, and Other Fallen Flowers*, 62–63, 77.

145. *Historic Hillsboro, a Walking Tour Guide*; Michael Jenkinson, *Ghost Towns of New Mexico: Playthings of the Wind* (Albuquerque: University of New Mexico Press, 1967), 144–48; see also "Hillsboro," http://www. ghosttowns.com.

146. Jenkinson, *Ghost Towns of New Mexico*, 143.

147. *Sierra County Ghost Towns*, pamphlet (Las Cruces: Rural Economic Development through Tourism Project, New Mexico State University Cooperative Extension Service, n.d.); Moynahan, *Soiled Doves, Sportin' Women, and Other Fallen Flowers*, 64.

148. Varney, *New Mexico's Best Ghost Towns*, 111; Florin, *Ghost Towns of the West*, 630.

149. Florin, *Ghost Towns of the West*, 652; miscellaneous undated news clipping, Prostitution File, Silver City Museum; Varney, *New Mexico's Best Ghost Towns*, 135; Evans, *Madam Millie*, 74.

150. Elliott West, "Scarlet West: The Oldest Profession in the Trans-Mississippi West," *Montana Magazine* (Spring 1981), 18.

151. Sherman and Sherman, *Ghost Towns and Mining Camps of New Mexico*, 156M; "Mogollon, New Mexico," *Wikipedia*, http://en.wikipedia.org/wiki/ Mogollon,_New_Mexico.

152. "Mogollon, New Mexico"; "Mogollon—Once a Miner's Lady," in *Forever Frontier: The Visitor's Guide to Southwestern New Mexico and Eastern Arizona* (Silver City, N.Mex.: Glenwood Gazette, 2005); Sherman and Sherman, *Ghost Towns and Mining Camps of New Mexico*, 156M; Joan Mazzio, "Mogollon—A Seven Mile Ghost Town," http://www. SouthernNewMexico.com.

153. Sherman and Sherman, *Ghost Towns and Mining Camps of New Mexico*, 79E, 1660, 224–25W; Looney, *Haunted Highways*, 60; Varney, *New Mexico's Best Ghost Towns*, 74; Florin, *Ghost Towns of the West*, 662.

154. Sherman and Sherman, *Ghost Towns and Mining Camps of New Mexico*, 225–26W; Varney, *New Mexico's Best Ghost Towns*, 74.

155. *Sierra County Ghost Towns*; see also "Chloride, New Mexico," http://www.ghosttowns.com/states/nm/chloride.html.

156. Sherman and Sherman, *Ghost Towns and Mining Camps of New Mexico*, 42C.

157. Looney, *Haunted Highways*, 151.

158. *Historic Chloride, a Guide to a Classic, Old West Ghost Town*, pamphlet (Las Cruces: Rural Economic Development Through Tourism Project, New Mexico State University Cooperative Extension Service, n.d.).

159. Mike J. Pappas, *Raton: History Mystery and More* (Raton, N.Mex.: Coda, 2003), 17–18; "Raton New Mexico Historic Downtown Walking Tour," http://www.raton.info/historicfirstst.htm.

160. Raton New Mexico Walking Tour of the Downtown Historic District; author's interview with Eleanor Smith, Trinidad, Colorado, December 1980.

161. Pappas, *Raton*, 17; Florin, *Ghost Towns of the West*, 615.

162. Bob L'Aloge, *Knights of the Sixgun: A Diary of Gunfighters, Outlaws, and Villains of New Mexico* (Las Cruces, N.Mex.: Yucca Tree Press, 2d printing, 1993), 112.

163. Ibid., 112–14; Case 819, Territory of New Mexico, *Socorro County v. Susan Yonkers*, March 1886, New Mexico State Archives and Records Center, Santa Fe.

164. L'Aloge, *Knights of the Sixgun*, 115, 120; Case 819, Territory of New Mexico, *Socorro County v. Susan Yonkers*.

165. "Gallup, New Mexico," *Wikipedia*, http://en.wikipedia.org/wiki/Gallup,_New_Mexico; author's interview with Eleanor Smith, Grand Junction, Colorado, 1999; Varney, *New Mexico's Best Ghost Towns*, 35.

166. Sherman and Sherman, *Ghost Towns and Mining Camps of New Mexico*, 7A.

167. Ibid., 13B.

168. "La Belle," http://www.ghosttowns.com; Jim B. Pearson, "Life in La Belle," *New Mexico Historical Review* 45 (1970), 153–54; Lee Myers, "An Experiment in Prohibition," *New Mexico Historical Review* 40 (1965), 304–5. Nearly the same story places Phenix, formerly called "Eddy," outside of Carlsbad. Writer Lynn Perigo states that founder Charles B. Eddy required that all property deeds prohibit liquor from being sold on the premises. In answer, one B. A. Nymeyer platted Phenix, outside the city limits, for saloons, which quickly evolved into gambling dens and brothels. Raids were what caused Ed Lyle and sixteen prostitutes to depart for Globe, Arizona, in 1895. See Lynn I. Perrigo, "Oasis on the Pecos: The Town of Eddy and Early Carlsbad," http://www.carlsbadnm.com/mhayes/perrigo.htm.

169. *Durango Democrat*, September 9, 1905, p. 1, col. 1.

170. MacKell, *Brothels, Bordellos, and Bad Girls*, 235; Evans, *Madam Millie*, 127.

Chapter Seven

1. Kevin Halleran, "Wasatch Mountains," http://www.media.utah.edu/ UHE/w/WASATCHMOUNTAINS.html; Jeffrey Nichols, *Prostitution, Polygamy, and Power: Salt Lake City, 1847–1918* (Chicago: University of Illinois Press, 2002), 9.

2. Alan Edwards, "Now & Then: Street's History Is Big Selling Point for Ogden," *Deseret News*, April 9, 2003, http://www.findarticles.com/p/ articles/mi_qn4188/is_20030409/ai_n11390783; Nichols, *Prostitution, Polygamy, and Power*, 14–17.

3. Nichols, *Prostitution, Polygamy, and Power*, 25; U.S. Bureau of the Census, *Seventh Census of the United States, 1850* (Washington, D.C.: National Archives and Records Administration, 1850); Hal Schindler, "The Oldest Profession's Sordid Past in Utah," *Salt Lake Tribune*, http:// www.sltrib.com.

4. John Mount, "The Lost and Forgotten History of Johnstone's Army, the Utah War, and Camp Floyd 1857–1861," Utah Civil War Association, http:// www.utcwa.org/floyd.html; Schindler, "The Oldest Profession's Sordid Past in Utah"; Harold [Hal] Schindler, "Utah War Broke Hold Mormons Had on Utah," http://www.sltrib.com; U.S. Bureau of the Census, *Eighth Census of the United States, 1860* (Washington, D.C.: National Archives and Records Administration, 1860).

5. Nichols, *Prostitution, Polygamy, and Power*, 25–27; John S. McCormick, "Red Lights in Zion: Salt Lake City's Stockade," *Utah Historical Quarterly* 50, no. 2 (Spring 1982), 170.

6. *Deseret News*, September 4, 1872, p. 12, col. 1.

7. Nichols, *Prostitution, Polygamy, and Power*, 28.

8. Ibid., 28.

9. Ibid., 29.

10. McCormick, "Red Lights in Zion," 173; Nichols, *Prostitution, Polygamy, and Power*, 54–58.

11. Thomas G. Alexander and James B. Allen, *Mormons and Gentiles: A History of Salt Lake City*, Western Urban History Series, vol. 5 (Boulder, Colo.: Pruett, 1984), 118; Nichols, *Prostitution, Polygamy, and Power*, 55–56.

12. Nichols, *Prostitution, Polygamy, and Power*, 47–48.

13. Janelle Biddinger Hyat, "Scholar: Study of Prostitution in Utah Must Address Polygamy," *Ogden Standard Examiner*, August 23, 1998, http:// www.polygamyinfo.com/media%20plyg%2045standardex.htm.

14. Nichols, *Prostitution, Polygamy, and Power*, 1.

15. Schindler, "The Oldest Profession's Sordid Past in Utah."

16. Nichols, *Prostitution, Polygamy, and Power*, 35.

17. McCormick, "Red Lights in Zion," 173.

18. Alexander and Allen, *Mormons and Gentiles*, 118, 148.

19. Nichols, *Prostitution, Polygamy, and Power*, 58; *Ogden Standard Examiner*, April 5, 1894, p. 2, col. 2.

20. U.S. Bureau of the Census, *Twelfth Census of the United States, 1900* (Washington, D.C.: National Archives and Records Administration, 1900); *Salt Lake Herald*, June 6, 1909, p. 7, col. 3; Schindler, "The Oldest Profession's Sordid Past in Utah"; McCormick, "Red Lights in Zion," 174.

21. *Salt Lake Herald*, February 7, 1908, p. 10, col. 4.
22. *Salt Lake Herald*, June 6, 1909, p. 7, col. 4; *Park Record* (Park City, Utah), July 28, 1922, Utah Digital Newspapers, http://www.lib.utah.edu/digital/unews.
23. Nichols, *Prostitution, Polygamy, and Power*, 59–62.
24. Ibid., 83.
25. McCormick, "Red Lights in Zion," 169.
26. Ibid., 172.
27. Ibid., 173–74.
28. Ibid., 171.
29. Schindler, "The Oldest Profession's Sordid Past in Utah."
30. McCormick, "Red Lights in Zion," 171.
31. Schindler, "The Oldest Profession's Sordid Past in Utah."
32. McCormick, "Red Lights in Zion," 171.
33. Nichols, *Prostitution, Polygamy, and Power*, 84–85.
34. Edwards, "Now & Then."
35. Nichols, *Prostitution, Polygamy, and Power*, 139.
36. Ibid., 48; Alexander and Allen, *Mormons and Gentiles*, 148; McCormick, "Red Lights in Zion," 173.
37. Schindler, "The Oldest Profession's Sordid Past in Utah"; *Davis County Clipper*, July 17, 1908, p. 3, col. 3.
38. Jami Balls, "History of the Stockade and Salt Lake's Red Light District," Utah History to Go, http://www.historytogo.utah.ogv/places/olympic_locations/stockade.html.
39. McCormick, "Red Lights in Zion," 174; Nichols, *Prostitution, Polygamy, and Power*, 143.
40. Schindler, "The Oldest Profession's Sordid Past in Utah"; Hyat, "Scholar"; McCormick, "Red Lights in Zion," 176.
41. Nichols, *Prostitution, Polygamy, and Power*, 77 n. 97; U.S. Bureau of the Census, *Thirteenth Census of the United States, 1910* (Washington, D.C.: National Archives and Records Administration, 1910); U.S. Bureau of the Census, *Twelfth Census of the United States, 1900*; Jan MacKell, *Brothels, Bordellos, and Bad Girls: Prostitution in Colorado 1860–1930* (Albuquerque: University of New Mexico Press, 2004), 98 (this printing cited unless otherwise noted).
42. "Queen of Ogden's Underworld," *Ogden Standard Examiner*, March 11, 1902, p. 6, col. 2; Richard C. Roberts and Richard W. Sadler, *A History of Weber County* (Salt Lake City: Utah State Historical Society, 1997), 182; for the birth of the child, see U.S. Bureau of the Census, *Thirteenth Census of the United States, 1910*.
43. *Ogden Standard Examiner*, December 14, 1899, p. 4, col. 1; U.S. Bureau of the Census, *Twelfth Census of the United States, 1900*.
44. Whether the London Ice Cream Parlor's name was related to Dora's pseudonym is unknown. City of Ogden and National Register of Historic Places Walking Tour, Ogden, Utah.

45. *Ogden Standard Examiner*, March 11, 1902, p. 6, col. 2. When Ethel Topham died in California in 1986, it was noted that her mother's maiden name was "Long." State of California, *California Death Index, 1940–1997* (Sacramento: Center for Health Statistics, State of California Department of Health Services, 1997). Thomas Topham died in 1906 in Ogden. Nichols, *Prostitution, Polygamy, and Power*, 77 n. 97.

46. City of Ogden and National Register of Historic Places Walking Tour; *Ogden Standard Examiner*, June 27, 1908, p. 5, col. 2; Schindler, "The Oldest Profession's Sordid Past in Utah"; McCormick, "Red Lights in Zion," 178.

47. McCormick, "Red Lights in Zion," 176.

48. Schindler, "The Oldest Profession's Sordid Past in Utah"; Nichols, *Prostitution, Polygamy, and Power*, 143; Roberts and Sadler, *A History of Weber County*, 183; U.S. Bureau of the Census, *Thirteenth Census of the United States, 1910*.

49. Schindler, "The Oldest Profession's Sordid Past in Utah"; McCormick, "Red Lights in Zion," 177; Nichols, *Prostitution, Polygamy, and Power*, 143, 149; Hyat, "Scholar."

50. McCormick, "Red Lights in Zion," 179.

51. Nichols, *Prostitution, Polygamy, and Power*, 147; McCormick, "Red Lights in Zion," 177.

52. Nichols, *Prostitution, Polygamy, and Power*, 147.

53. Ibid., 147–48.

54. Ibid., 148.

55. McCormick, "Red Lights in Zion," 177; Schindler, "The Oldest Profession's Sordid Past in Utah"; Hyat, "Scholar."

56. Schindler, "The Oldest Profession's Sordid Past in Utah."

57. Balls, "History of the Stockade and Salt Lake's Red Light District"; McCormick, "Red Lights in Zion," 178; Schindler, "The Oldest Profession's Sordid Past in Utah."

58. Schindler, "The Oldest Profession's Sordid Past in Utah"; Hyat, "Scholar"; Nichols, *Prostitution, Polygamy, and Power*, 149.

59. Nichols, *Prostitution, Polygamy, and Power*, 149–51.

60. Ibid., 151–54.

61. Hyat, "Scholar"; McCormick, "Red Lights in Zion," 176; Utah Third District Court, *Territorial Criminal Case Files Index, 1882–96* (Provo, Utah: MyFamily.com, 2003).

62. U.S. Bureau of the Census, *Thirteenth Census of the United States, 1910*; McCormick, "Red Lights in Zion," 178.

63. City of Ogden and National Register of Historic Places Walking Tour.

64. U.S. Bureau of the Census, *Thirteenth Census of the United States, 1910*.

65. McCormick, "Red Lights in Zion," 172, 180; U.S. Bureau of the Census, *Thirteenth Census of the United States, 1910*.

66. Nichols, *Prostitution, Polygamy, and Power*, 157–58; Schindler, "The Oldest Profession's Sordid Past in Utah."

67. Schindler, "The Oldest Profession's Sordid Past in Utah."

68. Erna Von R. Owen, "Woman's Vote in Utah," http://www.fax.libs.uga.edu/suff/1f/suffragette_material_form_harpers.txt; Hyat, "Scholar"; Nichols, *Prostitution, Polygamy, and Power*, 159.

69. Nichols, *Prostitution, Polygamy, and Power*, 50, 159–60; Utah Third District Court, *Territorial Criminal Case Files Index, 1882–96*.

70. Schindler, "The Oldest Profession's Sordid Past in Utah."

71. *Salt Lake Tribune*, September 28, 1911, p. 1, col. 1.

72. McCormick, "Red Lights in Zion," 181; Hyat, "Scholar."

73. Nichols, *Prostitution, Polygamy, and Power*, 60, 157, 165–66; City of Ogden and National Register of Historic Places Walking Tour; U.S. Bureau of the Census, *Fourteenth Census of the United States, 1920* (Washington, D.C.: National Archives and Records Administration, 1920); Ancestry.com, *California Passenger and Crew Lists, 1893–1957* (online database) (Provo, Utah: Generations Network, 2006); U.S. Bureau of the Census, *Fifteenth Census of the United States, 1930* (Washington, D.C.: National Archives and Records Administration, 1930); State of California, *California Death Index, 1940–1997*.

74. Alexander and Allen, *Mormons and Gentiles*, 149; McCormick, "Red Lights in Zion," 181; Schindler, "The Oldest Profession's Sordid Past in Utah."

75. *Carbon County News*, March 12, 1914, p. 1, col. 1.

76. Nichols, *Prostitution, Polygamy, and Power*, 187.

77. Balls, "History of the Stockade and Salt Lake's Red Light District"; Alexander and Allen, *Mormons and Gentiles*, 282; Edwards, "Now & Then."

78. Schindler, "The Oldest Profession's Sordid Past in Utah"; Mount, "The Lost and Forgotten History of Johnston's Army."

79. Nichols, *Prostitution, Polygamy, and Power*, 26.

80. Ibid., 26.

81. Orson F. Whitney, *History of Utah*, vol. 2 (1870), chap. 17, http://www.ancestry.com.

82. Halleran, "Wasatch Mountains."

83. George A. Thompson, *Treasure Mountain Home: Park City Revisited* (Salt Lake City: Dream Garden Press, 1993), 88.

84. Cheryl Livingston, "Mother Rachel Urban, Park City's Leading Madam," in *Worth Their Salt: Notable but Often Unnoted Women of Utah*, edited by Colleen Whitley (Logan: Utah State University Press, 1996), 124–27.

85. Raye Carleson Ringholz, *Diggings & Doings in Park City*, 5th ed. (Park City, Utah: Self-published, 1983), 47.

86. Ancestry.com, *Utah Death Index, 1905–1951* (online database) (Provo, Utah: Generations Network, 2003).

87. U.S. Bureau of the Census, *Fourteenth Census of the United States, 1920*; Livingston, "Mother Rachel Urban," 124–26.

88. Jay Moynahan, *Remedies from the Red Lights* (Spokane, Wash.: Chickadee, 2000), 14; Ringholz, *Diggings & Doings in Park City*, 64; Livingston, "Mother Rachel Urban," 124.

89. Livingston, "Mother Rachel Urban," 126–27.

90. Ibid., 125; Ringholz, *Diggings & Doings in Park City*, 65.

91. Livingston, "Mother Rachel Urban," 128; Ringholz, *Diggings & Doings in Park City*, 65.

92. Livingston, "Mother Rachel Urban," 128.

93. Ancestry.com, *Utah Death Index, 1905–1951*; George A. Thompson, *Treasure Mountain Home: Park City Revisited* (Salt Lake City: Dream Garden Press, 1993), 88.

94. Halleran, "Wasatch Mountains"; Muriel Sibell Wolle, *The Bonanza Trail: Ghost Towns and Mining Camps of the West* (Chicago: Sage Books, 1953), 372; *Salt Lake Tribune*, February 24, 1878, p. 4, col. 4; Nichols, *Prostitution, Polygamy, and Power*, 27; Lambert Florin, *Ghost Towns of the West* (Superior, Neb.: Superior Publishing for Promontory Press, 1970), 361.

95. Edwards, "Now & Then"; U.S. Bureau of the Census, *Ninth Census of the United States, 1870* (Washington, D.C.: National Archives and Records Administration, 1870); Roberts and Sadler, *A History of Weber County*, 182; Nichols, *Prostitution, Polygamy, and Power*, 30.

96. City of Ogden and National Register of Historic Places Walking Tour.

97. Edwards, "Now & Then"; *Deseret News*, September 4, 1872, p. 12, col. 1, Utah Digital Newspapers, http://www.lib.utah.edu/digital/unews; Nichols, *Prostitution, Polygamy, and Power*, 29.

98. Hyat, "Scholar."

99. Nichols, *Prostitution, Polygamy, and Power*, 29.

100. Hyat, "Scholar."

101. Nichols, *Prostitution, Polygamy, and Power*, 29.

102. Ibid., 52–53; *Salt Lake Tribune*, March 17, 1887, p. 4, col. 1; *Deseret News*, September 13, 1890, 17, and *Salt Lake Tribune*, January 9, 1896, 8, Utah Digital Newspapers, http://www.lib.utah.edu/digital/unews.

103. *Salt Lake Tribune*, October 16, 1898, 8, Utah Digital Newspapers, http://www.lib.utah.edu/digital/unews.

104. City of Ogden and National Register of Historic Places Walking Tour.

105. *Ogden Standard Examiner*, February 12, 1904, 1, and *Millard County Progress*, January 26, 1912, 3, Utah Digital Newspapers, http://www.lib.utah.edu/digital/unews; "Ogden's Historic 25th Street," http://www.historic25.com/history.htm.

106. Schindler, "The Oldest Profession's Sordid Past in Utah"; Roger D. Launius, "World War II in Utah," in *Utah History Encyclopedia*, http://www.media.utah.edu/UHE/w/WWII.html.

107. Roberts and Sadler, *A History of Weber County*, 354.

108. Ibid., 355–56.

109. Edwards, "Now & Then."

110. Gary Lee Walker, "Recollections of the Duchesne Strip," *Outlaw Trail Journal*, 2–4, magazine clipping, no volume number, no date, Regional Room, Uintah County Library, Vernal, Utah.

111. Ibid., 3; "Gusher (Moffat)," undated, untitled manuscript, Uintah County Library.

112. Walker, "Recollections of the Duchesne Strip," 4.

113. Aldon Rachele, "The Strip a Rough, Wild Town of the Old West," *Vernal Express*, June 15, 1983, 35:3; "A Lawless Land," undated, untitled news clipping, Uintah County Library.

114. Walker, "Recollections of the Duchesne Strip," 5–6.

115. Fred Mazzulla and Jo Mazzulla, *Outlaw Album*, 12th ed. (Denver: A. B. Hirschfeld Press, August 1979), 26; Doris Karren Burton with

Dr. Thomas G. Kyle, *Queen Ann Bassett Alias Etta Place* (Vernal, Utah: Burton Enterprises, 1992), 31.

116. Richard Patterson, *Butch Cassidy: A Biography* (Lincoln: University of Nebraska Press, 1998), 180. A second photograph of Etta, posing in Bolivia with Butch and Sundance, is too small and blurry to discern any real features. "Etta Place," *Wikipedia*, http://en.wikipedia.org/wiki/Etta_Place.

117. Richard F. Selcer, "The Women Who Loved the Wild Bunch," *Wild West Magazine* (December 1994), 50.

118. Lula Parker Betenson as told to Dora Flack, *Butch Cassidy, My Brother* (Provo, Utah: Brigham Young University Press, 1976), 121.

119. Patterson, *Butch Cassidy*, 180.

120. Anne Meadows, *Digging Up Butch and Sundance* (New York: St. Martin's Press, 1994), 97 (cited as "1st ed." from this point).

121. Patterson, *Butch Cassidy*, 180; W. Paul Reeve, "Just Who Was the Outlaw Queen Etta Place?" *History Blazer* (May 1995), http://www.historytogo.utah.gov/Utah.

122. Kirby cited in Patterson, *Butch Cassidy*, 178.

123. Kerry Ross Boren and Lisa Lee Boren, "Inlaws & Outlaws: The Family Origins of Butch Cassidy, the Sundance Kid, and Etta Place," http://www.prospector-utah.com/butch.htm.

124. "Etta Place," *The Past Times* (newsletter), http://www.fortlincoln.com/Article%202.htm; Boren and Boren, "Inlaws & Outlaws." The Frewens' presence at the ranch is verifiable in the 1880 census, and the brothers were born in England. U.S. Bureau of the Census, *Tenth Census of the United States, 1880* (Washington, D.C.: National Archives and Records Administration, 1880).

125. "Ancestry World Tree Project: My Tree by David Robarts," http://www.ancestry.com; Patterson, *Butch Cassidy*, 89; Robert Redford, *The Outlaw Trail: A Journey Through Time* (New York: Grosset and Dunlap, 1978), 185.

126. Boren and Boren, "Inlaws & Outlaws"; Patterson, *Butch Cassidy*, 179; Meadows, *Digging Up Butch and Sundance*, 1st ed., x; Patterson, *Butch Cassidy*, 311 n. 36. Ernst and Buck cited in "Ancestry World Tree Project."

127. Patterson, *Butch Cassidy*, 180, 313 n. 50; Michael Rutter, *Wild Bunch Women* (Gulford, Conn., and Helena, Mont.: Twodot, an Imprint of the Globe Pequot Press, 2003), 58. The speculation that Etta worked at Fannie's appears to be based mostly on the fact that other Wild Bunch women such as Laura Bullion and Annie Rogers also came from there. Selcer, "The Women Who Loved the Wild Bunch," 54.

128. U.S. Bureau of the Census, *Twelfth Census of the United States, 1900.*

129. Patterson, *Butch Cassidy*, 63, 178; "Ancestry World Tree Project: My Tree by David Robarts." In fact, many historians believe Butch and Etta courted before she met Sundance. See "Etta Place," *Wikipedia*.

130. Meadows, *Digging Up Butch and Sundance*, 1st ed., 122; Boren cited in Patterson, *Butch Cassidy*, 178–79, 312 n. 37; U.S. Bureau of the Census, *Twelfth Census of the United States, 1900*; Gail Drago, *Etta Place: Her Life and Times with Butch Cassidy and the Sundance Kid* (Plano: Republic of Texas Press, 1996), 52–53.

131. "Etta Place," *The Past Times*.

132. Patterson, *Butch Cassidy*, 179; Daniel Buck and Anne Meadows, "Etta Place: A Most Wanted Woman," http://www.ourworld.compuserve.com/homepages/danne/etta.htm.

133. Redford, *The Outlaw Trail*, 185; James D. Horan, *The Wild Bunch* (New York: Signet Books, 1958), 113.

134. Patterson, *Butch Cassidy*, 98.

135. Betenson, *Butch Cassidy, My Brother*, 121, referring to Pearl Baker, *The Wild Bunch at Robbers Roost* (Lincoln: University of Nebraska Press, 1971).

136. Patterson, *Butch Cassidy*, 98, 178; Baker, *The Wild Bunch at Robbers Roost*, 173.

137. Patterson, *Butch Cassidy*, 100, 289 n. 32; Reeve, "Just Who Was the Outlaw Queen Etta Place?"

138. Patterson, *Butch Cassidy*, 45; "Etta Place," *Wikipedia*.

139. Burton with Kyle, *Queen Ann Bassett Alias Etta Place*, 32.

140. Patterson, *Butch Cassidy*, 81, 103.

141. Ibid., 109; Charles Kelly, *The Outlaw Trail: A History of Butch Cassidy and His Wild Bunch*, rev. ed. (Lincoln: University of Nebraska Press, 1996), 152.

142. Some say Etta decided to join up with Butch and Sundance because they scored only $50 after their robbery at Tipton, Wyoming, in 1901. Etta apparently figured she should start masterminding the robberies for a better profit. Newspaper Enterprise Association, *The Good Housekeeping Woman's Almanac* (New York: United Feature Syndicate, 1977), 501.

143. Patterson, *Butch Cassidy*, 181–83; "Etta Place," *Wikipedia*.

144. Patterson, *Butch Cassidy*, 185.

145. Meadows, *Digging Up Butch and Sundance*, 1st ed., 37.

146. Baker, *The Wild Bunch at Robbers Roost*, 193; Drago, *Etta Place*, 158; Rutter, *Wild Bunch Women*, 64; Meadows, *Digging Up Butch and Sundance*, 1st ed., 37; Patterson, *Butch Cassidy*, 185. Records from Tiffany's show that a James Ryan—one of Butch's aliases—did purchase a gold watch for $40.10 on February 4, 1901. Buck and Meadows, "Etta Place: A Most Wanted Woman."

147. Patterson, *Butch Cassidy*, 186. Butch posed as Etta's brother, Jim Ryan. "Etta Place," *Wikipedia*.

148. "Etta Place," *The Past Times*.

149. Meadows, *Digging Up Butch and Sundance*, 1st ed., 5.

150. Ibid., 6, 11–12, 54.

151. Meadows, *Digging Up Butch and Sundance*, 1st ed., 39; "Etta Place," *Wikipedia*; Patterson, *Butch Cassidy*, 202–7.

152. Anne Meadows, *Digging Up Butch and Sundance*, 2d ed. (Lincoln: University of Nebraska Press, 2003), 79.

153. Patterson, *Butch Cassidy*, 202–7. Many historians have placed Etta at this robbery, but if Sundance's letter is correct, she was no longer in Bolivia at that time. Others, such as Richard Patterson *(Butch Cassidy)*, think she returned to America between December 1905 and early 1906.

154. Even if this is true, it seems highly unlikely that with an attack of appendicitis Etta could withstand horseback rides, stages, trains, steamships, and months of travel to reach Denver. Patterson, *Butch Cassidy*, 209.

155. Meadows, *Digging Up Butch and Sundance*, 1st ed., 97, 121.

156. Betenson, *Butch Cassidy, My Brother*, 169.

157. Selcer, "The Women Who Loved the Wild Bunch," 53; Betenson, *Butch Cassidy, My Brother*, 186; Patterson, *Butch Cassidy*, 228, 235; Rutter, *Wild Bunch Women*, 59; "Etta Place," *Wikipedia*.

158. Meadows, *Digging Up Butch and Sundance*, 1st ed., 44, 121; "Etta Place," *Wikipedia*; Burton with Kyle, *Queen Ann Bassett Alias Etta Place*, 41.

159. *Millard County Progress*, January 11, 1918, p. 7, col. 2.

160. Jim Smiley, "Jim Smiley's Trap Line," *Fur News and Outdoor World* (September 1920), 19.

161. Meadows, *Digging Up Butch and Sundance*, 1st ed., 97, 110, 121, 189, 202; "Etta Place," *Wikipedia*; Patterson, *Butch Cassidy*, 179.

162. Patterson, *Butch Cassidy*, 179; Meadows, *Digging Up Butch and Sundance*, 1st ed., 122–23.

163. Patterson, *Butch Cassidy*, 180.

164. Burton with Kyle, *Queen Ann Bassett Alias Etta Place*, 9–12. It should be noted that there is no known official description of Ann Bassett, only photographs of her. Reeves, "Just Who Was the Outlaw Queen Etta Place?"

165. Reeve, "Just Who Was the Outlaw Queen Etta Place?"

166. Ibid.; "Etta Place," *The Past Times*; Burton with Kyle, *Queen Ann Bassett Alias Etta Place*, 15.

167. Burton with Kyle, *Queen Ann Bassett Alias Etta Place*, 26.

168. Reeve, "Just Who Was the Outlaw Queen Etta Place?"

169. Patterson, *Butch Cassidy*, 183; Meadows, *Digging Up Butch and Sundance*, 1st ed., x.

170. Burton with Kyle, *Queen Ann Bassett Alias Etta Place*, 32, 37–40; Reeve, "Just Who Was the Outlaw Queen Etta Place?"

171. Burton with Kyle, *Queen Ann Bassett Alias Etta Place*, 41. Interestingly, Frank couldn't bring himself to scatter Ann's ashes at Brown's Park and kept her cremains in the trunk of his car until he died in 1963. Family eventually buried the ashes at an unmarked spot in the park. Reeve, "Just Who Was the Outlaw Queen Etta Place?"

172. Patterson, *Butch Cassidy*, 312, n. 37; "Etta Place," *Wikipedia*; Meadows, *Digging Up Butch and Sundance*, 1st ed., 120; Burton with Kyle, *Queen Ann Bassett Alias Etta Place*, 32; Reeve, "Just Who Was the Outlaw Queen Etta Place?"

173. Willis cited in Reeve, "Just Who Was the Outlaw Queen Etta Place?"; Patterson, *Butch Cassidy*, 235; Rutter, *Wild Bunch Women*, 60; Meadows, *Digging Up Butch and Sundance*, 1st ed., 120.

174. Walker, "Recollections of the Duchesne Strip," 10; Doris Karren Burton, *Behind Swinging Doors: A Colorful History of Uinta Basin* (Vernal: Utah County Library, with funds by Utah Humanities Council, 2001), 301–3.

175. Edwards, "Now & Then"; Ronald G. Watt, *A History of Carbon County* (Salt Lake City: Utah State Historical Society, 1997), 364, 372; *Carbon County News*, March 12, 1914, 1:1.

176. *Davis County Clipper*, April 17, 1914, 3:3, and *Carbon County News*, December 31, 1914, 1:1; *Carbon News Advocate*, January 18, 1917, 3; *Davis County Clipper*, June 22, 1917, 3.

177. *Davis County Clipper*, June 22, 1917, 3.

178. Watt, *A History of Carbon County*, 372.

179. Frank A. Beckwith, unidentified article from the *Salt Lake Tribune*, March 5, 1950, Digital Collections, J. Willard Marriott Library, University of Utah.

180. Jody Tesch Sorenson, "Queen of the Desert: The Real Story of Mary Devitt Laird," courtesy Jay Moynahan, Spokane, Washington. Ms. Sorenson is Mary's great-great-niece. Correspondence with Janet Koski, Sioux Falls, South Dakota, May 21, 2007.

181. U.S. Bureau of the Census, *Tenth Census of the United States, 1880*; Sorenson, "Queen of the Desert"; correspondence with Janet Koski; Beckwith, unidentified *Salt Lake Tribune* article; Ancestry.com, *Utah Death Index, 1905–1951*.

Chapter Eight

1. *A Self-Guided Tour to Southern Wyoming*, pamphlet (Lander: Wyoming Travel Commission, n.d.).

2. Weddon and Huseas cited in Larry K. Brown, *The Hog Ranches of Wyoming: Liquor, Lust, and Lies under Sagebrush Skies* (Glendo, Wyo.: High Plains Press, 1995), 16–17.

3. "Fort Laramie National Historic Site," *Wyoming Visitor Magazine* (Summer–Fall 1996), 36.

4. *A Self-Guided Tour to Southern Wyoming*; "Fort Laramie National Historic Site," 45.

5. "Fort Laramie National Historic Site," 25.

6. Brown, *The Hog Ranches of Wyoming*, 27.

7. Michael Rutter, *Upstairs Girls: Prostitution in the American West* (Helena, Mont.: Farcountry Press, 2005), 38.

8. Brown, *The Hog Ranches of Wyoming*, 27.

9. Anne M. Butler, *Daughters of Joy, Sisters of Misery: Prostitutes in the American West 1865–90* (Chicago: University of Illinois Press, 1987), 62.

10. Brown, *The Hog Ranches of Wyoming*, 27.

11. Rutter, *Upstairs Girls*, 161.

12. Brown, *The Hog Ranches of Wyoming*, 29.

13. Anne Seagraves, *Soiled Doves: Prostitution in the Early West* (Hayden, Idaho: Wesanne, 1994), 124.

14. Brown, *The Hog Ranches of Wyoming*, 29.

15. Jay Moynahan, *Soiled Doves, Sportin' Women, and Other Fallen Flowers* (Spokane, Wash.: Chickadee, 2005), 45.

16. Butler, *Daughters of Joy*, 102. In the 1880 census, Sophie is identified as "Sophia Riccard," born 1853 in Indiana and living in Laramie City. U.S. Bureau of the Census, *Tenth Census of the United States, 1880* (Washington, D.C.: National Archives and Records Administration, 1880).

17. U.S. Bureau of the Census, *Tenth Census of the United States, 1880*; Brown, *The Hog Ranches of Wyoming*, 34.
18. Butler, *Daughters of Joy*, 100.
19. U.S. Bureau of the Census, *Tenth Census of the United States, 1880*.
20. Butler, *Daughters of Joy*, 104.
21. Ibid., 106.
22. Brown, *The Hog Ranches of Wyoming*, 27.
23. Max Evans, *Madam Millie: Bordellos from Silver City to Ketchikan* (Albuquerque: University of New Mexico Press, 2002), xi, 146.
24. *A Self-Guided Tour to Southern Wyoming*.
25. Butler, *Daughters of Joy*, 142.
26. *What to Do in Cheyenne, Wyoming*, pamphlet (Cheyenne, Wyo.: Greater Cheyenne Chamber of Commerce, 1986).
27. Larry K. Brown, "Petticoat Prisoners of Old Wyoming," *Wild West Magazine* (February 1998), 54.
28. Butler, *Daughters of Joy*, 100, 117 n. 17.
29. Ibid., 112.
30. Ibid., 45 n. 35, 61, 113, 117 n. 17.
31. U.S. Bureau of the Census, *Tenth Census of the United States, 1880*; Larry Underwood, *Love and Glory: Women of the Old West* (Lincoln, Neb.: USA Media, 1991), 115.
32. Underwood, *Love and Glory*, 121.
33. U.S. Bureau of the Census, *Tenth Census of the United States, 1880*; Butler, *Daughters of Joy*, 107.
34. Underwood, *Love and Glory*, 117.
35. Butler, *Daughters of Joy*, 107.
36. U.S. Bureau of the Census, *Tenth Census of the United States, 1880*.
37. Underwood, *Love and Glory*, 122.
38. U.S. Bureau of the Census, *Tenth Census of the United States, 1880*. See also appendix I in this volume.
39. Butler, *Daughters of Joy*, 109.
40. Rutter, *Upstairs Girls*, 10.
41. U.S. Bureau of the Census, *Tenth Census of the United States, 1880*.
42. Jan MacKell, *Brothels, Bordellos, and Bad Girls: Prostitution in Colorado, 1860–1930* (Albuquerque: University of New Mexico Press, 2004), 63 (this printing cited unless otherwise indicated).
43. U.S. Bureau of the Census, *Twelfth Census of the United States, 1900* (Washington, D.C.: National Archives and Records Administration, 1900).
44. "Fort Laramie National Historic Site," 47.
45. Butler, *Daughters of Joy*, 55, 100.
46. Ibid., 109. There is no record of an Annie St. Clair at the Colorado State Pen in Canon City. See Prisoner Records, Colorado State Penitentiary Archives, http://www.colorado.gov/dpa/doit/archives/pen/Snyder-Stout.htm.
47. Brown, "Petticoat Prisoners of Old Wyoming," 54–55.
48. Ibid., 56.
49. Ibid., 84.
50. MacKell, *Brothels, Bordellos, and Bad Girls*, 213.
51. *Fort Collins Weekly Courier* (Colorado), August 10, 1917, p. 5, col. 3.

52. "Fort Fetterman: Historic Site Takes You Back in Time," in *Converse County Visitor's Guide* (Douglas, Wyo.: Douglas Budget, ca. 1995), 29.

53. Brown, *The Hog Ranches of Wyoming*, 27.

54. Ibid.

55. Ibid.

56. Rutter, *Upstairs Girls*, 38.

57. Brown, *The Hog Ranches of Wyoming*, 27.

58. *A Self-Guided Tour to Southern Wyoming.*

59. U.S. Bureau of the Census, *Tenth Census of the United States, 1880.*

60. Undated pamphlet, publisher unknown, Clippings File, Rawlins Public Library, Rawlins, Wyoming.

61. *A Self-Guided Tour to Southern Wyoming.*

62. Brown, "Petticoat Prisoners of Old Wyoming," 55–56.

63. Evans, *Madam Millie*, 146–52.

64. Brown, *The Hog Ranches of Wyoming*, 28.

65. U.S. Bureau of the Census, *Ninth Census of the United States, 1870* (Washington, D.C.: National Archives and Records Administration, 1870).

66. Brown, *The Hog Ranches of Wyoming*, 34.

67. Butler, *Daughters of Joy*, 104.

68. U.S. Bureau of the Census, *Tenth Census of the United States, 1880.*

69. *Fremont County Pioneer Museum*, pamphlet (Lander: Wyoming Travel Commission, n.d.); "Fort Laramie National Historic Site," 36.

70. Rutter, *Upstairs Girls*, 21.

71. The *Billings Gazette* recorded Etta's presence in Billings at least twice: once when she divorced in September 1899 and again in December 1900 when her taxes were in arrears. "Vital Statistics Plus, 1882–1901, D-F," City of Billings, Montana, Web site, http://ci.billings.mt.us/DocumentView. asp?DID=1034.

72. Cathy Luchetti, *I Do! Courtship, Love, and Marriage of the American Frontier* (New York: Crown Trade Paperbacks, 1996), 80.

73. Brown, *The Hog Ranches of Wyoming*, 34.

74. Milt C. Riske, "Monument for Featherlegs," *Frontier Times*, September 1978, 27.

75. Brown, *The Hog Ranches of Wyoming*, 25.

76. "Girls of the Gulch: Ol' Mother Featherlegs," *Deadwood Magazine* (March–April 1997), http://deadwoodmagazine.com/archivedsite/Archives/ Girls_Featherlegs.htm.

77. Brown, *The Hog Ranches of Wyoming*, 25.

78. Rutter, *Upstairs Girls*, 39.

79. Brown, *The Hog Ranches of Wyoming*, 25.

80. "Girls of the Gulch."

81. Brown, *The Hog Ranches of Wyoming*, 25.

82. Riske, "Monument for Featherlegs," 27, 61; "Girls of the Gulch."

83. Ibid.

84. See "Mother Featherlegs—Prostitute Monument," http://www. roadsideamerica.com/attract/WYLUSfeath.html.

85. U.S. Bureau of the Census, *Tenth Census of the United States, 1880.*

86. Evans, *Madam Millie*, 143.

87. Brown, *The Hog Ranches of Wyoming*, 33.
88. U.S. Bureau of the Census, *Tenth Census of the United States, 1880.*
89. Brown, *The Hog Ranches of Wyoming*, 33.
90. Douglas Wyoming Court Records, November 24, 1887, to June 22, 1910, William L. Clements Library, University of Michigan, Ann Arbor.
91. Hillyer Best, *Julia Bulette and Other Red Light Ladies* (Sparks, Nev.: Western Printing, 1959), 20–22.
92. Butler, *Daughters of Joy*, 111.
93. Brown, *The Hog Ranches of Wyoming*, 34.
94. Brown, "Petticoat Prisoners of Old Wyoming," 84.
95. Harry Sinclair Drago, *Notorious Ladies of the Frontier* (New York: Dodd, Mead, 1969), 226.
96. Ibid., 224.
97. Kay Reynolds Blair, *Ladies of the Lamplight* (Leadville, Colo.: Timberline Books, 1971), 18; Drago, *Notorious Ladies of the Frontier*, 226.
98. Drago, *Notorious Ladies of the Frontier*, 226.
99. Blair, *Ladies of the Lamplight*, 19; Fred Mazzulla and Jo Mazzulla, *Outlaw Album*, 12th ed. (Denver: A. B. Hirschfeld Press, August 1979), 22.
100. Kate was also sometimes referred to as "Cattle Kate Maxwell." Drago, *Notorious Ladies of the Frontier*, 232.
101. Blair, *Ladies of the Lamplight*, 19.
102. Drago, *Notorious Ladies of the Frontier*, 226.
103. "Old West Legends, Complete List of Old West Scoundrels," *Legends of America*, http://www.legendsofamerica.com/WE-ScoundrelList.html; Blair, *Ladies of the Lamplight*, 19.
104. Blair, *Ladies of the Lamplight*, 20.
105. Butler, *Daughters of Joy*, 70 n. 18.
106. Drago, *Notorious Ladies of the Frontier*, 228–29.
107. Ibid., 228.
108. Blair, *Ladies of the Lamplight*, 20.
109. Mazzulla and Mazzulla, *Outlaw Album*, 22.
110. Drago, *Notorious Ladies of the Frontier*, 230–31.
111. Blair, *Ladies of the Lamplight*, 21.
112. Drago, *Notorious Ladies of the Frontier*, 227.
113. Blair, *Ladies of the Lamplight*, 21.
114. Brown, *The Hog Ranches of Wyoming*, 34.
115. Brown, "Petticoat Prisoners of Old Wyoming," 84.
116. Mazzulla and Mazzulla, *Outlaw Album*, 26; "Lesson 3: The Wild Bunch Women, Laura Bullion and Annie Rogers," http://www.Suite101.com; "Laura Bullion," http://en.wikipedia.org/wiki/Laura_Bullion; Donna Ernst, "True West Legends: The Wild Bunch Women," *True West Magazine* (August 1997), 31.
117. U.S. Bureau of the Census, *Twelfth Census of the United States, 1900*; "Laura Bullion."
118. "Laura Bullion." Author Donna Ernst says that Laura's mother also died in 1891. Ernst, "True West Legends: The Wild Bunch Women," 31.
119. "Lesson 3: The Wild Bunch Women."
120. "Laura Bullion."

121. U.S. Bureau of the Census, *Twelfth Census of the United States, 1900*.
122. "Lesson 3: The Wild Bunch Women."
123. Mazzulla and Mazzulla, *Outlaw Album*, 26.
124. Charles Kelly, *The Outlaw Trail: A History of Butch Cassidy and His Wild Bunch*, rev. ed. (New York: Bonanza Books, 1996), 281.
125. "Laura Bullion."
126. "Will Carver," http://en.wikipedia.org/wiki/William_Carver_(Wild_Bunch); "Dhaese Family Pictures," Ancestry World Tree Project, http://www.ancestry.com.
127. "Laura Bullion"; Ernst, "True West Legends: The Wild Bunch Women," 32.
128. "Laura Bullion."
129. "Woman Train Robber Held," *New York Times*, November 8, 1901, p. 2, col. 2.
130. Michael Rutter, *Wild Bunch Women* (Gulford, Conn., and Helena, Mont.: Twodot, an imprint of the Globe Pequot Press, 2003), 78.
131. "Laura Bullion"; Ernst, "True West Legends: The Wild Bunch Women," 32.
132. Ernst, "True West Legends: The Wild Bunch Women," 32.
133. "Lesson 3: The Wild Bunch Women."
134. "Laura Bullion."
135. MacKell, *Brothels, Bordellos, and Bad Girls*, 256.
136. Ibid., 212, 217.
137. Lambert Florin, *Ghost Towns of the West* (Superior, Neb.: Superior Publishing for Promontory Press, 1970), 495.
138. Evans, *Madam Millie*, 145; Rutter, *Upstairs Girls*, 19.

Chapter Nine

1. Jan MacKell, *Brothels, Bordellos, and Bad Girls: Prostitution in Colorado 1860–1930* (Albuquerque: University of New Mexico Press, 2004), 222 (this printing cited unless otherwise noted).
2. Miscellaneous news clipping dated June 25, 1978, Clippings File, Silver City Museum, Silver City, New Mexico; Max Evans, *Madam Millie: Bordellos from Silver City to Ketchikan* (Albuquerque: University of New Mexico Press, 2002), xvi.
3. International Sex Worker Foundation for Art, Culture, and Education (ISWFACE), *Tales of the Dumas Parlor House, Butte Montana: The Mining City's Last Brothel 1890–1982* (N.p.: ISWFACE, 1998), 16.
4. Richard Erdoes, *Saloons of the Old West* (Avenel, N.J.: Grammercy Books, a division of Random House Value, 1997), 202.
5. Lambert Florin, *Ghost Towns of the West* (Superior, Neb.: Superior Publishing for Promontory Press, 1970), 122; *Ghost Towns and History of the American West*, Chloride, Arizona, www.ghosttowns.com.
6. Debe Branning, *Sleeping with Ghosts! A Ghost Hunter's Guide to Arizona's Haunted Hotels and Inns* (Phoenix: Goldenwest, 2007, 3rd printing), 20, 49; see also photos at http://www.flickr.com.
7. Bennie Blake, "Women of the Back Streets: Jerome's Ladies of the Night," in *Experience Jerome and the Verde Valley: Legends and Legacies* (Sedona, Ariz.: Thorne Enterprises, 1990), 232.

8. "Shadowlands Haunted Places Index—Arizona," http://www.66.218.69/ search/cache?ei=UTF-8&p=prostitute+in+Arizona+history.

9. Ben T. Traywick, *Behind the Red Lights—History of Prostitution in Tombstone* (Tombstone, Ariz.: Red Marie's, 1993), 31.

10. "Bird Cage Theatre," *Wikipedia*, http://en.wikipedia.org/wiki/ Birdcage_Theater.

11. Joan Schuman, "Working Women," *Tucson Weekly*, June 1, 2003, http:// www.Tucsonweekly.com/gbase/CityWeek/Content?oid=47171; see photos at http://www.flickr.com; Branning, *Sleeping with Ghosts!*, 130.

12. See photos at http://www.flickr.com and http://www.legendsofamerica. com/AZ-RedGarter.

13. Fred Mazzulla and Jo Mazzulla, *Brass Checks and Red Lights* (Denver: Self-published, 1966), 3–4.

14. Perry Eberhart, *Guide to the Colorado Ghost Towns and Mining Camps*, 4th ed. (Columbus: Swallow Press, Ohio University Press, 1981), 329.

15. Crooked Creek Saloon and Eatery, "Who Is Rosie?" http://www. crookecreeksaloon.com/rosie.html.

16. MacKell, *Brothels, Bordellos, and Bad Girls*, 252.

17. *The Duchess and the Dirtwater Fox*, Internet Movie Database, http:// www.imdb.com.

18. MacKell, *Brothels, Bordellos, and Bad Girls*, 249.

19. See photos at http://www.flickr.com; Anne Seagraves, *Soiled Doves: Prostitution in the Early West* (Hayden, Idaho: Wesanne, 1994), 110.

20. Grace Roffey Pratt, "Charlie Bemis' Highest Prize," *Frontier Times* (Winter 1961), 26; Ancestry.com, *Prairie View Cemetery Inscriptions, Grangeville, Idaho* (online database) (Provo, Utah: MyFamily.com, 1999); see also University of Idaho Community Enrichment Program, "The World of Polly Bemis," http://www.uidaho.edu/LS/AACC/tour2002.htm.

21. Interview with Jack Mayfield, Oasis Bordello Museum, Wallace, Idaho, September 2006.

22. See photos at http://www.flickr.com.

23. Ibid.; *Historic Chloride, A Guide to a Classic, Old West Ghost Town*, pamphlet (Las Cruces: Rural Economic Development Through Tourism Project, New Mexico State University Cooperative Extension Service, n.d.); "Mogollon, New Mexico," *Wikipedia*, http://en.wikipedia.org/wiki/ Mogollon,_New_Mexico.

24. See http://www.ghosttowns.com; *Sierra County Ghost Towns*, pamphlet (Las Cruces: Rural Economic Development Through Tourism Project, New Mexico State University Cooperative Extension Service, n.d.); Lizzie McGrath display, McGrath's Bar & Grill, Albuquerque.

25. See photos at http://www.flickr.com.

26. Alan Edwards, "Now & Then: Street's Colorful History Is Big Selling Point for Ogden," *Deseret News*, April 9, 2003, http://www.findarticles. com/p/articles/mi_qn4188/is_20030409/ai_n11390783.

27. See photos at http://www.flickr.com.

28. "Girls of the Gulch: Ol' Mother Featherlegs," *Deadwood Magazine* (March–April 1997), http://deadwoodmagazine.com/archivedsite/Archives/ Girls_Featherlegs.htm.

INDEX

Page numbers in italic text indicate illustrations.

Abbott, Birdie, 434n105, 107
abortion, 3, 17, 33–34
abuse, 10, 17, 28, 30, 31, 32, 54, 88, 124, 150, 154, 180, 184, 195, 204, 234, 255, 256, 260, 338, 346, 348, 351, 358, 367, 368, 405n72
Adams, Jennie, 257, 259
advertising, 3; to bring women West, 133, 218, 288; for business, 26, 91, 92, 98, 114, 119, 124, 146, 155, 178, 197, 224, 237, 348; to lure women into prostitution, 5, 62, 117, 307, 309
Ahrens, Leola (Leo the Lion), 97, 158
Ah Toy, 9, 10
Airey, Josephine (Chicago Jo, Josephine Hankins, Josephine Hensley, Mary Welch), 199–203, 200, 204, 216, 421n33, 422n48
Alaska, 16, 26, 77, 109, 163, 279, 370
Albright, George, 24, 39n91
Albuquerque, NM, 5, 17, 25, 37, 38, 254, 255–62, 377
Alexander, Pauline, 347, 384
Allen, Clara, 85, 86, 87
American Federation for Sex Hygiene, 368
American Social Hygiene Association, 368
Anaconda, MT, 14, 224, 225, 234, 237
Anderson, Jack "White-Eye," 210, 213
Aspen, CO, 77, 129, 130
Averill, Jim, 359–62

Baca, Julian, 267, 367
Baker, Dorothy Josephine (Big Dorothy), 205, 206
Baldwin, Elias Jackson "Lucky," 116, 407n110
Baldwin, Verona (Fannie), 116, 117
Bannock (Bannack), MT, 194, 195, 197, 199, 208, 235
Banters, Jennie. *See* Bauters, Jennie
Barcelo, Gertrudis (Doña Tules, La Tules, Madam T., Madam Toolay), 251–54, 253
Barnard, Belle (Bernard, Birnard), 115, 116, 348
Bartlett, Bee, 307, 310, 311
Bassett, Ann (Ann Willis), 324, 329, 334, 335–36, 337, 445n164
Bassett, Josie, 324, 329
Bauters, Jennie (Belgian Jennie, Jennie Banters), 54–57, 56, 60, 370, 371
Beartown, MT, 216, 425n108
Behan, Johnny, 70, 72, 74, 82, 398n161
Belgian Jennie. *See* Bauters, Jennie
Bell, Verdie, 271, 272
Belmont, Merle, 434n105, 107
Bemis, Polly (Lalu Nathoy), 172–73, 174, 175, 375, 418n66
Big Alma (of Laramie, WY), xiv, 353
Big Dorothy. *See* Baker, Dorothy Josephine
Bignon, Minnie (Big Minnie), 71, 83
Billings, MT, 213, 246–47, 354, 448n71
Bird Cage Theatre (Tombstone, AZ), 29, 77–79, 83, 84, 371, 397n154, 399n200, 400n210

452

birth control, 33, 220

Bisbee, AZ, 75, 77, 81, 370; Bisbee Massacre, 84; Brewery Gulch, 75, 85, 86, 87; establishment of, 83–84; ordinances, 85, 86, 87

Blaylock, Celia Ann "Mattie" (Celia Ann Blaylock, Mattie Earp), 64, 67, 68, *69*, 71, 75, 396n133, 134, 397n146, 398n165

Blazes, Helen (Helen Smith), 299–300, 301, 307

Blonde Marie (in Tombstone), 6, 79–80, 197

Blonde Mollie (in Tombstone). *See* Bradshaw, Mollie

Boise, ID, 162–64, 375

Bonanza, CO, 22, 125, 146

Bonanza, ID, 175–76

Bothwell, Albert John, 359, 361

Boulder, CO, 3, 4 38, 94, 99, 211

Boulter, Charles, 346, 347

Bowen, Jane (Sage Hen), 136–37

Bowman, Sarah (the Great Western), 263–65

Bozeman, MT, 38, 196, 199, 209, 214–16

Bradshaw, Mollie (Blonde Mollie, Mollie Williams), 29

Brady, Ed, 353, 354

Brady, Mary, 353, 354

Bransford, John, 301, 302, 305, 306, 307, 308

Breckenridge, CO, 122, 123

Brown's Park (Brown's Hole), UT, 329, 334, 335, 445n171

Buena Vista, CO, 104, 146

Bullion, Laura (Clara Hays, Della Rose, Freda Arnold, Freda Bullion Lincoln, Laura Casey, Nellie Rose), 324, 362–66, *365*, 443n127, 449n118

Bunch, Lou, 119, *120*, 373, 378

Burden, Molly (Maggie Hall, Molly b'Damn, Molly Hall), 184–87, *187*, 375, 378

Burke, ID, 184, 188, 190

Burton, Blanche, 105, 373

Butch Cassidy. *See* Parker, Robert Leroy

Butte, MT, 7, 14, 18, 26, 28, 36, 197, 203, 204, 205, 218, 219–44, 245, 298, 368, 381, 429n210

Byrnes, Mollie (Belle Crafton), 203, 422n48

Calamity Jane. *See* Canary, Martha Jane

California, xiv, 8–10, 12–14, 16, 295

Canary, Martha Jane (Calamity Jane, Martha Burke, Mrs. R. S. Dorsett, Prairie Queen), *212*, 343; birth, 206–07, 208; daughter(s), 209, 211, 212, 213–14; death of, 213; as prostitute, 195, 208, 209, 210, 211, 213; and Wild Bill Hickok, 209, 213

Canyon Diablo, AZ, 39–40, 88

Carbon County, UT, 338, 340, 359, 377

Cardinal, CO, 122, 408n136

Caribou, CO, 121, 122

Carillo, Margarita, 34, 133

Carroll, Minnie, 260, 261, 262

Casper, WY, 126, 127, 361, 366, 377

Castle City, MT, 211, 212, 248

Cattle Kate. *See* Watson, Ella

Central City, CO, 118–21, 360, 373, 378

Cheyenne, WY, 124, 208, 210, 211, 345–51, 359, 377, 384

Chicago Jo. *See* Airey, Josephine

children: deaths of, 36, 342, 352; as prostitutes, 36; of prostitutes, 6, 10, 17, 31, 34, 83, 85, 87, 97, 116, 133, 141, 165, 171, 175, 178, 181, 207, 209–14, 220, 238, 246, 259, 269, 275, 281, 304, 310, 315, 334, 340, 347, 415n269, 439n42; taken care of by prostitutes, 24, 62, 108, 125, 150, 165, 170, 185, 263, 276, 279, 282, 405n72; as witnesses to prostitution, 3–4, 28, 88, 121, 159, 270, 301, 322

Chinese: and anti-Chinese sentiments, 9, 10, 14, 15, 16, 80, 173, 259; Chinese Exclusion Act, 13, 14; enslavement of, 8, 10–13, 16, 107,

162, 167, 172–73, 175, 218, 222, 234, 238, 357; immigration of, 8–10, 13; as prostitutes, 8–10, 12, 13, 16, 79, 80, 166, 167, 176, 194, 215, 220; Tongs, 8, 10, 13, 80
Chloride, AZ, 370
Chloride, NM, 287–88, 376
Clapper, Maria, 167, 168
Clifford, Georgie (Georgia Redmond, Stella Campbell), 89, 90
Clifford, Ruth, 224, 225, 241
Cockeyed Liz. *See* Enderlin, Liz
Coffey, Jules (Ecoffey), 209, 210, 342, 343
Colorado City (Old Colorado City), CO, 24, 34, 94, 98, 100–106, 195, 372, 373, 403n20
Columbus, NM, 293–94
Corinne, UT, 317–18, 319
courtesans, 9, 16, 17, 23, 40, 119, 175, 251, 354
Creede, CO, 103, 104, 135, 136, 152
crib girls, 23, 107, 124, 240, 308
Cripple Creek, CO, 7, 16, 18, 19, 34, 37, 77, 97, 98, 101, 103, 105, 117, 143, 150–61, 190, 242, 292, 351, 374
Crumley, Grant, 153, 157
Cusey, Millie (Madam Millie, Millie Cusey-Clark, Silver City Millie), 17, 18, 275–81, 285, 353, 368, 434n102, 109, 435n122

dance hall girls, 6, 20, 23, 28, 48, 119, 123, 124, 135, 139, 145, 165
Dangerous Dick the Terrapin (Dick Davis), 355, 357
Davis, Emma, 297, 298
Davis, Maude (Maude Davis Lay), 324, 329, 336
Davis, Nellie, 300, 343
Deadwood, SD, 68, 185, 210, 211, 212, 213, 356, 378
Dean, Juanita Marie "Sammie," 60–61
Decker, Clarabelle, 3–4
Deer Lodge, MT, 231, 244, 246
Deer Valley, UT, 314–15, 317, 377
DeLamar, ID, 170, 189

DeMarr, Emma (Matilda Turnross), 176, 297, 298, 299
Demonstrand, Marie, 225, 244
Denver, CO, 16, 18, 34, 36, 37, 97, 98, 100, 106–18, 146, 148, 154, 155, 159, 348, 362, 373, 407n115
DeVere, Pearl (Isabelle Martin), 18, 152, 154–55, 157, 374, 414n252
Diamond Tooth Lil. *See* Hildegard, Evelyn
Dimsdale, Thomas, 20, 22, 191, 192
Doña Tules. *See* Barcelo, Gertrudis
Douglas, Lil, 24, 62, 371
Downs, Arley, 50, 51, 52
drugs, 4, 16, 34, 90, 112, 155, 188, 203, 236, 348; as medicine, 18, 27, 70; recreational, 5, 38, 89, 103; used for suicide, 18, 37, 76, 115, 138, 157, 180, 188, 204, 220, 222, 223, 234
Duetsch, Billy (Dietz), 154, 414n252
Dumas Brothel (Butte, MT), 26, 228–34, 237, 244, 245, 376, 426n152, 427n159, 164, 173
Durango, CO, 139–41, 293
Dutch May. *See* Sutter-Peters, Annie Marie

Earp, Allie, 70, 71, 75, 398n157
Earp, Bessie (Nellie Bartlett Ketchum), 64, 67, 75, 396n133, 397n146
Earp, James, 397n137, 146
Earp, Josie. *See* Marcus, Sarah Josephine
Earp, Louisa (Louisa "Lou" Houston), 74, 75, 398n165, 173
Earp, Mattie. *See* Blaylock, Celia Ann "Mattie"
Earp, Morgan, 74, 75, 398n165
Earp, Virgil, 64, 68, 74, 75
Earp, Wyatt, 67, 68, 69, 70, 71, 74, 76–77, 396n134, 397n135, 150, 398n150, 407n110
Ecoffey, Jules. *See* Coffey, Jules
Ellis, Anne, 22, 160
Enderlin, Liz (Cockeyed Liz, Liz Spurgen), 37, 146
Evens, Laura, 27, 98, 126, 127, 148–50, 366, 373

Lewis and Clark, 2
Livingston, MT, 213, 215, 248–49, 376
Loma Parda, NM, 266–67, 376
London, Belle. *See* Topham, Dora
Longabaugh, Harry (Hiram BeBee,
    Sundance Kid), 324, 325, 326,
    327, 328, 329, 330, 331, 332, 333,
    334, 335, 443n116, 444n142, 153

Madam Millie. *See* Cusey, Millie
madams, 10, 23, 26, 60, 64, 79, 163,
    204, 232, 299, 302, 422n48;
    abuse by, 28, 31–32; Madam's
    Association (Trinidad, CO), 131;
    Madam's Rest Home (Trinidad,
    CO), 133; Madam's Trolley system
    (Trinidad, CO), 131, 133
Majors, Mamie, 101, 104, 105, 373
Marcus, Sarah Josephine (Josie Earp,
    Sadie Earp, Sadie Jo, Sarah
    Josephine Earp, Shady Sadie),
    64, 69, 70, 71, 73, 74, 407n110
marriage: and married men, 3, 4, 12,
    27, 130, 195, 209–10, 255, 268;
    and married prostitutes, 40,
    50, 97, 133, 142, 238, 275, 287,
    304, 310, 315, 347, 384, 385; of
    prostitutes, 16, 22, 32, 37, 57, 68,
    77, 108, 110, 112, 115, 128, 152, 143,
    144, 155, 159, 162, 163, 165, 167,
    170, 173, 196, 201, 211, 247, 251,
    264, 281, 291, 297, 298, 320,
    349, 372
Martin, Pablita (Paula Angel), 267–
    68, 432n64
Marysville, MT, 206–7
McDaniel, Laura Bell (Laura Bell Dale,
    Laura Bell Horton, Laura Berg),
    xv, 24, 100–103, 105, 373
McGrath, Lizzie, 257–60, 262, 377
McIntyre, Annie (Annie Morrow, Peg
    Leg Annie), 171–72
Miami, AZ, 92–93
military posts: Banning Committee
    of 1876, 354; and the closing of
    red light districts, 45, 60, 93,
    133, 247–48, 275, 293, 368, 369;
    Fort Collins, CO, 127, 134–35;

Fort Duchesne, UT, 323, 324,
    336; Fort Laramie, WY, 209, 210,
    341, 342, 344; Fort Pueblo, CO,
    94–95; Fort Union, NM, 266,
    267; prostitution at, 23, 43–44,
    48, 88, 93, 94, 161, 191, 254,
    262, 263, 275, 293, 295, 313, 341,
    342, 343, 345, 351, 353, 354; and
    venereal disease, 46, 247, 263,
    342, 368
Missoula, MT (Fort Missoula), 25, 216,
    217, 218, 376
Mogollon, AZ, 285–87, 376
Molly b'Damn. *See* Burden, Molly
Mora, Longino, 91, 92, 371
Mullan, ID, 184, 190
Murphy, Etta "Spuds," 95, 126, 127,
    366
Murray, ID, 32, 184, 185, 186, 187, 188,
    190, 375, 378

Naco, Sonora, 85, 87, 88
Nadeau family (of Butte, MT), 228,
    229, 230, 231, 241
Nash, Emma Lenore, 349–50
Nation, Carrie, 158, 219, 225, 426n138
Native Americans, 1, 2, 5, 33, 40, 47,
    70, 79, 85, 94, 95, 106, 162, 165,
    171, 173, 175, 196, 206, 234, 269,
    273, 276, 282, 287, 290, 323, 336,
    341, 342, 354, 417n66
Nevada, 163, 185, 196, 201, 205, 290,
    296, 333, 340, 421n16
Nevada City, MT, 194, 195, 208, 375
Nigger Lee. *See* Wilson, Lee
Nigger Liz (of Butte, MT). *See* Hall,
    Lizzie
No-Nose Maggie. *See* Laird, Mary Alice
    Ann Devitt

Oak Creek, CO, 141–44
Oasis Bordello (Wallace, ID), 177, 181,
    182, 183, 184, 375
Oatman, AZ, 3–4
Ogden, UT, 302, 304, 305, 309, 311,
    312, 319, 320, 321, 322, 377

Old Homestead (Cripple Creek, CO), 154, 155, 156, 157, 159, 374, 414n252, 253

Orchard, Sadie (Sarah Jane Creech), 24, 281–84, 376, 436n134, 143

Ouray, CO, 28, 136–37, 139

Park City, UT, 314–15, 317, 377

Parker, Robert Leroy (Butch Cassidy, George Capel, Jim Ryan, Santiago Ryan), 323, 324, 326, 327, 328, 329, 330, 331, 333, 334, 336, 358, 444n146, 147

Peg Leg Annie. *See* McIntyre, Annie

Perry, Lea, 24, 169, 170

Pershing, General John "Black Jack," 293, 294

Phelps, Mae, 131–32

Phenix, NM, 293, 437n168

Phoenix, AZ, 43, 44–46, 48, 58, 90, 93

Pickett, Lottie Ables (Sorrel Mike), 223–23

Piercen, Louise "Pee Wee" (Louise Tartar), 143–44, 412n221

Pinal, AZ, 75–76

Pinos Altos, NM, 270–71, 274, 281, 376

Place, Etta (Ethel Place, Etta Longabaugh, Hazel Tryon, Laura Etta Place Capel, Mrs. Longbow), 324–37, 364

Powers, Lillian (Fay Weston, Tiger Lil), 97–98, 405n67

Prescott, AZ, 27, 41–44, 68, 70, 77

Price, UT, 328, 330, 340

Prince, Eva, 152, 154, 157

prostitutes: and addiction, 28, 188; choosing profession, 4, 17, 85, 106, 246, 257, 263, 276, 313; deaths of, 27, 36–37, 131, 134, 137, 220, 234, 236; fines levied on, 24, 41, 45, 48, 49, 50, 59, 63, 64, 70, 71, 83, 87, 95, 99, 112, 133, 135, 138, 141, 143, 144, 147, 150, 158, 166, 169, 180, 183, 188, 193, 215, 216, 222, 224, 239, 241, 247, 252, 257, 271, 279, 280, 289, 297, 298, 299, 300, 302, 312, 314, 315, 320, 323, 343, 345, 348, 354, 361, 400; health exams imposed upon, 41, 59, 60, 83, 90, 158, 181, 248, 294, 299, 307, 308, 368; income of, 22, 79, 97, 234, 244; lifestyles of, 17, 219; and marriage, 8, 9, 16, 22, 27, 37, 38, 40, 57, 77, 97, 128, 152, 153, 170, 185, 287, 293, 371; numbers of, 4, 10, 44, 91, 97, 116, 117, 133, 138, 146, 149, 150, 158, 159, 166, 168, 191, 204, 205, 216, 218, 219, 220, 225, 241, 246, 275, 298, 309, 319, 351; personal hygiene of, 20, 62, 74, 181, 297, 368; typical work day of, 22, 170; as viewed by society, 147, 223

Pueblo, CO, 37, 94–97, 125, 126, 290, 366

Raton, NM, 289–90

Rawlins, WY, 345, 352–53, 359, 377

Ray, Mary Aline, 142–43

Rogers, Jennie (Jennie Calvington, Leah J. Wood, Leeah Fries, Leeah Friess, Leeah Tehme), 110–15, 117, 148, 407n115

Root, Candace, 152–53

Ruby City, ID, 165, 170

Salida, CO, 27, 36, 98, 100, 126, 144, 146, 147–50, 373

Salt Lake City, UT, 16, 23, 24, 112, 114, 176, 192, 193, 196, 207, 208, 295, 296–314, 320, 377, 411n184, 422n51

San Francisco, CA, 8, 9, 10, 12, 13, 14, 16, 172, 205, 226

Santa Fe, NM, 68, 74, 251–54, 376

Scott, Mollie (Mollie Forrest), 220, 222

Shepherd, Mollie, 41–43

Silks, Mattie (Martha Ready), 18, 37, 107–10, 114, 117, 148, 373, 405n63, 72

Silver City, ID, 7, 12, 165–70

Silver City, NM, 271–81

Silver Cliff, CO, 98, 125, 146

Silverton, CO, 129, 136–39

Six Mile Hog Ranch, WY, 342, 343